ISBN 978-0-428-09167-5
PIBN 11244410

ANNUAL REPORTS

BY THE OFFICERS OF THE

TOWN OF WATERTOWN

FOR THE

Three Hundred and Fourth Year of its Organization

YEAR ENDING DECEMBER 31, 1934

THE HAMPSHIRE, PRESS, INC.
Cambridge, Mass.
1935

SEE BACK OF BOOK FOR CONTENTS

TOWN OFFICERS FOR 1934

Selectmen

MAURICE H. O'CONNELL, *Chairman*

JAMES H. SHERIDAN, *Clerk*

EDWARD D. HOLLAND

Committee Assignments

MAURICE H. O'CONNELL

Highways, Sewers and Drains, Sidewalks, Dust Laying, Administration Building, Soldiers' Relief, State and Military Aid.

JAMES H. SHERIDAN

Police, Insurance, Contingent, Town Physician, Town Veterinarian, Weights and Measures, Outside Aid, Mothers' Aid.

EDWARD D. HOLLAND

Fire, Election Expenses, Inspector of Buildings, Tree Warden, Moth Department, Engineering, Poles and Wires, Workmen's Compensation, Street Lights.

Town Clerk

WILLIAM P. McGUIRE   Term expires 1936

Treasurer

HARRY W. BRIGHAM   Term expires 1935

Assessors of Taxes

EDWARD A. OATES, *Chairman*   Term expires 1935
EDWARD F. WRIGHT, *Secretary*   Term expires 1936
JOHN J. CURRAN   Term expires 1937

Collector of Taxes

FREDERICK J. COLBY   Term expires 1935

Auditor

WILLIAM W. NORCROSS, Jr.   Term expires 1935

Moderator

P. SARSFIELD CUNNIFF   Term expires 1935

School Committee

CHARLES F. J. HARRINGTON, *Chairman*
      Term expires 1935
FRANCIS A. KELLY, *Secretary*   Term expires 1937
HAROLD B. BLAZO   Term expires 1935
E. LOUISE RICHARDSON   Term expires 1936
HARRIE E. WAITE   Term expires 1936
ROSCOE F. DAUGHTERS   Term expires 1937
PATRICK A. MENTON   Term expires 1937

Trustees Free Public Library

CHARLES F. SHAW; *Chairman*   Term expires 1936
RUTH H. FURBER, *Secretary*   Term expires 1935
REV. EDWARD C. CAMP   Term expires 1936
FRED E. CRAWFORD   Term expires 1935
JOHN A. COLLINS   Term expires 1937
JOHN M. RUSSELL   Term expires 1937

Board of Health

EARL J. WYLIE, *Chairman*   Term expires 1936
EUGENE F. GORMAN, *Secretary*   Term expires 1937
GUY C. PESCE   Term expires 1935

Park Commissioners

WINTHROP G. ROCKWELL, *Chairman*	Term expires 1936
GEORGE B. WELLMAN, *Sec.*	Term expires 1937
ARTHUR L. MORSE	Term expires 1935

Water Commissioners

JOHN P. GALLAGHER, *Chairman*	Term expires 1936
ARTHUR C. FAGAN, *Secretary*	Term expires 1937
GEORGE J. GAFFNEY	Term expires 1935

Tree Warden

JOHN C. FORD	Term expires 1935

Constables

WALDO M. EMERSON	Term expires 1935
JAMES L. HADDIE	Term expires 1935
FRANK L. MAGUIRE	Term expires 1935
*ROY C. PAPALIA	Term expires 1935
**JAMES M. OGILVIE	Term expires 1935

Planning Board

MASSIS N. TOMASSIAN, *Chairman*	Term expires 1935
RONALD M. STONE, *Secretary*	Term expires 1936
WILFRED A. NORRIS	Term expires 1936
ERNEST M. SMALL	Term expires 1935
JOHN H. DARDIS	Term expires 1937

APPOINTED OFFICERS

Superintendent of Moth Department

JOHN C. FORD	Term expires January 1935

Registrars of Voters

JOHN A. LOYND, *Chairman*	Term expires 1936
WM. P. McGUIRE, *Clerk*	Term expires 1936
PATRICK D. GLEASON	Term expires 1937
WILLIAM S. HUGHES	Term expires 1935

*Appointed by Selectmen, September 28, 1934.
**Appointed by Selectmen, November 2, 1934.

Town Engineer
OTIS D. ALLEN

Superintendent of Streets
PIERCE P. CONDON

Keeper of Infirmary and Pound
GEORGE H. WHITE

Town Physician
MICHAEL J. KELLEY, M. D.

Inspector of Cattle and Town Veterinarian
HARRY W. JAKEMAN, V. M. D.

Inspector of Buildings
WILLIAM H. WILSON

Sealer of Weights and Measures
VICTOR M. ANDERSON

Agent for Burial of Deceased Soldiers
WILLIAM P. McGUIRE

Agent, Department of Public Welfare
DANIEL H. MURPHY

Fence Viewers
WILLIAM H. ILIFEE   JOHN S. WILSON
FRANK W. WATERHOUSE

Keeper of Lockup
JOHN F. MILMORE

General Agent, Board of Health
FRED W. BODGE

Superintendent of Cemeteries
VAN D. HORTON

Inspector of Plumbing
CHARLES M. HEWITT

Town Counsel

FRANCIS J. McNAMARA

Playground Commissioners

BERNARD S. McHUGH, *Chairman*	Term expires 1935
ARTHUR C. FAGAN	Term expires 1936
EDMUND P. HICKEY	Term expires 1937

Dog Officer

WARREN J. EASTMAN

Special Officers With Pay When on Duty

GEORGE H. WHITE	ARNOLD E. HOLMES
PATRICK J. QUINN	PATRICK J. VAHEY
WALTER E. RUNDLETT	JOHN J. HOGAN
JAMES B. MURPHY	ALLEN KIMBALL
ROBERT MULLEN	DANIEL J. SULLIVAN
	JAMES T. PHELAN

Finance Committee

JOHN A. COLBERT, *Chairman*	Term expires 1936
WILFRED J. PAQUET, *Secretary*	Term expires 1937
THOMAS E. DOYLE	Term expires 1937
LEO P. LANDRY	Term expires 1937
ARTHUR B. JONES	Term expires 1937
ANTHONY JULIAN	Term expires 1937
FELIX A. LEONARD	Term expires 1937
DANIEL J. MURPHY	Term expires 1937
MATTHEW W. J. CARLEY	Term expires 1935
STERLING R. CARRINGTON	Term expires 1935
*JESSE H. MASON	Term expires 1935
GROVER C. CODIE	Term expires 1935
DAVID E. FITZGERALD	Term expires 1935
RALPH C. GARDINER	Term expires 1935
**A. LESTER SHIPTON	Term expires 1935
***EDWARD C. HALL	Term expires 1936

ROBERT S. QUINBY, M. D.	Term expires 1936
WILLIAM G. GRUNDY	Term expires 1936
****EDMUND P. HICKEY	Term expires 1936
JAMES T. PHELAN	Term expires 1936
EDWARD C. WEBSTER	Term expires 1936

*Appointed in place of Roscoe F. Daughters, elected to School Committee.
**Appointed in place of J. Vincent MacDonough, resigned.
***Appointed in place of John M. Russell, elected Library Trustee.
****Appointed in place of Patrick A. Menton, elected to School Committee.

Public Weighers

THOMAS R. BLAKENEY	JOSEPH KEELEY
ROY M. EATON	DOUGAL McMILLAN
HAROLD R. PEVEAR	NATHAN B. DOLBIER
WM. CASEY	HUGH GODDARD
CHAS. CASEY	FRED SOUCEY
WALLACE J. GREEN	PERCY J. WALKER
H. DEAN YORK	JOHN RING
ALMON H. MACDONALD	JOHN STUART
HARRY W. PACKARD	ANTHONY FLYNN
FORREST E. J. GLIDDEN	LOUIS HIRSCH
FRANK G. LEONARD	MARTIN GILLERAN
JOSEPH McSHEFFREY	WM. F. BURNS
JAMES MURPHY	GEORGE McNAMARA
G. J. PRESTON	LEWIS L. BIRD
THOMAS JOSEPH McCUE	SAMUEL BAGDASARIAN
C. B. WENDELL	MISSAK DERDERIAN
C. G. OSGOOD	CHARLES KEISER
HUGH GOLDING	JOSEPH A. HOLBROOK

RALPH KNOX

Measurers of Wood and Bark

C. G. OSGOOD	C. B. WENDELL
WM. J. CASEY	CHARLES L. CASEY

HAROLD R. PEVEAR

RECENT COMMITTEE APPOINTMENT

Committee of Seven, to Study and Revise the Zoning By-Law, Appointed by Moderator P. Sarsfield Cunniff on May 1, 1934, under authority of vote passed at Town Meeting held on April 11, 1934, under Article 22:

> Francis J. McNamara, Town Counsel, 5 Lovell Road,
> William H. Wilson, Building Inspector, 61-A Phillips Street,
> Ernest M. Small, Planning Board, 42 Walnut Street,
> Ronald M. Stone, Planning Board, 100 Russell Ave.,
> Massis N. Tomassian, Planning Board, 71 Spruce St.,
> Wilfred A. Norris, Planning Board, 47 Emerson Rd.,
> John H. Dardis, Planning Board, 26 Hawthorne St.

POPULATION

The estimated number of inhabitants of Watertown for the year 1915, as shown by the State census, 16,615; police census, 18,040. Police census, January 1917, 20,055. Estimated population, January 1918, 20,500. Police census, January 1919, 21,500. United States census, January 1, 1920, 21,457. Estimated population, January 1922, 22,500. Estimated population, January 1923, 23,000. Estimated population, January 1924, 25,000. State census, April 1, 1925, 25,480. Estimated population, January 1926, 27,500. Estimated population, January 1927, 28,500. Estimated population, January 1928, 30,000. Estimated population, January 1929, 31,500. Estimated population, January 1930, 32,500. United States census, April 1, 1930, 34,913. Estimated population, January 1, 1933, 36,400. Estimated population, January 1, 1934, 36,500. Estimated population, January 1935, 36,500.

REPORT OF THE FINANCE COMMITTEE ON
APPROPRIATIONS

To the Annual Town Meeting, 1934

Monday Evening, March 26, 7:00 P. M.

FINANCE COMMITTEE

John A. Colbert	Arthur B. Jones	J. Vincent MacDonough
William G. Grundy	George O. Baxter	Roscoe F. Daughters
Partick A. Menton	Thomas E. Doyle	Grover C. Codie
James F. Phelan	A. Lester Shipton	Sterling R. Carrington
Dr. Robert S. Quimby	Leo P. Landry	Matthew W. J. Carley
John Russell	Wilfred J. Paquet	Ralph C. Gardiner
Edward C. Webster	Thomas F. Megan	David E. Fitzgerald

REPORT OF FINANCE COMMITTEE

March 6, 1934.

To the Citizens of Watertown:

The Finance Committee makes the following recommendations to the Annual Town Meeting, on Monday, March 26, 1934. The Committee has carefully studied each request for an appropriation. The budget for preceding years has been analyzed, and we have tried to measure both the needs of the various Departments and the ability of the property owner to pay taxes. We are of the opinion that the general retrenchment policy adopted by the Town of Watertown during 1933, should be continued during 1934. The amounts recommended in the following tables, will, we believe, warrant the efficient operation of all essential services of the Town.

Salaries

The Heads of Departments have recommended the return of salary cuts placed in effect during 1933, and also the elimination of voluntary contributions by Civil Serv-

11

ice employees. No Department Head that has appeared before us during the hearings on the budget has been able to substantiate this request with facts that would warrant such a recommendation by the Finance Committee. On the contrary, we realize that the employees of Watertown received their full base compensation during the first three years of the depression, while most citizens have had salary and income reductions during four years. It is believed by this Committee that the last group to be affected by decreased earnings should not be the first to have their decrease restored. We therefore recommend a continuation of the policy of appropriating only ninety per cent of the salaries of all civil service employees for the year 1934, and that no increases over 1933 salaries, or any yearly increments, be paid.

That the income of the citizens of Watertown has not increased to an extent to warrant enlarged appropriations, is shown by the following table:

Year	Anticipation Borrowings	Interest on Ant. Loans	Unpaid Ant. Loans on Dec. 31st	Unpaid real and personal taxes
1930	$1,300,000.00	$32,629.14	$400,000.00	$408,046.72
1931	1,550,000.00	28,348.28	550,000.00	561,322.28
1932	2,200,000.00	71,271.61	700,000.00	745,315.05
1933	1,750,000.00	52,742.15	750,000.00	683,195.55

In addition to the $683,195.55 of unpaid real and personal taxes on December 31st, $81,333.43 of other taxes were unpaid; Special Assessments of $27,534.52 unpaid, $38,560.59 of unpaid water revenue, and Tax Titles of $133,114.29 to be redeemed. The levy against real and personal estates in 1932 was $2,162,740.68, and in 1933 the levy was reduced to $1,825,860. In spite of this decrease, the unpaid debts of tax-payers to the Town on December 31st, 1933, as listed above, amounted to $963,-738.38, or approximately fifty per cent of the cost of running the Town during the year.

Federal Relief

During 1933, the Town of Watertown received considerable relief from the United States Government in the form of made work for unemployed persons in the Civilian Conservation Corps, the Civil Works Program, and in cash.

The Civil Works Program is being continued in 1934 and also the Civilian Conservation Corps, and the Federal Government has extended considerable assistance in the form of fuel. We have pending an application for $280,584 to be expended in a Public Works Program. These measures must provide some relief from our local welfare and relief burdens. The Finance Committee has noted a distinct drop in the number of cases aided, but the decline in dollars has not been too apparent. We fully expect a sharp drop in the cost of welfare and other relief during the year 1934.

We realize that the United States Government cannot continue this relief program indefinitely, and we recommend a conservation of our local resources, in order that we, as a community, may be in a position to go ahead rapidly when the proper time arrives.

The Public Works Program, when and if approved, will provide employment for some Department employees, and this must be considered by the Highway and Water Departments in planning their yearly activities.

In connection with the Government program, we have been asked to provide the sum of $25,000 for materials and tools for the Civil Works Administration, who will provide the labor. This committee recommends the appropriation of $17,795.98, to be expended as follows, when and if the Civil Works projects are approved: $8,111.98 by the Highway Department, $2,484.00 by the School Department, and $7,200.00 by the Water Department, as all these departments are engaged in this work.

Betterment Streets

This Committee has reported adversely on most recent requests for new construction, especially where betterments are to be assessed on taxpayers, unless the prop-

erty owners have been willing to assume these extra
costs. We have this year recommended the construction
of two Betterment Streets, Hill Street and Grandview
Avenue, and have included appropriations for the essential drainage. We do this only to provide some employment for Highway Department employees, who because
of the fact that the Department has been over-manned,
have been sharing the available work between them, with
resulting decreased compensation. Hearings on Hill Street
and Grandview Avenue have not been held at the time this
report is filed, and the Finance Committee therefore re-
serves the right to change its recommendations prior to
the Town Meeting, should the abuttors on these streets
object to their construction.

Welfare

It is difficult to determine the amount necessary for
Soldiers' Relief and Outside Aid at this period of the year.
The Finance Committee has therefore recommended
amounts smaller than the requests for appropriation. We
do not advocate a supplementary budget during the year,
but we believe that the postponement of the full yearly
appropriation on these items is for the best interests of
the Town.

New Clerks

As usual, we have requests for new clerks in various
Departments. We have recommended against the addition of any new clerks to the regular payroll of the Town,
as we believe there are already more clerks in the Administration Building than would be used by any business
organization performing similar tasks. We regret the
lack of co-operation between Department Heads in lending assistance to other Departments when unusual conditions arise, especially when the clerks in some Departments have little or nothing to do while others are in
need of extra help. We have recommended the purchase
of a billing machine by the Water Department, and fully
expect that all tax and water bills will be made in this

manner. We recommend that the Selectmen immediately designate some person now employed in the Administration Building, as Chief Clerk or Supervisor to co-ordinate the work of all offices.

Debt

During 1933, the Town voted to borrow $280,584.00 for a Public Works Program. Our application for this loan is now pending, and if authorized, will be borrowed during 1934. We recommend no further borrowings this year. We will pay off $216,000.00 of our bonded debt during 1934, and the Public Works borrowing will leave a net increase in our debt of $64,584.00.

If the recommendations contained in this report are adopted by the Town Meeting, it is our firm belief that every Department of the Town can function in an efficient manner, and that our tax rate can be further reduced.

As Chairman of the Finance Committee, I wish to commend the members on their splendid attendance, their fairness, and their excellent work on the various sub-committees.

Respectfully submitted,

JOHN A. COLBERT,

Chairman.

Voted: That the report of the Chairman of the Finance Committee be adopted as the Report of the Committee.

WILFRED J. PAQUET,

Secretary.

GENERAL ADMINISTRATION ($76,951.40)

Item	Detail	1933 Appropriation	1933 Expended	1934 Appro. Asked	1934 Committee Recommends
Moderator				$100.00	$90.00
Selectmen's Department:					
Selectmen's Salaries	$1,350.00				
Salary of Clerk	450.00				
Contingencies	800.00	$2,600.00	$2,386.43	2,800.00	2,600.00
Clerk's Department:					
Clerk's Salary	2,970.00				
Salary of Clerk	1,035.00				
Contingencies	660.00	4,600.00	4,595.57	5,200.00	4,665.00
Treasurer's Department:					
Treasurer's Salary	3,150.00				
Salary of Clerk	1,035.00				
Extra Clerk Hire	500.00				
Contingencies	1,450.00	7,185.00	6,331.57	7,270.00	6,135.00
Tax Title Foreclosures (See Art. 9):				6,150.00	2,000.00
Collector's Department:					
Collector's Salary	2,970.00				
Salary, First Clerk	1,260.00				
Salary, Second Clerk	945.00				
Extra Clerical Services	842.40				
Contingencies	1,500.00	10,549.40	10,450.26	8,778.25	7,517.40
Tax Sale Advertising				1,500.00	1,200.00
Recording Deeds				2,200.00	1,500.00
Assessors' Department:					
Assessors' Salaries	3,690.00				
Clerks' Salaries	4,313.00				
Contingent	2,000.00	10,803.00	10,798.30	12,389.00	10,003.00
Finance Committee		2,000.00	1,631.36	2,000.00	2,000.00
Legal Services:					
Salary of Town Counsel	1,800.00				
Contingencies	500.00	2,500.00	2,331.21	2,700.00	2,300.00

Item					
Town Clerk's Department:					
Town Clerk's Salary	3,150.00				
Salary, First Clerk	1,215.00				
Salary, Second Clerk	1,170.00				
Salary, Third Clerk	1,125.00				
Contingencies	1,500.00	8,160.00	8,019.33	8,900.00	8,160.00
Engineering Department:					
Salaries		12,000.00	12,000.00	13,400.00	12,060.00
Contingent		1,200.00	1,196.56	1,400.00	1,200.00
Used Car				200.00	200.00
Bion Expense		4,800.00	4,364.33	8,000.00	8,000.00
Registrars of Bs:					
Salary of four men at $90.00	360.00	360.00	360.00	400.00	360.00
Printing Voting lists	522.55	522.55	522.55	600.00	600.00
Town Hall:					
Salary of Janitor	1,440.00				
Labor	1,260.00				
Telephone operator	936.00				
Fuel	1,000.00				
Light	1,000.00				
Contingent	500.00				
Extension of Heat in Draughting Room	125.00	6,426.00	6,419.37	7,451.00	6,261.00
Planning Board		100.00	44.90	200.00	100.00

PROTECTION OF PERSONS AND PROPERTY ($233,169.65)

Item					
Police Department:					
Salaries:					
Chief	$2,880.00				
Lieutenants (3)	7,020.00				
Sergeants (4)	8,820.00				
Patrolmen (37)	72,630.00	$90,021.68	$89,425.48	$104,000.00	$91,350.00
Special Police		400.00	380.50	500.00	400.00
Janitor and Wagonman		1,642.50	1,642.50	1,825.00	1,642.50

		1933 Appropriation	1933 Expended	1934 Appro. Asked	1934 Committee Recommends
Clerk and Wagonman		1,642.50	1,642.50	1,825.00	1,642.50
Teletype		600.00	588.00	600.00	600.00
Replace Mtor Cycles		580.00	580.00	645.60	645.60
New 1934 Autos		500.00	500.00	1,156.00	1,156.00
Radio Equipment				525.00	525.00
Ordnance Equipment				1,100.00	1,100.00
Contingencies		3,800.00	3,643.00	1,000.00	1,000.00
Fire Department:					
Salaries:		96,399.00	96,323.05	106,510.00	96,323.05
Chief	2,8880.00				
Captains (3)	7,020.00				
Lieuts (4)	8,820.00				
Permanent Men (38)	75,164.05				
All Men (2)	279.00				
Spec. (1)	2,160.00				
Tires—Engine One				250.00	250.00
New Hose				1,500.00	1,500.00
Toilets and Repairs		4,860.00	4,860.00	3,500.00	2,000.00
Contingencies				6,000.00	4,000.00
New 750 Gallon Pump				9,000.00	No Appro.
Inspector of Buildings:		2,650.00	2,638.80	2,950.00	2,665.00
Salary of Inspector	2,340.00				
Salary of Clerk	225.00				
Contingencies	100.00				
Weights and Measures:		2,020.00	2,012.57	2,350.00	2,170.00
Salary of Sealer	1,620.00				
50 Gal. Auto	150.00				
Contingencies	400.00				
Gypsy and Brown Tail Mth:					
Salary of Superintendent		720.00	720.00	800.00	720.00
Salary of Clerk		427.50	427.50	475.00	427.50
Labor		2,000.00	1,999.94	4,000.00	2,000.00

Tree Warden:				
Salary of Tree Warden	900.00	900.00	1,000.00	900.00
Salary of Clerk	180.00	180.00	200.00	180.00
New Trees			1,000.00	400.00
Maintenance	4,000.00	3,999.81	5,000.00	4,000.00
C. W. A.	75.00	75.00		
Poles and Wires Department:				
Salary of ...or	2,880.00	2,880.00	3,200.00	2,880.00
Salary of Clerk	427.50	427.50	475.00	427.50
Assistant Clerk			380.00	No Appro.
Maintenance	10,178.00	10,177.84	10,000.00	1,400.00
...r				6,100.00
New 1934 Auto			816.80	6000
...e of Signal Room			5,545.00	865.00
Dog ...er	300.00	298.00	300.00	300.00

HEALTH AND SANITATION ($53,145.00)

Health Department:				
Salary of Agent	$2,880.00	$2,880.00	$3,200.00	$1,530.00
Salary of Clerk	1,035.00	1,035.00	1,150.00	1,035.00
Salary of ...es (3)	2,700.00	2,700.00	3,000.00	2,700.00
...us Diseases	22,600.00	22,337.32	22,600.00	20,000.00
Baby Clinic	440.00	440.00	140.00	440.00
Dental Clinic	2,500.00	2,498.88	2,500.00	2,500.00
Laboratory Maintenance	100.00	97.89	100.00	No Appro.
Contingent	1,275.00	1,272.94	1,400.00	1,000.00
Salary of Veterinarian	540.00	540.00	600.00	540.00
...on of Plumbing:				
Salary of ...or $2,250.00	2,350.00	2,349.79	2,600.00	2,350.00
...es 100.00				
Sewer Department:				
...on	3,400.00	3,398.83	3,050.00	3,050.00
Maintenance	15,000.00	14,993.31	15,000.00	15,000.00
Drainage	6,100.00	6,086.06	5,000.00	3,000.00

CARE AND LIGHTING OF HIGHWAYS ($215,884.00)

		1933 Appropriation	1933 Expended	1934 Appro. Asked	1934 Committee Recommends
Highway Department:					
Salaries:					
Superintendent	$3,240.00				
1st Clerk	1,350.00				
2nd Clerk	1,125.00				
Office Expense		5,715.00	5,715.00	6,350.00	5,715.00
ins		400.00	397.75	500.00	400.00
		8,719.56	8,719.56	7,284.00	7,284.00
Construction				44,552.00	No Appro.
Maintenance		61,690.35	61,682.80	75,000.00	65,000.00
Patching Streets C. W. A.				5,125.00	5,000 0
Stable Maintenance		13,900.00	13,894.09	15,000.00	12,000.00
Garbage		27,500.00	27,494.25	27,500.00	27,500. 0
Ashes and Paper		25,000.00	24,998.55	28,500.00	25,000.00
Dust Laying		3,015.09	3,015.09	12,000.00	5,000. 0
Betterment Streets (See Article 19)					
Special for Construction only:					
Grandview Ave. from Copeland St. to Gilbert Street				24,735.00	12,000.00
Hill St. from Fayette St. to Palfrey St.				9,900.00	4,335.00
Betterment Drainage (on above streets)				6,250.00	No Appro.
Gasoline Shovel				6,565.00	No Appro.
Gasoline Roller				717.00	650.00
New 1934 Auto					
Street Lights		41,500.00	41,397.84	41,500.00	40,000.00
ks		5,000.00	4,993.63	15,000.00	6,000.00

CHARITIES AND SOLDIERS BENEFITS ($189,419.73)

	1933 Appropriation	1933 Expended	1934 Appro. Asked	1934 Committee Recommends
Infirmary Department:				
Salary of Keeper	$900.00	$900.00	$900.00	$900.00
General Expense	5,040.00	5,036.17	4,929.73	4,929.73
Public Welfare Department:				
Salary of Agent	2,000.00	2,000.00	2,000.00	2,000.00

Salary of Visitor	1,080.00	1,080.00	1,200.00	1,080.00
Salary of Clerks (2)	1,620.00	1,620.00	2,700.00	1,620.00
Salary of Male Clerk	750.00	750.00	1,000.00	1,000.00
Investigators	2,160.00	2,160.00	2,400.00	2,160.00
Contingent	2,300.00	2,299.46	2,500.00	2,000.00
Outside Aid	220,000.00	218,506.62	5,000.00	100,000.00
Mother's Aid	31,521.48	31,108.73	35,000.00	30,000.00
Old Age Assistance	19,356.37	18,982.30	20,000.00	20,000.00
Town Physician	1,530.00	1,530.00	1,700.00	1,530.00
State Aid	1,800.00	1,775.00	2,200.00	2,200.00
Soldier's Relief and Military Aid	60,000.00	53,855.28	30,000.00	20,000.00

SCHOOLS AND LIBRARIES ($540,042.00)

School Department:				
General Control	$11,849.20	$11,849.08	$14,584.00	$12,275.00
Instruction — Salaries and Supplies, 1933	414,689.00	413,988.51	454,430.00	395,867.00
Instruction — Supplies			22,000.00	18,000.00
Operation	54,585.00	54,584.75	63,710.00	54,470.00
Maintenance	5,215.00	5,198.50	8,000.00	5,500.00
New Equipment	1,000.00	160.50	3,000.00	700.00
Miscellaneous	5,750.00	5,748.11	6,500.00	5,800.00
Evening School	3,000.00	2,989.43	3,500.00	3,120.00
Trade and Continuation	9,500.00	9,336.27	13,000.00	10,000.00
Transportation	1,500.00	1,448.00	1,500.00	1,500.00
Public Library:				
Salaries	21,780.00	21,758.02	25,250.00	21,810.00
Books, Periodicals and Binding	5,400.00	5,399.65	6,000.00	6,000.00
Maintenance	4,950.00	4,945.67	5,000.00	5,000.00

RECREATION ($9,600.00)

Park Department:				
Salary of Superintendent	450.00	450.00	450.00	450.00
Maintenance	2,000.00	2,000.00	4,500.00	2,500.00
Victory Field	2,000.00	1,999.79	3,000.00	2,000.00

	1933 Appropriation	1933 Expended	1934 Appro. Asked	1934 Committee Recommends
Tennis Courts	500.00	500.00	1,200.00	700.00
New Power Mower			455.00	No Appro.
Waterproof Grandstand			300.00	150.00
Playground Department:				
Salaries	2,000.00	2,000.00	3,640.00	2,000.00
Maintenance	1,500.00	1,492.27	1,600.00	1,500.00
New Equipment			2,050.00	300.00

PUBLIC ENTERPRISES ($45,008.33)

	1933 Appropriation	1933 Expended	1934 Appro. Asked	1934 Committee Recommends
Water Department:				
Salaries:				
Superintendent	$2,880.00			
1st Clerk	1,170.00			
2nd Clerk	932.40			
	$4,982.40	$4,982.40	$6,572.00	$4,982.40
Maintenance	34,551.68	34,548.41	69,932.53	34,551.68
Office Expense	1,900.00	1,898.23	3,920.25	2,125.25
Vacations	1,000.00	982.64	1,530.00	1,299.00
New 1934 Car			1,000.00	625.00
New 1934 Truck			1,200.00	1,200.00
Billing Machine			225.00	225.00

CEMETERIES ($13,050.00)

	1933 Appropriation	1933 Expended	1934 Appro. Asked	1934 Committee Recommends
Cemetery Department:				
Salary of Superintendent	1,800.00	1,771.50	2,000.00	1,800.00
Labor	8,000.00	7,992.96	8,000.00	8,000.00
Contingent	500.00	496.48	800.00	500.00
Avenues at Ridgelawn			3,800.00	No Appro.
Tombs and Tool House at Ridgelawn			2,500.00	2,500.00
Lowering Device and Greens			250.00	250.00

PUBLIC DEBT AND INTEREST ($331,000.00)

Town Debt (See Article 6)	243,000.00	243,000.00	216,000.00	216,000.00
Interest	130,000.00	129,230.57	130,000.00	115,000.00

UNCLASSIFIED ($84,369.75)

Pensions	13,527.45	13,123.15	13,600.00	13,600.00
Memorial Day (See Article II)	1,000.00	1,000.00	1,100.00	1,100.00
Insurance	4,651.01	4,624.60	10,611.50	10,611.50
Workmen's	2,821.79	2,443.42	5,000.00	5,000.00
Printing Town Reports	1,000.00	984.64	1,000.00	1,000.00
Headquarters for Veterans of Foreign Wars (See Article 12)	1,080.00	1,080.00	1,080.00	1,080.00
Headquarters Disabled American Veterans (See Article 13)				
Contingent	2,000.00	1,905.51	360.00	360.00
Reserve Fund	10,000.00	5,978.00	2,000.00	1,700.00
Unpaid Bills	2,278.82	2,238.88	10,000.00	10,000.00
County T. B. Assessment (See Art. 10)	24,207.55	24,207.55	317.04	317.04
Civil Works Projects (See Art. 17):			21,805.23	21,805.23
Highway Department			8,111.98	8,111.98
School Department			2,484.00	2,484.00
Water Department			7,200.00	7,200.00
	$1,936,396.38	$1,920,643.84	$2,217,482.91	$1,791,639.86

Article 5. See Tabulated Schedule of Appropriations.

Article 6. The Committee recommends the appropriation of $216,000.00 for that portion of the Town Debt which matures during the year 1934: $430.10 of this sum to be transferred from the Premium Account and the balance assessed on the polls and estates for the year 1934.

Article 9. See Tabulated Schedule.

Article 10. See Tabulated Schedule.

Article 11. See Tabulated Schedule.

Article 12. See Tabulated Schedule.

Article 13. See Tabulated Schedule.

Article 16. The Committee recommends no appropriation.

Article 17. The Committee recommends the following sums:

$8,111.98 for materials and labor to be expended by the Highway Department, if and when the projects are approved.

$2,484.00 for materials and labor to be expended by the School Department, if and when the projects are approved.

$7,200.00 for materials and labor to be expended by the Water Department, if and when the projects are approved.

Article 19. The Committee recommends the sum of $12,000.00. See Tabulated Schedule—Betterments.

Article 20. The Committee recommends no appropriation.

Article 21. The Committee recommends no apprpriation.

Article 22. The Committee recommends no appropriation.

Bonds Due in 1934

Schools	$119,000.00
Streets	38,000.00
Sewers and Drains	26,000.00
Water	7,000.00
Miscellaneous	26,000.00

Interest Payable in 1934

Schools	$39,088.75
Streets	3,746.25
Sewers and Drains	5,530.00
Water	596.25
Miscellaneous	10,600.00

RECORD OF THE TOWN CLERK

WARRANT FOR ANNUAL TOWN MEETING
ELECTION OF OFFICERS AND TOWN
MEETING MEMBERS
March 5, 1934

Commonwealth of Massachusetts.   Middlesex, ss.

To any Constable in the Town of Watertown, Greeting:

In the name of the Commonwealth of Massachusetts, you are hereby required to notify and warn the legal voters of the Town of Watertown to meet in their respective voting places in said Town:

PRECINCT 1—Coolidge School, Arlington Street.

PRECINCT 2—Hosmer School, Winthrop Street.

PRECINCT 3—East End Fire Station, Mt. Auburn St.

PRECINCT 4—Senior High School Columbia Street.

PRECINCT 5—Central Fire Station, Main Street.

PRECINCT 6—James Russell Lowell School, Lowell Avenue.

PRECINCT 7—Administration Building Main Street.

PRECINCT 8—Central Fire Station, Main Street.

PRECINCT 9—West Junior High School, Waverley Avenue.

PRECINCT 10—Browne School, Main Street

on Monday, the fifth day of March, 1934, at 8 A. M., to act on the following articles, viz.:

Article 1. To choose the regular Town Officers for the ensuing year, the following to be printed on and chosen by the official ballot, to wit: One Selectman for three years, who shall also be a member of the Board of Public

26

Welfare, Surveyor of Highways and Appraiser; one Moderator for one year; one Treasurer for one year; one Collector of Taxes for one year; one Auditor for one year; one Assessor of Taxes for three years; three members of the School Committtee for three years; two trustees of the Free Public Library for three years; one member of the Board of Health for three years; one Park Commissioner for three years; one Water Commissioner for three years; one Water Commissioner for one year (to fill vacancy); òne Tree Warden for one year; three Constables for one year; one member of the Planning Board for three years.

Also for the election of nine (9) Town Meeting Members for the three year term in each of the ten (10) voting precincts of the Town, and to fill the following vacancies: two (2) vacancies in term expiring in 1935, in Precinct Three; one (1) vacancy in term expiring in 1935, in Precinct Six; one (1) vacancy in term expiring in 1935, in Precinct Eight; one (1) vacancy in term expiring in 1935, in Precinct Nine; one (1) vacancy in term expiring in 1935, in Precinct Ten.

THE POLLS WILL OPEN AT 8 A. M. and WILL CLOSE AT 8 P. M.

You are also required to notify and warn the legal voters aforesaid to meet in the Administration Building, in said Town, on Monday, the fifth day of March, 1934, at 8:15 P. M., to act on the following article:

Article 2.   To choose all other necessary Town Officers in such manner as the Town may direct.

The consideration of further business under this warrant will be postponed until Monday evening, March 19, 1934, at 7. P. M., in the Senior High School Building, Columbia Street, or until such later time as the meeting may direct.

Article 3.   To hear the report of the Town Officers as printed and to hear the report of any committee heretofore appointed, and act thereon.

Article 4. To see what action the Town will take relative to the continuance, for the year 1934, of the Voluntary Contribution Agreement of Town employees relative to salaries and wages in force during the year 1933, or take any action relating thereto.

Article 5 To grant such sums of money as may be thought necessary for the uses and expenses of the Town for the ensuing year, direct how the same shall be raised, or take any action relating thereto.

Article 6. To see if the Town will vote to appropriate the necessary sum of money to pay that portion of the Town debt which matures on or previous to January 1, 1935, direct how the money shall be raised, or take any action relating thereto.

Article 7. To see if the Town will vote to authorize the Treasurer, with the approval of the Selectmen, to refund any or all of the revenue notes issued in anticipation of the revenue of the year 1934, in accordance with the provisions of Section 17 of Chapter 44 of the General Laws; any debt so incurred to be paid from the revenue of 1934.

Article 8. To see if the Town will vote to authorize the Treasurer, with the approval of the Selectmen, to refund any or all of the revenue notes issued in anticipation of the revenue of the year 1933, in anticipation of the provisions of Section 17, of Chapter 44 of the General Laws; any debt so incurred to be paid from the revenue of 1933.

Article 9. To see what method the Town will vote to adopt for the collection of taxes for the ensuing year, and to fix the compensation of the Collector, or take any action relating thereto.

Article 10. To see if the Town will appropriate a sum sufficient to pay the County of Middlesex as required by law on account of assessments levied on the town for its share of the principal of the Middlesex County Tuberculosis Hospital Funding Loan, Act of 1932, bonds maturing in 1934, issued in compliance with Chapter 10, Acts of 1932, also for any other indebtedness incurred and. outstanding under said Chapter 10, also for the town's share of the cost and interest on said bonds due in 1934, also for the town's share of the expense incurred under the provisions of Chapter 331 of the Acts of 1933 which provided for the settlement of certain claims of the Commonwealth against the Middlesex County Tuberculosis Hospital District, also for the care, maintenance, and repair of said hospital for 1933, and including interest on temporary notes issued therefor, in accordance with sections of Chapter 111 of the General Laws applicable thereto, and for all other expenses in connection therewith, determine how the money shall be raised, or in any way act thereon.

Article 11. To see if the Town will appropriate a sum of money for the rent of the Grand Army Hall, care of the grounds around the Soldiers' Monument, and to defray the expenses of decorating the graves of deceased soldiers on the next Memorial Day, and authorize Isaac B. Patten Post No. 81 G. A. R. to expend the same, direct how the same shall be raised, or take any action relating thereto.

Article 12. To see if the Town will vote to appropriate a sum of money to pay the cost of providing suitable headquarters for Burnham-Manning Post No. 1105, Veterans of Foreign Wars of the United States, direct how the money shall be raised, or take any action relating thereto. (Request of Burnham-Manning Post No. 1105, Veterans of Foreign Wars of the United States.)

Article 13. To see if the Town will vote to appropriate a sum of money to pay the cost of providing suitable headquarters for Watertown Chapter No. 14, Disabled American Veterans of the World War, direct how the money shall be raised, or take any action relating thereto. (Request of Watertown Chapter No. 14, Disabled American Veterans of the World War.)

Article 14. To see if the Town will vote to accept the provisions of Chapter 136, Section 21 to 25 inclusive, of General Laws, Tercentenary Edition, relative to certain sports and games permitted on the Lord's Day, or take any action relating thereto. (Request of Mrs. Mary Connors and others.)

Article 15. To see if the Town will vote to authorize the School Committee to sell a second-hand bookkeeping machine now in use in the School Department, or take any action relating thereto. (Request of the School Committee.)

Article 16. To see if the Town will vote to appropriate the sum of twelve hundred dollars ($1200.), to be expended by the School Committee for the purchase of a bookkeeping machine, or take any action relating thereto. (Request of School Committee.)

Article 17. To see if the Town will vote to appropriate the sum of twenty-five thousand dollars ($25,000.) to pay the cost of materials, trucking and all other necessary charges arising out of the conduct of Civil Works Administration projects, said sums to be expended under the direction of the Civil Works Administrator, or take any action relating thereto.

Article 18. To see if the Town will vote to offer the land owned by the Town of Watertown at the corner of Main and Church Streets now occupied by the Old Town Hall and other buildings to the Federal Government as a site for a post office building, or take any action relating thereto. (Request of G. Frederick Robinson and others.)

Article 19. To hear the report of the Selectmen relative to the laying out of the following-named streets, to wit:

Coolidge Hill Road, from Grove Street to accepted portion of Coolidge Hill Road;

Grandview Avenue, from Gilbert Street to Copeland Street;

Hill Street, from Palfrey Street to Fayette Street;

Nyack Street, from Belmont Street to dead end;
under the provisions of Chapters 82 and 80 of the General Laws, as amended, the latter providing for the assessment of betterments, and to see if the Town will vote to accept said streets, or any of them, as and for public ways, and will authorize the Selectmen to take by eminent domain, or acquire by purchase, or otherwise, any land necessary for said laying out, provide the sum or sums necessary to pay the cost or land damages therefor, and the cost of construction, direct how said money shall be raised, or take any action relating thereto.

Article 20.   To see if the Town will vote to appropriate the sum of one thousand dollars ($1,000.) to be paid as an annuity to the dependents of Gilbert Nichols, deceased, a former member of the Fire Department, said annuity to be paid in accordance with the provisions of Chapter 340 of the Acts of 1933, providing for an annuity to dependents of a fireman who is killed or dies from injuries received, while in the performance of his duty, or take any action relating thereto.

Article 21.   To see if the Town will vote to appropriate the sum of one thousand dollars ($1,000.) to be paid as an annuity to the dependents of Willard E. Streeter, deceased, a former member of the Fire Department, said annuity to be paid in accordance with the provisions of Chapter 340 of the Acts of 1933, providing for an annuity to dependents of a fireman who is killed or dies from injuries received, while in the performance of his duty, or take any action relating thereto.

Article 22.   To see if the Town will vote to appoint a committee consisting of the Town Counsel, the Building Inspector, and five members of the Planning Board to study and revise the Zoning By-law, and to appropriate the sum of one hundred dollars ($100.) to pay the cost of advertising, printing, hearings and expert advice, or take any action relating thereto. (Request of the Planning Board.)

Article 23.   To hear the report of the Planning Board relative to a petition of Joseph L. Doherty and others, for an amendment to the Zoning By-law, by altering the Zoning Map therein referred to, by changing certain property located at the corner of Main and Gleason Streets, as shown on Assessors' Plan of the Town of Watertown, Section 11, Block 23, Lot 28, Plan Lot 62-A and Section 11, Block 23, Lot 1, Plan Lot 62-B, from District 3-C (two-family residence district) to District 2-B (store purposes.)

Article 24.   To see if the Town will vote to accept a deed from Abby M. Gardner and Mabelle W. Dickinson for public purposes of a certain lot of land located on Winter Street, Watertown, containing approximately forty-five hundred twelve (4512) square feet, or take any action relating thereto.

And you will notify and warn the legal voters of the Town of Watertown to meet at the times and at the places herein specified, by leaving at every inhabitated house in Town a printed copy of this warrant, and also by posting copies of the same in ten or more conspicuous public places in Town, seven days at least prior to the time of said meeting.

Hereof fail not, and make return of this warrant, with your doings thereon, into the office of the Town Clerk on or before the time of said meeting.

Given under our hands this twenty-first day of February, A. D. 1934.

EDWARD D. HOLLAND,
MAURICE H. O'CONNELL,
JAMES H. SHERIDAN,

Selectmen of Watertown.

Officers' Return on Warrant

As required by the foregoing warrant, I have notified and warned the legal voters of the Town of Watertown to meet at the times and at the places herein specified, by leaving at every inhabited house in Town a printed copy of this warrant, and also by posting copies of the same in ten or more conspicuous public places in Town seven days at least prior to the time of said meeting.

JOSEPH W. REGAN, *Constable of Watertown.*

Attest: WILLIAM P. McGUIRE, *Town Clerk.*

Notices were mailed to the Town Meeting Members at least seven days prior to the Town Meeting of the proposed business to be considered at the meeting.

WILLIAM P. McGUIRE, *Town Clerk.*

ANNUAL TOWN MEETING, March 5, 1934

Precinct Officers

Precinct 1. Eugene L. Storey, Warden; Joseph J. Morley, Clerk. Inspectors: Frances C. Murphy, Pearl A. Baxter, Grace L. Cole, Lillian A. Sullivan, Helen L. Boudreau, Alfred T. Pennington. Counters: Guido F. Pugliese, Martin Wolohojian, George P. Ward.

Precinct 2. Arthur J. McCarthy, Warden, William B. Glidden, Clerk. Inspectors: Bernard A. Morley, Frederick O. Fitzgerald, Blanche H. Robinson, Mae F. Elwell, Ella Lane, Ralph Duley, Margaret J. O'Driscoll. Counters: Julia T. Coffey, Peter T. Coen, Roger S. Hubbard, Harry G. Elwell, Walter Glidden.

Precinct 3. Richard M. Hatch, Warden, John J. Ingerson, Clerk. Inspectors: Mabel C. MacNutt, Izolee H. Gardiner, Ernest K. Ingalls, Thomas Creamer, William J. Holland, Thomas J. Mulvahill. Counters: Arthur D. Wilkins, Marguerite Farrenkopf, Roger E. Mathews, Roy L. Cummings.

Precinct 4. Wm. M. Emerson, Warden, John B. Watson, Clerk. Inspectors: Mary V. Holland, Lavina Jensen, Roland B. MacDonald, Winifred M. Donnelly, James D. Hackett, Richard H. Gallagher. Counters: Amy F. Osborn, Elizabeth F. MacDonough, Francis M. Lightbody, Thomas A. McNiff, Emil K. Hall, Hugh A. McBreen.

Precinct 5. Joseph R. Cooney, Warden, Grace M. Olson, Clerk. Inspectors: Alice T. Withre, Walter R. Flagg, Grace E. Ward, Sadie E. Nichols, Margaret B. Walker, David F. Keefe. Counters: Lena Buchanan, Alice E. Sanger, Ann C. Wilson, Helen M. O'Brien, Cecelia Ford, Edward K. **Bacon.**

Precinct 6. Frederick Bell, Warden, Lester A. Murphy, Clerk. Inspectors: Madeline E. Van Dyke, S. Alice Youngman, Anne M. Davis, Katherine L. Landry, Rosalie Whelan, Theodore B. Robinson. Counters: Ruth E. Peppard, Agnes C. Luther, Isabelle B. Sweet, Lewis A. Reed, Charles V. Gerrish, Harold W. Duvall.

Precinct 7. Harry J. York, Warden, Walter J. McMullen, Clerk. Inspectors: Cynthia M. Watts, Marguerite MacDonald, Joseph H. Bussey, Ernestine P. Howe, Anna T. Hyde, Alexander Macdonald. Counters: Margaret E. Barry, Evangeline L. Johnson, Thomas F. Jennings, George E. LeFavor.

Precinct 8. Joseph D. McCall, Warden, Wallace A. Shipton, Clerk. Inspectors: Ruth E. Hall, Catherine Campbell, Esther Grace, Olive P. Thayer, Daniel J. Clifford. Counters: Mildred Fencer, Joseph W. Landers, Bertha M. Ryan, Joseph L. Coen, O. Charles Couture.

Precinct 9. James J. O'Connell, Warden, Frederick E. Owen, Clerk. Inspectors: Eleanor Mosman, Eva M. Eagleson, Edsel Tocci, Mary McElligott, Emma R. Roche, Harry E. Hill. Counters: Ralph O. Owen, Ernest Bullen, Josephine Barksdale, Domenic White.

Precinct 10. Charles A. McCarthy, Warden, Joseph S. Parent, Clerk. Inspectors: Anna V. Hughes, Mildred Upit, Hannah R. Farley, Ellen B. Lougee, Catherine R.

Hurley, Mollie E. Smith. Counters: Florence V. Haddie, Anna M. Keating, R. Frances Delaney, Bernard S. Smith, Gerard J. Riley, Leon M. Lamb.

The foregoing officers were sworn to the faithful performance of their duties by Town Clerk, Wm. P. McGuire.

The necessary ballots and paraphernalia for conducting the election were inspected by the election officers of the various precincts.

At 8 A. M. the meetings were called to order, the polls were declared open, and voting continued until 8 P. M. The ballots were counted and the result of the same was declared in the respective precincts.

The returns of votes cast in Precincts 1, 2, 3, 4, 5, 6, 7, 8, 9 and 10 were duly recorded in the record books of said precincts, and the ballot sheets and records were delivered to the Board of Registrars who proceeded to canvass the same with the following result, which was declared by the Town Clerk.

The following persons indicated by (*) were elected and were sworn to the faithful performance of their duties by Town Clerk, William P. McGuire.

Total Vote Cast 8,855

SELECTMAN, MEMBER OF BOARD OF PUBLIC WELFARE, SURVEYOR OF HIGHWAYS AND APPRAISER—For Three Years

Precincts	1	2	3	4	5	6	7	8	9	10	Total
Clarence G. Reynolds	229	433	545	748	415	500	557	248	213	302	4190
*James H. Sheridan	612	520	307	193	479	282	447	787	388	489	4504
Blanks	31	13	11	9	12	14	17	25	8	21	161

On March 8, 1934, petition was received by the Board of Registrars from Clarence W. Dealtry and others for recount of votes cast for Selectmen. The recount held on March 13, resulted as follows:

	1	2	3	4	5	6	7	8	9	10	Total
Clarence G. Reynolds	228	431	545	747	414	498	557	247	215	303	4185
*James H. Sheridan	612	521	308	193	479	284	447	788	389	488	4509
Blanks	32	14	10	10	13	14	17	25	5	21	161

MODERATOR—For One Year.

Precincts	1	2	3	4	5	6	7	8	9	10	Total
*P. Sarsfield Cunniff	577	539	335	276	506	316	520	797	371	522	4759
Hewitt G. Fletcher	235	394	506	667	374	464	466	223	211	264	3804
Blanks	60	33	22	7	26	16	35	40	27	26	292

On March 8, 1934, petition was received by the Board of Registrars from Clarence W. Dealtry and others for recount of votes cast for Moderator. The recount held on March 13, 1934, resulted as follows:

	1	2	3	4	5	6	7	8	9	10	Total
*P. Sarsfield Cunniff	572	540	335	280	504	317	522	802	375	524	4771
Hewitt G. Fletcher	232	394	505	663	376	463	464	217	210	262	3786
Blanks	68	32	23	7	26	16	35	41	24	26	298

TREASURER—For One Year

	1	2	3	4	5	6	7	8	9	10	Total
*Harry W. Brigham	618	755	746	858	717	700	830	806	473	642	7145
Blanks	254	211	117	92	189	96	191	254	136	170	1710

COLLECTOR OF TAXES—For One Year

	1	2	3	4	5	6	7	8	9	10	Total
*Frederick J. Colby	626	756	746	862	735	704	847	805	487	637	7205
Blanks	246	210	117	88	171	92	174	255	122	175	1650

AUDITOR—For One Year

	1	2	3	4	5	6	7	8	9	10	Total
*William W. Norcross, Jr.	598	731	737	863	698	687	818	783	475	614	7004
Blanks	274	235	126	87	208	109	203	277	134	198	1851

ASSESSOR OF TAXES—For Three Years

	1	2	3	4	5	6	7	8	9	10	Total
*William Bell	232	426	555	760	423	500	594	270	211	288	4259
John J. Curran	595	499	287	179	447	276	387	742	360	479	4251
Blanks	45	41	21	11	36	20	40	48	38	45	345

On March 7, 1934 a petition was received by the Board of Registrars signed by Eugene F. Gorman and others for recount of votes cast for Assessor; another petition signed by Clarence W. Dealtry and others was received on March 8, 1934. The recount held on March 13, 1934, resulted as follows:

	1	2	3	4	5	6	7	8	9	10	Total
William Bell	212	425	551	760	423	500	591	273	219	291	4245
*John J. Curran	619	501	291	178	451	275	391	739	355	477	4277
Blanks	41	40	21	12	32	21	39	48	35	44	333

SCHOOL COMMITTEE—For Three Years

	1	2	3	4	5	6	7	8	9	10	Total
*Charles O. Chase	243	423	548	744	414	484	564	249	224	301	4194
Roscoe F. Daughters	530	485	282	192	444	294	398	729	358	458	4170
Doris L. Erskine	233	396	530	748	397	493	548	236	211	275	4067
*Francis A. Kelly	552	501	293	182	461	286	411	769	354	472	4281
Patrick A. Menton	526	484	278	179	455	287	378	752	355	493	4187
*Frederick D. Shaw	242	434	547	745	418	475	580	245	212	295	4193
Blanks	290	175	111	60	129	69	184	200	113	142	1473

On March 7, 1934, a petition was received by the Board of Registrars signed by Florence F. McAuliffe and others for recount of votes cast for School Committee; on March 8, 1934 a petition signed by Francis J. McNamara and others was received, and on March 8, 1934, a petition signed by Clarence W. Dealtry and others was received. The recount held on March 13, 1934, resulted as follows:

Precincts	1	2	3	4	5	6	7	8	9	10	Total
Charles O. Chase	241	425	550	742	409	482	563	246	222	302	4182
*Roscoe F. Daughters	531	486	283	194	454	296	405	737	361	456	4203
Doris L. Erskine..	232	397	530	748	392	490	544	231	211	272	4047
*Francis A. Kelly	554	501	293	182	460	289	407	767	355	475	4283
*Patrick A. Menton	539	483	284	178	460	284	384	756	356	497	4221
Frederick D. Shaw	232	436	545	742	415	478	578	244	211	293	4174
Blanks	287	170	104	64	128	69	182	199	111	141	1455

LIBRARY TRUSTEES—For Three Years

	1	2	3	4	5	6	7	8	9	10	Total
*John A. Collins..	539	503	283	190	476	281	403	740	364	472	4251
Benjamin T. Loring	236	403	543	738	392	483	555	248	211	286	4095
*John M. Russell..	534	506	295	201	460	291	385	733	339	461	4205
Mosetta I. Vaughan	222	365	516	716	367	464	549	225	206	274	3904
Blanks	213	155	89	55	117	73	150	174	98	131	1255

On March 8, 1934, a petition was received by the Board of Registrars signed by Clarence W. Dealtry and others for recount of votes cast for Library Trustees. The recount held on March 13, 1934, resulted as follows:

	1	2	3	4	5	6	7	8	9	10	Total
*John A. Collins..	541	508	287	189	478	279	404	742	363	473	4264
Benjamin T. Loring	235	405	546	736	389	485	552	252	212	283	4095
*John M. Russell	537	507	291	203	457	288	388	733	342	462	4208
Mosetta I. Vaughan	218	362	517	709	370	465	550	227	204	275	3897
Blanks	213	150	85	63	118	75	148	166	97	131	1246

BOARD OF HEALTH—For Three Years

	1	2	3	4	5	6	7	8	9	10	Total
*Eugene F. Gorman	560	515	297	199	467	280	422	796	360	503	4399
Walter N. Secord	234	409	544	740	408	490	555	226	220	283	4109
Blanks	78	42	22	11	31	26	44	38	29	26	347

On March 8, 1934, a petition was received by the Board of Registrars signed by Clarence W. Dealtry and others for recount of votes cast for Board of Health. The recount held on March 13, 1934, resulted as follows:

	1	2	3	4	5	6	7	8	9	10	Total
*Eugene F. Gorman	560	517	297	194	467	282	422	794	359	505	4397
Walter N. Secord	235	407	546	744	408	488	555	228	222	283	4116
Blanks	77	42	20	12	31	26	44	38	28	24	342

PARK COMMISSIONER—For Three Years

Edmund P. Hickey 546 493 278 185 449 276 385 757 350 475 4194
*George B.
Wellman 247 418 552 747 418 495 592 257 225 295 4246
Blanks 79 55 33 18 39 25 44 46 34 42 415

On March 8, 1934, a petition was received from Joseph Hyde and others; also a petition signed by Clarence W. Dealtry and others for recount of votes cast for Park Commissioner. The recount held on March 13, 1934, resulted as follows:

Edmund P. Hickey 547 495 279 186 449 276 386 758 352 476 4204
*George B.
Wellman 246 417 553 746 418 495 591 260 226 294 4246
Blanks 79 54 31 18 39 25 44 42 31 42 405

WATER COMMISSIONER—For Three Years

*Arthur C. Fagan 556 486 279 179 456 268 405 752 367 515 4263
Edward C. Hall.... 236 417 557 755 412 508 571 260 212 269 4197
Blanks 80 63 27 16 38 20 45 48 30 28 395

On March 8, 1934, a petition was received by the Board of Registrars signed by Clarence W. Dealtry and others for recount of votes for Water Commissioner—3 year term. The recount held on March 13, 1934, resulted as follows:

*Arthur C. Fagan 558 490 279 177 455 269 405 753 368 515 4269
Edward C. Hall.... 234 414 559 756 413 507 572 256 212 267 4190
Blanks 80 62 25 17 38 20 44 51 29 30 396

WATER COMMISSIONER—For One Year.(to fill vacancy)

*George J.
Gaffney 562 498 295 193 481 283 397 761 359 474 4303
Norman D.
MacKay 231 409 537 741 391 495 575 244 211 288 4122
Blanks 79 59 31 16 34 18 49 55 39 50 430

On March 8, 1934, a petition was received by the Board of Registrars signed by Clarence W. Dealtry and others for recount of votes for Water Commissioner—1 year term. The recount held on March 13, 1934, resulted as follows:

*George J.
Gaffney 562 500 295 190 483 284 397 767 357 473 4308
Norman D.
MacKay 230 406 537 743 389 495 575 236 213 287 4111
Blanks 80 60 31 17 34 17 49 57 39 52 436

TREE WARDEN—For One Year

*John C. Ford 555 535 321 254 489 315 451 775 365 511 4571
Arthur L. Morse.. 238 378 516 684 385 465 533 241 214 275 3929
Blanks 79 53 26 12 32 16 37 44 30 26 355

On March 8, 1934, a petition was received by the Board of Registrars signed by Clarence W. Dealtry and others for recount of votes cast for Tree Warden. The recount held on March 13, 1934, resulted as follows:

*John C. Ford......	550	537	316	258	488	314	453	777	366	512	4571
Arthur L. Morse..	242	377	521	680	386	465	531	240	213	275	3930
Blanks ..:...............	80	52	26	12	32	17	37	43	30	25	354

CONSTABLES—For One Year

*Waldo P. Emerson	351	524	615	779	504	561	649	408	302	381	5074
*James L. Haddie	334	456	603	759	443	542	604	364	285	369	4759
*Frank L. Maguire	566	648	674	777	662	626	725	570	433	583	6444
Michael Spergiurio	537	466	214	165	370	237	344	624	286	387	3630
Blanks	828	804	483	370	739	422	741	1034	521	716	6658

PLANNING BOARD—For Three Years

*John H. Dardis..	533	467	277	182	461	275	401	742	350	472	4160
William W. Rugg	229	392	529	731	388	474	545	227	194	268	3977
Blanks	110	107	57	37	57	47	75	91	65	72	718

On March 8, 1934, a petition was received by the Board of Registrars signed by Clarence W. Dealtry and others for recount of votes cast for Planning Board. The recount held on March 13, 1934, resulted as follows:

*John H. Dardis..	528	466	279	181	461	273	402	747	349	468	4154
William W. Rugg	236	392	528	734	390	476	545	226	196	274	3997
Blanks	108	108	56	35	55	47	74	87	64	70	704

TOWN MEETING MEMBERS
PRECINCT ONE
Three Year Term—Vote for Nine

*Bagnall, James J.	15	Kimball Road	341
Barker, Forrest W.	23	Woodleigh Road	213
*Crupi, Vincent	5	Lyons Street	277
*Curran, Neil T.	826	Mt. Auburn St.	431
*Davenport, Alfred M.	88	Grove Street	296
*Diliberto, Paul C.	823	Mt. Auburn St.	316
*Fitzmaurice, Isabel M.	23	Irma Avenue	281
French, Gordon R.	8	Westland Road	210
Harting, Herbert C.	62	Templeton Parkway	251
*Hartnett, Patrick S.	766	Mt. Auburn St.	299
Kendall, Delbert W.	38	Kimball Road	206
Levine, Bernard I.	38	Brimmer Street	217
Lincoln, Ralph F.	106	Belmont Street	211
Papalia, Augustin	67	Crawford Street	185
Papazian, Aris B.	39	Prentiss Street	181
*Rose, William F.	12	Keenan Street	272
Smith, James B.	68	Templeton Parkway	268
Stevenson, Thomas J., Jr.	16	Maplewood Street	203
*Sullivan, William J.	21	Brimmer Street	314
Whittemore, Casper M.	149	Hillside Road	251
Blanks,			2625

PRECINCT TWO
Three Year Term—Vote for Nine

Bernard, Fred J.	42	Chauncy Street	252
*Burke, Charles T.	76	Spruce Street	306
*Der Bogosian, Kevork	21	Melendy Avenue	279
*Fairbanks, Franklin W.	44	Spruce Street	364
*Fairbanks, Katherine L.	44	Spruce Street	277
*Fallon, Walter L.	6	Porter Street	288
Fancy, Raymond A.	32	Spruce Street	214
Hannon, Owen E.	67	Hazel Street	205
Kavalgian, Aram	553	Mt. Auburn St.	196
MacKinnon, Hugh	160	School Street	249
McAuliffe, Florence F.	72	Spruce Street	199
McLaughlin, James	35	Hosmer Street	245
Meehan, George H.	31	Adams Street	275
Morrissey, John L.	56	Spruce Street	268
*Murray, John A.	184	School Street	321
*Oates, William F.	39	Hazel Street	386
O'Brien, James J.	11	Putnam Street	243
O'Driscoll, John C.	43	Fairfield Street	211
Parshley, Margaret K.	16	Dartmouth Street	140
Robley, George Harold	45	W. Boylston Street	220
Sanborn, Charles F.	12	Spruce Street	232
Stewart, James A.	164	School Street	243
*Sullivan, John J.	96	Boylston St., W.	321
Wallace, Mary E.	140	School Street	225
*Whittemore, Charlotte	11	Fairfield St.	296
Scattering,			1
Blanks,			2238

PRECINCT THREE
Three Year Term—Vote for Nine

*Beale, William R.	38	Carver Road	380
Boyle, James S., Jr.	5	Upland Road	227
Breslin, James E.	45	Shattuck Road	230
*Brooks, Eugene B.	97	Langdon Avenue	482
Buffum, Erving N.	33	Hillside Road	309
Comey, Elmer H.	23	Carver Road	306
Curtin, John C.	101	Langdon Avenue	286
*Finn, Stuart Thayer	104	Langdon Avenue	317
Hanlon, Bridget M.	10	Appleton Terrace	161
*Johnson, Carl W.	72	Winsor Avenue	501
Mahoney, Thomas F.	9	Rangeley Road	222
*Manchester, Lewis G.	197	Maplewood Street	373
*Mayo, E. Clark, Jr.	33	Commonwealth Road	384
O'Leary, Thomas F.	15	Upland Road	215
Perryman, Linda M.	11	Upland Road	152
Peterson, Hadar F.	21	Carver Road East	312
*Saunders, Abraham	93	Langdon Avenue	328
**Sheldon, Charles	311	School Street	340
Tracy, James E.	16	Appleton Street	199
*Tuck, Harold S.	73	Hillside Road	467
Blanks			1576

**Already a Town Meeting Member, in term expiring in 1936.

Town Meeting Member—One Year Term (To fill vacancies)

Halpin, William	22	Irma Avenue	272
*Melanson, Ernest J.	2	Upland Road	431
*Tyler, Earle S.	164	Maplewood Street	567
Blanks			456

PRECINCT FOUR

Three Year Term—Vote for Nine

*Bowen, Alma G.	265	Mt. Auburn St.	415
Brennan, John J.	247	Common Street	195
*Camp, Edward C.	25	Garfield Street	684
Danner, William A.	157	Common Street	198
*Donaldson, William	28	Centre Street	449
Donnelly, John F.	23	Grenville Road	172
Donnelly, Thomas J.	23	Grenville Road	162
Foster, Lucy C.	330	Mt. Auburn Street	240
Gray, Frank A.	20	Lincoln Street	392
Harcourt, Catherine A. E.	247	Mt. Auburn Street	355
*Iliffe, William H.	99	Bailey Road	483
*Johnson, Eric L.	87	Barnard Avenue	594
*Mason, Jesse H.	12	Walnut Street	430
*Mayo, Walter L.	50	Stoneleigh Circle	532
Oates, James M.	145	Russell Avenue	361
O'Brien, Thomas E.	42	Grenville Road	164
Tarbell, Elizabeth L.	18	Avon Road	321
*Weldon, Melvin V.	41	Columbia Street	499
*Whitehill, Edwin H.	42	Barnard Avenue	650
Blanks			1254

PRECINCT FIVE

Three Year Term—Vote for Nine

Berquist, Paul E.	4	Frank Street	325
*Burger, Francis J., Jr.	148	North Beacon Street	348
Cazmay, Thomas W.	15	Bay Street	323
Clement, Peter J.	17	Priest Road	271
*Colligan, Mary	5	Royal Street	393
*Comstock, Effie	103	North Beacon Street	377
*Corcoran, Frank	123	Arsenal Street	374
Galligan, Thomas J.	12	Palmer Street	316
*Godwin, Harold A.	120	Riverside Street	350
*Hall, Edward C.	65	Mt. Auburn Street	348
Jacobson, Earl W.	12	Ladd Street	224
Linehan, Ellen	13	Fletcher Terrace	250
MacGregor, William C.	14	Priest Road	230
Morris, Griffith E.	41	Irving Street	330
*Rooney, John F.	110	Riverside Street	372
Thibodeau, Ralph Joseph	83	Mt. Auburn Street	108
*Vahey, Ambrose P.	104	Riverside Street	348
*Vahey, James J.	104	Riverside Street	390
Whitney, Charles A.	15	Fifield Street	319
Wilber, Gifton M.	33	Paul Street	297
Blanks			1861

PRECINCT SIX

Three Year Term—Vote for Nine

*Blackall, James D.	24	Wolcott Road	434
*Blake, Thomas A.	56	Bradford Road	367
*Bobst, Frank T.	173	Lovell Road	414
*Bradford, Andrew D.	144	Lovell Road	467
*Bramhall, Charles W.	28	Hall Avenue	404
Crowley, Charles B. P.	111	Poplar Street	219
Dee, Patrick J.	33	Channing Road	232
*Dyer, Rufus A.	43	Hovey Street	367
*Eckert, William H.	12	Hall Avenue	363
*Gillis, Edward F.	176	Lovell Road	407
Harrington, Charles F. J.	9	Fairview Avenue	262
McCoubrey, John W.	83	Standish Road	221
McKeon, R. Kelsie	41	Hall Avenue	265
Morrissey, Richard C.	87	Standish Road	223
Murphy, Daniel J.	35	Channing Road	231
*Parsons, William	114	Carlton Terrace	359
Peppard, Matthew B.	120	Bellevue Road	136
Rooney, Henry J., Jr.	40	Carroll Street	204
Sheehan, Joseph H.	26	Bradford Road	238
Tessin, Fred G.	114	Lovell Road	165
Blanks			1186

Town Meeting Member—One Year Term (To fill vacancy)

*Geary, John J.	17	Bradford Road	353
Swimm, H. LeRoy	730	Belmont Street	330
Blanks			113

PRECINCT SEVEN

Three Year Term—Vote for Nine

*Beechler, Harry W.	49	Katherine Road	519
*Campbell, George C.	166	Church Street	574
Carroll, Joseph L.	69	Waverley Avenue	362
Cerqua, Nello	80	Winter Street	181
Corcoran, Mary C.	14	Palfrey Street	375
*Everett, Harold C.	114	Marshall Street	528
*Fish, Pierce L.	78	Marshall Street	505
Foley, Augustine A.	66	Spring Street	305
*Gibson, Ethel H.	25	Marion Road	382
*Gray, Arthur F.	20	Fayette Street	492
LeConti, Charles	152	Fayette Street	166
Murnaghan, Hugh J.	81	Summer Street	187
O'Halloran, Edward P.	107	Fayette Street	342
Papalia, Roy C.	191	Summer Street	188
*Perkins, Elias A.	73	Fayette Street	458
Simmons, Alonzo F.	166	Palfrey Street	374
*Skinner, Hiram L.	56	Marion Road	481
*Smith, Harry A.	52	Oliver Street	511
Blanks			2259

PRECINCT EIGHT
Three Year Term—Vote for Nine

*Andrews, Joseph W.	134	Main Street	628
*Coen, Thomas J.	9	Green Street Terrace	441
*Conroy, Robert L.	24	Bacon Street	460
*Costello, Maurice H.	57	Union Street	530
*Devaney, Dennis	72	Green Street	520
Evans, Albertina M.	73	Capitol Street	302
Evans, David A.	73	Capitol Street	342
*Gorman, William R.	24	Bacon Street	440
Grace, Frank S.	9	Jewett Street	253
Noden, David G.	102	Morse Street	251
Noden, Harold R.	108	Morse Street	254
Malley, Joseph A.	152	Pleasant Street	419
*McBride, Lawrence S.	47	Eliot Street	424
*McNamara, Edward G.	182	Main Street	472
Monahan, John P.	5	Myrtle Street	422
Thayer, Samuel G.	31	Morse Street	337
*Ward, Bernard L.	24	Cuba Street	458
Blanks			2587

Town Meeting Member—One Year Term (To fill vacancy)

*Dyer, Edward E.	62	Capitol Street	704
Blanks			356

PRECINCT NINE
Three Year Term—Vote for Nine

Carbone, Giovanni	26	Gertrude Street	214
Christofferson, Carl A.	3A	Hilltop Road	215
Cornetta, Anthony	151	Sycamore Street	225
*DeVoe, Stephen J.	101	Westminster Avenue	266
*Garland, William	58	Hillside Street	280
**Hill, Harry E.	36	Piermont Street	275
*Keyes, Herbert W.	63	Hillside Street	259
Lagerblade, August A.	4A	Hilltop Road	160
*MacDonough, M. Frances	28	Whitcomb Street	291
*Mahoney, John J.	28	Whitcomb Street	273
*Perkins, Joseph G.	158	Sycamore Street	335
Purchase, Bertram G.	11	Whitney Street	196
Russo, Carmine	100	Edenfield Avenue	191
Scaltreto, Tony	10	Sparkhill Street	121
*Swanson, Swan E.	361	Orchard Street	242
*Tocci, Carmine	240	Waverley Avenue	240
Blanks			1698

**Resigned, Mar. 13, 1934.

Town Meeting Member—One Year Term (To fill vacancy)

*Norton, Clinton	6	Hilltop Road	4
Scattering			5
Blanks			600

PRECINCT TEN
Three Year Term—Vote for Nine

*Campbell, Thomas F.	73	Waltham Street	410
Christensen, Fred J.	11	Wilmot Street	311

*Connors, Clarence L.	118	Rutland Street	390
*Connors, James E.	83	Rutland Street	368
*Dwyer, John M.	30	Stuart Street	441
*Fagan, Arthur C.	20	Emerson Road	430
Grimes, Ernest B.	13	Swett Court	225
*Hoey, Edward J.	9	Stuart Street	420
LaFort, William P.	430	Pleasant Street	227
*LeShane, Frank C.	18	Wilmot Street	353
Mattison, John E.	24	Charles Street	283
*Menton, Lucy A.	669	Main Street	424
*Newell, Caleb S.	42	Stuart Street	352
Norrish, William I.	23	Purvis Street	320
Scharff, Louis	16	Olcott Street	292
Stewart, Robert A.	19	Rutland Street	348
Blanks			1714

Town Meeting Member—One Year Term (To fill vacancy)

*Harrington, Michael J.	37	Gilbert Street	579
Blanks			233

TOWN MEETING MEMBERS BY VIRTUE OF THEIR OFFICES

Selectmen

Maurice H. O'Connell	20 Westminster Avenue
James H. Sheridan	76 Green Street
Edward D. Holland	16 Stearns Road

Town Clerk

Wm. P. McGuire   48 Green Street

Moderator

P. Sarsfield Cunniff   79 Marshall Street

Treasurer

Harry W. Brigham   2 Brigham Street

Collector of Taxes

Frederick J. Colby   86 Bailey Road

Auditor

William W. Norcross, Jr.   39 Spruce Street

Town Counsel

Francis J. McNamara   5 Lovell Road

Tree Warden

John C. Ford   24 Church Street

Chairman, School Committee

Charles F. J. Harrington   9-B Fairview Avenue

Chairman Library Trustees

Charles F. Shaw   62 Langdon Avenue

Chairman, Board of Health

Earle J. Wylie   128 Mt. Auburn Street

Chairman, Board of Assessors

Edward A. Oates   37 Hazel Street

Chairman, Planning Board
Massis N. Tomassian   71 Spruce Street

Chairman, Water Commissioners
John P. Gallagher   16 Hawthorne Street

Chairman, Park Commissioners
Winthrop G. Rockwell   13 Hawthorne Street

Chairman, Playground Commissioners
Bernard S. McHugh   19 Emerson Road

Representative in General Court
George H. Dale   654 Main Street

Finance Committee

John A. Colbert, Chairman	14 Appleton Terrace
Matthew W. J. Carley	48 Evans Street
Sterling R. Carrington	11 Stoneleigh Road
Grover C. Codie	99 Franklin Street
David E. Fitzgerald	34 Olcott Street
Ralph C. Gardiner	23 Commonwealth Road
*J. Vincent MacDonough	28 Whitcomb Street
Robert S. Quinby, M. D.	361 School Street
William G. Grundy	29 Carver Road
James T. Phelan	103 Chapman Street
Edward C. Webster	124 Marshall Street
**Roscoe F. Daughters	35 Knowles Road
***John M. Russell	96 Robbins Road
****Patrick A. Menton	669 Main Street
Thomas E. Doyle	76 Hillside Road
Leo P. Landry	72 Bradford Road
Wilfred J. Paquet, Secretary	95 Spruce Street
Arthur B. Jones	29 Carroll Street
Felix A. Leonard	30 Brimmer Street
Daniel J. Murphy	35 Channing Road
Anthony Julian	11 Carlton Terrace

WM. P. McGUIRE,
Town Clerk.

*Resigned—Ambrose Lester Shipton appointed to fill vacancy.
**Removed—Elected to School Committee. Jesse H. Mason appointed to fill vacancy.
***Removed—Elected to Library Trustees. Edward C. Hall appointed to fill vacancy.
****Removed—Elected to School Committee. Edmund P. Hickey appointed to fill vacancy.

Annual Town Meeting, Monday Evening, March 5, 1934

Meeting was called to order at 8.15 P. M. by Moderator P. Sarsfield Cunniff. Officers' returns on warrant were read by Town Clerk, Wm. P. McGuire.

Voted: To take up Article 2.

Article 2. To choose all other necessary Town Officers in such manner as the Town may direct.

Voted: That the Selectmen be and they are hereby authorized to appoint all Town Officers not chosen on the official ballot.

Voted: That this meeting be and is hereby adjourned until Monday evening, March 26, 1934, at 7.00 P. M., to meet in the Senior High School, on Columbia Street, Watertown, at which time and place all business called for in the warrant for the Annual Town Meeting of March 5, 1934, under Articles 3 to 24, inclusive, will come before the meeting for consideration and action.

Notice for Adjourned Town Meeting, Monday Evening, March 26, 1934

Notice is hereby given the legal voters of the Town of Watertown that the Town Meeting called for Monday evening, March 5, 1934, at 8:15 P. M., has been adjourned until Monday evening, March 26, 1934, at 7 P. M., to meet in the Senior High School Building, on Columbia Street, in said Town of Watertown, at which time and place all business called for in the warrant for the Annual Town Meeting of March 5, 1934, under Articles 3 to 24 inclusive, will come before the meeting for consideration and action.

And the legal voters of the Town of Watertown are hereby notified and warned to meet at the time and at the place herein specified, by posting copies of this notice in ten or more conspicuous places in Town, twenty-four hours at least prior to the time of said meeting, and also by causing a copy of the same to be published in a Watertown newspaper.

Given under our hands this fifth day of March, A. D. 1934.

P. SARSFIELD CUNNIFF, *Moderator.*
WM. P. McGUIRE, *Town Clerk.*

Clerk's Return on Notice

I have posted copies of the foregoing notice in ten or more conspicuous public places in Town, at least twenty-four hours prior to the time of said adjourned meeting, and have also caused a copy of the same to be published in a Watertown newspaper.

Notices were mailed to the Town Meeting Members at least twenty-four hours prior to the time of said Adjourned Town Meeting of the proposed business to be considered at the meeting.

WILLIAM P. McGUIRE, *Town Clerk.*

Record of Annual Town Meeting, March 26, 1934

Adjourned Town Meeting was called to order at 7.30 P. M. by Moderator P. Sarsfield Cunniff. Prayer was offered by Rev. Daniel C. Riordan, pastor of St. Patrick's Church. Clerk's return on notice for Adjourned Town Meeting was read by Town Clerk, Wm. P. McGuire.

Number of Town Meeting Members necessary for a quorum: 93; number present on March 26th: 259.

The Town Meeting Members present were sworn in by Town Clerk, Wm. P. McGuire, as follows:

"Having been elected Town Meeting Members, you and each of you severally, solemnly swear that you will faithfully perform the duties pertaining to that office, so help you, God."

Vacancies in Town Meeting Membership Filled

March 26th. Notice was received from the Chairman of Precinct 2 of the election of James Donovan, 11-A Fairfield Street, to fill one (1) vacancy in term expiring in 1935, caused by the election as Chairman of Assessors of Edward A. Oates, 37 Hazel Street.

Notice was received from the Chairman of Precinct 3 of the election of Elmer H. Comey, 23 Carver Road, to fill one (1) vacancy in term expiring in 1937, caused by Charles L. Sheldon, 311 School Street, being elected in three year term at 1934 Town Election, he already being a member in term expiring in 1936, Mr. Comey to serve until the 1935 Town Election.

Notice was received from the Chairman of Precinct 9 of the election of Roscoe F. Daughters, 15 Knowles Road, to fill one (1) vacancy in term expiring in 1936, caused by removal from the precinct of George H. Malley; also of the election of Harry E. Hill, 36 Piermont Street, to fill one (1) vacancy in term expiring in 1937, these two members to serve until the 1935 Town Election.

Article 3. To hear the report of the Town Officers as printed and to hear the report of any committee heretofore appointed, and act thereon.

Voted: That the reports of the Town Officers as printed in the Town Report for the year 1933 be and they are hereby accepted.

Article 4. To see what action the Town will take relative to the continuance for the year 1934, of the Voluntary Contribution Agreement of Town employees relative to salaries and wages in force during the year 1933, or take any action relating thereto.

132 in the affirmative, 104 opposed.

Voted: That all salaries be paid on the 1932 basis, that is, that the ten per cent salary cut, voluntary or otherwise, shall expire as of January 1, 1934.

Article 5. To grant such sums of money as may be thought necessary for the uses and expenses of the Town for the ensuing year, direct how the same shall be raised, or take any action relating thereto.

Record of Appropriations Voted at Adjourned Annual Town Meeting Held on March 26, 1934.

General Administration ($76,861.40)

Selectmen's Department:
Selectmen's Salaries	$1,350.00	
Salary of Clerk	450.00	
Miscellaneous	800.00	$2,600.00

Auditor's Department:
Auditor's Salary	$2,970.00	
Salary of Clerk	1,035.00	
Contingencies	660.00	4,665.00

Treasurer's Department:
Treasurer's Salary	$3,150.00	
Salary of Clerk	1,035.00	
Extra Clerk Hire	500.00	
Contingencies	1,450.00	6,135.00

Tax Title Foreclosures	2,000.00

Collector's Department (See Article 9):
Collector's Salary	$2,970.00	
Salary, 1st Clerk	1,260.00	
Salary, 2nd Clerk	945.00	
Extra Clerical Services	842.50	
Contingencies	1,500.00	7,517.40
Tax Sale Advertising		1,200.00
Recording Deeds		1,500.00

Assessors' Department:
Assessors' Salaries	$3,690.00	
Clerks' Salaries	4,313.00	
Contingent	2,000.00	10,003.00

Finance Committee		2,000.00
Legal Services:		
Salary of Town Counsel	1,800.00	
Contingencies	500.00	2,300.00
Town Clerk's Department:		
Town Clerk's Salary	3,150.00	
Salary, 1st Clerk	1,215.00	
Salary, 2nd Clerk	1,170.00	
Salary, 3rd Clerk	1,125.00	
Contingencies	1,500.00	8,160.00
Engineering Department:		
Salaries		12,060.00
Contingent		1,200.00
Used Car		200.00
Election Expense		8,000.00
Registrars of Voters:		
Salary of four men at $90.00 each		360.00
Printing Voting Lists		600.00
Town Hall:		
Salary of Janitor	1,440.00	
Labor	1,260.00	
Telephone Operator	936.00	
Fuel	1,000.00	
Light	1,000.00	
Contingent	500.00	
Extension of Heat in Draughting Room	125.00	6,261.00
Planning Board		100.00

Protection of Persons and Property ($254,191.60)

Police Department: 135 in favor, 101 opposed. Voted:

Salaries:		
Chief	3,200.00	
Lieutenants (3)	7,800.00	

Sergeants (4)	9,800.00	
Patrolmen (37)	80,700.00	101,500.00
Special Police		400.00
*Janitor and Wagonman		1,825.00
*Clerk and Wagonman		1,825.00
Teletype		600.00
Replace Motorcycles		645.60
New 1934 Autos		1,156.00
Radio Equipment		525.00
Ordnance Equipment		1,100.00
Contingencies		4,000.0C

*136 in favor, 80 opposed. Voted.

Fire Department: 144 in favor, 97 opposed. Voted: .

Salaries:		
Chief	3,200.00	
Captains (3)	7,800.00	
Lieutenants (4)	9,800.00	
Permanent Men (38)	83,000.00	
Call Men (2)	310.00	
Mechanic (1)	2,400.00	106,510.00

Tires—Engine One	250.00
New Hose	1,500.00
Toilets and Repairs	2,000.00
**Contingencies	4,000.00

**92 in affirmative, 122 opposed—To increase Contingencies to $6,000. Defeated.

Inspector of Buildings:		
Salary of Inspector	2,340.00	
Salary of Clerk	225.00	
Contingencies	100.00	2,665.00

Weights and Measures:		
Salary of Sealer	1,620.00	
50 Gallon Auto Measure	150.00	
Contingencies	400.00	2,170.00

Gypsy and Brown Tail Moth Department:

Salary of Superintendent	720.00
Salary of Clerk	427.50
Maintenance	2,000.00

Tree Warden's Department:

Salary of Tree Warden	900.00
Salary of Clerk	180.00
New Trees	400.00
Maintenance	4,000.00

Poles and Wires Department: 105 in the affirmative, 103 opposed. Voted:

Salary of Inspector	3,200.00
Salary of Clerk	427.50
Maintenance	1,400.00
Labor	6,100.00
New 1934 Auto	600.00
Maintenance of Signal Room	865.00
Dog Officer	300.00

Article 9. To see what method the Town will vote to adopt for the collection of taxes for the ensuing year, and to fix the compensation of the Collector, or take any action relating thereto.

Action taken in conjunction with Article 5.

Voted: That the same method for the collection of taxes be and is hereby adopted as was pursued last year, and that interest be charged on all taxes not paid on or before November 1, 1934, interest to be charged from the fifteenth day of October, 1934, at the rates per annum as provided by Chapter 59, Section 57 of the General Laws of 1930, and acts in amendment thereof. See Schedule for Appropriations under Article 5.

Article 20: To see if the Town will vote to appropriate the sum of one thousand dollars ($1,000.) to be paid as an annuity to the dependents of Gilbert Nichols, deceased, a former member of the Fire Department, said annuity to be paid in accordance with the provisions of Chapter 340 of the Acts of 1933, providing for an annuity to dependents of a fireman who is killed or dies from injuries received, while in the performance of his duty, or take any action relating thereto.

Action taken in conjunction with Article 5.

Voted: That the sum of seven hundred and fifty dollars ($750) be and is hereby appropriated to pay the amount due for the year 1934 for an annuity to the dependents of Gilbert Nichols, deceased, former member of the Fire Department, said sum to be payable in accordance with the provisions of Chapter 340 of the Acts of 1933.

Article 21. To see if the Town will vote to appropriate the sum of one thousand dollars ($1,000.) to be paid as an annuity to the dependents of Willard E. Streeter, deceased, a former member of the Fire Department, said annuity to be paid in accordance with the provisions of Chapter 340 of the Acts of 1933, providing for an annuity to dependents of a fireman who is killed or dies from injuries received while in the performance of his duty, or take any action relating thereto.

Action taken in conjunction with Article 5.

Voted: That the sum of seven hundred and fifty dollars ($750) be and is hereby appropriated to pay the amount due for the year 1934 for an annuity to the dependents of Willard E. Streeter, deceased, a former member of the Fire Department, said sum to be payable in accordance with the provisions of Chapter 340 of the Acts of 1933.

Voted: That this meeting be and is hereby adjourned until Tuesday evening, April 3, 1934, at 7.30 P. M.

Notice for Adjourned Town Meeting,
Tuesday Evening, April 3, 1934.

Notice is hereby given the legal voters of the Town of Watertown that the Town Meeting called for Monday evening, March 26, 1934 at 7.00 P. M. has been adjourned until Tuesday evening, April 3, 1934, at 7.30 P. M., to meet in the Senior High School Building on Columbia Street, in said Town of Watertown, at which time and place all business called for in the warrant for the Annual Town Meeting of March 5, 1934, from Articles 1 to 24 inclusive, will come before the meeting for consideration and action, with the exception of Articles 1, 2, 3, 4, 9, 20 and 21.

Notice is hereby given that motions to reconsider any or all action taken on salaries at Town Meetings held on March 26, 1934, under Article 5, will be offered at the meeting.

And the legal voters of the Town of Watertown are hereby notified and warned to meet at the time and at the place herein specified, by posting copies of this notice in ten or more conspicuous public places in Town twenty-four hours at least prior to the time of said adjourned meeting, and also by causing a copy of the same to be published in a Watertown newspaper.

Given under our hands this twenty-ninth day of March, A. D. 1934.

P. SARSFIELD CUNNIFF, *Moderator.*

WM. P. McGUIRE, *Town Clerk.*

Clerk's Return on Notice

I have posted copies of the foregoing notice in ten or more conspicuous public places in Town, at least twenty-four hours prior to the time of said adjourned meeting, and have also caused a copy of the same to be published in a Watertown newspaper.

Notices were mailed to the Town Meeting Members at least twenty-four hours prior to the time of said Adjourned Town Meeting of the proposed business to be considered at the meeting.

WILLIAM P. McGUIRE, *Town Clerk.*

Record of Adjourned Town Meeting,
Tuesday Evening, April 3, 1934

Meeting was called to order at 7.30 P. M. by Moderator P. Sarsfield Cunniff. Clerk's return on notice for Adjourned Town Meeting was read by Town Clerk Wm. P. McGuire.

Number of Town Meeting Members necessary for a quorum, 93; number present on April 3rd: 262.

The Town Meeting Members present were sworn in by Town Clerk Wm. P. McGuire, as follows:

"Having been elected Town Meeting Members, you and each of you severally, solemnly swear that you will faithfully and impartially perform the duties pertaining to that office, so help you, God."

Vacancy in Town Meeting Membership Filled

Notice was received from the Chairman of Precinct 1 of the election of James B. Smith, 68 Templeton Parkway, to fill one (1) vacancy in term expiring in 1936, caused by resignation of William R. Curran, 22 Templeton Parkway, this member to serve until the March 1935 Town Election.

Article 5. To grant such sums of money as may be thought necessary for the uses and expenses of the Town for the ensuing year, direct how the same shall be raised, or take any action relating thereto.

The following notice for reconsideration was filed on March 29, 1934, with the Town Clerk:

· "Watertown, Mass., March 29, 1934.

"Mr. Wm. P. McGuire,
    Town Clerk,
      Watertown, Mass.

"Dear Sir:

"Notice is hereby given that motions to reconsider any or all action taken on salaries at Town Meeting held on March 29, 1934, under Article 5, will be offered at the meeting.

"Respectfully yours,

(Signed) JOHN A. COLBERT,"

Record of Appropriations Voted Under Article 5
April 3, 1934

Health and Sanitation ($54,495.00

Health Department: 125 in favor, 105 opposed. Voted:

Salary of Agent	$2,880.00
Salary of Clerk	1,035.00
Salary of Nurses (3)	2,700.00
Contagious Diseases	20,000.00
Baby Clinic	440.00
Dental Clinic	2,500.00
Contingent	1,000.00

Cattle Inspection:

Salary of Veterinarian	540.00

Inspection of Plumbing:

Salary of Inspector	$2,250.00	
Contingencies	100.00	2,350.00

Sewer Department:

Construction	3,050.00
Maintenance	15,000.00
Drainage	3,000.00

Care and Lighting of Highways ($233,171.00)

Highway Department:

Salaries: 132 in the affirmative, 110 opposed. Voted:

Superintendent	$3,240.00	
First Clerk	1,350.00	
Second Clerk	1,125.00	5,715.00
Office Expense		400.00
Vacations		7,284.00
*Construction		28,672.00
Maintenance		65,000.00
Patching Streets, C. W. A.		5,000.00
Stable Maintenance		12,000.00
Garbage Collection		27,500.00
Ashes and Paper		25,000.00
Dust Laying		5,000.00

Betterment Street (See Article 19):

Hill Street, from Fayette Street to Palfrey Street—Special for Construction and Drainage on above street	4,950.00
New 1934 Auto	650.00
Street Lights	40,000.00
Sidewalks	6,000.00

*146 in favor, 22 opposed. Voted: That the sum of twenty-eight thousand, six hundred and seventy-two dollars ($28,672.00) be and is hereby appropriated for the purpose of paying the cost of construction of Irving Street from Mt. Auburn Street to Charles River Road; Marshall Street, from Mt. Auburn Street to Oliver Street; Morse Street, from Galen Street to Watertown Street.

Charities and Soldiers' Benefits ($189,959.73)

Infirmary Department:

Salary of Keeper	$900.00
General Expense	4,929.73

Public Welfare Department:

Salary of Agent	2,000.00

Salary of Visitor—127 in the affirmative, 99 opposed, Voted:	1,200.00
Salary of Clerks (2)—127 in the affirmative, 98 opposed. Voted:	1,800.00
Salary of Male Clerk	1,000.00
Investigators (2)—127 in the affirmative, 100 opposed. Voted:	2,400.00
Contingent	2,000.00
Outside Aid	100,000.00
Mothers' Aid	30,000.00
Old Age Assistance	20,000.00
Town Physician	1,530.00
State Aid	2,200.00
Soldiers' Relief and Military Aid	20,000.00

Schools and Libraries

School Department: Vote for Rollcall:

127 in favor, 94 opposed.

**General Control: Rollcall Vote:

129 in favor, 113 opposed. Voted. $13,700.00

**Moderator Cunniff appointed John A. Collins, Wm. W. Norcross, Jr., and Harold S. Tuck as counters and checkers for rollcall on General Control Appropriation in School Department.

Article 10. To see if the Town will appropriate a sum sufficient to pay the County of Middlesex as required by law on account of assessments levied on the Town for its share of the principal of the Middlesex County Tuberculosis Hospital Funding Loan, Act of 1932, bonds maturing in 1934, issued in compliance with Chapter 10, Acts of 1932, also for any other indebtedness incurred and outstanding under said Chapter 10, also for the Town's share of the cost and interest on said bonds due in 1934, also for the Town's share of the expense incurred under the provisions of Chapter 331 of the Acts of 1933 which provided for the settlement of certain claims of the Commonwealth against the Middlesex County Tuberculosis Hospital District, also for the care, maintenance and repair of said hospital for 1933, and including interest on temporary notes issued therefor, in accordance with sections of Chapter 111 of the General Laws applicable thereto, and for all other expenses in connection therewith, determine how the money shall be raised, or in any way act thereon.

Voted: That the sum of ten thousand dollars ($10,000) this being the Town's share of the principal of the Middlesex County Tuberculosis Hospital Funding Loan, Act of 1932 bonds maturing in 1934, be and the same is hereby appropriated, and that a further sum of three thousand, six hundred ten dollars and forty-eight cents ($3,610.48) be and hereby is appropriated on account of interest and other charges on account thereof. That a further sum of one thousand, six hundred sixty-seven dollars and sixty-seven cents ($1,667.67) be and hereby is appropriated for the Town's share of the expense incurred under the provisions of Chapter 331 of the Acts of 1933, which provided for the settlement of certain claims of the Commonwealth against the Middlesex County Tuberculosis Hospital District. That a further sum of six thousand, five hundred twenty-seven dollars and eight cents $6,527.08) be and hereby is appropriated for the Town's share of the net cost of care, maintenance and repairs of the Middlesex County Hospital, including interest on temporary notes issued therefor, in accordance with sections of Chapter 111 of the General Laws applicable thereto.

Article 19. To hear the report of the Selectmen relative to the laying out of the following-named streets, to wit:

Coolidge Hill Road, from Grove Street to accepted portion of Coolidge Hill Road;

Grandview Avenue, from Gilbert Street to Copeland Street;

Hill Street, from Palfrey Street to Fayette Street;

Nyack Street, from Belmont Street to dead end;
under the provisions of Chapters 82 and 80 of the General
Laws, as amended, the latter providing for the assessment of betterments, and to see if the Town will vote to
accept said streets, or any of them, as and for public ways,
and will authorize the Selectmen to take by eminent domain, or acquire by purchase, or otherwise, any land necessary for said laying out, provide the sum or sums of
money necessary to pay the cost or land damages therefor, and the cost of construction, direct how said money
shall be raised, or take any action relating thereto.

Report of the Selectmen on the Layout of Hill Street

TOWN OF WATERTOWN, MASS.

Selectmen's Office.

March 9, 1934.

After due notice as required by the provisions of Chapter 82 of the General Laws, we, the Selectmen of Watertown, met on the 3rd day of March, A. D. 1934, at 2.15
o'clock P. M., for the purpose of viewing the premises,
and on the 9th day of March A. D. 1934 at 8 o'clock P. M.
for the purpose of a public hearing of all parties interested, on a petition for the laying out of Hill Street as a
public way, and we, the Selectmen, upon consideration of
the matter, do hereby adjudge that public convenience
and necessity require that Hill Street be laid out as and
for a public way, in accordance with the following description, and as shown on a plan drawn by Otis D. Allen, Town
Engineer, and dated February 25, 1934.

Description—Hill Street

Beginning at a point of curvature on the southerly side
of Palfrey Street, four hundred eighty-eight and three-
tenths (488.3) feet, more or less, northwesterly from the
westerly line of Pearl Street, thence turning and extending westerly and southerly along a curved line having a

radius of fifteen (15) feet, twenty-four and seven tenths
(24.7) feet, more or less, to a point of tangency on the
easterly line of Hill Street; thence extending southwest-
erly along the easterly line of Hill Street, four hundred
twenty-one and four hundredths (421.04) feet, more or
less, to a point of tangency; thence turning and extending southerly and easterly along a curved line have a radius of fifteen (15) feet, twenty-three and nine tenths
(23.9) feet, more or less, to a point of curvature on the
northerly line of Fayette Street by land belonging to the
following-named persons whose ownership and assessable
frontages are herewith recorded, consecutively, namely,
Benjamin Rix et ux Anna M., one hundred twenty-two
and seven hundredths (122.07) feet; Thomas J. Crosby,
et ux, Catherine F., one hundred fifty-six and eight
tenths (156.8) feet, comprising two (2) lots, one (1)
of eighty-three and thirteen hundredths (83.13) feet, and
one of seventy-three and sixty-seven hundredths (73.67)
feet; Antonio Dinardo, et ux, Annina and Felice Digiovine,
et ux, Maria, one hundred (100) feet; thence turning and
extending northwesterly along the northerly line of Fayette Street, fifty (50) feet, more or less, to a point of curvature; thence turning and extending easterly and northerly along a curved line having a radius of fifteen (15)
feet, twenty-three and two tenths (23.2) feet, more or
less, to a point of tangency on the westerly line of Hill
Street; thence extending northeasterly along the westerly line of Hill Street, four hundred twenty-six and
thirty-two hundredths (426.32) feet, more or less, to a
point of curvature; thence turning and extending northerly and westerly along a curved line having a radius of
fifteen (15) feet, twenty-two and four tenths (22.4) feet,
more or less, to a point of tangency on the southerly line
of Palfrey Street; by land belonging to the following-
named persons whose ownership and assessable frontages
are herewith recorded consecutively, namely, Patrick J.
McDermott, one hundred fifteen (115) feet; Heirs or Dev-
isees of Bessie S. Wallace, Isaiah H. Wallace, Administra-

tor, sixty-six and five tenths (66.5) feet; Walter L. Hatch and Goldie B. Hatch, sixty-six and forty-two hundredths (66.42) feet; Margaret E. Barry, fifty (50) feet; Joseph P. Quinlan, fifty (50) feet; Alonzo F. Simmons, et ux, Lillian L., one hundred seven (107) feet; thence turning and extending southeasterly along the southerly line of Palfrey Street, fifty and two tenths (50.2) feet, more or less, to a point of curvature and also point of beginning.

The area enclosed by the above description comprises the limits of Hill Street, which is twenty (20) feet in width between parallel lines, extending from the southerly line of Palfrey Street to the northerly line of Fayette Street.

Said street is hereby laid out and the grades thereof established as shown on a plan entitled "Town of Watertown, Plan of Hill Street, to accompany description for acceptance under the Betterment Act, February 15, 1934, Otis D. Allen, Town Engineer," on file in the office of the Town Clerk, a copy of which is to be duly recorded in the South Registry District of Middlesex County with this order.

And it is therefore ORDERED that Hill Street be and is hereby laid out as and for a public way, under the provisions of Chapters 80 and 82 of the General Laws, and amendments thereto according to the foregoing description, and having considered the question of damages sustained by the owners of the lands across and through which said street has been laid out as aforesaid, we hereby determine that no damages have been sustained and none are awarded, other than as shown in the Schedule hereto annexed, and we further order and declare that said laying out is done under Chapter 80 of the General Laws providing for the assessment of betterments, and that the area comprising the several parcels described and set forth in said Schedule hereto annexed, will receive benefit or advantage other than the general advantage of the community from said laying out and that betterments are to be assessed for said laying out upon the parcels of land in said area described in said Schedule and as shown on a plan of said area drawn by Otis D. Allen, Town Engineer, dated February 15, 1934, and on file in the office of the Town Clerk of Watertown, a copy of which is to be duly recorded in Middlesex South District Registry of Deeds with this order, and the amount set opposite each of said described parcels is the amount estimated to be the betterment that will be assessed upon said described parcel.

MAURICE H. O'CONNELL,
JAMES H. SHERIDAN,
EDWARD D. HOLLAND,
Selectmen.

Selectmen's Office.

Watertown, Mass., April 13, 1934.

Whereas, at a Town Meeting held by the Town of Watertown, regularly called and duly warned and held on the 3rd day of April, A. D. 1934, at which meeting a quorum was present when Article 19 of the Warrant was before the meeting as follows:

"To hear the report of the Selectmen relative to the laying out of the following-named street, to wit

Hill Street:

under the provisions of Chapters 82 and 80 of the General Laws, as amended, the latter providing for the assessment of betterments, and to see if the Town will vote to accept said street, as and for a public way, and will authorize the Selectmen to take by eminent domain, or acquire by purchase, or otherwise acquire, any land necessary for said laying out, provide the sum or sums of money necessary to pay the cost or land damages therefor, and the cost of construction, direct how said money shall be raised, or take any action relating thereto."

An order of the Selectmen laying out Hill Street and the report of the Selectmen with reference to said laying out were read to the meeting, and upon motion duly made and seconded it was voted unanimously as follows:

"That the laying out of Hill Street as a public way, as appears in the report of the Selectmen be and is hereby accepted, and the Selectmen are hereby authorized to take the land described in said report as and for a public way."

And whereas, for the purpose of laying out Hill Street as and for a public way, it is necessary to acquire the several parcels of land which are included in the area described in said order of laying out as shown by a copy of said order and plan recorded herewith, and on file in the office of the Town Clerk of Watertown, and the owners, description and areas of each of said parcels are shown in said Schedule.

And whereas, the Selectmen were duly authorized to take said land, and an appropriation was made at said Town Meeting therefor.

Now therefore, it is ordered that the herein described parcels of land, all contained within the area described in the said order of laying out, be and the same are hereby taken for the purposes of a public way, including the easement in the land adjoining the location of said public way consisting of the right to have the land of the location protected by having the surface of the adjoining land slope from the boundary of the location, under the provisions of law authorizing the assessment of betterments, and all according to the plan referred to in said order of laying out, which said plan was duly filed in the office of the Town Clerk more than seven days prior to said Town Meeting.

And all trees upon the land so taken and all structures affixed thereto are not included in said taking.

And the owners and occupants of the land hereby taken and laid out as a public way are allowed until August 1,

1934, to take off and remove trees or structures affixed thereto.

And it is further ordered, upon the consideration of the question of damages sustained by the owners of the land hereby taken, that damages are estimated and awarded as shown on said Schedule.

Adopted:

> MAURICE H. O'CONNELL,
> JAMES H. SHERIDAN,
> EDWARD D. HOLLAND,
> > *Selectmen.*

Schedule

In said Schedule each parcel of land is described as of the first day of April next preceding the date of this order. The persons named in said Schedule are the supposed owners of record as of said first day of April, and in case said owner's name is not correctly stated, it is to be understood that said parcel is owned by owners unknown.

And the number of the lot set opposite each parcel in said Schedule is the number of the lot shown on a plan on file in the office of the Assessors of the Town of Watertown.

Schedule—Hill Street

Side of Street	Area Taken	Front-age	Estimated Betterment	Dam-ages	Owner Address	Lot No.
East	1279	122.07	$488.28	None	Benjamin Rix, et ux, Anna M.,158 Palfrey St., Watertown	3-25-3
East	831	83.13	332.52	None	Thos. J. Crosby, et ux, Catherine F., 15 Hill St., Watertown	3-25-1
East	737	73.67	294.68	None	Thos. J. Crosby, et ux, Catherine F., 15 Hill St., Watertown	3-24-3
East	737	73.67	294.68	None	Elizabeth M. Donahue, 11 Hill St., Watertown	3-24-16 -4
					Antonio Dinardo, et ux, Annina, 89-91 Fayette	

					St., Watertown .... 3_24_15_
					Felice Figiovine, et ux,
					Maria, 89_91 Fayette
East	1050	100.00	400.00	None	St., Watertown .... _5
					Patrick J. McDermott, 95 3_26_3_
West	1197	115.00	460.00	None	Fayette St., Watertown.. _6
					Heirs or Devisees of Bes_
					sie S. Wallace, Isaiah H.
					Wallace, Adm., 12 Hill
West	666	66.5	266.00	None	St., Watertown .... 3_26_4
					Walter L. Hatch, Goldie
					B. Hatch, 18 Hill St.,
West	664	66.42	265.68	None	Watertown .... 3_26_5
					Margaret E. Barry, 22 Hill 3_26_
West	500	50.	200.00	None	St., Watertown .... 6a_4
					Joseph P. Quinlan, 3_26-
					22 Hill Street 6_7B_
West	500	50.	200.00	None	Watertown .... _4
					Alonzo F. Simmons et Lil-
					lian L., 166 Palfrey St., 3_26_
West	111	107.	428.00	None	Watertown .... 7_3

For appropriation, see Schedule under Art. 5—Betterment Street.

Voted: That this meeting be and is hereby adjourned until Wednesday evening, April 11, 1934, at 7:30 P. M., to meet in the Senior High School Building, Columbia St.

Adjourned Annual Town Meeting, April 11, 1934
Notice for Adjourned Annual Town Meeting,
Wednesday Evening, April 11, 1934

Notice is hereby given the legal voters of the Town of Watertown that the Town Meeting called for Tuesday evening, April 3, 1934, at 7:30 P. M. has been adjourned until Wednesday evening, April 11, 1934, at 7:30 P. M., to meet in the Senior High School Building, on Columbia Street, in said Town of Watertown, at which time and place all business called for in the warrant for the Annual Town Meeting of March 5, 1934, from Articles 1 to 24, inclusive, will come before the meeting for consideration and action, with the exception of Articles 1, 2, 3, 4, 9, 10, 19, 20 and 21.

Notice is hereby given that motions to reconsider any or all action taken on salaries at Town Meeting held on

March 26, 1934, or on April 3, 1934, will be offered at the meeting.

Notice is hereby given that reconsideration will be asked on the vote passed under Article 5, appropriating the sum of thirteen thousand, seven hundred dollars ($13,700) for General Control in School Department.

And the legal voters of the Town of Watertown are hereby notified and warned to meet at the time and at the place herein specified, by posting copies of this notice in ten or more conspicuous public places in Town twenty-four hours at least prior to the time of said adjourned meeting, and also by causing a copy of the same to be published in a Watertown newspaper.

Given under our hands this fifth day of April, A. D. 1934.

P. SARSFIELD CUNNIFF, *Moderator,*
WM. P. McGUIRE, *Town Clerk.*

Clerk's Return on Notice

I have posted copies of the foregoing notice in ten or more conspicuous public places in Town, at least twenty-four hours prior to the time of said adjourned meeting, and have also caused a copy of the same to be published in a Watertown newspaper.

Notices were mailed to the Town Meeting Members at least twenty-four hours prior to the time of said Adjourned Town Meeting of the proposed business to be considered at the meeting.

WILLIAM P. McGUIRE, *Town Clerk.*

Record of Adjourned Town Meeting, April 11, 1934

Meeting was called to order at 7:30 P. M. by Moderator P. Sarsfield Cunniff. Clerk's return on notice for Adjourned Town Meeting was read by Town Clerk, Wm. P. McGuire.

Number of Town Meeting Members necessary for a quorum: 93; number present on April 11, 1934; 240.

The Town Meeting Members present were swe 'n in by Town Clerk, Wm. P. McGuire, as follows:

"Having been elected Town Meeting Members, you severally, solemnly swear that you will faithfully and impartially perform the duties pertaining to that office to the best of your ability, so help you, God."

Article 5. To grant such sums of money as may be thought necessary for the uses and expenses of the Town for the ensuing year, direct how the same shall be raised, or take any action relating thereto.

The following notice for reconsideration was filed on April 5, 1934, with the Town Clerk.

"Watertown, Mass., April 5, 1934.

"Mr. Wm. P. McGuire, Town Clerk,

Watertown, Mass.

"Dear Sir:

"Notice is hereby given that motions to reconsider any or all action taken on salaries at Town Meeting held on March 26, 1934, or April 3, 1934, under Article 5, will be offered at the meeting.

"Notice is hereby given that reconsideration will be asked on the vote passed under Article 5 appropriating the sum of thirteen thousand, seven hundred dollars ($13,700) for General Control in School Department.

"Very truly yours,

"JAC:AGM.   (Signed) John A. Colbert."

Record of Appropriations Voted at Adjourned Town Meeting, April 11, 1934

Schools and Libraries ($605,175.00)

	Voted:
School Department:	
General Control	$13,700.00
Instruction—Salaries and Supplies, 126 in favor, 101 opposed	468,860.00
Operation—115 in favor, 105 opposed, Voted:	58,815.00
Maintenance	5,500.00
New Equipment	700.00
Miscellaneous, 114 in favor, 101 opposed	6,400.00
Evening School, 120 in favor, 92 opposed	3,450.00
Trade and Continuation	10,000.00
Transportation	1,500.00
Public Library:	
Salaries	25,250.00
Books, Periodicals and Binding	6,000.00
Maintenance	5,000.00

Recreation ($9,850.00)

Park Department:	
Salary of Superintendent	500.00
Maintenance	2,500.00
Victory Field	2,000.00
Tennis Courts	700.00
Waterproof Grandstand	150.00
Playground Department:	
Salaries	2,200.00
Maintenance	1,500.00
Equipment	300.00

Public Enterprises ($52,085.25)

Water Department.	
Salaries:	
Superintendent	$3,200.00

1st Clerk	1,300.00	
2nd Clerk	1,030.00	$5,536.00
Maintenance		41,300.00
Office Expense		2,125.25
Vacations		1,299.00
New 1934 Car		625.00
New 1934 Truck		1,200.00

Cemeteries ($13,250.00)

Cemetery Department:
Salary of Superintendent	2,000.00
Labor	8,000.00
Contingent	500.00
Tombs and Tool House at Ridgelawn	2,500.00
Lowering Device and Greens	250.00

Public Debt and Interest ($331,000.00)

Town Debt (See Article 6)	216,000.00
Interest	115,000.00

Unclassified ($91,067.02)

Pensions	13,600.00
Memorial Day (See Article 11)	1,100.00
Insurance	10,835.37
Workmen's Compensation	5,000.00
Printing Town Reports	1,159.38
Headquarters for Veterans of Foreign Wars (See Art. 12)	1,080.00
Headquarters Disabled American Veterans (See Art. 13)	360.00
Contingent	2,450.00
Reserve Fund	10,000.00
Unpaid Bills	317.04
County T. B. Assessment (See Art. 10) April 3, 1934	21,805.23
Civil Works Projects (See Art. 17): Highway Department	10,000.00

School Department		2,800.00
Water Department		8,960.00

Special for Committee on Revision of Zoning
By-Law (See Art. 22)   100.00

Annuity for Dependents of Gilbert Nichols
(See Art. 20) March 26, 1934   750.00

Annuity for Dependents of Willard E. Streeter
(See Art. 21) March 26, 1934   750.00

April 11th. After Appropriations for Town Debt and Interest were voted by the meeting, motions were offered to reconsider the votes pertaining to salaries at previous meetings passed on March 26th and April 3rd, which had provided for a reduction of ten per cent (10%) in salaries as compared with the 1932 Appropriations for Salaries, and the meeting then proceeded to increase each salary account by ten per cent (10%) as voted and appearing in the Schedule of Appropriations under Article 5.

Notation. Appropriations indicated by star (*) were increased ten per cent (10%) from the amounts voted at Town Meetings held on March 26th and April 3, 1934.

Official Record of Appropriations Voted at Adjourned Annual Town Meetings, Held on March 26, April 3 and April 11, 1934

Article 5. Voted: That the following sums be and are hereby appropriated for the use of the various Town departments, as indicated in the following Schedule, for the current year beginning January 1, 1934.

General Administration ($82,264.00)

Moderator		
Selectmen's Department:		
*Selectmen's Salaries	$1,500.00	
*Salary of Clerk	500.00	
Miscellaneous	800.00	$2,800.00

Auditor's Department:
*Auditor's Salary	3,300.00	
*Salary of Clerk	1,150.00	
Contingencies	660.00	5,110.00

Treasurer's Department:
*Treasurer's Salary	3,500.00	
*Salary of Clerk	1,150.00	
Extra Clerk Hire	500.00	
Contingencies	1,450.00	6,600.00
Tax Title Foreclosures		2,000.00

Collector's Department (See Art. 9):
*Collector's Salary	3,300.00	
*Salary, 1st Clerk	1,400.00	
*Salary, 2nd Clerk	1,050.00	
*Extra Clerical Services	950.00	
Contingencies	1,500.00	8,200.00
Tax Sale Advertising		1,200.00
Recording Deeds		1,500.00

Assessors' Department:
*Assessors' Salaries	4,100.00	
*Clerks' Salaries	4,789.00	
Contingent	2,000.00	10,889.00
Finance Committee		2,000.00

Legal Services:
*Salary of Town Counsel	2,000.00	
Contingencies	500.00	2,500.00

Town Clerk's Department:
*Town Clerk's Salary	3,500.00	
*Salary, 1st Clerk	1,350.00	
*Salary, 2nd Clerk	1,300.00	
*Salary, 3rd Clerk	1,250.00	
Contingencies	1,500.00	8,900.00

Engineering Department:
*Salaries	13,400.00
Contingent	1,200.00
Used Car	200.00

*Registrars of Voters:
  *Salary of four men at $100 each   400.00
  Printing Voting Lists   600.00

Town Hall:
  *Salary of Janitor   1,600.00
  *Labor   1,400.00
  *Telephone Operator   1,040.00
  Fuel   1,000.00
  Light   1,000.00
  Contingent   500.00
  Extension of Heat in
    Draughting Room   125.00   6,665.00
  Planning Board   100.00

Protection of Persons and Property ($254,951.60)

Police Department, March 26, 1934:
  Salaries:
    Chief $3,200.00
    Lieutenants (3)   7,800.00
    Sergeants (4)   9,800.00
    Patrolmen (37)   80,700.00 $101,500.00
  Special Police   400.00
  Janitor and Wagonman   1,825.00
  Clerk and Wagonman   1,825.00
  Teletype   600.00
  Replace Motorcycles   645.60
  New 1934 Autos   1,156.00
  Radio Equipment   525.00
  Ordnance Equipment   1,100.00
  Contingencies   4,000.00

Fire Department: March 26, 1934:
  Salaries:
    Chief $3,200.00
    Captains (3)   7,800.00
    Lieutenants (4)   9,800.00
    Permanent Men (38)   83,000.00

Call Men (2)	310.00	
Mechanic (1)	2,400.00	106,510.00
Tires — Engine One		250.00
New Hose		1,500.00
Toilets and Repairs		2,000.00
Contingencies		4,000.00

Inspector of Buildings:
*Salary of Inspector	2,600.00	
*Salary of Clerk	250.00	
Contingencies	100.00	2,950.00

Weights and Measures:
*Salary of Sealer	1,800.00	
50 Gal. Auto Measure	150.00	
Contingencies	400.00	2,350.00

Gypsy and Brown Tail Moth Department:
*Salary of Superintendent	800.00
*Salary of Clerk	475.00
Maintenance	2,000.00

Tree Warden:
*Salary of Tree Warden	1,000.00
*Salary of Clerk	200.00
New Trees	400.00
Maintenance	4,000.00

Poles and Wires Department:
Salary of Inspector: March 26, 1934	3,200.00
*Salary of Clerk	475.00
Maintenance	1,400.00
Labor	6,100.00
New 1934 Auto	600.00
Maintenance of Signal Room	865.00
Dog Officer	300.00

Health and Sanitation ($55,540.00)

Health Department:
*Salary of Agent	3,200.00
*Salary of Clerk	1,150.00

*Salary of Nurses (3)		3,000.00
Contagious Diseases		20,000.00
Baby Clinic		440.00
Dental Clinic		2,500.00
Contingent		1,000.00

Cattle Inspection:
*Salary of Veterinarian $600.00

Inspector of Plumbing:

*Salary of Inspector	$2,500.00	
Contingencies	100.00	2,600.00

Sewer Department:

Construction	3,050.00
Maintenance	15,000.00

Drainage 3,000.00

Care and Lighting of Highways ($233,806.00)

Highway Department:
Salaries:

*Superintendent	3,600.00	
*1st Clerk	1,500.00	
*2nd Clerk	1,250.00	6,350.00
Office Expense		400.00
Vacations		7,284.00
Construction:		28,672.00

Irving Street, from Mt. Auburn St. to
Charles River Road, Marshall St. from
Mt. Auburn St. to Oliver St., Morse St.
from Galen St. to Watertown St.

Maintenance	65,000.00
Patching Streets, C. W. A.	5,000.00
Stable Maintenance	12,000.00
Garbage Collection	27,500.00
Ashes and Paper	25,000.00
Dust Laying	5,000.00

Betterment Street (See Art. 19):
Hill St., from Fayette St. to Palfrey St.
Special for Construction and Drainage
  (on above street)   4,950.00
New 1934 Auto   650.00
Street Lights   40,000.00
Sidewalks   6,000.00

Charities and Soldiers' Benefits ($190,360.14)

Infirmary Department:
  *Salary of Keeper   1,000.00
  *General Expense   5,060.14
Public Welfare Department:
  *Salary of Agent   2,000.00
  Salary of Visitor—April 3, 1934   1,200.00
  Salary of Clerks (2)—April 3, 1934   1,800.00
  Salary of Male Clerk—April 3, 1934   1,000.00
  Investigators (2)—April 3, 1934   2,400.00
  Contingent   2,000.00
  Outside Aid   100,000.00
  Mothers' Aid   30,000.00
  Old Age Assistance   20,000.00
*Town Physician   1,700.00
State Aid   2,200.00
Soldiers' Relief and Military Aid   20,000.00

Schools and Libraries ($605,175.00)

School Department:
  General Control $13,700.00
  Instruction — Salaries and Supplies   468,860.00
  Operation   58,815.00
  Maintenance   5,500.00
  New Equipment   700.00
  Miscellaneous   6,400.00
  Evening School   3,450.00
  Trade and Continuation   10,000.00

Transportation	1,500.00
Public Library:	
*Salaries	25,250.00
Books, Periodicals and Binding	6,000.00
Maintenance	5,000.00

Recreation ($9,850.00)

Park Department:	
*Salary of Superintendent	500.00
Maintenance	2,500.00
Victory Field	2,000.00
Tennis Courts	700.00
Waterproof Grandstand	150.00
Playground Department:	
*Salaries	2,200.00
Maintenance	1,500.00
New Equipment	300.00

Public Enterprises ($52,085.25)

Water Department:		
Salaries:		
*Superintendent	$3,200.00	
*1st Clerk	1,300.00	
*2nd Clerk	1,036.00	5,536.00
Maintenance		41,300.00
Office Expense		2,125.25
Vacations		1,299.00
New 1934 Car		625.00
New 1934 Truck		1,200.00

Cemeteries ($13,250.00)

Cemetery Department:	
*Salary of Superintendent	2,000.00
Labor	8,000.00
Contingent	500.00
Tombs and Tool House at Ridgelawn	2,500.00
Lowering Device and Greens	250.00

Public Debt and Interest ($331,000.00)

Town Debt (See Article 6)	216,000.00
Interest	115,000.00

Unclassified ($91,067.02)

Pensions	$13,600.00
Memorial Day (See Article 11)	1,100.00
Insurance	10,835.37
Workmen's Compensation	5,000.00
Printing Town Reports	1,159.38
Headquarters for Veterans of Foreign Wars (See Article 12)	1,080.00
Headquarters for Disabled American Veterans (See Article 13)	360.00
Contingent	2,450.00
Reserve Fund	10,000.00
Unpaid Bills	317.04
County T. B. Assessment (See Art. 10)	21,805.23
Civil Works Projects (See Art. 17)	
Highway Department	10,000.00
School Department	2,800.00
Water Department	8,960.00
Annuity for dependents of Gilbert Nichols (See Article 20)	750.00
Annuity for dependents of Willard E. Streeter (See Article 21)	750.00
Committee for Revision of Zoning By-Law (See Article 22)	100.00

Total Appropriations	$1,919,349.01

April 11th. Voted: That the sum of one million, nine hundred nineteen thousand, three hundred forty-nine dollars and one cent ($1,919,349.01) be and is hereby assessed on the polls and estates for the current year.

Article 6. To see if the Town will vote to appropriate the necessary sum of money to pay that portion of the

Town debt which matures on or previous to January 1, 1935, direct how the money shall be raised, or take any action relating thereto.

Action taken in conjunction with Article 5.

Voted: That the sum of two hundred sixteen thousand dollars ($216,000.) be and is hereby appropriated to pay that portion of the Town debt which matures during the year 1934.

Article 7. To see if the Town will vote to authorize the Treasurer, with the approval of the Selectmen, to refund any or all of the revenue notes issued in anticipation of the revenue of the year 1934, in accordance with the provisions of Section 17 of Chapter 44 of the General Laws; any debt so incurred to be paid from the revenue of 1934.

Voted: That the Treasurer be and he is hereby authorized, with the approval of the Selectmen, to refund any or all of the revenue notes issued in anticipation of the revenue of the year 1934, in accordance with the provisions of Section 17 of Chapter 44 of the General Laws; any debt so incurred to be paid from the revenue of 1934.

Article 8. To see if the Town will vote to authorize the Treasurer, with the approval of the Selectmen, to refund any or all of the revenue notes issued in anticipation of the revenue of the year 1933, in accordance with the provisions of Section 17 of Chapter 44 of the General Laws; any debt so incurred to be paid from the revenue of 1933.

Voted: That the Treasurer be and he is hereby authorized, with the approval of the Selectmen, to refund any or all of the revenue notes issued in anticipation of the revenue of the year 1933, in accordance with the provisions of Section 17 of Chapter 44 of the General Laws; any debt so incurred to be paid from the revenue of 1933.

Article 11. To see if the Town will appropriate a sum of money for the rent of the Grand Army Hall, care of the grounds around the Soldiers' Monument, and to defray the expenses of decorating the graves of deceased soldiers on the next Memorial Day, and authorize Isaac B. Patten Post No. 81, G. A. R. to expend the same, direct how the same shall be raised, or take any action relating thereto.

Action taken in conjunction with Article 5.

Voted: That the sum of eleven hundred dollars ($1100.) be and is hereby appropriated for the rent of the Grand Army Hall, care of the grounds around the Soldiers' Monument, and to defray the expenses of decorating the graves of deceased soldiers on the next Memorial Day, one thousand dollars ($1,000.) to be expended under the direction of Isaac B. Patten Post No. 81, G. A. R., and one hundred dollars ($100.) to be expended under the direction of Watertown Post No. 99, American Legion.

Article 12. To see if the Town will vote to appropriate a sum of money to pay the cost of providing suitable headquarters for Burnham-Manning Post No. 1105, Veterans of Foreign Wars of the United States, direct how the money shall be raised, or take any action relating thereto. (Request of Burnham-Manning Post No.1105, Veterans of Foreign Wars of the United States.)

Action taken in conjunction with Article 5.

Voted: That the sum of one thousand and eighty dollars ($1,080.) be and is hereby appropriated for rent of Headquarters for Burnham-Manning Post No. 1105, Veterans of Foreign Wars of the United States, to be expended under the direction of the Selectmen.

Article 13. To see if the Town will vote to appropriate a sum of money to pay the cost of providing suitable headquarters for Watertown Chapter No. 14, Disabled American Veterans of the World War, direct how the money shall be raised, or take any action relating thereto.

Action taken in conjunction with Article 5.

Voted: That the sum of three hundred and sixty dollars ($360.) be and is hereby appropriated for rent of Headquarters for Watertown Chapter No. 14, Disabled American Veterans of the World War, this money to be expended under the direction of the Selectmen.

Article 14. To see if the Town will vote to accept the provisions of Chapter 136, Sections 21 to 25 inclusive, of General Laws, Tercentenary Edition, relative to certain sports and games permitted on the Lord's Day, or take any action relating thereto. (Request of Mrs. Mary Connors and others.)

Indefinitely postponed.

Article 15. To see if the Town will vote to authorize the School Committee to sell a second-hand bookkeeping machine now in use in the School Department, or take any action relating thereto. (Request of School Committee.)

Indefinitely postponed.

Article 16. To see if the Town will vote to appropriate the sum of twelve hundred dollars ($1200.) to be expended by the School Committee for the purchase of a bookkeeping machine, or take any action relating thereto. (Request of School Committee.)

Indefinitely postponed.

Article 17. To see if the Town will vote to appropriate the sum of twenty-five thousand dollars ($25,000.) to pay the cost of materials, trucking and all other necessary charges arising out of the conduct of Civil Works Administration projects, said sums to be expended under the direction of the Civil Works Administrator, or take any action relating thereto.

Voted: That the sum of ten thousand dollars ($10,000.) be and is hereby appropriated for materials and labor to be expended by the Highway Department, if and when projects are approved under the direction of the Administrator of the E. R. A.

Voted: That the sum of twenty-eight hundred dollars ($2800.) be and is hereby appropriated for materials and labor to be expended by the School Department, if and when projects are approved under the direction of the Administrator of the E. R. A.

Voted: That the sum of eight thousand, nine hundred and sixty dollars ($8,960.) be and is hereby appropriated for materials and labor to be expended by the Water Department, if and when projects are approved under the direction of the Administrator of the E. R. A.

Article 18.   To see if the Town will vote to offer the land owned by the Town of Watertown at the corner of Main and Church Streets now occupied by the old Town Hall and other buildings to the Federal Government as a site for a post office building, or take any action relating thereto. (Request of G. Frederick Robinson and others.)

Indefinitely postponed.

Article 22.   To see if the Town will vote to appoint a committee consisting of the Town Counsel, the Building Inspector, and five members of the Planning Board to study and revise the Zoning By-law, and to appropriate the sum of one hundred dollars ($100.) to pay the cost of advertising, printing, hearings and expert advice, or take any action relating thereto. (Request of the Planning Board.)

Voted: That the Moderator be authorized to appoint a committee, consisting of the Town Counsel, Building Inspector and five members of the Planning Board to study and revise the Zoning By-Law, and to pay the cost of advertising, printing, hearings and expert advice, the sum of one hundred dollars ($100.) be and is hereby appropriated.

Committee Appointed by Moderator Cunniff on May 1, 1934:

Town Counsel, Francis J. McNamara, 5 Lovell Road,

Building Inspector, William H. Wilson, 61-A Phillips Street,

Planning Board: Ernest M. Small, 42 Walnut Street,

Ronald Stone, 100 Russell Avenue,

Massis N. Tomassian, 71 Spruce Street,

Wilfred A. Norris, 47 Emerson Road,

John H. Dardis, 26 Hawthorne Street.

Article 23. To hear the report of the Planning Board relative to a petition of Joseph L. Doherty and others, for an amendment to the Zoning By-Law, by altering the Zoning Map therein referred to, by changing certain property located at the corner of Main and Gleason Streets, as shown on Assessors' Plan of the Town of Watertown, Section 11, Block 23, Lot 28, Plan Lot 62-A and Section 11, Block 23, Lot 1, Plan Lot 62-B, from District 3-C (two-family residence district) to District 2-B (store purposes).

Indefinitely postponed.

Article 24. To see if the Town will vote to accept a deed from Abby M. Gardner and Mabelle W. Dickinson for public purposes of a certain lot of land located on Winter Street, Watertown, containing approximately forty-five hundred twelve (4512) square feet, or take any action relating thereto.

Voted: That the Selectmen be and they are hereby authorized on behalf of the Town to accept a deed from Abby M. Gardner and Mabelle W. Dickinson for public purposes of a certain lot of land located on Winter Street, Watertown, containing approximately forty-five hundred twelve (4512) square feet.

WILLIAM P. McGUIRE, *Town Clerk.*

Warrant for Party Primary Election, Tuesday, April 24, 1934

Commonwealth of Massachusetts.   Middlesex, ss.

To any Constable in the Town of Watertown, Greeting:

In the name of the Commonwealth of Massachusetts, you are hereby required to notify and warn the legal voters of said town who are qualified to vote in Primaries to meet in their respective voting places in said town:

Precincts 1, 2 and 3—East End Fire Station, Mt. Auburn Street.

Precincts 4 and 5—Senior High School Bldg., Columbia Street.

Precincts 5, 7 and 8—Administration Building, Main Street.

Precincts 9 and 10—West Junior High School Building, Waverley Avenue.

on Tuesday, the twenty-fourth day of April, 1934, at 2 P. M., for the following purposes:

To bring in their votes to the Primary Officers for the ELECTION of Candidates of Political Parties for the following offices:

District Member of State Committee for each political party for the Fifth Senatorial District; Fifty (50) Members of the Democratic Town Committee; Fifty Members of the Republican Town Committee; Five (5) Delegates to State Convention of the Democratic Party; Four (4) Delegates to State Convention of the Republican Party.

All the above candidates are to be voted for upon one ballot.

THE POLLS WILL BE OPEN FROM 2 P. M. TO 8 P. M..

And you will notify and warn the legal voters of the Town of Watertown to meet at the times and at the places herein specified, by leaving at every inhabited house in Town a printed copy of this warrant, and also by posting copies of the same in ten or more conspicuous public places in Town, seven days at least prior to the time of said meeting.

Hereof fail not, and make return of this warrant, with your doings thereon, into the office of the Town Clerk on or before the time of said meeting.

Given under our hands this sixth day of April, A. D. 1934.

MAURICE H. O'CONNELL,
JAMES H. SHERIDAN,
EDWARD D. HOLLAND,
Selectmen of Watertown.

Officers' Return on Warrant

As required by the foregoing warrant, I have notified and warned the legal voters of the Town of Watertown to meet at the times and at the places herein specified, by leaving at every inhabited house in Town a printed copy of this warrant, and also by posting copies of the same in ten or more conspicuous public places in Town seven days at least prior to the time of said meeting.

JOSEPH W. REGAN,
Constable of Watertown.

Attest: WM. P. McGUIRE, *Town Clerk.*

Record of Party Primary Election, April 24, 1934

The polls were opened at 2 P. M., and voting continued until 8 P. M., at which time the polls were closed.

The following election officers were present:

Precincts 1, 2 and 3. Eugene L. Storey, Warden; Joseph J. Morley, Clerk. Inspectors and Counters: William B. Glidden, Bernard Morley, Arthur J. McCarthy, Helen L. Boudreau, Mabel C. MacNutt, Pearl A. Baxter, Richard M. Hatch, William J. Holland.

Precincts 4 and 6.   Edith M. Beck, Warden, John B. Watson, Clerk. Inspectors and Counters: ·Lavinia Jensen, Ruth Peppard, Madeline E. Van Dyke, Katherine Landry, . S. Alice Youngman, Lester A. Murphy. Counters: From 9 P. M.: Waldo P. Emerson, Thomas A. Blake, Harry E. Youngman, Percy J. Van Dyke.

Precincts 5, 7 and 8.   Harry J. York, Warden, John T. Gleason, Clerk. Inspectors and Counters: Margaret Walker, Grace M. Olson, Ernestine P. Howe, Wallace A. Shipton, Daniel J. Clifford, Allan Kimball, Joseph H. Bussey, Joseph W. Andrews. Counters from 9:30 P. M., Daniel J. Walker, Lester E. Markham.

Precincts 9 and 10.   James J. O'Connell, Warden, Frederick E. Owen, Clerk. Inspectors and Counters: Frances Delaney, Mollie E. Smith, Anna V. Hughes, Emma R. Roche, Mildred Upit, Ellen B. Lougee.

DEMOCRATIC

(Total Vote Cast: 866)

STATE COMMITTEE—Fifth Middlesex District

Precincts	1-2-3	4-6	5-7-8	9-10	Total
P. Gerard Cahill of Waltham	12	12	13	8	45
James H. Sheridan of Watertown	150	90	232	103	575
Blanks	85	37	80	44	246

DELEGATES TO STATE CONVENTION

Watertown					
Michael F. Casey	34	23	35	22	114
*Charles P. Colligan	140	62	194	83	479
*Charles F. J. Harrington	80	96	96	72	344
*Edmund P. Hickey	68	33	192	70	363
Ralph W. Kearns .	13	11	61	12	97
Leo P. Landry	48	63	60	44	215
J. Vincent MacDonough	51	39	104	60	254
Florence F. McAuliffe	28	35	68	31	162
Edward G. McNamara	64	34	72	36	206
Daniel J. Murphy	50	45	78	34	207
*John A. Murray	144	46	85	48	323
James J. O'Brien	63	8	24	7	102
James Phelan	52	24	42	55	173
*James H. Sheridan	160	72	237	104	573
Blanks	240	104	277	97	718
*Elected					

DEMOCRATIC TOWN COMMITTEE

Precincts	1-2-3	4-6	5-7-8	9-10	Total
*A. A. Foley	124	93	153	99	469
*John H. Dardis	131	90	160	104	485
*John P. Gallagher	135	92	165	116	508
*Mary C. Corcoran	127	91	157	105	480
*Joseph Hyde	128	88	145	109	470
*Charles P. Colligan	154	99	167	116	536
*Sadie E. Nichols	131	92	148	103	474
*John J. Dugan	113	80	148	99	440
*Thomas J. Galligan	122	87	146	98	453
*Ellen Linehan	115	82	144	93	434
*J. Vincent MacDonough	132	90	155	115	492
*James E. Keenan	113	83	137	94	427
*Joseph G. Perkins	122	81	136	104	443
*John J. Mahoney	121	83	139	100	443
*John T. O'Connor	120	84	139	102	445
*Edmund P. Hickey	140	93	154	110	497
*Maurice H. Costello	125	87	143	107	462
*Florence F. McAuliffe	121	90	148	100	459
*Peter H. Duffy	128	82	138	93	441
*John C. O'Driscoll	134	85	137	90	446
*John P. Oates	155	98	152	108	513
*Edward A. Oates	152	98	145	101	496
*Daniel H. Murphy	135	84	144	99	462
*John J. Curran	151	89	138	95	473
*Isabel M. Fitzmaurice	115	79	136	88	418
*Neal T. Curran	138	82	139	91	450
*Mary McCarron	112	82	141	91	426
*Edward G. Cousineau	133	90	148	105	476
*Patrick A. Menton	150	101	154	118	523
*Warren J. Eastman	113	81	140	104	438
*Cornelius P. Delaney	127	88	139	100	454
*Michael J. Harrington	129	101	143	115	488
*Robert J. Carney	117	86	140	104	447
*Helen E. Murphy	117	85	140	89	431
*Effie Comstock	118	83	152	89	442
*Thomas F. Campbell	113	79	138	95	425
*Andrew E. McDermott	123	88	146	94	451
*John M. Russell	118	90	137	97	442
*Charles F. J. Harrington	123	102	140	99	464
*Edward F. Morley	123	83	140	95	441
*John P. Monahan	123	91	143	95	452
*Edward G. McNamara	127	92	142	110	471
*George J. Gaffney	120	87	141	94	442
*Edmund F. Jones	110	83	131	90	414
*Sadie A. Dugan	112	81	139	90	422
*John F. Collins	119	93	142	95	449
*William S. Andrews	128	85	148	107	468
*Leo P. Landry	0	1	1	4	6
Scattering	10	1	6	5	22
Blanks	6403	2815	9446	3026	21,690

*Elected

REPUBLICAN
(Total Vote Cast: 1023)

STATE COMMITTEE—Fifth Middlesex District

Precincts	1-2-3	4-6	5-7-8	9-10	Total
Madge Nourse Ray of Hudson	117	275	190	41	623
Scattering	0	1	0	0	1
Blanks	103	135	121	40	399

DELEGATES TO STATE CONVENTION

*George H. Dale	135	283	202	50	670
Clarence W. Dealtry	85	161	117	25	388
Irving E. Grundy	45	80	80	6	164
James L. Haddie	33	58	48	22	161
*Andrew T. Johnson	93	233	179	42	547
*Norman D. MacKay	99	201	142	53	495
*Elizabeth A. Perkins	100	245	221	32	598
Elizabeth L. Tarbell	56	145	85	8	294
Earle S. Tyler	117	142	101	35	395
Blanks	117	96	116	51	380

REPUBLICAN TOWN COMMITTEE—Group 1

James L. Haddie	7	28	13	5	53
Group 2					
*William H. Lucas	116	292	211	43	662
*George H. Dale	105	278	205	47	635
*Edward P. Furber	111	286	212	48	657
*Arnold Leonard	106	286	212	40	644
*Eric L. Johnson	113	298	214	49	674
*Clifford S. Lovell	114	285	205	41	645
*Andrew T. Johnson	107	277	198	44	626
*Ruth N. Hull	106	260	191	39	596
*David E. Fitzgerald	89	253	173	42	557
*Leon M. Lamb	93	283	203	46	625
*Eva L. Shipton	104	277	205	41	627
*Robert S. Quinby	111	282	195	38	626
*Harry G. Elwell	107	275	190	41	613
*Lester E. Markham	94	272	201	38	605
*Samuel G. Thayer	101	277	200	38	616
*William C. MacGregor	96	262	185	39	582
*Sylvester M. Loring	111	301	217	42	671
*Melvin V. Meldon	99	284	208	36	627
*Harold B. Blazo	108	292	215	42	657
*Harrie E. Waite	107	288	207	36	638
*Harold I. Hunt	100	265	191	48	599
*Ernest M. Small	105	271	193	39	608
*Margaret T. Boutelle	95	259	181	35	570
*Dickran H. Boyajian	88	245	169	38	540
*George C. Campbell	101	279	203	40	623

Precincts	1-2-3	4-6	5-7-8	9-10	Total
*Caleb S. Newell	98	260	182	41	581
*Clarence L. Frounfelker	92	282	195	40	609
*Elizabeth L. Tarbell	95	268	180	38	581
*Doris L. Erskine	106	293	204	41	644
*Edward C. Hall	106	281	198	40	625
*L. Bennett Turner	104	281	191	33	609
*Charles F. Sanborn	112	281	195	43	631
*Walter C. Stone	116	290	211	40	657
*James G. Grower	94	278	193	39	604
*Albert L. Partridge	112	270	186	35	603
*Ronald M. Stone	108	289	206	41	644
*Harold C. Everett	110	290	204	39	643
*William M. Emerson	104	272	193	41	610
*Roland B. Macdonald	102	272	186	37	597
*George B. Wellman	109	267	196	40	612
*Hewitt G. Fletcher	105	287	193	40	625
*W. Stanley Field	108	268	195	36	607
*Earle S. Tyler	107	267	184	43	601
*Ralph C. Gardiner	108	265	186	33	592
*Agnes G. Page	103	254	183	36	576
*Kevork Der Bogosian	89	246	171	33	539
*Norman D. MacKay	102	283	191	46	622
*Anthony Julian	92	252	183	39	566
*Guy C. Pesce	92	244	181	37	554
*Carmine Tocci	88	250	179	41	558

*Elected.

REPUBLICAN TOWN COMMITTEE
Group 3

	1-2-3	4-6	5-7-8	9-10	Total
Shahin A. Ajemian	44	64	59	15	182
Herbert C. Harting	47	73	58	23	201
Catherine A. E. Harcourt	52	99	69	16	236
Norman D. MacKay	45	78	56	22	201
Elizabeth A. Perkins	63	105	87	19	274
Clarence W. Dealtry	53	87	65	21	226
Earle S. Tyler	46	75	49	19	189
Charles F. Shaw	62	96	78	25	261
Wallace E. McCarthy	41	61	49	20	171
Carl W. Johnson	62	87	61	22	232
Charles J. Cassese	36	80	60	25	201
William I. Norrish	40	81	61	26	208
Bernice L. Campbell	51	78	66	18	213
Agnes G. Page	46	68	51	17	182
Harold S. Tuck	55	77	55	17	204
Frederick M. Balsor	38	57	49	18	162
Leland C. Bixby	47	99	73	21	240
Roland M. Stone	46	86	49	19	200
Nazzareno A. Toscano	39	58	57	18	172
Edward C. Hall	43	79	41	22	185
Ralph Joseph Thibodeau	36	63	51	13	163
Anthony Tocci	36	60	52	22	170
George B. Wellman	45	78	44	16	183
Winthrop G. Rockwell	49	102	79	24	254
William W. Rugg	50	94	72	24	240

Precincts	1-2-3	4-6	5-7-8	9-10	Total
Frederick Bell	47	91	64	24	226
Arthur L. Morse	48	95	76	23	242
Frank T. Bobst	37	66	47	14	164
William A. Eagleson	42	68	56	25	191
Ruth E. Hall	45	83	62	19	209
Leonard Owen	40	61	48	23	172
Roland B. Macdonald	44	87	44	16	191
Gardner F. Packard	43	81	62	21	207
Anne M. Davis	39	73	52	20	184
Delbert J. Kendall	43	65	52	17	177
Carl E. Withee	41	73	61	19	194
Blanks	4203	3977	3672	1325	13177

Result of count of votes cast at Party Primary for State Committees and Delegates to State Conventions was forwarded to the Secretary of the Commonwealth, and notices were sent to the Democratic and Republican Town Committes of the Delegates elected to State Conventions and members elected to Town Committees, also notices were sent to individuals elected as Delegates to State Conventions and as members of Town Committees.

WM. P. McGUIRE, *Town Clerk.*

Warrant for Town Meeting, Monday Evening, August 13, 1934

Commonwealth of Massachusetts.   Middlesex, ss.

To any Constable in the Town of Wttertown, Greeting:

In the name of the Commonwealth of Massachusetts, you are hereby required to notify and warn the legal voters of the Town of Watertown to meet in the Senior High School Building, Columbia Street, in said Town, on Monday evening, the thirteenth day of August, 1934, at 7:30 P. M., to act on the following articles, viz:

Article 1. To hear the report of any Committee heretofore appointed, and act thereon.

Article 2. To see if the Town will vote to provide by transfer or otherwise, such sums of money as may be necessary for the use of the various Town Departments for the balance of the current year, direct how the same shall be provided, or take any action relating thereto.

Article 3. To see if the Town will vote to appropriate the sum of $45,500. for the use of the Outside Aid Department, direct how the money shall be provided, or take any action relating thereto.

Article 4. To see if the Town will vote to appropriate the sum of $400. for the use of the Assessors' Department, direct how the same shall be provided, or take any action relating thereto.

Article 5. To see if the Town will vote to appropriate the sum of $500. for the use of the Tax Collector's department, direct how the same shall be provided, or take any action relating thereto.

Article 6. To see if the Town will vote to appropriate the sum of $1536. for the use of the Poles and Wires Department, direct how the same shall be provided, or take any action relating thereto.

Article 7. To see if the Town will vote to appropriate and provide by transfer or otherwise, for the use of the School Department, the sum of Four Thousand Eighty-four dollars, as follows:

From Instruction to General Control	$ 834.00
From Instruction to Operation	3,200.00
From Instruction to Unpaid Bills	50.00
Total	$4,084.00

or take any action relating thereto.

Article 8. To see if the Town will vote to appropriate the sum of $3,000. for the use of the Treasurer's Department, as follows:

Clerical Services	$ 250.00
Tax Titles	2,750.00
Total	$3,000.00

direct how the same shall be provided, or take any action relating thereto.

Article 9. To see if the Town will vote to appropriate the sum of $20,000, for the use of the Soldiers' Relief Department, direct how the money shall be provided, or take any action relating thereto.

Article 10. To see if the Town will authorize the Selectmen to purchase or take by right of eminent domain the tract of land containing approximately 180,557 square feet of land, more or less, located on Arlington Street, for Playground purposes, bounded as follows:—

Northerly by land now or formerly of Susan F. Brown, et al, and land now or formerly of Wilfred A. Norris, 453.77 sq. ft.

Easterly by land now or formerly of Herbert Coolidge, et al, 363.17 sq. ft.

Southerly by land now or formerly of Thomas O'Connell, and land now or formerly of Lillian P. Ellis, 409 sq. ft.

Westerly by Arlington St. 475 sq. ft.

Being shown on plan of land in Watertown by Aspinwall & Lincoln, Civil Engineers, dated November 7, 1929, appropriate a sum of money to pay the cost of the same, direct how the money shall be raised, or take any action relating thereto.

Article 11. To hear the report of the Planning Board relative to a petition and hearing of Joseph L. Doherty et al to change the Zoning By-law to affect the Zoning of a parcel of land shown on the Assessors' plan of the Town Section 11, Block 23, Lot 28, Plan Lot 62-B at the corner of Gleason and Main Streets from District 3-C (two family residence purposes) to District 2-B (store purposes). (Request of Planning Board.)

Article 12. To see if the Town will vote to appropriate the sum of $30,000. for the purchase of materials and supplies in connection with E. R. A. projects in the Engineering, Highway, Cemetery, Park and Public Buildings Department, direct how the money shall be provided, or take any action relating thereto.

Article 13. To see if the Town will vote to appropriate the sum of $92. to reimburse Edward D. Holland for expenses incurred for out of State trip to Washington in connection with the Public Works Program, or take any action relating thereto.

Article 14. To see if the Town will vote to appropriate the sum of $8200. to pay the cost of surfacing sidewalks prepared for finishing through C. W. A. appropriations during the year 1933, direct how the money shall be provided, or take any action relating thereto.

Article 15. To see if the Town will vote to appropriate $2100. necessary to pay the cost of employment of four (4) permanent operators for balance of year 1934 in connection with the Fire Alarm Signal System, direct how the money shall be provided, or take any action relating thereto.

Article 16. To see if the Town will vote to appropriate the sum of $200. for the use of Legal Service Contingent Department, direct how the money shall be provided, or take any action relating thereto.

Article 17. To see if the Town will vote to appropriate from the sum of $19,579.84 received from the City of Boston in payment of accounts with the Welfare Department, the sum of $16,664.10 for the payment of accounts due from the Welfare Department to the City of Boston for the years 1928 to 1932 inclusive, or direct how said money shall be raised, or take any action relating thereto.

Article 18. To hear the report of the Selectmen relative to the laying out of Quincy Street, as and for a public highway, from Palfrey Street to Fitchburg Street, direct how the necessary money may be provided to pay the cost of construction, or take any action relating thereto.

Article 19. To see if the Town will vote to appropriate the sum of $1800. to pay the cost of reconstruction of bridges, direct how the money shall be provided, or take any action relating thereto.

Article 20. To see if the Town will appropriate the sum of $275. for the purpose of changes in main heating system so that Fire Alarm Signal System may be operated independently after closing hours.

Article 21. To see if the Town will vote to amend the vote under Article 4 of the Town Meeting of December 18, 1933, so as to authorize the Treasurer with the approval of the Selectmen, to borrow from any source such sums of money as may be necessary to provide the sum of $20,000. appropriated to pay the cost of construction of sidewalks under the National Industrial Recovery Act, or take any action relating thereto.

Article 22. To see if the Town will vote to amend the vote under Article 5 of the Town Meeting of December 18, 1933, so as to authorize the Treasurer with the approval of the Selectmen, to borrow from any source such sums of money as may be necessary to provide the sum of $40,355. appropriated to pay the cost of construction of streets under the National Industrial Recovery Act, or take any action relating thereto.

Article 23. To see if the Town will vote to amend the vote under Article 6 of the Town Meeting of December 18, 1933, so as to authorize the Treasurer with the approval of the Selectmen, to borrow from any source such sums of money as may be necessary to provide the sum of $25,000. appropriated to pay the cost of construction of sewers and drains under the National Industrial Recovery Act, or take any action relating thereto.

Article 24. To see if the Town will vote to amend the vote under Article 7 of the Town Meeting of December 18, 1933, so as to authorize the Treasurer, with the approval of the Selectmen, to borrow from any source such sums of money as may be necessary to provide the sum of $25,000. appropriated to pay the cost of construction of water mains under the National Industrial Recovery Act, or take any action relating thereto.

Article 25. To see if the Town will vote to amend the vote under Article 8 of the Town Meeting of December 18, 1933, so as to authorize the Treasurer, with the approval of the Selectmen, to borrow from any source such sums of money as may be necessary to provide the sum of $135,000. appropriated to pay the cost of construction of an addition to the Senior High School, under the National Industrial Recovery Act, or take any action relating thereto.

Article 26. To see if the Town will vote to amend the vote under Article 10 of the Town Meeting of December 18, 1933, so as to authorize the Treasurer, with the approval of the Selectmen, to borrow from any source such sums of money as may be necessary to provide the sum of $35,229. appropriated to pay the cost of construction of an addition to the Main Branch of the Free Public Library, under the National Industrial Recovery Act, or take any action relating thereto.

And you will notify and warn the legal voters of the Town of Watertown to meet at the time and at the place herein specified, by leaving at every inhabited house in Town a printed copy of this warrant, and also by posting copies of the same in ten or more conspicuous public places in Town, seven days at least prior to the time of said meeting.

Hereof fail not, and make return of this warrant, with your doings thereon into the office of the Town Clerk on or before the time of said meeting.

Given under our hands this twentieth day of July, A. D. 1934.

MAURICE H. O'CONNELL,
JAMES H. SHERIDAN,
EDWARD D. HOLLAND,
                    Selectmen of Watertown.

Officers' Returns On Warrant

As required by the foregoing warrant, I have notified and warned the legal voters of the Town of Watertown to meet at the time and at the place herein specified, by leaving at every inhabited house in Town a printed copy of this warrant, and also by posting copies of the same in ten or more conspicuous public places in Town seven days at least prior to the time of said meeting.

JOSEPH W. REGAN,
Constable of Watertown.

Attest: WM. P. McGUIRE, *Town Clerk.*

. Notices were mailed to the Town Meeting Members at least seven days prior to the Town Meeting of the proposed business to be considered at the meeting.

WM. P. McGUIRE, *Town Clerk.*

Record of Town Meeting, Monday Evening, August 13, 1934

Meeting was called to order at 7:45 P. M., by Moderator P. Sarsfield Cuniff. Officers' returns on warrant were read by Town Clerk, Wm. P. McGuire.

Vacancies, Town Meeting Members:

Precinct 3: John McCree was appointed to fill a vacancy in term expiring in 1935; Hadar Peterson was appointed to fill a vacancy in term expiring in 1936.

Precinct 5: John J. Dugan was appointed to fill a vacancy in term expiring in 1935.

Precinct 8: John A. Kimball, Jr., was appointed to fill vacancy in term expiring in 1935; George Slamin was appointed to fill vacancy in term expiring in 1936.

Precinct 9: Through error Elizabeth D. Shriver and J. Vincent MacDonough were appointed to fill one vacancy in term expiring in 1936.

The counters reported that there were 171 Town Meeting Members present; number necessary for a quorum: 93.

The following shows representation from the various precincts:

Virtue of Office	15
Finance Committee	17
Precinct 1	11
Precinct 2	9
Precinct 3	14
Precinct 4	14
Precinct 5	13
Precinct 6	18
Precinct 7	18
Precinct 8	17
Precinct 9	15
Precinct 10	10
Total	171

Article 1. To hear the report of any Committee heretofore appointed, and act thereon.

No action.

Article 2. To see if the Town will vote to provide by transfer or otherwise, such sums of money as may be necessary for the use of the various Town Departments for the balance of the current year, direct how the same shall be provided, or take any action relating thereto.

Finance Committee recommended and it was—

Voted: That the sum of $76.61 be appropriated for a Mechanician in the Police Department from September 1st, this sum to be placed on the tax levy for the current year.

Article 3. To see if the Town will vote to appropriate the sum of $45,500. for the use of the Outside Aid Department, direct how the money shall be provided, or take any action relating thereto.

Finance Committee recommended and it was—
Voted: That the sum of $44,000. be appropriated for the use of the Outside Aid Department and that this sum be placed on the tax levy for the current year.

Article 4.   To see if the Town will vote to appropriate the sum of $400. for the use of the Assessors' Department, direct how the same shall be provided, or take any action relating thereto.

Finance Committee recommended and it was—
Voted: That the sum of $400. be appropriated for the use of the Assessors' Department, same to be placed on the tax levy for the current year.

Article 5.   To see if the Town will vote to appropriate the sum of $500. for the use of the Tax Collector's Department, direct how the same shall be provided, or take any action relating thereto.

Finance Committee recommended and it was—
Voted: That the sum of $100 be appropriated for the use of the Tax Collector's Department, said sum to be placed on the tax levy for the current year. Motion to increase this sum by $400. defeated.

Article 6.   To see if the Town will vote to appropriate the sum of $1536. for the use of the Poles and Wires Department, direct how the same shall be provided, or take any action relating thereto.

Finance Committee recommended and it was—
Voted: That the sum of $1,536. be appropriated for the use of the Poles and Wires Department, said sum to be placed on the tax levy for the current year.

Article 7.   To see if the Town will vote to appropriate and provide by transfer or otherwise, for the use of the School Department, the sum of Four Thousand Eighty-four dollars, as follows:

From Instruction to General Control .. $ 834.00
From Instruction to Operation 3,200.00

From Instruction to Unpaid Bills 50.00

Total $4,084.00

or take any action relating thereto.

Finance Committee recommended and it was—

Voted: That the sum of $4,084. be appropriated to be transferred from the Instruction Appropriation in the School Department to—

General Control .... $ 834.00
Operation 3,200.00
Unpaid Bills 50.00

Total $4,084.00

Article 8. To see if the Town will vote to appropriate the sum of $3,000.00 for the use of the Treasurer's Department, as follows:

Clerical Services .... $ 250.00
Tax Titles 2,750.00

Total $3,000.00

direct how the same shall be provided, or take any action relating thereto.

Finance Committee recommended and it was—

Voted: That the sum of $2,750, be appropriated for the Foreclosure of Tax Titles in the Treasurer's Department, this amount to be placed on the tax levy for the current year. Motion to appropriate $250. for clerical services defeated.

Article 9. To see if the Town will vote to appropriate the sum of $20,000. for the use of the Soldiers' Relief Department, direct how the money shall be provided, or take any action relating thereto.

Finance Committee recommended and it was—

Voted: That the sum of $20,000. be appropriated for the use of the Soldiers' Relief Department, this amount to be placed on the tax levy for the current year.

Article 10. To see if the Town will authorize the Selectmen to purchase or take by right of eminent domain the tract of land containing approximately 180,557 square feet of land, more or less, located on Arlington Street, for Playground purposes, bounded as follows:—

Northerly by land now or formerly of Susan F. Brown, et al, and land now or formerly of Wilfred A. Norris, 453.77 sq. ft.

Easterly by land now or formerly of Herbert Coolidge, et al, 363.17 sq. ft.

Southerly by land now or formerly of Thomas O'Connell, and land now or formerly of Lillian P. Ellis, 409 sq. ft.

Westerly by Arlington St. 475 sq. ft.

Being shown on plan of land in Watertown by Aspinwall & Lincoln, Civil Engineers, dated Nov. 7, 1929, —— appropriate a sum of money to pay the cost of the same, direct how the money shall be raised, or take any action relating thereto.

Indefinitely postponed.

Article 11. To hear the report of the Planning Board relative to a petition and hearing of Joseph L. Doherty et al to change the Zoning By-law to affect the Zoning of a parcel of land shown on the Assessors' plan of the Town, Section 11, Block 23, Lot 28, Plan Lot 62-B at the corner of Gleason and Main Streets from District 3-C (two family residence purposes) to District 2-B (store purposes). (Request of Planning Board.)

Indefinitely postponed.

Article 12. To see if the town will vote to appropriate the sum of $30,000 for the purchase of materials and supplies in connection with E. R. A. projects in the Engineering, Highway, Cemetery, Park and Public Buildings Departments, direct how the money shall be provided, or take any action relating thereto.

Finance Committee recommended and it was—

Voted: That the sum of $20,000. be appropriated for the use of the E. R. A. projects in the Engineering, Highway, Cemetery, Park and Public Buildings Departments, this sum to be placed on the tax levy for the current year, the same to be spent under the direction of the local Administrator of the E. R. A.

Article 13.   To see if the Town will vote to appropriate the sum of $92. to reimburse Edward D. Holland for expenses incurred for out of State trip to Washington in connection with the Public Works Program, or take any action relating thereto.

Finance Committee recommended and it was—

Voted: That the sum of $92.00 be appropriated to reimburse Edward D. Holland for expenses incurred in trip to Washington in connection with Public Works program, this amount to be placed on the tax levy for the current year.

Article 14.   To see if the Town will vote to appropriate the sum of $8200. to pay the cost of surfacing sidewalks prepared for finishing through C. W. A. appropriations during the year 1933, direct how the money shall be provided, or take any action relating thereto.

Finance Committee recommended and it was—

Voted: That the sum of $4,000. be appropriated to pay the cost of surfacing sidewalks prepared for finishing through C. W. A. appropriations during the year 1933, this amount to be placed on the tax levy for the current year.

Article 15.   To see if the Town will vote to appropriate $2100. necessary to pay the cost of employment of four (4) permanent operators for balance of year 1934 in connection with the Fire Alarm Signal System, direct how the money shall be provided, or take any action relating thereto.

Voted: That this matter be referred to the Selectmen for further investigation and report at a later meeting.

Article 16. To see if the Town will vote to appropriate the sum of $200. for the use of Legal Service Contingent Department, direct how the money shall be provided, or take any action relating thereto.

Finance Committee recommended and it was—

Voted: That the sum of $200. be appropriated for the use of Legal Service Contingent Department, this amount to be placed on the tax levy for the current year.

Article 17. To see if the Town will vote to appropriate from the sum of $19,579.84 received from the City of Boston in payment of accounts with the Welfare Department, the sum of $16,664.10 for the payment of accounts due from the Welfare Department to the City of Boston for the years 1928 to 1932 inclusive, or direct how said money shall be raised, or take any action relating thereto.

Finance Committee recommended and it was—

Voted: That the sum of $16,664.10 be appropriated for the purpose of paying accounts due from Welfare Department to the City of Boston for the years 1928 to 1932 inclusive, said payment to be made if and when the City of Boston pays to the Town of Watertown the sum of $19,579.84 due the Town of Watertown from the City of Boston for Welfare accounts for the years 1928 to 1932, inclusive, said sum ($16,664.10) to be placed on the tax levy for the current year.

Article 18. To hear the report of the Selectmen relative to the laying out of Quincy Street, as and for a public highway, from Palfrey Street to Fitchburg Street, direct how the necessary money may be provided to pay the cost of construction, or take any action relating thereto.

Indefinitely postponed.

Article 19. To see if the Town will vote to appropriate the sum of $1800. to pay the cost of reconstruction of bridges, direct how the money shall be provided, or take any action relating thereto.

Finance Committee recommended and it was—

Voted: That the sum of $1800. be appropriated to pay the cost of reconstruction of bridges, said sum to be placed on the tax levy for the current year.

Article 20. To see if the Town will appropriate the sum of $275. for the purpose of changes in main heating system so that Fire Alarm Signal System may be operated independently after closing hours.

Finance Committee recommended and it was—

Voted: That the sum of $275. be appropriated for the purpose of making changes in main heating system in the Fire Alarm Signal Room to provide for independent operation after closing hours, said sum to be placed on the tax levy for the current year.

Article 21. To see if the Town will vote to amend the vote under Article 4 of the Town Meeting of December 18, 1933, so as to authorize the Treasurer with the approval of the Selectmen, to borrow from any source such sums of money as may be necessary to provide the sum of $20,000. appropriated to pay the cost of construction of sidewalks under the National Industrial Recovery Act, or take any action relating thereto.

By a two-thirds vote the following motion was adopted:

Voted: That the vote under Article 4 of the Town Meeting of December 18, 1933, be amended by adding thereto the following: "said sum to be borrowed from any source by the Treasurer with the approval of the Selectmen."

Article 22. To see if the Town will vote to amend the vote under Article 5 of the Town Meeting of December 18, 1933, so as to authorize the Treasurer with the approval of the Selectmen, to borrow from any source such sums of money as may be necessary to provide the sum of $40,355. appropriated to pay the cost of construction of streets under the National Industrial Recovery Act, or take any action relating thereto.

By a two-thirds vote the following motion was adopted:

Voted: That the vote under Article 5 of the Town Meeting of December 18, 1933, be amended by adding thereto the following: "said sum to be borrowed from any source by the Treasurer with the approval of the Selectmen."

Article 23.   To see if the Town will vote to amend the vote under Article 6 of the Town Meeting of December 18, 1933, so as to authorize the Treasurer with the approval of the Selectmen, to borrow from any source such sums of money as may be necessary to provide the sum of $25,000. appropriated to pay the cost of construction of sewers and drains under the National Industrial Recovery Act, or take any action relating thereto.

By a two-thirds vote the following motion was adopted:

Voted: That the vote under Article 6 of the Town Meeting of December 18, 1933, be amended by adding thereto the following: "said sum to be borrowed from any source by the Treasurer with the approval of the Selectmen."

Article 24.   To see if the Town will vote to amend the vote under Article 7 of the Town Meeting of December 18, 1933, so as to authorize the Treasurer, with the approval of the Selectmen, to borrow from any source such sums of money as may be necessary to provide the sum of $25,000. appropriated to pay the cost of construction of water mains under the National Industrial Recovery Act, or take any action relating thereto.

By a two-thirds vote the following motion was adopted:

Voted: That the vote under Article 7 of the Town Meeting of December 18, 1933, be amended by adding thereto the following: "said sum to be borrowed from any source by the Treasurer with the approval of the Selectmen."

Article 25.   To see if the Town will vote to amend the vote under Article 8 of the Town Meeting of December 18, 1933, so as to authorize the Treasurer with the approval of the Selectmen, to borrow from any source such sums of money as may be necessary to provide the sum of $135,000. appropriated to pay the cost of construction of an addition to the Senior High School under the National Industrial Recovery Act, or take any action relating thereto.

By a two-thirds vote the following motion was adopted:

Voted: That the vote under Article 8 of the Town Meeting of December 18, 1933, be amended by adding thereto the following: "said sum to be borrowed from any source by the Treasurer with the approval of the Selectmen."

Article 26. To see if the Town will vote to amend the vote under Article 10 of the Town Meeting of December 18, 1933, so as to authorize the Treasurer, with the approval of the Selectmen, to borrow from any source such sums of money as may be necessary to provide the sum of $35,229. appropriated to pay the cost of construction of an addition to the Main Branch of the Free Public Library, under the National Industrial Recovery Act, or take any action relating thereto.

By a two-thirds vote the following motion was adopted:

Voted: That the vote under Article 10 of the Town Meeting of December 18, 1933, be amended by adding thereto the following: "said sum to be borrowed from any source by the Treasurer with the approval of the Selectmen."

WM. P. McGUIRE,
Town Clerk.

Warrant for State Primary.
Thursday, September 20, 1934

Commonwealth of Massachusetts. Middlesex, ss.

To any Constable in the Town of Watertown, Greeting:

In the name of the Commonwealth of Massachusetts, you are hereby required to notify and warn the legal voters of the Town of Watertown, who are qualified to vote in primaries, to meet in their respective voting places in said Town:

PRECINCT 1—Coolidge School, Arlington Street
PRECINCT 2—Hosmer School, Winthrop Street
PRECINCT 3—East End Fire Station, Mount Auburn Street
PRECINCT 4—Senior High School, Columbia Street
PRECINCT 5—Central Fire Station, Main Street
PRECINCT 6—James Russell Lowell School, Lowell Avenue
PRECINCT 7—Administration Building, Main St.
PRECINCT 8—Central Fire Station, Main Street
PRECINCT 9—West Junior High School, Waverley Avenue
PRECINCT 10—Browne School, Main Street

on Thursday, the twentieth day of September 1934, at 12 Noon for the following purposes:

To bring in their votes to the primary officers for the nomination of candidates of political parties for the following offices:

Governor, Lieutenant Governor, Secretary of the Commonwealth, Treasurer and Receiver-General, Auditor of the Commonwealth, Attorney General, Senator in Congress, Representative in Congress for the Ninth Congressional District, Councillor for Third Councillor District, Senator for Fifth Senatorial District, Three Representatives in General Court for Seventh Representative District, District-Attorney for Northern District, Clerk of Courts for Middlesex County, Register of Deeds for Seventh Middlesex District, One County Commissioner for Middlesex County, two Associate County Commissioners for Middlesex County, Sheriff for Middlesex County (to fill vacancy).

The polls will be open from Twelve (12) Noon to Eight (8:00) P. M.

And you will notify and warn the legal voters of Watertown to meet at the time and the places herein specified, by leaving at every inhabited house in Town, a printed copy of this warrant, and also by posting copies of the same in ten or more conspicuous public places in Town, seven days at least prior to the time of said meeting.

Hereof fail not, and make return of this warrant, with your doings thereon, in the office of the Town Clerk on or before the time of said meeting.

Given under our hands this seventh day of September, A. D. 1934.

MAURICE H. O'CONNELL,
JAMES H. SHERIDAN,
EDWARD D. HOLLAND,
Selectmen of Watertown.

Officer's Return On Warrant

As required by the foregoing warrant, I have notified and warned the legal voters of the Town of Watertown to meet at the times and at the places herein specified, by leaving at every inhabited house in Town a printed copy of this warrant, and also by posting copies of the same in ten or more conspicuous public places in Town seven days at least prior to the time of said meeting.

JOSEPH W. REGAN,
Constable of Watertown.

Attest: WM. P. McGUIRE, *Town Clerk.*

RECORD OF STATE PRIMARY,
SEPTEMBER 20, 1934

The polls were opened at 12:00 o'clock noon, and voting continued until 8:00 o'clock P. M., at which time the polls were closed.

The following election officers were present:

Precinct 1.

Eugene L. Storey, Warden; Joseph Morley, Clerk. Workers: Pearl A. Baxter, Frances C. Murphy, Helen L. Boudreau, Joseph L. Pennington, Frank L. Maguire, George P. Ward, Lillian Sullivan, Fred E. Lindo, Gordon R. French, John T. Dorney.

Precinct 2.

Arthur J. McCarthy, Warden; William B. Glidden, Clerk. Workers: Blanche H. Robinson, Mae F. Elwell, Ella S. Lane, Frederick O. Fitzgerald, Peter T. Coen, Warren T. Shanahan, Helen L. Morley, Richard J. Fontaine, Frank A. Fitzpatrick, Harry G. Elwell.

Precinct 3.

Richard M. Hatch, Warden; Frank H. Ingerson, Clerk. Workers: Thomas J. Mulvahill, Mabel C. MacNutt, Izolee H. Gardiner, Roy L. Cummings, Marguerite Farrenkopf, Stephen J. Foley, Arthur L. Watts, Ralph C. Gardiner, Walter J. O'Leary, Leon Caragulian.

Precinct 4.

William M. Emerson, Warden; John B. Watson, Clerk. Workers: Lavinia Jensen, Elizabeth MacDonough, Amy F. Osborn, Mary Holland, Francis Lightbody, Thomas A. McNiff, Waldo P. Emerson, Helen L. Walsh.

Precinct 5.

Joseph R. Cooney, Warden; Grace M. Olson, Clerk. Workers: Margaret Walker, Lena Buchanan, Walter R. Flagg, Ann C. Wilson, Patrick B. Ford, Alice E. Sanger, Sadie E. Nichols, Odo F. Hann.

Precinct 6.

Harold W. Duvall, Warden; Lester A. Murphy, Clerk. Workers: Anne M. Davis, Ruth E. Peppard, Agnes C. Luther, Lewis A. Reed, Charles V. Gerrish, Percy J. Van Dyke, Austin F. Chamberlin, James P. Plunkett.

Precinct 7.

Harry J. York, Warden; John Gleason, Clerk. Workers: Ernestine P. Howe, Margaret E. Barry, Alexander Macdonald, Percy M. Bond, Cynthia M. Watts, Anna T. Hyde, Marie Gildea, James F. O'Halloran.

Precinct 8.

Bernard Ward, Warden; Wallace A. Shipton, Clerk. Workers: Olive P. Thayer, Ruth E. Hall, Mildred Fencer, Esther Grace, Mary McCall, Daniel J. Clifford, Allan Kimball, Samuel G. Thayer, John McCann, Frederick T. Thayer.

Precinct 9.

Edmund P. Hickey, Warden; Frederick E. Owen, Clerk. Workers: Eva M. Eagleson, Eleanor Mosman, Emma Roche, James F. Keenan, Mary D. McElligott, Charles E. Cunniff.

Precinct 10.

Francis J. McCarthy, Warden; Ellen B. Lougee, Clerk. Workers: Mollie E. Smith, John E. Mattison, Donald J. MacDonald, Gerard John Riley, Anna V. Hughes, Mildred Upit, Bernard S. Smith, Joseph W. Burke.

RECORD OF STATE PRIMARY, SEPTEMBER 20, 1934

DEMOCRATIC
(Total Vote Cast: 4,083)

GOVERNOR

	1	2	3	4	5	6	7	8	9	10	Total
Charles H. Cole of Boston	155	154	145	68	89	124	101	208	71	104	1219
James M. Curley of Boston	366	377	168	79	295	156	173	465	218	312	2609
Frank A. Goodwin of Boston	18	25	8	6	15	8	19	17	16	17	149
Blanks	32	21	1	0	8	2	9	16	8	9	106

LIEUTENANT GOVERNOR

	1	2	3	4	5	6	7	8	9	10	Total
Joseph L. Hurley of Fall River	280	289	202	94	187	167	172	353	162	220	2126
Francis E. Kelly of Boston	211	239	98	54	190	103	105	270	120	177	1567
Blanks	80	49	22	5	30	20	25	83	31	45	390

SECRETARY

	Precincts										
	1	2	3	4	5	6	7	8	9	10	Total
Joseph Santosuosso of Boston....	251	192	148	71	149	119	127	230	120	155	1562
James P. Blake of Boston	26	35	6	1	15	11	13	39	12	15	173
John J. Buckley of Boston	74	116	50	24	71	51	55	129	48	73	691
James Joseph Dugan of Quincy..	14	22	5	2	13	3	10	25	6	11	111
John D. O'Brien of Boston	38	55	23	13	39	18	17	48	35	40	326
Clement A. Riley of Norwood....	23	23	7	8	12	8	12	28	11	20	152
William F. Sullivan of Boston....	62	56	33	15	52	33	26	76	36	50	439
Blanks	83	78	50	19	56	47	42	131	45	78	629

TREASURER

	1	2	3	4	5	6	7	8	9	10	Total
Charles F. Hurley of Cambridge	454	501	280	138	347	252	251	612	262	367	3464
Blanks	117	76	42	15	60	38	51	94	51	75	619

AUDITOR

	1	2	3	4	5	6	7	8	9	10	Total
Thomas H. Buckley, Abington....	277	323	203	105	235	184	190	392	177	258	2344
Leo D. Walsh of Boston	173	167	70	33	114	69	67	195	85	109	1082
Blanks	121	87	49	15	58	37	45	119	51	75	657

ATTORNEY GENERAL

	1	2	3	4	5	6	7	8	9	10	Total
Paul A. Dever of Cambridge	305	290	199	98	195	150	149	315	162	209	2072
John Martin Boyle of Boston....	64	73	23	9	55	24	31	80	34	54	447
Philip A. Chapman of Boston	32	41	14	15	20	36	16	38	19	28	259
Harold W. Sullivan of Boston....	85	109	46	21	83	49	63	166	57	76	755
Blanks	85	64	40	10	54	31	43	107	41	75	550

SENATOR IN CONGRESS

	1	2	3	4	5	6	7	8	9	10	Total
David I. Walsh of Fitchburg	355	385	229	109	243	203	208	466	200	275	2673
Edward P. Barry of Boston	110	107	60	30	100	55	46	112	65	90	775
William Donahoe of Boston	44	44	12	11	38	15	27	63	23	44	321
Blanks	62	41	21	3	26	17	21	65	25	33	314

CONGRESSMAN—Ninth District

	1	2	3	4	5	6	7	8	9	10	Total
Albert L. Brophy of Waltham....	100	98	65	39	84	65	82	161	71	128	893
Richard M. Russell of Cambridge	291	298	171	85	188	170	126	259	152	178	1918
Frank L. White of Newton	87	108	41	18	79	24	53	164	51	68	694
Blanks	93	73	45	11	56	31	41	122	39	67	578

COUNCILLOR—Third District

	1	2	3	4	5	6	7	8	9	10	Total
Timothy E. Carroll of Cambridge	134	155	71	36	116	64	87	182	82	101	1028
William J. Coughlan, Brookline	124	169	89	52	111	83	88	209	89	123	1137
Bernard M. Cronin of Boston......	46	34	8	7	23	19	20	45	16	35	253
John P. Hennessy of Cambridge	148	120	91	29	78	69	51	127	67	82	862
Blanks	119	99	63	29	79	55	56	143	59	101	803

SENATOR—Fifth Middlesex District

	1	2	3	4	5	6	7	8	9	10	Total
P. Gerard Cahill of Waltham	285	323	177	92	238	164	188	431	196	252	2346
Joseph A. O'Dea of Waltham....	153	151	71	31	94	68	57	128	68	98	919
Blanks	133	103	74	30	75	58	57	147	49	92	818

REPRESENTATIVES IN GENERAL COURT
Seventh Midlesex District (3)

	Precincts										
	1	2	3	4	5	6	7	8	9	10	Total
George C. Cousens of Waltham..	55	46	17	11	43	26	32	72	57	88	447
Thomas J. Flannery of Waltham	51	62	35	13	23	22	34	77	38	43	398
Leo P. Landry of Watertown	290	320	167	98	200	168	162	330	161	181	2077
Joseph M. Maher of Waltham....	56	44	23	6	39	10	21	47	28	58	332
Patrick A. Menton, Watertown..	267	331	181	89	282	185	195	423	208	359	2520
Joseph J. Monahan of Waltham..	219	160	103	76	186	108	118	351	104	171	1596
John A. Murray of Watertown..	370	454	224	91	294	184	181	418	188	225	2629
Joseph G. Randall of Waltham....	44	40	14	6	13	9	6	28	9	9	178
Blanks	361	274	202	69	141	158	157	372	146	192	2072

DISTRICT ATTORNEY—Northern District

	1	2	3	4	5	6	7	8	9	10	Total
James J. Bruin of Lowell	100	111	49	34	75	45	45	94	50	68	671
John A. Crowley of Lowell	67	86	41	14	59	35	65	117	52	55	591
John F. Daly of Cambridge	181	161	111	41	129	100	79	210	102	139	1253
Joseph M. Gavan of Cambridge	118	136	58	35	76	62	60	148	51	84	828
Blanks	105	83	63	29	68	48	53	137	58	96	740

CLERK OF COURTS—Middlesex

	1	2	3	4	5	6	7	8	9	10	Total
John J. Brennan of Somerville....	210	245	134	66	207	134	140	366	150	182	1834
Edward L. Ford of Cambridge....	183	192	103	48	107	90	88	170	87	144	1212
John D. Medeiros of Somerville..	65	52	18	7	13	17	18	27	20	12	249
Blanks	113	88	67	32	80	49	56	143	56	104	788

REGISTER OF DEEDS—Southern Middlesex District

	1	2	3	4	5	6	7	8	9	10	Total
John Gordon Duffy, Cambridge	292	273	152	66	191	145	134	344	151	194	1942
John T. Ford of Somerville..........	154	205	89	52	125	88	105	203	99	148	1268
Blanks	125	99	81	35	91	57	63	159	63	100	873

COUNTY COMMISSIONER—Middlesex

	1	2	3	4	5	6	7	8	9	10	Total
Thomas B. Brennan of Medford	185	195	120	67	157	119	133	275	134	174	1559
Robert F. Donovan of Somerville	190	212	91	34	137	79	80	232	89	119	1263
Louis F. Stuart of Somerville	62	52	22	7	20	27	22	43	23	35	313
Blanks	134	118	89	45	93	65	67	156	67	114	948

ASSOCIATE COMMISSIONERS—Middlesex County (2)

	1	2	3	4	5	6	7	8	9	10	Total
Charles R. Brunelle, Somerville.	127	104	40	29	74	44	56	108	62	83	727
Edward L. Harley of Lowell	89	92	30	17	61	39	42	88	44	48	550
Francis R. King of Lowell	59	61	22	16	46	23	35	61	39	34	396
Thomas Murray of Somerville....	240	297	162	70	197	153	139	348	153	202	1961
John A. Sweeney of Cambridge..	288	303	176	76	219	172	154	369	158	220	2135
Blanks	339	297	214	98	217	149	178	438	170	297	2397

SHERIFF—Middlesex County
(To fill vacancy)

	1	2	3	4	5	6	7	8	9	10	Total
Patrick J. Brennan of Cambridge	85	87	52	26	92	59	80	187	61	99	828
Michael DeLuca of Cambridge....	71	34	8	2	13	7	23	18	19	19	214
Charles P. Fox of Lowell	17	10	11	0	7	3	3	7	4	1	63
William R. Griffin of Lowell........	11	20	1	1	6	3	6	13	3	5	69
John C. Kelleher of Somerville..	32	42	35	13	51	38	33	91	38	56	434
Daniel P. Leahy of Cambridge....	46	35	30	13	20	32	21	39	27	27	290
Ralph W. Robart of Cambridge..	71	70	50	30	38	50	19	56	51	35	470
Patrick Henry Ryan, Somerville	17	21	9	7	28	13	13	41	16	29	194
William H. Walsh, Framingham	126	194	81	33	84	44	61	139	47	95	904
Blanks	95	64	45	23	68	41	43	115	47	76	617

REPUBLICAN
(Total Vote Cast: 2212)

GOVERNOR

	Precincts										
	1	2	3	4	5	6	7	8	9	10	Total
Gaspar G. Bacon of Boston	71	96	274	417	156	215	232	47	45	70	1623
Frank A. Goodwin of Boston........	43	65	37	48	59	88	62	45	34	56	537
Blanks	2	12	5	7	2	3	13	4	2	2	52

LIEUTENANT GOVERNOR

	1	2	3	4	5	6	7	8	9	10	Total
John W. Haigis of Greenfield....	98	150	299	464	215	289	288	83	69	114	2069
Blanks .,...................................	18	23	17	8	2	17	19	13	12	14	143

SECRETARY

	1	2	3	4	5	6	7	8	9	10	Total
Frederic W. Cook of Somerville..	99	150	300	461	211	287	286	77	71	117	2059
Blanks	17	23	16	11	6	19	21	19	10	11	153

TREASURER

	1	2	3	4	5	6	7	8	9	10	Total
Oscar U. Dionne of New Bedford	59	91	205	311	139	170	197	53	42	67	1334
Thomas M. Vinson, Winchester..	39	54	85	136	64	114	81	24	24	47	668
Blanks	18	28	26	25	14	22	29	19	15	14	210

AUDITOR

	1	2	3	4	5	6	7	8	9	10	Total
Elizabeth W. Pigeon of Boston	43	50	172	223	67	144	140	16	29	38	922
Elmer P. Atherton of Revere....	6	11	4	14	5	6	7	6	1	4	64
Alonzo B. Cook of Boston............	54	79	126	221	135	141	130	55	40	73	1054
Irma Adelaide Rich of Boston....	3	14	5	3	1	6	8	4	3	4	51
Blanks	10	19	9	11	9	9	22	15	8	9	121

ATTORNEY GENERAL

	1	2	3	4	5	6	7	8	9	10	Total
Joseph E. Warner of Taunton..	99	151	296	455	204	286	284	79	72	116	2042
Blanks	17	22	20	17	13	20	23	17	9	12	170

SENATOR IN CONGRESS

	1	2	3	4	5	6	7	8	9	10	Total
Robert M. Washburn of Boston	97	141	299	455	205	282	276	77	66	115	2013
Blanks	19	32	17	17	12	24	31	19	15	13	199

CONGRESSMAN—Ninth District

	1	2	3	4	5	6	7	8	9	10	Total
Robert Luce of Waltham	95	133	283	448	202	274	274	75	66	109	1959
Blanks ....:...............	21	40	33	24	15	32	33	21	15	19	253

COUNCILLOR—Third District

	1	2	3	4	5	6	7	8	9	10	Total
Frank A. Brooks of Watertown..	75	119	246	383	177	260	238	64	54	102	1718
Sylvester Kaufman of Brookline	4	5	2	0	4	4	5	2	1	2	29
Margaret McGill of Newton	11	7	26	37	8	10	26	8	6	3	142
Russell A. Wood of Cambridge..	15	17	24	40	18	23	19	10	9	14	189
Blanks	11	25	18	12	10	9	19	12	11	7	134

SENATOR—Fifth Middlesex District

	1	2	3	4	5	6	7	8	9	10	Total
George G. Moyse of Waltham......	95	140	287	441	203	274	264	77	70	110	1961
Blanks	21	33	29	31	14	32	43	19	11	18	251

REPRESENTATIVES IN GENERAL COURT
Seventh Middlesex District (3)

	1	2	3	4	5	6	7	8	9	10	Total
					Precincts						
Albert W. Bullock of Waltham....	79	107	245	391	170	234	231	61	56	92	1666
George H. Dale of Watertown....	75	125	249	408	181	251	255	74	56	94	1768
Arthur A. Hansen of Waltham	72	104	226	373	168	223	217	50	50	93	1576
Clyde C. Potter of Waltham......	42	54	106	116	70	104	79	35	30	38	674
Blanks	80	129	122	128	62	106	139	68	51	67	952

DISTRICT ATTORNEY—Northern District

	1	2	3	4	5	6	7	8	9	10	Total
Warren L. Bishop of Wayland....	100	144	300	451	206	285	285	72	69	114	2026
Blanks	16	29	16	21	11	21	22	24	12	14	186

CLERK OF COURTS—Middlesex

	1	2	3	4	5	6	7	8	9	10	Total
Ralph N. Smith of Arlington......	92	145	286	457	206	285	277	75	68	111	2002
Blanks	24	28	30	15	11	21	30	21	13	17	210

REGISTER OF DEEDS—Middlesex Southern District

	1	2	3	4	5	6	7	8	9	10	Total
Thomas Leighton of Cambridge	75	120	269	413	187	259	248	72	60	101	1804
George LeRoy Woods of Everett	25	24	17	26	19	27	28	6	10	12	194
Blanks	16	29	30	33	11	20	31	18	11	15	214

COUNTY COMMISSIONER—Middlesex

	1	2	3	4	5	6	7	8	9	10	Total
Smith J. Adams of Lowell	21	30	72	90	29	56	37	16	16	22	389
George H. Brown of Lowell	16	30	33	78	34	30	48	14	13	23	319
Wesley G. Collings of Everett....	8	6	9	15	10	17	13	4	5	5	92
Harry J. Gilmore of Medford	18	23	31	27	27	38	28	10	12	10	224
Francis F. Griffith of Somerville	9	15	10	10	17	21	8	8	4	6	108
Victor Francis Jewett of Lowell..	20	38	118	195	83	112	121	23	20	40	770
Blanks	24	31	43	57	17	32	52	21	11	22	310

ASSOCIATE COMMISSIONERS—Middlesex County (2)

	1	2	3	4	5	6	7	8	9	10	Total
John Alfred Brodbine of Malden	25	39	42	59	31	65	45	13	15	24	358
Robert D. Donaldson of Lincoln..	58	94	212	355	156	200	202	50	44	73	1444
Melvin G. Rogers of Tewksbury..	48	78	201	316	147	179	169	44	37	70	1289
Carroll E. Scott of Medford	36	58	66	62	44	80	57	29	23	31	486
Blanks	65	77	111	152	56	88	141	56	43	58	847

SHERIFF—Middlesex County
(To fill vacancy)

	1	2	3	4	5	6	7	8	9	10	Total
Howe Coolidge Amee, Camb'ge	3	9	17	19	8	13	17	4	1	8	99
Joseph G. Bates of Malden	3	7	8	6	4	3	7	8	5	3	54
Harry Dunlap Brown of Billerica	15	17	41	98	33	27	38	12	7	25	313
George Groombridge, Somerville	1	3	3	1	3	2	4	1	0	3	21
John W. Justice of Medford	2	1	4	1	1	3	1	0	0	2	15
Clarence P. Kidder, Cambridge	1	11	27	24	13	12	28	4	5	8	133
Joseph M. McElroy, Cambridge..	38	67	109	195	87	164	111	29	23	41	864
Ralph W. Robart of Cambridge	12	14	38	31	12	24	23	10	13	12	189
Wendell D. Rockwood, Camb'ge..	7	6	9	11	5	6	5	2	4	4	59
George A. C. Stone, Somerville..	5	9	6	8	5	9	6	3	4	2	57
Henry L. Walker of Medford......	13	12	36	55	37	32	36	8	11	13	253
Blanks	16	17	18	23	9	11	31	15	8	7	155

Result of count of votes cast at State Primary was forwarded to the Secretary of the Commonwealth.

WM. P. McGUIRE, *Town Clerk.*

WARRANT FOR STATE ELECTION,
TUESDAY, NOVEMBER 6, 1934
COMMONWEALTH OF MASSACHUSETTS

Middlesex, ss.

To any Constable in the Town of Watertown,
Greeting:

In the name of the Commonwealth of Massachusetts, you are hereby required to notify and warn the legal voters of the Town of Watertown, to meet in their respective voting places in said Town:

PRECINCT 1—Coolidge School, Arlington Street

PRECINCT 2—Hosmer School, Winthrop Street

PRECINCT 3—East End Fire Station, Mount Auburn Street

PRECINCT 4—Senior High School, Columbia Street

PRECINCT 5—Central Fire Station, Main Street

PRECINCT 6—James Russell Lowell School, Lowell Avenue

PRECINCT 7—Administration Building, Main Street

PRECINCT 8—Central Fire Station, Main Street

PRECINCT 9—West Junior High School, Waverley Avenue

PRECINCT 10—Browne School, Main Street

on Tuesday, the sixth day of November, 1934, at 8 o'clock in the morning for the purpose of giving in their votes for the following State, District and County officers, viz:

Governor; Lieutenant Governor; Secretary of the Commonwealth; Treasurer; Auditor; Attorney General; Senator in Congress; Congressman—Ninth District; Councillor, Third District; Senator, Fifth Middlesex District;

Representatives in General Court, Seventh Middlesex District (3); District Attorney, Northern District; Clerk of Courts, Middlesex County; Register of Deeds, Middlesex Southern District; one County Commissioner, Middlesex County; two Associate Commissioners, Middlesex County; Sheriff, Middlesex County (to fill vacancy).

Also for giving in their votes on the following questions:

Question No. 1 Law Submitted Upon Referendum after Passage. Shall a law described as follows:

This law amends General Laws, Chapter 131, as previously amended, by repealing Section 105-A thereof and adding thereto three new sections, 105-B, 105-C, and 114-A.

Section 105-B provides that whoever uses any trap or other device for capture of fur-bearing animals, which is not designed to kill such animal at once or take it unhurt and which is likely to cause continued suffering to an animal caught therein, shall be fined fifty dollars, but traps or other devices for protection of property, set not more than fifty yards from any building, cultivated plot, or enclosures used for rearing poultry or game birds, to the use of which the presence of vermin may be detrimental, are excluded from the application of this section.

Section 105-C provides for the submission to the voters at a municipal election in any city or town upon petition, of the question of whether the operation of Section 105-B shall be suspended or if it has been already suspended, of the question whether it shall again be operative in such city or town.

Section 114-A provides that the Commissioner of Conservation may suspend the operation of Section 105-B for a period not exceeding thirty days within any specified territory under the control of his department.

The law also provides for the submission, by the Selectmen to the voters at a special Town Meeting in the current year, upon petition, of the question as to whether the provisions of Section 105-B shall be suspended in any town; and which was approved by both branches of the General Court by vote not recorded, be approved?

To obtain a full expression of opinion, voters should vote on both of the following questions:

a. If a voter desires to permit the sale of any and all alcoholic beverages in this Town he will vote "YES" on both questions.

b. If he desires to permit the sale of wines and malt beverages only herein, he will vote "NO" on Question No. 1, and "YES" on Question No. 2.

c. If he desires to prohibit the sale of any and all alcoholic beverages herein, he will vote "NO" on both questions.

1. Shall licenses be granted in this Town for the sale therein of all alcoholic beverages (whisky, rum, gin, malt beverages, wines and all other alcoholic beverages)?

2. Shall licenses be granted in this Town for the sale therein of wines and malt beverages (wines and beer, ale and all other malt beverages)?

1. Shall the pari-mutuel system of betting on licensed horse races be permitted in this county?

2. Shall the pari-mutuel system of betting on licensed dog races be permitted in this county?

The vote on these questions will be "Yes" or "No."

And you will notify and warn the legal voters of the Town of Watertown to meet at the time and at the places herein specified, by leaving at every inhabited house in Town a printed copy of this warrant, and also by posting copies of the same in ten or more conspicuous public places in Town, seven days at least prior to the time of said meeting.

Hereof, fail not, and make return of this warrant, with your doings thereon, into the office of the Town Clerk, on or before the time of said meeting.

Given under our hands this nineteenth day of October, A. D. 1934.

MAURICE H. O'CONNELL,
JAMES H. SHERIDAN,
EDWARD D. HOLLAND,
Selectmen of Watertown.

The Polls will open at 8 A. M. and will close at 8 P. M.

Officer's Return on Warrant

As required by the foregoing warrant, I have notified and warned the legal voters of the Town of Watertown to meet at the time and at the places herein specified, by leaving at every inhabited house in Town a printed copy of this warrant, and also by posting copies of the same in ten or more conspicuous public places in Town seven days at least prior to the time of said meeting.

JOSEPH W. REGAN,
Constable of Watertown.

Attest: WM. P. McGUIRE, *Town Clerk.*

Record of State Election, November 6, 1934

The polls were opened at 8:00 o'clock A. M., and voting continued until 8:00 o'clock P. M., at which time the polls were closed.

The following election officers were present:

Precinct 1.

Eugene L. Storey, Warden; Joseph Morley, Clerk. Workers: Frances C. Murphy, Helen L. Boudreau, Pearl

A. Baxter, Lillian Sullivan, Mary Arone, Frank L. Maguire, Ernest Swanson, Grace L. Cole, Mary Pennington, Delbert J. Kendall, Charles V. Harney, Gordon R. French.

Precinct 2.

Arthur J. McCarthy, Warden; William B. Glidden, Clerk. Workers: Warren T. Shanahan, Ralph Duley, Blanche H. Robinson, Ada Drake, Margaret J. O'Driscoll, Roger S. Hubbard, Peter T. Coen, Patrick R. Burns, Frank A. Fitzpatrick, Frederick O. Fitzgerald, Helen L. Morley, Theodore F. Nielsen, Marshall L. Barnard, R. J. Fontaine.

Precinct 3.

Richard M. Hatch, Warden; John J. Ingerson, Clerk. Workers: Mabel E. Kimball, Roger E. Mathews, Mabel C. MacNutt, Thomas Creamer, Walter J. O'Leary, Arthur D. Wilkins, Ernest K. Ingalls, Izolee H. Gardiner, Frank J. Hynes, Thomas J. Mulvahill.

Precinct 4.

William M. Emerson, Warden; John B. Watson, Clerk. Workers: Amy F. Osborn, Lavina Jensen, Elizabeth F. MacDonough, Francis Lightbody, Margaret Skuse, Thomas A. McNiff, Helen L. Walsh, James D. Hackett, Mary V. Holland, Waldo P. Emerson.

Precinct 5.

Joseph R. Cooney, Warden; Grace Olson, Clerk. Workers: Margaret Walker, Lena Buchanan, Anne C. Wilson, Alice Sanger, Sadie Nichols, Helen O'Brien, John J. Keefe, Alice Withee, Grace Ward, E. K. Bacon.

Precinct 6.

Harold Duvall, Warden; Lester A. Murphy, Clerk. Workers: Gordon H. Robertson, Theodore B. Robinson, S. Alice Youngman, Corah W. Wohltman, Ruth Peppard, Mary G. Luther, Lewis A. Reed, Anne M. Davis, Arthur

B. Jones, Percy Van Dyke, Charles Jewell Brown, Charles B. P. Crowley, Matthew B. Peppard, Alvira Davis.

Precinct 7.

Harry J. York, Warden; John T. Gleason, Clerk. Workers: Walter J. McMullen, Marie Gildea, Evangeline L. Johnson, Ernestine P. Howe, Margaret E. Barry, Cynthia M. Watts, Ella M. Humphreville, Anna T. Hyde, Percy M. Bond, Alexander Macdonald.

Precinct 8.

Bernard M. Ward, Warden; Wallace A. Shipton, Clerk. Workers: Ruth E. Hall, Catherine Campbell, Mildred Fencer, Esther Grace, Olive P. Thayer, Frederick T. Thayer, John P. Monahan, Allan Kimball, Daniel J. Clifford, Dorothy M. Thayer, Mary McCall, Madeline C. Morgan, K. Gardiner Thayer, Thomas L. Hughes.

Precinct 9.

Edmund P. Hickey, Warden; Frederick E. Owen, Clerk. Workers: Eva M. Eagleson, Margaret D. Hayes, Edmund Tocci, Joseph J. Kelly, Charles E. Cunniff, Frances Delaney, Emma Roche, Marguerite R. Colby, Mary McElligott, Eleanor Mosman.

Precinct 10.

Francis J. McCarthy, Warden; Ellen Lougee, Clerk. Workers: Mildred Upit, Catherine Hurley, John E. Mattison, Anna V. Hughes, Mollie E. Smith, Donald J. Macdonald, Florence Haddie, Hannah Farley, Anna M. Keating, Gerard Riley, Bradford S. Wilson.

(Total Vote Cast: 12,706)

GOVERNOR

					Precincts						
	1	2	3	4	5	6	7	8	9	10	Total
John W. Aiken of Chlsea, Socialist Labor Party..	6	9	3	0	0	0	3	3	1	5	30
Gaspar G. Bacon of Boston, Republican	309	442	836	978	522	907	665	238	257	352	5506
James M. ... of Boston, Democratic	943	882	496	284	656	508	515	970	492	643	6389
Freeman W. Follett of Haverhill, Prohibition	0	0	0	1	1	1	0	1	0	3	7
Frank A. Goodwin of Boston, Equal Tax	35	81	37	25	51	62	40	54	40	66	491
Alfred Baker Lewis, Cambridge, Socialist Party	9	6	4	3	3	3	2	5	5	2	42
Edward Stevens of Boston, ...ist Party ...	11	16	3	0	1	0	3	3	4	1	42
Blanks	26	23	20	14	23	8	22	34	14	15	199

LIEUTENANT GOVERNOR

	1	2	3	4	5	6	7	8	9	10	Total
Elizabeth Donovan, N. Brookfield, Socialist Party	22	14	8	3	5	6	9	19	8	6	100
John W. Haigis of Greenfield, Republican	321	484	830	997	565	928	680	245	266	393	5709
Horace I. Hillis of Saugus, Socialist Labor Party	11	13	3	0	4	1	7	6	1	5	51
Joseph L. Hurley of Fall River, Democratic	913	883	534	291	658	537	523	976	503	658	6476
Florence L. Lawton of Worcester, Prohibition	0	5	3	1	3	3	3	7	4	6	35
Horace Riley of Boston, Communist Party	18	29	5	2	6	1	6	9	7	2	85
Blanks	54	31	16	11	16	13	22	46	24	17	250

SECRETARY

	1	2	3	4	5	6	7	8	9	10	Total
Walter Burke of New Bedford, Communist Party	23	36	8	4	4	2	8	6	13	4	108
Frederic W. Cook of Somerville, Republican	339	486	866	1014	584	967	692	291	286	409	5934
...ge L. ... Beverly, Soc'list Labor Party	16	13	2	2	3	2	3	10	4	6	61
Leslie A. Richards of So. ...y, Socialist Party	14	18	6	2	5	6	4	11	8	2	76
Joseph Santosuosso of Boston, Democratic	892	850	476	260	629	482	508	919	476	633	6125
William B. Taylor of ...ton, Prohibition	2	7	4	6	1	3	1	9	2	6	41
Blanks	53	49	37	17	31	27	34	62	24	27	361

On December 6, 1934, petition was received by the Board of Registrars for recount of votes cast for Secretary. The recount, held on December 10, 1934, resulted as follows:

SECRETARY

Walter Burke of New Bedford, Communist Party	22	36	8	4	4	2	8	6	13	4	107
Frederic W. Cook of Somerville, Republican	339	486	867	1014	585	968	692	292	286	411	5940
George L. McGlynn, Beverly, Soc'list Labor Party	16	13	2	2	3	2	3	10	4	7	62
Leslie A. Richards of So. Hadley, Socialist Party	14	18	6	2	5	6	4	11	7	2	75
Joseph Santosuosso of Boston, Democratic	892	850	475	260	628	481	508	916	478	639	6118
William B. Taylor of Plympton, Prohibition	3	7	4	6	1	3	5	10	2	6	47
Blanks	53	49	37	17	31	27	30	63	23	27	357

TREASURER

Oscar U. Dionne of New Bedford, Republican	253	390	726	916	502	807	603	218	227	345	4987
William R. Ferry of Newton, Prohibition	8	35	24	21	23	21	25	19	8	19	203
Thomas Gilmartin, Brookline, Soc. Labor Party	20	22	6	1	3	1	10	7	2	4	76
Charles F. Hurley of Cambridge, Democratic	966	926	602	349	697	624	565	1003	531	682	6945
Harry Maltzman of Boston, Socialist Party	13	17	9	1	6	5	5	10	5	2	73
Frederick S. Reynolds of Lynn, Communist Party	15	25	6	0	2	2	7	2	9	3	71
Blanks	64	44	26	17	24	29	35	49	31	32	351

AUDITOR

Henning A. Blomen, Cambridge, Soc. Labor Party	27	22	4	2	3	5	11	10	4	6	94
Thomas H. Buckley of Abington, Democratic	927	873	583	377	682	591	542	964	496	645	6680
Alonzo B. Cook of Boston, Republican	287	459	750	870	502	844	636	262	266	396	5272
Walter S. Hutchins of Greenfield, Socialist Party	16	17	12	3	33	9	9	9	6	4	118
Paul Skers of Worcester, Communist Party	17	24	3	0	2	2	6	4	7	2	67
Blanks	65	64	47	53	35	38	46	59	34	34	475

ATTORNEY GENERAL

Morris Berzon of Everett, Socialist Party	25	19	7	7	3	5	13	10	8	5	97
Paul A. Dever of Cambridge, Democratic	918	885	515	289	666	531	517	956	492	638	6407
Charles A. Flaherty of Saugus, Communist Party	17	31	6	1	1	1	6	7	9	5	89
George F. Hogan of Nahant, Prohibition	5	9	1	8	5	5	5	9	2	3	52
Fred E. Oelcher of Peabody, Socialist Labor Party	9	10	1	1	3	2	2	7	3	6	44
Joseph E. Warner of Taunton, Republican	309	463	843	984	553	916	671	257	271	397	5664
Blanks	56	42	26	20	21	29	36	62	28	33	353

SENATOR IN CONGRESS

| | Precincts | | | | | | | | | | |
	1	2	3	4	5	6	7	8	9	10	Total
Albert Sprague Coolidge, Pittsfield, Soc. Party....	17	27	6	6	7	9	10	14	7	6	109
W. Barnard Smith of Brookline, Prohibition	6	13	4	9	4	10	7	6	4	3	66
David I. Walsh of Fitchburg, Democratic	998	982	673	420	755	746	617	1021	547	704	7463
Robert M. Washburn of Boston, Republican	230	361	691	858	461	704	568	205	219	330	4627
Albert L. Waterman, Boston, Soc. Labor Party....	12	13	5	1	0	2	5	4	2	8	52
Paul C. Wicks of Greenfield, Communist Party....	16	21	4	1	2	2	6	2	7	2	63
Blanks	60	42	16	10	28	16	37	56	27	34	326

CONGRESSMAN—Ninth District

	1	2	3	4	5	6	7	8	9	10	Total
Robert Luce of Waltham, Republican	254	411	752	912	517	820	635	232	240	362	5135
Richard M. Russell of Cambridge, Democratic	1010	994	615	374	712	648	574	1018	539	688	7172
Blanks	75	54	32	19	28	21	41	58	34	37	399

COUNCILLOR—Third District

	1	2	3	4	5	6	7	8	9	10	Total
Frank A. Brooks of Watertown, Republican	369	522	847	1017	582	974	723	307	298	439	6078
William J. Coughlan of Brookline, Democratic	879	856	498	262	633	482	481	916	479	593	6079
Blanks	91	81	54	26	42	33	46	85	36	55	549

SENATOR—Fifth Middlesex District

	1	2	3	4	5	6	7	8	9	10	Total
P. Gerard Cahill of Waltham, Democratic	921	908	526	297	659	524	494	953	490	622	6394
George G. Moyse of Waltham, Republican	300	462	795	959	531	899	682	266	271	398	5563
Blanks	118	89	78	49	67	66	74	89	52	67	749

On November 9, 1934, petition was received by the Board of Registrars for recount of votes cast for State Senator, Fifth Middlesex District. The recount, held on November 14, 1934, resulted as follows:

SENATOR—Fifth Middlesex District

	1	2	3	4	5	6	7	8	9	10	Total
P. Gerard Cahill of Waltham, Democratic	922	907	524	296	651	521	494	954	490	620	6379
George G. Moyse of Waltham, Republican	301	465	798	960	537	902	682	263	271	400	5579
Blanks	116	87	77	49	69	66	74	91	52	67	748

Watertown, Mass., November 14, 1934.

The clerks of the Town of Watertown and City of Waltham, comprising the Seventh Middlesex District, met on ' ...er 14, 1934, at 11:00 A. M., in Administration Building, ...wn, and canvassed the returns cast for Representatives in General Court for said district. The result was as follows:

REPRESENTATIVES IN GENERAL COURT—Seventh Middlesex District
(Vote for Three)

Votes Cast in Watertown, November 6, 1934.

	1	2	3	4	5	6	7	8	9	10	Total
Albert W. Bullock of Waltham, Republican	260	380	725	905	498	812	612	219	225	346	4982
George H. Dale of Watertown, Republican	309	464	796	945	550	903	662	286	260	409	5584
Thomas J. Flannery of Waltham, Democratic	871	841	474	265	597	467	465	926	458	611	5975
Arthur A. Hansen of Waltham, Republican	247	358	700	889	501	778	609	216	220	348	4866
Leo P. Landry of Watertown, Democratic	919	916	528	311	634	592	535	944	502	626	6507
John A. Murray of Watertown, Democratic	919	969	541	319	649	544	539	929	493	626	6528
Blanks	492	449	433	281	342	371	328	404	281	295	3676

VOTES CAST IN WALTHAM FOR REPRESENTATIVES, NOVEMBER 6, 1934.

Albert W. Bullock of Waltham, Republican	6,233
George H. Dale of Watertown, Republican	5,549
Thomas J, Flannery of Waltham, Democratic	7,849
Arthur A. Hansen of Waltham, Republican	6,588
Leo P. Landry of Watertown, Democratic	6,523
John A. Murray of Watertown, Democratic	6,058
Blanks	4,367

TOTAL NUMBER OF VOTES CAST FOR REPRESENTATIVES IN WATERTOWN AND WALTHAM

Albert W. Bullock of Waltham, Republican	11,215
George H. Dale of Watertown, Republican	11,133

	Total
*Thomas J. Flannery of Waltham, Democratic	13,824
Arthur A. Hansen of Waltham, Republican	11,454
*Leo P. Landry of Watertown, Democratic	13,030
*John A. Murray of Watertown, Democratic	12,586
Blanks	8,043

*Elected.

DISTRICT ATTORNEY—Northern District

					Precincts						
	1	2	3	4	5	6	7	8	9	10	Total
Warren L. Bishop of Wayland, Republican	344	532	862	1008	574	951	725	304	274	424	5998
James J. Bruin of Lowell, Democratic	869	800	469	259	622	471	453	889	474	584	5890
Richard S. McCabe of Lexington, Independent	42	60	23	14	22	27	19	40	19	27	293
Blanks	84	67	45	24	39	40	53	75	46	52	525

CLERK OF COURTS—Middlesex County

	1	2	3	4	5	6	7	8	9	10	Total
John J. Brennan of Somerville, Democratic	911	836	537	280	652	532	503	957	493	642	6343
Ralph N. Smith of Arlington, Republican	273	439	778	981	550	891	661	250	256	386	5465
V. Philip Torgian of Cambridge, Socialist Party	58	101	23	6	7	10	16	13	16	9	259
Blanks	97	83	61	38	48	56	70	88	48	50	639

REGISTER OF DEEDS—Middlesex Southern District

	1	2	3	4	5	6	7	8	9	10	Total
John Gordan Duffy of Cambridge, Democratic	939	906	523	286	656	521	527	977	503	645	6483
Thomas Leighton of Cambridge, Republican	309	469	818	978	548	912	673	255	264	392	5618
Blanks	91	84	58	41	53	56	50	76	46	50	605

COUNTY COMMISSIONER—Middlesex County

	1	2	3	4	5	6	7	8	9	10	Total
Thomas B. Brennan of Medford, Democratic	929	866	536	293	655	527	531	975	499	651	6462
Earl C. Hamilton of Cambridge, Socialist Party	50	79	19	6	35	17	16	19	17	10	268
Victor Francis Jewett of Lowell, Republican	264	418	776	958	505	880	645	237	245	369	5297
Blanks	96	96	68	48	62	65	58	77	52	57	679

On November 9, 1934, petition was received by the Board of Registrars for recount of votes cast for County Commissioner—Middlesex County. The recount, held on November 14, 1934, resulted as follows:

RECOUNT FOR COUNTY COMMISSIONER—Middlesex County

Thomas B. Brennan of Medford, Democratic	928	865	538	296	657	528	531	976	499	651	6469
Earl C. Hamilton of Cambridge, Socialist Party	51	79	18	5	7	17	16	19	17	10	.239
Victor Francis Jewett of Lowell, Republican	264	419	777	957	531	878	646	236	245	369	5322
Blanks	96	96.	66	47	62	66	57	77	52	57	676

ASSOCIATE COMMISSIONERS—Middlesex County
(Vote for two)

Robert D. Donaldson of Lincoln, Republican	262	425	760	927	511	852	650	237	241	362	5227
Edward L. Harley of Lowell, Democratic	874	842	499	272	631	499	485	927	470	625	6124
Thomas Murray of Somerville, Democratic	873	818	507	269	619	504	490	907	468	595	6050
Alfred H. Pigott of Somerville, Socialist Party	53	58	13	4	9	9	15	16	14	10	201
Melvin G. Rogers of Tewksbury, Republican	242	389	738	921	503	834	620	223	230	353	5053
John D. Sexton of Somerville, Socialist Party	37	46	12	6	6	10	11	15	10	8	161
Blanks	337	340	269	211	235	270	229	291	193	221	2596

SHERIFF—Middlesex County (To fill Vacancy)

Donald P. Hurd of Somerville, Socialist Party	33	48	9	5	12	12	16	9	12	10	166
Joseph M. McElroy of Cambridge, Republican	331	490	798	954	566	898	682	256	258	399	5632
Ascania di Rago of Medford, Fusionist	15	14	2	2	0	3	9	20	7	3	75
Ralph W. Robart of Cambridge, Democratic	879	843	543	313	632	523	502	940	489	625	6289
Blanks	81	64	47	31	47	53	41	83	47	50	544

Question No. 1
LAW SUBMITTED UPON REFERENDUM
AFTER PASSAGE

Shall a law described as follows:—

This law amends General Laws, Chapter 131, as previously amended, by repealing section 105A thereof and adding thereto three new sections, 105B, 105C, and 114A.

Section 105B provides that whoever uses any trap or other device for capture of fur-bearing animals, which is not designed to kill such animal at once or to take it unhurt and which is likely to cause continued suffering to an animal caught therein, shall be fined fifty dollars, but traps or other devices for protection of property, set not more than fifty yards from any building, cultivated plot, or enclosures used for rearing poultry or game birds, to the use of which the presence of vermin may be detrimental, are excluded from the application of this section.

Section 105C provides for the submission to the voters at a municipal election in any city or town upon petition, of the question of whether the operation of section 105B shall be suspended or if it has been already suspended, of the question whether it shall again be operative in such city or town.

Section 114A provides that the Commissioner of Conservation may suspend the operation of section 105B for a period not exceeding thirty days within any specified territory under the control of his department.

The law also provides for the submission, by the Selectmen to the voters at a special town meeting in the current year, upon petition, of the question as to whether the provisions of section 105B shall be suspended in any town; AND WHICH WAS APPROVED BY BOTH BRANCHES OF THE GENERAL COURT BY VOTE NOT RECORDED, be approved?

	1	2	3	4	Precincts 5	6	7	8	9	10	Total
Yes	466	558	478	443	385	493	417	447	303	392	4382
No	254	233	381	466	316	396	340	256	158	262	3062
Blanks	619	668	540	396	556	600	493	605	352	433	5262

Question No. 2

INTOXICATING LIQUORS

To obtain a full expression of opinion, voters should vote on both of the following questions:

(a) If a voter desires to permit the sale of any and all alcoholic beverages in this city (or town) he will vote "YES" on both questions.

(b) If he desires to permit the sale of wines and malt beverages only herein, he will vote "NO" on question 1 and "YES" on question 2.

(c) If he desires to prohibit the sale of any and all alcoholic beverages herein, he will vote "NO" on both questions.

1. Shall licenses be granted in this city (or town) for the sale therein of all alcoholic beverages (whiskey, rum, gin, malt beverages, wines and all other alcoholic beverages)?

	1	2	3	4	5	6	7	8	9	10	Total
					Precincts						
Yes	783	896	625	447	583	701	538	793	468	608	6442
No	367	394	637	785	563	693	592	365	263	380	5039
Blanks	189	169	137	73	111	95	120	150	82	99	1225

2. Shall licenses be granted in this city (or town) for the sale therein of wines and malt beverages (wines and beer, ale and all other malt beverages)?

	1	2	3	4	5	6	7	8	9	10	Total
					Precincts						
Yes	760	894	647	536	580	769	541	800	467	615	6609
No	323	335	558	672	520	588	541	313	229	338	4417
Blanks	256	230	194	97	157	132	168	195	117	134	1680

Question No. 3

HORSE AND DOG RACING

1. Shall the pari-mutuel system of betting on licensed horse races be permitted in this county?

	1	2	3	4	5	6	7	8	9	10	Total
					Precincts						
Yes	875	958	734	609	671	805	651	837	541	697	7378
No	239	275	501	590	420	521	431	247	160	240	3624
Blanks	225	226	164	106	166	163	168	224	112	150	1704

2.   Shall the pari-mutuel system of betting on licensed dog races be permitted in this county?

| | Precincts | | | | | | | | | | |
	1	2	3	4	5	6	7	8	9	10	Total
Yes	687	756	465	380	493	560	500	684	425	555	5505
No	354	406	699	787	530	709	520	345	244	329	4923
Blanks	298	297	235	138	234	220	230	279	144	203	2278

ABSENT VOTERS' BALLOTS RECEIVED AND CAST

| | Precincts | | | | | | | | | | |
	1	2	3	4	5	6	7	8	9	10	Total
Ballots	0	3	4	12	3	0	5	3	0	2	32

The Selectmen made return to the Secretary of the Commonwealth as required by law of the foregoing result of votes cast in Watertown.

The Registrars of Voters made an amended return to the Secretary of the Commonwealth as required by law of the result of the recount of votes cast in Watertown for Senator—Fifth Middlesex District and for County Commissioner—Middlesex County.

Thomas J. Flannery, Leo P. Làndry and John A. Murray were declared elected Representatives in General Court, Seventh Middlesex District, and notices of their election were delivered to them by the City Clerk of Waltham, and forwarded to the Secretary of the Commonwealth.

The Registrars of Voters made an amended return to the Secretary of the Commonwealth as required by law of the result of the recount of votes cast in Watertown for Secretary of the Commonwealth.

WM. P. McGUIRE, Town Clerk.

Warrant for Town Meeting, Tuesday Evening, November 13, 1934

Commonwealth of Massachusetts. Middlesex, ss.

To any Constable in the Town of Watertown, Greeting:

In the name of the Commonwealth of Massachusetts, you are hereby required to notify and warn the legal voters of the Town of Watertown to meet in the Senior High School Building, Columbia Street, in said Town, on Tuesday evening, the thirteenth day of November, 1934, at 7:30 P. M., to act on the following articles, viz:

Article 1. To hear the report of any Committee heretofore appointed, and act thereon.

Article 2. To see if the Town will vote to provide by transfer or otherwise, such sums of money as may be necessary for the use of the various Town Departments for the balance of the current year, direct how the same shall be provided, or take any action relating thereto.

Article 3. To see if the Town will authorize the Treasurer, with the approval of the Selectmen, to borrow money on and after January 1, 1935, in anticipation of the revenue of the financial year beginning January 1, 1935, or take any action relating thereto.

Article 4. To see if the Town will vote to amend the By-laws of the Town by adding to Article 6 of the By-laws of the Town as adopted on March 14, 1910 and amendments thereto, the following:

1. The Collector shall have full power to assign any tax titles held by the Town upon the payment of the lawful charges to the Town thereon.

2. All assignments of tax titles shall be executed by the Collector in the name and on behalf of the Town:

or take any action relating thereto.

Article 5.   To see if the Town will vote to appropriate the sum of Fifty Dollars ($50.) for Cemetery Contingent for the remainder of the year 1934, direct how the same shall be provided, or take any action relating thereto.

Article 6.   To see if the Town will vote to appropriate the sum of Fifteen Hundred Dollars ($1500.) for the use of the Health Department for Contagious Diseases to complete their business for the ensuing months, direct how the same shall be provided, or take any action relating thereto.

Article 7.   To see if the Town will vote to appropriate the sum of Two Hundred Sixty-seven Dollars ($267.) for the use of the Poles and Wires Department, direct how the same shall be provided, or take any action relating thereto.

Article 8.   To see if the Town will vote to appropriate and provide by transfer or otherwise, for the use of the Highway Department, the following sums:

	Transfer From	*Transfer To*
Highway Maintenance		$9,950.00
Highway Stable		2,200.00
Highway Vacations	$ 119.06	
Highway Construction	3,000.00	
Ashes and Paper		2,000.00
Betterments	635.04	
Arlington Street	7,252.64	
Orchard Street	2,010.66	
	$13,017.40	$14,150.00

Article 9.   To see if the Town will vote to appropriate the sum of Five Hundred Dollars ($500.) for the use of the Assessors' Department, as follows:

$250 for Board of Tax Appeals case

250.00 for office expense

$500.00

direct how the same shall be provided, or take any action relating thereto.

Article 10. To see if the Town will vote to appropriate and provide by transfer or otherwise the sum of Two Hundred Ninety-five Dollars ($295.) for the use of the Police Department, or take any action relating thereto.

Article 11. To see if the Town will vote to appropriate and provide by transfer or otherwise the sum of One Thousand, Seven Hundred Ninety Dollars, Twenty-five Cents ($1,790.25) for the use of the Public Welfare Department, or take any action relating thereto.

Article 12. To see if the Town will vote to appropriaate Six Hundred Dollars ($600.) necessary to pay the cost of employment of four (4) permanent operators for the balance of year 1934 in connection with the Fire Alarm Signal System, direct how the money shall be provided, or take any action relating thereto.

Article 13. To see if the Town will vote to appropriate and provide by transfer or otherwise the necessary sum of money to pay the cost of equipment for an addition to the Main Street Public Library Building, direct how the same shall be raised, or take any action relating thereto.

And you will notify and warn the legal voters of the Town of Watertown to meet at the time and at the place herein specified, by leaving at every inhabited house in Town a printed copy of this warrant, and also by posting copies of the same in ten or more conspicuous public places in Town, seven days at least prior to the time of said meeting.

Hereof fail not, and make return of this warrant, with your doing thereon into the office of the Town Clerk on or before the time of said meeting.

Given under our hands this 26th day of October, A. D. 1934.

MAURICE H. O'CONNELL,
JAMES H. SHERIDAN, ...
EDWARD D. HOLLAND,
Selectmen of Watertown.

Officer's Return on Warrant

As required by the foregoing warrant, I have notified and warned the legal voters of the Town of Watertown to meet at the time and at the place herein specified, by leaving at every inhabited house in Town a printed copy of this warrant, and also by posting copies of the same in ten or more conspicuous public places in Town seven days at least prior to the time of said meeting.

JOSEPH W. REGAN,
Constable of Watertown.

Attest: WM. P. McGUIRE, *Town Clerk.*

Notices were mailed to the Town Meeting Members at least seven days prior to the Town Meeting of the proposed business to be considered at the meeting.

WM. P. McGUIRE.
Town Clerk.

Meeting was called to order at 8:00 P. M., by Moderator P. Sarsfield Cunniff. Officers' returns on warrant were read by Town Clerk, Wm. P. McGuire.

The counters reported that there were 102 Town Meeting Members present; number necessary for a quorum: 93. The following shows representation from the various precincts:

Virtue of Office 12
Finance Committee 16
Precinct 1 5

Precinct 2 10
Precinct 3 3
Precinct 4 9
Precinct 5 7
Precinct 6 10
Precinct 7 13
Precinct 8 9
Precinct 9 5
Precinct 10 3

Total 102

Article 1. To hear the report of any Committee heretofore appointed, and act thereon.

Committee on change of zoning by-laws stated that report will be made at the annual Town Meeting.

Article 2. To see if the Town will vote to provide by transfer or otherwise, such sums of money as may be necessary for the use of the various Town Departments for the balance of the current year, direct how the same shall be provided, or take any action relating thereto.

Finance Committee recommended and it was—

Voted: That the following sums be and are hereby appropriated for the use of the following departments and that the money be provided by transfer in accordance with the following schedule:

From

Election Expense .... $ 125.00
Interest 15.00
Fire, Salaries 600.00
Interest 3,574.20

$4,314.20

To

Printing Voting Lists .... $ 140.00
Fire, Contingent 600.00
Collector 416.20

Town Hall 808.00
Health, Contagious 2,000.00
Pensions 350.00

_____

$4,314.20

Article 3. To see if the Town will authorize the Treasurer with the approval of the Selectmen, to borrow money on and after January 1, 1935, in anticipation of the revenue of the financial year beginning January 1, 1935, or take any action relating thereto.

Voted: That the Town Treasurer, with the approval of the Selectmen, be and he is hereby authorized to borrow money on and after January 1, 1935, in anticipation of the revenue of the financial year beginning January 1, 1935, and to issue the note or notes of the Town therefor, payable within one year, any debt or debts incurred under this vote to be paid from the revenue of the financial year beginning January 1, 1935.

Article 4. To see if the Town will vote to amend the By-laws of the Town by adding to Article 6 of the By-laws of the Town as adopted on March 14, 1910 and amendments thereto, the following:

    1. The Collector shall have full power to assign any tax titles held by the Town upon the payment of the lawful charges to the Town thereon.

    2. All assignments of tax titles shall be executed by the Collector in the name and on behalf of the Town.:
or take any action relating thereto.

Voted: That the By-Laws of the Town be amended by adding thereto the following new chapter:

"CHAPTER XXIX.

Assignment of Tax Titles

    Section 1. The Treasurer shall have full power to assign any tax titles held by the Town, upon the payment of the lawful charges to the Town thereon.

Section 2. All assignments of tax titles shall be executed by the Treasurer in the name and on behalf of the Town."

Article 5. To see if the Town will vote to appropriate the sum of Fifty Dollars ($50.) for Cemetery Contingent for the remainder of the year 1934, direct how the same shall be provided, or take any action relating thereto.

Finance Committee recommended and it was—

Voted: That the sum of Fifty Dollars ($50.) be appropriated for the use of the Cemetery Contingent for the remainder of the year 1934, and that this sum be transferred from Interest Account.

Article 6. To see if the Town will vote to appropriate the sum of Fifteen Hundred Dollars ($1500.) for the use of the Health Department for Contagious Diseases to complete their business for the ensuing months, direct how the same shall be provided, or take any action relating thereto.

Indefinitely postponed. See Article 2.

Article 7. To see if the Town will vote to appropriate the sum of Two Hundred Sixty-seven ($267.) Dollars for the use of the Poles and Wires Department, direct how the same shall be provided, or take any action relating thereto.

49 in the affirmative, 46 opposed.

Voted: That the sum of Two Hundred Sixty-seven Dollars ($267.) be appropriated for the use of the Poles and Wires Department for the balance of the year, same to be transferred from Mothers' Aid Account.

Article 8· To see if the Town will vote to appropriate and provide by transfer or otherwise, for the use of the Highway Department, the following sums:

	Transfer From	Transfer To
Highway Maintenance		$9,950.00
Highway Stable		2,200.00
Highway Vacations	$ 119.06	
Highway Construction	3,000.00	

Ashes and Papers		2,000.00
Betterments.	635.04	
Arlington Street	7,252.64	
Orchard Street	2,010.66	
	$13,017.40	$14,150.00

Finance Committee recommended and it was—

Voted: That the sum of Twelve Thousand, Six Hundred Seventeen Dollars, Forty Cents ($12,617.40) be appropriated for the use of the Highway Maintenance, Highway Stable Maintenance, Ashes and Paper Departments, the same to be transferred as provided in the following schedule:

From

Highway, Vacations	$ 119.06
Highway, Construction	2,600.00
Betterments	635.04
Arlington Street	7,252.64
Orchard Street	2,010.66
	$12,617.40

To

Highway Maintenance	$8,817.40
Highway ,Stable Maintenance	2,000.00
Ashes and Paper	1,800.00
	$12,617.40

Article 9. To see if the Town will vote to appropriate the sum of Five Hundred Dollars ($500.) for the use of the Assessors' Department, as follows:

$250 for Board of Tax Appeals Case
250.00 for office expense

$500.00

direct how the same shall be provided, or take any action relating thereto.

Voted: That the sum of Seven Hundred Fifty Dollars ($750.) be appropriated for the use of the Assessors' Department, this sum to be transferred from Interest Account in accordance with the following schedule:

From

Interest Account	$750.00
	$750.00

To

Board of Tax Appeals Case	$500.00
Office Expense	250.00
	$750.00

Article 10.   To see if the Town will vote to appropriate and provide by transfer or otherwise the sum of Two Hundred, Ninety-five Dollars ($295.) for the use of the Police Department, or take any action relating thereto.

Finance Committee recommended and it was—

Voted: That the sum of Two Hundred, Ninety-five Dollars ($295.) be appropriated for the use of the Police Department and transfer made in accordance with the following schedule:

From

Police, Salaries	$ 95.00
Police, Radio Equipment	200.00
	$295.00

To

Police, Special Police	$ 95.00
Police, Contingent	200.00
	$295.00

Article 11.   To see if the Town will vote to appropriate and provide by transfer or otherwise, the sum of One Thousand, Seven Hundred Ninety Dollars, Twenty-five Cents ($1,790.25) for the use of the Public Welfare Department, or take any action relating thereto.

Finance Committee recommended and it was—

Voted: That the sum of One Thousand, Seven Hundred Ninety Dollars, Twenty-five Cents ($1,790.25) be appropriated for the Public Welfare, Old Age Assistance and Public Welfare Contingent, same to be provided by transfer in accordance with the following schedule:

From

Public Welfare, and Mothers' Aid	$1,790.25
	$1,790.25

To

Public Welfare, and Old Age Assistance	$1,402.33
Public Welfare, Contingent	387.92
	$1,790.25

Article 12. To see if the Town will vote to appropriate Six Hundred Dollars ($600.) necessary to pay the cost of employment of four (4) permanent operators for the balance of year 1934, in connection with the Fire Alarm Signal System, direct how the money shall be provided, or take any action relating thereto.

Voted: That the sum of Six Hundred Dollars ($600.) be appropriated to pay the cost of employment of four (4) permanent operators for the balance of the year 1934, in connection with the Fire Alarm Signal System under the direction of the Poles and Wires Department, and to pay the cost of same, the sum of Six Hundred Dollars ($600.) be and is hereby transferred from Interest Account to Fire Alarm Signal System Account.

Article 13. To see if the Town will vote to appropriate and provide by transfer or otherwise the necessary sum of money to pay the cost of equipment for an addition to the Main Street Public Library Building, direct how the same shall be raised, or take any action relating thereto.

Finance Committee recommended and it was—

Voted: That the sum of Four Hundred Dollars ($400.) be appropriated to pay the cost of equipment for an addition to the Main Street Public Library Building, this sum to be provided by transfer from the Highway Construction Account.

WM. P. McGUIRE,

Town Clerk.

REPORT OF THE SEALER OF WEIGHTS AND MEASURES

To the Honorable Board of Selectmen,

Gentlemen:

The following report of the Sealer of Weights and Measures, for the year 1934, is respectfully submitted.

Sealing Fees Collected	$310.64
Adjustment Charges	6.70
Total	$317.34

Scales	Adjusted	Sealed	Not Sealed	Condemned
Platforms, over 5,000 lbs.	—	22	—	2
Platforms, 100 to 5,000 lbs.	4	79	—	6
Counter, 100 lbs. or over	2	19	—	2
Counter, under 100 lbs.	7	83	—	7
Spring, 100 lbs. or over	—	34	—	10
Spring, under 100 lbs.	13	167	—	21
Computing, under 100 lbs.	24	141	—	7
Personal Weighing (slot)	—	23	—	1
Prescription	—	22	1	3

Weights

	Adjusted	Sealed	Not Sealed	Condemned
Avoirdupois	20	566	—	6
Apothecary	—	256	—	20
Metric	—	75	—	2
Capacity Measures				
Liquid	—	270	—	1
Oil Jars	—	139	—	—
Ice Cream Cans	—	400	—	—
Automatic Measuring Devices				
Gasoline Pumps	—	49	—	4
Gasoline Meters	18	153	—	3
Kerosene Pumps	—	4	—	1
Oil Measuring Pumps	—	95	—	—
Oil Meters	—	7	—	—
Quantity Stops on Pumps	16	379	—	—
Grease Measuring Devices	—	51	—	6
Linear Measures				
Yard Sticks	—	13	—	3
Taxi Meter	—	1	—	—
Cloth Measuring Devices	—	3	—	—
Totals	104	3051	1	105

Commodity Trial Weighings

	Total Tested	No. Correct	Under	Incorrect Over
Bread	183	164	7	12
Beans	18	6	12	—
Butter	121	110	9	2
Coal (Paper Bags)	8	1	—	7
Coal (In Transit)	3	1	1	1
Dry Commodity	90	88	2	—
Flour	67	40	27	—
Fruits and Vegetables	11	2	2	7
Liquids	2	2	—	—
Lard	48	48	—	—
Meats and Provisions	45	35	4	6

Potatoes	26	14	6	6
Totals	622	511	70	41

Inspections

Pedlars' Licenses	31
Coal Certificates	30
Marking of Bread	180
Clinical Thermometers	24
Pedlars' Scales	31
Oil Jars	469
Retest of Gasoline Pumps	17
Court Case	1

4 Special Town Licenses issued by the Director of Standards.

Respectfully,

VICTOR M. ANDERSON,

Sealer of Weights and Measures.

REPORT OF WIRE DEPARTMENT

Watertown, Mass., January 15, 1935

To the Honorable Board of Selectmen:

Gentlemen:

The report of the Poles and Wires Department for the year ending December 31, 1934 is herewith submitted.

Due to the customary annual practice of renewing and relocating poles in the various sections of the town by the Edison Electric Illuminating Company and the New England Telephone and Telegraph Company, many alterations were necessitated on our aerial lines of the Fire Alarm and Police Signal Systems. The necessary wires, cross-arms, equipment and fittings were installed which were required by these changes. Many of these installations entailed the transfer of police and fire alarm boxes.

During the past year thirteen tappers were transferred to new locations. New underground cable, essential to the proper working of the signal system, was installed in the duct lines on Galen Street, from Hunt Street to the Central Fire Station on Main Street. Also on Arsenal Street from Patten Street to the Central Station. The necessary connections were made and the lines are now in working order.

All signal boxes, both fire alarm and police, were painted, oiled and examined periodically throughout the year, to insure their proper performance. However, there is an opportunity for improvement in the system by retiring some of the older type boxes and replacing them with modern equipment. It was necessary to replace two underground cable boxes which were destroyed by automobile collisions.

Four operators were appointed by the Board of Selectmen to take care of the work at the Signal Room. This work was performed by firemen detailed to temporary duty until these appointments were made. The appointees assumed work on November 27th. They have been thoroughly instructed in their duties and are now operating on regular schedule.

In order to perfect our lines it will be necessary to replace many miles of ragged, weather-beaten wires throughout the town. Equipment and crossarms which have greatly deteriorated from the elements must also be replaced.

The street lights received careful attention. All notifications that street lights were not burning were immediately reported to the Edison Company and broken and burned out lamps were promptly replaced.

Relative to interior wiring, 832 permits for wiring in dwellings and industrial plants were issued. This wiring necessitated over 3500 inspections, as many of the jobs had to be inspected three or four times. The fees for the permits amounted to $416.00, which amount was handed to the Town Treasurer. Approximately 300 permits to turn on current were issued to the Edison Electric Illum inating Company.

I wish to express to the Board of Selectmen my appreciation for their co-operation during the past year. I also extend thanks to the heads of the various departments, to the Gamewell Company, the Edison Electric Illuminating Company and the New England Telephone and Telegraph Company for the courtesies they have shown me during the past year.

Respectfully submitted,

PATRICK J. VAHEY,
Inspector of Wires.

REPORT OF TREE WARDEN

January 15, 1935.

To the Honorable Board of Selectmen:

Gentlemen:

The report of the Tree Warden for the year 1934 is herewith submitted.

During the year a great deal of pruning was done to the street trees where the branches overhung the highways and sidewalks and were a danger to life and property. Dead and dangerous branches were also removed, and many trees which were a menace to public safety were cut down. New growth on many trees was also trimmed, in order to properly shape the trees and stimulate growth. Tree guards were repaired and those guards which were beyond repair were removed. Where the guards were removed new guards were placed, if required for the protection of the trees.

The Edison Company was notified whenever their wires came in contact with the town trees in such a way as to injure the trees. On notification they gave prompt attention to their wires and co-operated with the work of the department in every way.

Many young trees which had either died or made unsatisfactory growth, were removed and new trees set out in their place. There are many more replacements to be made and this work should be attended to this spring. Tree guards were placed around all the new trees which were set out this past year.

A great deal of help was given the Tree Warden Department this past year by the E. R. A. They assisted in the removal of many large and dangerous trees and also in the pruning of tall trees. The wood from the work of the department was delivered at the Town Infirmary and distributed by the Welfare Department to needy cases.

A great many of our public shade trees are infested with various pests, such as elm bark beetle, elm leaf beetle, aphis, etc., and if the ravages of these pests are not checked now it will mean a much greater expenditure later on, and perhaps the loss of many valuable shade trees.

I wish to thank the Board of Selectmen and the Edison Electric Illuminating Company for the cordial co-operation extended to me in the work of the Department during the year.

Respectfully submitted ,

JOHN C. FORD,
Tree Warden.

REPORT OF MOTH DEPARTMENT

Watertown, Mass., January 15, 1935.

To the Honorable Board of Selectmen:

Gentlemen:

The report of the Superintendent of the Moth Department for the year ending December 31, 1934, is herewith submitted.

The work of suppressing the gypsy and browntail moths was carried on in the usual way. In the fall and winter months egg clusters and nests were destroyed wherever found. This work was followed in the late spring and early summer by extensive spraying.

The gypsy moth is much more prevalent now than it has been for some time and the State Conservation Department is requesting co-operation from all municipalities in the extermination of this pest.

Not only should the work of suppressing the gypsy and browntail moths be carried on extensively this coming year, but the ravages of the elm leaf beetle and the aphis should also be checked, as these pests are doing a great deal of damage to our trees. Spraying is the best known method of fighting the elm leaf beetle, so a great deal of spraying should be done this ensuing year.

Elm bark beetle is infesting our elms and there is also a great deal of danger from the Dutch Elm disease. In order to protect our valuable trees it will be necessary to give strict attention to this work. Destruction of the trees will not only cause an outlay of a great deal of money for the planting of young trees, but valuable trees, which can never be replaced, will be absolutely destroyed if neglected.

Respectfully submitted,

JOHN C. FORD,
Superintendent of Moth Department.

REPORT OF INSPECTOR OF BUILDINGS

Watertown, Mass., January 3, 1935.

To the Honorable Board of Selectmen:

Gentlemen:

I herewith respectfully submit the following report of Permits issued from this office for the year ending December 31, 1934.

Whole number issued, 186. Probable cost of same, $345,080. as follows:

9	One Family Houses	$46,000.00
13	Garages	3,190.00
5	Store Additions	8,825.00
3	Service Stations	20,500.00
1	Office Building	8,000.00
6	Storage Buildings	10,750.00
1	Receiving Tomb	2,500.00
1	Lunch Room	1,000.00
1	Carmen's Lobby	10,000.00
1	Public Library Addition	30,000.00
1	School Addition	130,000.00
100	Alterations	74,315.00
		$345,080.00

1 Boiler Installation
5 Fireworks Stands
17 Razing Permits
20 Signs
1 Awning

Respectfully submitted,

WILLIAM H. WILSON,

Inspector of Buildings.

REPORT OF DOG OFFICER

To the Honorable Board of Selectmen:

Watertown, Massachusetts.

Gentlemen:

I herewith submit my annual report as Dog Officer for the year ending December 31, 1934.

There were 743 dogs licensed.

There were 132 dogs killed. '

There were 27 dogs returned to their owners.

Posters containing regulations and licensing of dogs were posted as required.

An active campaign was conducted the entire year collecting license fees.

Under the existing conditions, I consider the results gratifying.

I thank the Police and the various Town Officials for their co-operation.

WARREN J. EASTMAN,

Dog Officer.

Your attention is called to the following remarks:

There is a new provision in the revised laws which becomes effective January 1, 1935 which requires dog officers to seek out, catch and confine, all unlicensed dogs. For this an officer is entitled to 50 cents per day, not to exceed six days, for each dog so confined. This is payable by the owner, if known, directly to the dog officer. If no owner is found after six days, the dog is to be sold or destroyed. In this case, the officer is entitled to $3.00 for detention, and $1.00 for each dog destroyed. Such expenditures will be reimbursed by the County, but must be paid, in the first instance, by the Town.

REPORT OF THE PLAYGROUND COMMISSION

December 17, 1934.

To the Honorable Board of Selectmen:

The report of the Superintendent of Playgrounds covering every phase of the activity, is hereby submitted as the report of the Playground Commission for the year 1934:

I respectfully submit the annual report of the Superintendent of Playgrounds for the year 1934.

The playground season opened July 9th and closed August 31st. The playground apparatus was transferred from Victory Field to the lot of land at the corner of Lowell and George Streets, and this playground was made ready for the opening day. Horseshoes, checkers and paddle tennis sets as well as baseball equipment were furnished to each playground.

Playground activities consisted of the forming of baseball leagues for the boys. These leagues were composed of four classes: First Midgets—12 years and under: Second Midgets—10 years and under; Juniors—14 years and under; and Seniors—16 years and under. Inter-playground competition in checker tournaments, horseshoe elimination contests, and track meets held the interest of the boys of all ages. The athletic activities enjoyed by the girls were batball, baseball and track.

Handiwork and sewing were very popular among the girls and many useful as well as ornamental articles were made. A new activity, wood carving, was introduced and interested boys and girls alike. The carving out of lawn ornaments, comic strip characters, curtain pulls and animals was the chief interest of many. Wood carving, if properly fostered and encouraged, should prove highly successful in future playground activities.

Playground "Days," namely "Freak Day," "Play Day," "Pet Day," and "Party Day," stimulated enthusiasm among the little folks. Entertainments and parades on these "Days" drew a large attendance.

One main exhibition was held at Victory Field. The presence of a large number of adults and the interest shown by them in the accomplishments of their children, justified the time and effort spent by the instructors in achieving a successful closing.

If attendance is any criterion of success in a recreational season, and it would seem that it is, the season just passed through was tremendously successful. The playgrounds had an average weekly attendance of about 7000 children while the bathing beach accommodated daily from 400 to 600 bathers.

Recommendations

Keeping in mind the end for which playgrounds were established, namely that children might play in safety, I would recommend that the swing frames at the Parker, Hosmer and Bemis Playgrounds be replaced by new ones. The present apparatus at the Parker and Hosmer Playgrounds has been in use about ten years and is decidedly unsafe. The wood swing structure at the Bemis Playground is insecure and unsteady and leaves the children liable to injury. I would advise the acquisition of the land adjacent to the Bemis Playground to increase the playing area. At present it is nothing more than a baseball diamond. I would recommend the erection of a suitable storehouse in which to store equipment during the off-season. I would advise the building of permanent bath houses with toilet facilities for the bathing beach. The present houses are in a disreputable state and will hardly be more useful for another season. I would strongly advise the continuance of Saltonstall Park, or some part of it, as a playground, as this is a playground which is largely frequented by the children during the season and if they were denied the use of it, they would be obliged to look elsewhere for recreation.

In conclusion, I wish to thank the members of the Playground Commission, the instructors and other Town officials and citizens for their co-operation and assistance in making the Summer of 1934 a successful recreational season in Watertown.

JOSEPH W. ANDREWS, Supt.
BERNARD S. McHUGH, Chairman
ARTHUR C. FAGAN,
EDMUND P. HICKEY, Secretary

Watertown Playground Commission.

REPORT OF TOWN VETERINARIAN

1934

To the Honorable Board of Selectmen:

Gentlemen:

My annual report as Town Veterinarian and Inspector of animals is respectfully submitted.

During the year there have been a larger number of dog bite cases reported than usual. These reports have been made to me by the Board of Health, Police Department or State Division of Livestock Disease Control. A total of 324 visits has been made investigating these bite cases to ascertain whether or not the animals inflicting the injuries were affected with rabies. A state law requires that such animals be kept under a quarantine or observation period of two weeks.

There have been six positive cases of rabies in the Town during 1934. One of these cases was in a Chow dog of unknown ownership. It attacked, as far as could be determined, 14 other dogs of which 5 developed the disease and died. The remaining 9 had been vaccinated or were given treatment and did not develop rabies. 35 visits were made in connection with this outbreak, quarantining exposed dogs and making periodic examinations of them. In addition 6 visits were made to the Police Station to examine stray dogs picked up by the Police.

Inspection of all properties in the Town on which farm animals are kept has been carried out and certification of health and sanitary conditions made to the State Authorities, a copy being furnished the owners. Following the detection of tuberculosis in cattle by means of the tuberculin test a careful inspection and check-up has been made to see that proper disinfection and cleansing of the premises has been carried out.

Twenty three visits were made to the Town barn to treat or examine Town horses. Considering the age of most of these animals very little trouble has been encountered due largely to the care and attention given to them by the employees at the Town barn.

No outbreaks of infectious diseases in animals other than rabies have occurred during the year.

In carrying out the duties of my office I wish to express appreciation of the co-operation and helpful attitude taken by all Town Officials and Employees.

H. W. JAKEMAN, V. M. D.

Town Veterinarian and Inspector of Animals.

REPORT OF INFIRMARY DEPARTMENT

To the Honorable Board of Public Welfare:

Gentlemen:

I herewith submit my report as Keeper of the Infirmary for the year ending December 31, 1934.

Total number of inmates have been forty-four, thirteen, have been removed to another place of support, eight, secured employment, two, were transferred to the Tewksbury State Hospital, one to the Westboro Hospital, one, to the Saint Elizabeth Hospital, one, to the Holy Ghost Hospital, one, to the Boston Psychopathic Hospital, one, to the Bridgewater Hospital, one, to the Waltham Hospital, and one, died.

The average age of our inmates is sixty-eight; we have fifteen inmates at the present. The general health of our inmates has been very good. Only a small acreage of land was tilled and planted, which kept us supplied with fresh vegetables only a part of the time, any surplus was sold.

The inmates during the past few months who have been able to work, have been sawing and cutting wood which was brought in by the Tree Warden and distributed by the Welfare Department to the needy poor.

Our Infirmary needs to be painted and should be done this coming year. It should have two coats of paint. New gutters are absolutely necessary; when it rains, the water not carried off by the conductors runs down the side of the house owing to the leaky condition of the gutters.

I would also recommend that a shelter of some sort or a covered piazza be built to protect the inmates from the hot rays of the sun.

I earnestly request that a wire fence be built around the Infirmary grounds to protect our lawn and grounds from the general public who make it a common thoroughfare. It will also safeguard the school children and our feeble inmates from accidents that are liable to occur under the existing conditions. Auto drivers also try to make the grounds a Public Highway driving over the grounds both day and night.

Considerable painting and repairs should be made in the interior of the Infirmary.

I wish to thank the visitors who have made gifts to the inmates. I wish to thank the Watertown Emblem Club for their gifts at Christmas which brought much sunshine to all the inmates.

I wish also to thank the members of the Epworth League for their song service which was held up to mid-year.

Our Town Physician Dr. M. J. Kelley has carefully attended to the wants of our inmates who have been ill.

We welcome visitors during reasonable hours. In closing I wish to thank your Honorable Board for your kind and courteous attention.

GEORGE H. WHITE,

Keeper.

FEDERAL EMERGENCY RELIEF ADMINISTRATION

As the Emergency Relief Administrator for the Town of Watertown, I wish to present a resume of the activities engaged in, their relation to relieving some of the tax burden through the placement of potential and actual Welfare and Soldiers' Relief cases and other unemployed, and also by making much needed new installation, necessary repairs, and providing for maintenance of town facilities.

During the calendar year of 1934, a total of $490,000.00 was disbursed for wages only, $27,400.00 for materials purchased under C. W. A., $14,000.00 by the War De-, partment, and $33,000.00 by town appropriation.

The following items amounting to $148,550.00 all have a direct bearing on taxes as regular town maintenance items, and will effect a saving on taxes for years to come:

12,250 feet of new drainage was installed in various sections of the town when it was necessary, owing to insufficient drainage, at a labor cost of $50,700.00. There is still 1100 feet to be completed for which projects have been allowed.

4850 feet of new water mains were installed to take the place of worn-out, clogged and inadequate piping, increasing circulatory flow for better fire protection and manufacturing service. Labor cost was $13,000.00.

A thorough renovation of all schools has been in progress during the entire year at a labor cost of $48,000.00. When this work is completed, all necessary major repairs will have been made. This work included painting, roofing repairs, waterproofing and repointing, brick and mason work. replacing broken glass, and repairing school equipment.

Approximately eight miles of gravel walks and street gutters have been regraded and placed in a safe condition at a cost of $24,000.00.

On public buildings, such as the Legion Home, Central Fire Station, West End Library, necessary repairs were made. A portion of the old Town Hall was converted into a repair garage for police cars. All of this was done at an outlay of $4,000.00.

Another maintenance item which has recently been provided is for the cleaning of all open and closed water shed drains on which no work has been done for many years. When this is completed, faster drainage will result and the present tendency of streets flooding will be eliminated. A total of $7,200.00 has been spent to Dec. 31, 1934.

Arlington and Common Street Cemetery fences have been cleaned and painted at a cost of $750.00.

New street signs were painted at a cost of $900.00.

Other projects that are still in operation or have been completed are:

Town Playgrounds—on which $87,000.00 has been spent in labor, for improvements and beautification. Included in this is the work being done in Saltonstall Park. This will show a vast improvement this Spring, when finally seeded and planted with new trees and shrubbery.

On Ridgelawn Cemetery the old stone wall has been rebuilt, all roads regraded and covered, and at the present time, we are removing a large ledge providing for more burial lots.

Five new professional tennis courts are provided at Victory Field; also a Dug-out for the use of players.

The Tree Warden is removing all dead trees and dangerous limbs on town property with E. R. A. labor and we have just provided more men to assist in removing Brown Tail Moths and other tree pests. .

The C. W. A. and E. R. A. projects at Watertown Arsenal comprise a total of ninety-five items, forty-six of which have been completed. The work consists of reconditioning and rehabilitating buildings in stand-by conditions and of cleaning and rust-proofing some $8,000,000. worth of stand-by machinery. The work on buildings consisted of repairs to roofs, cleaning and painting structural steel, interior painting, remodeling, painting and water-proofing brick work, plastering and repairs to steam, electric and water lines.

The maximum number of Watertown employees engaged in CWA projects was 861, fourteen of whom were women. The total paid in wages to these employees was $118,303.07. Sixteen thousand seven hundred eighty dollars ($16,780.00) CWA funds and $3,766.90 War Department funds, a total of $20,546.80 was expended for materials during the same period. The CWA projects were first approved by the ERA for Massachusetts in December, 1933, and were discontinued on April 30, 1934.

On December 31, 1934, there were 249 employees on ERA projects approved by the Town of Watertown for work at the Arsenal. These projects were first approved in May, 1934, and there has been expended for wages up to December 31, 1934, $62,704.05. During the same period there was expended for materials approximately $10,000., all of which was allotted by the War Department.

Female employment is provided by making clothing, household linens, etc., for distribution through the Welfare Department. Over $22,000. has been paid to sewers and knitters. All material except findings, is provided by E. R. A. Assistants were furnished to the Library to recatalog and rebind worn-out books.

In order to provide employment for so-called "white collar men," we are using engineers for landscaping, new zoning maps, Assessors' maps and block plans.

A census of all under 21 years of age is being taken to assist the School Department in their estimates for pre-school night school and other educational purposes.

Assistant playground instructors were furnished during the vacation period.

We have just recently organized a Community Center Project with E. R. A. allotments providing for four centers to furnish much needed instruction for part time amusement to those who have no money to provide it. This is for special benefit of the younger class out of school and unable to procure work. In this project are offered athletics, tap and ballroom dancing, games of all kinds, and many other forms of useful occupation of idle time. We are indebted to the School Department for their support in providing necessary quarters. A dance orchestra is also provided for furnishing music through the E. R. A.

A concert orchestra under the direction of Mr. Robert MacDonald (who is paid by E. R. A. funds), comprised of over 40 volunteer musicians has given several very excellent exhibitions of musical talent to the public.

A project for making and repairing toys to be used in pre-school centers has been presented for approval.

Clerical help is also provided to the National Re-employment Bureau in the Chamber of Commerce.

Our present allotment of $43,000. per month is an increase of $20,000. since May 1st when E. R. A. began. This provides for the employment of 758 men and 97 women, of which 315 men and 36 women and their dependents would be on the Welfare Roll, and 60 ex-Service men would be drawing on Soldiers' Relief.

MAURICE H. O'CONNELL,

E. R. A. Administrator

Chairman, Board of Selectmen.

REPORT OF PLANNING BOARD

The Planning Board met on March 17th, 1934, and organized as follows: Massis N. Tomassian, Chairman, Ronald M. Stone, Secretary, and Wilfred A. Norris, John H. Dardis, and Ernest M. Small, members.

At the request of the Planning Board the Chairman of the Board of Selectmen, as E. R. A. Administrator, secured E. R. A. funds for the preparation of a Use Map of the town by the engineering department. This map will be of much value to the Planning Board and the Town as it will show the use to which each building in the Town is being put.

Present two-family districts in which a large majority of houses are one-family houses should be changed to one-family districts to give home owners proper protection. Any further increase of two-family houses in such districts will not only reduce the revenue in taxes but increase the expenses of the town.

At a Town Meeting held in March it was voted to appoint a committee consisting of the Town Counsel, Building Inspector and the five members of the Planning Board to study and revise the present Zoning By-laws of the Town and voted to appropriate $100.—— to be used as payment for expert advice and incidental expenses.

The committee secured the services of Mr. Edward T. Hartman, Mass. State Consultant of Planning, to study and rewrite our present Zoning By-laws in order to make them conform to new legislation and modern zoning practice. The new By-laws are now ready and after a hearing will be presented to the Town Meeting for action.

A hearing was held relative to a change of Zoning lines at the corner of Main and Gleason -Sts. on petition of Joseph Doherty and others. After hearing the tremendous opposition that appeared, it was voted to recommend no change to the Town Meeting.

ıA joint meeting was held at the Administration Building with the Waltham Planning Board for the purpose of discussing Zoning along town boundary lines.

It was agreed to prepare plans and make a study for the purpose of zoning for the same classes of homes along the boundary lines of Watertown and Waltham.

In January 1935 the Town Counsel informed the Planning Board of an adverse decision in the Superior Court to action brought by the Building Inspector for enlargement of a non-conforming building located at School and Mt. Auburn Streets.

The Planning Board and Town Counsel felt that the interests of the town required an appeal from the decision and so voted. If this decision is not reversed it will seriously affect Watertown and every town in Massachusetts that is operating under modern Zoning By-laws. It will mean that an existing non-conforming building can be enlarged at the will of the owner by merely complying to the building laws.

Respectfully submitted,

MASSIS N. TOMASSIAN, *Chairman*
RONALD M. STONE, *Secretary*
JOHN H. DARDIS
WILFRED A. NORRIS
ERNEST M. SMALL

Planning Board.

REPORT OF TOWN PHYSICIAN

January 19, 1935.

To the Honorable Board of Selectmen:

Watertown, Mass.

Gentlemen:

I respectfully submit my report for the year ending December 31, 1934.

During the year 2253 examinations, consultations and visits to homes were made. As you will note the duties of Town Physician have increased somewhat in the past year.

The Police Department has rendered valuable assistance in transferring patients to the various hospitals by ambulance and cruisers.

I thank the Honorable Board of Selectmen and the heads of the various departments for their co-operation.

Respectfully,

M. J. KELLEY, M. D.,
Town Physician.

WATERTOWN

MASSACHUSETTS

PUBLIC SCHOOLS

The Ninety-Seventh Annual Report

OF THE

SCHOOL COMMITTEE

AND THE

Fifty-Fourth Annual Report

OF THE

SUPERINTENDENT OF SCHOOLS

1934

THE HAMPSHIRE PRESS, INC.
CAMBRIDGE, MASS.
1935

SCHOOL COMMITTEE

CHARLES F. J. HARRINGTON,
          Chairman   Term expires 1935

HAROLD B. BLAZO	Term expires 1935
E. LOUISE RICHARDSON	Term expires 1936
HARRIE E. WAITE	Term expires 1936
ROSCOE F. DAUGHTERS	Term expires 1937
FRANCIS A. KELLY	Term expires 1937
PATRICK A. MENTON	Term expires 1937

WILFRED H. PRICE,
Superintendent of Schools.

Office, Administration Building

Office Hours

8:30 to 9:30 A. M., except Saturday
4 to 5 P. M., except Wednesday and Saturday

Watertown, Mass., January 10, 1935.

In School Committee: Voted: That the report of the Chairman and the report of the Superintendent of Schools be accepted and adopted as the annual report of the School Committee of the Town, and voted to print for distribution the report of the School Committee.

E. LOUISE RICHARDSON,

Secretary Pro Tem.

FINANCIAL STATEMENT

Receipts and Expenditures for
Year Ended December 31, 1934

Receipts

Appropriations	$568,925.00	
Smith-Hughes Fund	86.73	
		$569,011.73

Expenditures

General Control:		
Superintendent and enforcement of Law	$8,600.00	
Clerks	2,900.00	
Attendance Office Expense	616.80	
Office Expense	1,219.83	
Telephones	915.95	
		14,252.58
Instruction:		
Salaries	$444,037.26	
Books and Supplies	17,999.92	
		$462,037.18
Operation:		
Salaries	$34,357.25	
Supplies	2,062.10	
Light and Power	9,200.13	
Fuel	13,781.06	
School Halls	899.30	
Water	1,710.94	
		$62,010.78
Maintenance		$4,632.95
New Equipment		$697.05
Miscellaneous:		
Salaries of Physicians & Nurses	$6,000.00	
Health Supplies and Sundries	345.63	
		$6,345.63

Evening School:
Salaries	$2,894.90	
Supplies	102.20	
		$2,997.10

Trade Schools and Continuation School	$9,536.41
Transportation	$1,416.00
	$563,925.68
Smith-Hughes Fund	86.73
	$564,012.41
Unpaid Bills	50.00
	$564,062.41
Unexpended Balance	4,949.32
	$569,011.73

Treasury Receipts

Tuition:
State Wards	$1,412.65
Continuation School, cities and towns	32.24
Continuation & Trade School reimbursements	4,573.74
Sight saving class	231.98

Hall Rent		994.50
Senior-High School		
Stamps sold	$ .15	
Chemistry breakage	18.42	
Books and Supplies	52.46	
		71.03

Miscellaneous:
Damage, telephones, books, etc.	11.12
Evening Schools	110.00
Americanization Reimbursement	314.71

Continuation School Reimbursement 502.45
   (Home School)
Sight-Saving Class Reimbursement 500.00

$8,754.42
General School Fund $48,890.36

$57,644.78

REPORT OF THE SUPERINTENDENT

To the School Committee:

In accordance with your custom, I am submitting herewith a report upon the conditions of the schools for the year 1935. This is the ninety-seventh in the series of School Committee reports and the twenty-seventh that has been written by the present incumbent.

Educational conditions throughout the country in general remain unchanged, and it is needless for me to attempt to discuss major topics of current educational interest and importance. Every magazine and newspaper of note in our country has dealt with the educational problems that face our public schools and our educators.

Enrollments in the public schools have increased everywhere. More children are demanding educational opportunities and the new requests and new demands are coming from the pupils of secondary school level for whom training is more expansive and whose demands are more difficult to meet.

The raising of the compulsory school age to sixteen or eighteen years, the elimination of child labor, N. R. A. and other governmental regulations, have liberated from employment a class of boys and girls for whom our educational program must be formulated in our secondary and vocational schools.

These schools, in these particular fields must guide students in the understanding of the economic order in which they have been living and must aid them to a better knowledge of their own interest, aptitudes, and abilities, and a wiser selection of fields of service in which they may labor with profit both to themselves and to society.

Educators and laymen alike are of the opinion that there is an imperative need of constructing an educational program suitable to the new change of social order. This program must be comprehensive since education must touch the life of every growing child at every point of his social life and civic contact. Some critics are loth to accept our present educational organizations and educational procedures, claiming that they have proved inadequate in the training of our youth. It is generally concluded that our educational system has been the bulwark of our democracy in creating wholesome ideals and patriotism. Hasty change of an educational system that has given us effective service in the past is not wise and does not necessarily indicate progress until we know where we are going.

Neither you or I have any definite conception of the tremendous social and economic developments that lie just ahead. A careful study of the devastating effects of rapidly changing social and economic influences at work upon our schools must be made and the educational offerings revised to conform to the new readjustment.

The schools will have a tremendous responsibility in interpreting and perpetuating the advances made in this period of re-adjustment. The new education calls emphatically for the development of the program of studies and the activities of the school in a direction that will yield greater returns in the development of character and citizenship. We should fearlessly clear the curriculum of such matter that has no immediate social or economic value and include in our curriculums materials that will create in our boys and girls desirable attitudes toward citizenship and life.

There are many phases of school work that should be covered by this report. To this end, I have asked the high school principal and several of the directors and supervisors to submit to me a report of their work. I am therefore including a portion of their reports as a part of my annual report.

REPORT OF HIGH SCHOOL MASTER
Edwin H. Whitehill

The year 1935 marks the three hundredth anniversary of public secondary education in America, for in 1635, one year before the founding of Harvard College, was opened the Public Latin School in Boston, an institution still one of the foremost of its kind in the United States, and still existing for the one definite purpose of preparing boys for entrance to higher institutions. From this beginning in one of the original towns of Massachusetts Bay Colony has spread throughout our country the idea of free public secondary training until at the present time there are 23,550 public high schools with an enrollment of 4,399,422 pupils. Nor has the growth in numbers, exceedingly rapid during the twentieth century, been more startling than the expansion of the curriculum. In 1635 education of the secondary grades was largely for the training of boys for the Christian ministry, a purpose also recognized in the founding of Harvard College, hence a study of ancient languages plus a little mathematics and a little ancient history was deemed sufficient. Today the emphasis in education is being placed, and rightly so, on preparation for daily living in a world infinitely more complex in its organization, its relationships and its problems than the citizens of the town of Boston in 1635 could have dreamed.

Eighty years ago, in the fall of 1853, in the old Phillips Building 52 pupils under William Webster as master entered the first session of the Watertown High School. Twelve years later the School Committee felt the need of

larger accommodations for the High School, which at that
time numbered less than fifty pupils, and suggested making available for the school a hitherto unused and unfinished room on the second floor. The Chairman concludes
the recommendation with this interesting statement: "If
the alteration is made in the second story the town will
never be obliged to erect a building expressly to receive
the High School." In view of the fact that construction is
now under way of an addition to the second "building expressly to receive the High School' since that report was
written, it is evident that there was little realization of
the future destiny of what was then a rural farming community.

The present facilities for a greatly expanded curriculum
have kept pace with the growth in numbers and the variety of legitimate interests created by a greatly diversified
population. Whereas there is still a demand that it shall
be possible for a pupil to be prepared for any higher institution of learning in New England or even beyond the
borders of that section, there is also an ever growing call
for training in such practical arts as shall fit the pupil to
earn a living. But still more important is it in these un-
certain days that there shall be instruction in the funda-
mental virtues that lead to clean living, sound character
and a respect for law that shall make for good citizenship
in the community, the state, and the nation as well as for
a better international understanding. To this end we feel
that a careful study of our present curriculum should be
made with a view to its revision and expansion to meet
these needs.

A class of 292 pupils was graduated in June, the largest
on record. Of these, 25 have entered higher institutions,
largely by certificate as the number of colleges granting
admission by this method or by some modification of the
examination system is increasing. At the present time
the whole question of admission to college, including the

state teachers colleges, is undergoing investigation and the near future may see some modification by existing methods.

Continued satisfactory reports are coming in of the work of our graduates in higher institutions, while many of those who have finished their college career are making noteworthy achievements in their chosen fields.

Mr. Morton H. Cassidy in April was appointed to a position in the Hyde Park High School and much to the regret of us all entered upon the work there at the opening of the summer term. Mr. Cassidy by his thorough scholarship, his enthusiasm for his subject, his originality and resourcefulness had made the department of Biology one of the best and most widely known in New England

There is nothing of unusual importance in the life of the school for the past year to report. The daily work of the school has gone on with the usual attention and care in all departments. More pupils than ever before are taking part in the extra-curricular activities which include the musical organizations, athletics, and clubs.

Pupils in the school have co-operated to some extent with outside organizations in projects of mutual benefit. Our Band in conjunction with the Champion Legion Band gave a concert in the early part of the year which was in itself sufficient justification for the employment of Mr. Chick as bandmaster. Miss Bisbee's orchestra concert was of the usual high order and reflected great credit on her leadership. The usual Senior and Middler plays were given under the direction of Miss Griffith who also directed, in November, a short play given before the Watertown Woman's Club in recognition of the interest in the school shown annually by the scholarship awarded by the Woman's Club.

With the completion of the addition to the building a return to one session will solve some of the difficult problems now confronting us. We are looking forward with anticipation to a return to a normal school day and the improved facilities promised.

This report would not be complete without an expression of appreciation for the devoted service rendered to the School by Miss A. May Frost, who retired in June in accordance with the Tenure Law of 1914. Miss Frost was much more than a teacher of Latin; she was a sympathetic teacher of developing boys and girls. Her personal influence extended beyond the classroom to the lives and the interests and the homes of those whom she taught. Her work was her consuming passion and to it she gave her best and from it she parted with extreme regret. Her colleagues, the hundreds who have been her pupils, and all who have known her will join in wishing for her many years of happy memories and useful service in other fields.

REPORT OF PHYSICAL EDUCATION DEPARTMENT

Sally T. Biggane, Supervisor

The work of my department is functioning in a very efficient manner. Pupil leadership is one phase of our work which merits comment. Because of the fact that worthy use of leisure time is so essential today, pupil leadership, which furthers this, is considered an important part in our physical education program. You will find these leaders in the classroom of the elementary school conducting the physical education lesson each day. On the playground or in the playroom during the recess periods, you will find the captains as leaders taking charge of the games and play. In the Junior and Senior High Schools, the leaders are given an opportunity to help in the extra-curricular program of sports after school.

The physical instructors in the Junior and Senior High Schools co-operate with the nurses by weighing the underweight pupils each month and checking up on their health habits personally. This information is passed on to the doctor for his special examination in May.

Posture is always one of our most important objectives. Special postural examinations are given three times during the year in every grade throughout the school system. Pupils with serious defects are sent to the hospital clinics for further help.

It is a pleasure to see the grounds around the schools gradually being turned into adequate play spaces for the children. I hope that they will be made into safe places as well, by the addition of fences.

REPORT OF SCHOOL CAFETERIAS
Marion P. Keep, Supervisor

The Watertown School Department Cafeterias are in operation in the Senior High School, which has an enrollment of 1124 pupils, in the East Junior High School with 703 pupils, and in the West Junior High School with 908 pupils,—a total enrollment of 2735 students. More than two-thirds of the students and about one hundred teachers patronize the school cafeterias.

Lunch is prepared and served in each school daily. Because of the two-platoon system in the Senior High School, a mid-afternoon lunch is served in addition.

The daily luncheon offers: soup, made entirely from fresh vegetables, meat stock, or, in case of chowders, whole milk (absolutely no canned soups, with the exception of tomato, are used) ; a hot special (meat or fish plus potato and vegetable) salads, sandwiches (a choice of three kinds, plus dark bread and butter), salad rolls, milk, desserts (prepared in the cafeteria kitchens), ice cream, cookies, fruit and candy.

A great deal of painstaking effort is spent in preparing wholesome and well-balanced menus which will provide appetizing food and food rich in vitamin content. The menus are changed not only daily but weekly, thus offering variety from which to choose one's lunch.

In spite of increased cost of foods, the cafeteria management has been able, through careful planning and wise buying, to continue to serve all luncheon dishes at the very moderate prices first established, five and ten cents, including even the daily hot plate. Any child can, therefore, for the small sum of ten or fifteen cents, secure an appealing, hearty and nutritious noon meal.

REPORT OF INDUSTRIAL ARTS DEPARTMENT
John Black, Director

The number of pupils in the several departments have remained about the same this past year. Personal contact with each instructor has been made weekly.

The work of the sixth grades have continued with a few changes in projects.

A new course of study for woodworking in the Junior High Schools has been completed. This course is planned to co-ordinate the several subjects related to woodworking.

West Junior High School. During the past year a large storage cabinet has been built. This cabinet will allow each pupil an individual locker to store his work. Several lawn chairs painted in bright colors have been completed.

The sheet metal shop has built several metal frames for home work benches. The material for these benches is furnished by the pupils. At very little expense they have built a practical work bench. Work of this kind is encouraged by the writer because it will encourage pupils to make better use of their leisure time.

The print shop has been kept busy with the "Broadcaster."

East Junior High School. The print shop has been enlarged and renovated and is now a cheerful place to work.

Both woodworking shops and the print shop are working to capacity.

Senior High School. The machine shop will have the two new lathes completed for the fall term of school. There are a few difficult patterns to be finished. Several repair jobs requiring welding have provided practical experience in the art of welding. Tables, book cabinets and miscellaneous articles have been made for the several elementary schools in the wood shop. The electrical shop is overcrowded. This course is very popular. Tracings and blueprints for the Junior High woodworking course were furnished by the drafting room. The Print Shop is taking care of the general printing for the schools.

As this report is being written the echo of the steam shovel tells us our new annex is under way. The new shops will allow for larger classes.

There is a need for a new course in auto ignition. There will be practically no expense for this equipment as most of the equipment will be donated. The present sheet metal and electrical shop could be used for this course.

REPORT OF DRAWING SUPERVISOR
Florence H. Russell, Supervisor

It is gratifying to be able to say that the results of the instruction given during the past year have attained the usual standard despite the fact that we have cut the cost of supplies to less than that of previous years.

The full-time week allotted to Miss Farley, Elementary Assistant, relieved me of some of my fourth grade teaching, giving me opportunity to supervise the Senior High School classes and make any adjustments necessary to develop a strong progressive course in art, throughout the system.

In the Junior High Schools, there has been no change in the teachers of drawing, but an increase in the number of classes, making full programs for these teachers.

A new course of study of a more permanent form was given to the Junior High art teachers in September. This is such, that new problems may be added to it from time to time. Group meetings with these teachers enabled us to commence the year well.

The removal of the lockers from the drawing room at the West Junior High was accomplished during the summer, giving added blackboard space, which is being used to advantage.

The Broadcaster, the school publication in this building is a fine example of applied art.

Those who witnessed the operetta given in March at the West Junior High saw a worthy use of trained ability in good art and good music. In coming years when the margin of leisure will be greatly extended, it will be important that these future citizens have abundant resources for making the most wholesome use of their increased leisure through ability to appreciate the fine arts.

The Exhibition of Art from the elementary and junior high schools given last May at the Francis Hall School, gave the public an opportunity to see the great value of art education as a unifying influence for other school subjects. It was largely attended by parents and friends as well as by supervisors and teachers from other cities. There were over one hundred and fifty mounts, as well as one hundred chalk drawings from the easel classes.

I feel that exhibitions such as this, as well as those held from time to time at the Public Library are well worth while, as they not only place our work before the public but stimulate interest among the pupils.

In closing may I thank the parents for their splendid co-operation in supplying material for the easel classes which we could not have otherwise obtained. Also I thank the Manual Training Department for easels constructed.

Lastly, may I thank the teachers for their untiring effort in upholding the standard of work I endeavor to maintain.

REPORT OF MUSIC DEPARTMENT
Rena I. Bisbee, Supervisor

The general program of music in our Watertown schools was about the same for the year 1933-34 as for the past few years. Certain variations are necessary each year because of conditions in different buildings, and when there are extra public assemblies or entertainments for which chorus and orchestra are needed, the music schedule has to be adapted to these.

From the very first year in school our chief endeavor is to make the child love music, know how to listen to it and enjoy active participation at first with the voice and later add the playing of some instrument|. It seems to the supervisor that there is an increased interest in vocal music among the older boys and girls. This change is noticeable in the Junior High Schools as now there are more who volunteer for special group work or are willing even to sing solos. Since the voices of pupils at this age are in a transitional stage (especially those of the boys) it has often been difficult to make the right appeal for overcoming a certain diffidence about singing.

Another encouraging feature is the size of the volunteer chorus at the High School. Many late applicants had to be refused admission because better work can be done with a group that is not too large. If the High School program permitted, a second chorus or a mixed glee club could be formed, as it is now, the boys' glee club meets out of school hours. They are doing some intensive work preparatory to giving a whole evening's program.

While on the subject of the High School, mention should be made of the operetta given on December eleventh, for All School Night. Beside the talented soloists, a selected chorus and orchestra showed what can be done by such young musicians.

The High School Orchestra and Band concert last March showed great advancement in both organizations. From the orchestra, eight pupils had the honor of being admitted to the New England High School Festival Orchestra which met at Hampton Beach, N. H. last May. The band formed one of the units at the State Festival in Melrose earlier that month. Among the special activities this Fall was the playing by the orchestra on Parents' Night.

Mr. Chick reports that the band has played for three out of town football games beside the home games. They have also furnished music for different organizations here in town on special occasions. The joint concert by the Legion and High School bands, under the leadership of Arnold Chick has become an annual event.

/The two Junior High School orchestras have a large registration. A "symphony" group has been formed, taking the most advanced players from both schools. This rehearses after school hours. A band at the West Junior High School is soon to be started.

Several of the grammar schools have orchestras, under the supervision of Mrs. Drew, assistant supervisor of music. These orchestras made their first public appearance at the Christmas assemblies.

Speaking of school assemblies, it is gratifying to have the parents attend in even greater numbers each year. They find these entertainments well worth while. The Christmas and patriotic musical programs have become a special feature in our schools and are anticipated by many interested friends.

Now that there is a community orchestra and a community chorus, our High School graduates can go into these and continue with ensemble music. Reports from the boys and girls going to college tell of prominent places in the musical organizations of their respective schools. Some will make music a profession and others will find it the happiest way to spend leisure time.

REPORT OF SCHOOL NURSES

Number of pupils examined by Physicians		5408
Number of pupils having defects		920
Nose and throat	617	
Heart (functional and organic)	83	
Nutrition	79	
Postural defects	192	
Skin	56	
Number of pupils having defective vision		240
Number of pupils having defective hearing		55
Number of individual inspections		25500
Number of home visits		1264
Number of first aid treatments		1154
Number of visits to clinics		44
Number of pupils tested by State Clinics:		
Chadwick		157
Retarded		61

The Chadwick Clinic conducted by the Massachusetts Department of Public Health in May 1934, re-examined 157 pupils and reported 152 improved. 12 pupils were discharged, requiring no further check-up. Children in need of special treatment were approved by the Clinic and sent to Health Camps through donations from local organizations.

Through follow-up work and home co-operation, urgent defects have been cared for.

The promotion of the health of our school population continues to receive the interested attention of Principals and Teachers.

MARY C. CARNEY,
SUSAN M. HARDING,
ALICE JOHNSON,
School Nurses.

REPORT OF THE ATTENDANCE AND
CERTIFICATING DEPARTMENT

During the year ending December 31, 1934, the Supervisors of Attendance investigated sixteen hundred and ninety-five cases of reported non-attendance. Of these cases three hundred and twenty-four were found to be caused by truancy and seventy due to the indifference and neglect of the parents. It was necessary to resort to the courts in only two cases. One boy was committed to the Middlesex County Training School and one case is still pending in the court.

This year the Supervisors of Attendance in co-operation with the School Nurses took over the work of caring for and clothing needy children. This work is supported by the voluntary contributions of all the school employees under the name of the School Welfare Fund. Approximately two hundred children have been given shoes, clothing, eyeglasses and in a few emergency cases medical care.

The certificating office issued four hundred and seventy-four certificates to employed minors during the year, fifty-nine boys were issued newsboys licenses.

JOSEPH L. CARROLL,
FRANCIS M. CAVERLY,
Supervisors of Attendance.

In conclusion I desire to express my appreciation to the School Committee for their loyal support and to the school teachers for their hearty co-operation in carrying out the work of the schools.

Respectfully submitted,

WILFRED H. PRICE,
Superintendent.

Enrollment by Grades, January 1, 1935
Compared with January 1, 1934

	1934	1935
Kindergarten	415	394
Grade 1	638	630
Grade 2	596	610
Grade 3	565	590
Grade 4	589	582
Grade 5	565	585
Grade 6	531	546
Grade 7	535	522
Grade 8	510	546
Grade 9	471	504
Grade 10	460	420
Grade 11	345	388
Grade 12	274	277
Post Graduate	38	24
Special Classes	149	124
Sight-saving class	10	11
	6691	6753
Continuation School	8	2
	6691	6653

SUMMARY OF STATISTICS
Teachers, January 1, 1934

Number of Principals	9
Number of teachers in high school	42
Number of teachers in junior high schools	61
Number of teachers in elementary schools	125
Number of special teachers and supervisors	13

Teachers, January 1, 1935

Number of Principals	9
Number of teachers in high school	∕
Number of teachers in junior high schools	62
Number of teachers in elementary schools	121
Number of special teachers and supervisors	12

Pupils

Pupils enrolled, school year 1933-34	6895
Average daily attendance	6230
Average membership	6662
Enrolled January 1, 1935	6755
Enrolled January 1, 1934	6699
Enrolled January 1, 1933	6570
Enrolled January 1, 1932	6493
Enrolled January 1, 1931	6280
Enrolled January 1, 1930	6110
Enrolled January 1, 1929	5674
Enrolled January 1, 1928	5204
Enrolled January 1, 1927	4568
Enrolled January 1, 1926	4260

REPORT OF THE CHAIRMAN OF THE SCHOOL COMMITTEE

To the School Committee and Citizens of Watertown:

Having been duly authorized by the unanimous vote of the School Committee, on December 5, 1934, to prepare a report which, with the report of the Superintendent, is to be considered a report of the School Committee for the year 1934, the Chairman herewith respectfully presents his report This report has been submitted to the Committee and after due consideration, unanimously approved.

Budget

The stringency of the times requires careful and conscientious handling of all public funds by those entrusted with the expending of same. Your School Committee has carefully and thoughtfully administered the budget this year. We are pleased to report that there is a balance of $4,949.32, which has been returned to the Town. This saving is the result of rigid economy consistent with efficiency. It has been the desire of your Committee to steer a middle course in the matter of economy rather than to acquiesce to radical demands in this direction or to completely ignore the will of those people who desire the amplification of public expenditures for education in order that some particular hobby may be included in the curriculum, or to ignore the will of the people who chose them to carry out their will. Your Committee subscribes to a philosophy of government which prescribes that it is the duty of public officials to determine the will of those whom they represent and having once determined it, follow that will unswervingly. With this thought in mind, when the question of restoring salaries to their normal levels presented itself, it was determined that the Committee would instruct its Chairman to follow the will of the Town Meeting Members, as expressed by their vote on an article in the Warrant, calling for an expression of opinion with respect to the restoration of salary cuts. The majority of the Town Meeting voted to restore salaries to their 1932 levels; therefore, your Chairman proceeded accordingly to insure the appropriation of sufficient funds to carry out this purpose. It becomes our duty to report that adequate money was appropriated and salary cuts were restored. A reasonable appropriation was also received to be used for payment of salaries to those absent for a limited time on account of sickness. We feel certain that the generosity of the townspeople is appreciated in full by the School Department employees because of the loyalty and thorough concept of duty displayed, almost without exception, by those employed in this Department. Adequate money was appropriated to continue the automatic increment guaranteed to teachers by contract at the time of employment. For the past two years, the initial date of this increment has been January first rather than September first, in order that the appropriation might coincide with the fiscal year of the Town.

In addition to the balance above mentioned, your Committee transferred from the **Instruction Account** **$4,084** to make up a deficiency within the school budget and to meet obligations contracted in the previous year; $834.00 of this amount was transferred to General Control to meet the unpaid..expense of the Accounting equipment; $3,-200.00 was transferred to the Fuel Account to take care of excess fuel used because of the unusually cold winter; $50.00 was transferred to Unpaid Bills to reimburse the Attendance Officers for expenses contracted by them, with the approval of the Committee but unpaid because of a deficiency in the budget of last year. Gross savings, as a result of the changes in instruction and supervision, together with the replacement of teachers, has resulted in a saving to the Town in excess of $12,000.00 on an annual basis with no impairment of efficiency.

Teachers

The total teaching personnel has been reduced by two through the merging of classes and the abolition of position of Elementary Supervisor. The usual resignations made it possible to accomplish this saving without the discharge of a single teacher. Further reduction in the teaching personnel could probably be accomplished, without impairment of the educational facilities of the Town, by abandonment of the Junior High School System.

The appointment and re-appointment of teachers consumed the full time of the Committee at several meetings as it was deemed advisable, in view of certain unpleasant experiences, comments and inuendos, to carefully consider the references, qualifications, marks and any other data pertaining to the record of a teacher or applicant for teaching position in our system and to permit only those thoroughly qualified to continue as employees of the Department. Your Committee, acting on the suggestion of the Chairman, has authorized the appointment of a subcommittee of two with the Superintendent ex-officio to consider a more intelligent system for determining the relative merits and qualifications of applicants for teaching positions. Mr. Menton and Miss Richardson were appointed as the sub-committee, to report in February, 1935.

Your Committee discontinued the practice of paying transportation charges incurred by certain student teach- .ers, who are permitted to observe and train in our system. It was the feeling of the Committee that this was an unwarranted expense, particularly in view of the fact that we were offering our facilities without charge to such students.

Supervisory Program

The Supervisory Staff has been reorganized and revised, as recommended by the Columbia Survey. It became apparent to your Committee that some individuals designated as supervisors and receiving extra compensation as such were, in reality, traveling teachers. Therefore, they were so designated and their salaries adjusted accordingly. Comment, justifying this change, will be found on Page 106, Item 4 of the Columbia Survey.

The position of Elementary Supervisor has been abolished and the work formerly handled by the incumbent is now being carried on by the Superintendent and the Principals of the various schools, with monthly reports to the full Committee. This change has worked out satisfactorily, according to our Superintendent. The former Elementary Supervisor has been assigned to teaching in the fourth grade and accepted that assignment, filling a vacancy as a result of a resignation. This change saves the Town $3,000.00 annually.

Economic conditions have made unnecessary the maintenance of Continuation School as a separate unit because of the reduced number of pupils. Therefore, your Committee has merged the Continuation School pupils with the regular Junior High School classes and have saved the three hundred dollars formerly allotted to the Continuation School teacher because of the fact that he was already receiving maximum compensation as a Junior

High School teacher and is now able to handle these pupils. as members of his regular classes.

The duties of the Supervisor of Drawing have been enlarged and revised. This Supervisor now directs the drawing throughout the system. We believe this to be a progressive step in view of the intricacies of this subject.

The athletic activities have been rearranged and new coaches assigned to undertake the work of handling the teams. The present plan is being carefully watched and the results will be studied by your Committee.

The Supervisor of Industrial Arts is now in charge of all industrial arts work within the system and also supervises manual training. He is required to report periodically to the Superintendent and the School Committee. This Supervisor has been requested to "give more attention to the relationship of the content of the industrial arts courses to the actual needs of the pupils of Watertown," as recommended by the Columbia Survey.

Curriculum Revision

There has been an unusual increase in the number of pupils assigned to the Industrial Arts course, which leads to one of two conclusions: that either the pupils reaching the Senior High School have not been properly prepared for subjects requiring a higher standard of intelligence or they are not receiving sufficient guidance at the Junior High Schools in the matter of selecting other courses, which are of greater educational value and conducive to better mental development. The latter conclusion is supported by a written report from the Superintendent of Schools, from which we quote verbatim: "Replies were received from each of the three High School Masters relative to the mode of procedure employed in assigning pupils to the Industrial Arts courses, to the effect that courses of study in the grades from seven to twelve are submitted to the individual pupils and they are assigned to relative courses according to their choice. We assume that teachers of Vocational Guidance will exert a certain influence on the pupil, according to his choice of career." The Superintendent was asked by your Chairman for an opinion as to the possibility of students now assigned to Industrial Arts courses to profitably undertake work in other courses but his reply to this inquiry contains no opinion or recommendation. The cost of the Industrial Arts Department, together with expenditures for trade school education outside of Town, is altogether out of proportion to the cost of other courses. According to figures submitted by the Superintendent, this type of education has reached the staggering cost of approximately $43,000.00, nearly ten per cent of the total instruction and supply budget. It is hoped by your Committee that, with proper guidance, more pupils will be diverted to other courses as they are capable of undertaking the work.

With the unanimous permission of the School Committee, your Chairman proposes to again make an effort to prevail upon the Legislature to amend the law which compels the inclusion of Industrial Arts courses in the curriculum of our Senior High School. Should his efforts be successful, it would be possible to dispense with these courses and offer to the pupil interested in trade work an opportunity in one of the adjoining communities in which are located trade schools. If the law above referred to is changed, Watertown can effect a considerable saving and offer better opportunities to those interested in trade school work. Those pupils not interested in trade work but unable to keep up with the regular work of the other courses may then be assigned to smaller classes where they should receive more individual attention.

Your Committee gave some thought to the revision, merging or elimination of various courses at the Senior High School, but in view of the approaching retirement of the present Principal, it was thought wise to allow the matter to rest until the new Principal was appointed, at which time it would be possible to consider with him the most desirable procedure towards reorganization.

Junior High School System

During the past year, your Chairman consulted with various educators, who advanced the opinion that the educational results of the Junior High School system have not warranted the additional expense required for the operation of this system. In view of these opinions, your Committee has consented to the appointment of a sub-committee, composed of Mr. Kelley, Mr. Daughters and the Superintendent ex-officio, to study this matter and to make recommendations, as a result of their deliberations, to the full Committee in February, 1935.

It should be noted that in the University City of Cambridge and our neighboring Town of Brookline, the Junior High School System was never adopted and it is the opinion of the majority of those connected with the School System of these communities that education has not suffered within the community.

Buildings and Building Construction

Chapters III and IV of the Columbia Survey deal extensively with the existing buildings and the anticipated building requirements of the Town, based on the continuance of the Junior High School System. The recommendations, as to location of proposed buildings, are well conceived. Your Committee considers it inadvisable to accept the survey plan in its entirety until such time as the sub-committee on Junior High Schools shall have reported and the report has been exhaustively considered by the School Committee. The Chairman believes that future school buildings in the Town should be all fireproof construction rather than the Type B classification of the American Institute of Architects, as recommended by the Survey in Chapter III. The reason for this difference in opinion is that the initial cost of erecting fireproof construction is but slightly greater than the Type B construction above referred to, but the difference in cost will be absorbed by the saving in upkeep and insurance in a few years' time. The difference in fire insurance cost alone would be twenty cents per hundred dollars of value annually. Your Committee has voted to recommend to the Town Meeting the substitution of a new fireproof, twenty-five room building in place of the present Phillips and Francis Schools. As recommended on Page 43 of the Columbia Survey, the new school should be constructed to permit enlargement on a scientific basis. Immediately, upon the completion of this new building, the Grant School, which is more than fifty years of age, should be abandoned and the Town re-districted to permit the maximum use of the new building and to relieve congestion in some of the present elementary schools, as well as the West Junior High School. The Columbia Survey criticizes some of our past building committees and it is the opinion of your present School Committee that future buildings should be built under the jurisdiction of the School Committee acting as a building committee. This arrangement will prevent interference with the progressive planning of the School Committee by a non-cooperative building committee.

In the matter of the addition to the Senior High School, your School Committee, in joint session with the Building Committee, recommended the elimination of the proposed small auditorium or study hall and the substitution, therefor, of class rooms. This request, however, was disregarded by the Building Committee, over the strenuous objections of the Chairman of the School Committee, who informed the Building Committee that adequate auditorium facilities were already provided in the present building and that the School Committtee objected to lowering the standard of specifications for the sake of building an unnecessary room. During the discussion concerning the addition, the question was raised as to whether or not the

Junior High School System was to be continued in the Town and your Chairman advised the Building Committee of the existence of a sub-committee studying this plan and suggested that, in event of a report favoring the abolition of the Junior High School System, the present Senior High School facilities might prove inadequate, unless the space assigned to the new auditorium was devoted to class rooms. The authority for this statement is based on a written report to your Chairman by the Superintendent under date of November 28, 1934, in which he states, "it would appear to me that if the numbers that are already in the ninth grade were transferred to the Senior High School, the building would be too small to accommodate the same even with the new addition." We trust this incident demonstrates the wisdom of building future schools under the jurisdiction of the School Committee.

This idea was called to the attention of the Town in 1932 by Francis A. Kelly in his report of that year.

Building Maintenance

It seems appropriate to call to the attention of the Town the matter of building maintenance on which there has been expended a constantly reducing amount. During the past three years, the average amount appropriated for the work has been $5,500.00 as against approximately $16,-00000 for 1931 It is self-evident that, to maintain buildings valued at approximately $2,000,000 this amount is entirely insufficient. It, therefore, became necessary for your School Committee to accept the assistance of the Federal Government and the Welfare Department in order to properly maintain your school property. The total labor and material received from this source for the years 1933 and 1934 amounted to approximately $50,000.00. Much of the work undertaken by the Federal Government allotment could have been avoided had the Town appropriated an adequate amount yearly to maintain their public buildings. Your Committee respectfully recommends more careful consideration of this problem in the future. It might appear from the fact that there is a small balance in the maintenance account that the points above made are not well taken but if it is considered that practically no labor is included in the maintenance expenditures this year, together with the fact that maintenance supplies have been curtailed on account of Federal allotments unforeseen when the budget was contemplated, this balance is easily understood.

Purchase of Supplies

Your Committee decided that the purchase of supplies under our present organization should be made by a sub-committee of the School Committee, consisting of the Chairman, and Secretary, together with the Superintendent. All supplies bought during the past year have been purchased from the lowest responsible bidders after competitive bids from at least three interested concerns. We are convinced that the Town saved considerable money as a result of this procedure and we recommend the continuance of the plan but with more careful attention to the matter of specifications, which will enable all bidders to compete on the same basis. The Superintendent has been asked to submit complete data on this subject at an early meeting. It has been the purpose of your Committee to purchase only those supplies which will be used during the current fiscal year, as far as possible, which policy has been in keeping with the ideas of the Finance Committee and the Town Meeting.

Reports of Committees

The sub-committee appointed to revise the rules and regulations governing the conduct of the Schools completed its work and submitted to the full Committee its report, which, after discussion and revision, was adopted unanimously. The new rules are to be printed and distributed in the near future.

The Committee appointed to prepare regulations governing the rental of the School Halls has also reported and the report has been accepted.

Both of these committees have worked long and arduously and presented to the full Committee reports which were most intelligent and satisfactory.

There has been a marked improvement in the conduct of the business administration of the School Department, due to the installation of an Accounting System. The information required by the Committee on short notice is more easily obtained than under the former accounting system.

We call attention to the fact that the eight thousand dollar Columbia Survey has guided us in many important changes and recommendations covered by this report.

Various members of the Committee have consulted with prominent educators whose assistance and advice have been invaluable. We feel that the remarks, complimentary to the conduct of the educational system in Watertown, as expressed by Commissioner of Education, Payson Smith, on the occasion of his recent visit here, give testimony to the progressive and intelligent handling of school affairs by your present Committee.

Conclusion

The School Committee expresses its thanks to the employees of the School Department and to the citizens of Watertown for their consideration and assistance in the administration of the affairs of the schools during a most trying and difficult economic era.

Your Chairman expresses his appreciation and gratitude to the School Committee for honoring him with the Chairmanship during the past year, and for the cooperation and assistance rendered.

With all sincerity, the Chairman wishes to express to the Finance Committee his appreciation of the fair, considerate and courteous treatment accorded him in the presentation of the school budget.

Your Committee pledges itself to carry forward for the balance of its term, the plans and ideals which it is hoped will improve our educational system.

Respectfully submitted,

CHARLES F. J. HARRINGTON,
Chairman of the School Committee.

AVERAGE MEMBERSHIP AND NUMBER OF TEACHERS FOR THE PAST TEN YEARS, INCLUDING THE HIGH SCHOOL AND EXCLUDING THE CONTINUATION SCHOOL

	1925	1926	1927	1928	1929	1930	1931	1932	1933	1934
Average membership for school year ending June	3889	4055	4643	5112	5202	6005	6192	6393	6541	6662
Number of teachers	138	152	165	180	201	225	231	242	250	246

AVERAGE MEMBERSHIP AND NUMBER OF TEACHERS FOR THE PAST TEN YEARS IN THE SENIOR HIGH SCHOOL

	1925	1926	1927	1928	1929	1930	1931	1932	1933	1934
Average membership	477	493	537	604	695	739	799	956	1052	1100
Number of teachers	21	25	27	30	32	33	35	44	44	44

School	High	Junior High	Elementary	Total	High	Junior High	Elementary	Total	High	Junior High	Elementary	Total	High	Junior High	Elementary	Total	No. days in session
Senior High	1152			1152	1044			1044	1100			1100	183819			183819	176
East Junior		688		688		641		641		672		672		112895		112895	176
West Junior		890		890		823		823		868		868		144844		144844	176
Browne			456	456			408	408			442	442			71273	71273	175
Coolidge			748	748			683	683			731	731			73194	73194	175
Hosmer			955	955			883	883			940	940			154090	154090	175
Lowell			713	713			608	608			673	673			106353	106353	175
Parker-Grant and Marshall Spring			718	718			660	660			709	709			115040	115040	174
Francis-Phillips			575	575			480	480			525	525			83520	83520	174
	1152	1578	4165	6895	1044	1464	3722	6230	1100	1540	4020	6660	183819	257739	603470	1045028	174

GRADUATION EXERCISES
The Senior High School
Watertown, Massachusetts

AUDITORIUM
Friday, June 15, 1934   8:00 P.M.

PROGRAM

PROCESSIONAL, The Conqueror   *Corey*
Orchestra

IN SPAIN   *di Chiara*
Chorus and Orchestra

PRAYER
Rev. James C. Simpson

THE HEAVENS ARE DECLARING   *Beethoven*
Chorus

ADDRESS
Mr. James Roosevelt

MINNEHAHA, Indian Serenade   *Loring*
Chorus

PRESENTATION OF DIPLOMAS,
Mr. Charles F. J. Harrington, Chairman of School Committee

MASSACHUSETTS STATE SONG   *Bunting*
Chorus and Orchestra

RECESSIONAL, The Captain General   *Louka*
Orchestra

CLASS OF 1934

College

Helen Adess
Gerard Thomas Amirian
Lois Arline Ayers
Harry Bahadurian
Mary Alison Belding
Murray Earl Berringer
Kenneth Thomas Bird
Donald Alfred Boylan
George Warren Bramhall
Elizabeth Barbara Brooks
Francis Xavier Callahan
Barbara Louise Coburn
†George Earl Dale
*Joseph Edward DeAngelo
Zaven Richard Diran
Arthur Clinton Fagan
*Ernest Emilio Falbo
Alphonso William Finocchio
Thomas Fabien Gately
Joseph James Guidrey
*John Joseph Hagenbuch
Norair Nishan Hagopian
†August Warren Hanson
Nathaniel Hawthorne
Peter Ianniello
*Robert Pierce Kelley
Evelyn Gertrude Kelly
*Kenneth Eugene Keyes
Myles King
Clinton Wayland Kline
†Dorothy Knott
Dorothy Madeline Landry
Ruth Claire Landry
George Thomas Larkin
*Robert Nelson Larson
Anna Helen Lund
Isabelle Carol McBrayne
Thomas Francis Maher
Roger Sherman Mason
Philip McLaughlin
Alice Rose Miller
Richard Charles Minasian
Jean Lucille Morrissey
Clare Murdock
*Maude Louise Newell
Robert Linsdell Newell
Helen Winifred Nolan
Reuben Allan Noroian
*Eben John O'Brien
Paul Newton Otto
Edward James Reid
Richard Rockett

†*John Griffin Rote, Jr.
Barbara Elizabeth Russell
Harry Sevastos Samaras
Joseph Henry Sheehan
*Rose Marion Sheridan
Henry Simone
Sumner Grant Starbird
†John William Thompson
Peter James Tsolas
†Joseph Daniel Wallace
†Althea Virginia Weldon
Helen Elizabeth Wheeler
Herbert Alan Wiley, Jr.
†Serpouhi Rose Young

General

Reidar Lars Anderson
Melvin Boyd Barker
Charlotte Elizabeth Beers
Robert Edward Bond
John Joseph Busconi
Theodore Walter Bussey
Francis Joseph Callan
Alice Ferguson Campbell
John James Cassidy, Jr.
Walter Thomas Chamberlain
Arlene Ida Chevrette
Edward Archie Chevrette
John Brewster Clark
Laurence Joseph Connors
Alfred Mortimer Davenport
Assunta Didomenico
Paul Revere Emery
Robert Spence Ewart
Herbert Lauder Fairbanks
Madeline Stiles Fairbanks
Vincenzo Falco
Allen Hibbard Fisk
Mary Theresa Foisy
†Elizabeth Follansbee
Nicholas Joseph Fontano
†Jennie Lucy Mary Franchi
Anthony Frissore
Eunice Pauline Gordon
†Ardys Myrl Gray
Charles Daniel Hallman
Barbara Lefie Hicks
Harry Kritzman, Jr.
Alexander Lavrakas
Marion Louise Leary
Helen Louise Lordan
†Elizabeth Dimond Lovejoy
Rita Hurley MacDonald
John Alfred Mansfield

Edward Paul Martin
Leo Martin
Nubar Martin Mazmanian
James Joseph McDonnell
Rita Gertrude McElligott
Evelyn May McElhiney
Joseph Francis McElroy
Donald James McKinnon
Helen Mary Michalak
John Joseph Molloy
Beatrice Mary Moreau
Ivan Phillip Morel
George Lee Mosnicka
Thomas Joseph Muldoon
Carolyn Wilma Myott
William Francis Oates
John Ovoian
Josephine Joan Papalia
Alfred Henry Parlee
Archer William Parquette, Jr.
Lloyd John Davidson Peacock
Effie Willma Peterson
Gueido Petrino
Charles Edgar Phillips
Albert Edward Pratley, Jr.
Virginia Burton Ring
Vincent James Sansone
Doris Madeline Scott
Frederick Charles Shay
Robert Edgar Simmons
†John Mansfield Sjostedt
Ralph Oscar Sjostedt
Karl Eugene Soukikian
Harry Stepanian
†George Asadoor Surabian
Siranoush Martha Tashjian
Hilda Myrtle Theurer
Mardiros Vahan Tovmassian
George Kimball Walker
William Albert Wilke
Edward Nelson Zacheus

Commercial

Grace Adrienne Alemian
Eleanor Terese Arone
Hope Avtgis
†Irving Garland Babcock
Grace Jane Baird
Virginia Mary Bazarian
Marian Beauchamp
Marian Louise Beehner
Grace Roberta Bernado
Edna Florence Berry
Rose Boujicanian
Eleanor Gertrude Brett
Margaret Brusellis

Elsie Rosamond Burbank
Marjorie Eleanor Carter
  Bythewood
Catherine Elizabeth Campbell
Jeannette Mildred Caouette
Mary Rita Carney
Frances Rita Cerqua
Erle LeRoy Chase
William Albert Chevoor
Viola Rose Chrakian
Vito Mario Cirillo
Marie Cecelia Collins
Santa Susan Mary Crupi
Dora Yolanda Eleanor D'Alanno
Alice Dedeian
Lawrence DeGiso
Lea Anna DiPrato
Mildred Elizabeth Dorley
Josephine Dostoomian
Frances Ann Drinkwater
Eleanor Eva Fitzgerald
Sophie Flecca
Mary Alice Garabedian
Elton Kevork George
Elizabeth Gray
†Margaret Hagopian
Edith Reed Haines
†Mary Virginia Harney
Ann Elizabeth Hillier
Leo Paul Holland
Louise Frances Iodice
Mildred Irene Jordan
Catherine Juliano
Marion Mary Kalajian
Helen Mary Kander
Helen Rita Kelley
Evelyn Marie Knox
Mary Elizabeth Lee
Hildegard Bertha Lenander
Ellen Gertrude Lyons
Marion Florence MacArthur
Celia Gladys Madanian
Rose Pampic Mazmanian
†Mary Pauline McCollom
Cora Christina Munroe
Cathryne Mary Murphy
Constance Grace Natoli
Doris Muriel Noden
Rosalie Noden
Hazel Olivene Peters
Helen Edith Powers
Rita Cecelia Rady
Nicolena Riselli
Mary Rosenske
Herbert William Ruhr

Mildred Elsie Russo
Mary Cornelia Rustic
Lily Rose Safer
Hilda Bessie Sanger
Robert William Santos
Mary Ruth Saupp
Elsie Henrietta Scott
Eileen Clare Shaughnessy
Olive Virginia Shea
Ralph Francis Simonetti
Helen Marie Stanley
Sophie Loring Stanton
Helen Winifred Strayhorn
Beatrice Surabian
Mary Jane Swift
George Tashjian
Francis Louise Dorothea Thomson
Josephine Pollyanna Treggiari
Elvira Philomena Treglia
James Vartanian
Nancy Grace Walsh
James Wareing
Emil Weretelnyk
Thelma Alice Westgate
†Doris Marie Wilkins
Helen Theresa Wyss

Household Arts

Mary Dorothy Corazzini
June Isabel Gregoire
Rose Elizabeth Grossi
Bertha Mae Mandelle
Mary Ann Morrison
Frances Mary Paone
Rose Clara Pascuzzi
Susie May Simmons

Industrial Arts

Norman Sidney Abbott
Jack Vahan Ananian
Austin Frederick Andrews
George Herbert Armstrong

David Wendell Ballantine
Stephen Condon Barker
William Thomas Barksdale
Joseph Harry Berberian
Joseph Anthony Berinato
Armand Boudakian
Joseph Anselm Burgess
†Clement Joseph Carbone
†James Michael Carney
Louis Albert Ciccotelli
John Francis Colleran
Leslie James Connelly
Arthur George Corazzini
Robert Patrick Cram
Nathan Curry Dolbier
Alphonse Esposito
John Philip Giordano
Dominic Joseph Guzzetti
Wilfred Ringer Harlow
Leslie Albert Hertach
Charles Francis Holland
Joseph Thomas Lawson
Edward Raymond LeBlanc
Frank Chester LeShane, Jr.
Kenneth Paul Lowney
Dominic Lupo
Mathew Magliocca
Anthony Joseph Mantenuto
James Edward McCassie
John Joseph Moran
Michael Francis Mungillo
Michael Natale
Adam Anthony Operacz
Henry Della Paolera
Mgrdich Missak Parsekian
John Perry
Nicholas Vincent Riselli
Richard Bernard Sheer
Walter Herbert Slayton
†Paul Peter Toscano
Stanley Werren
Philip Earl Wildman

*Members of Cum Laude Society
†Neither absent nor tardy for 3
years

Sixty-Seventh Annual Report

OF THE

BOARD OF TRUSTEES

OF THE

FREE PUBLIC LIBRARY

OF THE

TOWN OF WATERTOWN

MASSACHUSETTS

1934

THE HAMPSHIRE PRESS, INC.
Cambridge, Mass.
1934

198

REPORT OF THE TRUSTEES OF THE
FREE PUBLIC LIBRARY, WATERTOWN

To the Citizens of Watertown:

The report of the Librarian relative to the administration of the Library during the past year shows it to have been one of progress. The Trustees, in behalf of the citizens whom they represent, desire to express to her and a devoted staff of assistants full appreciation for their work.

Yearly new problems appear and new demands are made upon our Library resources. How well and completely these have been met is apparent in the Librarian's review of the year's work. Circulation of books remains at a high level per capita while the cost per book circulated is extremely low. The three branch libraries meet the demands of their adjacent book-loving populations in constantly increasing volume and usefulness.

From its founding, the Watertown Public Library has taken and maintained a position in the front rank of similar institutions in the Commonwealth, both in its efficient administration and in its expanding service to the community. This position could not have been achieved without the constant and continued support of the Town itself as expressed by its regular annual appropriations and by special appropriations for useful additions to the library facilities. That its investment has been, and continues to be, of the most enduring kind must be constantly evident to our citizens.

In this report of the Chairman special mention should be made of the construction work now in progress at the Main Library building. This was made possible by a special appropriation made by the Town in 1934 together with a contingent Federal grant of money. The work involves a long needed addition to the library stacks for the storage of books and also the construction of an adequate office for the Librarian. By changes in the basement areas better arranged work rooms are provided and more adequate facilities made available for staff use. Changes in the heating and lighting system were also necessary. Completion of this construction will add much to the usefulness of this centre of the Town's library work.

A comprehensive plan for the Main Library has been prepared for the Trustees by the architects in charge of the present alterations. This plan contemplates the eventual duplication of the present westerly wing for the easterly side of the Library, and a new and dignified main entrance in the centre of the building. This is for the future, as the finances of the Town may permit, or as some benefactor may provide.

The increasing use of the North Branch indicates the desirability of soon equiping for library use the additional room, there located, which is not now used. The Trustees have plans ready to make the necessary changes when the Town can provide the funds to make them.

The Library budget for 1935 will be presented to the Town in its usual modest proportions. Additional plant requires additional maintenance, and a small increase in that expense will be asked for. Our book appropriation is held to the 1934 level. The appropriation for salaries as presented makes provision for the normal annual increase for those of the staff who have not yet reached the maximums established, by vote of the Trustees, some years ago.

At the last Town Meeting of 1934 a special appropriation of $400 was made as that portion of the total expense immediately necessary in connection with the Main Library addition now under construction. To complete the proper equipment for the building when finished, will require an additional appropriation of $2,000. This sum will be requested under the provisions of a special article in the Town Warrant for the next Annual Town Meeting.

In closing my term of office as Chairman of the Trustees, I wish to express to my Trustee associates, to the Librarian and to each member of the Library organization, my deep appreciation of their co-operation during the past year.

This institution, for the guidance and operation of which we are jointly responsible, holds an honorable and useful place in the municipal life of the Town. It is loved by its many users and respected by all. With such standards, confidently it passes to another year of usefulness and service.

Respectfully submitted,

CHARLES F. SHAW,
Chairman.

REPORT OF THE LIBRARIAN

To the Trustees of the Watertown Free Public Library:

Gentlemen:

Although the circulation of books for home use this last year shows a slight decrease from that of 1933 this is not surprising. In the dark days of 1932 and 1933 people used libraries as never before and now a reflection of the present unsettled conditions is showing in the circulation of practically all libraries. This reaction is temporary and not serious as the figures will show. In 1934 we circulated 402,773 volumes, 18,086 less than in 1933, and it is interesting to note that the loss is almost entirely in adult fiction and in the school collection. Evidently people have less time for pleasure reading and our changed plans, because of the alterations to the library, partly account for the loss in school circulation.

There seems to have been an increased use of the library for reference purposes and more requests for information have come over the telephone. For the statistics of circulation from the different libraries, and by classes of books, I refer you to the tables which have been compiled.

The two smaller branches have shown a very encouraging increase in circulation both to adults and young people. The North Branch circulated 51,827 books from one small room. The book shelves are filled to capacity and at busy times the room is too crowded to work efficiently, especially on the days when there is a story hour. The heating problem would be lessened if an oil burner could be installed but this is not practical with our present heating system. I trust that this building can be altered at an early date so that we can look forward to a still larger increase in the work at this branch. It is in a growing community.

During the year we have added 4,151 books to the Library, 210 of which were gifts. This is an increase of 254 over the number added in 1933. We have, however, to report that 2,381 books have been lost or discarded during the year which is 1,037 more than the year before. This is but the natural result of the heavy use of the books during the last few years. Many more books should be withdrawn because the information in them has been superseded. Two thousand and one hundred seventy-five books had to be rebound.

The Library has co-operated with the E R A and during the year had several workers doing book repairing, typing and cleaning. In co-operation with the Recreation Committee hobby groups have met at the East Branch. At present there are three of these groups and others are in the process of formation. There is also a boy's stamp club, two other boys' clubs and two clubs of girls under the leadership of a college student helper. All the leaders of these groups and clubs and the people they secure to talk to them are volunteers.

This year we have been unable to pay for story tellers but members of the staff have conducted some very fine story hours. At some they have told the stories, for others they have secured outside talent. At the Chinese story hour Dr. Hsieh, from the Friends of China Society, talked to about three hundred children. With him were two Chinese children in native costume. Sculpture and book contests have been held. A summer reading club helped to stimulate the reading of good books during the vacation period and many exhibits of the children's own handiwork have helped to make the young people feel that the Library is theirs.

The Charles River Library Club, at a meting held in our Library last May, appointed a committee on library radio broadcasting. Miss Mead and I were members of this committee. A series of seven broadcasts on library service were given over Station WEEI from October 22 to December 10. These broadcasts covered various features of library work, such as:

The Service the Public Library offers the Community.

How to get the most from your Public Library.

Hobbies to ride and how the Public Library can help in the fun.

A business man takes stock of his Public Library.

How Libraries introduce good books through story-telling.

How your Public Library can help you to prepare for Christmas.

A general survey of Public Library service.

This venture was unique in that no group of libraries, as far as we know, has undertaken co-operative broadcasting. As one of the programs was written by our staff and broadcast by Miss Mead and as we had a hand in preparing other programs we feel an especial interest in the reactions to this venture. Later the Club may go on the air again with book reviews.

The alterations of the Library did not start until months later than we anticipated therefore our plans have been changed somewhat. Last month we moved from our school department and workroom in the basement. We have no idea when our next move will be made or where we will move to but we will have to hold ourselves in readiness to do what is necessary as the need arises. Progress depends upon the weather, to a large extent, and as the heating system is to be changed it may necessitate some curtailment of service but we hope that it will not be necessary to close the Library. The staff will have much to bear in the next four months but we trust that the services to the public will not be too much impaired and that the new arrangements, when they are completed, will meet with their approval.

There have been no changes on the staff during the year but we have granted leaves of absence to two members of the staff because of illness in their families. Members of the staff have attended meetings of the American Library Association, the Massachusetts Library Club, and the Charles River Library Club.

At the October meeting of the Massachusetts Library Club one of the speakers said: "Libraries are glorified university extensions," and that "leisure will be a cannon loose on the deck unless we prepare for it." Libraries will have an important part in providing means of profitably filling the leisure time, which is surely coming with the shorter working week.

Appropriations for our Library have increased since the time, often referred to as "the good old days," but people often fail to think of the increased advantages offered in these days. They think of the expense in the aggregate without realizing that for every inhabitant of the town it costs only 4.7 cents a day to give educational opportunities to over 6,800 young people, that the highways and byways were cared for, eliminating the PWA and ERA projects, for a little more than 2 cents a day per inhabitant and that the same inhabitants receive police and fire protection for a little less than 2 cents a day, while for this "glorified university extension" for people from the picture book age up, the town appropriates 28 one hundredth of a cent a day, or less than 2 cents a week, for each man, woman and child of the Town.

In preparing the budget for 1935 may I ask you to bear these facts in mind and may I also express my appreciation of the co-operation I have received from you and from my staff, of whom I have received many expressions of approbation from the public they serve.

Respectfully submitted,

LYDIA W. MASTERS,

Librarian.

APPENDIX A

Circulation Statistics for 1934

Circulation by Classes	Adult	Junior	Juvenile	Total	Percentage
Periodicals	6,394	1,203	7,144	14,741	3.67
Philosophy, religion and folklore	3,291	256	6,898	*10,445	2.60
Biography	6,043	2,215	3,897	12,155	3.02
History	4,010	1,486	8,059	13,555	3.37
Georgraphy and travel	5,154	1,109	11,306	17,569	4.37
Social scences	4,961	430	1,409	6,800	1.70
Natural sciences and medicine	3,119	1,229	9,803	14,151	3.51
Useful arts	3,653	1,622	3,459	8,734	2.11
Recreative arts	1,352	576	1,953	3,881	.96
Music	1,101	98	571	1,770	.46
Fine arts	2,244	114	966	3,324	.88
Language and literature	10,188	1,240	30,579	#42,007	10.43
Books in foreign languages	2,905			2,905	.72
Fiction	155,993	48,969	45,774	250,736	62.25
	210,408	60,547	131,818	402,773	100.00
Main Library	99,494	19,288	32,738	151,520	
East Branch	77,440	25,847	40,389	143,676	
North Branch	28,208	9,404	14,215	51,827	
West Branch	4,867	6,008	11,372	22,247	
Schools	399		33,104	33,503	
	210,408	60,547	131,818	402,773	

* Of these 5,074 were folklore.
\# Of these 23 026 were readers.

APPENDIX B

American Library Association Form for Uniform Statistics
Annual Report for the Year ended December 31,1934

Name of Library ....Free Public Library of
Town ....Watertown, Massachusetts
Name of Librarian ....Lydia W. Masters
Date of founding 1868
Population served ....34,913 (census)
Assessed valuation $53,168,110
Library appropriation per capita....$1.039
Terms of use ....Free for lending and reference.
Number of agencies ....Main Library, branches, 2; sub-
        branch, 1; schools, 11; rooms, 67
Number of days open during year..302
Hours for lending
    Main Library ....72 (10 mos.), 66 (2 mos.)
    East Branch ....52 (10 mos.), 46 (2 mos.)
    North Branch 30
    West Branch 20

FINANCIAL STATEMENT

Receipts

Town appropriation	$36,250.00
Special for equipment	400.00
	$36,650.00

Expenditures

Books and periodicals	*$4,529.81
Binding	1,469.87
Salaries:	
Library service	22,055.44
Janitor service	3,187.00
Heat, light and water	2,123.71
Building maintenance and repairs	908.59
Supplies	785.09
Other maintenance	1,190.94
Special for equipment	396.00
TOTAL EXPENDITURES	$36,637.45
Balance returned to Town	12.55
	$36,650.00
Book fines returned to the Town	$1,269.82

* See also amounts expended from Funds

INCOME FROM ENDOWMENT FUNDS

	Balance 1933	Received 1934	Total	Amount expended	Balance
Barry Fund	$ 9.89	$ 35.63	$ 45.52	$ 35.75	$ 9.77
Mead Fund	115.45	85.21	200.66	84.30	116.36
Pierce Fund	271.57	44.71	316.28	9.00	307.28
Pratt Fund	7.69	350.00	357.69	350.00	7.69
	$404.60	$515.55	$920.15	$479.05	$441.10

BOOK STOCK

	Adult	Juvenile	Total
Number of volumes at the beginning of the year	60,540	15,360	75,900
Volumes added during the year	2,368	1,783	4,151
Gifts and exchange, included above 210			
Number of volumes lost and withdrawn during the year	957	1,424	2,381
Total number at the end of the year	61,951	15,719	77,670
Number of periodicals and newspapers, currently received: Titles			153
Copies			265

USE

	Adult	Juvenile	Total
Number of fiction lent for home use	Adult	Juvenile	Total
Main Library	70,267	27,586	97,853
East Branch	57,811	36,505	94,316
North Branch	23,438	13,943	37,381
West Branch	4,468	8,629	13,097
Schools	9	8,080	8,089
Percent fiction of total volumes lent			62.25
Total number of volumes lent for home use			
Main Library	99,494	52,026	151,520
East Branch	77,440	66,236	143,676
North Branch	28,208	23,619	51,827
West Branch	4,867	17,380	22,247
Schools	399	33,104	33,305
Total	210,408	192,365	402,773

Decrease in circulation from that in 1933	18,086
Circulation per capita	11.5
Expenditure per volume circulated	$.08
Number of pictures lent for home use	2,936

REGISTRATION

	Adult	Juvenile	Total
Number of borrowers registered during the year	2,302	1,710	4,012
Total number of registered borrowers	7,293	4,494	11,787

STAFF

Number of staff, library service (reckoning part time service to make whole units	16
Janitor service	2

REPORT OF THE BOARD OF ASSESSORS

The Board of Assessors hereby submit its annual report for the year 1934.

The Assessors were very much pleased to make the announcement of the 1934 tax rate of $33.80, or a reduction of $.40 over the 1933 rate.

The total valuation for 1934 is $53,168,110.00, or a reduction of $219,600.00 over 1933. This decrease was due principally to the falling off of building, and adjustments in assessments which were necessary in the judgment of the Assessors, for the best interest of the Town.

We do not look for an increase in valuation for 1935, but we do expect a substantial decrease.

The assessment date for 1935 is January 1st instead of April 1st as in previous years. The "Form of List" previously filed between April 1st and May 15th must be filed on or before February 15th. The date for filing applications for abatement of real estate and personal property is changed from December 31st to December 1st.

During 1934, one case was brought before the Board of Tax Appeals on residential property which was settled in favor of the Town.

We again wish to impress upon the taxpayers that the tax rate is actually made at the Town Meeting. The Assessors cannot control the amount of money being expended locally, but hope through the assistance of the taxpayers to reduce the tax rate for 1935.

The following is a list of State, and County taxes and valuations for the year 1934.

Respectfully submitted,

EDWARD A. OATES, *Chairman,*
EDWARD F. WRIGHT,
JOHN J. CURRAN.

Requirements for State, County and Town

Grants and Appropriations

State Tax	$78,100.00
County Tax	77,696.74
Metropolitan Planning	287.99
Metropolitan Parks	27,918.18
Metropolitan Water	86,299.42
South Metropolitan Sewerage	48,853.67
Charles River Basin	4,695.41
Abatement of Smoke Nuisance	278.83
Canterbury Street Highway	109.70
Land Taking State Highway (Revere)	1,126.19
West Roxbury, Brookline Highway	150.93
Ocean Avenue, Revere	436.02
Ways in Malden, Braintree, Weymouth and Hingham	5.50
B. E. Deficiency (Rental Payments)	2,266.06
B. E. Deficiency	27,861.97
Boston Metropolitan District Expense	133.48
Street Betterments	21,058.64
Sidewalks	4,227.39
Interest on Street Betterments	7,464.53
Interest on Sidewalk Assessments	1,861.21
Moths	283.00
	391,114.86
Town Grants	1,517,114.44
	1,908,229.30
Income Tax	119,012.28
Total Requirements	1,789,217.02
Overlay	42,760.37
Total Commitment, 1934	1,831,977.39

Valuations

Buildings exclusive of land	$38,734,800.00	
Land exclusive of buildings	9,736,485.00	
		$48,471,285.00
Personal Estate		4,696,825.00
		$53,168,110.00

Additional December Assessments

Personal Estate	1,525.00

Total valuation including additional		$53,169,635.00
Decrease in valuation of Real Estate including December Assessments	$389,150.00	
Increase in valuation of Personal Estate including December Assessments	166,375.00	
Total decrease in valuation including Dec. Assessments	$222,775.00	

Tax Rate of 1934, $33.80

Total Poll Abatements

For the year 1932	$1,268.00	
For the year 1933	2,124.00	
For the year 1934	122.00	
		$3,514.00

Total Abatements on Real and Personal Property

For the year 1931	$1,681.50	
For the year 1932	6,876.78	
For the year 1933	15,530.48	
For the year 1934	13,234.09	
		$37,322.85

Total Abatement on Street and Sidewalk Interest

For the year 1932	$2.31	
For the year 1933	.35	
	——	$2.66

Total Abatements on Moth Tax

For the year 1932	$1.86	
For the year 1933	.50	
	——	$2.36

Motor Vehicle Excise

Total valuation of motor vehicle excise for 1934	$1,871,030.00

Total Abatements on Motor Vehicle Excise

For the year 1932	$3,810.79	
For the year 1933	2,547.83	
For the year 1934	2,834.88	
	————	$9,193.50

REPORT OF TOWN COUNSEL

January 15, 1935.

To the Honorable Board of Selectmen,
Administration Building,
Watertown, Massachusetts.

Gentlemen:

I submit my report as Town Counsel for the year 1934.

The usual routine of the office in advising the various departments in legal matters, preparation of votes of Town Meeting and borrowings, and preparation and approval of contracts and other matters of detail, have received the necessary attention.

Many novel questions have been submitted for opinions in connection with projects carried out in co-operation with the Federal Government, including the Civil Works Administration, the Emergency Relief Administration and the Public Works Administration.

The interests of the Town have been protected in all Court actions and the following cases are now pending in the Middlesex Superior Court against the Town of Watertown:

#100613—Beatrice Benger vs. Town of Watertown.

#91218—Agnes Bouchie, p.p.a. vs. Town of Watertown.

#89194—Louise Cafarella vs. Town of Watertown.

#64935—Morris Cohen vs. Town of Watertown.

#88771—Hazel Feeley vs. Town of Watertown.

#99201—Mary Janikian vs. Town of Watertown.

#84847—Philomena Murgia vs. Town of Watertown.

#94423—Martha E. Murphy vs. Town of Watertown.

#74154—Susan A. Quinlan vs. Town of Watertown.

#93743—Antonio Villante vs. Town of Watertown.

There are also pending in the Middlesex Superior Court the case of William H. Wilson, Inspector of Buildings vs. John Millian, a petition in equity for the enforcement of the Zoning By-Law, and cross actions between the Town of Watertown and the City of Worcester and the Town of Watertown and the City of Lowell, in connection with reimbursement of expenditures of the Welfare Department.

There are now pending in the Suffolk Superior Court the following actions against the Town of Watertown:

Eli Zalinger vs. *Town of Watertown*

Max S. Ginsberg vs. *Town of Watertown*

There is now pending in the Second District Court of Eastern Middlesex, at Waltham, the case of *Angelina Raymond* vs. *the Town of Watertown*.

I have appeared for the Assessors of the Town of Watertown in numerous cases before the Board of Tax Appeals and it is my recommendation that special counsel be employed by the Assessors to defend appeals from their assessments and that a real estate expert be retained under an annual retainer fee to assist the Assessors in maintaining their assessments in these cases.

Answers of the Town of Watertown as trustee in actions by creditors against employees of the Town have been prepared and filed in twenty cases.

I have appeared before the Industrial Accident Board in defending the Town against claims by employees for Workmen's Compensation.

Many claims against the Town have been settled for small amounts by the Selectmen upon my advice.

A petition for a writ of mandamus was filed in the Supreme Judicial Court by Elmer H. Comey, Hadon F. Peterson, Harold S. Tuck, Ethel A. Tuck, Walter W. Whitehill, Pearl I. Whitehill, Lewis G. Manchester, Grace Peterson, Herbert W. Howard, Ethel L. Comey, Rufus A. Dyer, Jet B. Dyer, John W. Coombs, Carrie C. Coombs, and Olava Anderson against the Selectmen of the Town of Watertown, to compel the Selectmen to call a Special Town Meeting for the purpose of presenting to the voters of Watertown at large the questions involved in the petition for referendum on votes at the Annual Town Meeting, whereby appropriations were made for the payment of salaries during the year 1934. This petition for a writ of mandamus resulted from the refusal of the Selectmen to act upon a petition alleged to have been signed by 126 voters of the Town, which petition was denied by the Selectmen. I appeared before the Supreme Judicial Court in all preliminary matters in connection with this petition. Upon the trial of the case before an Auditor appointed by the Supreme Judicial Court and upon confirmation of the Auditor's Report to the Supreme Judicial Court, a single Justice of that Court entered a decree dismissing the petition with costs to the petitioners, and execution for costs against the petitioners was issued and the amount of the costs paid to the Treasurer of the Town of Watertown.

The demands upon the Town Counsel by the various Town departments have increased during each year of my service in that office.

I wish to thank the Town officers and the various departments for their co-operation during the year.

Respectfully submitted,

FRANCIS J. McNAMARA,
Town Counsel.

SELECTMEN'S REPORT

The Selectmen herewith submit their annual report for the fiscal year ending December 31, 1934.

The year 1934 has indeed been a trying one for the citizens of our Town, who, in many cases, have suffered severe financial reverses. Homes have been lost and many are receiving aid through our Public Welfare Department. Despite all this, our financial statement is proof that the Town is in a healthier condition than it has been for many years.

Under P. W. A., as a result of application made by the Town through the Selectmen, agreements were executed by the Selectmen for the acceptance of a 30% grant for five projects, namely—construction of Mt. Auburn St., from Beacon Square to Russell Ave., and Walnut Street; construction of School Street from Carver Road to Belmont St.; also drainage for the following streets: Bailey Road, Elm St., Franklin St., Harnden Ave., Hunt St., Chestnut St., Olney St., Riverside St., Summer St., and Union St.

Sidewalks were also constructed under P. W. A, as follows: Lloyd Rd., Mt. Auburn St., Hunt St., Sycamore St.,

Appleton St., Dartmouth St., Woodleigh Rd., Arlington St., Prentiss St., Brimmer St., Keenan St., Francis St., St. Mary's St., School St., Maplewood St., Commonwealth Rd., Winsor Ave., Belmont St., Hillside Rd., Edgecliffe Rd., Upland Rd. The addition to the Senior High School and the addition to the Main Public Library were also P. W. A. projects.

On all P. W. A. projects, the contracts have been let in accordance with the P. W. A. Regulations and the work on most of the projects is now under way.

Under C .W. A., superseded by E. R. A., in April, a large amount of important work was carried on, for the details of which the Selectmen refer you to the E. R. A. Administrator's report.

The Selectmen commend the Superintendent of Streets and the Town Engineer and their respective departments for their assistance in carrying out the many details in connection with the C. W. A., P. W. A., and E. R. A. projects.

The committee of ten citizens appointed by the Selectmen one year ago have given unselfishly of their time in an unbiased investigation of all applicants for or receiving relief through the Welfare Department. Much credit should be given to Agent Daniel H. Murphy and his staff for the efficient manner in which they have conducted the department with fairness to the Town and to the applicants in all Public Welfare cases.

Many sidewalks have been built during the past year, as a result of which the Town has benefitted and property owners have had the opportunity of improving their property.

The various departments, including Police, Fire and Town employees, are to be complimented on the spirit which they have shown in co-operating with the Selectmen.

In conclusion, the Selectmen wish to thank the various department heads who have worked in the best interests of all residents of the Town during the past year.

Respectfully submitted,

MAURICE H. O'CONNELL,
JAMES H. SHERIDAN,
EDWARD D. HOLLAND,
Selectmen of Watertown.

REPORT OF BOARD OF PUBLIC WELFARE

Outside Aid

The past year shows a large reduction in the aid granted by the Welfare Department in Temporary Aid cases. The case load reached a peak of 343 cases and was reduced to 202 cases at the closing of the year.

A total of 573 applications for aid were filed at the Welfare Department and a large number of these applicants were given employment on the E. R. A. projects. Due to the co-operation given by the E. R. A. and the close supervision of Welfare cases by the department a saving of $74,617.47 has been made in 1934. In some cases supplementary relief has been granted to those employed on the E. R. A. at $12.00 per week and medical aid and assistance given to those injured while working on the E. R. A.

Department investigators have made 1,037 investigations and 205 re-investigations of those employed on E. R. A. and 118 investigations on C. C. C. boys who had completed their term of enrollment. These investigations have been in addition to a total of 3,454 regular welfare investigations.

A total of $101,124.09 has been collected by the Treasurer from the State and other Cities and Towns and turned in to Treasury Receipts.

The E. R. A. Sewing Unit completed 12,814 finished articles and the handling and distribution of same was taken care of by the Welfare Department. Soldiers' Relief, E. R. A., Welfare and Outside Social Agencies received their quota of the goods.

United States Government commodities consisting of pork, veal, butter, cheese, rice, potatoes, cabbage, canned roast beef, hamburg and stew meat have been distributed in large quantities to aid recipients, E. R. A. workers and private charities.

The expenses of the Welfare Department have been -curtailed this year while neighboring cities and towns show an increase in expenses for aid and relief granted.

A total of $27,660.05 has been paid the past year, divided as follows: $12,251.83 to hospitals for injuries, sickness and confinement cases; $4,171.02 to the Commonwealth of Massachusetts for patients at the State Infirmary at Tewksbury and for State Wards in the care of the Division of Child Guardianship; $11,237.20 has been paid to other cities and towns for Watertown settlements now residing elsewhere.

The Welfare Advisory Committee has held a number of meetings during the year and the department wishes to thank its members for their advice and assistance.

The Department again wishes to thank those who have donated clothing, fuel, etc., especially the Teachers Association, Knights of Columbus, St. Vincent de Paul Society, Massachusetts Catholic Women's Guild and the Telephone Operators of the Newton North Exchange and other private organizations for assistance given to this department.

The unemployment situation remains about the same and if not for the E. R. A. the department would have had a bigger burden this winter than at any previous time.

Old Age Assistance

This aid is granted under Chapter 118-A of the General Laws and is given to deserving citizens 70 years of age and over who have resided in Massachusetts for the past 20 years and who have not more than $300 in cash or a $1,500.00 equity in their home. The assistance given is supervised by the Welfare Department visitor who makes quarterly calls to the homes of the recipients and a total of 468 calls has been made during the past year.

There are at present 77 cases receiving this assistance which shows an increase over the past year. A total of $10,551.37 has been collected from the State and other cities and towns and returned to Treasury Receipts. The department expects a greater increase in the Old Age Assistance for the coming year.

Mothers' Aid

The aid as distributed under Chapter 118 to mothers with dependent children in their own homes has shown a decrease during the past year. The aid granted is sufficient to maintain mothers and their children in their own homes. The aid is supervised by a visitor who makes quarterly calls to the home of each recipient. The total visits made to these homes was 209.

At present there are 35 mothers with 137 dependents receiving this form of aid and no increase is anticipated for the coming year.

During the past year a total of $16,473.36 has been turned back to Treasury Receipts from bills rendered to the State and other cities and towns.

Respectfully submitted,

DANIEL H. MuRPHY,
Agent.

REPORT OF THE COLLECTOR OF TAXES

I respectfully submit the following report relative to the collection of taxes and assessments for the year 1934.

1931 TAXES

Real and Personal

Balance outstanding Jan. 1, 1934	$1,800.88	
Disclaimed Tax Titles	13.71	
Adjustment	.58	
		$1,815.17
Abatements granted during 1934	$1,681.50	
Credit by Tax Titles	133.67	
Total Credits		$1,815.17

1932 TAXES

Real and Personal

Balance outstanding Jan. 1, 1934	$71,435.79	
Disclaimed Tax Titles	1,899.63	
Refunds	452.50	
Adjustments	37.51	
		$73,825.43
Abatements granted during 1934	$5,993.70	
Credit by Tax Ttitles	52,796.93	
Paid to Treasurer during 1934	15,034.80	
		$73,825.43

1932 POLL TAXES

Balance outstanding Jan. 1, 1934	$1,274.00	
Adjustment	3.00	
		$1,277.00
Abatements granted during 1934	$1,268.00	
Paid Treasurer during 1934	9.00	
Total Credits		$1,277.00

1932 Old Age Assistance

Balance outstanding Jan. 1, 1934	$628.00
Adjustment	5.00
	$633.00
Abatements granted during 1934	$631.00
Paid to Treasurer during 1934	2.00
Total credits	$633.00

1932 Motor Vehicle Excise

Balance outstanding Jan. 1, 1934	$3,831.30
Refunds	8.17
	$3,839.47
Abatements granted during 1934	$3,810.79
Paid Treasurer during 1934	14.84
Total Credits	$3,825.63
Balance outstanding Jan. 1, 1935	$13.84

1933 TAXES

Real and Personal

Bal. outstanding Jan. 1, 1934	$703,860.33
Committed in 1934	159.03
By Refunds	2,690.44
Disclaimed Tax Titles	1,946.82
Tax Title Abatement	1,368.00
By Adjustments	997.47
	$711,022.09
Abatements granted during 1934	$14,778.64
Credit by Tax Titles	168,393.26
Paid to Treasurer during 1934	520,083.69
Total Credits	$703,255.59
Balance outstanding Jan. 1, 1935	$7,766.50*

1933 POLL TAXES

Bal. outstanding Jan. 1, 1934	$2,359.00	
Committed May 1, 1934	78.00	
By Adjustments	1.00	
		$2,438.00
Abatements granted during 1934	$2,124.00	
Paid to Treasurer during 1934	242.00	
Total Credits		$2,366.00
Balance outstanding Jan. 1, 1935		$72.00

1933 Old Age Assistance

Balance outstanding Jan. 1, 1934	$1,220.00	
Committed May 1, 1934	39.00	
By Adjustments	78.00	
		$1,337.00
Abatements granted during 1934	$1,218.00	
Paid to Treasurer during 1934	119.00	
Total Credits		$1,337.00

1933 Motor Vehicle Excise

Balance outstanding Jan. 1, 1934	$5,518.78	
Committed January 17, 1934	712.54	
Committed March 14, 1934	37.10	
Refunds	110.88	
		$6,379.30
Abatements granted during 1934	$2,547.83	
Paid to Treasurer during 1934	3,468.10	
Total Credits		$6,015.93
Balance outstanding Jan. 1, 1935		$363.37

1934 TAXES

Real and Personal

Original Commitment	$1,831,977.39	
December Commitment	51.55	
Total Commitment		$1,832,028.94

Refunds   2,356.78
                                                    ───────────
                                                   $1,834,385.72

Abatements granted during 1934 $13,233.69
Paid to Treasurer during 1934 $1,201,204.33
Total Credits   ───────────── $1,214,438.02
                                                    ───────────
Balance outstanding Jan. 1, 1935 $619,947.70

1934 POLL TAXES

Original Commitment
  June 20, 1934 $21,212.00
Committed Sept. 13, 1934   322.00
Committed Dec. 31, 1934   120.00
Total Commitment   ───────────── $21,654.00
Abatements granted during 1934 $122.00
Paid Treasurer during 1934   19,136.00
Total Credits   ───────────── $19,258.00
                                                    ───────────
Balance outstanding Jan. 1, 1935 $2,396.00*

1934 Motor Vehicle Excise

Original Commitment
  March 20, 1934 $27,755.30
Committed Aug. 6, 1934   16,630.73
Committed Dec. 12, 1934   5,284.05
                                 ─────────────
Total Commitment $49,670.08
Cash Refunds   995.46
                                 ───────────── $50,665.54
Abatements granted during 1934 $2,834.88
Paid to Treasurer during 1934   41,909.94
Total Credits   ───────────── $44,744.82
                                                    ───────────
Balance outstanding Jan. 1, 1935 $5,920.72

* There is a small unlocated difference which had not
been discovered at the time the report went to print.

1934

TOTAL PAYMENTS TO TREASURER

BY COLLECTOR OF TAXES

1932 Real and Personal Taxes		$15,034.80
Interest on above	$1,311.09	
1932 Poll Taxes		9.00
1932 Old Age Assistance		2.00
1932 Motor Vehicle Excise		14.84
Interest on above	1.18	
1933 Real and Personal Taxes		520,083.69
Interest on above	18,169.37	
1933 Poll Taxes		242.00
Interest on above	1.52	
1933 Old Age Assistance		119.00
Interest on above	.02	
1933 Motor Vehicle Excise		3,468.10
Interest on above	63.10	
1934 Real and Personal Taxes		$1,201,204.33
Interest on above	2,055.22	
1934 Poll Taxes		19,136.00
Interest on above	.07	
1934 Motor Vehicle Excise		41,909.94
Interest on above	98.06	
Total Taxes		$1,801,223.70
Total Interest	$21,699.63	21,699.63
Total Taxes and Interest		$1,822,923.33
By Receipts from Statement of Liens and Redemption Certificates		$548.00
By Receipts from unapportioned Sidewalk Assessments		68.00
By Receipts from apportioned Sidewalk Assessments paid in advance		1,222.59

By Receipts from apportioned Street Betterments paid in advance	4,912.05
By Receipts from Interest on Sidewalk and Street Betterment Assessments	104.93
By Receipts from Tax Sale Advertising and Fees	3,930.72
Total paid Treasurer during 1934	$1,833,709.62

FREDERICK J. COLBY,

Collector of Taxes for the Town of Watertown.

Approved: W. W. NORCROSS, Jr., *Auditor.*

December 31, 1934

ANNUAL REPORT

OF THE

AUDITOR

OF THE

TOWN OF WATERTOWN

FOR THE

YEAR ENDING DECEMBER 31, 1934

THE HAMPSHIRE, PRESS, INC.
Cambridge, Mass.
1935

AUDITOR'S REPORT

I herewith present the annual report of the Financial transactions of the Town of Watertown, for the year ending December 31, 1934.

The various funds in charge of the Town Treasurer belonging to the Trustees of the Public Library have been examined and found correct.

I have certified the cash of the Town Treasurer and Tax Collector and found it correct.

Periodical examinations of the Tax Collector's Outstanding Accounts have been made and checked against the Controlling Account in my office.

Respectfully submitted,

W. W. NORCROSS, Jr.
Town Auditor.

Watertown, Mass.

Then personally appeared the foregoing subscriber, W. W. Norcross, Jr. who made oath that the foregoing statement subscribed by him are true.

WM. P. McGUIRE,
Justice of the Peace.

Receipts

Taxes, Real Estate and Personal

1932	$11,846.30
1933	505,830.13
1934	1,182,694.01

Polls

1932	9.00
1933	242.00
1934	19,136.00

Old Age Assistance

1932	633.00
1933	1,337.00

Motor Excise

1932	14.84
1933	3,468.10
1934	41,909.59

From State

Corporation, Income, Street Railway		
Bank, etc.	172,672.06	
		$1,939,792.03

Special Assessments

Moth	303.49	
Sidewalks		
Added to Tax Bills	4,118.76	
Unapportioned	68.00	
Paid in Advance	1,222.59	
Streets		
Added to Tax Bills	21,084.91	
Paid in Advance	4,879.43	
		$31,677.18

Tax Titles		$194,340.42
Accounts Receivable		
Town Clerk	5.12	
Dog Officer	180.00	
Weights and Measures	48.43	
Health	6,942.54	
Public Welfare	101,124.09	
Schools	1,758.72	
Cemetery	5,505.63	

Water Rates	187,151.69	
Water Charges	1,393.97	
		$304,110.19
State and County Aid to Highways		$5,705.88

Loans

Temporary, Anticipation of		
Revenue	$1,265,000.00	
Highway Construction, P.W.A.	28,000.00	
Sewers and Drains P.W.A.	16,000.00	
Sidewalks P.W.A.	11,000.00	
Senior H.S. Add'n. P.W.A.	115,000.00	
Library Add'n. P.W.A.	29,000.00	
Premium on Bonds	932.70	
		$1,464,932.70

Interest

Taxes	$21,698.78	
Special Assessments		
Sidewalks	1,957.18	
Streets	8,733.59	
Paid in Advance	105.52	
Tax Titles	12,948.98	
Accrued on Bonds	361.88	
Trust Funds		
Cemetery Perpetual Care		
Fund	1,581.66	
Potter Memorial Gate Fund	15.10	
Library Trust Funds	479.05	
Templeton Fund	97.64	
		$47,979.38
Sewer Deposits		1,373.00
Dog Fund		1,665.00
School Dept., Smith-Hughes Fund		86.73

Miscellaneous Receipts

Ashes and Paper	3.15
Collector, costs	3,936.30
Collector, statements	543.00
Fireworks permits	9.50
Fire loss	223.85
Fire Department	51.00
Health Dental Clinic	123.91
Licenses	485.50
Plumbing Permits	576.00
Highway, Garbage	2,795.04
Damages	10.00
Infirmary, Produce	73.20
Middlesex County, Dog licenses	1,222.78
Military Aid	190.50
Poles and Wires, Permits	416.00
Damages	11.37
Polics, Fines	873.92
Hackney Licenses	15.00
Damages	15.10
Public Library, Fines	1,466.45
Old Books	19.90
School, Evening	110.00
Trade and Continuation	5,076.19
Americanization	314.71
State Wards	1,412.65
Damages	7.12
Selectmen, Licenses	14,336.38 -
Sidewalks	27.97
State Aid	1,747.00
Town Clerk	2,067.56
Water, Junk	6.00
Weights and Measures, Fees	254.53
Licenses	100.00

$38,521.58

Refunds

Boston Elevated	24.01	
Court Costs	57.95	
Mothers' Aid	55.50	
Old Age Assistance	100.91	
Outside Aid	168.23	
Schools	134.04	
Soldiers' Relief	356.75	
State Aid	20.00	
Tax Titles	81.88	
Emergency Relief	19,627.29	
		$20,626.56
		$4,050,810.65
Cash on hand January 1, 1934		130,337.66
		$4,181,148.31

Payments

General Government

Selectmen	$2,616.94
Auditor	5,002.16
Treasurer	6,392.37
Tax Title Foreclosures	1,920.00
Collector	8,715.21
Tax Sale Advertising	1,466.40
Recording Deeds	1,717.95
Assessor's	11,538.98
Board of Tax Appeals	133.48
Finance Committee	1,663.96
Legal Services	2,452.44
Town Clerk	8,811.68
Engineering Department:	
Salaries	13,400.00
Contingent	1,199.90
Used Car	198.40
Election Expense	7,457.88

Registrars, Salaries	400.00
Printing Voting Lists	739.25
Town Hall	7,472.04
Planning Board	71.00

Protection of Persons and Property

Police Department:

Salaries	101,087.30
Mechanician	76.61
Special Police	590.00
Janitor and Wagon-man	1,700.00
Clerk and Wagon-man	1,825.00
Teletype	588.00
Replace Motor Cycles	645.60
New 1934 Autos	1,156.00
Contingent	4,948.50
Radio Equipment	220.50
Ornance Equipment	1,099.25

Fire Department:

Salaries	105,700.72
Contingent	4,600.00
Tires, Engine One	245.86
New Hose	1,500.00
Toilets and Repairs	1,983.82
Fire Alarm Signal System, Heating	275.00
Inspector of Buildings	2,942.05
Weights and Measures	2,348.28

Moth Department:

Superintendent	800.00
Clerk	475.00
Maintenance	1,999.99

Tree Warden Department:

Salary	1,000.00
Clerk	200.00
New Trees	400.00
Maintenance	3,999.96

Poles and Wire Department:

Inspector	3,200.00
Clerk	475.00
Maintenance	1,399.51
Labor	6,361.62
New 1934 Auto	600.00
Maintenance of Signal Room	858.74
Signal Room Salaries	600.00
Special	1,533.17
Dog Officer	296.00

Health and Sanitation:

Health Department

Agent	3,200.00
Clerk	1,150.00
Nurses	2,880.00
Contagious	21,713.62
Contingent	1,300.00
Baby Clinic	428.38
Dental Clinic	2,489.92
Inspector of Cattle	600.00
Inspector of Plumbing	2,584.42
Sewer, Construction	3,046.23
Sewer, Maintenance	14,996.83
Drainage	2,996.81
Sewers and Drains, P.W.A.	3,408.26

Highways

Highway Dept.

Salaries	6,350.00
Office Expense	386.68
Construction	25,666.06
Betterments	4,314.96
Maintenance	73,817.08
C.W.A. Patching	4,996.16
Civil Works Projects	9,990.68
Stable Maintenance	13,999.32
Stable Special	499.68
Vacations	7,164.94

New 1934 Auto	650.00
Construction P.W.A.	27,446.26
Bridge Repairs .	1,779.10
Ashes and Paper	26,799.90
Garbage Collection	27,493.81
Dust Laying	4,991.98
Street Lights	40,000.00
Arlington Street	35.00
Sidewalks	5,999.72
Sidewalks, Special	3,998.09
Charities and Soldiers Benefits:	
Public Welfare:	
Agent	2,000.00
Visitor	1,200.00
Clerks	1,800.00
Male Clerk	1,000.00
Investigators	2,400.00
Contingent	2,366.83
Outside Aid	144,040.20
Outside Aid, Special	14,690.20
Mothers' Aid	27,758.12
Old Age Assistance	21,396.24
Infirmary Department:	
Keeper	1,000.00
General Expense	5,059.20
Town Physician	1,700.00
State Aid	1,465.00
Soldiers' Relief and	
Military Aid	36,664.22
Schools and Libraries	
School Department:	
General Control	14,252.58
Instruction	462,171.22
Operation	62,010.78
Maintenance	4,632.95
New Equipment	697.05
Miscellaneous	6,345.63

Evening	2,997.10
Trade and Continuation	9,536.41
Transportation	1,416.00
Smith-Hughes Fund	86.73
C. W. A.	1,251.38
Civil Works Projects	2,799.24
Public Library:	
Salaries	25,242.44
Books, Periodicals and	
Bindings	5,999.68
Maintenance	4,999.33
Equipment for Addition	396.00
Trust Fund Income	479.05
Recreation	
Park Department:	
Superintendent	500.00
Maintenance	2,500.00
Victory Field	1,998.78
Tennis Courts	700.00
Waterproofing Grandstand	79.58
"Delta" McGlauflin Bequest	365.50
C. W. A.	25.07
Playground Department:	
Salaries	2,200.00
Maintenance	1,499.23
New Equipment	300.00
Unclassified	
Pensions	13,812.66
Nichols Annuity	750.00
Streeter Annuity	750.00
Memorial Day	1,100.00
Insurance	10,750.64
Workmen's Compensation	3,093.03
Executions	3,684.59
Printing Town Reports	1,159.38
Headquarters V.F.W.	1,080.00
Headquarters D.A.V.	270.00

Contingent	2,329.13
Unpaid Bills	367.04
Holland Expense	92.00
E. R. A.	19,988.43

Enterprises and Cemeteries
Water Department:

Salaries	5,536.00
Office Expense	2,122.66
Maintenance	41,297.28
Civil Works Projects	8,960.00
Vacations	1,299.00
New 1934 Car	624.00
New 1934 Truck	1,200.00

Cemetery Department:

Superintendent	2,000.00
Labor	7,999.38
Contingent	547.89
Tool House	2,500.00
Lowering Device and Greens	244.50

Interest and Debt:

Interest	86,017.64
Town Debt	216,000.00

State and County Taxes:

County Tax	77,696.74
County Hospital Assessment	21,805.23
State Taxes and Assessments	278,523.35
Soldiers Exemptions	131.88
Temporary Loans	1,515,000.00
Premium	713.16

Trust Funds:

Potter Memorial Gate Fund	10.00
Templeton Fund	97.64
Deposited in Cemetery Perpetual Care Fund	1,604.00

Refunds:

Water Department	193.42	
Charged to Estimated Receipts	159.24	
Tax Refunds		
Real and Personal	5,638.48	
Poll	4.00	
Old Age Assistance	1.00	
Motor Excise	1,114.51	
Special Assessments	125.10	
Dog Fund	1,516.80	
		$3,908,206.95
Cash on hand Dec. 31, 1934		272,941.36
		$4,181,148.31

General Government
Selectmen

Appropriation for 1934 $2,800.00

Expenditures

Avery, Daniel, services	$ 3.00
Carters Ink Co., carbon paper	2.11
Comm. of Public Safety, license	2.90
Eaton, Leroy S., printing	18.00
Gibbs Express Co., expressage	.35
Graphic Press, The, printing	150.72
Hawes Electric Co., installing Clock	30.00
Hobbs & Warren Inc., supplies	.77
Holland, Edw. D., salary	500.00
Kelly, Timothy, spray	20.00
Lydston, W. W., cleaning inkwells	6.65
Main Street Garage, taxi	9.00
McAdams, Wm. M. L., supplies	2.12
McGuire, Wm. P., salary	500.00
Middlesex County Selectmen's Assoc., dues	4.50

Mooney, Fred R., supplies	5.00
New Eng. Tel. & Tel. Co., service	141.84
O'Connell, Maurice H., salary	500.00
P. O. Dept., postage	75.48
Royal Typewriter Co., rental of Type.	18.00
Sheridan, James H., salary	500.00
Tribune-Enterprise, The, advt. and printing	126.50
Total Expenditures	$2,616.94
Transferred to Revenue	183.06
	$2,800.00

Auditor

Appropriation for 1934	$5,110.00

Expenditures

Allen-Wales Adding Mch. Co., ribbon and maintenance	$ 19.50
Blake & Rebhan, supplies	16.50
Boston Belting & Ribbon Co., Linoleum for files	7.00
Cameron, Florence, salary	996.00
Dimond Union Stamp Works, seal	5.50
Eaton, Leroy S., printing	64.35
Graphic Press, The, printing	85.75
Gray Gift Shop, supplies	8.10
Hawes Electric Co., desk lamp	9.10
Hobbs & Warren, supplies	1.68
Kee Lox Mfg. Co., supplies	6.34
LaRhette, Elizabeth, salary	99.00
Lydston, W. W., rep. inkwells	2.50
Comm. of Mass. Director of Accounts, supplies	25.59
Mass. Mun. Auditor's & Comp. Ass'n, dues	2.00

Mooney, Fred R., supplies	13.55
Municipal Finance Officers' Assoc., dues	10.00
New Eng. Tel. & Tel. Co., service	57.73
Norcross, Jr., W. W., salary	3,300.00
Norcross, Jr., W. W., notary fee	5.00
Norton, E. L., supplies	11.70
Pascoe, George T., supplies	12.04
P. O. Dept., postage	2.00
Standard Maintenance Co., maintenance of typewriter	8.00
Ward's, supplies	3.60
Watertown Sun, advertisement	126.00
Watertown Tribune-Enterprise, The, advertisement	57.50
Winston Co., John C., book	2.13
Yawman-Erbe Mfg. Co., filing cabinet	44.00

Total Expenditures	$5,002.16	
Transferred to Revenue	107.84	
		$5,110.00

Treasurer

Appropriation for 1934	$6,600.00

Expenditures

Am. Railway Express, expressage	$ 2.87
Boston Herald Traveler, advt.	8.00
Boston News Bureau, advertising	32.50
Brigham, H. W., salary	3,500.00
Burroughs Adding Mch., service	10.40
Dimond Union Stamp Works, rep. stamps	3.75
Easterbrook, Dorothy, Clerical Ser.	88.50
Easton, Leroy S., printing	6.90
Farnham, Alice, clerical services	261.00

Fletcher, Hdw. Co., keys	.40
Graphic Press, The, printing	82.85
Gray Gift Shop, supplies	6.45
Haseltine, H. L., supplies	4.25
Kiley, Margaret E., bond	286.50
LaRhette, Elizabeth, clerical ser.	6.00
Lydston, W. W., cleaning inkwells	.25
Comm. of Mass., Director of Accts., supplies	4.11
Comm. of Mass., certification	155.00
Mattison, Gertrude, salary	1,150.00
McGlauflin, B. Fay, insurance	85.62
Miller Bryant-Pierce Co., supplies	10.00
Morley, Joseph, clerical services	18.00
New Eng. Envelope Co., envelopes	27.75
New Eng. Tel. & Tel. Co., service	57.73
New Eng. Towel Supply Co., service	4.20
Pascoe, George T., supplies	3.03
P. O. Dept., postage	273.25
Safford, Howard, clerical services	36.00
Sherman Envelope Co., supplies	68.17
Simonds, supplies	2.69
Standard Maintenance Co., maint. of Typewriter	8.00
Todd Sales Co., The, checks	81.20
Union Market Nat'l. Bank, rent of box	11.00
Webber, Harold, clerical services	96.00

Total Expenditures	6,392.37	
Transferred to Revenue	207.63	
		$6,600.00

Treasurer, Tax Title Foreclosure

Appropriation for 1934	$2,000.00	
Additional Appropriation	2,750.00	
		$4,750.00

Expenditures

Land Court, tax title foreclosure 1,920.00
_____

Total Expenditures	1,920.00
Transferred to Revenue	2,830.00

$4,750.00

Collector's Department

Appropriation for 1934	$8,200.00
Additional Appropriation	100.00
Transferred Town Meeting	416.20

$8,716.20

Expenditures

Allen-Wales Adding Mch. Ribbon and maintenance	15.00
Beverly, Mary E., salary	1,050.00
Blake & Rebhan Co., bookbinder	11.75
Colby, F. J., salary	3,300.00
Colby, F. J., incidentals	39.30
Cunniff, M. F., salary	1,400.00
Dimond-Union Stamp Wks., stamps	17.70
Eaton, Leroy S. ,printing	59.55
Fairbanks & Co., J. L., supplies	5.75
Graphic Press, The, printing	176.02
Gray Gift Shop, supplies	25.60
Haseltine, H. L., supplies	2.75
Hobbs & Warren, supplies	35.50
Keystone Envelope Co., envelopes	5.96
Leighton, Thos., recording	6.50
Lindbladh Co., binding books	45.25
Lydstom, W. W., cleaning inkwells	1.00
Maryland Casualty, bonds	30.00
Mass. Comm. of., Dept. of Corp. & Taxation, supplies	24.19
McGlauflin, B. Fay, insurance	85.62

Moran, Marie, salary 950.00
New Eng. Towel Supply Co., service 6.00
New Eng. Tel. & Tel. Co., service 115.53
Norton, E. L., supplies 16.08
Pascoe, George T., supplies 3.79
P. O. Dept., postage 242.77
Safford, Howard, clerical services 315.90
Standard Maintenance Co., maint. of
    typewriter 16.00
Stone, Edwin L., bond 628.00
Walsh, Catherine, clerical services 83.70

Total Expenditures	$8,715.21	
Transferred to Revenue	.99	
		$8,716.20

Collector, Tax Sale Advertising

Appropriation for 1934	$1,200.00	
Transferred from Reserve Fund	266.40	
		$1,466.40

Expenditures

Safford, Howard, clerical services	32.40	
Watertown Sun, The, advt.	550.50	
Watertown Tribune-Enterprise, The, advertising	883.50	
Total Expenditures	$1,466.40	$1,466.40

Collector, Recording Deeds

Appropriation for 1934	$1,500.00	
Transferred from Reserve Fund	420.10	
		$1,920.10

Expenditures

Leighton, Thos., recording tax deeds	1,717.95	
Total Expenditures	1,717.95	

Transferred to Revenue 202.15
—————— $1,920.10

Assessors' Department

Appropriation for 1934 $10,889.00
Additional Appropriation 400.00
Trans. Town Meeting 250.00
—————— $11,539.00

Expenditures

Applin, L. L., transfers	344.20
Ass'n. of Mass. Assessors, dues	3.00
Assessor's Auto Tax Service, tax tables	2.00
Bell, William, salary	284.70
Butter's Express, expressage	3.30
Cassidy, Martin H., postage	2.64
Conroy, Robert C., supplies	1.70
Curran, John J., salary	1,081.96
Curtis 1000 Inc., envelopes	44.63
Dimond-Union Stamp Works, stamp	3.00
Doyle, Marguerite A., salary	939.00
Eaton, Leroy S., printing	655.40
Flaherty, Marie E., salary	1,100.00
Gillis Office Supply Co., supplies	2.00
Graphic Press, The, printing	299.25
Gray Gift Shop, supplies	29.10
Haselting, H. L., supplies	2.75
Hobbs & Warren, Inc., supplies	1.48
Kerivan, Helen F., salary	1,400.00
Lafond & Co., A. W., poll tax bills	113.20
Mass. Comm. of., Bd. of Tax Appeals, books	15.50
MacDonald, A. D., taxi	202.50
New Eng. Tel. & Tel. Co., service	173.25
Oates, Edw. F., salary	1,366.67
Pascoe, George T., supplies	8.42

P. O. Dept., postage	495.26
Prefixt Forms Co., tax bills	105.00
Railway Express Agency, expressage	2.12
Royal Typewriter Co., repairs	4.50
Standard Maintenance Co., maint. of typewriter	25.50
Wakefield Item Co., printing	.75
Walsh, Mary E., salary	1,350.00
Watertown Bindery, binding books	37.53
Watertown Sun, The, advertising	16.00
Watertown Tribune-Enterprise, advertising	16.00
Wright, Edw. F., expenses	30.00
Wright, Edw. F., salary	1,366.67
Wright, Harold, services	10.00

Total Expenditures	11,538.98	
Transferred to Revenue	.02	
		$11,539.00

Assessor's, Board of Tax Appeals

Trans. Town Meeting	$500.00

Expenditures

Brooks, Everett M., photos	107.32
Chase, Cedric G., photos	11.36
Leighton, Thos., copies	14.80

Total Expenditures	133.48	
Balance carried forward	$366.52	
		$500.00

Finance Committee

Appropriation for 1934	$2,000.00

Expenditures

Ditto Co., supplies	11.41
Eaton, Leroy S., printing	15.20

Graphic Press, The, printing	1,261,85	
Norcross, Jr., W. W., services	300.00	
Ward's, supplies	75.50	
	———	
Total Expenditures	1,663.96	
Transferred to Revenue	336.04	
	———	$2,000.00

Legal Services

Appropriation for 1934	$2,500.00	
Additional Appropriation	200.00	
	———	$2,700.00

Expenditures

Belleville, Wm. J., serving writ	4.00
Damon Co., Inc., supplies	7.15
Dubois Co., H. W., supplies	8.65
Lawyers Co-op. Pub. Co., subs.	8.50
Leighton, Thos., recording	56.88
Lorman, Gerald E., services	4.25
McKenna, Jas. H., services	2.25
McNamara, Francis, salary	2,000.00
McNamara, Francis J., expenses	6.00
Middlesex County Clerk, certified copy	.75
Moro, Rose L., clerical services	56.00
Nally, J. Edw., supplies	11.00
New Eng. Tel. & Tel. Co., services	57.76
Ransom's Taxi, taxi services	2.15
Sheehan, Henry F., shorthand reporter	209.10
Shepard's Citations, subs.	13.00
White, Edith M., report	1.00
Worcester County Deputy Sheriff, services	4.00

Total Expenditures	$2,452.44	
Transferred to Revenue	247.56	
	———	$2,700.00

Town Clerk

Appropriation for 1934 $8,900.00

Expenditures

American City, subs.	2.00
Benjamin, Alma R., salary	1,250.00
Dimond-Union Stamp Works, stamp	2.00
Davenport, A. M., flowers	6.00
Dow Mfg. Co., supplies	20.00
Gibbs Express Co., expressage	.35
Graphic Press, The, printing	163.49
Griffith, Mary C., salary ·	1,300.00
Hamilton Supply Co., type. keys	2.50
Haseltine, H. L., supplies	2.75
Hobbs & Warren, supplies	3.15
Howard Clock Co., repairs	6.75
Industrial Stationery Co., binder	2.00
Jordan Marsh Co., window boxes	5.85
K. & F. Stapling Mch., staples	1.50
Lydston, W. W., cleaning and repairing inkwells	10.60
Maloney, Wm. J., services	12.00
McCarthy, Helena, clerical services	417.00
McGuire, Wm. F., salary	3,500.00
Meagher, Annie G., salary	1,187.03
Mooney, Fred R., supplies	72.27
Moran, Thos. F., posting notices	2.00
Morris Ireland Safe Co., services	5.00
Munson Supply Co., typewriter keys	4.00
Murphy, P. B., printing	3.00
New Eng. Tel. & Tel. Co., services	217.25
Pascoe, Geo. F., supplies	20.45
Physicians, return of births	41.00
Post Index Co., supplies	12.75
P. O. Dept., postage	57.28
Ross, David, services	15.00

Standard Maintenance Co., maint.
of typewriter 23.00
Suburban Distributing Co., distrib-
uting warrants 120.00
Undertakers, returns of deaths 46.50
Watertown Bindery, binding 37.25
Watertown Sun, The, advt. 118.46
Watertown Tribune-Enterprise,
advertising 109.50
York, Harry J., services 12.00

Total Expenditures 8,811.68
Transferred to Revenue 88.32
——————— $8,900.00

Engineering Department, Salaries

Appropriation for 1934 $13,400.00

Expenditures

Allen, Otis D., salary 3,200.00
Cook, Herbert C., salary 1,700.00
Dwyer, Thos., salary 2,300.00
Fitzgerald, Francis, salary 1,150.00
Hetherington, Walter, salary 1,150.00
Milmore, Fred F., salary 1,150.00
Stanley, Herbert, salary 1,150.00
Sullivan, Jas., salary 1,600.00

Total Expenditures 13,400.00 $13,400.00

Engineering Department, Contingent

Appropriation for 1934 $1,200.00

Expenditures

Allen, Otis D., garage rent and
incidentals 85.85
American City Magazine, subs. 2.00

Boston Janitors Supply Co., supplies 2.00
Bruning Co., Chas., supplies   291.24
Burroughs Adding Mch. Co., ribbon
    and inspection   5.20
Busconi Oil Co., gas   66.73
Butler, George F., supplies   8.70
Derry, Inc., supplies   25.00
Fletcher Hdw. Co., supplies   8.65
Gray Gift Shop, supplies   6.85
Hayes Service Station, supplies and
    auto rep.   77.94
Howell, Wm. D., auto repairs   259.28
Land Court, plans   .60
Lord, H. D., map   9.80
Lyons, John F., insurance   11.13
Mass. Comm. of. Reg. of Motor
    Vehicles, registration   6.00
McGlauflin, B. Fay, insurance   56.90
Middlesex Linen Supply Co., service 30.00
Middlesex Reg. of Deeds, blue prints 2.62
New Eng. Tel. & Tel. Co., service   161.21
O'Connell & Lee Mfg. Co., stakes   76.20
Roads & Streets, subs.   3.00
Thorp & Martin, supplies   2.50
Spaulding-Moss Co., supplies   .50

Total Expenditures	1,199.90
Transferred to Revenue	.10

$1,200.00

Engineering Department, Used Car

Appropriation for 1934 $200.00

Expenditures

Frost Motors, Inc., car   175.00
Kelter, George A., making trunk   23.40

Total Expenditures   198.40

Transferred to Revenue   1.60

                       $200.00

Election Expense

Appropriation for 1934	8,000.00	
Trans. Town Meeting	125.00	
		$7,875.00

Expenditures

Beatty, Richard, services	66.00
Bond's, lunches	117.60
Bruning, Co., Chas.	21.85
Campbell, Lillias J., lunches	8.40
Carroll, Francis, services	20.00
Corcoran, John, services	10.00
Coakley, Timothy, lunches	4.40
Dolan, Bessie C., services	297.00
Driscoll, John, services	30.00
Eaton, Leroy S., printing	74.30
East Jr. High School Cafeteria, lunches	5.30
Emerson, Wm. M., services	17.00
Fletcher Hdw. Co., supplies	5.70
Foisy, Hubert, services	30.00
Folino, F. F., lunches	2.00
Garfield, James C., lunches	12.45
Graphic Press, printing	1,208.18
Hand & Radley, lunches	3.00
Hartson, Wm., services	30.00
Hearthstone Lunch, lunches	2.50
Hebert & Co., Wm., repairs	38.75
Hughes, Jas. F., printing	26.50
Irma Lunch, lunches	3.65
Jack-O-Lantern, lunches	5.85
Jerry's Grill, lunches	1.70
Kelley, Jas. R., services	30.00
Kosticks, lunches	3.00

Loynd, John A., services	5.00
Mackins Lunch, lunches	22.90
MacArthur, John G., lunches	6.60
McAndrews, D. J., lunches	7.80
McGuire, Wm. P., incidentals	3.25
Moran, Thos., services	72.00
Mooney, Fred R., supplies	37.55
Nally, Mrs. Mary A., trucking	10.00
O'Leary & Tracy Folding Chair Co., tables	19.50
Parquette Folding Chair Co., chairs	29.50
Pay-Roll election officers	4,130.00
Rand, Claude A., lunches	4.00
Ross, David ,services	78.00
Splendid Cafeteria, lunches	18.60
Steward, S. C., lunches	332.70
Suburban Distributing Co., Del. warrants	235.20
Town Grill, lunches	3.55
Town Diner, lunches	20.55
Tracy, Thos. F., chair rental	1.00
Union Bookbinding Co., binders	6.50
Victoria Spa, lunches	2.50
Watertown Bindery, binding	12.00
Watertown Sr. High School Cafeteria, lunches	12.95
Watertown Tribune-Enterprise, The, printing	138.40
West Jr. High School Cafeteria, lunches	11.95
White, Peter J., carpenter work	165.75

Total Expenditures	7,462.88	
Transferred to Revenue	412.12	
		$7,875.00

Registrars of Voters

Appropriation for 1934		$400.00

Expenditures

Gleason, Patrick, salary	100.00	
Hughes, Wm. S., salary	100.00	
Lloynd, John A., salary	100.00	
McGuire, Wm. P., salary	100.00	
Total Expenditures	400.00	$400.00

Printing Voting Lists

Appropriation for 1934	600.00	
Trans. Town Meeting	140.00	
		$740.00

Expenditures

Graphic Press, printing	739.25	
Transferred to Revenue	.75	
		$740.00

Town Hall

Appropriation for 1934	$6,665.00	
Trans. Town Meeting	808.00	
		$7,473.00

Expenditures

Acme Window Cleaners, service	75.00
Boston Belting & Rubber Corp., sup.	22.25
Boston Con. Gas. Co., service	58.54
Boston Janitors Supply Co., supplies	11.75
Brown, Chas. Jewell, supplies	18.00
Busconi Oil Co., oil	1,630.50
Cassidy, Frank E., radiator	90.00
Connors, Anna, salary	1,040.00
Dolge Co., C. B., disinfectant	4.69
Donaldson, Wm., repairs .	4.50

Duffy, Peter, salary	1,400.00
Eastern Products Co., supplies	11.91
Edison Elec. Ill. Co., service	1,061.17
Fletcher Hdw. Co., supplies	29.15
Fort Hill Paper Co., supplies	98.50
Gilbert Howe Gleason Co., repairs	14.08
Gibbs Express Co., expressage	.35
Gillis Office Supply Co., supplies	1.50
Gingras, E. P., repairs	2.50
Glover Co., L. M., supplies	69.20
Hawes Elec. Co., supplies	11.30
Holmes, C. E., repairs	1.50
Hoover Co., repairs	2.60
Kent Co., supplies	2.62
Kleenaire Kemikils Co., disinfectant	3.00
Landry Electric Co., repairs	6.75
Lawn Mower Grinding, repairs	3.60
Masury-Young Co., wax	12.85
Moran, Thos., salary	1,600.00
New Eng. Tel. & Tel. Co. service	57.73
Petroleum Heat & Power Co., repairs	85.20
Proctor, S. E. & R. C., supplies	16.50
Sullivan, Jas. H., oil	.80
Walker & Pratt Mfg. Co., lawn signs	9.00
Waterman, Chas. A., cleaning equip.	15.00

Total Expenditures	7,472.04	
Transferred to Revenue	.96	
		$7,473.00

Planning Board

Appropriation for 1934 $100.00

Expenditures

Dardis, John H., expenses	1.50
Garafalo, Helen T., clerical services	20.00

Mass. Federation Planning Board, sub.	30.00
Norris, Wilfred A., expenses	1.50
Reuter, A. L., typing	2.00
Tomassian, Massis N., expenses	1.50
Watertown Sun, The, advt.	10.00
Watertown Tribune-Enterprise, advertising	4.50
Total Expenditures	71.00
Transferred to Revenue	29.00
	$100.00

PROTECTION OF PERSONS AND PROPERTY

Police Department, Salaries

Appropriation for 1934	$101,500.00	
Trans. Town Meeting	95.00	
		$101,405.00

Expenditures

Boyle, Edw. J., salary	2,200.00
Burke, Jas. J., salary	2,200.00
Burke, Jas. P. (Lieut.) salary	2,600.00
Callahan, Pat'k. J., salary	2,200.00
Carnes, Wm. W., salary	2,200.00
Clinton, George M., salary	2,200.00
Cullen, Thos. J., salary	2,200.00
Devaney, Thos. W. (Sergeant) salary	2,450.00
Donnelly, Andrew J. (Sergeant) salary	2,450.00
Farrell, George J., salary	2,200.00
Flaherty, Walter F., salary	2,200.00
Gilfoil, Jos. H., salary	2,200.00
Gleason, John F., salary	2,200.00
Glidden, Chas. H., salary	2,200.00

Hanley, Lawrence C., salary	2,200.00
Hanlon, John J., salary	2,200.00
Harrington, Jos. C., salary	2,200.00
Higgins, John A., salary	2,200.00
Igoe, Jas. M. (sergeant) salary	2,450.00
Igoe, John J. (sergeant) salary	2,450.00
Kimball, Russell J., salary	2,200.00
Listen, Edw. J., salary	2,194.00
Long, John J., salary	2,200.00
Loughlin, Jos. J., salary	2,200.00
Mannix, Frank L., salary	2,200.00
McGeever, John F., salary	2,200.00
McNamara, John E. (Lieut.) salary	2,600.00
Milmore, John F. (Chief) salary	3,200.00
Munhall, Wm. H., salary	2,200.00
Murphy, Edw. P., salary	2,200.00
Murray, Edw. A., salary	2,200.00
Nally, Francis A., salary	2,200.00
Norton, Edmund H., salary	2,200.00
Owens, Richard J., salary	2,200.00
Parker, Harold A., salary	2,200.00
Perkins, Arthur F., salary	2,104.00
Perkins, Louis, salary	1,724.00
Reilly, Jas. M., salary	174.87
Reilly, Jos. J. (Lieut.) salary	2,600.00
Savage, Steward E., salary	2,200.00
Shea, Chas. E., salary	2,200.00
Shea, Jas. E., salary	2,200.00
Shea, Wm., salary	1,490.43
Stead, Jos .P., salary	2,200.00
Walsh, Jos. A., salary	2,200.00
Welsh, Henry L., salary	2,200.00

Total Expenditures	$101,087.30	
Transferred to Revenue	317.70	
		$101,405.00

Police Dept., Mechanician

Appropriation for 1934 $76.61

Expenditures

Clinton, George M., salary	76.61	$76.61

Police Dept., Janitor and Wagon-man

Appropriation for 1934 $1,825.00

Expenditures

Holmes, Arnold E., salary	1,170.00	
Ryder, Thos., salary	530.00	
Total Expenditures	1,700.00	
Transferred to Revenue	125.00	
		$1,825.00

Police Dept., Clerk and Wagonman

Appropriation for 1934 $1,825.00

Expenditures

Garafola, Francis, salary	1,825.00	$1,825.00

Police Dept., Special

Appropriation for 1934	400.00	
Trans. from Reserve Fund	95.00	
Trans. Town Meeting	95.00	
		$590.00

Expenditures

Kimball, Allan, service	10.00	
Murphy, Jas., service	365.00	
Oates, Bernard, service	5.00	
Sullivan, Daniel J., service	210.00	
Total Expenditures	590.00	$590.00

Police Dept., Teletype

Appropriation for 1934 $600.00

Expenditures

New Eng. Tel. & Tel. Co., service   588.00
Transferred to Revenue   12.00
                      $600.00

Police Dept., Replace Motorcycles

Appropriation for 1934 $645.60

Expenditures

Crandall Hicks Co., motorcycles   645.60 $645.60

Police Dept., New 1934 Auto

Appropriation for 1934 $1,156.00

Expenditures

Taylor Chevrolet Co., Auto   1,156.00 $1,156.00

Police Dept., Radio Equipment

Appropriation for 1934   525.00
Trans. Town Meeting   200.00
                      $325.00

Expenditures

Roskin Distributors, police radio   220.50
Transferred to Revenue   104.50
                      $325.00

Police Dept., Ordnance Equipment

Appropriation for 1934 $1,100.00

Expenditures

Iver Johnson Sporting Goods Co.,
     guns   791.25

Malloy, Jos. T., belts, holsters, etc.   308.00

Total Expenditures	1,099.25
Transferred to Revenue	.75

$1,100.00

Police Dept., Contingent

Appropriation for 1934	4,000.00
Trans. from Reserve Fund	750.00
Trans. Town Meeting	200.00

$4,950.00

Expenditures

American Building Works Co., Inc., lumber	2.00
American Gear Co., parts	6.69
Arlington Street Garage, auto repairs	9.77
Arrow Products Co., safety belts	18.00
Autographic Reg. Co., supplies	13.97
Auto Welding Co., welding	2.50
Ball, A. T., supplies	3.00
Barrabee Service Stores, supplies	233.50
Bleachery Fuel Co., fuel	182.74
Boston Auto Elec. Service, repairs	15.74
Boston Con. Gas Co., service	62.88
Brookline Auto Body Repair, auto rep.	3.00
Bunker Hill Press, supplies	2.50
Busconi Oil Co., gas	2,303.41
Butler, Geo. F., supplies	1.50
Carpenter Co., W. D., disinfectant	27.50
Chase, Cedric G., pictures	6.99
Central Auto Parts Co., auto parts	1.30
Claflin, Walter A., Co., supplies	6.10
Clinton, George M., auto parts	19.88
Colonial Beacon Oil, supplies	4.80
Comstock, A. H., laundry	10.00
Conroy, Robert L., supplies	30.26

Consolidated Expanded Metal Co.,
    repairs   14.40
Coolidge Sq. Service Station, auto
    supplies   18.44
Crandall Hicks Co., supplies   13.02
Cup Container Service Co., supplies   45.00
Daley Plumbing & Heating Co., rep.   32.70
East Watertown Hdw. Co., supplies   .45
Eaton, Leroy S., printing   18.00
Eaton Products Co., auto parts   1.69
Edison Elec. Ill. Co., service   297.76
Elliott Co., W. R., supplies   7.00
Everett Bros., Inc., auto repairs   16.95
Fletcher Hdw. Co., supplies   13.35
Gallagher, Herman J., plumbing rep.   50.00
Gamewell Co., supplies   47.34
Garden City Laundry, laundry   3.03
Gatchell Glass Co., repairs   3.00
Gibbs Express Co., expressage   1.05
Gingrass, E. P., carpenter work   16.50
Glover Co., Inc., L. M., disinfectant   10.00
Goding, Herbert, repairs   1.35
Grants Express, expressage   .35
Grant Motor Co., auto parts   20.90
Graphic Press, The, printing   137.16
Gray Gift Shop, supplies   3.85
Hawes Electric Co., Instal. light and
    switch   8.57
Hewitson & Co., R. T., supplies   8.59
Higgins, Mrs. M. A., services   15.00
Howe & Co., tubes   3.39
Hutchinson, Leroy, sub.   1.50
Hyman, J., auto repairs   12.75
International Magazine Co., sub.   4.00
Iver Johnson Sporting Goods Co., sup.   17.23
Kimball, C. S., auto supplies   5.85
Koehler Mfg. Co., supplies   40.00

Lauricella, A., lunches	209.43
Linsky & Bros., M., badges	15.25
Malloy, Jos. T., supplies	7.00
Manning, Jos. J., elec. work	10.00
Mass. Gas & Elec. Light, tubes	4.01
McAdams, Wm. M. L., supplies	31.74
McArdel, H. B., supplies	11.20
McBridge, T. J., auto repairs	1.50
McDonald Tire & Battery Station, battery rental	3.25
Mullen, George J., registration fee	4.00
Munhall, Wm. H., auto plates and gas	11.50
Murray, Edw. A., expenses	1.10
National Boston Lead Co., lead	31.80
New Eng. Police Revolver League, fees and supplies	19.17
New Eng. Tel. & Tel. Co. service	236.05
Newton Glass Co., glass	3.20
O'Brien, D. J., supplies	3.60
Parisian Dye House, cleansing	6.00
Penn. Oil Co., oil	134.20
Perlmutter, Dr. Sam'l M., service	5.00
Quirk Co., Edw., auto repairs	46.36
Railway Express Agency, expressage	2.25
Reed Co., Thos. W., supplies	9.00
Reilly, Jos. J., license	2.00
Riley, & Co., curtain	.75
Rockin Distributors, radio repairs	1.10
Smith & Wesson, reblueing revolver	5.00
Standard Auto Gear Co., auto repairs	94.65
Stevens, A. J., supplies	6.00
Stevens, Samuel S., supplies	1.59
Standard Maintenance Co., Maint. of typewriter	15.50
Sullivan, Jas. H., gas	7.36
Taylor Chevrolet, repairs	30.00
Tierney, Mrs. C., matron	5.00

Tydol Service Station, gas	1.94
United Motor Service, auto repairs	1.05
Waltham Buick Co., repairs	1.80
Waltham, City of, Bd. for lockup	3.00
Water Dept., service	23.20
Watertown Lumber Co., Inc., lumber	21.88 ·
Watertown Sq. Chevrolet, repairs	10.30
Watertown Tire Co., auto repairs	41.57
Yanco, Harry, aut oparts	10.00

Total Expenditures	4,948.50	
Transferred to Revenue	1.50	
		$4,950.00

Fire Dept., Salaries

Appropriation for 1934	$106,510.00	
Trans. Town Meeting	600.00	
		$105,910.00

Expenditures

Armstrong, Frank, salary	1,101.37
Barry, Wm. J., salary	1,945.21
Bates, Arthur C. (call man), salary	155.00
Blackburn, Chas., salary	2,200.00
Burgess, Arthur, salary	2,200.00
Clifford, Clarence, salary	2,200.00
Costello, Jerome (Lieut.), salary	2,450.00
Dardis, Jas., salary	2,200.00
Devaney, Jas. F., salary	2,200.00
Devaney, John J. (Lieut.), salary	2,450.00
Donnelly, Bernard P., salary	2,200.00
Dwyer, Paul, salary	2,200.00
Flanagan, Jas., salary	2,200.00
Ford, Ernest B., salary	2,200.00
Ford, Jas. E., salary	2,200.00
Gildea, J. Jos., salary	692.45
Gildea, John, salary	2,200.00

Gilfoil, George (Lieut.), salary	2,450.00
Higgins, Edmund P., salary	2,200.00
Hillier, Samuel, salary	2,200.00
Hunter, John, salary	2,200.00
Kelley, Albert P., salary	2,200.00
Kelley, John J. (Capt.), salary	2,600.00
Kirwan, Francis M., salary	2,200.00
Laughrea, Giles, salary	2,200.00
Mackin, Walter, salary	2,200.00
Maloney, Jas. J., salary	1,945.21
Maloney, Thos. (Lieut.), salary	2,450.00
Maloney, Wm. E., salary	2,200.00
Mann, Chas., salary	2,200.00
Mannix, Albert, salary	2,200.00
McElhiney, Bertram, salary	2,200.00
McElroy, Wm. C. (Capt.), salary	2,600.00
McManus, Frank, salary	2,200.00
McNicholas, Peter, salary	2,200.00
Mee, Gerald (Mechanician), salary	2,400.00
Mee, Jos. T., salary	2,200.00
Murphy, Jas. B. (call man), salary	155.00
Murphy, Jas. T., salary	2,200.00
Murphy, Jeremiah, salary	2,200.00
Murphy, Raymond (Capt.), salary	2,600.00
Nichols, Gilbert, salary	16.25
O'Hearn, John W. (Chief), salary	3,200.00
O'Leary, John J., salary	1,946.85
O'Reilly, Jas. M., salary	2,200.00
Quirk, John P., salary	2,200.00
Robbins, Benj., salary	2,200.00
Streeter, Willard, salary	16.25
Sullivan, John P., salary	1,945.21
Vahery, John T., salary	2,200.00
White, Geo. E., salary	2,181.92

Whittemore, Carroll, salary   2,200.00

Total Expenditures	$105,700.72
Transferred to Revenue	209.28

                 $105,910.00

Fire Dept., Contingent

Appropriation for 1934	4,000.00
Trans. Town Meeting	600.00

                 $4,600.00

Expenditures

Aetna Metal Products, supplies	9.05
American Fire Equip. Co., supplies	240.57
Appliance Engineering Corp., ser.	3.48
Ashton-Deveer, Inc., chains	10.40
Atmus Co., E. B., repairs	6.19
Baker, Frank G., supplies	3.00
Barrett, A. B., supplies	29.96
Belvidere Laboratories, supplies	14.40
Bleachery Fuel Co., fuel	144.21
Bishop Mfg. Co., Robert, supplies	37.06
Boston Con. Gas Co., service	196.10
Boston & Maine R.R. Co., freight	.50
Brookline Auto Body Repair Co., repairs	38.00
Buckminster Co., Geo. H., supplies	55.16
Burnham Laboratories, supplies	5.90
Camera & Gift Shop, supplies	13.48
Carlstrom, K. S., rep. clock	5.00
Central Auto Parts Co., supplies	32.44
Chase Handle Co., supplies	16.73
Claflin Co., Walter A., supplies	13.44
Comstock's Home Laundry, laundry	38.65
Continental Soap Co., supplies	34.00
Cooper, Arthur, comforter	3.00
Eagle Oil & Supply Co., supplies	11.25

East Watertown Hdw. Co., supplies   1.35
Eaton, Leroy S., cards   8.40
Edison Elec. Ill. Co., service   404.75
Flaherty Co., Wm. H., aut orepairs   15.76
Fletcher Hdw. Co., supplies   151.05
Fire Engineering, subs.   2.00
Fort Hill Paper Co., supplies   11.00
Fraser, W. H., laundry   67.83
Gabriel Son & Co., Sam'l., copies of
     fire chief   1.46
Gamewell Co., supplies   20.00
Goding, Herbert, plumbing repairs   6.75
Grant's Express, expressage   2.85
Grant Co., W. T., supplies   1.80
Gray Gift Shop, supplies   23.19
Green & Swett Co., supplies   104.32
Gregg & Sons, Geo. H., supplies   7.00
Halpins Welding Shop, welding   1.00
Harvey Sales & Service Co., auto parts   4.77
Hawes Electric Co., repairs   18.16
Hinkley, O. E., rep. lock and keys   5.50
Hood Rubber Product Co., supplies   295.48
Hub Auto Parts Co., repairs   4.00
Jackson Electric Co., elec. rep.   14.50
Johnston Co., J. G., replating   26.65
Kelly, Timothy, wreaths   30.00
Kleenaire Kemikils, disinfectant   4.50
Lauricella, A., oakite   .90
Leonard Fuel Co., fuel.   29.25
Lewandos, laundry   138.83
Littlefield-Greene Corp., equip.   1.14
Lux-Fyre Freez Co., recharging, etc.   37.30
Mass. Comm. of., Women's Reformatory
     sheets, etc.   37.90
Mass. Comm. of, State Prison,
     mattress   9.25
Mass. Comm. of, brooms and mops   16.00

Maxim Motor Co., auto parts	370.09
McCarthy Co., Justin A., supplies	12.35
McElhiney, Oscar, painting	20.00
McLenas, supplies	22.47
Met. Ice Co., fuel oil	415.71
Mine Safety Appliance Co., supplies	36.93
Morse & Sons, Andrew J., gates	43.00
National Fire Protection Asso., dues	10.00
New England Fireman, subs.	6.00
New Eng. Tel. & Tel. Co., service	351.00
Nonantum Coal Co., coal	91.40
Noyes Co., Ira S., disinfectant	10.00
O'Hearn, John W., incidentals	5.31
Ohio Chemical & Mfg. Co., inhalator cylinders refilled	16.00
O'Leary, John, making over mattresses	20.00
Otis Bros. & Co., supplies	20.30
Parmenter & Sons, J. W., rugs	49.33
Pioneer Publishing Co., sub.	6.75
Pittsburg Plate Glass Co., glass	34.98
Pray & Sons, John H., linoleum	44.63
Quirk & Co., Edw. S., tires	34.22
Railway Express, expressage	2.04
Reformatory for Women, pillow cases	6.49
Sentry Products Co., supplies	5.17
Snap-on Tools, Inc., wrenches	14.55
Sorenson, Soren, tailor rep.	7.75
Standard Auto Gear Co., plugs	2.70
Standard Oil Co., gas	363.06
Waterproof Paint & Varnish, paint	30.21
Watertown Letter Shop, multigraph.	2.25
Watertown Lumber Co., lumber	53.07
Watertown Public Market, supplies	4.55
Watertown Tire Co., supplies	12.08
Webster's Express, expressage	.70

Wolfson, Daniel, reimbursing for auto
    repairs   8.30

Total Expenditures	4,600.00	$4,600.00

Fire Dept., Tires—Engine One

Appropriation for 1934 $250.00

Expenditures

McDonald Tire & Battery Station,
    tires   179.68
Quirk & Co., Edw. S., tires   66.18

Total Expenditures	245.86	
Transferred to Revenue	4.14	
		$250.00

Fire Dept., New Hose

Appropriation for 1934 $1,500.00

Expenditures

American Fire Equip. Co., hose $1,500.00 $1,500.00

Fire Dept., Toilets and Repairs

Appropriation for 1934 $2,000.00

Expenditures

Baker Co., Frank G., repairs   6.55
Fletcher Hdw. Co., supplies   28.63
Gallagher, Herman J., plumbing   1,227.00
Green & Co., S. B., supplies   6.67
Hawes Electric Co., installing lights
    and switches   23.18
LaPietro, Amellio, plastering and
    patching   16.90
Metal Clad Doors, Inc., partitions   105.00
Morris, G. E., reefing supplies   61.90
Titus, L. C., carpenter work   12.11

Waterproof Paint & Varnish, paint 14.05
Watertown Lumber Co., lumber 11.33
Watertown Tile Co., tiling 445.00
Yawman & Erbe Mfg. Co., furniture 25.50

Total Expenditures 1,983.82
Transferred to Revenue 16.18

$2,000.00

Fire Alarm Signal System, Heating

Appropriation for 1934 $275.00

Expenditures

Cassidy, Frank E., heating $275.00 $275.00

Inspector of Buildings

Appropriation for 1934 $2,950.00

Expenditures

Eaton, Leroy S., printing 34.30
Ford, Anna R., salary 250.00
New Eng. Tel. & Tel. Co., service 57.75
Wilson, Wm., salary 2,600.00

Total Expenditures 2,942.05
Transferred to Revenue 7.95

$2,950.00

Weights and Measures

Appropriation for 1934 2,350.00

Expenditures

Anderson, Victor, salary 1,800.00
Brogle, Albert P., garage rent 60.00
Crandall, Leroy H., supplies 16.41
Fletcher Hdw. Co., supplies 1.60
Hayes Service Station, service 19.30

Hobbs & Warren, supplies	70.98	
Mass. Comm. of, Registry of Motor Vehicles, registration	2.00	
McGlauflin, B. Fay, insurance	7.60	
New Eng. Tel. & Tel. Co., service	57.75	
Scale Journal, subs.	2.00	
Service Station Maintenance Co., supplies	154.65	
Standard Maintenance Co., typewriter	38.50	
Veeder-Root Co., meas. machine	29.91	
Watertown Tire Co., gas and rep.	72.58	
Wilbur, Gifton, services	15.00	
Total Expenditures	2,348.28	
Transferred to Revenue	1.72	
		$2,350.00

Gypsy and B. T. Moth Supt.

Appropriation for 1934		$800.00

Expenditures

Ford, John C., salary	$800.00	$800.00

Gypsy and B. T. Moth, Clerk

Appropriation for 1934		$475.00

Expenditures

Ford, Anna, salary	$475.00	$475.00

Gypsy and B. T. Moth, Maintenance

Appropriation for 1934		$2,000.00

Expenditures

Bartlett Tree Expert Co., spraying	200.00	
Brewer & Co., Inc., chemicals	90.72	
Central Auto Parts Co., supplies	.45	
Coombs Motor Co., auto parts	2.15	
Fletcher Hdw. Co., supplies	.30	

Foley, A. A., auto repairs	5.00
Hayes Service Station, auto repairs	6.30
Hose Stay-Put Tool Co., supplies	9.30
MacDonald, auto repairs	2.00
Main St. Garage, gas	3.99
New Eng. Tel. & Tel. Co., service	28.88
New Eng. Towel Supply Co., service	1.40
Pay-Roll, weekly	1,559.75
Standard Maintenance Co., maint. of typewriter	2.00
Sullivan, Jas. H., gas	39.40
Taylor, Julia T., service	43.75
Watertown Tire Co., gas	4.60

Total Expenditures	1,999.99	
Transferred to Reserve	.01	
		$2,000.00

Tree Warden Dept., Salary

Appropriation for 1934		$1,000.00

Expenditures

Ford, John C., salary	$1,000.00	$1,000.00

Tree Warden Dept., Clerk

Appropriation for 1934		$200.00

Expenditures

Ford, Anna, salary	$200.00	$200.00

Tree Warden Dept., New Trees

Appropriation for 1934		$400.00

Expenditures

Fish & Co., Chas. R., trees	200.00	
Payroll, weekly	200.00	
Total Expenditures	$400.00	$400.00

Tree Warden, Maintenance

Appropriation for 1934 $4,000.00

Expenditures

Coombs Motor Co., supplies	.36
Fletcher Hdw. Co., supplies	79.36
Foley, Chas. A., use of land	20.00
Ford, John C., incidentals	22.50
Frost Insecticide Co., supplies	11.00
Hinkley, O. E., supplies	.70
Main St. Garage, gas	89.81
Mesiter's, auto repairs	5.05
New Eng Tel. & Tel, Co., service	28.87
New Eng. Towel Supply Co., service	1.40
O'Connell & Lee Mfg. Co., stakes	60.00
Payroll, weekly	3,451.78
Proctor, S. E. & R. C., supplies	48.00
Railway Express Agency, expressage	1.28
Standard Maintenance Co., maintenance of typewriter	2,00
Sullivan, Jas. H., gas	131.05
Taylor, Julia, clerical services	43.75
Watertown Lumber Co., lumber	.60
Watertown Tire Co., gas	2.45

Total Expenditures	3,999.96	
Transferred to Revenue	.04	
		$4,000.00

Poles and Wires Dept., Inspector

Appropriation for 1934 $3,200.00

Expenditures

Vahey, P. J., salary $3,200.00 $3,200.00

Poles and Wires Dept., Clerk

Appropriation for 1934 $475.00

Expenditures

Ford, Anna, salary	$475.00	$475.00

Poles and Wires Dept., Maintenance

Appropriation for 1934	'	$1,400.00

Expenditures

American Oil Products Co., oil	2.70
Barrabee Service Stores, supplies	3.55
Brookline Auto Body Repair Co,, repairs	55.00
Busconi Oil Co., gas	171.55
Butler, George F., supplies	.35
Butter's Express Co., expressage	1.00
Conroy, Robert L., supplies	.60
DiBenedetto, John, auto repairs	2.50
Dorley Motor Co., auto repairs	1.75
Eaton, Leroy S., printing	7.80
Edison Elec. Ill. Co., service	11.78
Electrical Contracting, subs.	2.00
Fletcher Hdw. Co., supplies	14.58
Gamewell Co., repairs	119.85
General Elec Supply Corp., supplies	38.63
Gingras, E. P., filing saw	.50
Globe Gas Light Co., torch	6.50
Grant's Express, expressage	2.70
Graphic Press, The, printing	18.00
Hawes Elec. Co., supplies	2.02
Hinkley, O. S., keys	1.75
Jackson New Eng. Sash & Door Co., glass	2.75
Kelter, George A., supplies	3.00
Kendall Mill Supply, ladder	10.60
Lydston, W. W., cleaning inkwells	2.60
MacPhail, M. Malcolm, rep. clock	8.00
Maloney's Service Station, Jim, gas	.83
Main St. Garage, repairs	139.63

Mass. Comm, of, registration	6.00
Mass. Gas & Elec. Light Supply Co., parts	2.53
McAdams, Wm. M. L., supplies	3.27
McDermott, F. A., supplies	30.85
New Eng. Municipal Sig. Ass'n., dues	8.00
New Eng. Tel. & Tel. Co., service	98.55
New Eng. Towel Supply Co., service	1.40
P. O. Dept., postage	2.00
Smith, Wm. L., dues	2.00
Standard Maintenance Co., maintenance of typewriter	. 2.75
State Examiner of Electricians, renewal license	1.00
Summer St. Garage, auto repairs	77.71
Taylor, Julia T., clerical services	62.50
Vahey, Pat'k J., garage rent and expenses	72.70
Waterproof Pnt. & Varnish Co., paint	32.50
Watertown Supply Co., polish	.40
Webster's Express, expressage	1.50
Webster Elec. Instrument, repairs	5.75
Wetmore-Savage Elec. Supply Co. supplies	355.58

Total Expenditures	1,399.51	
Transferred to Revenue	.49	
		$1,400.00

Poles and Wires Dept., Labor

Appropriation for 1934	$6,100.00	
Trans. Town Meeting	267.00	
		$6,367.00

Expenditures

Payroll, weekly	6,361.62	
Transferred to Revenue	5.38	
		$6,367.00

Poles and Wires Dept., New 1934 Auto

Appropriation for 1934 $600.00

Expenditures

Beacon Motor Co., Inc., car $600.00 $600.00

Poles and Wires Dept., Maintenance of Signal Room

Appropriation for 1934 $865.00

Expenditures

Arman Vahe Radio & Record, tube	2.00
Bishop Mfg. Co., Robert, supplies	17.00
Conroy, Robert L., supplies	.70
Edison Elec. Ill. Co., service	580.84
Fletcher Hdw. Co., supplies	5.55
Fort Hill Paper Co., supplies	10.00
Gamewell Co., supplies	22.55
Gray Gift Shop, supplies	10.25
Hawes Elec. Co., supplies	81.74
Kendall Mill Supply, supplies	29.70
McLean's, shades	5.10
Perkins, E .A., carpenter work	24.50
Sheridan, T. F., supplies	.70
Standard Oil Co. of N. Y., oil	17.83
Weston Elec. Instr. Corp., supplies	50.28

Total Expenditures	858.74	
Transferred to Revenue	6.26	
		$865.00

Poles and Wires Dept., Special

Appropriation for 1934 $1,536.00

Expenditures

Fletcher Hdw. Co., supplies	.40
Master Plumbers' Supply Co., pipe	2.09
Mass. Gas & Elec. Light Co., supplies	.90

Payroll, weekly	177.05	
Snyden Co., Jas., cable	152.13	
Simplex Wire & Cable Co., wire	1,200.60	
	————	
Total Expenditures	1,533.17	
Transferred to Revenue	2.83	
	————	$1,536.00

Poles and Wires Dept., Signal Room Salaries

Transferred Town Meeting		$600.00

Expenditures

Fitzpatrick, Frank, salary	150.00	
McEnaney, Arthur, salary	150.00	
O'Connell, Daniel E., salary	150.00	
Sheridan, Thos., salary	150.00	
	————	
Total Expenditures	600.00	$600.00

Dog Officer

Appropriation for 1934		$300.00

Expenditures

Eastman, Warren J., disposing of dogs and salary	296.00	
Transferred to Revenue	4.00	
	————	$300.00

HEALTH AND SANITATION

Health Dept., Agent

Appropriation for 1934		$3,200.00

Expenditures

Bodge, Fred W., salary	2,882.39	
Canzanelli, Dr. Pericles, salary	317.61	
	————	
Total Expenditures	$3,200.00	$3,200.00

Health Dept., Clerk

Appropriation for 1934		1,150.00

Expenditures

Farnham, Alice, salary	720.02	
Morse, Marjorie, salary	429.98	
Total Expenditures	$1,150.00	$1,150.00
		1,150.00

Health Dept., Nurses

Appropriation for 1934		3,000.00

Expenditures

Agemian, Rose, salary	1,044.41	
Drummey, Irene, salary	160.00	
Kirker, Agnes, salary	924.41	
Sullivan, Helen, salary	751.18	
Total Expenditures	$2,880.00	
Transferred to Revenue	120.00	
		$3,000.00

Health Dept., Contagious Diseases

Appropriation for 1934	$20,000.00	
Trans. Town Meeting	2,000.00	
		$22,000.00

Expenditures

Agemian, Rose, service	6.57
Belmont, Town of, care	85.00
Bodge, Fred W., incidentals	11.60
Boston, City of, care	811.35
Boston Dispensary, service	114.10
Brigham Hosp., Peter Bent, care	40.86
Broadbent Co., Chas. W., supplies	28.30
Burnitol Mfg. Co., supplies	3.94

Channing Home, care	107.15
Dimond-Union Stamp Works, stamps	2.75
Donovan, W. F., service	12.00
Drummey, Irene K., service	9.86
Eaton, Leroy S., printing	8.20
Fletcher Hdw. Co., supplies	.80
Grant, Mrs. Rae, service	43.00
Graphic Press, The, printing	17.25
Holland, Mary, services	68.60
Jakeman, Dr. Harry W., ser. & sup.	271.00
King, Dr. A. E., service	109.00
Kirker, Agnes, service	11.57
Kurkjian, John, service	102.00
Lakeville, State San., board	166.00
LeShane, Richard, service	4.00
Lyons Drug Store, supplies	20.47
MacGregor Instrument Co., Repairing Instrument	1.50
Marena, Horold B., service	10.00
Marena, Russell D., service	5.00
Mass., Comm. of, Dept. of Public Welfare, care	183.00
Mass., Comm. of, board	284.00
Mass. Eye & Ear Infirmary, care	170.87
Mass. Memo. Hospital, board	3,687.05
Mead & Wheeler Co., supplies	3.57
Middlesex County San., board	8,823.00
Newton, City of, care	45.00
No. Reading State San., care	1,050.00
Perlmutter, Dr. Samuel, service	37.00
Pine Tree Press Co., printing	27.50
Pitman-Moore Co., supplies	182.20
Plymouth, Town of, care	284.70
Railway Express Agency, expressage	3.27
Ransom's Taxi, service	5.45
Rockwell, Winthrop G., ambulance	25.00
Rust Craft Publishing Co., cards	24.35

Rutland State San., care	2,358.10
Secord, Dr. Walter N., services	490.00
Sharp & Dohne, vaccine	178.20
Simonds, supplies	1.00
Sline, Wm. H., services	5.00
Sullivan, Helen, services	5.84
Tarjan, Harry, services	5.50
Vouros, Gregory, Reimb. salary, account scarlet fever	10.00
Waltham, City of, care	41.00
Waltham Hospital, board	1,623.15
Watertown Sun, The, advt.	3.00
Wilcox, Wm. A., services	10.00
Various Persons, donations of blood	75.00

Total Expenditures	$21,713.62	
Transferred to Revenue	286.38	
		$22,000.00

Health Dept., Baby Clinic

Appropriations for 1934	$440.00

Expenditures

Biller, Dr. A. L., services	$50.00
Gray Gift Shop, supplies	5.75
New Eng. Electrotype Co., engraving	15.00
Pine Tree Press Co., printing	6.50
Pitman-Moore Co., supplies	1.13
Lavrakas, Dr. R. C., services	150.00
Silverstein, Dr. Louis, services	200.00

Total Expenditures	428.38	
Transferred to Revenue	11.62	
		$440.00

Health Dept., Dental Clinic

Appropriation for 1934	$2,500.00

Expenditures

Crimmings Co., J. J., needle	$1.50
Donahue, Dr. Jas., services	532.80
Drummey, Irene, Salary	650.67
Eaton, Leroy S., printing	26.20
Garhart Specialty Co., supplies	31.10
Gray Gift Shop, supplies	6.45
Hood Co., John, supplies	4.41
Keefe, Dr. Owen, services	201.60
Kelley, Dr. Chas. E., services	504.00
Lyons Drug Store, supplies	1.00
Sullivan, Helen, salary	293.23
VanBeslar, Dr. H., services	201.60
White Dental Mfg. Co., S. S., supplies	35.36

Total Expenditures	$2,489.92	
Transferred to Revenue	10.08	
		$2,500.00

Health Dept., Contingent

Appropriation for 1934	$1,000.00	
Trans. Reserve Fund	300.00	
		$1,300.00

Expenditures

Bodge, Fred W., incidentals	$11.00
Bostitch Sales C., supplies	5.25
Boston El. Railroad, car tickets	5.00
Builder's Finish & Hardware Co., ventilator	4.25
Donaldson, Wm., carpenter work	6.30
Eaton, Leroy S., printing	37.88
Farnham, Alice, petty cash	10.00
Gordon Supply Co., service	8.37
Gray Gift Shop, supplies	9.29
Hawes Electric Co., repairs	7.00
Hobbs & Warren, supplies	20.43

Howell, Wm. D., auto repairs	485.35
Maloney's Service Sta., Jim, gas	1.58
Mass. Agriculture College, Babcock inspection	2.50
Mass. Comm. of registration	6.00
McAdams Inc., Wm. M. L., supplies	31.00
McGlone's Express Co., expressage	.35
Middlesex Linen Supply Co., service	6.00
Morse, Arthur. L., base for cabinet	12.62
Municipal San., subs.	2.00
New Eng. Tel. & Tel. Co., service	163.59
No. Brighton Filling Sta., repairs	.50
Pine Tree Press Co., supplies	31.80
P. O. Dept., postage	25.00
Railway Express Agency, expressage	6.01
Science Service, subs.	1.00
Standard Maintenance Co., maint. of typewriter	6.00
Thayer, Samuel G., disposing of animals	205.00
Thomas Co., Arthur H., repairs	26.00
United Refrigeration Service, rep.	9.45
Watertown Tire Co., gas	153.48

Total Expenditures $1,300.00

           $1,300.00

Cattle Inspector and Town Veterinarian

Appropriation for 1934   **$600.00**

Expenditures

Jakeman, Harry W., salary   600.00

           $600.00

Inspector of Plumbing

Appropriation for 1934   **$2,600.00**

Expenditures

Graphic Press, The, printing	$37.00
Gray Gift Shop, supplies	6.84
Hewitt, Chas. M., salary	2,500.00
Hewitt, Chas. M., incidentals	3.50
New Eng. Tel. & Tel. Co., service	28.88
Watertown Tire Co., gas	3.20
Winston Co. John C., supplies	5.00

Total Expenditures	$2584.42	
Transferred to Revenue	15.58	
		$2,600.00

Sewer Dept., Construction

Appropriation for 1934	$3,050.00

Expenditures

Leonard, B., bldg. manhole	6.00
Pay Roll, weekly	2,981.93
Waltham Coal Co., pipe	20.16
Watertown Bldrs. Supply Co., pipe	38.14

Total Expenditures	$3,046.23	
Transferred to Revenue	3.77	
		$3,050.00

...... Sewer Dept., Maintenance

Appropriation for 1934		$15,000.00
Boston Ring & Gasket Co., supplies	$4.43	
Brake & Elec. Service Co., supplies	19.76	
Gar Wood Industries Inc., supplies	.75	
Hackett Bros. Co., supplies	1.15	
Harris, Chas. A., supplies	95.15	
Healey, Edw. P., renting		
excavating bucket	30.00	
Hood Rubber Co., rubber boots	22.60	
Leonard, B., bldg. manholes	12.00	

Mack Motor Truck Co. rental of magneto	2.50	
McCarty & Co., Chas. J., supplies	275.60	
Parker-Danner Co., supplies	47.10	
Pay Roll, weekly ·	14,315.58	
Waltham Coal Co., pipe	28.80	
Watertown Bldrs. Supply Co., supplies	141.41	
Total Expenditures	$14,996.83	
Transferred to Revenue	3.17	
		$15,000.00

Drainage

Appropriation for 1934		$3,000.00

Expenditures

Boston & Maine R. R., pipe privilege	$12.00	
Leonard, B., bldg. manholes	30.00	
Pay Roll, weekly	2,913.71	
Puritan Iron Works, grates	41.10	
Total Expenditures	$2,996.81	
Transferred to Revenue	3.19	
		$3,000.00

Sewer and Drains—P.W.A.

Appropriation for 1934		$25,000.00

Expenditures

Condon, Corp., John P., pipe, drains, etc.	$3111.38	
Pay Roll weekly	296.88	
Total Expenditures	$3,408.26	
Balance carried forward	21,591.74	
		$25,000.00

HIGHWAYS

Highway Dept., Salaries

Appropriation for 1934 $6,350.00

Expenditures

Condon, P. P., salary	$3,600.00
Regan, Esther, salary	1,500.00
Kelly, Sadie, salary	1,250.00
Total Expenditures	$6,350.00

       $6,350.00

Highway Dept., Office Expense

Appropriation for 1934 $400.00

Expenditures

Graphic Press, The, printing	$150.09
Gray Gift Shop, supplies	65.52
McAdams, Wm. M. L., supplies	18.10
New Eng. Tel. & Tel., service	115.54
Pascoe, George, supplies	4.50
Russell Inc., Chas B., supplies	1.50
Ward's, supplies	2.15
Watertown Sun, The, advt.	6.00
Watertown Tribune-Enterprise, The advertisement	19.00
Yawman & Erbe, supplies	4.28
Total Expenditures	$386.68
Transferred to Revenue	13.32

       $400.00

Highway Dept., Construction

Appropriation for 1934	$28,672.00
Trans. Town Meeting	3,000.00

       $25,672.00

Expenditures

Beacon Auto Parts Co., parts	$5.00
Beech Auto Parts Co., Inc., parts	5.00
Condon Corp., John P., concrete	14,392.00
McCarty & Co., Chas. J., supplies	12.00
Nonantum Coal Co., coal	87.22
Pay Roll, weekly	11,164.84
Total Expenditures	$25,666.06
Transferred to Revenue	5.94
	$25,672.00

Betterments

Appropriation for 1934	$4,950.00	
Trans. Town Meeting	635.04	
		$4,314.96

Expenditures

Condon Corp., John P., gravel	377.30	
Eastern Asphalt & Oil Co., asphalt	328.86	
General Crushed Stone Co., crushed stone	299.96	
Leonard, B., bldg. manholes	48.00	
Pay Roll, weekly	3,151.99	
Waltham Coal Co., supplies	8.06	
Waltham Lime & Cement Co., brick	100.79	
Total Expenditures	$4,314.96	
		$4,314.96

Highway Dept., Maintenance

Appropriation for 1934	$65,000.00	
Trans. Town Meeting	8,817.40	
		$73,817.40

Expenditures

A & J Auto Ignition Co., supplies	$93.13
Alemite Co. of N. E., supplies	18.57
Alexander Supply Co., supplies	21.10
American Bitumuls Co., supplies	15.95
American Oil Products Co., oil	371.32
Antonio, D., trucking	353.80
Atmus Co., auto repairs	17.01
Auto Car Sales & Service Co., auto repairs	276.93
Auto Welding Co., welding	22.75
Baker Co., Frank G., supplies	17.89
Barrabee Service Stores Inc., supplies	55.95
Beacon Auto Machine Co., repairs	40.00
Beatrice A., garage rent	391.00
Beatrice, J., trucking	250.76
Boston Automotive Elec., repairs	29.12
Boston Ring & Gasket Co., supplies	56.19
Brake & Elec. Service Co., auto parts	20.50
Brunswick Auto Supply, auto parts	10.90
Buffalo-Springfield Roller, repairs	120.05
Busconi Oil Co., gas	2,799.06
Butler, George F., supplies	1.70
Butter's Express expressage	13.45
Carbone, John, trucking	177.10
Carpenter-Morton Co., lettering	1.00
Central Auto Parts Co., repairs	25.54
Chase-Parker & Co., chain	26.55
Chas. River Sand & Gravel Co., sand	73.62
Claflin Co., Walter A., supplies	1.40
Comm. Chevrolet Co., parts	4.15
Condon, Pierce P., incidentals	13.50
Condon, Corp. John P., trucking	1,253.85
Coombs Motor Co., auto parts	44.59

Cords Piston Ring Sales Co., rings	24.70
Cotton, K. B., supplies	66.95
Dance Co., Inc., cable	3.50
Duff Spring Co., supplies	147.70
Dunns Drug Store, supplies	7.68
Durna, Jas. H., auto repairs	480.35
Dyer Bros., prestone	2.95
Eastern Asphalt & Oil Co., asphalt	274.20
Eaton Products Inc., supplies	6.60
Edison Elec. Ill. Co., service	43.16
Fay Co., C. E., auto repairs	138.54
Field & Son., Walter, gaskets	2.40
Fletcher Hdw. Co., supplies	623.58
Four Wheel Drive Sales Co., repairs	682.09
Gallagher Inc., John J., pipe	120.96
Gar Wood Industries, bolts	.75
Garchell Glass Co., Inc., glass	8.65
General Auto Parts Co., parts	21.76
General Crushed Stone Co., crushed stone	191.81
General Motors Truck Co., auto parts	38.48
Gingras, E. P., filing hand saws	36.75
Good Roads Mchy. Co., supplies	2.40
Grants Express Co., expressage	.50
Graphic Press, The, printing	18.00
Gulf Refining Co., spray	1.50
Hawes Electric Co., parts	6.16
Hayes Service Station, repairs	1.60
Heil Co., supplies	31.35
Holmes, C. E., grinding lawn mower	1.75
Hobbs Co., Clinton E., chains	233.20
Hood Rubber Products So., repairs	5.67
Hub Auto Parts Co., auto repairs	8.92
Hyman, J., auto repairs	18.00
Kendal Mill Supply Co., supplies	140.20
Kiley, Margaret E., insurance	8.50

Linscott Supply Co., mirrors	2.88
MacDonald, A. D., rep. auto	7.04
Mack Motor Truck Co., supplies	365.26
Maher's Grill, lunches	5.50
Mass., Comm. of, registration	38.00
Mass. Gas & Elec. Light Supply Co., supplies	7.61
Master Plumbers Sup. Inc., supplies	17.41
McCarty Co., Inc., Chas. J., supplies	128.13
McDonald Tire & Battery Sta., sup.	45.90
Monarch Mfg. Co., supplies	36.70
Municipal Street Sign Co., signs	26.18
New Eng. Tel. & Tel. Co., service	178.82
Newton Glass Co., glass	7.50
Nonantum Coal Co., coal	343.16
O'Brion-Russell & Co., insurance	17.11
O'Connell & Lee Mfg. Co., lumber	288.05
Pay Roll, weekly	59,307.00
Penn. Oil Co., supplies	79.27
Perkins, P. I., supplies	91.10
Proctor, S. E. & R. C., supplies	162.18
Quinn, P. J., garage rent	55.00
Quirk & Co., Edw. S., auto repairs	267.00
Railway Express Agency, expressage	8.97
Ramono, S., supplies	146.20
Riley & Co., supplies	1.52
Rubin Louis, garage rent	190.00
Silver Lake Rep. Shop, auto repair	27.32
Standard Auto Gear Co., supplies	70.80
Standard Maintenance Co., maint. of typewriter	10.60
Sullivan, Jas. H., gas	381.83
Sullivan, Wm. H., trucking	246.50
Summer St. Garage, auto repairs	364.17
Theurer, Otto, trucking	61.20
Traffic Equipment Co., traffic	

beacons	259.60	
Waltham Lime & Cement Co., cement	105.00	
Waltham Supply Co., supplies	.63	
Waterproof Paint & Varnish Co., paint	69.68	
Watertown Excavating Co., trucking	92.80	
Watertown Lumber Co., lumber	60.16	
White Co., The, auto repairs	152.45	
Yancy, Harry, auto repairs	71.11	
Total Expenditures	$73,817.08	
		$73,817.08

Highway Dept., Vacations

Appropriation for 1934	$7,284.00	
Trans. Town Meeting	119.06	
		$7,164.94

Expenditures

Pay Roll, weekly	$7,164.94	
		$7,164.94

Highway Dept., Patching Sts., C.W.A.

Appropriation for 1934		$5,000.00

Expenditures

Condon Corp., John P., concrete	$2,803.50	
Pay Roll, weekly	2,192.66	
Total Expenditures	$4,996,16	
Transferred to Revenue	3.84	
		$5,000.00

Highway Dept., Stable Maintenance

Appropriation for 1934	$12,000.00	
Trans. Town Meeting	2,000.00	
		$14,000.00

Expenditures

Baker, Frank G., sheet metal	.60
Edison Elec. Ill. Co., service	206.27
Green & Co., S. B., supplies	10.60
Hackett Bros. Co., supplies	3.15
Heaney Mfg. Co., supplies	85.44
Kendall Mill Supply Co., supplies	80.88
Keith, J. C., supplies	47.50
Linscott Supply Co., supplies	29.49
McCarty Inc., Chas. J., supplies	16.24
McLean's, oil stove	4.75
New Eng. Tel. & Tel. Co., service	57.76
O'Connell & Lee Mfg. Co., lumber	98.00
Ogden & Thompson, feed	2,897.75
Pay Roll, weekly	10,133.63
Proctor, S. E. & R. C., supplies	326.16
Walker & Pratt Mfg. Co., grate	1.10

Total Expenditures	$13,999.32	
Transferred to Revenue	.68	
		$14,000.00

Highway Dept., Stable Special

Transferred from Reserve Fund	$500.00

Expenditures

Ogden & Thompson, feed	$499.68	
Transferred to Revenue	.32	
		$500.00

Highway Dept., Garbage Collection

Appropriation for 1934	$27,500.00

Expenditures

American Oil Products Co., oil	$15.74
Autocar Sales & Service Co., repairs	46.41
Beatrice, A., garage rent	300.00

Busconi Oil Co., gas	1,636.78
Dover Stamping & Mfg. Co., supplies	172.80
Fletcher Hdw. Co., supplies	5.25
Globe Rubber Works, gaskets	8.06
McCarty & Co., Chas. J., supplies	10.20
Pay Roll, weekly	25,168.57
Quirk & Co., Edw. S., tires	100.00
Rubin, Louis, garage rent	30.00

Total Expenditures	$27,493.81	
Transferred to Revenue	6.19	
		$27,500.00

Ashes and Paper

Appropriation for 1934	$25,000.00	
Trans. Town Meeting	1,800.00	
		$26,800.00

Expenditures

American Oil Products Co., oil	$15.74
Beatrice, A., garage rent	300.00
Beatrice, Jos., trucking	17.70
Busconi Oil Co., gas	1,454.88
Condon Corp., John P., trucking	52.20
Coombs Motor Co., supplies	.63
Four Wheel Drive Sales Co., supplies	68.60
Keith, J. C., supplies	13.00
Mack Motor Truck Co., auto repairs	210.32
McCarty & Co., Chas. J., supplies	21.60
Pay Roll, weekly	24,279.52
Quirk & Co., Edw. S., tires	175.00
Rubin, Louis, garage rent	30.00
Sullivan, Wm H., trucking	17.40
Watertown Excavating Co., trucking	34.80
Watertown Tribune-Enterprise,	

The, printing	106.01
Yanco, Harry, supplies	2.50

Total Expenditures	$26,799.90	
Transferred to Revenue	.10	
		$26,800.00

Dust Laying

Appropriation for 1934	$5,000.00

Expenditures

Eastern Asphalt & Oil Co., asphalt	$300.69
Pay Roll, weekly	4,522.35
Riverside Sand & Gravel Co., sand	168.94

Total Expenditure	$4,991.98	
Transferred to Revenue	8.02	
		$5,000.00

Highway Dept., New 1934 Auto

Appropriation for 1934	$650.00

Expenditures

Taylor Chevrolet Co., car	$650.00	
		$650.00

Highway Dept., C.W.A. Projects

Appropriation for 1934	$10,000.00

Expenditures

Builders Iron Foundry, supplies	$24.08
Butler, Geo. F., supplies	6.30
Carters Ink Co., supplies	6.25
Chain Link Fence Co., fence	87.13
Condon Corp., John P., trucking	1,090.40
Eaton, Leroy S., printing	4.20
Fletcher Hdw. Co. supplies	720.19
Gallagher Inc., John J., supplies	3.53

Gray Gift Shop, supplies	21.50
Halenza, H. C., expenses	30.00
Halperin Co., Inc., A. E., supplies	42.00
Harvey Co., Arthur C., supplies	4.22
Hood Rubber Co., boots	3.40
Kendall Mill Supply Co., supplies	531.50
McCarthy Inc., Chas. J., jute	297.70
Middlesex County, House of Correction, supplies	22.00
O'Connell & Lee Mfg. Co., lumber	25.95
Riverside Sand & Gravel Co., sand and stone	97.69
Royal Typewriter Co., Inc., service	6.00
Sheperd Worsted Mills, needles	3.24
Sullivan, Jas H., gas	48.40
Sullivan, Wm. H., trucking	1,044.00
Waltham Coal Co., coal	1,397.74
Waltham Lime & Cement brick	1,777.39
Waterproof Paint & Varnish Co., paint	3.20
Watertown Bldrs. Supply Co., pipe	1,721.65
Watertown Lumber Co., lumber	10.35
Wheeler Co., Asahel, white lead	3.87
White Iron Works, C. M., manhole covers	936.80
Wright, Harold, expenses	20.00
Total Expenditures	$9,990.68
Transferred to Revenue	9.32
	$10,000.00

Highway Dept., Construction P.W.A.

Balance brought forward	$40,355.00

Expenditures

Condon Corp., John P., contract	$26,942.67

Pay Roll, weekly	503.59	
Total Expenditures	$27,446.26	
Balance carried forward	12,908.74	
		$40,355.00

Highway Dept., Bridge Repairs

Appropriation for 1934		$1,800.00

Expenditures

Pay Roll, weekly	$268.93	
Watertown Lumber Co., lumber	1,530.17	
Total Expenditures	$1,799.10	
Transferred to Revenue	.90	
		$1,800.00

Street Lights

Appropriation for 1934		$40,000.00

Expenditures

Edison Elec. Ill. Co., service	$39,958.41	
Hawes Elec. Co., globes	17.84	
Healey, Jas. H., traffic bell	23.75	
Total Expenditures	$40,000.00	
		$40,000.00

Sidewalks

Appropriation for 1934		$6,000.00

Expenditures

Chas. River Sand & Gravel Co., gravel	$78.68	
Dance Co. Inc., supplies	3.42	
Fletcher Hdw. Co., supplies	74.85	
Pay Roll, weekly	5,407.80	
Riverside Sand & Gravel, sand	68.50	

Waltham Lime & Cement, cement　　366.47

Total Expenditures	$5,999.72	
Transferred to Revenue	.28	
		$6,000.00

Sidewalks, Special

Appropriation for 1934	$4,000.00

Expenditures

Fletcher Hdw. Co., lamp black	$38.70	
Pay Roll, weekly	3,446.93	
Riverside Sand & Gravel Co., sand	74.60	
Waltham Lime & Cement Co., cement	414.18	
Watertown Lumber Co., lumber	23.68	
Total Expenditures	$3,998.09	
Transferred to Revenue	1.91	
		$4,000.00

Arlington Street

Balance brought forward	$1,713.76	
Received from State and County	5,705.88	
	$7,419.64	
Trans. Town Meeting	7,252.64	
		$167.00

Expenditures

Storey, Thorndike, Palmer & Dodge, legal services	$25.00	
Water Dept., service	10.00	
Total Expenditures	$35.00	
Transferred to Revenue	132.00	
		$167.00

CHARITIES AND SOLDIERS BENEFITS

Public Welfare Dept., Agent

Appropriation for 1934		$2,000.00

Expenditures

Murphy, D. H., salary	$2,000.00	
		$2,000.00

Public Welfare, Visitor

Appropriation for 1934		$1,200.00

Expenditures

LeBonte, Mrs. M. M., salary	$1,200.00	
		$1,200.00

Public Welfare Dept., Clerks

Appropriation for 1934		$1,800.00

Expenditures

Ford, Grace H., salary	$900.00	
Hanley, Mary A., salary	900.00	
Total Expenditures	$1,800.00	
		$1,800.00

Public Welfare Dept., Male Clerk

Appropriation for 1934		$1,000.00

Expenditures

Glynn, J. F., salary	$1,000.00	
		$1,000.00

Public Welfare Dept., Investigators

Appropriation for 1934		$2,400.00

Expenditures

Delaney, C. P., salary	$1,200.00	

Hyde, J. E., salary	1200.00	
Total Expenditures	$2,400.00	
		$2,400.00

Public Welfare Dept., Contingent

Appropriation for 1934	$2,000.00	
Trans. Town Meeting	387.92	
		$2,387.92

Expenditures

Allen Bros. Corp., badges	$18.12
Burroughs Adding Mch. Co., maint. of machine	5.75
Butler, George F., supplies	1.25
Delaney, C. P., expenses	360.00
Dimond-Union Stamp Works, ribbon	1.00
Eaton, Leroy S., printing	224.15
Fletcher Hdw. Co., supplies	26.95
Hinkley, O. E., keys	.75
Hobbs & Warren, supplies	74.81
Hyde, Jos. E., expenses	360.00
LaBonte, Mrs. M. M., expenses	105.70
Linsky & Bros., M., badges	4.50
McAdams, Wm. M. L., supplies	74.69
Mooney, Fred R., supplies	247.66
Murphy, D. H., expenses	451.00
New Eng. Tel. & Tel. Co., service	186.50
Postindex Co. Inc., supplies	28.56
Potter Press, printing	31.00
Standard Maintenance Co., maint. of typewriter	18.20
Under Elliott Fisher Co., rent of typewriter	25.00
Waltham Woodenware & Paper Co., supplies	56.74

Watertown Tribune-Enterprise,
The, advertisement   4.00
Yawman & Erbe Mfg. Co., file
and chair   60.50

Total Expenditures $2,366.83
Transferred to Revenue 21.09

          $2,387.92

Public Welfare Dept., Outside Aid

Appropriation for 1934 $144,000.00
Refunds   62.50

          $144,062.50

Expenditures

Abrahamian, Manoog, rent	12.50
Abrahamian, Zartig, rent	12.50
Akillian Bros., groceries	902.50
Albord Bros., rent	303.25
Andrews Milk Co., milk	321.32
Andrews, W. S., burials	192.00
Antoni Bruno, rent	102.50
Argento, Jos., rent	3.00
Atlantic & Pacific Tea Co., groceries	3,556.65
Assarian, Harry, rent	150.00
Ayers, Elizabeth E., board	65.15
Bacon, Dr. G. S., services	35.00
Barbanti, Philip, rent	62.50
Barbato, Cesare, rent	33.00
Barker, Mrs. Emma C., rent	44.00
Barmakian, H. N., rent	7.50
Baratta, Anthony, rep. shoes	18.65
Barnstable, Town of, aid	216.06
Barton ,W. G., rent	37.50
Belmont, Town of, care	296.50
Beverly, City of, aid	541.50
Biller, Dr, Albert L., services	12.00

Billerica, Town of, aid	5.20
Blaikie, Albert L., rent	63.00
Bleachery Fuel Co,, fuel	1,382.50
Bliefling, Eliza A., rent	29.00
Boccadora, Ida, rent	50.00
Boccadora, S., rent	403.00
Boyajian, Paul rent	12.50
Bollivar, Mrs. May, rent	10.00
Borghette, J. Joyce, rent	22.00
Boston Mutual Life Ins. Co., rent	37.50
Booth Hosp., Evangeline, care	83.50
Boston City Hospital, care	3.92
Boston Dispensary, care	25.00
Boston Tuberculosis Assoc., board	70.00
Boylston Pharmacy, supplies	2.50
Brackett, Mary E., rent	150.00
Braintree, Town of, aid	172.36
Bresnahan, B. J., rent	175.50
Brighton Co-op Bank, rent	75.00
Browne, Robert A., rent	287.50
Buda, Joseph, rent	10.00
Bunnell, S. W., rent	25.00
Burger, Dr. Francis J., service	8.00
Burns, John T. & Sons, rent	325.00
Busconi, Jos. J., rent	137.50
Busconi Oil Co., range oil	564.22
Butler, George F., medicine	322.60
Calden, Mrs. Wm., board	3.00
Cambridge, City of, aid	2,559.72
Cambridge Hospital, care	783.75
Cambridge Savings Bank, rent	11.00
Cammarra, Mrs. A., rent	12.50
Canzanelli, Dr. Pericles, service	140.00
Caragulian, G. H., rent	175.00
Carney, Mrs. Mary, board	240.00
Carter Clothing Co., clothing	61.98
Caruso, P., groceries	397.50

Caruos, Vincenzo, rent	16.00
Cash, weekly disbursements	30,933.22
Catholic Charitable Bureau, care	50.00
Cavalen, Rose, rent	15.00
Cerqua's Market, groceries	6,736.05
Charakian, Santay, rent	35.00
Chelsea, City of, aid	2,008.57
Children's Hospital, care	64.50
Chisholm, Chas., rent	25.00
Churakian, Ginter, rent	38.75
Ciccotteli, Tony, rent	75.00
Cippia, Carmen, rent	12.50
Claflin, Walter A., medicine	68.59
Cleary The Druggist, medicine	2.65
Clifford, N. E., rent	50.00
Colligan, Nellie M., rent	137.50
Collins, Mary J., board	103.41
Collins, John C., rent	12.00
Conlin, Mrs. Thos., board	133.77
Connolly, Thos. J., rent	533.00
Condon, Mrs. Hannah, rent	220.00
Conti, Dominick, rent	36.00
Convalescent Home of, (Children's Hosp.), board	9.00
Corazzini, John, rent	15.00
Costa Ambulance Coach, service	40.00
Cotter, Michael, rent	362.50
Couture, Mrs. Alice, rent	300.00
Crosby, Mrs. Catherine, rent	76.50
Cunniff, John F., rent	300.00
Cunniff, P. Sarsfield, rent	64.00
Cunningham, Mrs. Alice, rent	17.50
D'Amico, J., rent	20.00
D'Americo, Alexandro, rent	12.50
Darvishian, K., rent	162.50
Deignan, J. F., rent	12.00
Derarakilian, Melkor, board	500.00

Devoe, S. J., rent	62.50
DeWires Sons, T. A., groceries	753.00
DiBlasio, Nicolo, rent	137.50
Diliberto, C., groceries	2,014.00
Diliberto, Frank, groceries and rent	981.00
Divecchio, Vincenzo, rent	125.50
Donald, W. J. rent	19.50
Donohue Ellen rent	25.00
Dow T. R. rent	12.50
Drosdik Dr. Vincent, services	73.50
Dunn's Drug Store, supplies	259.45
Durnan, Jr., Jas. H., rent	475.00
Dwyer, Mrs. Michael, rent	150.00
Dwyer, Paul T., rent	130.00
Dyer & Co., rent	315.65
East Wat. Realty Co., rent	437.25
Eastman, Warren J., moving	1,110.00
Economy Grocery Store, groc.	5,309.64
Egizio, Frank, rent	9.00
Egleston Shoe Stores, shoes	290.15
Elbag, Mrs. Nazly, rent	6.25
English, S., rent	366.25
European Market, groceries	300.00
Faneuil Co-op Bank, rent	37.50
Fanning, Bertha, board	260.70
Farese, John, rent	12.50
Federal Co-op Bank, rent	50.00
Ferguson, Thos., rent	62.50
Ferrera Bros., Inc., groceries	585.00
Ferrins, J. W., rent	52.00
Fifteen Associates Realty Tr., rent	87.50
First National Stores, groceries	4,910.00
Fisher, M. W., rent	36.00
Fiske, Alice J., rent	25.26
Fitzgerald, Mrs. Bridget, rent	45.00
Fitzpatrick, Peter, rent	25.00
Flaherty, Wm., rent	37.00

Flecca, Catherine, rent	60.00
Fletcher Hdw. Co., supplies	8.30
Ford, John P., rent	12.50
Ford, Mrs. Lilla M., board	101.14
Fotis, Peter, rent	8.00
Fowler Shoe Repair Co., rep. shoes	14.50
Framington, Town of, aid	20.00
Friend Bros. Food Shop, supplies	43.68
Gabriel, Harry, rent	25.00
Gallagher, Catherine, rent	168.00
Gallagher, Hannah, rent	33.66
Garofalo, Frank, groc. and rent	168.00
Garafoni, Nicola, rent	12.50
Garaway, Herbert J., rent	65.00
Gavin, Mrs. Bridget, rent	97.50
Gavin, Jennie A., rent	33.00
Gentile, Oteri, rent	27.00
Geyikian, Arthur S., rent	12.00
Gilbridge Co., Howard F., supplies	18.00
Giles, George A., rent	37.50
Given, Susan D., rent	2.50
Gloucester, City of, aid	53.50
Gorman, Chas. J., rent	328.00
Gorman, Dr. Eugene F., service	12.00
Grand Market, groceries	512.00
Grand Meat Market, groceries	21.00
Greenlaw, D. M., board	115.00
Guzzetti, Mary, rent	12.00
Hackett Bros. Co., groceries	2,130.27
Hadjinlian, H., rent	12.50
Hall, Edw. C., rent	275.00
Hamilton, Mrs. W. S., rent	16.00
Handy, Mrs. Cora, board	104.00
Harris, Chas., clothes	926.70
Hart, George, eye glasses	6.90
Harvard Univ. Dental School, service	18.50
Hazel Market, groceries	4.00

Herligh Bros. Co., milk	29.88
Holland, Mary J., rent	12.50
Holy Ghost Hospital, care	2,904.98
Hood & Sons, H. P., milk	502.37
Hopewell, Frank B., rent	46.00
Household Fuel Corp., coal	1,769.85
Howard, F. H., rent	239.00
Huntington, Collis P., (Memo Hosp.), X-rays	31.00
Iannelli, Nicholas, rent	52.50
Inferrera, G., rent	66.00
Inferrera, Stephen, rent	91.00
Kane Cab Co., taxi	1.15
Keefe Jos. H. burial	100.00
Keefe Jos. P. rent	210.00
Kelley, Dr. Charles E., service	237.00
Kelley, Mrs. John, rent	12.50
Kelley, Dr. Jos. M., rent and service	295.50
Kelley, Dr. M. J., service and rent	529.28
Kelley, Mrs. Mary, rent	62.50
Kelley, Mrs. Rebecca, rent	12.50
Kevorkian, Leo, rent	11.00
Khederian, Garaged, rent	240.00
Krause, Wm. H., arch supports	5.00
LaFayette Bros., service	2.00
Lauricella, A., groceries	342.00
Lawrence, City of, aid	54.00
Leacy, H. M., moving	92.00
Lee, Town of, aid	776.53
LeFort, Mary S., rent	62.50
Leonard Fuel Co., fuel	233.75
Lewis, Viola, board	371.25
Lexington St. Drug Co., medicine	19.95
Lexington, Town of, aid	108.00
Libernini, Rose, rent	30.00
Liljeholm, Elizabeth, board	425.00
Lincoln Market, groceries	76.00

Lloyd Pharmacy, medicine	.75
Lopez, Mrs. Nancy, rent	25.00
Lovell, Eva B., rent	275.00
Lynch, Mary, care	47.00
Lyndonville Creamery, milk	275.50
Lyons Drug Store, medicine	1.25
MacDonald, A. D., rent	152.15
MacDonald, Mary, rent	45.00
MacDougall, D. L., rent	240.00
MacFarland, Agnes M., rent	250.00
MacIntosh Coal Co., John, coal	169.70
Mackins Lunch, meals	21.60
Madden, J. F., rent	25.50
Mager & Gougelman, eye glasses	15.00
Magnusson, John, rent	25.00
Manhattan, Market, groceries	22.00
Maher, Patrick, rent	30.00
Major, Daniel A., rent	75.00
Malden, City of, aid	298.29
Malkin Motor Freight Co., trucking	229.77
Maloney, Mrs. M., rent	87.50
Mancini, Antonio, rent	12.50
Manoogian, I. F., rent	50.00
Mantenuto, P., rent	112.50
Manzelli, D., rent	12.50
Marcocio, Guy, rent	100.00
Marrone, John, groceries	178.00
Martin, Jos. L., rent	12.50
Martino, Patsy, rent	50.00
Marvel Cash Market, groceries	263.00
Marvel Market, groceries	523.50
Mass. Comm. of, Div. of Child Guardianship, aid	1,906.40
Mass. Comm. of, Dept. of Public Welfare, aid	1,600.12
Mass. Comm. of, Pondville Hosp., care	270.00

Mass. Comm. of, Rehabilitation Sec. artificial limb	75.00
Mass. Comm. of, State Infirmary, aid	517.00
M. & R. Dietetic Laboraties, supplies	16.67
Mass. Eye & Ear Infirmary, service	331.32
Mass. Gen. Hospital, service	1,285.97
Mass. Memo. Hospital, care	27.00
McAteer, Mrs., rent	72.00
McCafferty, Abbie J., rent	21.50
McCree, John, rent	435.00
McNally, Alice, rent	12.50
McDonouth, Mary, rent	69.00
McGettigan, John, groceries	31.00
McKillips, C. W., (Estate of), rent	10.00
McMahon, P. T., rent	50.00
Medford, City of, aid	757.81
Meehan, Mrs. Patrick, rent	137.50
Melorian, Mary S., rent	12.50
Merchants Co-op Bank, rent	12.50
Merullo, Mrs. Margaret, rent	40.00
Messier & Centebar, groceries	1,098.00
Middleborough, Town of, aid	329.95
Michell, Clara M., rent	307.50
Monahan & Kellett, moving	16.00
Moriggi, Anthony, rent	9.00
Morse, A. G., rent	**22.00**
Mosca, Sabatino, rent	12.50
Murphy, Garland, rent	9.75
Murphy, Mrs. Margaret, board	240.00
Nally, Mary C., moving	16.00
Nally, T. F., moving	133.00
Nashua Mfg. Co., trucking	3.00
Nelson Drug Co., medicine	1.20
Netto, Pauline, rent	43.75
Newcomb, Jas. G., rent	20.00
Nicholson, A. M., rent	14.00
Noble's Milk Co., milk	3.52

Nonantum Coal Co., coal	281.30
No. Cambridge Co-op Bank, rent	112.50
Oakland Pharmacy, medicine	5.80
O'Brien, Margaret, rent	11.50
O'Connell & Lee Mfg. Co., lumber	21.46
O'Halloran, Mrs. Josephine, rent	42.14
Oliveri, Felice, groceries	212.00
Olivieri, Felix, rent	31.25
Oliveri, M., rent	12.50
Oteri, Anthony, rent	9.00
Otis Bros. Co., shoes, etc.	1,756.83
Pallotta, H., rent	12.50
Paone, Chas., rent	497.50
Paone, Jerry, rent	30.00
Papalia, Carmello, rent	275.00
Papazian, Mrs. A., board	30.00
Paramount Laundry Co., laundry	35.93
Parkinson's Milk, milk	809.32
Parmakian, Jas., rent	45.00
Parsekian, Araxy, board	365.00
Pascuzzi, Louis, rent	87.50
Pasquale, Albert, rent	12.50
Pearce, Ida E., rent	162.00
Peard, John V., rent	12.50
Perimian, John, rent	261.25
Pesce, Dr. Guy C., services	210.00
Peterson's Market, groceries	647.00
Piantedosi, John, rent	12.50
Piscatelli, Nichols, rent	80.00
Porter, Anna J., rent	12.50
Proto, Mrs. Catherine, rent	100.00
Purdy, Mrs., rent	52.09
Quincy, City of, aid	314.66
Quirk, John P., rent	137.50
Quirk, Dr. Thomas C., service	5.00
Ransom's Taxi, taxi service	61.05
Ray's Market, groceries	1,333.50

Real Estate Managers, Inc., rent	25.00
Regan, John F., rent	156.25
Reliance Co-op Bank, rent	140.00
Revere, City of, aid	271.68
Rich, T., rent	9.00
Riley & Co., supplies	682.50
Rizza, Jos., rent	62.50
Rizzutto, Guiseppe, rent	40.50
Roberts, Margaret, rent	50.86
Rodd, A. A., rent	144.50
Rosenberg's Inc., shoes	1,095.05
Roubian, Martin, rent	144.00
Russo, Felix, rent	62.50
Russo, Giordino, rent	12.50
Ryan, William, rent	129.75
Saghbazarian, K., rent	75.00
Sahagian, Vahan, rent	12.00
Salvatore, Sala, rent	50.00
Salvitti, Antonio, rent	37.50
Saugus, Town of, aid	238.99
Scarfaretti, A. R., rent	137.50
Scharff, L., rent	12.50
Schindler, John H., service	29.50
Sellew, Merle F., rent	31.26
Shamon, Helena H., rent	80.00
Sharkey, Jas. W., rent	62.50
Sheridan's Market, groceries	4,796.50
Srigfriedt, E. E., rent	43.75
Simond's, medicine	56.65
Simone, Mrs. J., rent	17.25
Somerville, City of, aid	367.28
Sottile, Nunziata, rent	12.50
Southern Middlesex Health Assoc., care	280.00
Splendid Cafeteria, lunches	24.50
Springfield, City of, aid	484.33
Squires, Jr., Harry P., rent	12.50

Stanley, N. H., rent	200.00
Star Market, groceries	1,860.50
Stearns, George M., rent	12.50
Stidstone, Edith, board	934.95
Stone, Edwin L., rent	12.50
St. Elizabeth's Hospital, care	3,227.24
St. Luke's Home, care	6.00
Sudbury, Town of, aid	53.00
Sullivan, Florence, rent	37.50
Sullivan, Jas. H., range oil	196.95
Sullivan, Mrs. John, rent	36.00
Sullivan, Wm. H., trucking	10.00
Summer St. Market, groceries	23.50
Sutherland, Mrs. Fred, rent	15.75
Taverna, Anna, rent	25.00
Taylor's Drug Store, medicine	7.50
Taylor, Mrs. Julia, rent	29.25
Technology Ambulance Service,	7.00
Teresian Hospital, service	35.00
Testa, Fred, rent	12.50
Thomas, Wm. H., burial	15.00
Tocci, Carmine, rent	87.50
Takmanian, Mary, rent	41.50
Todino, John, rent	15.00
Tomasetti, G, rent	762.13
Tomasetti's Market, groceries	355.00
Tomasian, M., rent	12.50
Tsicoulias, A. A., rent	8.00
Tufts College Dental School, service	17.50
Tutunjian, Anna, rent	150.00
Tutunjian's Market, groceries	459.00
Valchus, Attilio, rent	25.00
Valentino's Market, groceries	1,312.50
Vincini, Eugenio, rent	51.00
Vincini, Peter, rent	37.50
Volunteer Co-op Bank, rent	30.00
Waltham, City of, aid	670.20

Waltham Hospital, care	922.60
Waltham Woodenware & Paper Co., bags	76.93
Watertown Coal Co., coal	20.70
Watertown Co-op Bank, rent	181.50
Watertown District Nursing, service	125.25
Watertown Ideal Market, groeeries	3,017.50
Watertown Lumber Co., lumber	32.18
Watertown Savings Bank, rent	127.50
Watertown Shoe Store, shoes	136.81
White & Co., C. W., trusses	33.26
White's Market, groceries	784.50
White & Clean Laundry, laundry	8.79
Whiting's Milk Co., milk	27.80
Winchell, Ida, board	624.46
Woodland, Chas., milk	542.68
Worcester, City of, aid	639.04
Workingman's Co-op Bank, rent	43.75
Yerarde, Peter, rent	47.25
Zulalian, T. B., rent	150.00

Total Expenditures	144,040.20	
Transferred to Revenue	22.30	
		$144,062.50

Public Welfare Dept., Outside Aid Special

Appropriation for 1934		$16,664.10

Expenditures

Boston, City of, aid	14,690.20	
Transferred to Revenue	1,973.90	
		$16,664.10

Public Welfare Dept., Mothers' Aid

Appropriation for 1934	$30,000.00
Refunds	16.50
	30,016.50

Trans. Town Meeting   2,057.25

                                                        $27,959.25

Expenditures

Abe's Cash Market, groceries	4.00
Andrews Milk Co., milk	165.52
Atlantic & Pacific Tea Co., groceries	3.00
Belmont, Town of, aid	570.83
Bleachery Fuel Co., coal	46.50
Boston Dispensary, care	7.00
Burger, Jr., Dr. Francis J., service	3.00
Butler, George F., medicine	19.88
Cambridge Hospital, care	3.00
Caruso, James, rent	300.00
Cash, weekly disbursements	22,417.19
Children's Hospital, care	10.00
Claflin & Co., Walter, supplies	1.45
Diliberto, C., groceries	7.00
Diliberto, F., groceries	97.00
Drosdik, Vincent A., Dr., service	5.00
First National Stores, groceries	497.00
Germanio, Mrs., rent	336.00
Gorman, Dr. Eugene, service	5.00
Hadjinlian, Hagop, rent	300.00
Hart, George, eye glasses	7.00
Hood & Sons, H. P., milk	52.03
Household Fuel Corp., coal	115.15
Kelley, Dr., J. M., services	26.00
Kelley, Dr., M. J., services	55.30
Lahey Clinic, supplies	8.15
Leonard Fuel Co., fuel	22.90
Lexington St. Drug Store, supplies	.50
Lyndonville Creamery, milk	99.64
Mass. Gen. Hospital, service	91.50
Mass. Eye & Ear Infirmary, services	32.20
Newton, City of, aid	421.33
Nonantum Coal Co., coal	6.00

Potter Press, The, printing	16.30
Ransom's Taxi, taxi	4.75
Riverside Trust, rent	140.00
Rosenberg's Inc., shoes	2.60
Simond's, supplies	6.84
St. Elizabeth's Hospital, care	122.80
Tutunjian Market, groceries	6.00
Waltham, City of, aid	716.67
Winter Hill Co-op Bank, rent	324.00
Woodland, Chas. L., milk	682.09

Total Expenditures	27,758.12	
Transferred to Revenue	201.13	
		$27,959.25

Public Welfare Dept., Old Age Assistance

Appropriation for 1934	$20,000.00	
Trans. Town Meeting	1,402.33	
Refunds	18.00	
		$21,420.33

Expenditures

Andrews, Wm. S., burial	100.00
Belmont, Town of, aid	93.33
Billerica, Town of, aid	92.00
Bleachery Fuel Co., fuel	3.80
Boston, City of, aid	163.33
Bourne, Town of, aid	94.01
Brookline, Town of, aid	293.33
Burger, Dr. Francis, Jr., service	10.00
Busconi Oil Co., range oil	4.50
Butler, Dr. Alfred W., service	2.00
Butler, Dr. D. M., service	5.00
Butler, George F., medicine	2.50
Cambridge, City of, aid	447.33
Cash, weekly disbursements	18,534.08
Claflin, Walter A., medicine	4.50

Gorman, Dr. Eugene F., service	2.00
Gregg, Geo. H., burial	100.00
Grogan, Dr. T. F., service	35.00
Holbrook, Town of, aid	320.00
Holy Ghost Hospital, care	114.00
Kelley, Dr. M. J., services	96.00
Lee, Town of, aid	321.00
Leonard Fuel Co., fuel	1.75
Mass. Eye & Ear Infirmary, service	12.50
Mass. Gen. Hospital, care	11.45
Perlmutter, Dr. Samuel, service	4.00
Putnam, Dr. Frank W., services	34.00
Quirk, Dr. Thos. C., services	20.00
Riley, Gerard, transportation	3.00
Rockwell, Winthrop G., burial	100.00
St. Elizabeth's Hospital, care	31.50
Somerville, City of, aid	243.33
Waltham Hospital, care	64.50
Watertown District Nursing Ass'n. services	32.50

Total Expenditures	21,396.24
Transferred to Revenue	24.09

$21,420.33

Infirmary Dept., Keeper

Appropriation for 1934	$1,000.00

Expenditures

White, Geo. H., salary	$1,000.00	$1,000.00

Infirmary Dept., General Expense

Appropriation for 1934	$5,060.14

Expenditures

American Oil Products Co., oil	480.00
Barry, Beale & Co., F. W., supplies	2.50
Bay State Mattress Co., bedding	44.00

Boston Con. Gas Co., service	111.53
Butler, Geo. F., medicine	15.70
Centebar's, groceries	839.84
Claflin Co., Walter A., medicine	14.15
Edison Elec. Ill. Co., service	144.24
Fletcher, A. C., seeds	45.52
Fletcher Hdw. Co., supplies	30.56
Fowler Shoe Repai rCo., rep. shoes	11.60
Gould Oil Burner Co., cleaning burner	5.00
Grey Co., Thos. J., supplies	2.50
Gumpert Co., Inc., S., groceries	4.75
Hackett Bros. Co., Inc., groceries	245.78
Hughes, Wm. S., groceries	21.60
Jordan Marsh Co., supplies	150.58
Kelley, Dr. Jos. M., services	2.00
Lyndonville Creamery Assoc., milk	356.96
Malone, Bernard, rent of team and horses	42.00
Mass. Comm. of, Div. of Blind, mops	3.95
Mass. Gen. Hospital, care	2.00
McLean's, supplies	.50
McLellan Stores Co., supplies	41.99
New Eng. Tel. & Tel. Co., service	51.41
Nonantum Lumber Co., lumber	20.72
O'Brien, Eugene, hot bed sashes	40.00
Otis Bros. Co., shoes	6.45
Payroll, weekly	1,304.14
Post Rd. Tobacco Co., tobacco	50.76
Reformatory for Women, supplies	14.50
Raymond's Inc., supplies	50.70
Robinson Co., R. L., lumber	12.60
Smith Co., A. M., supplies	220.30
Speedo-Strong-Sales Co., supplies	1.75
Standard Brands, Inc., supplies	41.94
State Prison, supplies	22.30
Warren Soap Mfg. Co., soap	15.75
Watertown, Town of, water	78.90

Webster-Thomas Co., groceries	255.15
White & Co., C. W., supplies	1.69
White, George H., wet wash	250.89

Total Expenditures	5,059.20	
Transferred to Revenue	.94	
		$5,060.14

Physician

Appropriation for 1934		$1,700.00

Expenditures

Kelley, Dr. M. J., salary	$1,700.00	$1,700.00

State Aid

Appropriation for 1934	$2,200.00	
Refunds	20.00	
		$2,220.00

Expenditures

Payroll, monthly	1,465.00	
Transferred to Revenue	755.00	
		$2,220.0u

Soldiers' Relief and Military Aid

Appropriation for 1934	$40,000.00	
Trans. from Reserve Fund	4,000.00	
Refunds	256.75	
		$44,256.75

Expenditures

Burger, Francis J., Dr., services	3.00
Bleachery Fuel Co., fuel	12.75
Butler, George F., medicine	4.80
Cambridge, City of, trucking	2.50
Cambridge Hospital, care	50.00
Children's Hospital, care	21.50
Eames, Erle W., Dr., services	10.50

Garabedian, Harry, supplies	4.00
Graphic Press, The printing	7.50
Faulkner Hospital, care	91.00
Haggart, A. G., rep. brace	2.75
Household Fuel Corp., coal	20.75
Kelley, Dr. M. J., service	168.00
Kelley, Dr. Jos. M., services	3.00
LaFayette Bros., service	2.00
Leonard Fuel Co., fuel	27.50
Maguire Coal Co., M. J., fuel	2.50
Mass. General Hospital, care	70.69
Mass. Memo. Hospital, care	72.00
MacIntosh Coal Co., John, fuel	15.40
Monahan & Kellett, moving	15.00
Nally, Thos. F., moving	15.00
Nonantum Coal Co., fuel	16.25
Payroll, weekly	18,089.75
Payroll (Highway Dept.), weekly	17,467.37
Pittsfield, City of, aid	199.91
Postindex Co., Inc., forms ·	1.85
Ransom's Taxi, taxi	8.75
Simond's, supplies	.90
St. Elizabeth's Hospital, care	118.80
Sharon, Town of, aid	2.50
Waltham Hospital, care	136.00
Total Expenditures	36,664.22
Transferred to Revenue	7,592.53

$44,256.75

SCHOOL AND LIBRARIES

School Dept., General Control

Appropriation for 1934	$13,700.00
Trans. Town Meeting	834.00

$14,534.00

Expenditures

Allen-Wales Adding Mch. Co., sup.	1.18
Burroughs Adding Machine Co., bookkeeping machine	835.00
Bruce Publishing Co., subs.	3.00
Carroll, Jos., salary	1,900.00
Carroll, Jos. L., expenses	316.80
Carter-Rice & Co., supplies	33.50
Caverly, Francis, salary	1,700.00
Caverly, Francis, expenses	300.00
Durgin, Margaret W., salary	1,700.00
Gray Gift Shop supplies	53.65
Groom & Co., Thos., supplies	1.10
Howell, Wm. D., auto repairs	179.92
McGlauflin, B. Fay, insurance	13.19
New Eng. Publishing Co. subs.	3.00
New Eng. Tel. & Tel. Co., service	915.95
O'Toole, Anna, salary	1,200.00
P. O. Dept., postage	74.00
Price, Wilfred, salary	5,000.00
Dept. of Supt. of the National Education Assoc., year book	2.00
Watertown Bindery, binding	12.00
Wright & Potter Printing Co., printing	8.29

Total Expenditures	$14,252.58	
Transferred to Revenue	281.42	
		$14,534.00

School Dept., Instruction

Appropriation for 1934	$468,860.00	
Trans. Town Meeting	4,084.00	
	464,776.00	
Refunds	134.04	
		$464;910.04

Expenditures

Abbott, Sara, salary	1,900.00
Ackers, Pauline, salary	970.00
Adams, Alfred S. salary	2600.00
Adams, H. Bernice, salary	1,650.00
Albee, Lillian, salary	652.00
Allyn Lillian L., salary	1,650.00
Ambrose, Katherine, salary	850.00
Andrews, Joseph, salary	480.00
Badger, Louise G., salary	1,650.00
Banks, Pauline, salary	1,650.00
Bassett, Jennie M., salary	1,778.40
Bassett, Charlotte, salary	1,800.00
Beeten, Claire E., salary	1,650.00
Beeten, Claire, salary	30.00
Bentley, E. Mae, salary	1,650.00
Biggane, Sally T., salary	2,294.00
Bisbee, Rena I., salary	2,200.00
Black, John, salary	8,000.00
Blake, May A., salary	1,800.00
Blake, Thomas, salary	480.00
Blossom, Ellen C., salary	1,800.00
Brereton, A. Eleanor, salary	1,650.00
Brooks, Pauline, salary	400.00
Brown, Harriet, salary	899.00
Brown, Harriet, salary	32.00
Burgess, Lilla, salary	25.00
Burke, M. Alice, salary	1,600.00
Burke, Ruth E., salary	1,300.00
Byron, Mary R., salary	1,900.00
Cahill, Anna M., salary	960.00
Carey, Mary, salary	1,650.00
Carver, Alice M., salary	1,897.50
Cassidy, Morton, salary	1,040.00
Caterina, Helena, salary	1,400.00
Chase, Sarah M., salary	1,800.00

Chick, Arnold, salary	350.00
Chick, Arnold, salary	25.00
Colbert, Edw. B., salary	2,000.00
Collins, Margaret F., salary	1,800.00
Condon, Mary M., salary	1,479.00
Connor, Eleanor B., salary	1,594.00
Craig, John F., salary	2,600.00
Crocker, Margaret, salary	1,600.00
Daly, Helen J., salary	1,650.00
Davis, Mary T., salary	1,650.00
Dedian, Angel, salary	449.95
Denning, Dorothy F., salary	1,300.00
Dooley, Gertrude, salary	1,535.00
Dorney, Nellie A., salary	148.50
Drake, Mabel G., salary	1,800.00
Dresser, Mabel H., salary	1,635.00
Drew, Jessie P., salary	1,750.00
Dunbar, Eunice, salary	1,650.00
Durell, Chas. P., salary	3,069.00
Dwyer, Catherine, salary	400.00
Edwards, Josephine W., salary	1,650.00
Eagan, Mary, salary	1,300.00
Eisenhauer, Hugh J., salary	2,600.00
Ellis, Cyril F., salary	2,500.00
Farley, Helen M., salary	1,564.00
Farnham, Helen H., salary	404.25
Farwell, Willard G., salary	2,500.00
Finnegan, Mary, salary	400.00
Finnerty, Marion E., salary	1,600.00
Flagg, Augusta E., salary	1,650.00
Fletcher, Gene E., salary	1,650.00
Flynn, Jean, salary	1,255.00
Foley, Julia M., salary	1,500.00
Frank, Mildred H., salary	1,770.00
Frost, A. May, salary	1,140.00
Fulton, Leah M., salary	1,745.00
Galen, Catherine M., salary	1,197.26

Gallagher, Alice C., salary	1,297.50
Gartland, Harriet, salary	1,100.00
Gearin, Margaret M., salary	1,650.00
Gibbs, Dorothy, salary	1,650.00
Gibbs, Dorothy, salary	26.00
Gifford, Joanna J., salary	1,650.00
Gilligan, Mary H., salary	1,650.00
Goodhue, Winifred L., salary	1,650.00
Gould, Carolyn F., salary	1,650.00
Gray, Bertha M., salary	1,800.00
Gray, L. Jane, salary	1,782.00
Greeley, Julia W., salary	1,800.00
Griffith, Pearl, salary	1,900.00
Grimes, Jr., George, salary	2,000.00
Grosvenor, Lucy E., salary	1,900.00
Gruener, Adele, salary	1,650.00
Gutheim, Ruth, salary	1,650.00
Gutheim, Ruth, salary	26.00
Halberg, Irene, salary	1,500.00
Hall, Barbara, salary	400.00
Hamilton, Grace W., salary	1,900.00
Hammill, Catherine, salary	1,493.00
Hamor, Ruth E., salary	1,650.00
Hannabell, Mildred E., salary	1,650.00
Hardy, Alberta, salary	915.00
Harley, Gladys M., salary	1,400.00
Harrigan, Kathleen, salary	1,650.00
Harrington, Gertrude, salary	800.00
Hartnett, Elanor, salary	1,739:20
Haszard, May K., salary	1,745.62
Hayes, Helen F., salary	1,640.00
Hennessy, Julia F., salary	1,645.00
Higgins, Elizabeth, salary	1,300.00
Hill, Hazel, salary	1,185.00
Hillen, Ethel A., salary	1,650.00
Hilliard, Pearl M., salary	1,650.00
Hodge, Alice M., salary	1,871.50

Holman, Wm. O., salary	2,494.60
Howard, John R., salary	1,840.00
Howard, Mary S., salary	1,650.00
Howe, Walter, salary	25.00
Lindbladh, Ruth, salary	25.00
Hughes, Rose, salary	1,300.00
Hughes, Sally, salary	1,645.88
Hutchinson, Edythe F., salary	1,800.00
Hynes, Rose E., salary	1,650.00
Jacobs, Edith, salary	1,900.00
Jeffers, Harriett M., salary	1,800.00
Jenkins, Winifred E., salary	1,800.00
Johnson, Esther C., salary	1,900.00
Keating, Franklin P., salary	2,631.82
Keene, Irving C., salary	2,576.00
Keep, Marion P., salary	2,200.00
Kehoe, Katherine T., salary	1,550.00
Knox, Mary H., salary	1,641.00
Kelman, A. Robert, salary	2,600.00
Kemp, Anna M., salary	1,743.00
Kenney, Harold S., salary	2,100.00
Kent, I. Elliot, salary	2,300.00
Kinchla, Ruth, salary	900.00
Lagerquist, Bernice, salary	955.00
Lagerquist, Helen O., salary	1,645.00
Landin, Walter E., salary	2,500.00
Lane, Susan, salary	1,800.00
Learned, Edna A., salary	1,650.00
Learned, Edna, salary	8.00
Libby, Gladys M., salary	1,650.00
Liston, John J., salary	1,700.00
Lusk, Mildred H., salary	1,600.00
Lyons, Emma, salary	1,500.00
Lyons, Frances A., salary	1,632.50
Lyons, Helen R., salary	1,625.00
MacCurdy, Elmo D., salary	2,600.00
Macurdy, Louise B., salary	1,650.00

MacGregor, Helen D., salary	1,400.00
MacKenzie, Ella, salary	1,900.00
MacPherson, Mabel, salary	1,800.00
Malley, Jos., salary	2,075.50
Mansfield, Gertrude, salary	1,800.00
Mathews, Mary F., salary	1,700.00
Maurice, Juste, salary	25.00
McBreen, Eleanor, salary	930.00
McCarthy, Chas., salary	819.00
McCarthy, Marion, salary	1,232.00
McDermott, Winifred, salary	1,400.00
McDonough, Elizabeth, salary	1,650.00
McElroy, Vera, salary	1,650.00
McEnaney, Ann E., salary	990.00
McHugh, Katherine ,salary	1,200.00
McKinney, Gladys E., salary	1,900.00
McLaughlin, Helen, salary	1,000.00
McMahon, Katherine R., salary	1,641.75
McManus, Helen, salary	36.00
McManus, Helen E., salary	1,649.00
McMullen, Anastasia U., salary	1,800.00
McNally, Alice, salary	1,900.00
McNealy, John, salary	1,500.00
McNulty, Francis, salary	1,800.00
Mehann, M. Winifred, salary	1,616.74
Melen, Margaret, salary	774.00
Mitchell, Arthur J., salary	2,300.00
Moody, Harold L., salary	1,800.00
Mooney, Francis X., salary	2,800.00
Moore, Harris W., salary	2,285.00
Morrison, Maria P., salary	2,520.75
Muldoon, Marion, salary	1,000.00
Morse, Mildred I., salary	1,800.00
Moynihan, Mary H., salary	1,900.00
Murphy, Beatrice A., salary	1,800.00
Murray, Mary F., salary	1,600.00
Murray, Mary F., salary	12.00

Murray, Susan E., salary	1,270.00
Murray, Susan, salary	6.00
Nelson, Earl C., salary	3,100.00
O'Brien, Helen G., salary	1,500.00
O'Brien, Madeleine, salary	1,300.00
O'Brien, Jr., Thos., salary	1,600.00
O'Brien, Jr., Thos., salary	120.00
O'Neil, Mary Lyons, salary	1,800.00
O'Toole, Wm. E., salary	2,100.00 ·
Packard, Norma B., salary	1,650.00
Parker, Leila M., salary	1,650.00
Patterson, Agnes M., salary	840.00
Phelan, Julia, salary	1,400.00
Poole, Elaine D., salary	1,645.00
Prendergast, Winifred, salary	480.00
Putnam, Walter L., salary	3,400.00
Quackenbush, M. Theresa, salary	1,650.00
Quirk, Marjorie, salary	125.00
Raferty, Elizabeth, salary	1,300.00
Randall, Freda J., salary	1,812.40
Randlett, Rena D., salary	1,900.00
Ranney, Lurena, salary	1,778.40
Reed, Ethel L., salary	1,200.00
Reed, Lucy D., salary	1,653.00
Reid, Ethel E., salary	1,800.00
Reid, Mabel C., salary	1,650.00
Ricker, Ethel A., salary	1,804.00
Ricker, Ida A., salary	1,721.90
Rideout, Grace E., salary	1,650.00
Riley, Evelyn, salary	1,400.00
Riley, Evelyn, salary	27.00
Riley, Isabel, salary	1,650.00
Riley, Isabel, salary	27.00
Roberts, Katherine, salary	1,686.00
Robinson, Thos. D., salary	1,500.00
Rockwood, Catherine A., salary	1,200.00
Rooney, Edward, salary	400.00

Rowe, Edna P., salary	1,741.00
Rowe, Edna P., salary	28.00
Russell, FlorenceH ., salary	2,040.00
Ryan, Gertrude, salary	25.00
Rynne, Ann V., salary	1,650.00
Rynne, Ann V., salary	28.00
Sanborn, Alice L., salary	1,645.88
Sanderson, Lucy F., salary	1,900.00
Sargent, Mabel P., salary	1,800.00
Sawyer, Erald L., salary	3,100.00
Scannell, Louise M., salary	1,100.00
Secord, Muriel C. ,salary	1,641.75
Selian, Alice, salary	1,595.00
Semple,,Agnes, salary	1,900.00
Severance, Elizabeth, salary	1,888.00
Shay, Esther, salary	1,500.00
Sheridan, Elizabeth, salary	1,650.00
Singiser, Marian, salary	774.00
Slattery, Catherine, salary	1,382.76
Slattery, Mildred D., salary	1,600.00
Small, Virginia, salary	1,650.00
Smith, Gertrude M., salary	1,788.00
Smith, Ona L., salary	1,650.00
Smith, R. Glenn, salary	2,664.00
Smith, Madeline, salary	1,200.00
Smith, Rose, salary	1,900.00
Snow, Lucile, salary	1,650.00
Standish, Helen M., salary	960.00
Storey, Helen, salary	1,400.00
Striley, C. Harold, salary	3,100.00
Stuber, Wava M., salary	1,600.00
Sturdy, Ruth, salary	1,900.00
Sullivan, Gertrude, salary	1,400.00
Sullivan, Mary, salary	400.00
Sweet, Marion E., salary	1,900.00
Sullivan, Margaret E., salary	800.00
Sullivan, Margaret L., salary	2,500.00

Taylor, Catherine, salary	1,100.00
Thayer, Helen A., salary	1,900.00
Thompson, Doris ,salary	1,600.00
Thulin, Ruth, salary	1,393.00
Thurston, Charlotte, salary	1,449.00
Thurston, Charlotte, salary	25.00
Tierney, Edna M., salary	1,500.00
Timper, Alma L., salary	1,550.00
Timper, Alma L., salary	24.00
Tobin, Catherine, salary	1,080.00
Tozier, Carrie M., salary	1,882.00
Treadwell, Dorothy E., salary	1,650.00
Tynan, Gertrude, salary	1,641.74
Tynan, Gertrude, salary	23.00
Ulmer, James, salary	25.00
Urquhart, Mildred, salary	1,650.00
Vahey, Eleanor M. ,salary	1,355.00
Vahey, Eleanor, salary	24.00 .
Vahey, Ruth, salary	1,200.00
Vanier, Ella L., salary	1,800.00
Wanamaker, Evelyn, salary	1,650.00
Ward, Anna B., salary	1,800.00
Ward, Edwin H., salary	2,840.00
Ward, Jr., John H. R., salary	2,500.00
Ward, Josephine G., salary	1,645.00
Wetsell, Doris, salary	994.45
Wetsell, Doris, salary	28.00
Wheeler, C. Arthur, salary	3,410.00
Wheeler, Sarah R., salary	1,750.00
Whitaker, Grace E., salary	1,650.00
White, Belle S., salary	1,750.00
White, Bernard, salary	520.00
White, Bernard, salary	120.00
White, Margaret, salary	1,400.00
Whitehille, Edwin, salary	4,000.00
Wilcox, Ella M., salary	1,650.00
Wilcox, Ella M., salary	28.00

Winning, Gladys E., salary	1,800.00
Woodbury, Madeline A., salary	1,761.45

Substitutes

Ambrose, Katherine, salary	76.50
Angell, Beulah, salary	38.00
Andren, Mrs. Ann, salary	226.50
Boyajian, Charlotte, salary	12.00
Brewin, Eleanor, salary	5.40
Brigham, Catherine L., salary	27.00
Brown, Eileen, salary	30.00
Burgess, Esther C., salary	31.40
Buxton, Mrs. Frances, salary	108.90
Chaffe, Mrs. Maria K., salary	87.00
Chamberlin, Viola, salary	21.60
Conroy, Louise, salary	2.50
Daley, Elizabeth, salary	115.00
Deleberta, Rose, salary	5.40
Donnelly, Janete, salary	10.00
Dowling, Paul E., salary	48.60
Driscoll, Mrs. Katherine	187.80
Dwyer, Catherine, salary	29.25
Fall, Ruth, salary	154.80
Ford, Patrick, salary	12.00
Freethy, Virginia, salary	18.90
Frounfelker, Lorraine, salary	52.30
Gough, Anna, salary	126.90
Hall, Barbara, salary	21.60
Hammill, Elizabeth, salary	81.60
Jessup, Percy, salary	5.40
Linfield, Beatrice, salary	142.00
Maloney, John J., salary	18.00
Manning, Mrs. W. H., salary	294.00
McCarthy, Claire, salary	5.00
McCoubrey, Mrs. John W., salary	113.50
McDermott, Mrs. F. A., salary	690.25
Mealy, Gertrude, salary	6.00

O'Brien, John, salary	2.70
Peterson, Nathalie, salary	16.20
Prendergast, Winifred, salary	597.60
Quirk, Marjorie, salary	22.00
Slayton, Mary, salary	6.00
Sullivan, Mary, salary	15.75
Toscano, Mrs. Anna, salary	14.50
Ward, Alice, salary	50.75
Whitcomb, Sarah, salary	15.75

Supplies

Adona Co., The, supplies	2.75
Air Reduction Sales Co., supplies	41.39
Allyn & Bacon, books	640.89
Amberg File & Index Co., supplies	1.30
American Book Co., books	456.00
American Education Press, subs.	31.20
American Library Assoc., book	1.00
American Professions, supplies	92.00
American Type Founders Sales, supplies	344.58
American Viewpoint Society, books	53.83
Appleton Century Co. D., books	168.83
Arlo Publishing Co., books	5.82
Automatic Electric Heater, supplies	3.88
Babb & Co., Edw. E., supplies	1,525.64
Barnes & Noble Inc., books	26.04
Baker & Taylor Co., books	37.73
Beaudette & Co., supplies	55.90
Beckley-Cardy Co., books	35.26
Birchard & Co., C. C., music	14.95
Bobbs-Merrill Co., books	17.66
Boston Blue Print Co., supplies	81.15
Bostitch Sales Co., staples	2.00
Boston Music Co., music	33.50
Boston & Maine R.R., freight	.50
Bradley Co., Milton, supplies	1,397.09

Brine Co., Jas. F., supplies	4.05
Brine Co., Jas. W., supplies	13.74
Bruce Publishing Co., supplies	9.88
Butter's Express Co., expressage	.70
Cambosco Scientific Co., supplies	114.97
Carter & Co., John, supplies	4.96
Chandler & Farquhar Co., tools	85.37
Centebar, groceries	317.76
Carter-Rice & Co., supplies	238.44
Central Scientific Co., supplies	66.72
Chick, Arnold, music	5.00
Child Health Assoc., records	2.50
Chesterton, Co., A. W., supplies	39.75
Claflin Co., Walter A., supplies	.30
Classroom Teacher Inc., printer	18.92
Clear Type Publishing Co., book	2.61
College Entrance Board, books	6.50
Cosmo Press, Inc., supplies	11.11
Creative Educational Society, printer	20.05
Central Engraving Co., line plates	10.26
Cincinnati Electrical Co., supplies	.51
Dept. of English, books	1.25
Dick Co., A. B., supplies	250.26
Dietzgen Co., Eugene, supplies	57.03
Dico Laboratories, supplies	8.22
Ditto Inc., supplies	38.25
Dutton & Co., E. P., books	1.50
Fischer, Inc., Carl, music	44.43
Fletcher Hdw. Co., supplies	271.86
Gaylord Bros. Inc., supplies	2.15
Garden City Publishing Co., books	1.72
Globe Book Co., supplies	60.69
Gibbs Express Co., expressage	.35
General Biological Supply, supplies	25.26
Gilpatric, Wilbur D., supplies	498.22
Ginn & Co., books	1,023.58
Gray Gift Shop, supplies	130.30

Gregg Publishing Co., supplies	3.44
Hackett Bros., groceries.	217.47
Hammett Co., J. L., supplies	792.71
Harcourt, Brace & Co., books	226.11
Harper & Bros., books	27.84
Harvey Co., Arthur C., supplies	277.35
Hawes Electric Co., supplies	285.13
Heath & Co., D. C., books	568.83
Hobbs & Warren, books	1.08
Holden Patent Book Cover Co., binders	26.69
Holt & Bugbee Co., lumber	66.73
Homeyer & Co., Chas. W., music	1.56
Horace Partridge Co., supplies	91.43
Houghton, Mifflin Co., supplies	308.56
Hoyt, William, supplies	3.30
Iroquois Publishing Co., supplies	61.40
Jacobs, Walter, music	6.40
Jordan Marsh Co., supplies	48.70
Keith, Walter B., diplomas	99.75
Kenney Bros & Wolkins, supplies	94.10
Laidlaw Bros., books	29.58
Lippincott Co., J. B., books	102.05
Little Brown Co., books	100.67
Library of Congress, supplies	5.65
Lyons & Carnahan, books	65.12
Macmillan Co., books	286.71
Makepeace, Inc., B. L., supplies	14.47
Manual Arts Press, printing equip.	3.40
Mass. Bible Society, bibles	2.25
Mass. Teachers Federation, music	4.00
McAdams, Wm. M. L., supplies	154.88
McCarthy-Morris Co., supplies	8.75
McGraw-Hill Book Co., books	8.07
McIntosh Publishing Co., books	61.22
Mentzer-Bush Co., books	35.19
Merrill Co., Chas. E., books	33.16

Morrison, Maria P., postage	35.00
Morton, A. Lucy, engros. diplomas	76.50
Multistamp Co., stencils	26.27
Noble & Noble, books	.80
Newton Music Co., records	6.00
Nolan Co., W. L., books	3.50
Oxford Book Co., books	35.65
Prentice-Hall, books	98.53
Public School Publishing Co., books	6.38
Railway Express Agency, expressage	5.44
Raynham Bleachery, supplies	25.05
Remington Rand Inc., supplies	176.83
Roosevelt, James, graduation paper	50.00
Row-Peterson & Co., books	12.88
Sanborn & Co., Benj. H., books	151.35
Science Service, subs.	7.00
Scott-Foresman & Co., books	248.96
Scribner's Sons Co., Chas., books	74.13
Shaw-Walker, supplies	4.62
Silver-Burdett & Co., books	43.12
Singer Sewing Machine Co., supplies	8.76
South-Western Publishing Co., books	86.21
Standard Oil Co., oil	5.77
South Bend Lathe Works, emery grinder	1.60
Standard Maintenance Co., maintenance of typewriters	46.26
Standard Office Machine Co., varnish	1.08
Star Market Co., groceries	230.45
Thorp & Martin, cases	5.25
Teachers College, questionnaires	3.12
University Publishing Co., books	59.57
University Trust Co., books	452.01
Wahn Co., George H., supplies	83.99
Waltham Foundry Co., castings	33.09
Ward's, supplies	3.00
Watertown Electric Co., supplies	58.65

Watertown Lumber Co., lumber	395.81
Weldon, H. J., supplies	24.00
Welles Publishing Co., subs.	65.00
Wensell & Co. ,supplies	40.36
Wheeler Publishing Co., books	5.85
White Co., R. H., supplies	63.56
Wilkinson & Co., A. J., tools	168.54
Westland & Co., Wm., supplies	16.00
Wild & Stevens, supplies	9.54
Wiley & Sons, John, books	7.36
Wilson Co., H. W., books	11.85
Winston Co., John C., books	172.48
Wood Co., A. M., lumber	488.74
Woodland, Chas. L., milk	55.21
Woolworth Co., F. W., supplies	17.75
World Book Co., books	135.82
Wolkins Co., Henry S., supplies	1,562.71
Yawman & Erbe Mfg. Co., supplies	9.16

Total Expenditures	462,171.22	
Transferred to Revenue	2,738.82	
		$464,910.04

School Dept., Operation

Appropriation for 1934	$58,815.00	
Trans. Town Meeting	3,200.00	
		$62,015.00

Expenditures

Beatty, Richard, salary	1,700.00
Beigh, Albert, salary	70.00
Burns, Michael, salary	1,584.74
Carroll, Francis, salary	790.62
Corcoran, John, salary	834.91
Cornick, Adolphus, salary	1,700.00
Couture, Herman, salary	1,900.00
Doherty, James, salary	1,363.95

Dowd, Jas., salary	1,500.00
Driscoll, John, salary	1,883.39
Duffy, Mrs. Mary, salary	948.35
Dwyer, Mrs. Delia, salary	931.54
Foisy, Hubert, salary	1,900.00
Grant, Mrs. Rae, salary	950.00
Harrington, Jas., salary	1,800.00
Hartson, Wm., salary	1,900.00
Kelly, Jas. R., janitor service	102.50
Kerens, Grace, salary	23.65
Kerens, John, salary	212.82
Leach, Hubert, salary	36.68
LeShane, Richard, salary	1,500.00
Manning, Delia, salary	950.00
McElhiney, Geo., salary	300.00
Monahan, John, salary	60.00
Quinn, Terence, salary	1,500.00
Ross, David, salary	2,500.00
Ross, John J., salary	2,000.00
Sullivan, Mrs. Florence, salary	16.60
Touchette, Anna M., salary	950.00
Tracy, Annie, salary	950.00

Supplies

American Oil Products Co., oil	570.84
A. P. W. Paper Co., supplies	36.75
Bleachery Fuel Co., fuel	12,618.05
Boston Con. Gas Co., service	985.24
Butter's Express, expressage	18.00
Carroll, Francis, service	5.00
Chesterton Co., A. W., supplies	296.10
City Fuel Co., fuel	203.18
Corcoran, John, janito rservice	228.00
Doherty, James, service	15.00
Dowd Co., H. J., towels	130.00
Dowd, James, janitor service	332.00
Eagle Oil & Supply Co., supplies	121.52

Edison Elec. Ill. Co., service	8,187.38
Fletcher Hdw. Co., supplies	74.87
Foisy, Hubert, janitor service	25.00
Gidley, Samuel, gas	.96
Hackett Bros. Co., supplies	5.75
Hartson, Wm., service	5.00
Hawes Electric Co., parts	41.89
Jenney Mfg. Co., gas and oil	123.32
Kelly, Jas. B., janitor service	102.50
Loughlin, Jos., service	3.00
Mass. Comm. of, State Prison, sup.	74.08
Masury-Young Co., oil	29.88
Met. Ice Co., fuel oil	319.49
Murphy, Edw. P., service	5.00
Raynham Bleachery, supplies	18.60
Ross, John J., janitor service	178.80
Ryan Co., L., supplies	20.00
Standard Charcoal Co., charcoal	55.00
State Chemical Co., supplies	702.89
Stone & Forsyth Co., towels	395.00
Watertown S un,The, advt.	5.00
Watertown Tribune-Enterprise, The, advertisement	9.50
Water Dept., water service	1,710.94

Total Expenditures	62,010.78
Transferred to Revenue	4.22
	$62,015.00

School Dept., Maintenance

Appropriation for 1934	**$5,500.00**

Expenditures

Airway Branch of Boston, vacuum cleaner	71.55
Allen Shade Holder Co., shades	100.36
Allston Elec. Welding Co., welding	68.00

Atlantic Flag Pole Co., flag pole   122.00
Babb & Co., Edw. E., supplies   39.16
Baker, Frank G., door linings   7.00
Barnes & Jones, rep. damper regu-
     lators   147.64
Blair, Herman A., tuning piano   3.00
Brookline Auto Body Repair,
     auto repair   4.50
Blum Oil Burner Service, repairing   13.50
Chesterton Co., A. W., water paint   224.25
Dick Co., A. B., cleaning Mimeo.   6.00
Fletcher Hdw. Co., supplies   242.68
Stanley Freeman Co., E., supplies
     and repairs   432.10
Gardella, Primo, setting glass   4.00
General Electric Co., repair motor   24.50
Griffiths Saw Co., Albert, saws   13.85
Hales, Alfred W., cleaning clocks   12.00
Sidney W. Hall, repairs   5.60
Hawes Electric Co., repair clock   46.98
Hinkley, O. E., making key   .25
Holmes Co., C. C., plumbing parts   68.96
Gilbert Howe Gleason Co., Installing
     vacuum heating pump   18.07
Hughes, Wm. H., electric repairs   3.65
Ideal Mower Sales & Service, sup.   6.60
International Business Machine Co.,
     repairs   23.20
Johnson Service Co., repairs   139.50
Kenney Bros. & Wolkins, supplies   16.71
Lawn Mower Grinding Co., grinding   18.10
MacDonald, John, setting glass   12.00
Mass. Commonwealth of, State Prison,
     supplies   23.10
Mass. Gas & Elec. Supply, repairs   10.10
Master Plumbers Supply, Inc., supplies 92.60
Masury-Young Co., supplies   7.66

McGlauflin, B. Fay, insurance	13.20
McLean's, shade roller	.30
McWhirter, A. L., tuning piano	3.00
Narragansett Mfg. Co., keys	10.82
New Eng. Laundries, laundry	9.92
Newton Glass Co., glass	21.27
Nonantum Lumber Co., lumber	17.59
Pink, Jos. A., plumbing repairs	91.25
Powers Regulator Co., repairs to heating system	155.55
Quality Saw Co., saws filde	42.55
Ross, David, garage rent and service	561.92
Singer Sewing Mch. Co., parts	.88
Smith Co., H. B., grate bars	96.00
Standard Elec. Times, repairs	287.53
Standard Maintenance Co., maintenance of typewriters	912.80
Stone & Forsyth Co., fixtures	22.80
Vance, Alvin, recaneing	41.25
Vaughan Co., W. C., supplies	22.60
Vose Piano Co., tuning	12.00
Walker & Pratt Mfg. Co., grate bars	93.00
Watertown Lumber Co., post, etc.	74.09
Watertown, Town of (Health Dept.), permit for plumbing	4.00
Watertown Wall Paper, supplies	1.85
Webster's Express, expressage	1.60
White & Clean Laundry, laundry	14.92
Whitney, Chas. A., plumbing	87.34
Worcester, Ralph H., repairs	3.75

Total Expenditures	$4,632.95	
Transferred to Revenue	867.05	
		$5,500.00

School Dept., New Equipment

Appropriation for 1934	$700.00

Expenditures

Hammett Co., J. L., sand table	20.20
Kenney Bros. & Wolkins, chair, desks	66.25
Kenney, Horace S., chair desk	5.00
Royal Typewriter Co., typewriter	60.00
Wolkins Co., Henry S., lockers	545.60
Total Expenditures	$697.05
Transferred to Revenue	2.95
	$700.00

School Dept., Miscellaneous

Appropriation for 1934	$6,400.00

Expenditures

Carney, Mary, salary	$1,500.00
Harding, Susan M., salary	1,500.00
Johnson, Alice, salary	1,500.00
Kelly, Dr. Edw. J., salary	500.00
Toppan, Dr. Albert B., salary	500.00
Zovickian, Dr. H., salary	500.00

Supplies

Babb & Co., Edw. E., supplies	4.34
Carney, Mary, expenses	14.11
Claflin Co., Walter, supplies	72.74
French, Lucile G., carfare	39.98
Harding, Susan M., carfare & expenses	4.00
Johnson, Alice, carfare	8.60
Keating, Franklin P., carfare	9.10
Kelley, Timothy, sprays	11.00
Nelson, Earl C., expenses	33.20
Newton Music Store, music	.90
Noden, Elizabeth R., transportation	21.45
O'Toole the Florist, spray	5.00
Price, Wilfred H., expenses	1.00
Tilbert, Elizabeth F., transportation	74.25

Whitehill, Edw. H., incidentals 45.96

Total Expenditures $6,345.63
Transferred to Revenue 54.37

$6,400.00

School Dept., Evening

Appropriation for 1934 $3,450.00

Expenditures

Andren, Ann, salary	$144.00
Andrews, Jos., salary	81.00
Banks, Pauline, salary	87.00
Batchelder, Edw. P., salary	57.00
Burns, Mrs. Mary, salary	81.00
Corcoran, John, salary	135.60
Doherty, James, salary	6.00
Downey, Mary, salary	138.00
Ford, Patrick B., salary	57.00
Geary, Mrs. Cecelia, salary	144.00
Harrigan, Kathleen, salary	3.00
Hillen, Ethel, salary	87.00
Hunt, Mrs. Frances R., salary	36.00
Kaveny, John P., salary	72.00
Keep, Marion P., salary	144.00
Kelley, John Francis, salary	48.00
Kelley, Jr., John J., salary	138.00
Lyons, Helen, salary	138.00
Maloney, John, salary	138.00
McCann, Beatrice, salary	135.00
McDonald, Donald, salary	138.00
Mitten, Helen E., salary	$138.00
Mellen, Margaret, salary	57.00
Nelson, Earl C., salary	230.00
Paquette, Charlotte, salary	138.00
Ross, John J., salary	135.60
Shaw, Carolyn W., salary	2.70

Smith, Rose C., salary	135.00
Tierney, Edna M., salary	51.00

Supplies

American Book Co., books	16.73
Babb & Co., Edw. E., supplies	21.60
Bradley Co., Milton, supplies	6.88
Chandler School, books	12.71
Ginn & Co., books	21.98
Gregg Publishing Co., books	8.96
Wolkins Co., Henry S., supplies	13.34
Total Expenditures	$2,997.10
Transferred to Revenue	452.90
	$3,450.00

School Dept., Trade and Continuation

Appropriation for 1934	$10,000.00

Expenditures

Boston, City of, tuition	$1,126.47
Middlesex County, tuition	44.00
Lynn, City of, tuition	24.40
Newton, City of, tuition	8,156.93
Somerville, City of, tuition	146.16
Waltham, City of, tuition	38.45
Total Expenditures	$9,536.41
Transferred to Revenue	463.59	$10,000.00

School Dept., Transportation

Appropriation for 1934	$1,500.00

Expenditures

Lovell Bus Lines, transportation	$1,416.00
Transferred to Revenue	84.00
	$1,500.00

School Dept., Smith-Hughes Fund

Received from State		$86.73

Expenditures

Keating, Franklin P., salary	48.18	
Woodbury, Madeline A. ,salary	38.55	
Total Expenditures	$86.73	$86.73

School Dept., C. W. A.

Balance brought forward	$1,251.99

Expenditures

Eagle Cornice & Skylight Co., pitch	140.00
Fletcher Hdw. Co., supplies	223.33
Gatchell Glass Co., supplies	7.50
Kendall Mill Supply Co., paint	234.25
McAdams, Wm. M. L., supplies	18.83
McElroy, B. H., renting printing equip.	60.00
McNamara, J. H., supplies	14.25
Morris, G. E., renting roofing equip.	75.00
O'Connell & Lee Mfg. Co., lumber	48.93
Patent Scaffolding Co., scaffolding	273.00
Travers-Sandell, waterproofing	114.95
Watertown Bldrs. Supply Co., supplies	31.86
Watertown Lumber Co., lumber	9.48
Total Expenditures	$1,251.38
Transferred to Revenue	.61
	$1,251.99

School Dept., Civil Works Projects

Appropriation for 1934	$2,800.00

Expenditures

Baxter, Geo. O., plumbing supplies	66.25
Chapman & Soden Co., pitch	121.52

Fletcher Hdw. Co., supplies	973.71
Harvey Co., Arthur C., supplies	57.15
Kendall Mill Supply Co., paint	80.40
Lally & Co., Jos. M., scaffolding	25.00
Master Plumbers Supply Co., supplies	38.61
McElroy, B. H., rent of equip.	120.00
McNamara, J. H., supplies	16.95
Morris, G. E., rent of equip.	200.40
Patent Scaffolding Co., scaffolding	390.83
Smith, B. W., repairing ladders	14.45
Travers-Sandell, waterproofing	375.50
Watertown Bldrs. Supply Co., supplies	97.22
Watertown Lumber Co., lumber	221.25

Total Expenditures	2,799.24	
Transferred to Revenue	.76	
		$2,800.00

Public Library, Salaries

Appropriation for 1934		$25,250.00

Expenditures

Blazo, Elsa, salary	600.00
Brask, Antoinette, salary	220.50
Clark, J. L., salary	900.00
Coffey, John, salary	15.50
Collins, Beatrice C., salary	123.38
Courtney, Minnie C., salary	1,600.00
Crockford, Chas., salary	28.00
Gillmett, Mabel C., salary	1,055.99
Greene, Katherine B., salary	1,500.00
Halfyard, Allan, salary	25.00
Hanson, Evelyn, salary	140.63
Hinkley, W. H., salary	57.00
Hotz, Mary B., salary	92.90
Kelly, James, salary	200.00
Kelley, Rose, salary	600.00

Knowles, Mary G., salary	1,100.00
Leedham, Wm., salary	66.00
Litch, Ruth E., salary	1,358.33
Madden, Esther E., salary	1,000.00
Mannix, Bernard, salary	1,400.00
Martin, Doris G., salary	1,500.00
Masters, Lydia W., salary	3,000.00
Mead, Corinne, salary	1,800.00
Moore, Eleanor L., salary	1,800.00
Pollock, Chas., salary	399.98
Sama, Mary, salary	6.00
Sellon, Walter, salary	51.50
Shattuck, Sarah, salary	1,400.00
Smith, Helen, salary	376.90
Smith, Laura, salary	28.85
Wellington, Jos. H., salary	57.00
Wetsell, Mildred, salary	138.98
White, Ruth C., salary	1,100.00
York, Mary E., salary	1,500.00
Total Expenditures	$25,242.44
Transferred to Revenue	7.56
	$25,250.00

Public Library, Books, Periodicals and Bindings

Appropriation for 1934 $6,000.00

Expenditures

American Book Co., books	19.77
American Historical Assoc., subs.	5.00
American Library Assoc., books	2.25
Art Education Press, Inc., supplies.	3.47
Baker & Taylor, subs.	13.18
Beckely-Cardy Co., books	79.62
Berberian Bookstore, books	16.92
Bookshop for Boys and Girls, books	37.17
Boston Herald Travelers Corp., papers	14.40

Boy Scouts of America, manuals	1.12
Civil Service Book Co., book	1.00
Clark Co., Chas. W., books	75.82
Cox Book Co., carol books	18.52
Frontier Press Co., supplies	15.50
Friedman's, books	3.83
Ginn & Co., supplies	114.83
Goldberger Agency, Herman, subs.	71.45
Hale, Cushman & Flint, supplies	3.13
Handicrafter, The, subs.	**2.00**
Heath & Co., D. C., books	42.04
Houghton & Mifflin, books	89.77
Huntting Co., H. R., books	82.02
Ideal Bookshop, Inc., books	8.00
Internat'l Ttext book Co., supplies	2.64
Jr. Literary Guild, books	113.85
Karr, Jean, books	4.75
Keystone View Co., supplies	5.19
Leary-Stuart Co., books	3.15
Library Book House, books	608.69
Maynard, Katherine, supplies	4.00
Minot, John Clair, books	939.90
Nat'l Biblophile Service, books	1.60
New Eng. Historic Genealogical Society, dues	5.00
New Eng. News, books	153.59
Noble & Noble, supplies	11.23
Nolan Co., W. L., supplies	5.50
Old Corner Bookstore, books	5.50
Personal Book Shop, books	1,281.97
Rand-McNally Co., atlas	5.93
Rebuilt Bookshop, books	2.17
Ritter, Clement V., books	24.82
Roemer, Inc., A. H., books	27.62
Row-Paterson & Co., books	7.12
Salmond, Eloise F., books	2.50
Schoenhof Book Co., books	21.42

Scribners Sons, Chas., supplies	27.00
Silver-Burdett & Co., books	11.20
Small & Hanson, books	103.80
Smith, N. T., supplies	22.90
Spaulding's Bookshop, Mary, books	3.15
Trustee of Public Reservations, Mass.	
Landscape survey	1.00
Union Library Assoc., books	17.09
University Society, Inc., books	17.59
Van Nostrand Co., Inc., books	4.73
Wagner Co., R. W., books	69.75
Watertown News Co., transcript	68.88
Watertown Sun, The, subs.	6.00
Watertown Tribune-Enterprise, The, subs.	6.00
Wells Bindery, L. A., binding	1,469.87
Whitman & Co., Albert, books	129.88
Wilson Co., H. W., books	79.45
Womrath's Inc., A. R., books	2.44

Total Expenditures	$5,999.68	
Transferred to Revenue	.32	
		$6,000.00

Public Library, Maintenance

Appropriation for 1934	$5,000.00

Expenditures

American Cleaning Co., window cleaning	$41.28
American Library Assoc., dues	5.00
A. M. Archer & Co., supplies	24.75
Art Education Press, supplies	4.15
Baker, Frank G., rep. leak	43.75
Baker & Taylor, books	19.36
Barnard & Co., F. J., supplies	2.69
Bell, Edw. L., maps	1.50

Boston Con. Gas Co., service	13.23
Boston Mill Remnants Co., supplies	20.00
Bowker Co., R. R., books	1.25
Brae Burn Nursery, shrubs	14.70
Brestol Co. House of Correction, mats	12.40
Butter's Express, expressage	6.35
Cameron, W. R., sharpening lawn mower	3.00
Cook Chairs, Inc., refinishing library furniture	201.50
Crawford, Ward S., refilling fire extinguisher	1.50
Crown Shade & Screen Co., roller	1.25
Direct Stores, Inc., posters	4.75
Donaldson, Wm., repairs	183.55
Eastern Products Co., supplies	6.00
Eaton, Leroy S., printing	238.47
Edison Elec. Ill. Co., service	930.90
Emulso Corp., metal polish	2.00
Farm Service Stores, Inc., sheep dress.	4.50
Federal Chemical Co., wax	18.60
Fidelity Specialty Co., supplies	15.30
Fletcher Hdw. Co., supplies	34.08
Gaylord Bros., supplies	428.53
Gifford Supply Co., supplies	43.13
Goding, Herbert, plumbing repairs	15.50
Green's Paste Works, supplies	8.68
Hall, Sidney W., labor	16.45
Hawes Electric Co., elec. repairs	23.55
Holcomb Mfg. Co., supplies	6.86
Holliston Mills, Inc., supplies	40.65
Hotz, Mary B., services	30.80
Household Fuel Co., fuel	1,062.08
Huntting Co., H. R., supplies	4.24
Internat'l Engineering Works, lockers	79.38
Library Art Club, supplies	6.00
Library of Congress, cards	85.42

Lord, H. D., map	9.80
Lydston, W. W., cleaning and rep.	
ink-wells	18.40
Mason, Ralph W., wreaths	6.00
Mass., Comm. of, Dept. of Correction,	
supplies	5.34
Masters, Lydia W., incidentals	84.72
Masury-Young Co., supplies	7.95
McArdle, H. B., supplies	218.60
McElhiney, Eldon E., painting	23.60
Meister Co., D. A., supplies	2.00
Met. Ice Co., fuel oil	99.05
Minneapolis-Honeywell Reg. Co.,	
repairing clock	8.50
Nat'l Education Assoc., subs.	5.00
New Eng. Tel. & Tel. Co., service	229.88
Peabody, C. A., supplies	2.81
Photographic History Service, supplies	18.28
Railway Express Agency, expressage	14.16
Remington-Rand, Inc., supplies	6.65
Riveto Mfg. Co., supplies	2.91
Smith Corona Typewriter, L. C.,	
platen and typewriter	34.50
Snow Iron Works, W. A., fence	148.00
Spencer Mfg. Co., S. M., supplies	14.92
Stone & Forsythe Co., supplies	18.14
Supremacy Pen & Ink Co., supplies	4.00
Titus, L. C., repairs	6.50
Valois, Albert, expenses	247.65
Wadsworth Howland Co., supplies	1.64
Ward's, supplies	8.15
Water Dept., service	18.45
Wells Bindery, L. A., binding	1.70
Whitford, E. A., chair glides	17.50
White Co., R. H., supplies	7.45
Total Expenditures	$4,999.33

Transferred to Revenue	.67	
		$5,000.00

Public Library, Equipment for Addition

Transferred Town Meeting		$400.00

Expenditures

Gaylord Bros., equipment	$396.00	
Transferred to Revenue	4.00	
		$400.00

Library Trust Fund Income

Balance brought forward	$6.33	
Income received	479.05	
		$485.38

Expenditures

Clarke Co., Chas. W., books	7.50	
Goldberger Agency, Herman, magazines	350.00	
Masters, Lydia W., celebration expense	9.00	
Minot, John Clair, books	39.30	
Nolan Co., W. L., books	22.50	
Personal Book Shop, books	11.25	
Scribner's Sons, Chas., books	22.50	
Small & Hansen, books	17.00	
Total Expenditures	$479.05	
Balance carried forward	6.33	
		$485.38

RECREATION AND UNCLASSIFIED

Park Dept., Superintendent

Appropriation for 1934		$500.00

Expenditures

Mosman, Arthur D., salary	$500.00	$500.00

Park **Dept., Maintenance**

Appropriation for 1934 $2,500.00

Expenditures

Barrabee Service Stores, Inc., truck and bus cases	$117.30
Eaton, Leroy S., printing	6.60
Fletcher Hdw. Co., supplies	6.40
Goding, Herbert, plumbing repairs	.40
Hayes Service Station, repairs	33.60
Jenney Mfg. Co., gas	128.19
Lawn Mower Grinding Co., grinding	9.20
Lloyd, Francis G., paint	2.85
Pascoe, George T., typewriter	65.00
Payroll, weekly	2,036.95
Roberts, H. D., dump truck	70.00
Rockwell, Winthrop G., incidentals	3.11
Thompson-Durkee, bubbler	3.80
Sherwood, W. V., lettering	9.00
Watertown Tire Co., auto repairs	3.10
Watertown Water Dept., service	4.50

Total Expenditures $2,500.00 $2,500.00

Park **Dept., Victory** Field

Appropriation for 1934 $2,000.00

Expenditures

Bailey-Stewart Co., instal. pilot top	$1.10
Boston Cons. Gas Co., service	33.20
Butter's Express, expressage	.35
Edison Elec. Ill. Co., service	8.85
Fletcher Hdw. Co., supplies	15.54
Fuller & Son Lumber Co., G., score board	3.19
Green & Co., S. B., cement	20.15
Hawes Electric Co., parts	5.25

Iver Johnson Sporting Goods Co., bases	11.50
Jenney Mfg. Co., gas	22.40
Lawn Mower Grinding Co., grinding	4.00
New Eng. Toro Co., supplies	53.76
Payroll, weekly	1,755.05
Proctor, S. E. & R. C., grass seed	17.50
Watertown Lumber Co., lumber	20.84
Watertown Water Dept., service	26.10

Total Expenditures	$1,998.78	
Transferred to Revenue	1.22	
		$2,000.00

Park Dept., Tennis Courts

Appropriation for 1934	$700.00

Expenditures

Goding, Herbert, supplies	$ .61	
Iver Johnson Sporting Goods Co., supplies	77.20	
McMurtry, Fred'k, gravel	102.00	
New Eng. Toro Co., repairs and supplies	45.71	
Pay Roll, weekly	466.23	
Watertown Water Dept., service	8.25	

Total Expenditures	$700.00	
		$700.00

Park Dept., Waterproofing Grand Stand

Appropriation for 1934	$150.00

Expenditures

Morris, G. E., labor	$79.58	
Transferred to Revenue	70.42	
		$150.00

Park **Dept., C.W.A.**

Balance brought forward		$27.40

Expenditures

Proctor, S. E. & R. C., picks and handles	$25.07	
Transferred to Revenue	2.33	
		$27.40

Park **Dept., "Delta" McGlauflin Bequests**

Balance brought forward		$476.25

Expenditures

Breck & Sons, Jos., plants	$35.50	
Theurer Contracting Co., Otto A., curbing	330.00	
Total Expenditures	$365.50	
Balance carried forward	110.75	
		$476.25

Playground Dept., Salaries

Appropriation for 1934		$2,200.00
Andrews, Jos., salary	$219.00	
Callan, Mary, salary	80.00	
Carroll, Jr., Maurice, salary	104.00	
Daughters, Robert T., salary	11.00	
Donnelly, Jr., Andrew J., salary	40.00	
Ford, Patrick B., salary	96.00	
Garaway, Mrs. Mary B., salary	88.00	
Gostos, Evelyn V., salary	80.00	
Gough, Anna M., salary	96.00	
Grimes, Albert, salary	80.00	
Harrington, Ruth, salary	80.00	
Harris, Jr., John J., salary	70.00	
Holland, Francis, salary	88.00	
Knapp, Warren D., salary	80.00	

Linehan, Marie, salary	80.00
Maloney, Hugh, salary	77.00
McBreen, Patricia, salary	77.00
McBridge, Lawrence S., salary	40.00
McCarron, Mrs. Mary, salary	88.00
McElligot, Mary C., salary	70.00
Milmore, Mary L., salary	80.00
Mulvahill, Grace R., salary	96.00
Regan, James, salary	104.00
Riley, Gerard J., salary	96.00
Shriver, Mrs. Elizabeth, salary	70.00
Sullivan, Lillian A., salary	70.00
Vahey, Jr., Thos F., salary	40.00

Total Expenditures	$2,200.00	
		$2,200.00

Playground Dept., Maintenance

Appropriation for 1934	$1,500.00

Expenditures

Andrews, Jos. W., services	$15.50
Berry Hdw. Co., supplies	1.35
Brine Co., Jas. W., supplies	30.75
Callan, Mary, incidentals	2.90
Cleary, the Druggist, supplies	16.95
Dwyer, Frank, gas	9.59
Ellis & Sons Co., W. H., towing float	50.00
Fletcher Hdw. Co., supplies	10.16
Gough, Anna M., supplies	1.05
Grant Co., W. T., supplies	.79
Gray Gift Shop, supplies	1.15
Grosvenor & Co., W. J., repairs	71.25
Harris, Chas. A., bathing suits	14.00
Jackson New Eng. Sash & Door, door and frome	4.75
Kearns Service Station, gas	8.44

McCarthy-Morris Co., supplies	65.65	
Mulvihill, Grace, incidentals	2.00	
Pay Roll, weekly	1,168.00	
Shriver, Mrs. Elizabeth D., incidentals	2.50	
Taylor's Typewriter Exchange, ribbon	1.00	
Woolworth Co., F. W., supplies	21.45	
Total Expenditures	$1,499.23	
Transferred to Revenue	.77	
		$1,500.00

Playground Dept., New Equipment

Appropriation for 1934		$300.00

Expenditures

Ellis & Son Co., W. H., floatstage	$300.00	
		$300.00

Pensions

Appropriation for 1934	$13,600.00	
Trans. Town Meeting	350.00	
		$13,950.00

Expenditures

Andrews, John, pension	$600.00
Brown, Vernon S., pension	1,100.00
Burke, Martin, pension	584.24
Burke, Wm., pension	63.70
Coleman, Wm. F., pension	1,100.00
Doyle, Jas., pension	782.50
Ferrins, Jas. W., pension	747.26
Flaherty, Michael, pension	782.50
Howard, Wm. A., pension	1,000.00
Lane, Ward, pension	1,100.00
Lawn, Thos., pension	747.26
Maguire, Peter, pension	912.90

Murphy, Thos. J., pension	1,100.00	
Oliveto, Frank, pension	912.90	
Perkins, Louis, pension	196.90	
Stanley, Thos., pension	1,300.00	
Walsh, Patrick, pension	782.50	
Total Expenditures	$13,812.66	
Transferred to Revenue	137.34	
		$13,950.00

Nichols Annuity

Appropriation for 1934		$750.00

Expenditures

Nichols, Sadie, annuity	$750.00	
		$750.00

Streeter Annuity

Appropriation for 1934		$750.00

Expenditures

Streeter, Katie C., annuity	$750.00	
		$750.00

Memorial Day

Appropriation for 1934		$1,100.00
Patten, Isaac B., G.A.R. Post No. 81	1,100.00	
		$1,100.00

Insurance

Appropriation for 1934		$10,835.37

Expenditures

McElhiney, Eldon E., painting	$140.00	
O. W. Meserve Printing, printing	18.75	
O'Brion, Russell Co., insurance	9,996.52	

Petroleum Heat & Power Co., overhauling burner	83.87
Wright, Edw. F., insurance	511.50

Total Expenditures	$10,750.64	
Transferred to Revenue	84.73	
		$10,835.37

Workmen's Compensation

Appropriation for 1934	$5,000.00

Expenditures

Bardezbanian, Seragan, injury	$118.86
Biller, Dr. Albert, service	41.00
Branch, Dr. Byron, x-ray	15.00
Burns, Michael, injury	64.29
Butler, George F., supplies	21.22
Cambridge, Hospital, care	23.60
Colligan, John, injury	138.08
Doyle, John P., service	5.50
Dept. of Industrial Accidents, examination	10.00
Gallagher, Mrs. Annie, settlement	624.00
Gorman, Dr. Eugent F., service	16.00
Greene, Dr. David D., service	10.00
Higgins, Patrick J., injury	468.00
Kelley, Francis W., injury	170.94
Kelley, Dr. M. J., service	410.00
Kirker, Mrs. Agnes, injury	122.82
McGuire, Wm. P., incidentals	.50
McHugh, John, injury	25.72
Moloney, Dr. Albert M., service	10.00
Myerson, Dr. Abraham, service	25.00
Pesce, Dr. Guy C., service	13.00
Quirk, Dr. Thos. C., service	15.00
Ransom's Taxi, service	10.00
Rogers, Dr. Wm. A., services	10.00

St. Elizabeths Hospital, care	5.00
Sheehan, Gerald, injury	630.81
Welsh, Chas. D., injury	4.00
White & Co., C. W., anklet truss	1.69
Wylie, Dr. Earl J., service	64.00
York, Dr. Robert S., service	19.00

Total Expenditures	$3,093.03	
Transferred to Revenue	1,906.97	
		$5,000.00

Printing Town Reports

Appropriation for 1934		$1,159.38

Expenditures

Hampshire Press	$1,159.38	
		$1,159.38

Headquarters V.F.W.

Appropriation for 1934		$1,080.00

Expenditures

Tomasetti, Gregory, rent	$1,080.00	
		$1,080.00

Headquarters, Disabled American Vet.

Appropriation for 1934		$360.00

Expenditures

Skinner Hiram L., rent	$270.00	
Transferred to Revenue	90.00	
		$360.00

Contingent

Appropriation for 1934		$2,450.00

Expenditures

Berquist, Paul, auto repairs	$25.00	
Bigelow-Kennard Co., elec. fixtures	32.00	
Bond, Harold E., winding town clock	25.00	
Bond, Harol, ringing bell	10.00	
Boston Blue Print Co., blue print	.91	
Boston Elevated R. R., license	4.00	
Brae Burn Nursery, pruning shrubs	39.38	

Carter's Ink Co., supplies	3.83
Cate, Richard L., painting flag pole	10.00
Connors, Anna, services	6.00
Dimon-Union Stamp Works,, stamps	3.15
Edison Elec. Ill. Co., service	5.00
Graphic Press, The, printing	7.00
Heshion, Frank J., claim	6.85
Ingalls, Ernest K., singing bell	12.50
Karalekas, Stella J. & Steven G., claim	79.00
Keating, Mrs. Anna, switchboard operator	42.00
Kelly, Dr. E. J., services	25.00
Kelley, Dr. M. J., services	100.00
Kelley, Timothy, land damages	22.00
Kelley, Timothy, flowers	10.00
Lawyer's Co-op Publishing Co., book	15.00
Leighton, Thos., registering and recording	26.25
Lombard, Dr. Herbert L., services	25.00
Martin, Laura H., claim	250.00
Mass., Comm. of, Dept. Cor., flag	6.91
McAdams Inc., Wm. M. L., supplies	14.65
McGuire, Wm. P., incidentals	6.73
McNamara, Francis J., witness fees	64.00
Mooney, Fred R., supplies	12.60
Moran, Marie, switchboard operator	148.50
Murray, Hugh R., painting and gilding clock faces on Unitarian church	75.00
Muscara, James and Rose, settlement	200.00
New Eng. Tel. & Tel. Co., service	127.63
Parsekian, Veronica, settlement	354.91
P. O. Dept., postage	21.92
Reformatroy for Women, flag	6.91
Royal Typewriter Co., maint. of machinery	24.00

Shipton, Wallace A., ringing bell	3.00
Sprague, Mrs. Anna, settlement	50.00
Stewart, Mrs. Robert A., settlement	25.00
Thomas, W. H., plastering	21.00
Valas, Nellie, Alexander & Francis, injuries	200.00
Watertown Sun, The, advertisement	6.50
West Publishing Co., books	150.00
York, Dr. Robert S., service	25.00

Total Expenditures	$2,329.13	
Transferred to Revenue	120.87	
		$2,450.00

Reserve Fund

Appropriation for 1934	$10,000.00

Expenditures

Collector, Tax sale advt.	$266.40
Collector, recording	420.10
Health contingent, Transfer	300.00
Highway, Stable special, Transfer	500.00
Police, special, Transfer	95.00
Police, contingent, Transfer	750.00
Soldiers Relief, Transfer	4,000.00

Total Expenditures	$6,331.50	
Transferred to Revenue	3,668.50	
		$10,000.00

Unpaid Bills

Appropriation for 1934	$367.04

Expenditures

Carroll, Jos. L., auto expenses	$25.00
Caverly, Francis, auto expenses	25.00
Kelley, Dr. M. J., services	100.00
Lyndonville Creamery, milk	40.65

New Eng. Tel. & Tel. Co., service   176.39
_____

    Total Expenditures $367.04
_____
                        $367.04

Holland Expense

Appropriation for 1934 $92.00

Expenditures

Holland, Edw. D., expenses to
  Washington $92.00
_____
                        $92.00

E. R. A.

Appropriation for 1934 $20,000.00

Expenditures

Acme Window Cleaners, cleaning
  windows $25.00
Berger & Sons, C. L., repairs   44.00
Bleachery Fuel Co., charcoal   5.00
Boston Structural Steel Co., supplies 142.00
Brown, Chas. Jewell, labor   115.70
Bruning Co., Chas., supplies   165.10
Burroughs Adding Mch. Co., service 6.60
Busconi Oil Co., gas   515.83
Carbone, John, trucking   1,025.80
Chain Link Fence Co., fence parts 8.83
Concrete Steel Co., steel bars   27.00
Condon Corp., John P., trucking 1,316.60
Condon Corp., John P., concrete 1,827.00
Dick Co., A. B., supplies   6.55
Direct Stores, paint   14.42
Downey, Mary F., supplies   8.20
Dunn's, supplies   71.45
Durable Wire Rope Co., wire   13.54
Eagle Cornice & Skylight

Works, pitch	28.34
Eaton, Leroy S., printing	24.90
Field & Son Inc., W. W., repairs on boiler	335.95
Fletcher Hdw. Co., supplies	1,242.01
Gaylord Bros., supplies	38.50
General Crushed Stone Co., stone	77.46
Graphic Press, The, printing	1.50
Gray Gift Shop, supplies	30.27
Grosvenor & Co., W. J., metal	182.00
Halenza, H. C., expenses	48.50
Harris, Chas. A., gloves, etc.	34.30
Hayes Service Station, auto repairs	20.10
Hawes Electric Co., iron	5.50
Howell, Wm. D., repairs and storage	33.05
Highway Pay Roll, weekly	6,278.35
Kendall Mill Supply, supplies	863.35
Keystone Driller Co., shaft	12.60
Koplow Trimming Co., supplies	98.96
Lawn Mower Grinding Co., grinding	3.50
Leighton, Thos., blue prints	1.31
MacDonald, Robert, music	61.31
McNamara Inc., J. H., concrete	154.00
Nonantum Lumber Co., lumber	162.21
Paris, Gertrude H., supplies	15.95
Patent Scaffolding Co., renting scaffolding	179.67
Perkins, E. A., garage doors	65.90
Romano, Samuel, trucking	474.00
Royal Typewriter Co., maintenance of machine	30.00
Singer Sewing Mch. Co., supplies	169.45
Smith, B. W., ladder	31.50
Snow Iron Works, W. A., strainer	1.75
Spaulding-Moss Co., ribbon	1.05
Sullivan, Jas. H., gas	126.08
Sullivan, Wm. H., trucking	1,316.60

Taylor Typewriter Co., maintenance 7.50
Travers-Sandell Inc., waterproofing 104.50
Waltham Coal Co., cement 29.40
Waltham Lime & Cement, cement · 1,149.47
Ward's, supplies 8.10
Waterproof Paint & Varnish Co.,
   paint 39.87
Watertown Bldr's Supply Co., pipe 547.93
Watertown Letter Shop, printing 4.00
Watertown Lumber Co., lumber 149.67
Watertown Shoe Store, rubber
   boots 183.85
White Iron Works, C. M., manholes 241.60
Wright, H. F., carfares 34.00

Total Expenditures	$19,988.43
Transferred to Revenue	11.57

                                  $20,000.00

ENTERPRISE AND CEMETERIES

Water Dept., Salaries

Appropriation for 1934 $5,536.00

Expenditures

Rundlett, Walter, salary	$3,200.00
Bright, Emma L., salary	1,036.00
Rundlett, Laura, salary	1,300.00
Total Expenditures	$5,536.00

                                    $5,536.00

Water Dept., Office Expense

Appropriation for 1934 $2,125.25

Expenditures

American City Magazine, subs. $4.00
Boston Janitors Supply Co., supplies 2.00

Bruning Co., Chas., supplies	207.49
Eaton, Leroy S., printing	23.30
Gray Gift Shop, supplies	61.85
Groom & Co., Thos., supplies	8.20
Hughes, James F., supplies	103.75
Hutcheson Co., blue prints	12.12
Johnson, Edwin, salary	874.92
McArdle, H. B., supplies	3.45
McDermott, F. A., supplies	8.40
New Eng. Adding Mch. Co., repairs	5.70
New Eng. Tel. & Tel. Co., service	232.29
New Eng. Towel Supply Co., service	9.75
Pequossette Press, printing	160.00
P. O. Dept., postage	281.74
Standard Maintenance Co., maintenance of typewriter	12.00
Underwood Elliott Fisher Co., typewriter	108.00
Ward's, supplies	3.70

Total Expenditures	$2,122.66	
Transferred to Revenue	2.59	
		$2,125.25

Water Dept., Maintenance

Appropriation for 1934	$41,300.00

Expenditures

American Oil Products Co., gas	$182.98
Boston & Maine R. R., freight	32.45
Buffalo Pipe & Foundry, supplies	164.25
Builders Iron Foundry, pipe	48.26
Busconi Oil Co., gas	442.88
Chesterton Co., A. W., supplies	262.74
Conroy, Robert L., supplies	17.25
Durnan, Jr., Jas. H., auto repairs	7.00
Dwyer, Frank A., greasing truck	5.50
Edison Elec. Ill. Co., service	87.19

Eureka Pipe Co., couplings	2.49
Everett Bros. Inc., expressage	.35
Field & Son Inc., Walter W., auto repairs	100.15
Fletcher Hdw. Co., supplies	152.47
Gingrass, E. P., grinding lawn mower	5.00
Green & Co., S. B., supplies	48.31
Gulf Refining Co., oil	43.80
Halpin's Welding Shop, spring cleaners	9.75
Hauck Mfg. Co., supplies	109.73
Hawes Elec. Co., switch	1.10
Hayes Service Station, repairs	68.20
Hersey Mfg. Co., meter parts	1,306.12
Hopkins, John J., sharpening picks	154.95
Hughes, Wm. H., elec. fixture	4.75
Hurley Motor Repair Service, repairs	168.23
Hydraulic Development Corp., Hydro-Tite	106.00
Hyman, J., auto repairs	2.50
Jenney Mfg. Co., gas	174.48
Johnson, Edwin, salary	737.31
Kearns Service Station, service	195.80
Kendall Mill Supply, supplies	34.50
Kennedy Valve Mfg. Co., valves	1,073.36
Lead Lined Iron Pipe Co., pipe	58.19
LeBaron Co., E. L., iron castings	179.78
Leonard Fuel Co., coal	104.30
Linde Air Products Co., The, supplies	2.60
Ludlow Valve Mfg. Co., valves	17.45
Lyons, John F., insurance	222.00
Macauley & Sons, D., drills dressed	5.70
MacIntosh Coal Co., John, coal	81.35
Mass., Comm. of, registration	12.00
Master Plumbers Supply Inc., coupling	.24

McDermott, A. E., insurance	206.10
McDermott, F. A., supplies	72.75
McDonald Tire & Battery, service	2.50
Meister Co., D. A., oak wedges	4.00
Mueller Co., supplies	5.91
Nally, T. F., storage	15.00
Nat'l. Boston Lead Co., supplies	10.70
Neptune Meter Co., gaskets	44.60
New Eng. Brick Co., grinding clay	2.00
New Eng. Tel. & Tel. Co., service	57.77
Nonantum Coal Co., coal	65.50
Northeastern Express Inc., expressage	1.00
Oates, Edw. A., insurance	195.50
Ogden & Thompson, straw	11.76
Otis Bros. Co., supplies	69.00
Parker-Danner Co., lantern globes	50.11
Pay Roll, weekly	33,287.08
Pittsburgh Plate Glass Co., glass	6.00
Railway Express Agency, expressage	.51
Red Hed Mfg. Co., couplings	53.38
Rundlett, Walter E., garage rent	62.00
Shutt, George L., tires	62.00
Standard Auto Gear Co., supplies	.43
Sullivan, Jas. H., kerosene	117.61
Sumner & Dunbar, supplies	260.16
Thompson-Durkee Co., supplies	83.59
Watch City Chevrolet ,repairs	5.00
Watertown Brake & Elec. service supply	33.80
Watertown Tire Co., auto repairs	11.35
White Co., The, auto repairs	57.11
Woodward & Tyler, insurance	9.60
Total Expenditures	$41,297.28
Transferred to Revenue	2.72
	$41,300.00

Water Dept., Vacation

Appropriation for 1934		$1,299.00

Expenditures

Pay Roll, weekly	$1,299.00	
		$1,299.00

Water Dept., Civil Works Projects

Appropriation for 1934		$8,960.00

Expenditures

Boston & Maine R. R., freight	$51.57
Builders Iron Foundry, supplies	562.13
Caldweel Co., George A., supplies	93.35
Chesterton Co., A. W., globes	397.80
Eureka Pipe Co., Inc., couplings	.54
Hopkins, John J., sharpening picks	28.75
Kendall Mill Supply, supplies	76.15
Kennedy Valve Mfg. Co., gates	579.60
LeBarron Foundry Co., E. L., castings	205.47
Ludlow Valve Mfg. Co., hydrants	1,162.82
Measter Co., D. A., supplies	.48
Nat'l. Boston Lead Co., pipe	15.52
Parker Danner Co., repairs	3.00
Red Hed Mfg. Co., unions	285.75
Sullivan, Jas. H., gas	71.92
Warren Pipe Co of Mass., pipe	5,425.15

Total Expenditures	$8,960.00	
		$8,960.00

Water Dept., New 1934 Car

Appropriation for 1934		$625.00

Expenditures

Watch City Chevrolet Co., car	$624.00	
Transferred to Revenue	1.00	
		$625.00

Water Dept., New 1934 Truck ..

Appropriation for 1934		$1,200.00

Expenditures

White Co., The, truck	$1,200.00	
		$1,200.00

Cemetery Dept., Supt.

Appropriation for 1934		$2,000.00

Expenditures

Horton, Van D., salary	$2,000.00	
		$2,000.00

Cemetery Dept., Labor

Appropriation for 1934		$8,000.00

Expenditures

Pay Roll, weekly	$7,999.38	
Transferred to Revenue	.62	
		$8,000.00

Cemetery Dept., Contingent

Appropriation for 1934	$500.00	
Trans. Town Meeting	50.00	
		$550.00

Expenditures

Brae Burn Nursery, shrubs	$9.00
Brown, Chas. J., milorganite	25.00
Eaton, Leroy S., printing	24.01
Fletcher Hdw. Co., supplies	128.66
Goding, Herbert, plumbing repairs	.87
Gray Gift Shop, supplies	5.75
Gree & Co., S. B., cement and pea stone	70.98
Halpins Welding Shop, welding	3.00

Hobbs & Warren, supplies	8.65
Holmes, C. E., grinding	9.55
Horton, Van D., carfares	40.29
Kelter, Geo. A., sharpening picks	1.20
LeShane, Frank C., trucking	12.50
Manning Sales Co., supplies	27.50
Mason, Ralph W., planting flower beds	50.00
McGlauflin, B. Fay, insurance	6.67
Meister Co., D. A., sharpening picks	13.75
New Eng. Tel. & Tel. Co., service	68.98
Railway Express Agency, expressage	.94
Thompson-Durkee Co., supplies	2.88
Watertown Water Dept., service	11.40
Watertown Lumber Co., boards	19.51
Webb Mfg. Co., F. W., valve	3.80
Wollrath & Sons Inc., flowers	3.00

Total Expenditures	$547.89	
Transferred to Revenue	2.11	
		$550.00

Cemetery Dept., Tomb and Tool House

Appropriation for 1934	$2,500.00

Expenditures

Atherton, Walter & Carroll, architects	$150.00	
Sack Inc., Hdw. supplies	50.00	
Tocci Construction Co., contract	2,300.00	

Total Expenditures	$2,500.00	
		$2,500.00

Cemetery Dept., Lowering Device and Greens

Appropriation for 1934	$250.00

Expenditures

Nat'l. Casket Co., lowering device and greens	$244.50	
Transferred to Revenue	5.50	
		$250.00

INTEREST AND MATURING DEBT

Interest

Appropriation for 1934	$115,000.00	
Trans. Town Meeting	4,989.20	
		$110,010.80

Expenditures

Coupons on bonds	$59,561.25	
Discount on notes	22,579.41	
Noyes, H. K., interest on abatements	47.25	
Various persons, int. on prepaid taxes	3,829.73	
Total Expenditures	$86,017.64	
Transferred to Revenue	23,993.16	
		$110,010.80

Town Debt

Appropriation for 1934		$216,000.00

Expenditures

Bonds paid	$216,000.00	
		$216,000.00

TAXES

County Taxes

Appropriation for 1934		$77,696.74

Expenditures

Middlesex, County of	$77,696.74	
		$77,696.74

County Hospital T. B. Assessment

Appropriation for 1934 . $21,805.23

Expenditures

Middlesex, County of $21,805.23

$21,805.23

State Taxes and Assessments

Appropriation for 1934 $278,523.35

Expenditures

State Tax	$78,100.00
Metropolitan Planning	.287.99
Metropolitan Parks	27,918.18
Metropolitan Water	86,299.42
South Metropolitan Sewerage	48,853.67
Charles River Basin	4,695.41
Abatement of Smoke Nuisance	278.83
Canterbury St. Highway	109.70
Land Taking State Highway (Revere)	1,126.19
W. Roxbury, Brookline Highway	150.93
Ocean Ave., Revere	436.02
Ways in Malden, Braintree, Weymouth and Hingham	5.50
B. E. Def. (Rental Payments)	2,266.06
Boston Elevated	27,861.97
Boston Met. Dist. Expense	133.48

Total Expenditures $278,523.35

$278,523.35

Executions

Expenditures

Cabral, Mary, settlement	$770.63
Moran, Hannah (Bernard J. Killion, Atty.), settlement	250.00
Paquet, Wilfred, Atty. for Edw. J. Liston, settlement	500.00
Riccio, Mary, (Thos. A. Flannegan Atty.), settlement	163.96
United Fiscal Corp., settlement	2,000.00

Total Expenditures and Charged
to Revenue $3,684.59

$3,684.59

BALANCE SHEET,

ASSETS

Cash on hand, Dec. 31, 1934		$272,941.36
Collector's Petty Cash		500.00
Taxes		
1933 Real and Personal	$6,113.52	
1933 Poll	72.00	
1934 Real and Personal	603,698.05	
1934 Poll	2,400.00	
1932 Motor Excise	13.84	
1933 Motor Excise	363.37	
1934 Motor Excise	5,921.07	
		$618,581.85
Special Assessments		
Moth, 1934	$115.00	
Assessments added to tax bills		
Sidewalks 1934	1,970.38	
Streets 1933	194.81	
Streets 1934	9,772.97	
Committed Interest		
Sidewalks 1933	5.78	
Sidewalks 1934	843.25	
Streets 1933	99.84	
Streets 1934	3,547.65	
Unapportioned Sidewalk		
Assessments	271.85	
		$16,821.53
Departmental Accounts Receivable		
Poles and Wires	$153.96	
Weights and Measures	46.63	
Health	5,140.16	
Sewer	2,866.18	
Highway	583.33	
Public Welfare	57,767.97	

DECEMBER 31, 1934

LIABILITIES

Temporary Loans in Anticipation of Revenue		$500,000.00
Potter Memorial Gate Fund		197.27
Sewer Deposits		2,535.00
Premiums on Loans		649.64
Cemetery, Sale of Lots Fund		3,265.00
Overlays, reserved for abatements:		
Levy of 1933	$15,384.58	
Levy of 1934	29,404.28	
		$44,788.86
Overlay Reserve		$27,829.32
Motor Excise Tax Revenue		6,298.28
Special Assessment Revenue		16,821.53
Tax Title Revenue		172,512.77
Departmental Revenue		67,430.98
Water Revenue		41,040.70
Unexpended Balances Forward		
Assessors, Board of Tax Appeals	$366.52	
Sewer and Drains, P.W.A.	21,591.74	
Highway, Construction P.W.A.	12,908.74	
Sidewalks, P.W.A.	20,000.00	
Land Taking, Church St.	50.00	
Mt. Auburn St. Bldg. Line	500.00	
High School Add'n. P.W.A.	135,000.00	
Library Trust Fund Income	$6.33	
Public Library Add'n. P.W.A.	35,229.00	
Park, Delta	110.75	
Change of Zoning By-Law	100.00	
Water Mains, P.W.A.	25,000.00	

ASSETS (Continued)

School	587.75	
Cemetery	285.00	
		$67,430.98
Water Department		
Rates	$40,520.26	
Charges	520.44	
		$41,040.70
Tax Titles		$172,287.21
Tax Titles possessions		225.56
Federal Aid		81,584.00
Soldiers Exemptions		131.88
Overlay 1932 (deficit)		3,288.78
		$1,274,833.85

DEFERRED REVENUE ACCOUNTS

Apportioned Sidewalk assessments not due $26,150.02

Apportioned Street assessments not due $101,115.87

LIABILITIES (Continued)

	————	$250,863.08
Excess and Deficiency		$140,601.42

$1,274,833.85

DEFERRED REVENUE ACCOUNTS

Apportioned Sidewalk assessments

due in		
1935	$4,062.00	
1936	4,031.40	
1937	3,960.82	
1938	3,857.10	
1939	3,520.13	
1940	2,821.66	
1941	2,333.53	
1942	1,550.29	
1943	13.09	
	————	$26,150.02

Apportioned Street assessments

due in	
1935	$20,335.76
1936	19,123.09
1937	18,210.07
1938	16,261.15
1939	12,854.99

ASSETS (Continued)

DEBT ACCOUNT

Net Funded or Fixed Debt $1,482,000.00

LIABILITIES (Continued)

1940	8,315.30	
1941	4,505.66	
1942	1,476.82	
1943	33.03	
		$101,115.87

DEBT ACCOUNT

Refunding Loan 1906	$4,000.00
East End School Loan	2,000.00
Surface Drainage Loan 1916	12,000.00
High School Land Loan 1917	3,000.00
Hosmer School Loan 1919	25,000.00
Spring St. Drain Loan 1919	15,000.00
N. Beacon St. Bridge Loan 1919	15,000.00
Sewer and Drains 1920	16,000.00
Athletic Field Loan 1920	6,000.00
Drainage Loan 1921	17,000.00
West End School Loan 1921	84,000.00
High School Plans 1923	4,000.00
High School Land 1923	13,000.00
Land Taking Loan 1923	11,000.00
High School Loan 1924	310,000.00
Playground Loan 1925	6,000.00
High School Equipment 1925	36,000.00
Coolidge School Add'n. 1925	66,000.00
Sewer Construction Loan 1925	2,000.00
N. End. School Loan 1926	70,000.00
Street Construction Loan 1926	14,000.00
Pavement Loan 1926	6,000.00
W. J. High School Add'n. 1927	24,000.00
Sewer Loan 1927	6,000.00
StreetC onstruction Loan 1927	12,000.00
Hosmer School Addition 1928	44,000.00
Arsenal Street Loan 1928	40,000.00
Water Mains 1928	9,000.00

ASSETS (Continued)

TRUST ACCOUNTS

Trust Funds, Cash and Securities $68,303.33

LIABILITIES (Continued)

Sewer Loan 1928	23,000.00
W. Elementary School 1929	130,000.00
Sewer Loan 1929	2,000.00
School Loan 1930	50,000.00
Drainage Loan 1930	2,000.00
Drainage Loan 1931	8,000.00
Adm. Bldg. Loan 1931	172,000.00
Fire Alarm Sig. System 1932	24,000.00
Sidewalks P.W.A. 1934	11,000.00
Street Construction P.W.A. 1934	28,000.00
Sewer and Drains P.W.A. 1934	16,000.00
Senior H. School Add'n. P.W.A. 1934	115,000.00
Public Library Add'n. P.W.A. 1934	29,000.00

$1,482,000.00

TRUST ACCOUNTS

Asa Pratt Library Fund	$12,260.44
Meade Library Fund	3,116.36
Pierce Library Fund	1,307.28
Barry Library Fund	1,009.77
Templeton Fund	2,500.00
Martha Sanger Fund	710.59
Cemetery Perpetual Care Fund	47,398.89

$68,303.33

UNPAID BILLS

The following are all the unpaid bills sents to the Auditor:

Contingent

M. J. Kelley, M. D., professional services	$35.00

Engineering Department

New England Tel. & Tel. Co.	22.33

Fire Department

Metropolitan Ice Co.	$32.50	
Town of Watertown—Water Dept.	83.15	
		$115.65

Health Department

Gordon Supply So.	.15	
William D. Howell	24.90	
Samuel G. Thayer	16.00	
Watertown Tire Co.	14.24	
		$55.29

Police Department

Consolidated Gas Co.	$5.89	
Mass. Gas & Elec. Light Supply Co.	3.78	
A. Lauricella	41.85	
		$51.52

Street Lights

Edison Electric Ill. Co.	352.15

Town Hall

DuBois Soap Co.	$19.50
Boston Consolidated Gas Co.	6.74
Hawes Electric Co.	10.80
Boston Janitor's Supply Co.	3.75
Edison Electric Ill. Co.	201.53
F. J. Lowes	52.50

Kendall Mill Supply	41.78	
Busconi Oil Co.	246.72	
		$583.32

Workmen's Compensation

M. J. Kelly, M. D.		8.00
Total unpaid bills		$1,223.26

Respectfully submitted,

W. W. NORCROSS, Jr.,

Auditor.

INDEX TO REPORT OF TOWN AUDITOR

1934 POLL TAXES UNPAID
At Close of Business, December 31, 1934

Alwis, William, Coolidge Avenue
Amichetti, Luigi, 190 Walnut Street
Amiralina, Hagop, 116 Nichols Avenue
Amodee, Anthony, 204 Orchard Street
Anastasi, Stephen, 108 Pleasant Street
Anderson, James R., 71 Commonwealth Road
Anderson, Charles, 143 Boylston Street
Andrews, Paul, 106 Cypress Street
Andrews, William E., 44 Cypress Street
Anesti, Emil, 37 Crawford Street
Arcese, Andrew, 47 Waltham Street
Arena, Frank, 8 Bostonia Avenue
Arian, Mihran, 524 Mt. Auburn Street
Arian, Richard, 524 Mt. Auburn Street
Armenyan, Richard, 71 Putnam Street
Armstrong, Edward, 63 Evans Street
Arslanian, Amenag, 186 Boylston Street
Arslanian, Joseph, 6 Hosmer Street
Atamian, Artin, 234 Boylston Street
Attenazio, Anthony, 20 Perry Street
Aucoin, Bradford, 19 Jewett Street
Aucoin, Harold, 19 Jewett Street
Aucoin, Thomas, 19 Jewett Street
Aucoin, Wilfred, 19 Jewett Street
Auerback, Ernest, 480 Belmont Street
Avery, Daniel, 61 No. Beacon Street
Bailey, Otis S., 54 Edenfield Street
Baker, Eben H., 32 Paul Street
Baker, John, 47 Crawford Street
Balestieri, Artillo, 49 Hall Avenue
Balestieri, Thomas, 49 Hall Avenue
Barker, Stephen C., 95 Evans Street
Barranzo, Salvatore, 300 Arlington Street
Bartlett, Joseph W., 51 Hall Avenue
Barton, Lee, 42 Mt. Auburn Street
Barton, Ray, 24 Palmer Street
Basile, Joseph, 231 Arlington Street
Basilio, Felix, 7 Hearn Street
Basmajian, Ruben, 56 Quimby Street
Bazarian, Avedis, 133 Dexter Avenue

Bazarian, Panos, 48 Hazel Street
Bazarian, Sarkis, 16 Hazel Street
Beauregard, Frank, 268 Arlington Street
Becker, Herman F., 71 Edenfield Avenue
Bedig, Charles, 15 Elton Avenue
Bedigian, Leo, 19 Chauncy Street
Betie, Sherman, 12 Bancroft Street
Belcher, Thomas, 37 Morton Street
Bellis, Harold J., 56 Putnam Street
Bennet, Ernest, 138 Main Street
Berry, Herbert, 75 Marion Road
Beswick, George, 34 Hillside Street
Binks, Joseph S., 139 Morse Street
Binks, Joseph, 139 Morse Street
Blake, Peter T., 720 Mt. Auburn Street
Bleiler, Charles J., 23 Palmer Street
Bloomerberg, William W., 18 Jewett Street
Blue, James, 25 New Lexington Street
Boardman, Peter, 18 Melandy Avenue
Boghogian, Vartan, 23 Nichols Avenue
Bosogian, Simon, 19 Melandy Avenue
Bohannon, Francis, 57 Fitchburg Street
Bold, John J., 35 Cross Street
Bold, John M., 126 Putnam Street
Boothby, Vinal, 52 Spring Street
Boothby, Warren, 10 Dunton Road
Boris, Felix, 6 Lyons Street
Bortolotti, Anthony, 11 Laurel Street
Botti, Emillio, 224 Arlington Street
Boudakian, Vartan, 34 Cypress Street
Boudrout, Joseph, Jr., 182 Pleasant Street
Bouregeois, William F., 172 Walnut Street
Boyajian, Hagop, 73 Crawford Street
Boyle, James, 5 Upland Road
Bracken, Francis M., 69 Hillside Road
Bracken, Frank A., 69 Hillside Road
Breen, John, 25 Fairfield Street
Brigugliu, Anthony, 32c Royal Street
Brooks, Benjamin, 33 Bancroft Street
Brown, George F., 7 Bostonia Avenue
Brown, Karl H., 37 Chester Street
Brown, Richard H., 91 Orchard Street
Bryant, Robert, 196 Summer Street
Bryant, Richard, 47 Carver Road

Buckley, John, 30 Chauncy Street
Buckley, William J., 4 Eliot Street
Burdett, James B., 81 Boylston Street
Burke, John, 45 Lexington Street
Burke, Stephen, 47 Morse Street
Burke, Thomas, 83 Arsenal Street
Burns, John, 543 Mt. Auburn Street
Burr, Robert, 20 Carver Road
Burstein, Albert, 79 Orchard Street
Butler, Edward H., 17 Derby Road
Butt, George H., 74 Prospect Street
Cabral, Frank, 51 Edgecliff Road
Cabral, John, 51 Edgecliff Road
Caccavaro, George, Lyons Street
Cairo, Enrico, 213 Watertown Street
Callanan, Martin L., 146 Pleasant Street
Callaway, Timothy, 152 Hillside Road
Callera, Angelo, 18 Myrtle Street
Cameron, Daniel, 193 Boylston Street
Campagna, Joseph, 32 Lloyd Road
Campbell, Earl, 23 Avon Road
Cannon, P. Francis, 27 Gilbert Street
Capabianco, Antonio, 209 Arlington Street
Capone, Edward, 33 Laurel Street
Carneclli, Guy, 224 Arlington Street
Carr, Harold, 6 Washburn Street, Newton
Caruso, Daniel, 68 Forest Street
Case, Charles, 294 Belmont Street
Castagnola, Joseph, 87 Sparkhill Street
Castellano, Dominic, 12 Francis Street
Cavanaugh, Patrick, 8 Pearl Street
Cavanaugh, Thomas, 9 Melville Terrace
Cawley, John J., 298 Waverley Avenue
Chacrion, Arthur, 27 Fairfield Street
Chadwick, Bernard H., 467 Pleasant Street
Chadwick, Henry W., 467 Pleasant Street
Chakanian, George, 6 Hosmer Street
Chaplin, Charles, 42 Mt. Auburn Street
Charles, George, 72 Edgecliff Road
Childs, Bradley, 27 Adams Street
Chipman, John, 15 Irma Avenue
Choolgian, John, 48 Salisbury Road
Choolgian, Marvin, 48 Salisbury Road
Christopher, Arnold, 31 Oakland Street

Clark, Guy P., 34 Waverly Avenue
Clark, Robert F., 28 Marshall Street
Clark, John J., 12 Oliver Road
Cleverley, Ralph, 32 Sunnybank Road
Clouttiero, Lawrence, 163 Winsor Avenle
Colacito, Ernest, 27 Pleasant Street
Cole, Victor, 11 Channing Road
Cololla, Augustine, 11 Irma Avenue
Coleman, John, 61 No. Beacon Street
Collins, Michael, 502 Main Street
Concannon, Edmund, 106 Summer Street
Connelly, David, 2 Kimball Road
Connelly, Joseph S., 4 Adams Street
Connors, Edward, 16 Hunt Street
Connors, Michael J., 52 Spring Street
Constanza, Antonio, 15 Howard Street
Conti, Albert, 104 Arlington Street
Coole, Simeon, 36 Howard Street
Coombs, Herbert W., 158 Lovell Road
Coote, Edward, 8 Melville Terrace
Corbett, Leo M., 32 Watertown Street
Cordeiro, Aires, 78 Dexter Avenue
Corr, Joseph H., 30 Oakland Street
Corrazzino, Antonio, 14 Clarendon Street
Costa, Vincent, 33 Carroll Street
Cote, Alfred, 522 Pleasant Street
Cousineau, Edward, 716 Mt. Auburn Street
Craig, Allen D., 139 Church Street
Crescitelli, Angelo, 90 Edenfield Avenue
Crescitelli, Edward, 90 Edenfield Avenue
Crockford, Charles, 29 Hunt Street
Crosby, John J., 34 Hawthorn Street
Crosby, Raymond, 110 Poplar Street
Crowley, James, 46 Spruce Street
Crowley, Jerry, 9 Hudson Street
Crupi, Salvatore, 11 Keith Street
Cummins, John, 8 Bemis Street
Cunningham, Arthur, 17 Adams Street
Cunningham, Arthur M., 21 Hillcrest Circle
Curtis, William, 157 Galen Street
Cushing, Bruce, 57 Hovey Street
Cyr, Rudolph, 122 Nichols Avenue
Dacey, William C., 51 Commonwealth Road
Dadgian, John, 123 Putnam Street

Dalano, Antonio, 88 Arlington Street
Daley, Frank, 129 Winsor Avenue
Dame, Roy, 13 Oakland street
Danforth, Calvin, 161 Galen Street
Danforth, Ralph, 12 Royal Street
Darakjian, George, 17 Hazel Street
Davis, John A., 17 Brimmer Street
Davis, Michael D., 108 Belmont Street
Dawson, William J., 12 Arlington Street
DeCosy, Charles, 51 Fairfield Street
DeFelice, Joseph, 230 Westminster Avenue
DeGiso, Samuel, 9 Hazel Street
DeJulio, Santi, 118 Fayette Street
Delaney, John C., 897 Belmont Street
Delano, Chauncey, 41 Beacon Park
Delucato, James, 42 Dartmouth Street
DeMarco, Nichols, 196 Fayette Street
Dembow, Sherlock W., 32 Palfrey Street
Demitros, James, 36 Clarendon Street
Denarawski, Antonia, 36 Howard Street
DePrenio, Carmine, 16 Waverley Avenue
DerBoghosian, Paul, 119 Dexter Avenue
Derick, Earl F., 93 Boylston Street
DeStanfo, Joseph, 12 Warren Street
Devine, Charles J., 52 Commonwealth Road
Devine, Walter J., 52 Commonwealth Road
Delvin, Sylvester, 86 Franklin Street
DiBacco, Dominick, 6 Sexton Street
Dickey, Robert A., 44 Grenville Road
Digiacomandrea, Joseph, 88 No. Beacon Street
DiMartins, Matthew, Perkins Institute
Dion, Francis X., 59 Cypress Street
Donabed, Elias, 121 School Street
Donald, Harvey, 94 Lexington Street
Donofrie, Frank, 10 Chadbourne Road
D'Onofrio, Joseph, 11 Bostonia Avenue
Donavon, John, 55 Keenan Street
Dormady, Edward, 168 Waverley Avenue
Dorsi, Fred, 18 Myrtle Street
Dostoonian, Rueben, 150 Nichols Avenue
Doucette, Leo, 21 Olney Street
Dougan, James L., 8 Summer Street
Dougan, James R., 8 Summer Street
Douglas, George W., 70 Salisbury Road

Doughty, James, 37 Quimby Street
Doyle, John, 344 Belmont Street
Doyle, John, 41 Cuba Street
Drago, John, 11A Dartmouth Street
Drago, Joseph, 11A Dartmouth Street
Drew, James F., 359 Arlington Street
Drudy, Thomas, 32 Templeton Parkway
DuBois, Wilfred, 157 Spruce Street
Dudley, George E., 17 Spruce Street
Duff, Alexander, 42 Woodleigh Road
Duffy, John, 503 Main Street
Dukakis, Nicholas, 225 Arlington Street
Dunbar, Arthur R., 141 Marshall Street
Dunn, Martin T., 175 Spruce Street
Dupuis, Charles J., 29 Frank Street
Durso, Nicholas, 535 Mt. Auburn Street
Duvall, John W., 179 Waverley Avenue
Eagles, Charles, 59 Mt. Auburn Street
East, Cyril, 271 Pleasant Street
Eastman, Elmer C., 168 Walnut Street
Edgar, J. Harold, 28 Holt Street
Edward, Charley, 212 Waverley Avenue
Elms, George O., 158 Lovell Road
English, Angelo, 9 Spring Court
Enis, John, 157 Galen Street
Esposito, James, 18 Chandler Street
Essayan, Leon, 16 Porter Street
Esterbrook, Kimball, 32 Springfield Street
Evans, Robert A., 76 Prospect Street
Faga, Richard, 42 Clarendon Street
Farber, August, 55 Dartmouth Street
Faria, Manuel, 72 Hillside Road
Farley, George, 34 Cottage Street
Farraher, John, 5 Ladd Street
Farraher, Martin J., 571 Main Street
Farrell, John, 9 Winter Street
Farrell, Michael F., 137 Morse Street
Farrell, Paul, 137 Morse Street
Feeney, William, 22 Eliot Street
Field, Earl C., 10 Middlesex Road
Fifield, Mark L., 127 Lexington Street
Files, Addison E., 126 Chapman Street
Firgio, Ralph, 60 Prentiss Street
Fitzgerald, Dennis L., 92 Fayette Street

Fitzgerald, Joseph, 144 Dexter Avenue
Fitzpatrick, James, 410 Belmont Street
Flaherty, Thomas, 33 Forest Street
Flamburis, George, 137 Templeton Parkway
Foley, Patrick, 212 Arlington Street
Forbes, Harry E., 25 Morton Street
Fournier, John, 27 Adams Street
Freeman, Harold R., 48 Capitol Street
Fundeklian, Alexander, 18 Lloyd Street
Furlong, John J., 83 Watertown Street
Gallagher, Edward T., 11 Purvis Street
Gallagher, Norman, 180 Summer Street
Gallant, John, 9 Winter Street
Galvin, Patrick, 150 Brookline Street
Gameson, Edward W., 272 No. Beacon Street
Gardener, Everett, 123 Pleasant Street
Garvey, Thomas, 141 Galen Street
Gaudette, Claude, 28 Francis Street
Germanio, Henry, 45 Riverside Street
Gibbons, Michael, 6 Washburn Street
Gildea, John Joseph, 8 Theurer Park
Giragosian, Malcolm, 57 Bigelow Avenue
Gleason, William, 175 School Street
Glover, Charles G., 45 Dartmouth Street
Gloyd, Charles O., 114 Riverside Street
Glynn, Andrew, 51 Main Street
Glynn, Leo C., 16 Cross Street
Gobron, Arthur, 27 Channing Street
Goldsmith, Fred W., 73 Main Street
Graham, William T., 28 Richards Street
Gray, Edwin W., 532 Mt. Auburn Street
Gray, Franklyn, 154 Cypress Street
Green, Joseph E., 126 Walnut Street
Greenwood, George, 28 Adams Street
Gulesian, Joseph, 203 School Street
Gullason, Charles, 79 Dexter Avenue
Gullason, Roland, 79 Dexter Avenue
Gulo, Simon, 204 Boylston Street
Hale, Joseph, 26 Fifield Street
Halfyard, Allen W., 11 Dunton Road
Halios, George, 30 Wells Avenue
Halligan, James, 41 Keenan Street
Hancock, Walter J., 5 Hancock Street
Hanley, George S., 24 Waltham Street

Hannon, James J., 59 Boyd Street
Hansen, Evon, 710 Belmont Street
Hanson, David, 29 Lincoln Street
Hanson, John E., 29 Lincoln Street
Harrington, Jerome, 50 Hovey Street
Harrington, Michael J., 65 Bacon Street
Harris, Bruce, 474 Arsenal Street
Harris, Silas M., 476 Arsenal Street
Harvey, Roland T., 64A Westminster Avenue
Hastie, James, 153 Summer Street
Hauswerth, Albert J., 298 Waverley Avenue
Hawkins, Lloyd, 19 Morse Street
Haynes, Harry E., 64 Union Street
Hennessey, John, 23 French Terrace
Hession, Joseph, 11 Bancroft Street
Hever, Frank, 83 Pleasant Street
Hickey, John, 168 School Street
Hiemenz, Herbert J., 2 Bellevue Terrace
Hill, Acon, 38 California Street
Hiltz, William, 59 Locke Street
Hiltz, William E., 59 Locke Street
Hindilian, James, 16 Irma Avenue
Hindilian, Percy, 16 Irma Avenue
Hoban, John, 67 No. Beacon Street
Hoffman, Jay S., 28 Hillside Street
Hogan, Daniel, 7 Putnam Street
Hogan, Leo, 7 Putnam Street
Horan, John, 93 Riverside Street
Hotz, Theodore, 13 Laurel Street
Howes, Ernest, 256 No. Beacon Street
Hurley, Michael, 14 Fuller Road
Hyde, Harry, 214 Arlington Street
Iannelli, Patsy, 259 Lexington Street
Ingham, Benjamin, 537 Mt. Auburn Street
Iodice, William, 124 School Street
Iozzo, Bassilo, 808 Mt. Auburn Street
Irwin, Clifton, 80 Hillside Road
Jacobs, John, 100A School Street
Jenner, Harry, 185 Summer Street
Jepson, Percy W., 27 Palfrey Street
Johnson, Mike, 31 Melendy Avenue
Johnson, Parker, 50 Bailey Road
Jones, Arthur, 20 Center
Joyce, Joseph, 131 Worcester Street

Kavooghian, Jacob, 542 Mt. Auburn Street
Kay, Ernest, 234 No. Beacon Street
Keany, Joseph M., 30 Maple Street
Keany, Michael F., 30 Maple Street
Kearns, Michael, 15 No. Park
Keating, Thomas H., 187 School Street
Keefe, Cornelius H., 7 Cuba Street
Keefe, Henry, 215 Dexter Avenue
Keefe, James, Jr., 148 Boylston Street
Keefe, Jason, 172 Walnut Street
Kelley, Daniel, 35 Morse Street
Kelley, Edward, 109 Chapman Street
Kelly, Francis F., 45 Elton Avenue
Kelly, John, 37 Melendy Avenue
Kelly, Joseph, 26 Melendy Avenue
Kennedy, Lester, 240 Waltham Street
Kenney, John J., 133 Galen Street
Keough, John C., 187 Arsenal Street
Kerens, John, 24 Green Street
Kergian, Anoosh, 137 School Street
Kachadoorian, John, 43 Dartmouth Street
Kachjian, George, 217 Dexter Avenue
Kane, John J., 2 Derby Road
Karibian, Charles, 6 Hosmer Street
Karsian, Mike, 92 Cypress Street
Kezerian, John, 65 Putnam Street
Kherlakian, Avedis, 63 Elton Avenue
Kinchla, Timothy, 23 Maple Street
Kinder, William, 47 Quincy Street
Kinosian, Sarkis, 57 Quimby Street
Kivlin, Joseph, 12 Fifth Aveune
Klenjian, Hagop, 95 Nichols Avenue
Klustian, Richard, 79 Bigelow Avenue
Kondakian, Levon, 61 Crawford Street
Krantz, George, 370 Charles River Road
Krian, Paul, 77 Bigelow Avenue
Kulick, Felix, 520 Pleasant Street
Kurkjian, Peter, 60 Laurel Street
LaCamrie, Plarza, 33 Dartmouth Street
Lahey, John J., 68 Edenfield Avenue
Lake, James, 11 Avon Road
Lama, Niccolo, 56 Prentiss Street
Lamorticello, James, 11 Forest Street
Larkin, William R., 202 Sycamore Street

LaSpade, Joseph, 46 Westminster Avenue
Lavine, Clarence, 26 Dexter Avenue
Lavoy, Henry Jr., 404 Pleasant Street
Leary, Frank, 802 Mt. Auburn Street
LeBlanc, John, 24 Dexter Avenue
Lees, George, 46 Quincy Street
Lehan, Daniel J., 73 Evans Street
Lehman, Paul W., 139 Church Street
Lembo, Charles J., 176 Walnut Street
Leonard, John, 141 Galen Street
Leonard, Walter, 59 Olney Street
Lillejholm, Sidney P., 40 Garfield Street
Little, Albert, 36 Middlesex Road
Locke, Richard, 6 Bromfield Street
Lockhart, Harold C., 53 Edenfield Avenue
Lucas, Leonard, 173 School Street
Luther, Francis J., 307 Waverley Avenue
Lyman, Bernard, 201 Watertown Street
Lynch, Francis, 91 Langdon Avenue
MacArthur, Ralph E., 344 Arlington Street
MacDonald, John, 45 Gilbert Street
MacDonald, Louis, 86 Prentiss Street
MacDonald, Roderick, 29 Prescott Street
MacDonald, Ronald S., 10 Jewett Street
MacDonald, William F., 33 Bigelow Street
MacDougall, John D., 34 Hovey Street
MacGillivary, Daniel, 502A Main Street
MacInnis, Joseph Mark, 323 Arlington Street
Macken, Edward L., 137 Langdon Avenue
MacLeod, John J., 41A Parker Street
MacQuarrie, Bartelle E., 2 Kimball Road
Maguire, Hubert, 78 Arsenal Street
Mahoney , Thomas, 22 Whitcomb Street
Mahoney, William, 15 Charles Street
Malley, George K., 15 Green Street Terrace
Malone, John T., 150 Irving Street
Maloney, Charles A., 35 Boylston Street
Maloney, Paul, 43 Oakland Street
Mannarino, Guy, 33 Dexter Avenue
Manning, John, 142 Galen Street
Mansell, Joseph, 49 Cypress Street
Marchant, Clifford, 53 Mt. Auburn Street
Marchant, Edward, 129 Arsenal Street
Marchant, Ernest, 44 Morton Street

Marchant, Freeman, 137 Morse Street
Marchese, Vincent, 35 Oakland Street
Marco, Ralph J., 12 Sheldon Road
Mariano, Antonio, 8 Hearn Street
Marozza, Sabatian, 35 Howard Street
Marshall, Richard K., 3 Ladd Street
Martinez, Edward, 30 Malden Street
Matthew, Leonard, 154 Worcester Street
Matthews, Mittford M., 64 Commonwealth Road
Mattison, Robert E., 6 Chapman Street
Mazza, Charles C., 7 Hearn Street
McArthur, Clarence, 24 Dexter Avenue
McCabe, William, 69 Templeton Parkway
McCann, John J., 116 Main Street
McCann, Leo F., 116 Main Street
McCassie, Linwood, 10 Jewett Street
McClure, George, 109 Spring Street
McCool, Hugh, Jr., 53 Gilbert Street
McCue, Thomas J., 293 No. Beacon Street
McDonald, Alphonso, 116 Summer Street
McDonald, Bertram, 422 Mt. Auburn Street
McDonald, James A., 43 Edenfield Avenue
McDonald, John A., 34 Williams Street
McDowell, Charles D., 54 Salisbury Road
McDowell, Lewis D., 54 Salisbury Road
McEllen, John, 170 Summer Street
McEllen, Michael, 14 Fifth Avenue
McEmery, William, 16 Fifield Avenue
McEnaney, Arthur J., 113 Boylston Street
McGarrity, John J., 22 Carver Road
McGivern, Frank J., 5 Hilltop Street
McGonnell, Howard E., 820 Mt. Auburn Street
McGovern, John, 352 Arlington Street
McGrady, Charles, 29 Harrington Street
McGrail, John H., 16 Ladd Street
McGrath, Charles, 54 Parker Street
McHugh, Joseph, 137 Galen Street
McHugh, Patrick, 14 Theurer Park
McIntyre, Andrew, 90 No. Beacon Street
McIntyre, Angus, 42 Cypress Street
McIsaac, Joseph, 83 Morse Street
McKay, Donald C., 127 Church Street
McKay, John, 47 Hovey Street
McLaren, James, 808 Mt. Auburn Street

McCann, Thomas F., 94 Elm Street
McMaster, William H., 28 Laurel Street
McKee, William, 41 Elton Avenue
McNichol, Charles, 391 School Street
McStay, Patrick C., 39 Spring Street
McSweeney, Dan, 14 Fletcher Terrace
Melansen, Leonard, 169 Edenfield Avenue
Mercurio, Salvatore, 37 Prentiss Street
Meredith, Henry, 7 Summer Street
Merrulo, Pasquale, 42 Westminster Avenue
Meuse, Arthur, 34 Hawthorne Street
Middleton, W. Irving, 115 Barnard Avenue
Miller, Arlis, 43 Riverside Street
Miller, Dominick, 238 Arlington Street
Minasian, Charles, 37 Keenan Street
Minasian, Kay, 20 Wilson Street
Minesian, Hagop, 94 Nichols Avenue
Monohan, George H., 10 Union Street
Mongine, Joseph J., 74 Forest Street
Montague, Louis, 116 Walnut Street
Moore, Walter, 168 Walnut Street
Moran, Francis, 56 Gilbert Street
Moran, Leon J., 223 Watertown Street
Moran, Paul C., 56 Gilbert Street
Morash, Charles E., 55 Hazel Street
Morrisey, Richard, 64 Elton Avenue
Morizio, Salvatore, 137 Lexington Street
Morley, Patrick, 20 Hersom Street
Morris, Lewis, 22 Putnam Street
Mosca, Carlo, 65 Cottage Street
Mulhern, John H., 12 Theurer Park
Mullen, Joseph, 145 Galen Street
Mullenger, Lester, 169 Worcester Street
Murdock, David W., 176 Boylston Street
Murdock, Edward, 113 Chapman Street
Murphy, Charles A., 217 Orchard Street
Murphy, Edward A., 16 Belknap Terrace
Murphy, Edward, 36 Concord Road
Murphy, Henry J., 36 Cross Street
Murphy, James F., 98 Riverside Street
Murphy, John, Jr., 66 California Street
Murray, John F., 79 Dexter Avenue
Murray, William J., 531 Mt. Auburn Street
Najarian, Leon, 35 Porter Street

Nafratis, Demetra, 217 Arlington Street
Naretti, Pasquale, 24 Edgecliff Road
Negoghosian, Neshin, 16 Chauncy Street
Nelson, Francis E., 28 Partridge Street
Nelson, Otto N., 3 Locke Street
Neshanian, Murad, 89 Bigelow Avenue
Neshe, Peter, 28 Francis Street
Niccols, Henry, 29 Fairview Avenue
Nigohosian, Garabed, 203 Boylston Street
Nocurra, John, 29 Churchill Street
Norcross, James, Rev., 101 Standish Road
Normanda, Louis, 38 Boyd Street
Norton, Nelson, 1 Hilltop Road
Notargiacomo, Albert, 73 Springfield Street
Nuvirian, Carl, 25 Oak Street
Nuvirian, Peter, 25 Oak Street
Oatley, Augustus W., 29 Adams Street
O'Brien, Patrick H., 34 Union Street
Oderwald, John F., 350 School Street
O'Donnell, Frederick A., 15 Churchill Street
O'Donnell, John J., 14 Maplewood Street
Ogar, Arthur C., 46 Cuba Street
O'Hanian, Hagop, 52 Dartmouth Street
O'Hanian, Nishan, 52 Dartmouth Street
O'Hara, James J., 123 Edenfield Avenue
Olivetto, James, 29 Dewey Street
Olson, Walter H., 68 Bradford Road
O'Neil, Henry J., 11 Eliot Street
O'Neil, Thomas, 68 Elton Avenue
Ounjian, Mihran, 49 Laurel Street
Ounjian, Samuel, 49 Laurel Street
Panosian, Steven S., 31 Porter Street
Panosian, Steve, 31 Porter Street
Parent, Theodore, 7 Hearn Street
Parker, Harold, 14 Washburn Street
Parker, Homer C., 149 Common Street
Parkhurst, Albert, 581 Pleasant Street
Parry, Jeremiah, 102 Cypress Street
Parsons, Wesley, 129 School Street
Paskerian, Kregor, 117 Boylston Street
Pelargonio, Albert, 209 Arlington Street
Pelargonio, Mario, 209 Arlington Street
Pelky, Charles L., 48 Carroll Street
Perkins, David, 13 Oakland Street
Perkins, David, 13 Oakland Street

Perkins, Robert E., 111Hillside Road
Perry, Max, 10 Hovey Street
Peterson, Joseph, 15 Rangley Road
Piantedosi, Benjamin, 21 Homer Street
Piantedosi, Cosmo, 24 Cushman Street
Plaisted, George P., 114 Main Street
Poillucci, Antonio, 46 Dartmouth Street
Poillucci, Frank, 46 Dartmouth Street
Poillucci, Gus, 7 Yukon Avenue
Procippio, Paul, 8 Myrtle Street
Putney, Charles, 98 Waverley Avenue
Quinn, Horace A., 52 Edgecliffe Road
Ralph, Francis, 144 Dexter Avenue
Ralphlian, Casper, 28 Laurel Street
Raymond, Dominic, 8 Bostonia Avenue
Raymond, Joseph, 8 Bostonia Avenue
Reardon, Martin, 4 Jewett Street
Reardon, Patrick, 475 Pleasant Street
Reason, James E., 114 Waltham Street
Reagon, Richard, 40 Maple Street
Remarcho, Panfile, 12 New Lexington Street
Restingo, Dominic, 231 Arlington Street
Revane, Michael T., 8 Adams Street
Reynolds, George E., 176 Summer Street
Recardi, John, 93 Arlington Street
Riccio, Anthony, 125 Arsenal Street
Riccio, Frank, 125 Arsenal Street
Riccio, Joseph, 28 Clarendon Street
Rice, Henry W., 30 Hawthorne Street
Rice, Fred W., 44 Woodleigh Road
Rigdon, Elwin, 819 Mt. Auburn Street
Rizza, Joseph, 114 Forest Street
Rizza, Joseph Jr., 114 Forest Street
Roach, John H., 162 Spruce Street
Robb, Robert L., 36 Hardy Avenue
Robinson, Herbert, 25 Palmer Street
Roche, Vieateaur, 100 Pleasant Street
Rogers, Charles W., 70 Poplar Street
Rogers, Francis, 112 Forest Street
Rooney, Denis, 37 Cuba Street
Rooney, James E., 6 Winthrop Street
Rooney, Phillip, 23 Fifth Street
Rose, Roderick F., 86 Prentiss Street
Rosoff, Abraham, 328 Arlington Street

Rowan, Charles H., 8 Sidney Street
Rufo, Joseph, 16 Myrtle Street
Ruggiero, William, 8 Swetts Court
Russell, Benjamin, 297 Mt. Auburn Street
Russell, Frank, 8 Hardy Avenue
Russo, Antonio, 36 Prescott Street
Russo, Carmona, 100 Edenfield Avenue
Russo, Paul, 21 Hudson Street
Russo, Sam, 29 Waverley Avenue
Rutledge, Paul F., 70 Chapman Street
Ryan, Thomas, 43 Bigelow Avenue
Sacco, Roy, 38 Ridgecliff Avenue
Sacco, Charles A., 184 Summer Street
Sahagian, Vahan, 49 Crawford Street
Sanders, James L., 14 Fayette Street
Santo, Aliano, 36 Cottage Street
Santoro, Maurice, 61 Prentiss Street
Sarafian, Nishan, 205 Boylston Street
Sargent, John, 53 Hazel Street
Sarkisian, Adam, 11 Nichols Avenue
Sarkisian, Krikr, 47 Hazel Street
Sauguinett, Pack A., 876 Belmont Street
Savory, Robert, 225 Common Street
Sawyer, Kingsley, 84 Marion Road
Secord, Arthur, 179 Spruce Street
Serafino, Victor, 466 Arsenal Street
Shannahan, Henry, 136 Cypress Street
Shannahan, Warren, 136 Cypress Street
Sharkey, John E., 14 Templeton Parkway
Shea, Bartholomew, 128 Walnut Street
Shea, Edward, 116 Putnam Street
Shea, George, 66 Edenfield Avenue
Shea, John J., 142 Galen Street
Silvaggi, Libertore, 14 Warren Street
Sinourian, Simon, 24 Keenan Street
Sim, William, 43 Marshall Street
Sirianni, Joseph, 89 Elm Street
Sirianni, Louis, 89 Elm Street
Sirr, Bernard J., 24 Palmer Street
Skinner, Leslie, 104 Spring Street
Slavin, Harry, 11 Morton Street
Smith, Herbert, 46 Bridge Street
Smith, Walter I., 6 Oliver Road
Sowers, Alfred H., 14 Katherine Street

Sparks, Lester D., 23 Stuart Street
Sperguiro, Frank, 29 Coolidge Hill Road
Stanley, Henry, 58 Elton Avenue
Stanley, Nazareth, 58 Elton Avenue
Stapanian, George, 51 Quincy Street
Stevens, John, 156 Summer Street
Stidstone, John, 35 Hosmer Street
Stiriti, Frank, 93 Arlington Street
Stiriti, Joseph, 93 Arlington Street
Studley, Arthur, 14 Alden Road
Studerer, Walter, 27 Charles Street
Sullivan, Asa, 21 Water Street
Sullivan, Michael, 17 Melendy Avenue
Sullivan, Thomas, 27 Elton Avenue
Surabian, George, 72 Prentiss Street
Swanson, Ernest, 10 Keenan Street
Sweeney, William, 21 Oak Street
Tarjian, Jacob, 143 School Street
Terzian, Nazareth, 142 Nichols Avenue
Tasta, Alexander, 116 Forest Street
Tattrie, David, 56 Spring Street
Taverna, Carmine, 38 Berkeley Street
Thiesing, Herman, 15 California Park
Thimot, Moses, 78 Springfield Street
Thomag, Peter, 32 Concord Street
Thulin, Ralph C., 14 Chester Street
Tiberio, Carmine, 35 Churchill Street
Tiberio, Joseph, 27 Churchill Street
Tillot, Harry, 62 Prentiss Street
Tobin, Peter, 23 Maple Street
Tocci, Bragio, 22 Lyons Court
Tomasian, Setrak, 119 Dexter Avenue
Tomassetti, Frank, 25 Pleasant Street
Tomassian, Jacob, 61 Cypress Street
Tomelli, Tony, 89 King Street
Toomey, Michael, 781 Mt. Auburn Street
Torres, Maurice, 32 Whitney Street
Tracy, Thomas, 14 Fletcher Terrace
Tracy, William, 14 Fletcher Terrace
Transente, Michael, 59 Warren Street
Turbini, Joseph, 19 French Terrace
Tuscher, William R., 196 School Street
Tuttle, H. George, 42 Porter Street
Twohig, James, 90 No. Beacon Street

Tyler, Guy, 128 School Street
Tyler, Clifford, 22 Patten Street
Vacca, Nick, 15 Keenan Street
Vahey, John, 531 Mt. Auburn Street
Vance, Alvin, 8 Fletcher Terrace
Verkas, Alexander, 144 Pleasant Street
Velente, Joseph, 22 No. Beacon Street
Venerriano, Dominic, 350 Arlington Street
Venetzian, Jasper, 35 Cypress Street
Vincent, Arthur, 15 Adams Street
Viola, Savatore, 10 Berkley Street
Visella, Cesare, 50 Arsenal Street
Vivanian, Harry, 23 Cottage Street
Voney, Joseph, 189 Pleasant Street
Vrock, Rocco, 72 Olcott Street
Wade, John J., 153 Arsenal Street
Walker, Charles, 32 Templeton Parkway
Wall, Michael, 142 Galen Street
Walace, Frank, 120 Bellevue Road
Walsh, Edward, 4 Adams Street
Walsh, James J., 159 Langdon Avenue
Ward, George, 64 Elton Avenue
Waterman, Elwell J., 156 Spruce Street
Whalen, John B., 173 Worcester Street
White, Henry J., 53 Myrtle Street
White, John Russell, 17 Green Street
White, Rosario, 151 Arsenal Street
Whitney, Edwin O., 6 Melvin Terrace
Whittemore, Earl, 50 Marion Road
Willis, Arthur E., 573 Main Street
Woodbury, Lowell, 154 Orchard Street
Youvanian, Yervant, 17 Howe Street
Fries, Arvad, 18 Wolcott Street ,49 Parker St. Present)
Davis, William, 554 Belmont Street
Davishian, Charles, 15 Porter Street
Achmakjian, James, 23 Cottage Street
Adamo, Joseph Jr., 46 Edenfield Avenue
Agresta, Nicholas, 66 Forest Street
Alemsherian, Milkan, 9 Kondabian Street
Bracken, James, 69 Hillside Road
Bracken, John, 69 Hillside Road
Cairo, Emilo, 81 Boyd Street
Carlin, William, 87 Templeton Parkway
Cate, Ray L., 434 Mt. Auburn Street

DerBoghosian, K., 67 Laurel Street
Field, Richard, 10 Sunnybank Road
Kerrigan, John, 11 Oakland Street
Kerrigan, Thomas, 26 Paul Street
Lindsey, Robert, 56 Forest Street
Marchant, John, 129 Arsenal Street
McCormick, John, 92 Waltham Street
McCormick, John A., 92 Waltham Street
McGuire, William, 9 Winters Street
McMillan, Richard, 137 Templeton Parkway
Meehan, Patrick, 162 Spruce Street
Morrison, Sarsfield, 73 Spruce Street
Mullen, Patrick, 13 Beechwood Avenue
Murdock, William, 113 Chapman Street
Murphy, John A., 36 Laurel Street
Paddock, George B., 9 Loyd Street
Pollucci, Joseph, 7 Yukon Avenue
Polucci, Rocco, 108 Dexter Avenue
Quinn, Thomas, 46 No. Beacon Street
Quint, Leo, 8 Derby Road
Raphalian, Solomon, 13 Brimmer Street
Russo, Peter, 28 Forest Street
Sanders, Frank R., 174 No. Beacon Street
Sheenan, Leo, 203 Summer Street
Sperguiro, Michael, 29 Coolidge Hill Road
Stanley, Henry, 58 Elton Avenue
Stone, Selwyn, 734 Belmont Street
Arone, Lawrence, 25 Norseman Avenue
Arslanian, Joseph, 6 Hosmer Street
Aubrey, Ernest, 47 Commonwealth Road
Bagnall, John W., 13 Olcott Street
Baker, Irving, 163 Fayette Street
Balt, Anthony, 73 Boyd Street
Barkman, Gerard, 9 Gertrude Street
Benpamian, Harry J., 21 Boylston Street
Berry, Herbert, 75 Marion Road
Blanchette, Robert, 87 Arsenal Street
Bortone, Ernest, 984 Belmont Street
Boudakian, Haig, 34 Cypress Street
Boylan, James, 74 Fitchburg Street
Boyle, James S., Jr., 5 Upland Road
Bracken, Frank A., 69 Hillside Road
Brant, Francis J., 46 Union Street
Brennan, Bartholomew, 227 Lexington Street

Bresnahan, Joseph T., 82 Dexter Avenue
Bristol, Donald, 221 Common Street
Britton, Edward J., 42 Mt, Auburn Street
Brown, Leslie R., 115 Common Street
Buccadora, Salvatore, 308 Main Street
Buckley, Frances E., 30 Chauncey Street
Buckley, Joseph, 30 Chauncey Street
Buckley, William F., 30 Chauncey Street
Bugey, Walter K., 82 Carroll Street
Burke, James J., 51 Olney Street
Burke, Joseph, 51 Olney Street
Burke, Thomas F., 78 Chestnut Street
Burke, Walter E., 105 Pleasant Street
Caccavaro, Gerald, 36 Oakland Street
Callahan, Patrick J., 20 Oakland Street
Camerato, Carmine, 23 James Street
Campbell, Hecton, 15 Carlton Terrace
Campbell, James, 65 Bacon Street
Campbell, Paul R., 23 Oakland Street
Campbell, William, 102 Winsor Avenue
Cappellucci, Pantoline, 105 Pleasant Street
Cappucci, Mike, 23 Bostonia Avenue
Carcio, Joseph, 24A Norseman Avenue
Carey, William P., 44 Merrill Road
Casey, Herbert, 129 Langdon Avenue
Cate, Ray L., 434 Mt. Auburn Street
Caterino, Natale, 7 Nichols Avenue
Cavanaugh, Bartholomew, 547 Main Street
Chamberlain, Raymond S., 76 Irving Street
Chebookian, Harry, 157 Nichols Avenue
Clancy, Martin, 284 No. Beacon Street
Coffee, John, 47 Kondazian Street
Colligan, Albert, 5 Royal Street
Colligan, John J., 5 Royal Street
Consalarg, Joseph, 272 Palfrey Street
Cooper, John H., 57 Prospect Street
Corcoran, John, 491 Main Street
Coughlin, Jeremiah, 73 Union Street
Covino, Angelo, 226 Westminster Avenue
Covino, Sam, 226 Westminster Avenue
Crockford, William E., 29 Hunt Street
Dacey, John F., Jr., 62 California Street
Dadaian, Hamper, 212 Boylston Street
Daniels, Harry, 7 Bellevue Terrace

DeFilippis, Paul, 14 Lyons Court
Deldon, John, 175 Fayette Street
Delfino, Charles, 267 Palfrey Street
Delorey, James, 19 Oakland Street
Deloria, Charles M., 34 Melendy Avenue
Derhovanesian, Israel, 138 Forest Street
Desmond, Cornelius F., 57 Lexington Street
DeStefano, Tony, 29 Dewey Street
Diegnan, Patrick, 19 Adams Street
Doherty, Daniel, 12 Sunset Road
Donnelly, John F., 23 Grenville Road
Donovan, M. Augustus, 363 Arlington Street
Donovan, William, 22 Theurer Park
Doyle, Michael, 68 California Street
Driscoll, Dan A., 43 Fairfield Street
Ducharme, Leonard, 80 Edgecliffe Road
Dugan, James P., 62 Capitol Street
Dunderdale, Henry F., 224 Warren Street
Dunderdale, John J., Jr., 224 Warren Street
Dunne, James, 58 Morse Street
Dunphy, James P., 45 Grenville Road
Durgin, Clifton K., 32 Charles River Road
Duvall, Edwin, 179 Waverley Avenue
Dwyer, Michael J., 485 Main Street
Dymaza, Edmund V., 1 Oakley Road
Eastman, Earl, 28 Howard Street
English, Felix, 52 Crawford Street
English, James, 40 Pequosette Street
English, Joseph E., 40 Pequosette Street
Farese, Carmen, 264 Warren Street
Farese, John, 264 Warren Street
Farrenkoff, Joseph T., 122 Langdon Avenue
Fay, George, 122 No. Beacon Street
Feltch, Benjamin, 15 Quincy Street
Fifield, Albert L., 154 School Street
Files, Walter W., 12 Hardy Avenue
Flaherty, John, 48 Pearl Street
Flamburis, Harry, 137 Templeton Parkway
Flanagan, George, 543 Mt. Auburn Street
Flannery, John J., 826 Mt. Auburn Street
Flynn, Bart, 104 Morse Street
Flynn, George, H., 539 Mt. Auburn Street
Flynn, William B., 53 Gilbert Street
Fogarty, Edward, 543 Mt. Auburn Street

Foley, George C., 78 Putnam Street
Forbes, John F., 21 Eliot Street
Fraser, Herbert, 176 Spruce Street
Freeman, Leslie J., 488 Main Street
Friend, James R., 41 Fitchburg Street
Garito, Joseph, 145 Galen Street
Gaylord, John F., 13 Patten Street
Gingeria, Joseph, 20 Perry Street
Gould, George D., 11 Francis Street
Grassia, Ralph V., 35 Williams Street
Gray, Charles R., 358 Arlington Street
Green, John C., 34 Melendy Avenue
Gulesian, Samuel N., 46 Salisbury Road
Guzzetti, Guiseppe, 12 Berkeley Street
Hammond, Harold T., 72 Salisbury Road
Hannon, Edward J., 137 Morse Street
Hanrahan, Charles, 780 Belmont Street
Hanrahan, Francis, 543 Mt. Auburn Street
Harrington, Joseph R., 68 Bradford Road
Harris, Charles, 127 Evans Street
Hartung, Paul G., 27 Maplewood Street
Hastings, Leon W., 138 Orchard Street
Haughey, Edward F., 343 School Street
Henderson, Lawrence W., 101 No. Beacon Street
Hoban, John, 67 No. Beacon Street
Holland, J. Edward, 16 Stearns Road
Holmes, Clinton E., 94 Union Street
Hughes, Frank L., 41 Paul Street
Hughes, John, 114 Main Street
Hurley, Arthur J., 19 Locke Street
Hurley, John, 46 Watertown Street
Hynes, John L., 29 Boylston Street
Igoe, Henry, 27 Edenfield Avenue
Jardine, Archibald, 48 Watertown Street
Jelladian, Charles, 17 Dartmouth Street
Jelladian, Aram, 17 Dartmouth Street
Johnson, Allen, 342 School Street
Johnson, Jacob, 78 Dexter Avenue
Johnston, James A., 172 Howard Street
Jones, Sidney, 13 Summer Street
Kasparian, Kaspar, 77 Templeton Parkway
Keefe, Arthur C., 7 Cuba Street
Keefe, John, 133 Galen Street
Kelch, Edward J., 166 Hillside Road

Kelley, Edward J., 316 Mt. Auburn Street
Kelley, John O., 21 Capitol Street
Kenney, Francis J., 9 No. Park Street
Kenney, William, 11 Middlesex Road
Kapasian, Harry, 49 Hazel Street
Karakanian, Charles, 16 Hazel Street
Karakanian, Krikor, 16 Hazel Street
Kilcoyne, Eugene J., 56 Putnam Street
Kinney, Edward, 81 Commonwealth Road
Knight, Wallace S., 38 Cypress Street
Koch, John L., Jr., 372 Main Street
Kurkian, Derian, 47 Hazel Street
LaCamera, Samuel, 220 Arlington Street
Lakis, Stephen, 25 Prentiss Street
Lanctoto, Joseph E., 46 Copeland Street
Lapero, Gabriel, 63 Elm Street
Larribee, Frank L., 51 Boyd Street
Leonard, Andrew, 105 Rutland Street
Leonard, Benedict, 63 Hillside Road
Leonard, John, 11 Oakland Street
Leonard, John J., 105 Rutland Street
Leone, Daniel, 141 Galen Street
LeRoy, Arthur, 22 Royal Street
Lincoln, Walter, 106 Belmont Street
Lindahl, Francis C., 20 Prescott Street
Lindahl, Frederick, 20 Prescott Street
Little, Richard K., 15 Edenfield Avenue
Livoti, George R., 129 Evans Street
Lombardo, Joseph L., 94 Putnam Street
Lopez, Richard F., 484 Main Street
Lopez, Richard F., Jr., 484 Main Street
MacDonald, Charles, 38 Franklin Street
MacDonald, James D., 38 Franklin Street
MacDonald, John A., 27 Howard Street
MacDonald, Thomas R., 16 Richards Road
MacDonald, William, 56 Putnam Street
MacMahon, William H., 67 Lincoln Street
Magrath, Herbert, 46 Wilmot Street
Mahan, Herny, 44 Eliot Street
Mahan, William E., 44 Eliot Street
Maher, Joseph, 11 Olcott Street
Mailly, George, 20 Prescott Street
Major, Edwin M., 35 Eliot Street
Malloy, Edward A., 7 Chandler Street

Malloy, George, 7 Chandler Street
Mannix, Edward F., 9 Prescott Street
Mannix, Frank L., 9 Prescott Street
Martin, Albert, 14 Winthrop Street
Martocchio, John, 42 Forest Street
Marvin, William A., 151 Nichols Avenue
Marvin, Walter T., 151 Nichols Avenue
Mastrangelo, Louis, 169 Winsor Avenue
Maunus, William, 181 Walnut Street
Maxwell, Earl O., 39 Pearl Street
May, Kenneth H., 7 Grenville Road
Mazza, Carmen, 66 Ralph Street
Mazza, Peter, 8 Hearn Street
McCabe, William C., 83 Bradford Road
McCarthy, James, 6 Churchill Street
McCarthy, John J., 4 Maplewood Street
McCarthy, Thomas, 33 Bacon Street
McCarthy, Timothy J., 164 Hillside Road
McCormack, Joseph, 8 Adams Street
McDonald, Daniel, 425 Main Street
McElroy, Joseph, 37 Hunt Street
McGough, Edward, 24 Upland Road
McInnis, John A., 97 Evans Street
McIntyre, Francis M., 42 Cypress Street
McIntyre, John J., 42 Cypress Street
McIntyre, Raymond, 42 Cypress Street
McIntyre, Ronald, 42 Cypress Street
McLaughlin, John, 162 Hillside Road
McLellan, Daniel, 49 Mt. Auburn Street
McLellan, John R., 49 Mt. Auburn Street
McMann, Thomas F., 94 Elm Street
McNamara, James J., 11 Upland Road
Meehan, Joseph D., 11 Edenfield Avenue
Meehan, Richard J., 14 No. Beacon Street
Melone, Francis J., 10 Summit Road
Melvin, Irving Albert, 24 Marshall Street
Mendall, Lewis R., 65 Union Street
Mercer, John, 467 Pleasant Street
Merullo, James, 69 Forest Street
Merrill, William E., 65 Riverside Street
Minehan, Cornelius, 48 Irving Street
Mirable, Vito, 305 Mt. Auburn Street
Monahan, John, 5 Myrtle Street
Monahan, William J., 68A Edenfield Avenue

Mondlick, Solomon, 26 Edgecliff Road
Moony, Frank E., 227 No. Beacon Street
Moore, Lawrence, 16 Dunton Road
Moriarty, Clayton, 8 Kimball Road
Morgan, Leo M., 166 Spruce Street
Morley, John J., 10 Wells Avenue
Morrisey, Thomas, 486 Main Street
Mulhern, Joseph B., 12 Theurer Park
Mullen, Paul V., 13 Beechwood Avenue
Mulrain, Edward, 522 Pleasant Street
Murdock, Lorenzo, 198 Boylston Street
Murgia, John, 10 Lowell Street
Murphy, James A., 125 Langdon Avenue
Murphy, Joseph, 66 California Street
Murray, James J., 435 Mt. Auburn Street
Needham, Harry R., 128 Grove Street
Nichols, Parson H., 34 Oakley Road
Nilson, James, 44 Chauncey Street
Nizzari, Jerry, 144 Highland Avenue
O'Brien, James F., 146 Langdon Avenue
Odian, Charles, 115 Dexter Avenue
O'Donnell Alfred M., 21 Morton Street
O'Donnell, James A., 14 Churchill Street
O'Donnell, James A., Jr., 14 Churchill Street
O'Donnell, John H., 12 Bacon Street
O'Dowd, Edwin J., 149 Weverley Avenue
O'Gara, Joseph, 483 Main Street
Papandrea, Thomas, 186 Summer Street
Papazian, Bedros, 39 Prentiss Street
Paquette, Hewey, 155 Nichols Avenue
Parkinson, Frederick, 37 Prescott Street
Paul, Kenneth D., 286 Belmont Street
Peck, Ernest J., 147 Dexter Avenue
Perley, Ronald, 168 Walnut Street
Peterson, Albert 49 Prescott Street
Piantedosi, Jerry, 112 Forest Street
Piantedosi, Joseph, 183 Fayette Street
Pierce, Charles, 86 Prentiss Street
Pilon, Victor, 141 Pleasant Street
Pitelli, Joseph, 50 Edgecliffe Road
Poillucci, Joseph, 24 Dartmouth Street
Quinn, Edward M., Jr., 29 French Street
Quinn Francis, 46 No. Beacon Street
Rattigan, John, 27 Chapman Street

Ready, Leo, 25 Morton Street
Reardon Edward, 39 Spring Street
Reardon James A,. 4 Jewett Street
Reid, Daniel, 23 Chapman Street
Rice, Dominic, 35 Cottage Street
Richardson, Frederick G., 26 Adams Street
Riley, Edward, 26 Middlesex Road
Riley, Paul B., 549 Main Street
Roberts, Harold, 38 Bostonia Avenue
Roche, Charles J., 14 Royal Street
Roche, James P., 54 Capitol Street
Romano, Edward, 26 Clarendon Street
Rooney, Edward D., 110 Riverside Street
Rooney, John B., 110 Riverside Street
Rooney, John F., 110 Riverside Street
Rooney, Leo, 110 Riverside Street
Rose, William F., 12 Keenan Street
Rosen, Herbert, 124 Hillside Road
Rosen, Nils, 124 Hillside Road
Rosetta, John, 20 Cross Street
Russo, Joseph, 21 New Lexington Street
Russo, Matthew, 53 Laurel
Russo, Matthew, Jr., 53 Laurel Street
Ryan, Vincent A., 121 Pleasant Street
Salvitti, Greto, 75 Putnam Street
Sawyer, Bertram E., 15 Sheldon Road
Scanlan, William E., 395 School Street
Scott, John, 596 Pleasant Street
Scott, Herbert, 32 Olney Street
Shaughnessy, Daniel B., 25 Hosmer Street
Shaw, Bartlett M., Jr., 141 Common Street
Shaw, Elmer A., 36 Irving Street
Shaw, Elmer W., 36 Irving Street
Shaw Thomas A., 36 Irving Street
Shea, John, 56 Salisbury Road
Shea, John, 56 Salisbury Road
Shedd, Daniel W., 133 Waltham Street
Sheehan, Francis, 108 Summer Street
Sheehan, Jeremiah, 250 Main Street
Sheehan, Leo, 203 Summer Street
Shields, Matthew, 141 Galen Street
Shutt, Charles J., 141 Morse Street
Skahill, Peter J., 123 No. Beacon Street
Smith, Chester, 92 No. Beacon Street

Smith, Francis E., 92 No. Beacon Street
Smith, Herbert, 10 Winter Street
Smith, John, 46 Irving Street
Smith, John H., 262 Main Street
Smith, Wendell, 81 Edenfield Avenue
Smith, William H., 92 No. Beacon Street
Stanchfield, Azier, 19 Irma Avenue
Stanchfield, Earle, 19 Irma Avenue
Stanley, Herbert, 58 Elton Avenue
Stevenson, William, 196 Pleasant Street
Stewart, Arthur G., 44 Grenville Road
Stratton, Ralph R., 26 Richards Road
Sullivan, John, 35 Fifield Street
Sullivan, John H., 166 Common Street
Sullivan, John J., 96 Boylston Street
Sullivan, Joseph, 65 Lowell Avenue
Sullivan, Timothy, 65 Lowell Avenue
Sweeney, Leon C., 11 Cottage Street
Sweeney, William J., 25 Russell Avenue
Tessmer, Frank R., 74 Morse Street
Todd, John C., 158 Waverley Avenue
Torangeau, Nelson, 13 Adams Street
Troianni, Pasquale, 52 Ralph Street
Tucker, Walter W., 354 Arlington Street
Vahey, Michael B., 123 No. Beacon Street
Vahey, Thomas F., 238 No. Beacon Street
Valentino, George, 11 Norseman Avenue
Vanderwoude, Simon, 103 Arsenal Street
Varner, Curtis L., 31 Langdon Avenue
Veno, Thomas H., 148 Langdon Avenue
Viering, Bernard J., 26 Quincy Street
Waldron, Raymond, 28 Capitol Street
Wallen, Alfred, 40 Porter Street
Walsh, Leo F., 63 Union Street
Walter, Randall, 7 Cottage Street
Walton, William, 39 Irma Avenue
Ward, James F., 44 Melandy Avenue
Watkins, Walter, 137 Galen Street
Watson, George W., 42 Maplewood Street
Wemple, Robert G., 4 Adams Avenue.
Wentworth, John J., 73 Piermont Street
Wessels, Edward, 18 Maple Street
White Dominick, 308 Main Street

Whitewat, David Sterling, 156 Belmont Street
Whyte, Harry, 27 Lloyd Road
Willson, Donald R., 176 Waverley Avenue
Wilson, Philip, 55 Phillips Street
Wood, Horace, 23 Irving Street
Woodman, Richard E., 72 Bradford Road
Woolf Otto, 170 Lovell Road
Zaino, Albert, 51 Crawford Street
Rizza, Anthony, 114 Forest Street
Paris, Sherman B., 67 Winsor Avenue
Hagopian, Hagop, 32 Quimby Street
Bixby, Charles, 229 Common Street
Quinn Clarence M., 73 Spring Street
Grimes, George E., Perkins Institute
McGuire, Patterson, 33 Franklin Street
Taverna, Salvatore, 38 Berkeley Street
Small, Clifford T., 21 Longfellow Road
Leedham, Ira, 51 Quirk Street
McCarthy, Michael J., 18 Wolcott Road
Milne, Thomas A., 63 Maplewood Street
Randall, Lewis J., 377 Arlington Street
Holmes, Philip B., 37 Franklin Street
Phillips, Arthur J., 33 Phillips Street
Sheehan, Daniel P., 13 Lloyd Road
Shamgochian, Ohan, 146 Melendy Avenue
Shea, John R., 298 Waverley Avenue
Crook, William, 21 Bromfield Street
Corazzini Armond, 81 Cypress Street
DeFilippis, Natalino, 14 Lyons Court
Woodruff, James, 22 Arden Road
Frederick, Holmes W., 21 Carver Road
Hayes, John J., Jr., 61 Church Street
Head, Edwin, 50 Quimby Street
Johnson, Roy G., 35 Upland Road
McDonnell, Patrick, 16 Ladd Street
McHugh, Thomas, 55 Mt. Auburn Street
Proctor, George, 74 Pearl Street
Raphalian, Reuben, 28 Laurel Street
Rodgers, Anthony, 70 Paplar Street
Scalzi, Ralph, 124 Fayette Street
Sheridan, Patrick, 57 Cottage Street
Stillisano, Michele, 39 Cuba Street
Teehan, Maurice, 12 Royal Street
Todino, Elviro, 16 Gleason Street

Walsh, Richard D., 27 Kimball Road
Young, Hebron E., 60 Hillside Street
Smith, Herbert W., 169 Standish Road
Flamburis, James D., 137 Templeton Parkway
Dambrosio, Joseph, 85 Arlington Street
Sullivan, Edgar B., 34 Hersom Street
Hannon, Michael, 42 Maplewood Street
Butler, Thomas J., 85 Dexter Avenue
O'Brien, Thomas, 417 School Street
Cave, Raymond C., 116 Winsor Avenue
Gilman, Louis, 65 School Street
Davis, Wilbert, 106 Cypress Street
Davis, William J., 17 Brimmer Street
Amerian, Kurken, 123 Nichols Avenue
Hayes, John J., 467 Main Street
Hayes, John J., Jr., 467 Main Street
Raphaelian, Alex, 123 Putnam Street
Dorron, Clifford J., 16 Waverley Avenue
Comfort James, 5 Partridge Street
White, William A., 42 Edenfield Avenue

1934 UNPAID EXCISE TAXES
At Close of Business December 31, 1934
Committed March 19, 1934

*Paid since close of books—Verified to February 19, 1935

Abramo, Joseph, 39 Coolidge Avenue	$2.89
Aigiro, Catherine, 11 Dewey Street	10.28
Anderson, Grace E., 134 Standish Road	3.86
Anderson, Harry J., 71 Arlington Street	2.00
Andrews, Paul V., 106 Cypress Street	3.21
Anstatt, Richard A., 22 Bradford Road	7.39
Arena, Frank, 8 Bostonia Avenue	2.00
Armstrong, Albert M., 29 Chandler Street	5.46
Arnold, Wilhemina, 3A Carver Road	5.46
Arone, Lawrence, 25 Norseman Avenue	2.00
Arslanian, Dick, 115 Dexter Avenue	4.42
Bakarian, Albert, 377 Arlington Street	3.54
Barranco, Salvatore, 300 Arlington Street	6.75
Barry, James H., 111 Worcester Street	2.00
Bohanon, Martha T., 53 Fitchburg Street	2.00
Botti, Alfred, 224 Arlington Street	2.25
Bruce, Robert, 16 Prospect Street	8.68

Bunnell, Stuart, 40 Marshall Street	9.96
Burbank, A. P. W., 44 Katherine Road	2.00
Burke, George M., 52 Spring Street	5.79
Butler, Thomas W., 98 Westminster Avenue	5.79
Callahan, Daniel F., 76 Fayette Street	10.61
Canady, Oscar M., 17 Main Street	3.21
Canty, Irene, 54 Channing Road	20.57
Carey, Alice E., 269 No. Beacon Street	10.61
Casgrain, Natalie, 16 Ocean Ave., Beverly	4.18
Cavicchi, John, 8 Fifth Avenue	4.82
Coffey, John E., 50 Putnam Street	2.00
Cohen, Nathan, 90 Edenfield Avenue	4.82
Cooper, John H., 160 Sycamore Street	2.00
Costanzo, Guido, 39 Mt. Auburn Street	2.00
Coughlin, John F., — St. Mary's Street	7.39
Cousineau, Delia, 716 Mt. Auburn Street	2.57
Craig, Charles A., 105 Franklin Street	2.00
Crane, Berg H., 39 Frank Street	4.18
Crosby, Anna B., 146 Hillside Road	5.79
Cushing, Bruce E., 57 Hovey Street	3.85
Darling, Dorothy B., 18 Concord Road	9.64
Daumer, Charles, 38 Porter Street	10.61
*DeFelice, John A., 40 Melendy Avenue	2.25
Delano, Iola E., 41 Beacon Park	8.04
Doyle, Charles L., 344 Belmont Street	2.00
Duffy, James L., 503 Main Street	10.93
Dwyer, Frank A., 295 Main Street	7.39
English, Dorothy, 40 Pequosette Street	3.54
Evans, Robert A., 76 Prospect Street	2.25
Farese, Louis, 264 Warren Street	3.21
Farrar, James E., 278 Newtonville Ave., Newtonville	4.82
Files, Addison E., 126 Chapman Street	2.00
*Files, Walter W., 12 Hardy Avenue	4.82
Gallagher, Thomas H., 126 Worcester Street	2.25
Gately, Mildred E., 36 Bacon Street	3.54
Gilmour, Ernest B., 94 Lovell Road	13.82
Gorman, William F., 41 Cuba Street	2.25
Green, Benjamin A., 126 Walnut Street	4.18
Grundman, Harold G., 42 Chapman Street	16.73
Hegarty, Thomas H., 18 Bradford Road	3.54
Hancock, Walter J., 5 Winter Street	2.25
Hanley, Rita L., 22 Waltham Street	2.00
Hannon, Margaret, 137 Morse Street	2.94
Hanrahan, James F., 780 Belmont Street	12.53

Harrington, Jerome C., 50 Hovey St.	5.14
Harris, Charles W., 127 Evans St.	8.68
Hartnett, Edward, 15 Copeland St.	4.50
Hartnett, Josephine A., 5 Royal St.	5.46
Hartshorn, Fred, 33 Prentiss St.	2.00
Hipple, Lowell B., 231 Common St.	7.39
Hovanesyan, Barbara, 180 Walnut St.	7.39
Hunter, Charles L., 54 Union St.	5.46
Hurley, John F., 433 Main St.	3.21
Jacqueson, Russell, 11 Yukon St.	4.71
Joy, Marjorie M., 165 Worcester St.	8.04
Ladd, Evelyn, 90 Robbins Rd.	8.04
Lamond, John F., 18 Rosedale Rd.	2.00
Lane, Edwin S., 65 Templeton Pkwy.	2.25
Lehan, Carolyn, 73 Evans St.	2.89
Lindahl, Fred, 20 Prescott St.	4.18
Lopez, Agnes C., 484 Main St.	5.89
Luderer, Lillian, 27 Charles St.	4.00
Maher, Joseph M., 10 Wells Ave.	5.14
Maloney, Charles A., 35 Boylston Street	2.25
Mannaniro, Guy, 37 Dexter Ave.	3.86
Martocchio, Bros., Inc., 42 Forest St.	64.60
Marzilli, Antonio, 70 Westminster Ave.	3.21
McCarthy, George E., 24 Louise St.	13.89
McConnell, Clarence, 368 Mt. Auburn St.	3.86
McConnell, William, 14 Wilmot St.	6.43
McCue, Mary C., 293 No. Beacon St.	4.82
McDonald, Margaret, 57 Church St.	4.82
McDougall, Elizabeth A., 23 Oakland Street	2.00
Meehan, Joseph D., 11 Edenfield Ave.	2.25
Monahan, Helen, 68A Edenfield Avenue	2.00
Mooney, George E., 134 Westminster Ave.	2.00
Moore, Donald W., 194 Palfrey St.	2.57
Mortell, John, 17 Keenan St.	7.71
Murnaghan, Cecelia, 199 Palfrey St.	2.00
Murphy, Jeremiah F., 136 Orchard St.	3.86
Nahigian, Olga A., 25 Quimby St.	6.43
Nardella, Waldo, 234 Arlington St.	3.86
O'Leary, Florence M., 52 Copeland St.	3.21
O'Leary & Tracy Chair Co., 125 Spring St.	4.82
Owen, Frederick E., 2 Hillside St.	2.57
Paul, Kenneth D., 286 Belmont St.	7.71
Peck, William C., 109 Boyd St.	5.79
Phillips, Carl, 133 Templeton Pkwy.	2.25

Piantedosi, Antonio, 16 New Lexington St.	3.21
Piantedosi, Joseph, 183 Fayette St.	8.04
Pierce, Charles, 537 Mt. Auburn St.	9.64
Piscopo, Catheleen D., 27 Gleason Street	2.00
Ranney, Mabel, 114 Fayette St.	13.50
Riley, William J., 74 Olcott St.	3.54
Roach, Anthony T., 15 Green Street Terrace	16.39
Robinson, Herbert E., 25 Palmer St.	5.14
Rolland, Joseph, 33 Springfield St.	2.36
Rollins, Katherine M., 61 Eliot St.	16.39
Russell, Elizabeth, 304 School Street	4.50
Serafini, Victor, 466 Arsenal St.	2.00
Shanahan, Henry W., 136 Cypress St.	17.67
Stone, Elewellyn, 734 Belmonst St.	3.86
Sullivan, Edward J., 363 Carver Rd.	3.21
Sullivan, Lawrence, 31 Fitchburg St.	7.72
Sullivan, Leo E., 60 No. Beacon St.	2.57
Sweeney, Edward J., 6 Acton St.	2.00
Sylvester, E. Robert, 14 Cypress St.	2.57
Tattrie, Jennie M., 52 Spring St.	4.50
Tuttle, Henry G., 42 Porter St.	2.00
Uberti, William, 52 Crawford St.	4.18
Valentino, Alphonse, 11 Norseman Ave.	2.89
Volante, Lena, 20 Merryfield Ave.	4.50
Volante, Ralph, 26 Quincy St.	2.00
Walsh, Herbert J., 14 Chester St.	2.00
Whitney, Charles A., 15 Fifield St.	2.00
Willis, W. Jean, 573 Main St. .:...	4.18
Wolchojian, Martin, 46 Elton Ave.	5.46
Zaino, Frank P., Jr., 25 Norseman Ave.	3.21
Zirhut, Alan H., 29 Robbins Rd.	8.04

Committed August 6, 1934

Alexander, Grace, 324 Arlington St.	2.00
*Alford, James A., Jr., 485 Main St.	3.37
Alvin, Arthur, 13 Fifth Ave. .:...	7.66
Arone, Lawrence, 15 Keith St.	3.13
Bartoli, Mary, 16 James St.	3.22
Beattie, Grace B., 32 Olcott St.	2.78
Bedding, Grace M., 100 Fayette St. ....:	2.14
Bellis, Christina, 56 Putnam St.	2.00
Benson, Frank W., 105 Union St.	2.94
Bernsdorf, George E., 174 School St.	3.13
Biddescombe, Frank C., 146 Pleasant Street	3.22

Blanchett, Robert T., 87 Arsenal Street	4.93
Blue, Mary L., 25 New Lexington Street	2.00
Boccadaro, Ida, 308 Main St.	3.86
Botti, Melle, 18 Merryfield Ave	2.78
Bottomley, Arthur O., 53 Carroll St	2.00
*Boyajian, Gazaros, 52-A Melendy Ave	3.75
Boyajian, Nazareth, 40 Laurel St	19.01
Boyd, May L., 42 Porter St	2.00
Breen, John J., 6 Putnam St.	6.03
Bresnahan, Thomas J., 17 Cushman Rd., Brighton	2.00
Bristol Donald D., 221 Common St.	4.29
Brooks, Benjamin J., 33 Bancroft St.	7.50
Brown, Herbert G., 147 Morse St	2.00
Brown, Jennie L., 115 Common St	2.35
Buccheri, Mary, 346 Arlington St.	8.30
Buckley, John J., 30 Chauncey St	2.00
*Burke, Francis J., 40 Eliot St.	2.57
*Burke, James, 111 Harnden Ave.	3.82
Burke, Walter E., 105 Pleasant St.	2.00
Caferelli, Arthur J., 105 Pleasant St	2.00
Callahan, William, 146 Pleasant St	2.00
Campbell, Esther N., 15 Carleton Ter	8.30
Carva, Joseph, 41 Quirk Street	5.24
Casella, James J., 32 Oakland St.	2.00
Chakalas, George P., 21 Berkeley St.	2.00
Chatel, Edward J., 95 Brookline St., Boston	2.00
Christopher, Dorothy, 541 Main St.	4.82
Ciavardone, James V., 10 St. Mary	2.89
Clark, Benjamin, 81 Mt. Auburn St.	2.00
Clark, John J., 12 Oliver Rd.	6.16
Coakley, Ellen, 293 Lexington St.	20.63
Coffey, Anna, 47 Kondazian St.	2.00
Coffey Margaret, 47 Kondazian St.	2.00
Coleman, Helen E., 293 Lexington St.	2.00
Condon, William F., 64 Dexter Ave.	4.69
Connors, Catherine, 141 Galen Street	2.00
Conroy Walter, 32 Templeton Pkwy	2.00
Consolasi, Joseph, 272 Palfrey St.	2.00
Consolidated Marble Works, 94 Putnam St.	4.31
Conte, Bartolomeo, 104 Arlington St.	2.00
Cooper, John H., 160 Sycamore St.	3.53
Couture, Joseph H., 42 Carroll St.	2.00
Covell, Joseph, 99 Westminster Ave.	2.00
Coveno, Angelo, 266 Westminster Avenue	2.41

Cram, James W., 41 Eliot St.	2.00
Crosby, John J., 34 Hawthorne St.	11.35
Currey, John L., 24 Louise St.	2.95
Davis, Alice J., 106 Cypress St.	2.14
Dedekian, Deran, 138 Nichols Ave.	5.77
DeFilippo, Geraldina, 70 Westminster Ave.	21.21
DeLorie, John L., 19 Oakland St.	2.06
DeQuattro, James, 38 Dartmouth St.	2.00
Derounian, Susan et al, 19 Chauncey St.	2.00
DeStefano, Nicholas, 27 Dewey St.	2.35
DiPasquale, Francesco, 88 Arlington St.	6.15
Divanian, Harry, 278 No. Beacon St.	2.00
*Donovan, Edward M., 13 Olney St.	2.00
Downer, Stuart B., 303 Waverley Avenue	2.66
Doyle, Joseph, 11 New Lexington St.	2.00
Dozois, Mildred J., 9 Rutland St.	2.06
Ducharme, Mae A., 80 Edgecliffe Rd.	2.00
Duvall, Edwin H., 179 Waverley Ave.	3.43
East, Cyril A., 271 Pleasant St.	17.83
Edes, Dorothy M., 160 Summer St.	2.00
Evans, Robert A., 76 Prospect St.	2.00
Farley, Florence, 95 Lexington St.	12.53
Feidermann, Henry, 174 Orchard St.	3.21
Femino, John, 900 Harrison Ave, Boston	3.82
Field, Albert L., 154 School St.	7.48
Figliolini, Anthony, 73 Springfield Street	8.84
Files, Addison E., 126 Chapman St.	2.17
Flamburis, George, 137 Templeton Pkwy.	2.00
Flynn, Bartholomew F., 104 Morse St.	2.00
Fogarty, Edward J., 543 Mt. Auburn St.	2.00
Foley, Richard F., 42 Winsor Ave.	15.77
*Fostie, Emil, 50 Cypress St.	2.00
Fowler, James H., 477 Congress St., Portland, Me.	33.56
Freeman, Mary A., 488 Main St.	9.89
Fundeklian, Antonio, 16 Lloyd Rd.	2.24
Gildea, Leo J., 18 Fifield St.	2.06
Goodrow, Albert, 616 Arsenal St.	2.14
Gould, Blanche, 29 Lawrence St.	3.62
Gregory, Maud, 12 Bancroft St.	5.36
Hall, Charles J., 9 Harnden Ave.	2.57
Hancock, Walter J., 5 Winter St.	7.17
Hanrahan, James F. Jr., 780 Belmont St.	15.43
Hard, T. Oliver, 35 Upland Rd.	13.39
Harper, Clayton C., 146 Robbins Rd.	2.00

Harris, Charles W., 127 Evans St.	7.24
Harrington, Paul, 37 Gilbert St.	2.00
Harris, Jessie E., 165 Worcester St.	2.00
Hartung, Paul G., 27 Maplewood St.	4.56
Henault, Clover, 80 Hillside Ave.	2.99
Hinsman, James R., 35 Lawrence St.	3.13
Holmes, William J., 6 Howe St.	2.66
Huggan, Arthur A., 69 Hillside Rd.	20.20
Hughes, James, 113 Arsenal St.	2.00
Iodice, William, 124 School St.	3.85
Jacqueson, Russell, 11 Yukon Ave.	2.78
Johnson, Charles L., 343 School St.	2.06
Jones, Arthur D., 29 Carroll St.	1.86
Kasparian, Lillian, 77 Templeton Pkwy.	8.19
Keough, John C., 187 Arsenal St.	2.00
Kerkian, Takookie, 47 Hazel Street	3.13
Kilcoyne, Josephine F., 56 Putnam St.	3.62
Kilonis, John D., 57 Mt. Auburn Street	2.68
Kivell, Thomas F., 15 Longfellow Rd.	6.51
Kusick, James, 44 Brimmer St.	2.00
Lamond, John, 18 Rosedale Rd.	8.68
Larrabee, Frank L., 51 Boyd St.	2.00
Lawrence, James F., 24 Louise St.	11.26
Leonard, Paul W., 63 Hillside Rd.	2.80
Lindahl, Frank, 26 Prescott St.	2.00
Livoli, Louis, 130 Charles River Rd.	2.35
Lopez, Agnes, 484 Main St.	17.89
Lundahl, Frank, 26 Prescott St.	2.00
Lynch, John C., 32 Richards Rd.	4.82
Lyons, Nora A., 50 Evans St.	2.14
MacDonald, Catherine, 29 Keenan St.	2.00
MacDonald, Edna M., 35 Chapman St.	2.00
MacDougall, Clifford R., 195 Watertown St.	2.14
Malone, Francis J., 10 Summit Rd.	3.00
Maloney, Pauline, 105 Winsor Ave.	2.65
Maloy, William P., 36 Piermont St.	5.14
*Manning, Mary L., 234 Mt. Auburn St.	2.00
Manning, Mary V., 28 Purvis St.	2.78
Marchese, Bernice M., 35 Oakland St.	2.00
Margosian, Harry, 14 Adams Ave.	2.57
Marshall, Allister F., 153 Pleasant St.	2.00
Martocchio Bros. Inc., 42 Forest St.	21.00
Martocchio Trucking Co., Inc., 42 Forest St.	15.67
Mastrangelo, Louis, 169 Winsor Ave.	2.78

McCarthy, John J., 4 Maplewood Ave.................................... 4.00
McGary, Percy E., 495 Mt. Auburn St........................... 12.64
*McCourtie, Althea M., 135 Evans St............................ 6.37
McCue, Mary C., 273 No. Beacon St.................................... 6.75
McGivern, Frank J., 5 Hilltop Rd............................ 2.00
McHugh, Margaret A., 55 Mt. Auburn St............................ 2.00
McLellan, John R., 45 Mt. Auburn St............................ 4.25
McNeill, Daniel F., 188 Washington St., Newton................ 2.57
Meduri, Frank, 26 Arsenal St........................... 3.53
Meehan, Dorothy M., 11 Edenfield Ave............................ 4.69
Meehan, Joseph D., 11 Edenfield Ave............................ 2.00
Merlino, Agostino, 21 Ralph St............................ 4.00
Minasian, Hagop, 95 Nichols Ave............................ 2.99
Minasian, Karikin S., 20 Wilson Ave............................ 15.00
Miner, Kenneth H., 25 New Lexington St............................ 4.10
Mirabile, Vito, 305 Mt. Auburn St............................ 6.99
Mooney, George F., 134 Westminster Ave........................... 4.82
Moore, Marion C. T., 291 Mt. Auburn St............................ 2.78
Moran, Crohane J., 41 Fairfield St............................ 2.57
Morris, Charles L., 22 Putnam St............................ 3.75
Mortell, John, 17 Keenan St............................ 2.68
Moulton, Catherine H., 95 Church St............................ 2.57
Mullay, James H., 15 Purvis Street 11.56
Murray, Charles F., 11 Irma Ave............................ 2.00
Nahigian, John S., 37 Poole St., Medford............................ 2.66
Nally, Thomas F., 25 Bancroft St............................ 5.58
Nardella, Anthony, Arlington St............................ 3.64
Normine, John B., 66 Prentiss St............................ 2.00
North, Margaret H., 37 Garfield St............................ 4.88
Oates, Edward A., 37 Hazel St............................ 3.21
O'Donnell, George C., 112 No. Beacon St............................ 6.43
O'Hannesian, Barbara, 180 Walnut St............................ 5.78
O'Leary, Florence M., 58 Copeland St............................ 3.13
Panosian, Sarkis S., 31 Porter St............................ 2.00
Parray, Alice E., 26 Louise St............................ 8.36
Pasqualetto, Gilbert, 42 Forest St............................ 2.00
Perry, Maxim J., 10 Hovey St............................ 7.07
Peterson, Albert G., 49 Prescott St............................ 2.00
Peterson, Alfonso E., 49 Prescott St............................ 2.00
Pickens Roscoe A., 117 Common St............................ 3.43
Pilon, Victor A., 141 Pleasant Street 2.00
Prelack, Ethel, 68 Edgecliffe Road 5.58
Pyne, Mary E., 104 Waverley Ave............................ 3.21
Quinn, Horace A., 52 Edgecliffe Rd............................ 12.86

Rand, Helen M., 176 E. Boylston St..	2.00
Rich, Anthony, 66 Sparkhill	2.00
Rigdon, Elvin B., 819 Mt. Auburn St..	2.89
Riley, Nina L., 16 Middlesex St.................................	12.00
Ristango, Domenico, 231 Arlington St.......................	19.15
Robinson, Frank C., 25 Palmer St..............................	3.37
*Robinson, Gladys M., 25 Palmer St...........................	5.58
Roche, Emily M., 14 Royal St.................................	2.00
Rooney, Edward D., 110 Riverside St...........................	2.00
Rooney,Eugene, 23 Fifth Ave................................	2.00
Russo, Antonio, 249 Lexington Street	17.68
Ryan, William J., 37 Belmont St...............................	3.21
Shaw, Florence M., 141 Common St.............................	6.37
Shaw, Russell W., 36 Irving St...............................	2.00
Shaw, Thomas, 36 Irving St..................................	2.00
Shea, Charles E., 70 Salisbury Rd.............................	2.00
Shedd, Charlotte, 91 Standish Rd..............................	5.07
Sheridan, Thomas F., 5 Theurer Pk.............................	2.68
Shields, Peter, 229 Arsenal St................................	7.24
Silver, Cyril G., 10 Hillside Rd..............................	2.00
Smith, Chester E., 82 Edgecliffe Rd............................	2.14
Smith, George F., 92 No. Beacon St.	2.95
Smith, Gladys M., 54 Hersom St..............................	2.89
*Stefaniak, Peter J., 38 Dartmouth St.........................	3.43
Stratton, Ralph R., 26 Richards Rd............................	2.24
Surabina, George M., 72 Prentiss St...........................	2.00
Sylvester, E. Robert, 14 Cypress St...........................	2.14
Tattrie, Jennie M., 52 Spring St..............................	3.13
Taurson, Rose M., 504 Arsenal St.............................	2.00
Torres, John R., 234 Summer St..............................	2.35
Troungeau, Nelson, 13 Adams St..............................	4.93
Vahey, Ruth P., 238 No. Beacon St............................	3.13
Valentino, George, 11 Norseman Ave...........................	2.00
Veiring, Bernard, 164 Edenfield Ave...........................	2.57
Verros, Costas D., 13 Porter St...............................	10.28
Volante, Lena, 20 Merryfield Ave.............................	8.30
Volante, William A., 20 Merryfield Ave........................	6.64
Vrock, Rocco, 72 Olcott St...................................	3.62
Walsh, Clement G., 30 Quincy St..............................	5.14
Watertown Excavating Co., 200 Summer St.....................	64.93
Welch, Perley B., 8 Purvis St................................	4.50
Wemple, Robert, 4 Adams Ave................................	2.00
Williams, George F., 157 Spruce St...........................	2.14
Willson, Donald R., 176 Waverley Ave.........................	2.41

Wright, Edward F., 44 Fayette St.	12.77
York, Charles A., 275 Main St.	2.68
Zeller, George A., Watertown Arsenal	22.91

Committed December 12, 1934

*Abadesa, Vincent, 106 Common Street	$2.00
*Achorn, William O., 722 Mt. Auburn St.	5.49
*Adams, Chester A., 146 School St.	2.00
*Adess, Milton, 22 Kimball Rd.	4.82
*Akillian, George, 535 Mt. Auburn St.	2.00
Albee, Herbert L., 44 Cypress St.	2.00
*Alberico, Jerry, 19 Howard St.	2.00
Allen, Victor E., 106 Boylston St.	2.00
American Radiator Co., 240 Mt. Vernon St.	2.00
*Ames, Harvey L., 178 Palfrey St.	2.00
*Amiralian, Mary S., 24 Fairfield St.	3.37
*Amos, Agnes, 129 Dexter Ave.	6.32
Amrock, Stephen J., 119 Summer St.	2.00
Anderson, Julia, 78 Marion Rd.	7.61
Andrew, Victor, 25 Cottage Place	4.00
Andrews Milk Co., 43 Franklin St.	6.11
*Androski, Joseph C., 133 Lexington St.	2.00
*Androski, Stanley C., 133 Lexington St.	3.42
*Arakelian, Charles B., 29 Merryfield Ave.	12.38
*Argento, Joseph, 81 Elm St.	2.00
Armstrong, Charles, 69 Walnut St.	2.46
*Armstrong, George R., Jr., 6 Winthrop St.	3.69
*Arnold, Howard M., 30 Carver Rd.	4.00
Arone, Joseph, 23 Dewey St.	2.00
*Arone, Lawrence, 6 Keith St.	2.00
*Arzoomanian, Robert, 12 Porter St.	2.68
Aufiero, Vencenzo, 57 Crawford St.	2.00
*Avedian, Robert, 7 Porter St.	2.00
Averill, Victor W., 185 Spruce St.	2.00
*Ayers, J. Robert, 207 Common Street	2.00
*Ayers, J. Robert, 20 7Common St.	2.00
Bagley, Dudley, 146 Hillside Rd.	2.00
Bailey, Alice, 82 Dexter Ave.	7.02
*Bailey's Cleansers & Dyers, Inc., 30 Washburn St.	2.68
Baker, George E., 69 Poplar St.	8.43
Baker, Helen M., 106 California St.	2.09
*Baker, Stanley H., 38 Eliot Street	2.00
Barbanti, Charles, 27 Charles St.	2.00
*Barbato, Peter, 11 French St.	2.00

*Barber, Charles E., 12 Walnut St.	8.63
*Barnes, Richard M., 28 Hovey St.	5.15
*Barrett, Kathryn C., 506 Main St.	13.32
Bartholdi, John J., 211 Common St.	9.78
*Bartholomew, Leslie S., 52 Beechwood Ave.	6.12
*Bazarian, Peter, 526 Mt. Auburn St.	2.00
*Becklund, Elmer C., 177 Highland Ave.	2.74
Bennett, Philip S., 23 Olcott St.	4.00
*Benzer, Chester C., 383 School St.	2.00
*Bechner, Alfred W., 38 Kimball Road	4.69
Bernsdorf, George E., 174 School St.	2.00
*Berquist, John H., 197 Arsenal St.	7.10
*Betzold, Edward M., 109 Church St.	5.68
*Bigelow, Julia T., 22 Patten St.	2.00
*Bigham, Carl A., 35 Edenfield Ave.	2.00
Bird, Lewis L., 307 Arsenal St.	2.41
Bishop, John J., 108 Chapman St.	4.87
Black, Edward, 78 Main St.	2.00
Black, Simon S., 84 Edgecliffe Rd.	7.50
Blair, Joseph H., 60 Church St.	2.41
Black, Helena R., 56 Bradford Rd.	2.00
*Blessington, H. Arthur, 7 Laurel St.	7.65
*Boghosian, Arto, 34 Irma Ave.	2.00
Bolduc, Ludger, 105 Arsenal St.	2.00
Bolesiy, Dan, 74 Edgecliffe Road	5.63
*Bond, Herman L., 45 Parker St.	2.00
*Borghetti, Anthony, 133 Arsenal Street	2.25
*Borghetti, John F., 133 Arsenal St.	2.33
*Boris, Felix A., 6 Lyons Street	2.00
*Botti, Emilio, 25 Merrifield Ave.	2.00
*Boujicanian, Arsen, 343 Arlington St.	11.38
*Boujicanian, Hagop M., 343 Arlington St.	2.00
*Boyden, Mabel M., 181 Standish Rd.	2.00
Boyle, Robert M., 25 Beechwood Ave.	2.00
*Boynton Alvah B., 750 Belmont St.	2.00
Brackett, Augusta N., 51 Fayette St.	4.00
Branch, Harold R., 7 Bromfield St.	2.00
Brant, Francis J., 46 Union St.	2.00
Brenan, Mary S., 47 Hovey St.	2.43
*Brennan, John P., 41 Elton Ave.	3.00
Brennan, Mary A., 129 School St.	4.00
Brochu, Joseph, 28 Copeland St.	2.00
*Brock, Elaine W., 81 Robbins Rd.	2.00
Brown, Gilbert L., 870 Belmont St.	6.32

Brownell, Earle S., 124 Galen St.	2.00
*Bryant, Joseph W., 141 Bellevue Rd.	8.25
Buckley, John J., 30 Chauncey St.	2.00
Bullen, Ralph F., Jr., 225 Arsenal St.	2.00
*Burke, Edmund W., 76 Spruce St.	2.00
Burke, James J., 51 Olney St.	8.51
*Burns, Frank D., 206 No. Beacon St.	2.00
Burns, George V., 63 Eliot St.	7.07
Burns, James S., 11 Cushman St.	6.32
Busconi, Joseph, 40 Quimby St.	4.41
Butler ,Lillian M., 19 Derby Rd.	2.00
Butler, Thomas W., 98 Westminster Ave.	6.81
Button, George D., 817 Mt. Auburn St.	2.00
Caccavaro, Anna, 6 Lyons St.	2.62
*Caferelli, Americo, 164 Walnut St.	4.15
Calarese, John B., 96 Putnam St.	2.00
*Calden, William H., 52 Morse St.	2.00
*Calkins, Walter W., 76 Poplar St.	7.23
Callahan, Arthur, 9 Derby Rd.	2.68
*Canady, Lois J., 73 Spruce St.	2.89
*Cannalonga, Vito, 133 Arsenal St.	2.00
Capone, Abgelo, 28 Hudson St.	2.57
Capone, William A., 19 New Lexington St.	4.00
*Carew, Mary K., 26 Wolcott Rd.	5.15
Carey, Ethel Barbara, 40 Fitchburg St.	7.71
Carlstrom, Carl S., 55 Pequosette St.	2.01
*Carpenter, Roy B., 64 Lowell Ave.	2.00
Carroll, Frederick, 53Shattuck Rd.	10.92
Caruso, Anthony, 68 Forest St.	4.01
Caruso, Laurence, 68 Forest St.	13.26
Caruso, Mary, 87 Summer St.	2.00
Caruso, Pasquale, 87 Summer St.	2.00
*Cavanough, William J., 10 Lawrence St.	2.00
*Cawley, Agnes G., 85 Edenfield Ave.	2.00
Cazmay, Thomas W., Jr., 14 Birch Rd.	9.93
*Chamberlain, Hilda M., 129 Worcester St.	2.00
Chamian, Agop, 121 Dexter Ave.	2.00
Chase, Alice F., 1573 Commonwealth Ave., Brighton	2.01
*Chase, Charles O., 6 Patten St.	8.43
*Chase, Sarah M., 66 Bates Rd.	2.00
*Christie, Thomas G., 11 Melendy Ave.	2.00
*Christopher, Speror, 10 Kondazian St.	2.00
Clair, Basil E., 121 Chapman St.	2.00
Clark, Gladys M., 15 Bostonia Ave.	2.00

*Clark, Harold B., 74 Spruce St.	2.00
Clayton, Edward, 16 Bostonia Ave.	2.24
*Clayton, Robert F., 202 Maplewood St.	3.91
*Clear, Edward J., 18 Stuart St.	2.00
Clericuzio, Esther, 11 Hazel St.	2.24
*Clinton, Elizabeth K., 30 Templeton Pkwy.	2.79
Coffin, Alice G., 24 Beacon Pk.	2.00
*Colburn, Horace E., 66 Morse St.	2.00
*Cole, Victor B., 11 Channing Rd.	2.68
*Coleman, Warren, 38 Wilmot St.	2.00
*Colleran, Joseph P., 18 Palmer St.	2.00
*Colligan, Elmer E., 24 Church Street	10.60
*Comates, Peter, 111 Riverside St.	2.00
Condon, William F., Jr., 64 Dexter Ave.	4.17
*Conner, Stephen, 119 Evans St.	11.08
*Connors, Joseph P., 83 Rutland St.	2.00
*Cooke, Edmund W., 53 Carver Rd.	3.75
*Corazzini, Armondi, 31 Cypress Street	2.00
*Corazzini, Fred, 31 Cypress St.	4.42
*Corazzini, Pasquale, 115 Putnam St.	2.00
Corcoran, Edmund, 65 Palfrey St.	2.00
*Corcoran, Norma H., 15 Chauncey St.	3.21
*Corsi, Bernardo, 28 Waverley Ave.	11.06
*Cosse, George, 7 Whitney St.	13.34
*Costanzo, Guido, 16 Cross St.	2.00
*Costello, Patrick J., 193 Arsenal St.	2.00
*Courtney, Frank E., 33 Franklin St.	2.00
*Couture, Joseph H., 42 Carroll St.	4.83
*Coyne, Ellen M., 68 Commonwealth Rd.	5.62
*Cream Fried Cake Co., 19 Brooks St., Brighton	9.47
*Creaser, Lester J., 12 Carleton Terrace	5.63
Crescitelli, Arthur, Edenfield Ave.	2.00
*Cronk, Milton G., 20 Washburn St.	3.18
*Crossley, Victor A., 50 Prentiss St.	2.28
*Crossman, Everett S., 34 Gertrude St.	2.00
*Crowell, Martha Reiman, 146 Spruce St.	3.85
Crupi, Joseph R., 11 Keith St.	2.00
Cunningham, R. Telfer, 24 Channing Rd.	7.10
*Curren, Maurice, 240 Waltham Street	2.00
*Curwen, Reginald, 12 Dunton Rd.	11.06
*Cushing, Andrew F., 29 Fifield St.	6.43
Daley, James H., 8 Gay Rd.	15.56
*Dalton, Mary A., 207 No. Beacon St.	2.00
Daly, Wyncliff F., 120 No. Beacon St.	2.00

Dansie, Thomas, 29 Piermont St..........	2.00
*Daughters, Mary H., 15 Knowles Rd..........	15.50
*Daughters, Roscoe F., 15 Knowles Rd..........	5.14
Davenport, Alfred M., 88 Grove St..........	4.17
Davis, Herbert N., 12 Watertown St..........	2.00
*Davis, Russell W., 33 Stearns Rd..........	8.51
Days, James, 155 Spruce St..........	2.00
DelPapa, Angelo, 16 Cottage St..........	2.00
*DeRounian, Edward, 14 Hosmer St..........	2.00
*Deschenes ,Arthur J., 36 Upland Rd..........	2.00
DeMarco, Anthony, 99 Spring St..........	2.00
Denny, Robert E., 37 Kondazian St..........	2.00
Dependable Operators Corp., 416 Arsenal St..........	6.42
Derderian, Margaret F., 208 Common St..........	8.35
*Derderian, Setrak, 216 Common St..........	16.28
*Deschenes, Arthur J., 36 Upland Rd..........	4.55
Deveau, Andrew, 754 Mt. Auburn Street	2.00
*Dexter, Evans K., 101 Lovell Rd.	11.57
*DiBacco, Santo, 78 School St..........	2.00
Dickey, Robert A., 44 Grenville Rd..........	2.01
*DiDonato, Antonia, 23 James St..........	2.00
*Diliberto, Joseph, 749 Mt. Auburn St..........	11.06
*Dodakin, Charles A., 73 Evans St..........	3.21
*Dodge, Waldo E., 191 Maplewood St..........	8.43
*Doe, William A., 16 Russell Ave..........	7.84
Dolan, Charles H., 98 Franklin St..........	2.00
*Dolbier, Charles, 99 Boyd St..........	2.00
*Dolbier, Charles B., 99 Boyd St..........	2.00
*Dolbier, Walter H., 174 Waverley Ave..........	2.00
Dominick, Antonio, 105 Winsor Ave..........	2.00
*Donald, William H. et Charles H. Glidden, 114 Riverside..	2.25
Donovan, John J., 11-A Fairfield St..........	9.47
Doonan, Herbert J., 12 Birch Rd..........	15.56
*Doria, Elvira, 73 Dexter Ave..........	2.00
*Dracos, Charles G., 55 Kondazian St..........	2.00
Drago, Elizabeth V., 11-A Dartmouth St..........	2.00
*Drake, William A., 23 Hardy Ave..........	3.37
Dubois, Eugene, 86 Boylston St..........	2.25
Dudley, G. Walter, 17 Spruce St..........	2.00
Dunderdale, John J., 224 Warren St..........	2.00
*Dunham, Charlotte D., 34 Merrill Road	4.00
Dunlap, Helen A., 32 Olcott St..........	2.81
*Dunston, Hubert W., 48 Whitney St..........	2.46
Durnan, Patrick F., 17 Melendy Ave..........	2.01

Dwyer, Paul, 74 Springfield St.	2.00
Dyer, Thomas F., 101 Langdon Ave.	2.57
*Eagle-Picher Lead Co., 11 Wharf St., Boston	9.74
Eagleson, Walter B., 61 Hillside St.	2.00
*Eason, A. Russell, 72 Palfrey St.	7.71
Eastman, Elmer C., 168 Walnut St.	4.00
Eastman, Warren J., 44 Olcott St.	4.34
Eaton, Leroy S., 144 Winsor Ave.	10.32
*Eaton, Woodrow J., 64 Hillside Rd.	2.00
Ebert, Paul J., 41 Prospect St.	2.00
*Elasqua, Anthony, 151 Nichols Ave.	2.00
Elbag, Anne, 29 Coolidge Hill Rd.	2.00
Eleftherion, Mike, 200 Arlington St.	2.00
Ellis, Dorothy A., 28 Bradford Rd.	2.89
*Emerton, Fred D., 83 Forest St.	4.00
*Emery, George H., 41 Wilmot St.	2.00
Emery, Paul R., 41 Wilmot St.	2.00
Emery, Robert, 77 Dexter Ave	5.78
English, Dorothy H., 40 Pequosette St.	2.00
*Eoksuzian, George, 158 Boylston St.	2.68
*Erickson, Henry F., 26 Cypress St.	2.00
Erskine, Doris L., 91 Common St.	6.03
Eshelman, John W. Sons, 244 No. Queen St., Lancaster, Pa.	7.90
Evans, Robert, 206 Pleasant St.	2.01
Fahlstrom, Anna M., 104 Beechwood Ave.	2.68
*Fairbanks, Burtis F., 384 Charles River Rd.	8.80
*Fairbanks, Franklin G., 44 Spruce St.	8.03
*Fairbanks, Ralph W., 374 Charles River Rd.	2.00
Fairmont Creamery Co. of Maine, 35 Commercial St., Boston	7.10
*Fallon, Margaret E., 6 Porter St.	2.00
Farese, Angelo, 16 Gleason St.	10.97
Farese, Teresa, 264 Warren St.	2.00
*Farley, Florence, 95 Lexington St.	2.00
*Farrenkopf, August E., 17 Thurston Rd.	7.71
Fay, Elizabeth M., 167 Waverley Ave.	2.00
*Feehan, Peter E., 10 Oliver Rd.	2.00
Feloretos, James, 29 Hearn St.	2.00
Ferguson, Thomas P., 118 Summer St.	2.00
*Ferraro, Frank, 67 Prentiss St.	2.00
*Ferraro, Napoleon, 67 Prentiss St.	2.00
*Field, Robert F., 104 Church St.	5.79
*Files, Addison E., Jr., 222 Arlington St.	2.00
Files, Walter W., 12 Hardy Ave.	5.46

Fiske, Raymond M., 42 Maplewood St.	2.14
Fitzgerald, Herbert, 32 Laurel St.	2.00
*Fitzmaurice, John E., 23 Irma Ave.	2.00
Fitzpatrick, Joseph T., 28 Melendy Ave.	6.26
Flagg, Hubert W., 27 Piermont St.	4.69
*Flecca, Madeline, 182 Walnut St.	2.00
*Flecca, William G., 18 Norseman Avenue	2.00
Fleet, William H., 28 Gertrude St.	2.00
Flewelling, Robert, 7 Dexter Ave.	4.01
*Foley, Gerald A., 42 Winsor Ave.	9.47
*Foley, Michael F., 463 Main St.	3.35
Folino, Antonio F., 33 Morton St.	8.43
Ford, Ernest B., 738 Mt. Auburn St.	4.57
Foster, Mildred, 33 Lawrence St.	2.00
Fowler, Walter H., 72 Bradford Rd.	2.00
Francis, Hazel M., 36 Charles River Rd.	2.00
Frank, Russell W., 34 Adams St.	2.00
*Frazier, Freeman B., 184 Sycamore St.	2.00
*Fredericks, Louise, 26 Cypress St.	2.00
Fredette, Francis A., 107 Arsenal St.	2.00
Freeman, Harold R., 48 Capitol St.	2.00
*French, Gordon R., 8 Westland Rd.	8.51
French, Vaughn H., 20 Washburn St.	2.00
Frezza, Marco, 4 Swett Ct.	4.17
Friant, Merriman, 16 Belknap Terrace	3.62
*Fuller, Carl G., 87 Bradford Rd.	6.43
*Fuller, Francis B., 24 Hovey St.	2.00
Fuller, Myrtle E., Higgins Beach, Scarboro, Me.	5.68
Fundeklian, Alexander, 18 Lloyd St.	2.00
Gaffney, Cornelia, 28 Center St.	2.00
Gage, Charles R., 68 Bradford Rd.	2.00
*Gage, James M., 38 Standish Rd.	2.68
Gallagher, Richard, 20 Oakley Rd.	2.00
*Gandolfo, Vito C., 114 Dexter Ave.	2.00
*Garabedian, John, 80 Boylston St.	2.01
Garber, Rubin E., 185 Grove St.	2.00
Gardner, Burton, 158 Worcester St.	14.78
*Garofolo, Frank, 12 Linden St.	2.01
Gasper, John R., 435 Mt. Auburn St.	2.00
Gass, Elton B., 73 Walnut St.	4.00
*Gaudreau, Leo W., 11 Whitney St.	6.75
*Gavoor, Aram, Howe St.	2.57
Gaziano, Stella, 57 Warren St.	8.51
*Geiger, Bertha E., 364 Arlington St.	5.78

Geishecker, Philip, 120 Charles River Rd.	2.81
*Geoghegan, Eleanor, 78 Beechwood Ave.	2.57
*Gibson, Alice R., 55 Chapman St.	6.43
Giggey, Harold F., 11 Olcott St.	2.00
Gilberg, Henrik, 91 Bradford Rd.	2.00
*Gilbert, Laura E., 19 Malden St.	2.00
*Ginn, William E., 784 Belmont St.	2.95
*Giovanditti, Leonardo, 40 Melendy Ave.	2.25
*Glasheen, Agnes, 24 Capitol St.	2.09
Gleason, Dorothy, 40 Otis St.	2.00
Glickman, Edward B., 8 Oliva Rd., Brighton.	2.00
*Gloasa, William R., 375 Mt. Auburn St.	2.00
Godsoe, Clarence E., 156 Belmont St.	2.00
*Godwin, Harold A., 120 Riverside St.	4.28
*Gogwer, Leonard, 8 Mason Rd.	9.47
Goss, Annie, 263 Boylston St.	3.75
*Gostos, Evelyn V., 11 Patten St.	2.68
*Gould, Hiram, 11 Francis St.	2.00
*Gould Oil Burner Ser., 63 Orchard St.	9.72
*Graham, George C., Jr., 122 Barnard Ave.	2.00
Graham, Grace, 286 No. Beacon St.	2.00
Greeley, Viola, 83 Bradford Rd.	2.00
Green, Harry J., 31 Priest Rd.	2.74
Green, Hugh, 91 Mt. Auburn St.	2.00
*Green, William, 29 Priest Rd.	2.00
*Greene, Frederick, 35 Stearns Rd.	5.46
*Greene, James W., 74 Evans St.	9.00
*Greene, William J., 29 Priest Rd.	2.68
Greenwood, Anna, 93 California St.	2.00
*Greer, Lloyd E., 476 Mt. Auburn St.	4.89
*Gregoire, Wilfred G., 23 Gleason St.	2.00
*Griffith, Richard, 165 Summer St.	2.00
*Grimes, Wilfred P., 11 Swette Ct.	6.00
*Grundstrom, Carl W., 63 Church St.	2.00
Gulesian, Willis H., 46 Salisbury Rd.	2.00
Gullason, Rose A., 79 Dexter Ave.	2.00
*Gunter, Fred C., 53 Fairview Ave.	7.23
*Guy, Walter, 121 Marshall St.	2.00
*Guzzetti, James, 101 Arlington Street	2.78
*Haffey, Bernard, 85 Union St.	2.00
Hall, Dorothy M., 160 Summer St.	2.00
*Hall, Walter, 14 Beacon Pk.	2.00
*Hammond, Verna, 238 Bellevue Rd.	2.81
*Hampson, Peapeon, 10 Kimball Rd.	5.89

*Hannan, Theresa, 67 Hazel St.	2.00
*Hannem, Lillian M., 25 Adams St.	2.00
*Hannigan, Martin, 128 Summer St.	2.43
Hanson, David, 29 Lincoln St.	2.00
Hardy, Roland, 122 Charles River Rd.	8.51
*Harmenig, Amanda, 175 No. Beacon St.	5.68
*Harmon, Belma, 266 Belmont St.	3.37
*Haroian, Nishan, 14 Wells Ave.	2.00
Harrington, Joseph, 7 Woodleigh Rd.	2.00
Harrington, Michael, 37 Gilbert St.	7.87
*Harris, Franklin E., 12 Laurel St.	4.74
Hartenstein, Mae, 27 Boylston St. W.	2.00
Hartshorn, Marie, 33 Prentiss St.	2.00
*Havender, Harold, 244 No. Beacon St.	2.00
*Hawksworth, Clara, 17 Eliot St., Jamaica Plain	2.00
Hayden, Frances B., 32 Warwick Rd.	4.82
Hayes, John J., 467 Main St.	2.00
Hazelum, Mary, 43 Oakland St.	2.06
*Healy, Maurice, Purvis St.	12.75
*Heffernan, John E., 84 Charles River Rd.	4.42
*Hegarty, Richard, 91 Orchard St.	2.89
Henderson, Francis, 78 Carroll St.	9.47
*Hennessy, Anna, 14 Maplewood St.	2.00
Hernandez, Luis R., 99 Highland Ave.	3.08
*Hertach, Frederick, 125 Marshall St.	2.01
*Heshion, Frank J., 92 Fitchburg St.	10.60
*Hetherington, William, 712 Belmont St.	2.00
*Higgins, Anna F., 89 Galen St.	8.51
*Higgins, Edwin M., 18 Hovey St.	6.75
Hilliard, Raymond J., 38 Dartmouth St.	5.06
Hoffman, Jane B., 46 Hall Ave.	5.14
*Hogan, Helen B., 232 Common St.	22.16
*Hogan, Mary L., 232 Common St.	10.31
Holman, William O., 64 Westminster Ave.	2.00
Holmes, Arnold E., 8 Cross St.	2.00
*Holmes, Ralph A., 104 Beechwood Ave.	3.75
Hood, James H., Jr., 274 Common St.	2.00
Hopkins, Cleveland, 8 Chapman St.	2.00
Hovannesian, Mike, 97 Dexter Avenue	2.00
*Hovey, Mae E., 7 Harnden Ave.	2.00
*Howes, Alfred T., 28 Purvis St.	4.00
*Hoyt, George S., 38 Franklin St.	2.00
Huggan, Arthur, 69 Hillside Rd.	2.00
*Hughes, Michael G., 98 Pleasant St.	2.00

*Hughes, William H., 7 Purvis St.	11.06
Hullihen, Claris, 27 Bradford Rd.	2.00
Hunter, Bertha, 28 Irving St.	2.00
*Hutchings, Ferdinand, 7 Fletcher Terrace	2.00
*Hutchinson, Walter, 46 Brookline St.	2.00
Hynes, Theresa, 29 W. Boylston St.	2.00
Iannazzi, Angelo, 302 Arlington St.	2.00
*Ingalls, Edna P., 85 Poplar St.	7.90
Iodice, Michael, 75 Warren St.	2.24
*Irish, Herbert W., 35 Irving St.	5.39
Ives, Walton S., 133 Hillside Road	6.10
Jackson, Carl S., 40 Dexter Ave.	2.00
Jacqueson, Russell, 11 Yukon Ave.	2.00
*Jakeman, Alma C., 71 Lovell Rd.	11.41
James, Robert K., 154 Dexter Avenue	2.00
*Jannos, Lena, 58 Melendy Ave.	2.00
*Jardine, Catherine, 48 Watertown St.	2.00
*Jardine, Thelma, 469-A Pleasant St.	2.28
Jensen, Abe, 52 Arsenal St.	2.00
*Jester, Annie J., 3 Woodleigh Rd.	2.00
Johnson, Albert H., 18 Priest Rd.	2.00
*Johnson, Andrew T., 59 Palfrey St.	2.00
*Johnson, Ernest W., 510 Belmont St.	7.37
Johnson, Howard C., 72 Winsor Ave.	2.00
Johnston, George M., 219 Lexington St.	2.00
Jones, Arthur D., 29 Carroll Street	5.53
*Jones, Hattie L., 19 Edenfield Ave.	2.00
Julian, Anthony, 11 Carlton Terrace	5.36
*Kaderian, Garoferd, 127 Nichols Ave.	4.96
Kalustian, Elmas, 16 Hazel St.	2.41
Kasmouski, Evelyn, 42 Woodleigh Rd.	6.26
*Kaveny, John P., 13 Patten St.	11.57
*Keaney, William J., 4 Theurer Park	7.90
*Kearns, Martin H., 97 Galen St.	2.57
*Keany, George J., 69 Templeton Pkwy.	2.00
*Keddy, Kenneth S., 33 Eliot St.	2.00
Keefe, Agnes E., 24 Francis St.	3.21
Keefe, Arthur C., 7 Cuba St.	2.00
*Keefe, Mary F., 181 School St.	7.71
*Keefe, William J., 40 Maple St.	6.43
*Keenan, William M., 40 Dexter Ave.	2.25
*Kelley, Emma R., 372 Charles River Rd.	2.00
*Kelley, John J., 21 Frank St.	9.51
*Kelley, Marion D., 120 Walnut St.	2.00

Kelly, Bertha L., 7 Upland Road	2.00
Kelly, Daniel A., 35 Morse St.	2.00
*Kelly, John F., 9 Myrtle St.	2.00
*Kelly, Joseph L., 100 Capitol St.	4.42
*Kelly, Mary J., 26 Frank St.	8.99
*Kennedy, James G., 5 Marcia Rd.	7.90
*Kenney, Ethel H., 63 Parker St.	2.00
*Kenny, Maurice R., 49 Carroll St.	3.59
*Keough, Edward H., 189 Arsenal St.	6.43
*Kerr, Charles A., 9 Gay Rd.	5.57
*Kim, Homer T., 130 Charles River Rd.	7.10
Kinney, Eileen M., 81 Commonwealth Rd.	6.97
Kirk, James, Watertown Arsenal	2.25
*Kivlehan, Harold, 12 Fifth Ave.	2.00
Kivlehan, John J., 12 Fifth Ave.	3.69
Knowles, Olive D., 15 Langdon Ave.	2.00
Kuhn, Joseph R., 11 Richards Rd.	2.57
Kulegian, Kurken, 198 Arlington St.	2.28
*Lacey, William C., 96 Bradford Rd.	6.27
Lacoco, Alfred, 69 W. Boylston St.	2.00
*Laguff, John, Jr., 45 Hersom St.	2.09
Lanctot, Joseph E., 46 Copeland St.	2.00
*Landry, Roy A., 42 Salisbury Rd.	6.16
Lane, Francis H., 11 Gleason St.	6.37
LaRhette, John A., 9 Edenfield Ave.	2.00
LaRosa, Joseph, 17 Winter St.	2.57
*Larson, Frederick H., 39 Stearns Road	2.00
*Lavoy, Dorothy, 404 Pleasant Street	2.00
*Lawson, Alfred, 29 Ladd Street	2.00
*Lawson, Lynwood M., 340 School Street	2.00
*Leacy, H. Maynard, 111 Galen St.	6.03
Leahy, William W., Jr., 24 Westland Rd.	2.00
LeBlanc, Gertrude et Louis LaNormandin, 38 Boyd St.	13.79
*LeBlanc, Guy J., 10 California Pk.	3.37
LeBlanc, Robert, 10 California Pk.	2.00
*LeFort, David T., 134 Summer St.	2.00
*Leibing, Edward E., Bradford Rd.	2.97
Leonard, Paul W., 63 Hillside Rd.	2.00
LesCarbeau, Charles, Jr., 18 Dartmouth St.	2.00
*LeVally, Fred B., 21 Pequosette St.	2.09
*Lewis, Jacob P., 188 Orchard St.	3.86
*Lewis, Samuel L., 312 Pleasant St.	4.50
*Liljeholm, Sidney, 40 Garfield St.	2.00
Lillis, Almira M., 16 Howe St.	2.00

*Linen, Joseph F., 37 Melendy Ave.	2.00
*Linfield, Oliver S., 198 Palfrey St.	2.14
*Lingley, Blanch M., 44 Melendy Ave.	4.65
*Liston, John J., 34 Chauncey St.	7.71
Livoli, Louis, 20 Merrifield Ave.	6.41
Livoli, Paul, 302 Arlington St.	2.00
Lopez, Agnes C., 484 Main St.	3.08
Lopez, Raymond, 484 Main St.	2.00
Lord, Joseph A., 24 Elmwood Ave.	2.01
Loughlin, John T., 16 French St.	2.00
*Loughlin, Joseph T., 647 Main St.	2.00
Loumos, Lycargus A., 175 Lexington St.	2.00
*Lucason, Grace D., 13 Bromfield St.	4.29
Ludwin, Rebecca, 4 Winsor Ave.	2.68
*Lyman, Edward C., 6 Hovey St.	14.46
Lynch, John E., 321 Main St.	2.00
*Lyons, Bernard A., 11 Clayton St.	2.00
Lyons, Mary C., 32 Eliot St.	3.00
*Macaulay, Irene M., 15 Adams Ave.	5.90
*MacDonald, Alexander, 62 Marshall Street	3.94
*MacDonald, Herbert, 152 Cypress St.	4.98
MacDonald, Richard, 77 Putnam Street	2.81
*MacDonald, Robert, 24 Otis St.	2.00
*MacDonald, Walter, 24 Otis St.	4.31
*MacHugh, Elizabeth, 535 Pleasant St.	2.00
*MacInnes, Martin, 91 Spring St.	3.21
*MacIntosh Coal Co., John, 13 Church St.	10.84
*MacKay, Hector, 28 Dewey St.	2.00
*MacKay, Sadie, 166 Worcester St.	6.56
*Mackin, James H., 213 Watertown-Street	5.68
*MacLean, Malcolm D., 26 Dewey St.	2.00
*MacRae, Wilhelm, 83 Dexter Ave.	3.69
*Maguire, Joseph, 78 Arsenal St.	7.50
Maher, Lawrence K., 154 Dexter Ave.	2.00
*Maher, Patrick, 17 New Lexington St.	2.00
*Mahoney, Ellen, 9 Rangeley Rd.	2.00
*Mahoney, Joseph, 9 Rangeley Road	4.01
*Mahoney, William, 20 Bostonia Ave.	2.28
Malone, Francis, 10 Summit Rd.	2.00
*Maloney, James F., 75 Lexington St.	2.03
*Maloney, Ralph B., 75 Lexington St.	3.05
*Manasian, Kegan, 91 Dexter Ave.	3.75
Mannix, M. Frances 9 Prescott St.	11.06
*Mansell, Thomas, 49 Cypress St.	2.00

Manzelli, Attilio, 1016 Belmont St..	2.00
Manzelli, Domenico, 1016 Belmont St...............................	6.17
Marchant, Henry, 92 Nichols Ave.................................	2.00
*Marchant, Rose, 92 Nichols Ave................................	2.00
*Marotte, Charles, 18 Ladd St.................................	2.00
Martell, John, 17 Keenan St...................................	4.31
Martocchio Trucking Co., 42 Forest St........................	9.10
Mason, Ralph, 113 Mt. Auburn St..............................	2.25
*Maurer, Edward, 34 Laurel St................................	4.00
*Maxwell, William C., 172 Sycamore St.......................	2.68
*Maxwell, William, 36 California St..........................	2.46
Mayhew, Chester, 50 Hall Avenue	2.00
*Mayhew, William, 50 Hall Ave...............................	2.00
*Mayo, Walter L., 5 Stoneleigh Circle	12.53
Mayo, Franklin H., 78 Main St...............................	3.32
Mazza, Tony, 66 Ralph St....................................	2.00
*McAuliffe Co., Western Ave., Allston	21.76
*McCall, Joseph, 47 Green St................................	2.00
McCammon, Robert, 29 French St	2.00
McCann, William, 106 Summer Street	2.00
*McCarron, Edward T., 1 Capitol St..........................	2.89
McCarthy, John J., 38 Myrtle Street	2.00
*McCarthy, Marion, 29 Keenan St.............................	2.00
McCarthy, Mildred, 26 King St...............................	2.00
McCool, Elizabeth, 64-A Belmont St..........................	2.00
McDermott, Patrick, 97 Fayette Street	2.00
McDonald, Arthur, 69 Hovey Street	2.00
*McDonald, James, 42 Edenfield Ave..........................	2.00
McDonald, Patrick, 22 Oakland St............................	2.00
*McDonnell, John, 52 Cuba St................................	2.24
*McElhiney, George, 57 Prospect St..........................	2.00
*McGann, Delia J., 135 Edenfield Ave	3.21
*McGann, Patrick, 135 Edenfield Ave........................	2.00
McGarry, Percy E., 495 Mt. Auburn Street	16.07
*McGerigle, John T., 30 Union St............................	2.00
*McGirr, Mary A., 64 Elton Ave.............................	2.41
*McGirr, Samuel B., 64 Elton Ave...........................	2.00
*McHugh, Anna B., 77 Fayette St............................	13.88
*McHugh, Grace, 22 Belmont St...............................	2.00
McHugh, Sara, 90 School St..................................	2.00
McIntyre, Ronald, 42 Cypress St.............................	2.00
*McKay, Chloa R., 29 Hall Ave...............................	7.71
McKinnon, Charles, 55 Grendview Ave........................	2.00
*McKinnon, Daniel, 37 Harnden Avenue	3.21

*McKinnon, Louise, 87 Harnden Avenue	8.63
*McLaughlin, Eleanor, 27 Westland Road	4.29
McLellan, John R., 9 Oakland St.	2.00
*McLeman, Andrew, 28 Ladd Street	4.01
*McManus, Margaret, 192 Waverley Ave.	2.06
*McNamara, Edward C., 182 Main St.	2.19
*McSweeney, Bryan, 47 Spruce St.	11.08
*McWhirter, Alfred, 28 Parker St.	2.00
*Meda, Fred J., 129 Lexington St.	3.85
Mee, Gerald S., 8 Norseman Ave.	2.89
Meehan, George, 31 Adams St.	7.23
*Meehan, John J., 325 School St.	14.24
*Melbye, William, 44 Pequosette St.	8.83
Melvin, Albert, 24 Marshall St.	8.67
*Menghi, Hugh, 98 Standish Rd.	3.86
*Merchants Mutual Casualty Co., 18 Oliver St., Boston	9.80
*Mercier, Lawrence, 33 Fitchburg St.	5.22
Merlino, Agostino, 21 Ralph St.	2.00
*Merulla, Alfredo, 21 Hudson St.	2.00
Messier, Marion, 162 Orchard St.	2.00
*Messinger, Arthur, 34 Quincy St.	2.00
Middlesex Oli Co., 9 Myrtle St.	2.00
Middleton, W. Irving, Jr., 27 Wolcott Rd.	9.93
Midgley, George H., 19 Prentiss St.	8.51
Miller Charles, 25 Linden Way	2.00
Mills, Louis R., 17 Prescott St.	2.00
Mock, Louis F., Jr., 83 Barnard Ave.	9.05
*Moffat, Albert, 42 Arden Rd.	8.35
*Molito Michael A., 164 Orchard St.	2.89
Molloy, Mary G., 139 Winsor Ave.	2.00
Monahan, Ellen, 68-A Edenfield Ave.	2.00
Monti, John, 467 Pleasant St.	2.00
Moore, Arthur, 7 Chester St.	2.00
*Moore, Donald W., 194 Palfrey St.	2.00
*Moore, Lewis J., 29 Channing Rd.	2.00
Moran, Paul C., 56 Gilbert St.	4.15
Morgan, Chester D., 106 Morse St.	2.00
Morley, Edward, 38 Cypress St.	2.00
*Morrissey, Joseph J., 108 Winthrop St.	2.00
Morrell, Stephen, Watertown St.	2.04
*Moseley, Albion, 24 Marcia Road	6.32
Moulton, Catherine, 95 Church Street	2.00
*Mulkern, Matthew T., 7 Fairfield St.	2.00
*Mullaney, Bertram, 58 Wilmot St.	3.16

*Munhall, William H., 96 Charles River Rd.	4.17
*Murphy, James T., Jr., 589 Main St.	4.00
*Murphy John F., 137 Grove St.	2.00
*Murphy, Michael J., 69 Waverley Avenue	2.00
*Murphy, Nelli, 34 Francis Street	9.00
Murray, John F., 77 Putnam Street	2.00
*Murray, John J., 5 Harrington Street	2.00
Myrer, Wallace, 77 Putnam Street	2.00
*Nagle, Luke T., Jr., 392 Mt. Auburn Street	2.00
Nardelli, Saverio, 731 Main Street	9.23
Natale, Rose, 190 Walnut Street	2.00
Natale, Tillie, 26 Putnam Street	2.00
*Nazaretian, Krokor, 29 Hazel Street	2.00
*Nazaretian, Nicholas, 9 Hosmer Street	2.00
*Neagle, William H., 33 Richards Road	8.35
*Neese, W. Dewey, 5 Stearns Road	6.59
*Neiberg, Louis, 120 Spring Street	3.77
*Nelson, Ernest A., 22 Chauncey Street	2.57
*Newell, Wilfred L., 42 Stuart Street	6.97
Nichols, Leila, 700 Mt. Auburn Street	6.03
*Nielson, Knud B., 16 Wolcott Road	4.09
Nilsan, James G., 44 Chauncey Street	2.00
Nizzari, Jerry, 12 Adams Avenue	2.00
Noble, Gwendolyn F., 32 Russell Avenue	4.42
*Norbury, Albert E., 29 Paul Street	9.00
Norstrum, Ethel K., 74 Barnard Avenue	2.00
Notargiacomo, Anna, 50 Paul Street	15.10
Notargiacomo, Florence, 50 Paul Street	15.10
*Notargiacomo, Helen, 164 Edenfield Avenue	5.14
Norton, Jane O., 6 Hilltop Road	3.85
*O'Brien, Helen, 174 Spruce Street	2.28
*O'Brien, John H., 30 Birch Road	4.98
*O'Brien, Paul, 64 Forest Street	4.14
O'Brien, Richard, 64 Forest Street	2.00
O'Brien, William F., 194 Maplewood Street	5.06
O'Brien, William J., 70 Chapman Street	4.00
Ochs, Gertrude G., 1131 Commonwealth Ave., Allston	2.81
O'Connell, Mary K., 26 Westminster Avenue	7.90
*O'Connor, Agnes M., 48 Edenfield Avenue	2.00
O'Donnell, George C., 112 No. Beacon Street	14.14
O'Donnell, Henry, 12 Bacon Street	2.00
*O'Halloran, Mary F., 45 Mt. Auburn Street	3.37
O'Handley, Margaret T., et Elmer A. Shaw, 69 Green St.	2.00
O'Hara, James P., Jr., 123 Edenfield Avenue ....Re-reg.	2.00

*Oldford, James, 193 Lexington Street 2.00
*Orchard, Eldon F., 44 Quimby Street 6.43
O'Shea, George. C.; 41 Adams Avenue 2.00
*Osmond, Edward C., 19 Chapman Street 2.00
Otin, Marcel, 44 Edgecliffe Road 3.88
*Oxner, Cyril H., 132 Putnam Street 3.69
*Packard, Harry W., 26 Marshall Street 2.00
*Paige, Ruth M., 24 Norseman Avenue 2.00
*Panagas, Charles, 14 Chadbourne Terrace 2.00
Pane, Phillip, 61 Laurel Street 2.00
Panella, Joanne, 18 Upland Road 2.95
*Pano, Nick K., 23 Irma Avenue 7.23
*Panos, James, 25 Kondazian Street 4.15
*Pappas, Frances, 74 Belmont Street 4.65
Pappas, John C., 122 Belmont Street 5.68
Paramount Market, Inc., 319 Walnut Street, Newtonville.... . 6.30
*Parker, Mary A., 373 Main Street 6.17
*Parker, William S., 14 Washburn Street 2.00
Parkinson, Catherine, 37 Prescott Street 4.15
Parella, Joanne, 18 Upland Road 3.53
Partridge, Albert L., 54 Langdon Avenue 7.90
Patterson, George H., 67 Union Street 2.00
*Pearce, Oliver H., 28 Dexter Avenue 6.75
Pelletier, Peter J., 21 Paul Street 2.00
Perkins, David C., 13 Oakley Road 2.00
*Perkins, Homes C., 101 Marshall Street 7.61
Perkins, Joseph G., 158 Sycamore Street 2.00
*Perkins, Lena M., 37 Pearl Street 9.65
*Perkins, Ralph L., 194 No. Beacon Street 2.43
*Perry, Alessandro, 56 Westminster Avenue 3.35
*Perry, Ralph F., 125 Summer Street 2.43
*Pesce, Guy C., 293 Mt. Auburn Street 13.50
Peters, Calvin W., 125 Forest Street 2.00
*Peterson, Edward A., 47 Olcott Street 2.74
Phelan, James E., 14 Hillcrest Circle 5.46
Phelan, James T., 103 Chapman Street 4.69
*Phelps, George A., 217 Arsenal Street 2.41
*Phelps, Harold A., 217 Arsenal Street 5.30
*Phillips, Ernest, 22 Gilbert Street 6.00
*Phillips, Florence, 22 Gilbert Street 2.00
*Phillips, Thomas A., 15 Edgerly Road 5.06
Phipps, Frank L., 100 Langdon Avenue 2.00
*Piantedosi, Joseph, 25 Warren Street 2.00
*Pieterse, Clarence R., 55 Fayette Street 5.79

Pike, Charles W., 194 Pleasant Street	2.00
*Piantedosi, Antonio, 39 Quirk Street	2.41
*Pollard, Alice L., 12 Melendy Avenue	7.61
*Ponti, Andrew J., 36 Quincy Street	2.00
*Poor, Frank S., 31 Langdon Avenue	3.85
*Porter, Michael W., 45 Pequossette Street	2.19
Pouliot, Joseph, 231 No. Beacon Street	2.00
Powell, Marie R., 19 Carver Road	3.85
Powers, Patricia C., 126 Palfrey Street	18.74
*Pratt, George Arthur, 30 Spruce Street	17.68
*Prendergast, Winifred C., 784 Belmont Street	2.00
*Prendergast, John J., 12 Dana Terrace	2.84
*Prendergast, Peter E., 12 Dana Terrace	2.00
Priest, Frederick S., 74 Rutland Street	2.00
*Primpas, James N., 76 Belmont Street	10.50
Phitchard, Carleton F., 9 Merrill Road	3.16
*Proctor, Harold L, 50 Hovey Street	2.00
Pulsifer, Artemis B., 27 Hovey Street	5.25
*Purdy, Ruby A., 20 King Street	6.59
Purdy, Henry R., 33 Laurel Street	2.00
*Putney, Clarence M., 126 Westminster Avenue	2.00
*Quinlan, Arthur V., 68 Green Street	2.14
*Quinn, Everett J., 67 Lincoln Street	2.00
*Quirk, M. Marjorie, 22 Spruce Street	2.00
*Radio Fruit Co., 9 Oakley Road	11.25
*Raeke, Margaret G., 91 Spruce Street	2.00
Rand, Helen, 176 E. Boylston Street	2.00
*Rando, Anthony, 28 Waverley Avenue	2.14
*Rank, Charles W., 36 Hovey Street	10.77
*Ranney, Lurena M., 73 Winsor Avenue	9.47
*Ransom, Joseph, 72 Westminster Avenue	5.25
Ravanis, Nicholas, 97 Grove Street	3.18
Ravesi, John, 122 Chapman Street	2.00
Raymond, Fred S., 11 Chester Street	3.21
*Raymond, Howard C., 398 Mt. Auburn Street	8.51
Rayne, John E., 279 Pleasant Street	2.00
*Reardon, Norbert, Jr., 174 Lovell Road	2.00
Redding, Grace M., 100 Fayette Street	2.00
Regan, Joseph W., 81 Spring Street	3.37
Regan, Joseph, 77 Union Street	3.08
*Reid, Margaret M., 23 Chapman Street	3.21
Reiman, Herbert, 146 Spruce Street	2.00
*Reiman, Theodore, 146 Spruce Street	5.15
Reynolds, Frederic, 4 Carver Road	8.03

Riccio, Peter, 103 Arlington Street	2.00
*Richards, Harry, 50 Hillside Street	2.06
*Riley, Isabel F., 12 Carver Road	9.47
Risso, Eugene, 43 Cross Street	2.00
Ristagno, Dominick, 231 Arlington Street	4.02
Rix, Miriam, 158 Palfrey Street	4.74
Robbins-Bernard Co., 167 Mt. Auburn Street	2.41
Robbins, Harold M., et al, 167 Mt. Auburn Street	12.38
Roberts, Daniel, 124 Westminster Avenue	2.00
Roberts, Dexter, 738 Belmont Street	9.00
Roberts, Ulris, 46 Franklin Street	2.00
Robinson, Evelyn, 37 Adams Street	2.00
Robinson, Frank, 25 Palmer Street	2.01
Robinson, Gladys, 25 Palmer Street	9.47
Robinson, Herbert E., 25 Palmer Street	2.00
Roche, Emily, 14 Royal Street	2.00
Rodgers, Anthony G., 70 Poplar Street	4.93
Rogers, Chester, 144 Dexter Avenue	2.00
Rogers, Frank C., 112 Forest Street	7.90
Romano, Edward J., 26 Clarendon Street	2.00
Romano, Salvatore, 106 Elm Street	2.43
Rose, Adolph T., 82 Belmont Street	6.97
Rose, Raymond A., 538 Pleasant Street	6.75
*Rosoff, Misha, 326 Arlington Street	18.21
Rosoff, Nathaniel, 238 Arlington Street	6.32
Rossi, Harry, 235 Palfrey Street	2.00
Routen, Joseph S., 138 Orchard Street	2.00
*Rowe, Edna P., 34 Bates Road	9.37
Rudduck, Ellen G., 298 Mt. Auburn Street	2.00
Rudolph, James E., 120 Charles River Road	2.79
Rugg, Albert F., Jr., 17 Center Street	2.00
Rugg, William, 17 Center Street	2.00
*Rundquist, Florence, 17 Boylston Street	11.41
Russo, Antonio, 249 Lexington Street	7.37
Russo, Frank, 53 Laurel Street	4.69
Russo, Matthew, Jr., 53 Laurel Street	2.00
Rutherford, Jerome, 2 Clyde Road	4.41
*Ryan, Bertha, 121 Pleasant Street	2.00
Ryan, Richard, 45 Laurel Street	2.41
Ryerson, William G., 22 Palfrey Street	2.00
Saboigian, Haig, 58 Edgecliffe Road	2.00
Sacca, Rose, 38 Edgecliffe Road	2.00
Savill, Albert, 484 Main Street	4.00
Sands, George W., 46 Partridge Street	2.09

Sansone, Anthony T., 10 Merryfield Avenue	2.00
Saraf, Stephen M., 235 Boylston Street	2.00
Savage, Homer G., 63 Bradford Road	7.90
Saxe, Matthew H., 31 Bates Road	4.61
Scalia, Albert, 288 Common Street	18.16
Scalzi, Annie, 231 Palfrey Street	2.00
Scheirer, Herbert, 8 Appleton Street	5.04
Schnare, Alden, 269 E. Boylston Street	2.00
Schwendeman, George, 170 Maplewood Street	5.79
Scott, Gladys, 67 Capitol Street	2.00
Sears, Theodore, 262 Belmont Street	2.78
Seeds, Mildred, 96 Russell Avenue	2.68
Seferian, Avedis, 32 Fairfield Street	5.63
Sergi, Gaetano, 73 King Street	2.00
Sergi, Gliseppe, 73 King Street	4.00
Sessa, James W., 14 Bostonia Avenue	2.00
Sexton, John, 13 Hosmer Street	2.00
*Shahbazian, Nellie, 1063 Belmont Street	2.00
*Shallis, Herbert, 37 Pequosette Street	2.35
Shanahan, Henry, 136 Cypress Street	2.00
Shangochian, Megardich, 16 Laurel Street	2.00
*Sharpe, Evelyn, 28 Clyde Road	3.35
Shaw, Frederick D., 27 Oliver Street	11.41
*Shaw, N. Ferne, 45 Fitchburg Street	2.62
*Shea, Anna V., 102 Harnden Avenue	11.81
*Shea, Henry J., 5 Bellevue Terrace	16.81
Shelman, Samuel, 179 Watertown Street	2.00
Sheridan, Florence, 57 Cottage Street	2.09
Shurtleff, Arthur, 21 Fayette Street	2.00
Simone, Alman A., 29 Myrtle Street	4.09
Simpson, Alfreda, 165 Worcester Street	2.00
Simpson, Malvena J., 217 Common Street	6.32
*Sjostedt, John, 40 Hersom Street	6.18
*Skinner, Robert G., 137 Winsor Avenue	2.00
Slavin, William J., 11 Morton Street	2.00
Smith, Francis W., 26 Quincy Street	2.00
*Smith, Josephine, 83 Edenfield Avenue	2.00
*Smith, Lawrence, 16 Cross Street	2.41
*Smith, Lola A., 17 Fuller Road	5.99
*Smith, L. Orene, 229 Common Street	2.00
*Smith, Thomas, 428 Mt. Auburn Street	2.00
*Smith, Walter J., 41 W. Boylston Street	2.00
*Smyly, Wilfred J., 177 School Street	5.63
*Snow, Ernest, 312 Charles River Road	4.34

Snyder, William, Jr., 40 Fitchburg Street 3.37

Somerville Plumbing & Heating So., 78 Pentiss Street 8.83

Sorenson, Oswold F., 51 Patten Street............................... 2.68

*Spakowski, William, 327 Arlington Street 2.00

*Spinney, Isaac H., 74 Spruce Street 2.09

*Springfield Fire & Marine Insurance Co.,
    195 State Street, Springfield 2.84

Stadtman, Robert H., 106 Franklin Street 4.01

Standel, David I., 65 Morse Street 2.00

*Stanley, Nazareth, 58 Elton Avenue 2.00

*Stapleton, Roland J., 383 Arlington Street 3.37

Star Market Co., 24 Mt. Auburn Street 28.29

Stead, Edna M., 37 Channing Road 2.00

Stefaniak, Peter J., 38 Dartmouth Street 2.00

*Stephanis, Louis, 597 Mt. Auburn Street 4.49

Stevenson, Myron R., 20 Marcia Road 9.10

Stewart, William, 67 Marion Road 2.00

Stiles, Harry L., 74 Charles River Road 4.00

*Stokes, John F., 151 Waltham Street 3.69

*Stone, Edward J., 22 Hilltop Road 2.00

Stone, Helen E., 100 Russell Avenue 2.00

Stone, Winthrop, 126 Church Street 2.00

*Strangio, Elvira, 124 Fayette Street 2.00

Strati, Antonio, 23 Keenan Street 11.81

Stroup, J. Russell, 21 Templeton Parkway 4.15

Strout, Clarence F., 238 Main Street 2.00

Strout, Roy, 31 Merrill Road 12.75

*Stuart, David H., 92 Bellevue Road 4.50

Stuart, T. & Son Co., 70 Phillips Street 7.39

Studley, William O., 35 Cuba Street 2.00

Stumcke, Harry E., 38 Franklin Street 2.28

Sturdy, Ruth R., 31 Otis Street 9.47

Sullivan, Daniel J.,157Langdon Avenue 2.01

*Sullivan, DanielJ.,43Cypress Street 2.00

Sullivan, Edward F., 62 Pearl Street 5.15

Sullivan, Evelyn E., 194 Orchard Street 9.91

Sullivan, James H., 508 Main Street 2.00

*Sullivan, James H., Jr., 508 Main Street 2.00

Sullivan, John J., 96 Boylston Street 3.00

Sullivan, Marion R., 129 Morse Street 2.00

Sullivan, Walter S., 102 Fayette Street 9.10

Sullivan, William, 186 Waverley Avenue 2.10

Sutherland, George, 20 Putnam Street 2.00

*Sutton, Oliver, 271 Pleasant Street 2.00

*Swanson, Herbert, 60 Katherine Road	2.00
Sweeney, Leo H., 11 Palmer Street	2.00
Sylvester, Enio, 14 Cypress Street	2.00
*Tait, Norman R., 191 Waverley Avenue	2.00
*Tamburino, Thomas, 75 Dexter Avenue	2.00
Tarbell, Samuel K., 18 Avon Road	3.48
Tarris, Roy, 26 Louise Street	11.00
Tashjian, Vahe Stone, 12 Brimmer Street	3.37
Taubensee, Albert G., Watertown Arsenal	9.47
*Taverna, John, 19 Hersom Street	2.43
*Taylor, George A., 16 Bradford Road	2.00
*Taylor, Sydney D., 18 Melendy Avenue	2.00
*Terwilliger, Lillian W., 145 Common Street	19.84
*Terwilliger, Wynn M., 145 Common Street	5.36
Thayer, Edward E., 24 Charles Street	2.00
*Therkildsen, Harold, 70 Olcott Street	3.21
Theurer, Otto A., Contracting Co., Inc., 171 Watertown St.	4.82
*Thibodeau, Estelle M. J., 28 Chester Street	3.00
Thoburn, Thomas N., 37 Copeland Street	2.00
*Thollden, James O., 52 Hersom Street	8.67
*Thomas, Melvin H., 241 Waverley Avenue	2.00
Thompson, Irene C., 30 Richards Road	7.10
*Thorne, Carroll B., 17 Carver Road	2.00
Tocci, Carmine, 240 Waverley Avenue	3.00
Toland, Joseph A., 8 Chandler Street	2.00
Tombrink, Bernard E., 96 Hillside Road ....Re-reg	2.00
*Toomy, Mary, 122 Dexter Avenue	2.00
Torchio, Ralph, 7 Sawin Street	2.00
Toro, Joseph, 2 1New Lexington Street	2.00
*Torrielli, Lorenzo, 161 Edenfield Avenue	6.67
*Travia, Joseph, 17 Middle Street	4.42
Trohon, Herbert W., Jr., 48 Hovey Street	4.17
Trongeau, Nelson, 13 Adams Street	7.31
Troiano, Pasquale, 52 Ralph Street	2.00
Troy, Virginia M., 65 Gilbert Street	2.00
Tsacoyeanes, Konstantine, 181 Boylston Street	2.00
Tsolas, Peter, 41 Coolidge Hill Road	2.00
Tuttle, Henry G., 42 Porter Street	2.00
*Twist, John, 28 Copeland Street	2.00
*Tyler, Earles S., 164 Maplewood Street	6.75
Tyler, Hugh B., 7 Clayton Street	2.00
*Tyrrell Janet A., 15 Edgecliffe Road	2.00
*Tzannos, George, 58 Melendy Avenue	11.25
*Ulrich, Howard H., 10 Frank Street	2.00

*University Libraries, Inc., 690 Belmont Street 14.77
*Upham, Franklin M., 381 Arlington Street 2.00
Vernelli, Joseph, 11 Dewey Street 10.45
*Verner, Charles E., 47 Prescott Street 2.00
Verrill, Oliver W., 97 Carroll Street 2.00
*Vestal, Samuel C., 96 Russell Avenue 12.75
Viering, Dorothy G., 34 Quincy Street 2.00
*Vogel, Joseph A., 174 Worcester Street 2.00
Volante, Ralph, 24 Gertrude Street 4.50
Vrock, Rocco, 25 Olcott Street 2.00
*Vacca, Nick, 15 Keenan Street 2.00
*Vacca, Ralph C., 57 Cottage Street 2.00
Vahey, Ruth P., 238 No. Beacon Street 2.00
*Vahey, James A., 93 Hillside Road 7.31
*Vahey, Mary, 104 Riverside Street 2.09
*Vail, Norman F., 182 Maplewood Street 2.00
Valentino, George, 11 Norseman Avenue 2.00
Valchius, Mary J., 22 Belmont Street 2.00
Vaughan, James D., 26 Amherst Road 4.00
*Wakefield, George G., 48 Pearl Street 2.00
*Wallisch, William J., 81 Poplar Street 5.68
Walsh, Collin F., 109A Lexington Street 4.00
Walsh, James F., 12 Green Street 2.25
Walsh, Vivian E., 135 Evans Street 2.00
*Walston, Howard W., 15 Irma Avenue 2.43
*Walters, Norman L., 130 Nichols Avenue 2.00
*Wardwell, Myrtle E., 141 Hillside Road 2.00
*Warren, Ernest H., 852 Belmont Street 5.54
Warren, Grace M., 21 Keith Street 3.05
*Watertown Excavating Co., Inc., 200 Summer Street 66.93
*Watertown Lumber Co., Inc., Arsenal Street 2.00
Weigle, Fred B., 59 Bailey Road 2.00
*Welch, John J., Jr., 27 Quincy Street 6.82
Werner, Fred G., 114 Huntington Avenue, Boston 2.00
*Whalen, Mathilda, 121 Edenfield Avenue 2.00
*Wheeler, Bertell D., 162 No. Beacon Street 2.00
*Whitney, Carlton S., 14 Stoneleigh Circle 5.36
*Whyte, John, 56 Cuba Street 2.00
*Wiggin, Alfred P., 29 Channing Road 2.00
*Williams, James H., 30 Palfrey Street 2.00
*Williams, Norman G., 107 Worcester Street 2.35
Wilson, Coleman, 522 Pleasant Street 2.41
*Winslow, Elsie T., 289 Waverley Avenue 12.05
Winters, Charles T., 7 Harnden Avenue 4.00

*Wood, Wilbur H., 5 Bradford Road	5.46
*Woodland, Robert B., 58 Gilbert Street	2.65
*Wyss, Carl, 60 Winsor Avenle	2.00
*Wixon, Brenton, 12 Patten Street	2.06
*Yaghjian, Sarkis, 22 Templeton Parkway	13.52
York, Charles A., 275 Main Street	2.09
*York, Ernest, 252 School Street	5.22
York, Thomas A., 64 Whites Avenue	2.00
Young, George, 127 Worcester Street ....Re-reg.	2.00
*Young, Madeline, 175 Church Street	3.42
*Young, Samuel, 15 Broadway	5.30
Youngman, Sara A., 59 Bradford Road	2.00
*Yuchnevicz, Helen C., 18 Cottage Street	2.19
Zacheus, Edward N., 85 Robbins Road	2.00
Zalenski, Mabel G., 137 Lexington Street	2.65

1934 REAL AND PERSONAL TAXES REMAINING UNPAID AT THE CLOSE OF BUSINESS DECEMBER 31, 1934

*Paid since close of books—Verified to February 19, 1935

Abbott, Arthur S., et ux, 105 Palfrey Street	$220.71
Abrahamain, Roxey E., 255 Boylston Street	253.26
Abrams, Jack, Boston	215.23
Abrew, Francesco J., Burlington	211.25
Achorn, John J., et ux, 47 Maple Street	26.99
Adamo, Antonio, 468 Main Street	1.69
Aetna Mills Co.,	2,827.37
Aetna Mills Realty Co.	292.37
Agahigian, Henry, 329 Orchard Street	98.02
Agahigian, Mardiros, 329 Orchard Street	197.73
Ahlden, Ruben H., et ux, 110 Cypress Street	263.64
Ahlquist, Frederick E., 398 School Street	302.51
Aiello, Guiseppe, 21 Quirk Street	10.14
Aiello, Guiseppe et ux, 41 Quirk Street	103.09
Airasian, Sarkis et ux, 7 Porter Street	244.36
Ajamian, Hovsep, 98 Dexter Avenue	233.22
Ajamian, Joseph, 75 Elm Street	16.90
Ajamian, Mousek, 24 Lloyd Road	284.80
Ajamian, Rosie, 45 Quimby Street	227.77
Ajemian, Rose, 46 Concord Road	100.00
Akillian, Sarkis et Setrak, 50 Dexter Avenue	20.28
Alarie, Anne G., Mt. Auburn Street	84.50

Alarie, Heirs Elizabeth F., 220 Main Street 73.74
Alberico, Nunziata et al, 17 Howard Street 120.95
Alberico, Pietro et ux, 24 French Street 123.73
Alcock, Samuel, Belmont 251.81
Alcock, Samuel et ux, Belmont 241.67
Alemsherian, Melkon, 48 Dexter Avenue 33.80
Alexander, Daniel G., Cambridge 70.98
Alexander, Louis A., 264 No. Beacon Street 3.38
Alexander, Ruth R., 344 Mt. Auburn Street 392.08
Alexantrian, Mary, 9 Homer Street 243.36
Alger, Eliza A., 100 Pleasant Street 153.79
Alger, Phoebe P., 27 Fifield Street 265.33
Allen, Amelia F., 6 Carver Rd. East 175.19
*Allen, John K., et ux, 13 Rutland Street 133.51
Allen, Lillian E., 510 Belmont Street 267.02
Alt, Julia, Cambridge 10.14
Alteparmakian, Persape, 63 Elton Avenue 248.43
*Amaral, Conseico, East Cambridge 10.14
Amari, Gaspare et ux, 100 Summer Street............................ 60.55
Ambrose, James J. et ux, 51 Capitol Street 143.65
*Ambrosio, Pietro et ux, 56 Westminster Avenue 182.53
Ames, Etta C., 131 Mt. Auburn Street 101.40
Ananian, Garabed et al, 23 Crawford Street 275.47
*Ananian, Garabed H. et al, 568 Mt. Auburn Street 307.58
Ananian, Mariam, 18 Putnam Street 250.12
Anastasi, Heirs Pietro, 18 Bostonia Avenue 250.12
Anastasi, Peter, 18 Bostonia Avenue 287.30
Anderson, Axel, Spring Street 6.76
*Anderson, Broe J., 106 Hillside Road 278.01
Anderson, Margaret B., 21 Beacon Park 100.69
Anderson, Marie K., Waltham 219.70
*Anderson, Heirs Oscar E., 42 Barnard Avenue 302.51
Andrews, Austin H., 43 Franklin Street 1,292.85
Andrews, Mary A., 616 Mt. Auburn Street 8.45
Andrews Milk Co., 43 Franklin Street 373.49
Andrews, William S., 132 Main Street 10.14
Andrews, William S. et al, 132 Main Street 135.20
Andrsky, Charles et ux, 133 Lexington Street 97.17
Angel, Frank et ux, 214 Arlington Street 278.85
Angelo, Rocco et ux, 61 Spring Street 163.93
Anjoorian, Araxi C., 26 Adams Street 148.72
Anthony, Mary N., 248 Common Street 170.69
Antonian, Alexander S., 43 Crawford Street 60.51
Antramian, Jacob, 69 Elm Street 141.96

Aprahamian, Manoog, 99 Bigelow Avenue	8.45
Aprigian, Peter, 38 Cypress Street	79.10
Arcidiacomo, Maria N., 168 Fayette Street	69.69
Argento, Domenic, 68 Mt. Auburn Street	8.45
*Arlington Co-operative Bank, Arlington	158.86
Armenyan, Eugenie, 71 Putnam Street	238.29
Armstrong, Frank K. et ux, 34 Wilmot Street	90.34
Arno, Paolo, 24 Perry Street	84.50
Arone, Caroline, 79 Templeton Parkway	296.35
Arone, Domenico, 60 Prentiss Street	282.91
Arone, Elizabetta, 25 Norseman Avenue	212.94
Arone, Louis et al, 630 Mt. Auburn Street	6.08
Arone, Pasquale, et ux, 26 Keith Street	153.79
Aroutian, Artin et al, Trustees, 108 School Street	454.61
Aroutian, Artin M., 31 Melendy Avenue	243.36
*Asadoorian, Garabed D., 596 Mt. Auburn Street	10.14
Asadoorian, Sarkis, 29 Nichols Avenue	10.14
Asarian, Harry et ux, 48 Quimby Street	263.26
Aselbegian, Ariknaz et al, 10 Dartmouth Street	121.45
Aspegren, Carl H. et al, 96 Bradford Road	289.46
Asgardjian, Nargul, Watertown	27.04
Aston, Eleanor M., 106 Rutland Street	169.11
Atkinson, Thomas W. C., 56 Fitchburg Street	168.12
Atlantic Register Co., 2 School Street	2,220.66
Atwood, W. Elmer, 27 Merrill Road	290.66
Audella, Helen D., Boston	310.86
Avedion, Alice, 594 Mt. Auburn Street	10.14
Avery, James, No. Cambridge	10.14
Ayrazian, Munexar, 20 Concord Road	255.19
Baboian, Harry, 406 Mt. Auburn Street	8.45
Baboian, Rose, 710 Mt. Auburn Street	203.50
*Bachrach Incorporated, Hunt Street	2,330.51
Bagdasarian, P. A., 164 Belmont Street	16.90
*Bagnall, Anna Isabel, 15 Kimball Road	36.26
Bagnall, Earle E. et ux, 93 Highland Avenue	206.83
Bagnall, Earle E., 93 Highland Avenue	26.20
Baia, Luigi, 75 Boyd Street	241.67
Bailey, Pearl D., 15 Hilltop Road	154.45
Bake, Norma I., 104 Beechwood Avenue	268.71
*Baker, Emma C., 32 Commonwealth Road	78.47
Baker, Frank G., 7 Spring Street	3.38
Baker, Margaret E., 44 California Street	98.08
Balcom, Roy C., 32 Fitchburg Street	158.86
Balestrieri, Cresua T., 49 Hall Avenue	122.37

*Balian, Nazareth, 129 Winsor Avenue	114.00
Ball, Doris F., 58 Copeland Street	125.62
Bangs, J. Mitchell et ux, 64 Parker Street	229.84
Barbarossa, Sabino et ux, 35 Prescott Street	16.90
Barber, Helen Jane, et al, 32 Stearns Road	118.71
Barbonre, Soccorso, 47 Prentiss Street	48.15
Barbuto, Mary F., 334 Orchard Street	304.20
Barca, John, 42 Mt. Auburn Street	16.90
Barchard, Oliver W. et al, 17 Paul Street	245.05
Bardizbanian, Hasmig, et al, 30 Porter Street	245.05
Bardizbanian, Hasmig et al, 30 Porter Street	241.77
Bardizbanian, John M. et al, 33 Porter Street	260.67
Bardizbanian, Nishan et al, 12 Concord Road	245.05
Barker, George E. et ux, 91 Lovell Road	313.81
Baker, Luliona M. et al, 64 Commonwealth Road	143.56
Barksdale, Andrew H., 76 Brookline Street	96.53
Barmakian, Harutune, 142 Forest Street	126.75
Barnard, Simone, 77 Summer Street, Boston	233.22
Barnet, Bessie, Brighton	271.89
Barrett, Heirs Deborah, 550 Main Street	162.24
Barrett, Florence E., 44 Fitchburg Street	168.12
Barrett, J. Henry, 19 Commonwealth Road	3.38
Barrett, Peter P., Jr., 536 Main Street	645.58
Barry, Joanna J., 32 Bacon Street	180.83
Barton, William G. et ux, 9 Ladd Street	106.47
Baxter, Pearl A., 42 Kimball Road	246.74
Bayajian, Samuel et al, 32 Concord Road	250.12
Bazarian, Peter, 524 Mt. Auburn Street	282.23
Bazarian, Sarkis, 96 Nichols Avenue	3.38
Bean, Lena Marshall, 65 Robbins Road	24.44
*Beaudette, Ruth G., 35 Standish Road	287.79
Beck, Harry J., et'al, 60 Boylston Street	246.74
Becklund, Emil P., et ux, 177 Highland Avenue	15.99
Beckman, Ellen C., 68 Barnard Avenue	314.34
Bedigian, Mardiros B., et ux, 19 Chauncy Street	322.79
Bedrossian, Grace, 15 Chauncy Street	322.79
Bedrossian, Hagop H., 121 Galen Street	87.88
Bedrossian, Sarah H., 24 Union Street	265.33
*Bekerian, Aghasi, et al, 19 Lloyd Road	283.92
Belding, Anson W., 277 School Street	180.00
Bell, Hazel P., 20 Fitchburg Street	168.12
Bella, Tony et ux, Mary, Centerbrook, Conn.	558.05
*Bender, Anna Schoepfer, 189 Sycamore Street	5.00
Benger, Robert, 53 Wilmot Street	123.37

*Benjamin, Alma R., Trustee, 40 Katherine Road	70.54
Benjamin, Harold O., et ux, 46 Russell Avenue	248.43
Benjamin, Harry L., 68 Main Street	16.90
Bennett, Frances A., 50 Spruce Street	256.88
Bennett, Georgia A., 21 Alden Road	45.54
Benson, Oscar B., et ux, 43 Merrill Road	307.56
Berardine, Fred, 30 Perry Street	40.56
Berardino, Francesco, et ux, 184 Summer Street	50.00
Berardino, James, et ux, Catherine, 12 Cottage Street	75.07
Berberian, Arasky et Diran, 644 Mt. Auburn Street	6.76
Berg, Anna L., 5 Fairview Avenue	302.44
Bergman, G. Philip, 28 Standish Road	159.77
Bernabei, Salvatore, et ux, 16 Lyon Street	57.46
Berquist, Alice M., 4 Frank Street	85.55
Berry, Emile P., 7 Whitney Street	5.07
Berry, Emilie P., et al, 7 Whitney Street	285.98
Berry, Sarah H., et al, 31 Katherine Road	158.86
Beshgetourian, Mourad, et ux, 16 Concord Road	635.43
*Betcher, Charles W., et ux, 46 Carver Road East	300.82
Bettinger Enamel Corp., Pleasant Street	892.32
*Bevilacqua, Saturno, 51 Harrington Street	143.65
Bianco, Domenica, 20 French Street	157.17
Bigham, Carl A., et ux, 35 Edenfield Avenue	117.85
Bitchockjian, Harry, 536 Mt. Auburn Street	270.40
Bixby, Leland C., et ux, 45 Oliver Street	221.39
Bjorn, Gustave A., et ux, 19 Wilmot Street	77.91
Blair, Jennive, 60 Church Street	251.81
Blair, Margaret A., 2 Mt. Auburn Street	23.66
Blake, Edward, Merchants Row	6.76
Blake, Ralph J., et ux, 47 Standish Road	270.28
Bleifling, Eliza A., 54 Union Street	65.62
Boccodoro, Ida, 308 Main Street	228.18
Boccodoro, Salvatore, 11A Forest Street	40.08
Boccodoro, Salvatore, et ux, 11A Forest Street	749.15
Boerstler, Bessie M., 206 Maplewood Street	290.68
Bohne, Carl, et ux, 25 Grandview Avenue	155.84
Bonnano, Andrew, Boston	13.80
*Bonanno, Francesco, 80 Putnam Street	115.98
Bond, Edward J., et ux, 18 Lovell Road	295.96
Bond's Spa Inc., 18 Mt. Auburn Street	33.80
Borland, Joseph H., 94 Main Street	28.73
Baroian, Harry, 405 Mt. Auburn Street	8.45
Boschetto, Andrea, 103 Edenfield Avenue	335.19
*Boston Safe Deposit & Trust Co., Boston	-719.31

Boudreau, John I., et ux, 9 Theurer Park	310.56
Boudrot, Mary E., 100 Robbins Road	255.19
Boujoulian, Hamazash, et ux, 11 Chauncy Street	100.00
Bourque, Elzer M., et ux, 108 California Street	36.05
Boutelle, Eugene G., et ux, 15 Arden Road	119.84
Bowles, Emma A., 7 Summer Street	189.23
Bouajian, Gulania, 53 Quimby Street	200.73
Boyajian, Haig, 4 Bigelow Avenue	13.52
Boyajian, Sampad, 60 Bigelow Avenue	258.57
Boyd, Arthur R., et ux, 42 Porter Street	287.30
Boylan, Michael J., et ux, 74 Fitchburg Street	194.81
Boyle, Edward J., 616 Main Street	247.29
Boyle, William J., 7 Bostonia Avenue	155.48
Bracken, Mabel G., 17 Pequosette Street	245.05
Brackett, Mary E., 14 Hersom Street	130.13
Brady, Vera L., 89 Bailey Road	383.63
Braffit, Ada C., 48 Stuart Street	163.93
Branchaud, Anna Mary, 81 Orchard Street	321.10
Branco, Manuel R., Somerville	13.52
Brandolino, Camillo, 43 French Street	32.11
Brazilian, Aram, 636 Mt. Auburn Street	1.69
Brenen, Grace Strong, et al, 121 Poplar Street	314.34
Brenen, Mary Lovell, 45 Lovell Road	295.96
*Brennan, James J., 745 Mt. Auburn Street	234.91
Brennick, Anna M., et al, 92 Hovey Street	106.43
Brescia, Guiseppe, et ux, 30 Cypress Street	108.21
Brickley, John F., et ux, 208 No. Beacon Street	131.53
Bridgewater Savings Bank	444.09
*Brigandi, Stephen, 16 Cross Street	10.12
Briggs, Royal F., et ux, 848 Belmont Street	152.10
Brinkerhoff, Florence, 11 Parker Street	31.49
Brissin, Edna, 158 Belmont Street	16.90
Brochu, Lena, 28 Copeland Street	219.23
Brock, Lena E., 81 Robbins Road	241.73
Brock, Ralph O., 81 Robbins Road	5.07
Bronson, Burr B., et ux, 15 Brookline Street	67.60
Brooks, Frank A., et ux, 256 Common Street	305.89
Brooks, Helen W., 97 Langdon Avenue	202.80
*Brooks, John T., 638 Mt. Auburn Street	1.69
Brooks, William W., 18 Jewett Street	88.42
Brown, Bertha E., 148 Standish Road	288.26
*Brown, Cordelia A., 93 Russell Avenue	74.36
Brown, Gilbert L., et ux, 870 Belmont Street	279.06
Brown, Karl H., et al, 37 Chester Street	255.19

Brown, Katherine E., et al., 14 Maplewood Street	228.31
Brown, Heirs Lewis E., Arlington	236.60
Brown, Marguerite M., 103 Poplar Street	311.73
Brown, Mary F., 876 Belmont Street	635.44
*Brown, Milton S., 148 Standish Road	3.38
*Brown, Norman H., et ux, So. Boston	89.25
Brownell, Earle, 124 Galen Street	10.14
Brownell, William J., et ux, 726 Mt. Auburn Street	319.41
Bronow, Fannie, Mattapan	219.70
Bruce, Edward E., 26 Phillips Street	13.52
Bryant, Arthur P., 59 Garfield Street	4.39
Bryant, Caroline E., 59 Garfield Street	250.12
Bryant, Joseph W., Jr., et ux, 141 Bellevue Road	72.32
Buchanan, Blanche E., 117 Spring Street	118.01
Buckely, Ludwig W., et ux, 22 Robbins Road	150.00
Buda, Guiseppe, et ux, 23 James Street	147.03
Budding, Lillian M., 218 Belmont Street	294.06
Burg, Alice Claire, 227 Common Street	287.30
Burgess, Heirs Gertrude A., 19 Irving Street	239.98
Burgess, James B., 19 Irving Street	15.21
Burke, Mary A., 78 Chestnut Street	50.30
Burke, Susan, 51 Olney Street	118.30
*Burleigh, Charles M., et ux, 21 Hilltop Road	173.44
Burns, Heirs Joseph A., et ux, et al, 126 Main Street	209.56
Burns, Mary E., Newton	252.07
Burr, E. Florence, 12 Alden Road	283.92
Busby, Mary E., 144 Bellevue Road	106.92
Busconi, Carl, School Street	3.38
Busconi, Joseph, 575 Mt. Auburn Street	3.38
Busconi, Mary, 42 Quimby Street	824.98
*Bustin, Heirs Francis H., 93 Franklin Street	60.84
Butler, Alfred W., Lincoln	308.36
*Butler, Arthur F., et ux, 44 Phillips Street	167.02
Butler, George F., 45 Main Street	118.30
Butler, George F., et ux, 173 Mt. Auburn Street	295.75
Butler, Heirs Lillie, 19 Derby Road	289.44
Butters, Irene B., 281 Main Street	172.38
Butters, Lucinda, 269 Main Street	253.50
Cahalane, Julia, et al, Belmont	532.35
Cahill, Genevieve C., 47 Stuart Street	174.07
Caira, Agostino, 238 Palfrey Street	101.40
Caira, Antonio, et ux, 238 Palfrey Street	15.21
Caldaroni, Antonio, 118 Westminster Avenue	213.17
Calderoni, Antoio et ux, 187 Fayette Street	126.75

Calden, William H., 52 Morse Street 182.52
Calden, William H., et ux, 52 Morse Street 245.05
Callahan, John Francis, et al, 3 Grenville Road 382.34
Callahan, Patrick J., et ux, 56 Carver Road 316.03
*Callahan, Thomas J., et ux, 379 School Street 238.29
Callahan, Elizabeth G., 146 Pleasant Street 238.29
Stanley, Nazarit H., et al 385.32
Cambridge Trust Company, Cambridge 162.24
Cambridgeport Savings Bank 441.08
*Campagna, Argo, 755 Mt. Auburn Street 13.52
Campanini, Romeo, Lawrence 523.21
Campbell, Daniel, Prentiss Street 6.76
Campbell, Daniel T., West Somerville 25.48
Campbell, Emma F., 141 Winsor Avenue 278.85
*Campbell, Florence F., Conn. 419.58
Campbell, Joseph T., et ux, 125 Westminster Avenue 135.20
*Campbell, Lillias J., 115 Mt. Auburn Street 20.28
Campbell, Marion O., 164 Church Street 294.06
*Campbell, Percy C., 330 School Street 43.94
*Campbell, Wallace K., et ux, 12 Channing Road 282.73
Canady, Lois J., 75 Spruce Street 214.63
Canady, Oscar M., 18 Channing Road 1.69
Cannon, Patrick J., 27 Gilbert Street 214.92
Cannuli, Joseph, et ux, 11 Wheeler Court 84.50
Cantalupo, Jennie, 12 Lloyd Road 256.88
*Caoutte, Joseph T., et ux, 36 Bridge Street 91.26
Capone, Angelo, 28 Hudson Street 145.34
Caracostos, Mary, 8 Belknap Terrace 172.38
Caragulian, Araxi G., 404 Mt. Auburn Street 507.00
Caragulian, Garabed H., 404 Mt. Auburn Street 287.30
Carchia, John V., et ux, 118 Langdon Avenue 295.75
Carey, Paul W., 30 Morton Street 256.39
Carey, B. Evelyn, 44 Merrill Road 307.56
Carlson, August H., et ux, 145 Spruce Street 194.35
Carlstrom, Knut S., 55 Pequosette Street 10.14
Carlton, George E., et ux, 54 Merrill Road 287.23
Carney, Robert E., 49 Olney Street 118.30
Carpenter, Alice P., 64 Lowell Avenue 118.30
Carpenter, F. Scott, et ux, 102 Stoneleigh Road 286.99
Carr, Katherine A., 28 Springfield Street 246.61
Carroll, Cornelius J., et ux, 51 Harnden Avenue 277.16
Carroll, Frederick A., et ux, 53 Shattuck Road 417.43
*Carroll, Joseph E., 627 Mt. Auburn Street 33.80
Caruso, Anthony, 66 Forest Street 163.93

Caruso, Guisseppe, Waverley	20.28
Caruso, Vance R., et ux, 133 Fayette Street	253.50
Casey, Ruth R., 129 Langdon Avenue	248.43
Casey, William G., et ux, 11 Marcia Road	338.54
Cassesse, Charles J., 28 Fitchburg Street	168.12
Costellano, Fortunata, 12 Francis Street	272.09
Caterina, Tomaso, 85 Arlington Street	202.80
Caterina, Thomas, 91 Arlington Street	10.14
*Catton, Percy, 95 Barnard Avenue	10.14
Cavallaro, Philip, et al, King Street	10.14
*Cavalucci, Romano, et al, 331 Main Street	23.66
Cavanaugh, Florence I., 10 Emerson Road	218.40
Cavanaugh, John T., et ux, 545 Main Street	224.77
Ceglia, Vincenzo, et ux, et al, 33 Church Hill	169.00
*Central Auto Parts Co., 35 Galen Street	21.13
Cerqua, Nello, 181 Fayette Street	312.65
Chamberlain, Henry A., et ux, 116 Standish Road	295.70
Chamberland, Charles, 85 Putnam Street	267.02
Chamian, Karepe, et ux, 34 Cypress Street	179.14
Chandler, William S., 17 Merrill Road	3.38
*Chase, Ada B., 62 Robbins Road	255.19
Chase, Gertrude M., 5 Hall Avenue	230.84
Chase Company, L. C., 36 Pleasant Street	48.17
*Chase, Louis H., et al, 62 Robbins Road	11.83
Chase Lura E., 11 Irving Street	182.52
Chase, Paul Ellsworth, et ux, 33 Lincoln Street	206.18
Chelios, Charles, 447 Main Street	7.61
Chevoor, Mary B., 532 Mt. Auburn Street	253.50
Chin, Jimmie, 475 Main Street	3.38
Chinchinian, Paul, 24 Dartmouth Street	20.28
Chinchinian, Paul, et al, 24 Dartmouth Street	238.29
Chicchios, Sophia G., 124 Belmont Street	290.68
Chisholm, Charles M., et al, 23 Morton Street	241.18
Chopourian, Harry M., 504 Mt. Auburn Street	11.15
Chopourian, Minos, 504 Mt. Auburn Street	209.56
Chotilian, Apraham, et al, 27 Lloyd Road	246.74
Christofferson, Carl A., 3A Hilltop Road	6.76
Christopher, Frances, 121 Lexington Street	190.97
Christopher, Stelios, 101 Bigelow Avenue	10.14
Chuchian, Bedros, et al, 87 Templeton Parkway	379.78
Church, Barbara D., 74 Spruce Street	285.61
Church, Iva Gertrude, 122 Winsor Avenue	260.26
Ciampi, Veronica, 2 Putnam Street	274.78
Ciavardone, Ernesto, et ux, 8 St. Mary's Street	251.81

Ciavarro, Domenico, et ux, 23 Hearn Street	85.50
Ciccatelli, Antonio, 40 Waltham Street	64.28
Cioppa, Louise, Wellesley	267.02
Cipriano, Alfonso, Medford	15.21
Cirillo, Nicholas, et ux, 20 Edgecliffe Road	330.01
Cirino, Angelo, 121 Mt. Auburn Street	35.49
Clair, Michael James,121 Chapman Street	127.32
*Clapp, Philip F., et ux, 10 Winsor Avenue	302.51
Clark, Earl S., Boston	177.68
Clark, E. Everett, et ux, 11 Katherine Road	167.31
Clark, Gladys Marguerite, 15 Bostonia Avenue	160.55
Clarke, Maria, 22 Everett Avenue	145.35
*Clay, Heirs Cassius G., 94 Lexington Street	2.24
*Clifford, Marie E., 36 Hosmer Street	256.88
Clifford, Philip G., Boston	1,825.51
Clifford, Phillip G., Receiver	300.82
Clinton, Grace S., et al, 3 Whitney Street	255.19
Cloherty, Delia M., 14 Morse Street	275.47
Cody, Walter W., 250 Main Street	46.20
Coffey, Heirs John, 251 Pleasant Street	72.67
Coffey, Heirs Michael, 127 Fayette Street	118.30
Coffin,, Ernest L., et ux, 24 Beacon Park	158.86
Cohen, Benjamin, 84A Main Street	8.11
Cohen, Dexter S., 2A Mt. Auburn Street	3.38
Cohen, Frances R., 47 Capitol Street	175.76
Colbert, Laura R., 14 Appleton Terrace	212.94
Colby, Maurice D., Piermont Street	13.26
Cole, Harold A., 191 Maplewood Street	285.61
Coleman, Frederick T., et ux, 22 Edenfield Avenue	175.31
Coleman, Warren L., 38 Wilmot Street	175.76
Colesworthy, George B., 44 Adams Avenue	468.13
Colley, Charles B., et ux, 72 Carroll Street	261.95
*Colligan, Mary A., 5 Royal Street	130.13
Collins, Anna M., et al, 157 Galen Street	199.42
Collins, Caroline A., 43 Paul Street	174.07
*Collins, James P., 64 Carroll Street	183.27
Collins, John A., 43 Paul Street	160.55
Collins, Margaret W., 4 Avon Road	245.07
Collins, Ravenel L., 70 Beechwood Avenue	3.38
Collins, Thomas, et ux, 14 Gilkey Court	141.96
Collins, Walter W., et ux, 15 Sheldon Road	204.49
Collins, William J., et ux, 15 Edenfield Avenue	232.77
Colliton, Michael, et ux, 11 Arthur Terrace	109.85
Comick, Anna M., 50 Wilmot Street	143.65

*Commonwealth Co-operative Bank	273.78
Commonwealth Equities Corp.	236.60
Condon, John P., 145 Waverley Avenue	620.84
Condon, John P., Corp. 145 Waverley Avenue	277.16
Condon, Pierce P., Trustee	101.45
Connelly, Patrick H., et ux, 36 Edenfield Avenue	154.43
Connors, William H., 114 Rutland Street	162.35
Conrad, Emmeline F., 22 Olney Street	152.10
Conroy, Catherine, 24 Beacon Street	86.19
Consolazio, Anthony, 270 Palfrey Street	141.34
Constazo, Joseph M., 125 Mt. Auburn Street	6.76
Conti, Annie, 53 Riverside Street	147.34
Conway, Margaret M., 246 Boylston Street	246.74
Cooch, Mary E. B., 99 Robbins Road	282.23
Coon, Malvina J., 21 Palfrey Street	300.82
Cooper, Anson, et ux, 171 Maplewood Street	206.18
Corazzini, Anna Santoro, 27 Cypress Street	268.71
Corazzini, Elsie C., 25 Channing Road	288.58
Corazzini, Salvatore, et al, Main Street	52.39
Corcoran, David F., et ux, 132 Langdon Avenue	216.32
Corrigan, Ernest J., Trustee, Belmont	31.48
Corsetti, Guiseppe, et ux, 199 Lexington Street	135.20
Corsi, Bernardo, 215 Palfrey Street	42.25
Corsi, Tommaso, 112 Forest Street	88.80
Cosgrove Bakers Incorporated, 32 Crawford Street	437.71
Cosman, Frank T., 44 Morse Street	10.14
Costello, Ellen F., 36 Purvis Street	133.80
Cotter, Michael, 44 No. Beacon Street	246.74
Cotter, Michael, et ux, 44 No. Beacon Street	135.20
*Cotter, Timothy J., Mattapan	90.95
Cousbelis, Evanthia, 128 Westminster Avenue	278.79
Cousebelis, Louis, 684 Mt. Auburn Street	713.44
Couture, Alice M., 193 Pleasant Street	239.98
Couture, H. Joseph, et ux, 42 Carroll Street	204.80
Covino, Frank, 226 Westminster Avenue	16.90
Cox, Edward John, et ux, 51 Bailey Road	479.77
Coyne, Ellen M., 48 Commonwealth Road	292.37
*Crabtree, Constance H., Newton Centre	733.46
Craig, Amy L., 139 Church Street	261.95
*Craig, Irene, Boston	567.11
Craig, Samuel T., et ux, 41 Lowell Avenue	169.00
Cramer, Merrill E., et ux, 107 Common Street	313.50
Crawford, Calvin D., et al, Newtonville	15.21
Crawford, Mattie C., 30 Lincoln Street	429.26

Crawford, James E., et ux, 59 Carroll Street	229.84
Creeley, Heirs Oscar S., 128 Mt. Auburn Street	526.44
Crewe, Wiley D., et ux, 326 Charles River Road	282.23
*Critchett, Eleanor W., 35 Arden Road	535.87
*Critchett, Everett H., 35 Arden Road	2.54
Cronin, John W., et ux, 61 Shattuck Road	834.51
*Crowell, Warner R., 122 Garfield Street	329.55
Crowley, Charles F., Cambridge	23.66
Crowley, Joseph, et ux, 58 Bates Road	260.26
Crowley, Lillian G., 41 Stoneleigh Road	350.68
Crupi, Rosaria, 11 Keith Street	15.21
Cucinotta, Giovanni, Waverley	32.30
Cucinotta, John, Waverley	101.97
Cucinotta, Nunziata, Waltham	55.77
Cummings, Lawrence F., 34 Morton Street	236.11
Cummings, Roy L., 35 Upland Road	246.74
Cunniff, Heirs Catherine M., 79 Marshall Street	321.10
Cunniff, P. Sarsfield, 79 Marshall Street	270.40
Curcio, Theresa, 41 Fayette Street	280.54
Curran, Julia M., et al, 790 Mt. Auburn Street	290.68
Currie, Bessie, Hingham	297.83
Curtin, Edward A., et ux, 63 Carver Road	312.65
*Cusolito, Frederick, 123 Galen Street	33.80
Cutter Realty Corporation, Somerville	174.47
Cutting, A. Cora, 63 Commonwealth Road	295.75
Cutting, Flossie C., 9 Edith Avenue	243.36
Dailey, Edna M., 24 Oakley Road	331.24
D'Alanno, Antonio, 88 Arlington Street	6.76
Daley, Margaret J., 86 Edenfield Avenue	210.78
Daflino, Carmelo, 214 Waverley Avenue	6.76
Dalkranian, Krikor, 41 Melendy Avenue	148.72
Dalkranian, Nazareth K., 40 Laurel Street	187.59
Dallorso, Nicholas et ux, Providence, R. I.	13.52
Daly, Kathleen M., Waltham	263.64
Dalzell, Frederick W., 34 Oliver Street	226.46
D'Amico, Nicolas, et ux, 92 Putnam Street	219.70
D'Andrea, Vittorio, et ux, 23 Cottage Lane	158.42
Dane, Henry, 824 Mt. Auburn Street	64.22
Danner, Hazel G., 157 Common Street	236.60
Danskin, John F., et ux, 18 Hillside Road	261.95
Darakjian, Krikor, et ux, 29 Hazel Street	263.64
Dardis, James B., 26 Hawthorne Street	167.31
Dardis, Mary A., 26 Howthorne Street	145.34
Dasey, Elizabeth, Reading	260.60

Davenport, Alfred M,, 88 Grove Street	588.12
Davenport, Florence B., 88 Grove Street	50.70
Davey, Catherine, Trustee, 148 Robbins Road	376.88
Davison, Charles U., et ux, 15 Palfrey Street	2.70
Davitt, William, Atlantic	6.76
Davock, Mary E., 35 Stuart Street	167.31
Days, James, et ux, 155 Spruce Street	178.94
Dadekian, Baghdasar, 5 Louise Street	6.76
Dadekian, Baghader, et ux, 155 Dexter Avenue	248.43
Dadekian, Vartan, et al, 138 Nichols Avenue	326.06
Dee, Patrick J., et ux, 31 Channing Road	305.48
DeFelice, Giuseppe, et ux, 230 Westminster Avenue	15.21
DeFillipo, Josephine, 61 Langdon Avenue	241.67
DeFranco, Stella, Roslindale	262.59
Degeorgio, Pasquale, et ux, 146 Palfrey Street	245.05
DeGiacomo, Giacente et ux, 111 Evans Street	279.00
Degnan, Michael J., Belmont	393.59
Delleville, Antonio, et ux, 109 Arsenal Street	557.70
Delorey, John E., 141 Waltham Street	106.01
Deluca, James, et ux, 43 Loomis Avenue	148.72
Demarco, Joseph, et al, 99 Spring Street	50.70
Demirjian, Poline S., 216 Boylston Street	258.57
Demitrio, Mary, 34 Clarendon Street	160.30
DePrato, Urbano, 62 Bigelow Avenue	8.45
DeQuattro, Mary M., 38 Dartmouth Street	226.46
DerBedrosian, Lucia, 13 Putnam Street	241.67
DerBoghasian, Mardiros, 25 Nichols Avenue	8.45
DerBoghosian, Marion K., 21 Melendy Avenue	190.07
DerBoghosian, Mardiros, 13 Hosmer Street	239.98
Derderian, Missak, 208 Common Street	552.63
Derderian, Setrak, 216 Common Street	615.16
Deronde, Irena S., Cambridge	255.19
Descheneaux, Dorothy B., 158 Common Street	229.13
Descheneaux, George L., 158 Common Street	16.90
Deschenes, Arthur, 36 Upland Road	1.69
Desmond, Julia, 46 Eliot Street	147.03
Desmond, Richard, et ux, 87 Carroll Street	256.88
Dewire, Mabel G., et al, Somerville	456.30
*Dewire & Son, Thomas A., Somerville	32.11
*Dewire, Thomas A., Somerville	234.91
Dexter, Evans K., et ux, 101 Lovell Road	309.42
*DiBacco, Joseph, et ux, 4 Sexton Street	108.16
DiBlasio, Nicola, et ux, 51 Quimby Street	227.77
Dichter, Rietta R., 45 Maplewood Street	273.78

Dickensheid, Katherina, 30 Carver Road East	275.47
Didomenico, Allessandro, et ux, 92 Waltham Street	199.42
Didomenico, Alexander D., 92 Waltham Street	21.97
DiFraia, Maria, Trustee, Somerville	33.80
DiGiacomandrea, Domenico, et ux, 169 Fayette Street	82.81
Dilbarian, Dikran, 59 Templeton Parkway	328.97
Diliberto, Francesco, et ux, 749 Mt. Auburn Street	268.71
DiMarino, Michelle, 497 Pleasant Street	538.27
DiMascio, Raffaele, et ux, 86 School Street	194.35
Dinjian, Leo A., 17 Main Street	6.76
Diozzi, Julia L., Somerville	15.21
*DiPace, Elizabeth M., 9 Oakley Road	341.83
DiPietrantonio, Carmine, et ux, 63 Waltham Street	152.10
DiVecchio, Vincenzo, 129 Waltham Street	10.14
Dixon, Forrest W., 602 Belmont Street	345.07
Dobrowolski, Michael, et ux, East Cambridge	278.85
Dodd, Emma L., 6 Sunnybank Road	353.78
Dodge, Charles A., Heirs, 476 Mt. Auburn Street	574.60
Dodge, Ellery A., 73 Spring Street	3.04
Dohanian, Hagop M., et al, Somerville	304.20
Doherty, George, et ux, 25 Lovell Road	156.80
Donabed, Avedis B., et al, 121 School Street	245.05
Donahue, Charles F., et ux, 28 Robbins Road	259.79
Donohue, Paul James, 434 Mt. Auburn Street	329.52
Donahue, Thomas I., et ux, 71 Barnard Avenue	419.12
Donne, Nicola Delle, et ux, 175 Fayette Street	23.66
Donnelly, Bertha, 33 Hunt Street	145.34
Donnelly, John W., et ux, 37 Walnut Street	243.36
Donnelly, Margaret R., Malden	264.46
Donnelly, Mary E., 32 Bradford Road	289.46
Donavan, Lawrence E., Boston	505.59
Donavan, Mary E., et al, 18 Wolcott Road	282.15
Donavan, Mary J., 24 Theurer Park	297.82
Dosdoumian, Avedig, et ux, 148 Nichols Avenue	287.76
Doucakis, Andromacki, 223 Arlington Street	275.47
Doudakian, Steven, et al, 205 Boylston Street	231.53
Doyle, Mary, Newton Centre	289.47
Driscoll, James, et ux, Framingham	279.19
Dubois, Wilfred, 159 Spruce Street	167.11
Dudley, George W., et ux, 17 Spruce Street	297.44
Dudley, George W., et ux, 115 Spruce Street	197.73
Duest, Lydia M., 70 Hovey Street	126.75
Duff, Joseph L., 161 Lovell Road	282.23
Duffy, Mary E., 503 Main Street	57.46

Dugan, Sarah A., 158 No. Beacon Street	282.23
Duley, George E., et ux, 98 Spruce Street	221.39
Durbin, Joseph et ux, 24 Morse Street	57.73
Dunbar, Arthur R., 141 Marshall Street	190.97
Dunn, Joseph A., 279 Mt. Auburn Street	90.25
Durnan, James H., Jr., 79 No. Beacon Street	23.66
Durnan, James H., Jr., et al, 56 Melendy Avenue	253.50
Durnan, James H., 56 Melendy Avenue	141.96
Durnan, Heirs Nora, 44 Melendy Avenue	305.89
Durnan, Patrick, Melendy Avenue	3.38
Dwyer, Frank, 293 Main Street	3.38
Dwyer, Margaret M., 30 Stuart Street	174.07
Dwyer, Michael F., et ux, 485 Main Street	177.45
Dwyer, Winifred G., 24 Whitcomb Street	101.40
Dyson, Josephine H., 59 Orchard Street	276.47
Eagleson, Eva M., 60 Hillside Street	150.64
*Eagleson, William, 61 Hillside Street	196.61
Eagleson, William Sr., 60 Hillside Street	11.44
Eames, Lee, 12 Merchants Row	3.38
East Cambridge Savings Bank,	567.84
Eastman, Teresa A., 44 Olcott Street	162.24
East Watertown Realty	6.76
Eatough, George, et ux, 15 Auburn Court	143.65
*Eaton, Leona M., 64 Hillside Road	190.97
Eaton, Leroy S., 144 Winsor Avenue	128.44
Eaton, Leroy S., et ux, 144 Winsor Avenue	207.87
Eckland, Walter, et ux, 10 Purvis Street	29.93
Egan, William C., Cambridge	338.00
Eagleson, William, 61 Hillside Street	11.44
Ehrlich, Mary, Chelsea	336.31
Elacqua, Carmen, 264 Arlington Street	292.37
Emerson, Bessie M., 48 Walnut Street	190.97
Emerton, John, 85 Forest Street	138.58
English, Carmen, et ux, 25 Cottage Street	143.65
English, Enrico, 87 Summer Street	201.11
English, Sam, et ux, 129 Waverley Avenue	454.51
Eordekian, John, et ux, 194 Boylston Street	265.33
Erskine, Doris L., 91 Common Street	189.28
Erskine, Kenneth H., 91 Common Street	33.80
Erwin, Florence L., Winthrop	221.39
Essayan, Boghos, 64 California Street	250.12
Essayan, Kariken, 29 Boylston Street	3.38
*Esterberg, Herbert L., 17 Main Street	33.80
Evans, Josephine M., Arlington	526.58

Everett-Beechler Tire Co., 75 No. Beacon Street 10.82
*Everett, Lillian G., 122 Marshall Street 182.52
*Falco, Antonio, 167 Warren Street 10.14
Falco, Rose, 159 Lexington Street 892.72
*Falzarano, Louis, et al, 169 Walnut Street 8.45
Faneuil Co-operative Bank, Brighton 820.23
Farese, Angelo, 7 Maple Street 195.40
Farese, Angelo, et ux, 16 Gleason Street............................. 385.73
*Farese, Theresa, 264 Warren Street .:................................ 221.84
Farese, Vincenzo, 108 Forest Street 49.01
Farrell, Ellen Z., et al, 12 Rifle Court 89.57
Farrington, John, et ux, 43 Partridge Street 170.69
Farwell, Winifred D., 70 Robbins Road 255.19
Favuzza, Guiseppe, et ux, 129 Nichols Avenue 409.00
Fay, John J., 24 Putnam Street 234.91
Fazio, Michele, et al, Boston 234.91
Fenerjian, Khachadoor S., 170 Belmont Street 10.14
Ferrari, Andrew, 50 Prentiss Street 157.17
Ferraro, Napoleone, 38 Crawford Street 177.45
Ferry, Alice E., 16 St. Mary's Street 272.09
Fewkes, Charles H., et al, 53 Maple Street 106.47
Fierman, William, Edenfield Avenue 10.14
Files, Walter W., 12 Hardy Avenue 1.69
Fish, Jennie, M., 16 Templeton Parkway 313.65
Fisher, Edgar E., et ux, 30 Keenan Street 250.12
*Fisher, Martin W., Belmont 228.15
Fiske, C. Allen, et ux, 46 Arden Road 340.90
Fisk, Joseph H., Boston 606.71
Fitzgerald, Jerome V., et ux, 836 Belmont Street 253.50
Fitzgerald, Martin, et ux, 90 Fayette Street 163.93
*Fitzgerald, Rose A., 34 Olcott Street 177.45
Fitzgerald, Veronica E., 832 Belmont Street 184.21
*Fitzpatrick, James H., et ux, 33 Middlesex Road 406.60
Fitzpatrick, James J., 41 Maplewood Street 238.29
*Fitzpatrick, Mary A., 68 Dexter Avenue............................ 189.25
Flagg, Colon J. et ux, 35 Pequossette Street :.................... 114.92
*Flanagan, James E. et al, 25 Elliot Street.......................... 243.36
*Fleming, Robert, 165 Summer Street 106.47
*Fletcher, Ruth A., 10 Grenville Road 273.78
Flitcroft, Albert E., Chapman Street 16.90
Folino, Anna, 31 Morton Street ....:.................................. 239.49
Fontana, Antoietta, 29 Elmwood Avenue 158.37
Forand, Delphis C., 94 Lowell Avenue :............................. 463.06
Ford, Alexander C. et ux, 18 Wilmot Street 327.86

Ford, John C. et ux, 61 Green Street	82.81
Ford, Matilda E., 57 Emerson Road	184.60
Ford, Walter A. et ux, 158 Winsor Avenue	324.48
Forte, Vincenzo et ux, 173 Walnut Street	101.40
Foskett, Martha M., 129 Edenfield Avenue	150.15
Fowler, John W., 76 Olcott Street	257.67
Fowler & Son, Joseph, 16 Ladd Street	6.76
Franchi, Paolo et ux, 87 Arlington Street	177.45
Franchina, Paul F. G., 39 Morton Street	236.11
Frandesia, Pietro et al, 22 Cushman Street	180.83
Frappier, Ella M., 35 Elton Avenue	216.32
Fraser, Helen Chase, Washington, D. C.	10.14
French, Robert C., 46 Hersom Street	114.92
Frishchette, John J., 876 Mt. Auburn Street	8.46
Frye, Gustaf E., 80 Hillside Road	190.97
Fuller, Annie et al, 297 Waverley Avenue	121.68
Gale, Mary A., 35 Lovell Road	307.58
Galen Corporation, Maine	804.44
Gallagher, Agnes L., 111 Irving Street	150.41
Gallagher, Annie, 58 Whites Avenue	167.31
Gallagher, Gertrude C., et al, Cambridge	743.60
Gallagher, James M., 2 Maplewood Street	306.54
Gallagher, Thomas J. et ux, 40 Everett Avenue	193.66
*Gallarico, James, 783 Mt. Auburn Street	6.76
Galligan, Winifred C., 12 Palmer Street	257.98
Ganderizio, James, 102 Main Street	10.14
Gandolpho, Heirs Charles J., 114 Dexter Avenue	512.09
Gandolpho, Charles J., 114 Dexter Avenue	28.73
Gannazzi, Angelo, 213 Arlington Street	16.90
Gaqi, Andrew, 599 Mt. Auburn Street	50.70
Garabedian, Eliza M., 80 Boylston Street	245.05
Garabedian, Haig S., 1 Arden Avenue	388.99
Garabedian, Hovsep et ux, 20 Laurel Street	211.25
Garabedian, Kevork, Newton Upper Falls	89.57
Gardella, Frimo et ux, 6 Warwick Road	304.48
*Garfield, James C., 35 Main Street	30.42
Garafolo, Domenico, 308 Main Street	43.94
Garafolo, Frances, 12 Linden Street	136.89
Garafolo, Serafina, 29 Hillcrest Circle	367.31
Gartland, Mary C., 49 Olcott Street	227.04
*Garvey, Patrick J., 235 Arsenal Street	234.91
Gass, Samuel et al, Chelsea	1,608.88
Gavin, Jennie A., 66 Irving Street	878.11
Gavin, Margaret E., 25 Birch Road	275.97

Gaziano, Charles, 53 Warren Street	236.10
Gehring, William J., Boston	31.70
Geljookian, Kriker G. et ux, 48 Fairfield Street.....................	221.39
*Gentile, Amelia, Waltham	6.76
*Gentile, Dunate et al, Waltham	10.14
*Gentile, Joseph, 825 Mt. Auburn Street	8.45
Gentile, Luisella, 396 Main Street	267.02
*Geoghegan, Eleanor Mary, 41 Stuart Street	182.52
Geoghegan, Lawrence J., 41 Stuart Street	212.94
*Gethro, Anna T., 15 Katherine Road	158.86
*Gethro, George W., 15 Katherine Road	6.76
Geyekian, Arthur S., 82 Dexter Avenue	1,003.86
Geyikian, Steve, 354 Arsenal Street	6.76
Giacomandrea, Giovanni et ux, 47 Hosmer Street..................	236.60
Giannetto, Pasquale, 131 Grant Avenue	43.94
Gibson, Henry W., 14 Avon Road	4.06
Gibson, Ina E. P., 14 Avon Road	209.56
Gilberg, Henrick et ux, 91 Bradford Road	289.46
Gilbert, George F. et ux, 95 Barnard Avenue.........................	314.34
Gilbert, William B. et ux, 19-Malden Street	109.85
Giles, George A., Belmont	228.90
Gilfoil, Margaret, 26 Morton Street	212.94
Gill, Gordon S., 103 Common Street	231.53
Gilliatt, Gertrude A., 20 Commonwealth Road	275.47
Gillis, Loretto B., 176 Lovell Road	282.23
Gilmore, Katie M., 84 Garfield Street	1,144.68
Giorgiani, Joseph, 135 Spring Street	3.38
Giragosian, Herant M., 587 Mt. Auburn Street	3.38
*Giragosian, Henry M. et al, Brighton	331.24
Giuliano, Angelina, 143 Fayette Street	49.09
Given, Susan D., 531 Mt. Auburn Street	147.03
*Glidden, Mary C.	8.45
Glossa, William R. et ux, 375 Mt. Auburn Street....................	304.39
Glover, Charles A., South Lincoln	10.14
*Glynn, John F. et ux, 143 Irving Street..................................	248.43
Goldbank, Vosgerchian, 145 Mt. Auburn Street	33.80
Goldberg, Charles, 333 Main Street	30.42
Goldberg, Samuel H., 76 Main Street	72.67
Goldstein, Hyman, 52 Mt. Auburn Street	3.38
Goldthwaite, Dema D., 172 Bellevue Road	252.12
Gonsalo, Manuel A. et al, 72 Hillside Road	201.11
Goodsell, Carolyn W., 105 Garfield Street	614.63
Goodwin, Edward A., 134 Westminster Avenue	165.85
*Gorenstein, Sophie et al, Brighton	510.38

Gorman, Charles J., Boston 705.75

Gould, Alden W. et ux, 42 Wilmot Street 147.03

Grace, Frank S. et ux, 9 Jewett Street 155.48

Grant, Agnes et al, New York 32.34

Grant, Walter B., 32 Arsenal Street 77.74

Gray, Ralph E., 648 Mt. Auburn Street 27.04

Gray, Robert W., Cambridge 263.64

Green, Darby, 10 Hunt Street 481.65

Green, Russell A., 62 Maplewood Street 267.02

Greene, Cora I., 33 Stearns Road 331.24

Greene, Georgina F., 83 Franklin Street 183.52

Greene, Willard B., 222 Bellevue Road 345.07

Greenland, Fanny, 28 Gilbert Street 282.59

Greenwood, Wilfred C. et ux, 10 Chapman Street.............. 234.91

Griffin, Emma C., 74 Charles River Road.............................. 292.80

*Griffin, Mary E. et al, 362 Mt. Auburn Street.............. 327.86

Grillo, Santo et ux, 40 Loomis Avenue 183.09

Grimes, Lillian J., 74 Channing Road 317.56

Grinnell, William T., 14 Waverley Avenue 246.30

Griswold, L. D. 15.21

Grogan, Margaret C., 158 Russell Avenue............................ 324.48

Grower, James G. et ux, 30 Barnard Avenue 272.09

*Grund, Hedwig, Norton 189.28

Guarnieri, Fred L. et ux, 10 Elmwood Avenue....................... 145.34

Guberman, Hyman, Newton 687.36

Guerino, Jennie, Sparkill Street 6.76

Guidrey, Frances M., 26 Spruce Street 665.86

Gunderson, Robert A. et ux, 14 Clyde Road 295.75

Gustafson, John F., Watertown Street 3.38

Guzzetti, Guiseppe et ux, 101 Arlington Street.................... 405.60

Haartz, Mason Grower Co., 270 Pleasant Street 1,507.48

Haboian, Bedros et al, 105 School Street 417.43

Hadjinlian, Mary, 92 Nichols Avenue 27.56

Hadjinlian, Sarkis, 92 Boylston Street 282.23

Hagopian, Hagop, 8 Melendy Avenue 248.43

*Hagian, Sam, 561 Mt. Auburn Street 13.52

Hagopian, Karop H. et ux, 37 Melendy Avenue................... 100.00

Hall, Dorothy B., 14 Carroll Street 118.30

*Hall, Edward C., Jr., 63 Mt. Auburn Street 246.34

Hall, Edwin M., 30 Fuller Road 321.32

Hall, Eva B., 74 Barnard Avenue 150.75

Hallhaian, Jacob, 26 Galen Street 3.38

Hamilton, Charles E., Newton Centre 487.73

Hamlin, Cyril et al, 18 Watertown Street............................. 43.94

Hamm, M. Louise, Belmont	.607.64
Hammill, Catherine A., 66 Capitol Street	297.44
Hanlon, Bridget M., 10 Appleton Terrace	198.85
Hannon, Owen, 65 Hazel Street	238.25
Hannon, Mark et al, 59 Boyd Street	238.29
Hansen, Henry M., 129 Grove Street	251.16
Hanson, Mildred A., 60 Gilbert Street	236.60
Hanson, Mildred A., 42 Chapman Street	167.02
Hapgood, Theodore B., 68 Pearl Street	130.00
Hararis, Angelo et ux, 31 Kondazian Street	220.30
Harley, Bruce et ux, 178 Spruce Street	175.92
Harney, Mary, 38 Chauncy Street	241.67
Haroian, Arakel, 1A Crawford Street	16.90
Haroian, Daleta, 17 Kondazian Street	221.99
Harrington, Ralph E., South Sudbury	45.63
Harris, Arthur L., 45 Fairview Avenue	345.23
*Harris, Charles A., 12 Mt. Auburn Street	25.35
Harris, George C., 18 Fairfield Street	216.32
*Harris, Isaac et al, 37 Tremont Street	1,595.36
Harris, William S., 637 Mt. Auburn Street	1.69
*Hart, Ellen E., Brighton	12.31
Harting, Herbert C., 62 Templeton Parkway	546.32
Hartnett, Patrick, 766 Mt. Auburn Street	13.52
Hartnett, Elizabeth C., 766 Mt. Auburn Street	229.03
Hartung, Paul G., 62 Templeton Parkway	219.70
Harvard Trust Company, Cambridge	496.02
Harvey, Heirs Fannie, 16 Chestnut Street	74.47
Harvey, William M., et ux, 33 Warren Street	168.50
Haskell, Fred M. et ux, 227 Sycamore Street	68.65
*Hasle, Carl A., 114 School Street	52.26
*Haskell, Frank S., et ux, 28 Morse Street	49.56
Hatch, Walter L. et al, 18 Hill Street	37.20
Haughey, Helen Loretto, 343 School Street	175.76
Hauswirth, John J. et ux, 300 Waverley Avenue	255.19
Hawes, Anna McKay, 183 Mt. Auburn Street	319.41
*Hawes, Lena F., 31 Russell Avenue	255.00
Hawes, Otis L., 15 Main Street	117.62
*Hawkins, Alfred C., 26 Middlesex Road	394.60
Hawkins, William J. et ux, 271 Waverley Avenue	100.28
Hawthorne, Ruth L., 4 Carver Road East	398.84
*Hayes, Cornelius B. et ux, 77 Union Street	67.19
Hayes, Earl E. A., 18 Harrington Street	157.25
Haynes, Gladys D., 64 Union Street	135.20
Hayes, Maurice L. et al, 20 Alfred Road	240.34

Hayward, Hannah G., 40 Highland Avenue	50.70
Healey, John J., 503 Waltham Street	145.34
*Hegarty, Martin, Brighton	317.59
Henderson, Francis R. et al, Cambridge	6.76
Henderson, Maynard C. et ux, 207 Lexington Street	136.89
Hennelly, Walter L., Waltham	426.52
Hennessey, Thomas M., 1072 Belmont Street	13.52
Hennessey, Thomas M. et ux, 1072 Belmont Street	263.64
Hermanson, Hans, 44 Gilbert Street	147.03
Hershfield, Louis, Lawrence	963.30
*Heshion, Mary E., 90 Fitchburg Street	172.62
Hewitt, Agnes, 59 Capitol Street	190.97
Hewitt, Francis J., 55 Capitol Street	231.53
Hickey, Cornelius, 18 Irma Avenue	267.02
Hicks, Lefie C., 88 Riverside Street	196.04
Higham, Martha M., 370 School Street	277.16
Hill, Edward L., 48 Brookline Street	71.97
Hill, Elsa M., 700 Belmont Street	210.56
Hill, Oscar W., 700 Belmont Street	272.37
*Hillers, Charles A., 111 Charles Street	3.38
Hiller, George R., 28 Belmont Street	156.08
*Hillside Co-op. Bank, Medford	214.63
Hinckley, Lalia L., 119 Spruce Street	175.00
Hinckley, Ora E., 35 Mt. Auburn Street	13.52
Hjelmquist, Oscar et ux, 83 Bradford Road	142.08
Hodge, Charles H., 45 Bates Road	271.25
Hodges, Maude D., Malden	86.61
Hoffman, Helen B., 49 Bradford Road	160.88
Holbrook, Astrid S., 49 Chapman Street	143.90
Holbrook, Mabel A., 56 Olcott Street	159.65
Holland, Edward D., 16 Stearn Road	446.72
Holland, Mary A., 94 Galen Street	121.10
Holloway, Minnie C., 83 Barnard Avenue	365.04
Holmes, Austin H., 54 Fayette Street	106.47
Holmes, Clinton E., 94 Union Street	159.87
*Holmes, Emma W. S., Waverley	40.87
Holmes, Mary L., 272 Belmont Street	283.61
Holt, Charles P. et ux, 92 Standish Road	282.23
Hooban, Thomas J., 67 No. Beacon Street	109.85
Hopewell, Frank B. Tr., 36 Pleasant Street	1,885.31
*Hopkins, John J., 12 Frank Street	216.32
Hovagimian, 112 Laurel Street	136.89
Howard, Alvin, 145 Arsenal Street	3.38
*Howard, Helen G., 37 Russell Avenue	1.92

Howarth, Frank et ux, 89 Morse Street	64.79
Howe, Ernestine P., 58 Marshall Street	100.00
Howell, Edmund et ux, 12 Fitchburg Street	157.17
Howes, Flora A., 256 No. Beacon Street	165.62
Howes, Marie W., 28 Purvis Street	74.54
Hubbell, Phyllis A., Belmont	192.37
Hudson, Mary J., 24 Franklin Street	157.17
Hughes, Edward F., 20 Hawthorne Street	153.79
Hughes, Emily G., 7 Purvis Street	160.55
*Hughes, Flora M., 30 Grandview Avenue	109.85
*Hughes, Harry J., Grandview Avenue	5.07
Hughes, Joseph M. et ux, 10 Morton Street	263.15
Hughes, Heirs Margaret, 321 Main Street	341.58
Hughes, Heirs Mary A., 11 Royal Street	125.38
Hughes, Matilda V., Waltham	873.73
Hull, Ruth N., 47 Emerson Road	209.21
Hulten, Johan Hilmar et ux, 43 Carver Road	264.47
Hunt, John Joseph, 29 Chandler Street	64.76
Hunt, Murtagh, 26 King Street	226.46
Hurley, Arthur J. et ux, 19 Locke Street	317.54
Hurley, John, 164 Main Street	1.69
Hurley, John J., 6 Hosmer Street	239.98
Husselbee, Cyril et ux, 3 Summit Road	223.21
Hutchinson, Charles C., 18 Hovey Street	208.19
Hutton, Charles S., 694 Mt. Auburn Street	3.38
Hyde Park Savings Bank, Hyde Park	134.03
Hyman, Jacob, 2 Ladd Street	6.76
Hynes, Frank J., 4 Clyde Road	314.34
Iannazzi, Angelo, 302 Arlington Street	93.06
Iannelli, Nicola, 17 Winter Street	270.40
Igoe, Esther M., 16 Palmer Street	292.26
Ilacqua, Matteo et ux, 9 Myrtle Street	80.80
*Iliffe, William H., 99 Bailey Road	780.78
Inferra, Anton, 779 Mt. Auburn Street	40.56
*Inferra, Joseph, 103 Arlington Street	16.90
Inferra, Josephine, 781 Mt. Auburn Street	587.00
Ingalls, Harriette L., 30 Adams Avenue	442.78
Inglese, Gian F. et ux, 54 Crawford Street	47.73
Innocenzio, Pantolea, Newton	59.15
Iodice, Alfonso, 117 Warren Street	507.00
Iodice, Amodeo et al, 808 Mt. Auburn Street	200.17
Iodice, Clemente, 259 Lexington Street	23.66
Irish, Ernest C. et ux, 59 Bailey Road	451.23
*Ivans, Heirs Benjamin D., et al, 185 Devonshire St., Boston	65.48

Jacobson, Florence R. L., 52 Partridge Street	165.98
Jacobson, Martin B. et ux, 10 Gay Road	273.00
Jacobson, William, et al, 74 Main Street	101.40
*Jacques, Catherine, 65 Templeton Parkway	81.32
James, Anna E., 16 Wells Avenue	185.98
Janigian, Krikor, 96 Dexter Avenue	153.79
Jamikian, Asdour, et al, 26 Fairfield Street	241.67
Jarossi, Nicola, et ux, 31 Ralph Street	136.89
Jelladian, Garabed, et al, 15 Dartmouth Street	246.74
Jenkins, Walter L., et ux, 123 Spruce Street	194.59
Jennings, George K., et al, Allston	1,224.89
Jensen, John K., 572 Main Street	50.70
Jerossi, Nicola, et ux, Sparkill Street	6.76
Jewett, Alfred F., et ux, 27 Stoneleigh Road	344.76
Jigarjian, Hagop, et ux, 2 Appleton Street	197.73
Jiggerjian, Anna, 7 Dartmouth Street	224.77
Jiuliano, Michael, et ux, 157 Fayette Street	157.02
*Jobin, Theodore, 28 Chester Street	230.69
Johanson, Cecelia W., 40 Maplewood Street	344.32
Johansson, Ernest G., et ux, 37 Fairview Avenue	349.93
Johnson, Adele V., Somerville	268.71
Johnson, Agnes E., et al, 149 School Street	265.33
Johnson, Anna A., 44 Carver Road East	304.20
Johnson, Astrid L., 84 Bradford Road	269.18
Johnson, August, Somerville	251.81
Johnson, Carl E., 159 Palfrey Street	206.18
Johnson, Charles F., East Cambridge	231.53
Johnson, Grace O., 154 Common Street	505.39
Johnson, J. Erhard, 2 Belmont Street	40.56
Johnson, Louïse S., 130 School Street	267.02
Johnson, Nels A., et ux, 43 Pequosette Street	245.05
Johnson, Pauline Ames, 28 Sunnybank Road	338.00
Johnson, Roy C., Boston	206.18
Johnson, Vera Newbury, 18 Priest Road	279.48
Johnston, George D., et ux, 8 Amherst Road	334.62
Johnston, Harry E., 25 Wells Avenue	185.98
Jordan, Marie M., 23 Alden Road	275.47
Jordan, Stella L., 38 Chapman Street	150.41
Joseph, Palitia, So. Boston	270.80
*Joy, Cecelia M., et al, 43 Russell Avenue	65.71
Joyce,, Ellen, 23 Boyd Street	163.93
Joyce, John T., 634 Belmont Street	463.06
Joyce, Joseph J., et ux, 129 Worcester Street	146.43
*Joyce, Michael, 23 Boyd Street	170.69

Jucknavorian, Krikor, et al, 348 Arlington Street	245.05
Juiliano, Angelina, 145 Fayette Street	100.00
Juliano, Louis, et ux, 123 Fayette Street	98.92
Kalafatis, Varvara, 13 Porter Street	246.74
*Kalaijian, Matos B., 62 Lexington Street	176.76
Kandar, George, 43 Fuller Road	311.92
Kander, Edward D., 26 Brimmer Street	215.76
Kaplan, Bernard, et al	854.84
Kapralian, Horen, et ux, 31 Dewey Street	107.37
Kaprielian, Rapriel, 5 Nichols Avenue	3.38
Karageusion, Mike, 32 Quimby Street	20.28
Karaian, John S., et ux, 61 Boylston Street	241.67
Karagozian, Mike, 32 Quimby Street	185.55
*Karaian, Kourken, et al, 27 Prentiss Street	52.74
Karkashian, Hovannes, et ux, 77 Putnam Street	278.85
Karalekas, Stella J., et al, 99 Grove Street	258.19
Karamaian, Ohannes N., 16 Keith Street	114.92
Karonso, Ohn, 468 Main Street	8.45
Kashian, Jack, 90 Boylston Street	276.16
Kasper, Anna, 532 Pleasant Street	55.13
Katz, Benjamin, 17 Myrtle Street	25.35
Katz, Fannie, 17 Myrtle Street	194.35
Kaula, Henry J., et ux, 157 Lovell Road	200.00
Kavooghian, Jacob, et ux, 540 Mt. Auburn Street	216.57
Kazanjian, Hagop M., 105 School Street	23.66
Kazarosian, Bagdasaret, et ux, 152 Nichols Avenue	65.19
Keating, Anna M., 493 Main Street	273.09
Keddy, Thomas, 10 Mt. Auburn Street	1.69
Keefe, Albert, et ux, 349 School Street	268.71
Keefe, Charles E., 28 Arsenal Street	9.30
Keefe, Joseph, 174 Main Street	3.38
Keefe, Mary G., 14 Irving Park	691.21
Keefe, Owen, 8 Lincoln Street	6.76
*Keenan, Agnes B., 40 Dexter Avenue	145.75
Keenan, John W., Brighton	256.50
Kehyoian, Giragos, 69 Dexter Avenue	91.90
Keirce, Thomas P., 5 Holt Street	10.14
Keith, Lyde B., 17 Standish Road	287.79
*Keith, William J. A., et ux, 73 Standish Road	297.54
Kelch, Ellen T., 166 Hillside Road	197.73
Kelleher, Thomas, et ux, 33 Elmwood Avenue	194.32
*Kelley, Agnes J., 316 Mt. Auburn Street	377.82
Kelley, Annie M., care of Mary Torres	219.70
Kelley, Annie M., Dorchester	1.343.44

Kelley, Catherine L., 30 Springfield Street 247.30
Kelley, Charles B., 50 California Street 288.99
Kelley, Charles E., 10 Mt. Auburn Street 125.18
Kelley, Clara L., 122 Hillside Road 180.46
Kelley, Emma R., 374 Charles River Road 260.26
Kelley, Garrett, 280 Orchard Street 6.76
*Kelley, Georgia, 26 Winsor Avenue 290.68
Kelley, Harriet A., 39 Waverley Avenue 99.71
Kelley, Helen P., 35 Stoneleigh Road 334.62
Kelley, Herbert B., 105 Poplar Street 297.44
Kelley, James E., et ux, 50 Beacon Park 120.69
Kelley, James P., Waverley 436.02
Kelley, Joseph M., 98 Mt. Auburn Street 13.52
Kelley, Margaret, 35 Morse Street 314.34
*Kelley, Mary A., 24 Melendy Avenue 76.21
*Kelley, Mary J., 26 Frank Street 153.79
Kelley, Joseph, et ux, 48 Winter Street 118.30
Kelly, Maurice W., et al, 40 Bridge Street 97.66
Kelly, Michael, et ux, 49 Bancroft Street 170.64
Kelly, Michael J., et ux, 26 Maple Street 194.35
Kelly, Rebecca, 7 Upland Road 305.89
Kelly, Thomas J., et ux, 101 Lexington Street 99.00
Kelsey, Charles H., et ux, Belmont 42.68
Kennedy, Bertha E., 143 Watertown Street 177.45
Kennedy, Dorothy C., 23 Springfield Street 231.53
Kenney, Mary Evelyn, 81 Summer Street 114.92
Kenney, Patrick J., et ux, 133 Galen Street 206.18
Keohan, Leo E., et ux, 176 Orchard Street 143.59
*Keosseyan, Haig B., 18 Kimball Road 64.77
Keough, Edward H., 187 Arsenal Street 200.00
Kerkbeshian, Harry, et ux, 95 Dexter Avenue 214.63
Keville, Patrick J., 39 Chapman Street 201.07
Khederian, Garabed, 121 Nichols Avenue 618.42
Khederian, Mary, 125 Nichols Avenue 23.66
Kiely, James, 3 Theurer Park 322.10
Kilbride, William H., et ux, 136 Walnut Street 150.41
*Kiley, Margaret E., et al, 54 Chestnut Street 151.76
*Kilgore, Eva L., 135 Galen Street 25.00
Kimball, Charles, 115 Watertown Street 6.76
Kinder, Elizabeth, South Boston 165.62
Kinder, Sarah L., 10 Hillside Road 211.25
King, Anne J., 304 Mt. Auburn Street 140.82
*King, Myles L., et ux, 14 Partridge Street 226.46
*King, Norah T., 15 Partridge Street 129.53

Kirtley, Katherine, 240 Orchard Street 233.28
Kivell, Thomas F., 15 Longfellow Road 188.63
Kloongian, Hagop, et al, 112 School Street 27.04
Knapp, James C., et ux, 139 Langdon Avenue 270.89
*Kneeland, James P., 242 No. Beacon Street 82.0u
Knell, Walter W., 15 Everett Avenue 101.40
Knight, Mfg. Co., 36 Pleasant Street ....: 6.76
Knisell, Nellie P., 264 Common Street 446.03
Knox, George A., 63 Lexington Street 73.44
Koch, John L., 372 Main Street 108.16
*Kokotoff, Henry A., 5 Main Street 8.45
Kondazian, Minas S., Coolidge Hill Road 462.78
Konis, Efrasini, 9 Templeton Parkway 124.24
Kooyoumjian, Nishan, 44 Crawford Street 201.11
Kostarelos, Theresa P., 70 California Street 239.98
Kostick, John, 28 Mt. Auburn Street .... ̄67.60
Kougias, John, Roxbury 244.30
Kouzouian, Manoog, 404 Mt. Auburn Street 33.80
Kritzman, Benjamin, 140 Pleasant Street 204.49
Lafayette Lodge, No. 31, I.O.O.F., Watertown 54.08
LaFlamme, Arthur J., Cambridge 52.39
Lagerblade, Olgar E., 4-Hilltop Road 271.46
Lake, Albert F., 28 Paul Street 243.36
Lake, James, et al, 7 Avon Raod 287.30
*LaMarchia, Carmelo, Watertown 37.22
Landberg, Dorothy, 640 Mt. Auburn Street 16.90
Landry, Arthur N., et ux, 36 Hall Avenue 175.76
Landry, Charles F., et ux, 14 Quincy Street 185.95
Landry, Katherine L., 72 Bradford Road 355.28
Landry, Lean, 4 Pond Street 61.85
Lane, Mdg. Co., 38 Pleasant Street 84.50
Lang, William, 40 Mt. Auburn Street 16.90
*Lang, Katherine A., 22 Oakley Road 131.24
LaRhette, Allen R., 60 Stuart Street 153.79
Larrabee, Caroline A., et al, 40 Oakley Road 389.43
Larsen, Margaret E., 18 Hudson Street 75.31
LaSpada, Annie, 51 Lexington Street 218.68
Lauricella, Antonio, 106 Main Street 173.73
*Laverty, Anthony P., 730 Mt. Auburn Street 268.71
Lavrakas, Robert, 742 Mt. Auburn Street 10.14
Lawson, Agneta B., 100 Langdon Avenue 169.11
Lawton, Susan M., 39 Merrill Road 290.66
Leacy, Cecil M., 53 Galen Street 1,275.95
Leacy, Elizabeth, 111 Galen Street 295.75

*Leacy, Eugene S., et ux, 111 Galen Street	181.87
*Leahy, Abbie J., 38 Parker Street	81.15
Leary, Daniel J., et ux, 12 Stuart Street	165.62
Leave, Charles H., et ux, 42 Standish Road	287.79
Leavitt, Charles O., et ux, 111 Common Street	193.84
Leavitt Shirt Mfg. Co., Inc., 107 Spring Street	42.75
LeFort, Mary S., 134 Summer Street	243.36
Leighton, Harland P., 6 Morse Street	145.34
Lembo, Sebastiano, et ux, 176 Walnut Street	39.27
Lennartson, Josephine A., 27 Commonwealth Road	292.37
*Lennartson, Josephine A., et al, 27 Commonwealth Road....	324.48
Lembruno, Arcangelo, et ux, 47 Bridge Street	40.56
Leombruno, Pasquale, et ux, Brookline	267.24
Leonard, Adeline M., 248 Main Street	102.71
Leone, Antonio, et ux, 199 Boylston Street	191.81
Lepordo, Carlo, et ux, 13 Berkeley Street	182.52
Lepore, Guiseppe, et ux, 23 French Terrace	203.86
LeShane, Frank C., 18 Wilmot Street	40.63
LeShane, Richard, et ux, 615 Main Street	139.02
Leslie, Ethel M., 330 Mt. Auburn Street	200.00
Lester, Clarissa, et al, 28 Fuller Road	288.99
Lester, Clarissa M., 38 Bates Road	299.13
Letterio, Dominic, et ux, 38 Clarendon Street	46.94
Levesque, Martha M., 161 Mt. Auburn Street	40.56
Levine, Esther M., 38 Brimmer Street	233.22
*Lewis, George E., 18 California Park	61.23
Lewis, George M., et ux, 30 Palfrey Street	136.89
Lewis, Grace I., 50 Orchard Street	358.28
*L'Homme Dieu, Howard, et ux, 41 Standish Road	297.54
Lia, Annibale, et ux, 66 Prentiss Street	152.10
Lia, Louise M., 66 Prentiss Street	294.06
Lightbody, Dorothy H., 59 Robbins Road	245.36
*Liljcholm, Elizabeth P., 40 Garfield Street	258.57
Lilegren, A. Hjalmer, et ux, 20 Bradford Road	105.25
Lindahl, Maude Catherine, Prescott Street	16.90
Lindberg, Gustaf Adolf, 92 Bradford Road	245.62
Lindbadh, Clyda E., 340 School Street	657.41
Linehan, Susan C., 17 Bay Street	295.75
Lisanto, Vito, et Caterina, 12 Arsenal Street	20.28
Little, Nellie M., Warner, N. H.,	59.90
LoCascio, Robert, 10 Brimmer Street	251.81
London, Ida, 19 Channing Road	188.58
Longo, Consiglia, Somerville	15.21
Loomer, Pleamin F., Belmont	272.66

Looney, Mark E., et ux, 128 Summer Street	207.87
Lord, Hattie May, 45 Warren Street	80.67
Loring, Gustavus S., et ux, 137 Robbins Road	221.48
Loring, John G., 330 Charles River Road	277.16
Lorrey, Hilma, 71 Wilmot Street	30.66
Lovegren, Oscar P., 38 Gilbert Street	244.56
*Lovell, Eva B., 31 Katherine Road	3.38
Lovell, Heirs John S., 15 Mason Road	132.69
Lubets, Louis, 6 Bigelow Avenue	57.46
Lucas, Susie Dexter, 31 Otis Street	148.43
Lundgren, Victor, 36 Pleasant Street	91.26
Lush, Arthur J., et ux, 138 Common Street	324.48
Luther, Francis J., et ux, 307 Waverley Avenue	145.34
Lydon, Julia, So. Boston	259.07
Lynn Five Cents Savings Bank	374.85
*Lyons, William, Inc., Mt. Auburn Street	3.38
*Lyons, Mary Etta, 45 Robbins Road	121.90
Macarelli, Annie E., 82 Salisbury Road	321.29
MacCurdy, Elmo D., et ux, 100 Bradford Road	169.00
MacDonald, Alexander D., et ux, 62 Marshall Street	322.79
*MacDonald, Almon H., et ux, 22 Otis Street	175.74
MacDonald, Daniel L., et ux, 537 Main Street	651.65
MacDonald, Mary, 9 Cottage Street	91.26
MacDonald, Thomas F., et ux, 34 Gilbert Street	142.03
MacDougall, Donald L., et ux, 4 Concord Road	267.37
*MacIntosh, Walter H., et ux, 102 Robbins Road	234.91
*MacKay, John T., et ux, 2 Gill Road	145.34
Macken, Flora Saunders, Langdon Avenue	200.54
Mackin, Peter J., et ux, 50 Pearl Street	79.43
*MacKinnon, Margaret R., 138 School Street	22.07
MacLean, Alexander A., 60 Standish Road	249.73
MacLean, Roderick, Newton	266.38
*MacMillan, Adam J., 612 Mt. Auburn Street	33.80
MacMillan, Angus C., 183 Palfrey Street	169.00
MacNaughton, P. John, 170 Lovell Road	325.45
*Macurdy, Heirs Anna L., 43 Chester Street	194.35
Madanian, Jacob, 112 Dexter Avenue	18.59
Madanian, Phillip, et ux, 90 Dexter Avenue	231.53
Madden, Ellen, et al, 88 Poplar Street	129.28
*Madden, James F., 64 No. Beacon Street	27.04
Magnusson, Grace, 39 Piermont Street	113.68
Magrath, Edward J., 49 Merrill Road	273.76
Maguire, John J., et ux, 16 Partridge Street	162.24
Maguire, Mary, 72 Arsenal Street	114.92

Mahaney, William D., 16 Grenville Road	249.67
Maher, Frank, 107 Irving Street	270.40
Maher, John J., 7 No. Beacon Street	16.90
Maher, Ulick, et ux, 176 Spruce Street	187.07
Mahon, Margaret, Waltham	265.42
Mahoney, Daniel J., 40 Arsenal Street	135.20
*Mahoney, John J., et ux, 26 Pond Street	18.59
*Mahoney Associates Inc., 191 Arsenal Street	853.45
*Mailly, George, 20 Prescott Street	138.58
Malcolm, Heirs Blanche E., 109 Langdon Avenue	248.43
Malkasian, Peter O., 247 Boylston Street	181.22
*Malone, Francis J., et al, 8 Summit Road	250.12
Maloney, Annie C., 55 Morse Street	114.92
*Maloney, James, No. Beacon Street	3.38
*Maloney, Thomas F., et ux, 39 Green Street	47.45
Mancuso, John, 44 Clarendon Street	74.38
*Mangan, Thomas F., et ux, 12 Melendy Avenue	46.02
Maniaci, Carmelo, 76 Madison Avenue	70.98
Manjourides, Foteka, 21 Kondazian Street	242.27
Manning, Josephine F., 10 Clyde Road	231.48
Mannix, Mary F., 24 Middle Street	45.63
Manoogian, Almes, 253 Boylston Street	249.12
Manoogian, Bedros, et ux, 89 Dexter Avenue	107.97
*Manoogian, Harry, 49 Bigelow Avenue	248.43
*Manoogian, Harry, et ux, 137 School Street	219.70
Mantenuto, Mary G., 8 Pearl Street	269.83
Manuel, Gus, et al, 198 Arlington Street	239.98
*Manzelli, Josephine, 122 Waverley Avenue	252.06
Manzelli, Maria, 1016 Belmont Street	15.21
Marcantonio, Rocco, 33 Boylston Street	76.35
Marcantonio, Rocco, et al, 33 Boylston Street	100.00
Marchant, Arthur J., 97 Edenfield Avenue	12.66
Marchant, Arthur J., et ux, 97 Edenfield Avenue	137.92
Marchant, John P., et ux, 55 Maplewood Street	217.32
Marchant, Mary Alma, Boston	272.09
Marchese, Lorenzo, et ux, 33 Oakland Street	225.59
Marcocio, Gaetano, 41 Cypress Street	157.17
Mardirosian, Anahid, 144 School Street	56.60
Margosian, Alice, 12 Adams Avenue	341.38
Margosian, Victoria, 5 Appleton Terrace	192.66
Margosian, Victoria, et al, 7 Lloyd Road	229.34
Margosian, Victoria A., 7 Lloyd Road	192.54
*Mariano, Domenico, et al, Cambridge	8.45
Markarian, Manoog, et al, 62 Quimby Street	270.40

Markarian, Sarkis, 85 Bigelow Avenue	11.83
Markarian, Virginia, 49 Fairfield Street	231.53
Maroney, Catherine, 50 Salisbury Road	291.07
Marriott, Fred, 42 Union Street	970.06
Marrone, Frank, Boston	30.42
Marshall, Charlotte A., 125 Winsor Avenue	571.99
*Marso, Ralph J., et ux, 12 Sheldon Road	218.01
*Martin, Catherine C., et al, 683 Main Street	27.22
*Martin, Elizabeth F., 10 Winthrop Street	267.02
Martin, Laura H., 30 Channing Road	312.80
Martin, Margaret T., 17 Hilltop Road	58.01
Martin, Stanley, et al, 213 Dexter Avenue	10.14
Martini, Vincent, 819 Mt. Auburn Street	8.45
Martino, Pasquale, 18 Myrtle Street	183.42
Martocchio, Heira Pietro, 111 Warren Street	132.55
Marzilli, Fred, 37 Mt. Auburn Street	43.94
Maslowski, John, et ux, 12 Laurel Street	100.00
*Masoian, Aghavnie, 24 Laurel Street	211.25
Mason, Jane B., 56 Phillips Street	206.18
Mason, Ralph, 113 Mt. Auburn Street	16.90
Masson, George, et al, 19 Marion Road	168.23
Mastrodicasa, Constantino, 23 Berkeley Street	121.68
Mathews, George J., 55 Commonwealth Road	267.02
Mattison, John E., 24 Charles Street	121.39
Mattson, Vernon M., 65 Irving Street	311.54
Maxwell, Elsie M., Bedford	167.31
Mayer, Dorothy R., et al, 46 Wilmot Street	165.62
Mayer, Lucy C., 4 Grandview Avenue	145.34
Mayo, Everett C., et ux, 33 Commonwealth Road	133.71
Mayo, Harry Otis, 259 Mt. Auburn Street	74.36
Mazmanian, Elisha M., 74 Prentis Street	169.00
Mazza, Francesco, et ux, 12 Irma Avenue	65.06
Mazza, Giovanna, 8 Hearn Street	124.62
Mazza, James V., et ux, 48 Cottage Street	113.23
Mazza, James, et ux, 48 Cottage Street	15.21
Mazzucchelli, Virgini E., Dorchester	200.00
*Mazmanian, Nelson, 100 School Street	33.80
*McAteer, Peter, et ux, 60 Riverside Street	39.45
McAuliffe, Ethel M., 16 Fitchburg Street	164.74
McAvoy, Lawrence J., Somerville	295.27
McCabe, Margaret Ellen, 65 Boyd Street	280.10
McCafferty, Abbie J., Summer Street	150.75
McCall, Mary S. M., 45 Green Street	172.38
McCarthy, Agnes A., 30 Stuart Street	617.02

McCarthy, Francis J., 66 Lexington Street	236.60
McCarthy, John H., et ux, 81 Watertown Street	127.16
McCarthy, Margaret E., 30 Maplewood Street	346.92
McCarthy, Mary E., 43 Forest Street	70.98
McCarthy, Maureen, 49 Cypress Street	112.42
*McCollem, Guy E., 69 Lexington Street	253.50
McCool, Helen C., Watertown	10.14
McCool, Hugh M., et ux, 53 Gilbert Street	245.34
McCormick, Percy M., 470 Main Street	67.60
McCree, John, 52 Adams Avenue	512.38
McCue, Thomas Joseph, 293 No. Beacon Street	3.38
McCullagh, Arabella, et al, 162 Common Street	47.44
McCullough, Francis J., Medford	497.59
McCurdy, Katherine, 47 Fairfield Street	29.84
*McDermott, Andrew J., 40 Royal Street	256.88
McDonald, Clara J., 20 Hall Avenue	179.14
McDonald, Heirs Frank H., 69 Hovey Street	147.52
McDonald, Hugh J., 26 Arsenal Street	14.53
McDonald, Heirs James, 72 Pond Street	39.39
McDonald, Margaret A., 33 Bradford Road	269.18
McDonald, Michael A., et ux, 177 Sycamore Street	113.23
McDonald, Theresa A., et al, Somerville	218.01
McDonnell, Michael, 52 Cuba Street	39.98
McDonell, Theresa H., Cambridge	175.35
McDonough, Mary A., et al, 53 Boyd Street	178.58
McElhiney, Josephine, 19 Marshall Street	145.34
McElhiney, Laura B., 120 Riverside Street	160.36
McElroy, Joseph, et ux, 37 Hunt Street	148.72
McGann, Delia J., 135 Edenfield Avenue	60.31
*McGoldrick, Andrew M., 30 Merrill Road	99.79
McGowan, Paul G., 44 Upland Road	101.16
McGrath, Charles B., 135 Mt. Auburn Street	13.52
McGrath, Edward J., et ux, 37 Capitol Street	157.17
McGrath, Frank P., Brighton	8.45
McGready, Andrew, et ux, 119 Boyd Street	223.08
*McGuire, Julia A., 54 Chestnut Street	18.59
McHugh, Anna B., 77 Fayette Street	116.61
McHugh, Cecelia A., 1 Ladd Street	268.71
*McHugh, Frank J., 535 Pleasant Street	128.44
McHugh, John J., et ux, 90 School Street	206.18
McHugh, Patrick J., et ux, 15 Purvis Street	252.17
McHugh, Rose Anna, 1 Ladd Street	153.79
McKenna, Paul J., Springfield	296.00
McKenna, Hugh H., et ux, 35 Olney Street	94.28

McKenzie, Forbes L., et al, Trs., Waverley 468.13
McKenzie, Forbest L., 76 Lexington Street, Waverley 469.82
McKertick, Joseph, 191 Sycamore Street 8.45
McKillops, Heirs Catherine, 43 Riverside Street 449.54
McLaughlin, Annie A., 251 Common Street 573.73
McLaughlin, Ellen F., 162 Hillside Road 248.43
McLaughlin, Margaret C., 97 Poplar Street 310.04
McLauthlin, Elizabeth, et al, 51 Green Street 246.74
*McLean, John C., Somerville 422.74
McLellan, Edith M., et al, 79 Richard Road 1,860.65
McMahon, Margaret R., Newton 260.26
McMahon, Margaret, et Patrick T., Newton 282.23
McMahon, Patrick T., Newton 275.72
McManus, Jane K., 43 Morse Street 172.38
McNamara, Daniel F., et ux, 36 Capitol Street 155.48
McNamara, J. H. Inc., Allston 338.00
McNamara, John H., Allston 2,141.23
McNamara, Louise A., 5 Lovell Road 344.41
McNamara, Minnie, et al, 11 Upland Road 172.38
McNaught, Augusta, 31 Olney Street 138.58
McNicholas, Peter H., et ux, 14 Prescott Street 55.48
McQueeney, Catherine, et al, 71 Myrtle Street 161.20
McQuown, Margaret A., 115 Edenfield Avenue 26.09
McQuown, Thomas H., Heirs, 115 Edenfield Avenue 53.85
McSherry, Catherine F., 86 Forest Street 103.09
McSherry, James, et al, 86 Quirk Street 96.33
McVey, Catherine A., Brighton 87.88
McVey, Thomas, Brighton 42.25
McWhirter, Alfred L., et ux, 28 Parker Street 294.06
McWhirter, Ellen A., Heirs, 9 Patten Street 267.02
Mee, Heirs Annie, 11 Elton Avenue 158.86
Mee, Heirs Dennis, 716 Mt. Auburn Street 263.64
Meehan, Patrick, 162 Spruce Street 192.46
Megan, Emily A., 120 Lovell Road 318.64
Meister, David A. Co., Spring Street 8.45
Meister, Margaret H., 74 Church Street 115.09
*Melanson, Lillian A., 40 Paul Street 100.00
Melanson, Timothy H., Arlington 270.68
Mellen, Amy N., 15 Beacon Park 155.48
Meloian, Mary S., 31 Templeton Parkway 307.58
Meloian, Sarkis, 31 Templeton Parkway 4.23
Melvin, Albert H., 24 Marshall Street 102.77
Melvin, Albert I., 12 Flint Road 371.97
Merrullo, Jennie, 42 Westminster Avenue 128.00

Merz, Jessie M., Medford	218.01
Mesakian, Hagop, 91 Bigelow Avenue	263.64
Messier, Heirs Frederick W., 25 Olney Street	251.81
Messina, Vincenzo, et ux, 41 Bancroft Street	99.91
Metchear, Charles R., Stoneham	190.19
Metropolitan Ice Co., Somerville	5,767.13
Miami, Adoph, 83 Main Street	33.80
Michelson, Heirs Harriet E., 57 Spruce Street	219.70
Michon, Catherine, New Jersey	1,204.97
*Migliaccio, Emilio, 118 Edenfield Avenue	122.28
Migliaccio, Emilio, et ux, 145 Lexington Street	24.28
Mikaelian, Lucia, 36 Keith Street	216.32
Mikailian, Rose, 115 Dexter Avenue	307.58
Millard, Herbert E., 52 Hillside Road	216.32
Miller, Julia A., 107 Chapman Street	161.13
Mills, Abram, 24 Carroll Street	228.59
Milton, Axel Sigfrid, 20 Prospect Street	71.11
Minshull, Thora E., 102 Winsor Avenue	267.02
Minutoli, Frank, 69 Main Street	5.43
*Mirabile, John, 34 No. Beacon Street	8.45
Misserian, Novart N., Nichols Avenue	68.17
*Misakina, Hagop, 14 Wells Avenue	70.98
Misserian, Deran, et al, 72 Dexter Avenue	146.59
Mitchell, Margaret, Bristol, N. H.,	18.59
Mitchell, Mary A., 765 Mt. Auburn Street	197.22
*Mitchell, Philip W., et al, Brighton	120.00
Mitchell, Priscilla R., 40 Harnden Avenue	105.00
Moir, Laura C., 403 School Street	496.86
Molloy, Mary S., 54 Beechwood Avenue	231.53
*Monahan, Heirs Hugh, 5 Myrtle Street	118.30
*Monikus, Jacob, 71 Prentiss Street	250.12
Montgomery, Arthur B., 60 Merrill Road	9.30
Montgomery, Marion Louise, 60 Merrill Road	233.24
Moores, Heirs Wilhelmina B., 105 Spruce Street	25.35
Moomjian, Perooz, 39 Hosmer Street	236.60
Moomjy, Chemoon, 27 Crawford Street	206.18
Mooney, Alice, 28 Hunt Street	43.94
Mooney, Francis X., 25 Longfellow Road	155.53
Mooney, Frederick R., et ux, 36 Washburn Street	189.28
Mooradian, John, 159 Mt. Auburn Street	9.05
Mooradian, Minas, et al, 36 Quimby Street	127.62
Moore, Heirs Carrie, 12 Lincoln Street	300.82
Moore, Elizabeth G., 61 Marion Road	5.07
Moore, Frances B., 28 Appleton Street	260.26

*Moore, Herbert L., 149 Standish Road	294.06
*Moore, Irving B., 28 Appleton Street	3.38
Moore, Lawrence P., et ux, 16 Dunton Road	261.95
Moore, Reuben, et ux, 1086 Belmont Street	20.98
Moran, Eleanor, 386 Mt. Auburn Street	402.22
Moran, Michael, et ux, 92 Riverside Street	42.66
Moran, Patrick J., et ux, 56 Gilbert Street	189.56
Moran, Edward, School Street	3.38
Moreau, Marie, 223 Watertown Street	270.40
Morgan, James A., et ux, 32 Chandler Street	33.80
Morgan, James A., et ux, 32 Chandler Street	33.80
Moriggi, Antonio, et ux, 190 Summer Street	152.10
Morizio, Carmela, 161 Lexington Street	144.52
Morizio, Salvatore, 137 Lexington Street	267.20
Morley, Heirs Edward J., 115 No. Beacon Street	157.17
*Morris, Frederick A., et ux, 41 Lovell Road	273.78
Morris, Lydia E., 41 Irving Street	186.62
Morris, Millicent, Somerville	231.78
Morrissey, George L., 220A Waverley Avenue	67.60
Morrissey, Eleanor S., 87 Standish Road	295.59
Morrissey, Thomas C., et ux, 490 Main Street	597.92
Morrone, John, et ux, 379 Main Street	43.94
Morse, Alice G., 13 Avon Road	297.44
Morse, Arthur L., 24 Chapman Street	177.45
Morse, Heirs Henry L., 10 Harrington Street	140.00
Morse, Lottie W., 22 Chapman Street	145.34
Morse, Marjorie W., 24 Chapman Street	153.79
Mosca, Franco, 14 Spring Street	25.72
Mosca, John, et ux, 40 Bostonia Avenue	231.53
Mosca, Thomas, 16 James Street	15.21
*Mosely, Albion B., 24 Marcia Road	1.69
Mosely, Caroline E., 24 Marcia Road	280.54
Moshier, Sophia P., 468 Belmont Street	430.95
Mosman, Charles P., Highland Avenue	28.21
Mosman, Eleanor, 127 Highland Avenue	99.19
Mostowitz, Harold D., et al, 27 Mt. Auburn Street	6.76
Mostowitz, Helen J., 591 Main Street	187.84
*Moulton, Fred L., et ux, 169 Palfrey Street	177.45
Mourland, Jacob B., 50 Olcott Street	18.80
Muckjian, Leo, 228 Boylston Street	253.50
Mudirian, Garabed S., 94 School Street	100.00
*Mugridichian, Sarkis, et al, 26 Coolidge Hill Road	195.00
Murgedichian, Garabed, et ux, 125 Boylston Street	275.47
Mulcahy, Michael J., et ux, 375 Arlington Street	268.71

*Mullahy, Martin J., 8 Irving Park 238.29
Mullahy, Patrick, 8 Thurston Road 236.39
Mullen, Margaret M., Everett 126.75
Mullen, Walter E., 36 Belmont Street 125.66
Munyon, Daniel J., 79 Main Street 167.11
Munyon, Daniel J., et ux, Hawthorne Street 692.90
Munyon, John J., et ux, 34 Parker Street 108.44
Murless, Winiferd T., 40 Payson Road, Belmont 250.12
Murphy, Heirs Abbie E., 62 Prentiss Street 152.10
Murphy, Eugenia A., 125 Langdon Avenue 248.43
Murphy, Garland P., et ux, Cambridge 100.37
Murphy, Helen Gertrude, 226 Common Street 295.75
Murphy, James E., Belmont 245.75
Murphy, Lillian M., Belmont 618.91
Murphy, Heirs Margaret, Needham 185.90
Murphy, Mary A., 32 Myrtle Street 131.82
*Murphy, Mary T., Lowell Avenue 131.82
Murphy, Nora G., 98 Carroll Street 275.47
Murphy, Richard J., et ux, 12 Kimball Road 75.08
Murray, George F., 431 Mt. Auburn Street 253.69
Murray, Grace C., 2A Mt. Auburn Street 15.21
Murray, Irving F., et ux, 60 Fitchburg Street 158.86
*Murray, John A., et ux, 182 School Street 282.23
Murray, Mary W., 5 Harrington Street 126.75
Murray, Heirs Nora, 98 Galen Street 49.56
Murrin, John F., et ux, 31 Wilmot Street 8.89
Murtha, Ida T., 9 Partridge Street 157.17
Myra, Eber C., et ux, 27 Purvis Street 167.60
Nagle, Agnes M., 60 Hillside Road 185.90
Nahagian, John, 605 Mt. Auburn Street 84.50
Najarian, Eghia, et ux, 10 Coolidge Hill Road 226.46
Nally, Annie E., 83 Waverley Avenue 89.57
Nally, Patrick J., Sr., 69 Waverley Avenue 10.14
Nardella, Anthony, 71 Arlington Street 3.38
Naretti, Pasquale, Somerville 329.21
Natale, Paola, et ux, 41 Berkeley Street 60.84
Natale, Mazilda, Edenfield Avenue 21.33
Natick Trust Co., Natick 227.12
Natoli, Concetta, 52 Lovell Road.. 349.83
Natoli, Lawrence G., 125 Russell Avenue 824.72
Natoli, Lawrence G., et al, 20 Mt. Auburn Street 2,820.76
Natoli, John B., et al, 18 Mt. Auburn Street 687.83
Naum, Vangel, 47 Galen Street 27.04
*Nazareth, Mary, 128 Dexter Avenue 16.90

Neal, Paul W., et ux, Waltham Street 30.98
Neary, Martin J., et ux, Somerville 20.28
Nelson, Albert W., 22 Grenville Road 246.69
Nelson, Amanda C., 317 Common Street 50.12
Nelson, August E., 28 Partridge Street 202.80
Nelson, Fred W., 98A School Street 67.60
Nelson, Mina, 54 Lexington Street 223.08
Nelson, Palma M., 64 Wilmot Street 135.20
Netto, Walter A., et ux, Belmont 180.55
Neves, John, et ux, Cambridge 8.45
New England Laundries Inc., Winchester 3,145.09
New England Sash & Door Co., Inc., Pleasant Street 595.33
Newton Realty Corp., Newton 6.76
New Way Service Co., 89 Spring Street 236.60
Nichols, John B., 34 Oakley Road 541.38
Nicholson, Abby M., 426 Main Street 126.27
*Nicoli, Ermelinda, Somerville 20.28
Noble, Gwendolyn F., 32 Russell Avenue 348.14
Noden, Elizabeth R., 102 Morse Street 187.59
Noden, Julia G., 106 Morse Street 267.02
Nolan, John R., 32 Elmwood Avenue 66.08
Nonpleggi, Simone, Boston 6.76
Noon, Theodore W., Boston 108.50
Noren, Ernest Y., 10 Harnden Avenue 201.11
Norman, Alfrieda C., Boston 523.90
North, Patrick, et al, 2 Hosmer Street 121.24
Nylen, Thore F., et ux, 362 Arlington Street 74.82
Oakley Country Club, Belmont Street ......: 12,151.10
Oates, Mary A., 12 Dartmouth Street 212.94
Oates, Edward A., 443 Mt. Auburn Street 1.69
Oates, Walter J., et ux, 39 Hazel Street 239.98
O'Brien, Daniel J., 619 Mt. Auburn Street 3.38
O'Brien, Frank W., et ux, 31 Standish Road 253.99
O'Brien, James H., et ux, 201 Maplewood Street 267.02
O'Brien, John J., 51 Carroll Street 309.27
O'Brien, John J., et ux, 97 Standish Road 305.99
O'Brien, Lawrence M., et ux, 19 Hawthorne Street.............. 180.83
O'Brien, Margaret, 21 Churchill 194.35
O'Brien, Margaret L., 25 Avon Road 201.11
*O'Brien, Mary A., 144 Standish Road 302.51
O'Brien, Michael J., et ux, 17 Beechwood Avenue 239.98
O'Brien, Timothy J., et ux, 9 Birch Road 170.00
Ochab, Michael, et ux, 138 Edenfield Avenue 81.46
*O'Connell, Charles T., et ux, 104 Lovell Road 325.52

O'Connell, Mary E., 71 Green Street 219.70
O'Connell, Maurice H., et ux, 14 Westminster Avenue 204.09
O'Connell, Patrick H., et ux, 26 Westminster Avenue 238.12
O'Connell, Patrick J., et ux, 30 Frank Street 139.95
Odian, Mardiros G., et ux, 20 Wells Avenue 185.98
*O'Donnell, Richard P., et ux, 16 Carver Road 113.37
O'Donnell, Thomas, 12 Bacon Street 80.93
Ogilvie, Alma E. S., 75 Main Street 267.02
Ogilvie, James M., 75 Main Street 3.38
*O'Hanian, Charles N., 60 California Street 251.81
Ohanian, Mary M., et al, 33 Melendy Avenue 206.18
Ohannessian, Markar, et al, 62 Quimby Street 275.51
O'Hara, William J., 313 Common Street 261.25
Oikemus, Olga M., 102 Harnden Avenue 233.22
O'Keefe, Annie L., 118 School Street 240.43
Oldford, Harry J., et ux, 137 Westminster Avenue 158.37
Oldford, James M., 193 Lexington Street 61.12
O'Leary, Daniel M., 102 Rutland Street 169.11
Olivieri, Felice, Newton 54.08
*Oliver, Annie E., 672 Belmont Street 170.69
Olivieri, Felix, Newton 136.89
Olsen, Cora E., 15 Dwight Street 160.55
Olsen, Harold Olof, 24 Templeton Parkway 310.92
Olson, Ivar G., Boston 241.67
Onanian, Hovnan, et ux, 84 Putnam Street 219.70
Onanian, Jacob, 214 Weverley Avenue 6.76
O'Neil, Abbie C., et al, 38 Forest Street 16.90
Ongoonian, Antranig, 547 Mt. Auburn Street 196.84
Oransky, Murray, 87 Main Street 16.90
Osborn, Amy F., 36 Robbins Road 226.46
Osberg, Edward V., 9 Carroll Street 108.22
Osmond, Hedley, 19 Chapman Street 137.59
*Ostridge, Elizabeth A., 190 No. Beacon Street 84.15
O'Sullivan, Ella T., 30 Boyd Street 275.47
O'Sullivan, Patrick H., Cambridge 263.64
Oteri, Anthony, et al, 89 Elm Street 150.41
Otis, Ward M., et al, 15 Main Street 3,386.76
Ouderkirk, Mary A., 121 Spring Street 67.60
Owens, Richard J., et ux, 114 Walnut Street 216.32
Oxner, Lewis H., 153 Mt. Auburn Street 5.07
Pacifico, Carmeloa, 19 Hudson Street 138.58
Pacifico, Giovanni, 13 Hudson Street 212.94
Packard, Edward H., et ux, 12 Marion Road 220.95
Packard, Heirs Franklin, 22 Alden Road 199.42

Paddock, Esther, Dorchester	243.36
*Pagano, Nunzio, Cambridge	31.86
Palazzone, Michael, et ux, 42 Cypress Street	248.43
*Palazzone, Michell, 57 Cottage Street	92.08
Paleologos, Panagiotis, et al, 26 Berkeley Street	179.14
Pallone, Filippos, et al, 21 Waverley Avenue	37.51
Pallotta, Giovanni, 43 Cross Street	101.35
Pallotta, Orazio, et ux, 226 Palfrey Stree t	125.06
Panosian, Arakey S., 35 Porter Street	254.59
Paolera, Amelia Della, 21 Nichols Avenue	160.00
Paolera, Marcello D., 21A Nichols Avenue	199.00
Paone, Carmine, 24 Wheeler Lane	119.97
Paone, Ciriaco, 12 Wheeler Lane	319.22
Papalia, Domenick A., 117 Waverley Avenue	16.90
Papalia, Dominic A., et ux, 129 Waverley Avenue	251.81
Papazian, Aris B., 415 Mt. Auburn Street	8.45
Papazoan, Artin, et ux, 49 Melendy Avenue	162.24
Papazian, Louis, et al, 24 Kimball Road	311.82
Pappas, Frances S., 74 Belmont Street	300.82
Pappas, Peter C., et ux, 26 Warwick Road	207.86
Parisi, Francesca, et al, 27 Francis Street	127.76
Parisian Dye House Inc., 404 Main Street	906.69
Parker, Chester H., et ux, 17 Gleason Street	279.90
Parks, Irene A., 29 Hillside Road	118.52
Parks, Minnie, 127 Spruce Street	113.67
*Parquette, Archibald W., 48 Summer Street	3.38
Parquette, Mary C., 48 Summer Street	182.52
Parsekian, Sarkis, et al, 109 Nichols Avenue	16.90
Parsekian, Veronica M., 109 Nichols Avenue	13.52
Parsekian, Veronika, 109 Nichols Avenue	640.51
Parsons, Viola Rich, 14 Carleton Terrace	273.62
Paryianoglous, James, et ux, 27 Kondazian Street	146.99
Pascuzzi, Crocifissa, 170 Summer Street	37.18
Pascuzzi, Luigi ,170 Summer Street	23.66
Pascuzzi, Luigi, et ux, 170 Summer Street	116.61
*Pasquarosa, Linbertino, 29 Churchill	99.71
Patey, Walter G., et ux, 61 Walnut Street	298.44
*Paul, Teresa, 17 Hosmer Street	127.54
*Pease, Rebecca A., Cambridge	10.14
Peckham, Josephine S., 554 Belmont Street	377.49
*Peerless Pressed Metal Corp., 191 Arlington Street	202.80
*Pelkey, Charles L., et ux, 48 Carroll Street	234.91
Pendergast, George D. F., et ux, 71 Bromfield Street	189.28
*Pengeroth, Louise, 69 Chapman Street	301.79

Pennington, George H., et ux, 18 Brimmer Street 166.04
Pent, Arnold V., 67 Oliver Street 273.78
Pequosette Press, 17 Main Street 136.89
Perimian, Fermine, 77 Bigelow Avenue 113.73
Perimian, John, 77 Bigelow Avenue 3.38
Perkins, Annie M., 27 Elliot Street 238.29
Perkins, Elias A., 73 Fayette Street 204.49
Perkins, Thomas J., 31 Oliver Street ....: 111.46
Perry, Max, et al, 276A Orchard Street 3.38
Perry, Ralph F., et ux, 125 Summer Street 171.76
Peters, Andrew, 77 Watertown Street 302.51
Peters, Charlotte A., 10 Hillside Road 224.47
Peterson, Gustave, 47 Prescott Street 115.90
Peterson, Parnag, 473 Main Street 32.96
*Petre, George W., et ux, 71 Rutland Street 135.20
Philbrook, Earle S., 119 Poplar Street 310.54
Phillips, Thomas A., 597 Mt. Auburn Street 384.28
Piantedosi, Louisa, 25 Warren Street 257.30
Piantedosi, Michele, et ux, 183 Fayette Street 86.22
Piantedosi, Nicolina, 18 Cushman Street 273.78
*Piccolo, Marietta, 2 Watertown Street 485.27
Piers, Wesley, et ux, 50 Hall Avenue................................. 255.19
Pieterse, Agnes A., 55 Fayette Street 261.95
Pieterse, Albert S., 57 Fayette Street 106.47
Pilla, Peter, 199 Pleasant Street 126.14
Pillsbury, Benjamin O., et al, 232 Bellevue Road 6.76
Pillsbury, Blanche M., 232 Bellevue Road 314.34
Pinkham, Arthur F., et ux, 119 Robbins Road 328.38
Pino, Francesco, 49 Loomis Avenue 145.34
*Pino, Rosina, 25 Pleasant Street 10.14
*Pirella, Agnes, et al, 19 Hearn Street 22.25
Pisani, Edith Tarbell, 42 Winsor Avenue 89.91
Pisano, Sam, 33 Keenan Street 110.55
Piscatelli, Nicholas, 102 Pleasant Street 180.83
Piscatelli, Vincenzo, et al, 117 Pleasant Street 211.25
Pitts, Leo, et ux, 69 Boylston Street 74.63
Platon, Costas, et al, 295 Arsenal Street 39.50
Platt, Alonson E., et ux, 19 Parker Street 207.87
Plett, Henry A., et ux, 22 Standish Road 270.89
Pochi, Anesti, 10 Hosmer Street 248.43
Polihronis, Catina, 227 Arlington Street 300.82
Pollak, Sydney S., Boston 352.36
Poor, Mabel T., 31 Langdon Avenue 253.50
Portentoso, Nicolo, 162 Belmont Street 10.14

Porter, Charles J., et ux, 118 Putnam Street 200.00
Porter, George J., et ux, 138 Standish Road 71.90
Porter, Sarah A., 67 Emerson Road 58.83
Potter, Annabel S., 104 Barnard Avenue 320.91
Potter, C. W., Inc., 2 School Street 2,430.22
Potter, Mona Belle, 12 Walnut Street 677.69
Power, Sarah J., 11 Centre Street 161.21
Powers, Anna G., 27 Brimmer Street 275.47
Powers, Caroline I., 21 Paul Street 224.77
Powers, Fannie L., 1039 Belmont Street 140.27
Powers, Richard J., 21 Gilbert Street 164.22
Pratt, G. Arthur, et ux, 30 Spruce Street 307.58
Preble, Florence L., 17 Broadway 160.96
*Preble, Frank A., et ux, 744 Belmont Street 277.16
Preschia, Andrew, 69 Highland Avenue 27.04
Pretty, Rebecca, Medford 6.76
Priest & Company, 54 Bates Road 16.90
Principe, Giasue, 118 Edenfield Avenue 20.28
Prior, Matthew, et ux, 21 Patten Street 101.23
Pritchard, Carleton F., 9 Merrill Road 21.97
Pritchard, Carleton F., et ux, 9 Merrill Road 305.81
Pritchard, F. & Son Inc., 170 Common Street 255.19
Procopio, Paul, et ux, 8 Myrtle Street 109.85
*Pritchard, Frazer, et ux, 170 Common Street 299.13
Proctor, Emma S., 74 Pearl Street 223.08
Proodian, Surpouie, 90 Langdon Avenue 268.71
Prudential Insurance Co. of America, Boston 477.63
Prue, Grace M., Cambridge 238.22
Puccia, Joseph, 46 Maplewood Street 241.67
Puntonio, James, 63 Bigelow Avenue 13.52
*Puntonio, Vincenzo, et ux, 71 Bigelow Avenue 165.62
Purchase, Maude, 11 Whitney Street 285.98
Putney, Charles R., 98 Waverley Avenue 216.89
Puzo, Antonio, 39 Porter Street 219.70
Pyke, Heirs Susie A., 98 Hillside Road 39.60
*Querino, Basilio, et ux, Cambridge 10.14
Quimby, George Edward, 34 Middlesex Road 201.65
Quinby, Stella E., 361 School Street 212.94
Quinlan, William, et ux, 66 Green Street 51.81
Quinn, Edward J., et ux, 80 Belmont Street 284.16
*Quinn, Mary J., Trustee, 589 Main Street 225.00
Quinn, Mary L., 24 Longfellow Road 211.78
Quirk, James H., et ux, 22 Spruce Street 199.13
Quirk, John P., et ux, 57 Quirk Street 60.46

Quirk, Mary E., et al, 9 Adams Avenue	268.71
Quirk, Norma L., 149 Fayette Street	47.32
Raimondo, Domenico, 805 Mt. Auburn Street	959.92
Ramsay, Dorothy Towle, 15 Sunnybank Road	392.44
Ranaudi, Anna, Revere	21.97
Rand, Claude A., 632 Mt. Auburn Street	132.83
Rand, Caude Allen, et ux, 4 Edgecliffe Road	263.64
Rando, Felice, et al, 116 Irving Street	185.90
Ranney, James H., et ux, 142 Robbins Road	212.94
Raphaelian, Kasper, et ux, 11 Brimmer Street	224.77
Rattigan, Anna B., 77 Riverside Street	274.82
Rayne, George H., 279 Pleasant Street	31.90
Read, Marion H., et ux, 140 Church Street	250.12
Reagan, Emma B., 12 Sunset Road	138.00
Reagan, Margaret E., 111 Robbins Road	144.50
Redding, Grace, 51 Riverside Street	131.82
Reed, Ellen L., 12 Olney Street	141.96
Reid, Daniel B., No. Grafton	38.87
Reid, Laura I., 750 Belmont Street	65.00
Reid, Martin F., et ux, 23 Chapman Street	130.13
Reilly, Katherine M., 72 Standish Road	287.79
Reinhardt, Catherine F., 20 Watertown Street	229.84
Reitz, John A., 60 Standish Road	3.38
Reliance Co-operative Bank, Cambridge	705.97
Reynolds, John L., et ux, 45 Adams Avenue	224.68
Ricci, Domenica F., 105 Pleasant Street	753.74
Ricci, Salvatore, 10 Chadbourne Terrace	15.21
Ricci, Peter, 25 Nichols Avenue	25.35
Riccio, Peter, et al, 180 School Street	611.78
Rice, Addie L., No. Hanover	365.04
Rice, Harry, et ux, 136 Westminster Avenue	165.85
Rich, Everett B., Boston	187.59
Rich, Walter L, 472 Main Street	6.76
Richardson, Carlos A., New Britain, Conn.	76.20
Riley, Elizabeth A., 12 Carver Road	144.52
Ring, John M., et ux, 24 Chauncey Street	258.57
Riselli, Michele, et ux, 26 Irma Avenue	263.64
Riverside Trust Co., Watertown	268.71
*Riviccio, Luigi, et al, Quincy	15.21
Rizzo, Vito, East Boston	21.97
Rizzuto, Guiseppe, 5 Sexton Street	101.40
*Robbio, Tomaso, et ux, Cambridge	10.14
Roberts, Jessie R., 285 Arsenal Street	180.83
Robertson, Duncan W., et ux, Somerville	11.83

Robertson, Elijah B., et ux, 65 Hovey Street 83.22
Robinson, G. Frederick, 106 Mt. Auburn Street 1.69
Robinson, Heirs Grace, 106 Mt. Auburn Street 1,456.78
Robinson, Marguerite M., 25 Palmer Street 176.96
Rocco, Antonio, 825 Mt. Auburn Street 8.45
Roche, John J., et al, 152 Winsor Avenue 246.74
Roche, Michael J., et ux, 12 Royal Street 278.85
Roche, Priscilla, 21 Prescott Street 95.84
*Rodd, Grace M., 44 Bates oRad 200.00
*Rodd, Robert A., et al, 39 Franklin Street 261.95
Rodgers, Heirs Mary E., 70 Poplar Street 124.08
Rodman, Nathan M., Dorchester 451.23
Romano, Marie V., 21 Thurston Road 270.71
*Romano, Michele, et ux, 14 Adams Street 126.82
Romeo, Anthony, et al, 249 Waverley Avenue 226.46
Romeo, Heirs Carmelo, Belmont 54.20
Rooney, Bessie, Cambridge 174.07
Rooney, John F., 110 Riverside Street 6.76
*Rooney, William J., 115 Summer Street 138.58
Roper, John M., 36 Pleasant Street 67.60
Rorke, Mercedes J., New York 25.35
*Rosenfield, Louis, 6 Main Street 16.90
Rosi, Frank, 41 Quimby Street 200.73
Rosoff, Nathaniel, 326 Arlington Street 164.56
Ross, Marion Cooper, 119 Russell Avenue 460.49
*Ross, Thomas S., 45 Hillside Road 211.25
Rossi, Vitorio, et ux, 235 Palfrey Street 141.96
Rote, Julia A., 59 Adams Avenue 263.64
Routern, Joseph, 216A Waverley Avenue 1.69
Rugg, Emma C., 17 Centre Street 260.26
Rugg, William, 10 Mt. Auburn Street 16.90
Rugg, William W., et ux, 17 Centre Street 229.84
Ruggeri, Rosario, 188 Summer Street 3.38
Ruggiero, James, 6 Washburn Street 3.38
Russell, Bridget H., 154 Common Street 304.20
Russell, Emily B., 387 School Street 295.75
Russell, M. Louise, 96 Robbins Road 172.28
Russell, Nellie, 8 Hardy Avenue 167.31
Russell, Walter G., et ux, 42 Frank Street 147.03
Russo, Andrea, et ux, 40 Quirk Street 283.05
Russo, Antonio, et al, 221 Lexington Street 219.70
Russo, Fanny, 634 Mt. Auburn Street 8.45
Russo, Felix, 17 Oakland Street 382.64
Russo, Guiseppe, et ux, Waverley 16.90

*Russo, Lina, 53 Laurel Street	163.93
*Russo, Matteo, et ux, 53 Laurel Street	28.73
*Russo, Nicola, 22 Homer Street	214.05
Russo, Pietro, et al, 28 Forest Street	179.14
Russo, Antonio, et al, 249 Lexington Street	45.63
Russo, Samuel, et ux, 29 Waverley Avenue	260.26
Ruth, Emma F., 40 Upland Road	219.70
Ryan, Millard K., et ux, 25 Langdon Avenue	155.48
*Rydberg, Gustaf, et al, 137 Common Street	37.85
Ryder, Thomas, 74 Green Street	245.05
Sabatino, Ernest, et ux, 21 Francis Street	255.19
Sacca, Stefano, et ux, 145 Sycamore Street	174.07
*Saccento, Alfredo, Waltham	6.76
Safford, Howard F., et ux, 21 Centre Street	196.04
Saghbazarian, James, 133 Dexter Avenue	234.91
Sahagian, Krikor, 35 Kondazian Street	220.30
Salese, Gregory, 12 No. Beacon Court	224.77
Sallese, Pasquale, et ux, 103 Westminster Avenue	144.25
*Sallese, Salvatore, et ux, 12 No. Beacon Court	81.53
Salmon, Patrick F., Waltham	164.98
Salsbury, Lena, 21 Commonwealth Road	147.30
Sam, W. C., 212 Waverley Avenue	3.38
Samaras, John D., et ux, 111 Hillside Road	365.09
Sampson, Bessie S., 27 Woodleigh Road	265.33
Sampson, Helen M., 16 Frank Street	127.34
Samuelian, Armenag, et al, 36 Hazel Street	165.83
*Sanborn, Helen E., 1043 Belmont Street	102.80
Sands, John J., et ux, 189 Boylston Street	265.33
Sandstrom, Frank H., et al, 262 Belmont Street	40.37
Sanger, Charles W., et ux, 8 Fifield Street	155.48
Sansome, Anna, 121 Westminster Avenue	158.37
Sansone, Concetta, Trustee, 10 Merrifield Avenue	163.93
Santillo, Joseph, 294 Arlington Street	317.72
Santis Mfg. Co., 36 Pleasant Street	67.60
Santoro, Maurizio, 61 Pleasant Street	239.98
Saraf, Stephen, 235 Boylston Street	256.88
Sarkisian, Armenoosh et al, 1 Howe Street	245.05
Saunderson, Jennie F., 18 Middlesex Street	451.65
Savage, Jeremiah J. et ux, 142 Palfrey Street	5.07
*Savas, Maria, 25 Berkeley Street	12.95
Savino, James et al, 21 Keenan Street	270.40
Sawyer, Anson Earle, 9 Sheldon Road	184.21
Scalia, Diana, 121 Bellevue Road	315.74
Scalian, Julia, 248 Common Street	344.76

Scaltreto, Jane, 10 Sparkill Street	13.52
*Scannell, Charlotte V., 140 Hillside Road	265.33
Scanzillo, Joseph et ux, 90 Westminster Avenue	100.00
*Scarfotti, Agostino, 93 Arlington Street	91.27
Scarr, John et ux, 2 7Kimball Road	132.12
Scharff, Ethel, 16 Olcott Street	26.41
Scharff, Ethel, 16 Olcott Street	215.73
Scharff, Louis, 16 Olcott Street	3.72
Scheirer, Anna T., 8 Appleton Street	329.55
Scheirer, Herbert J., 8 Appleton Street	20.28
Schick, Jacob, 183 Grove Street	111.54
Schindler, John H., et ux, 13 Irving Park	153.79
Schroeder, William C., 70 Capital Street	3.38
Schutzer, Borgild E., 63 Edenfield Avenue	141.96
Schwabe, Oscar W., 64 Salisbury Road	80.22
Scifio, Rosalia, 24 Royal Street	207.87
Scollan, John J. et al, 96 Langdon Avenue	60.60
*Scott, Anna L., 49 Sycamore Street	87.88
Scott, Walter G. et al, 104 Hillside Road	165.79
Seale, Forest W., et ux, 13 Fifth Avenue	485.03
Secord, Fred, 65-A Dexter Avenue	11.83
Secord, Walter N., 80 Barnard Avenue	250.12
Seferian, Armenag, 23 Fairfield Street	243.36
Seferian, Avedis et al, 99 School Street	23.66
Seferian, Serope, 19 Fairfield Street	134.02
Seferian, Hagopian et ux, 32 Fairfield Street	223.08
Sellon, Walter A. et ux, 4 Sheldon Road	200.83
Semonian, Altoon A., 11 Howe Street	246.74
Seretelly, Euripedes M. et al, 95 Arlington Street	11.83
*Sergi, Guiseppe, 14 Bostonia Avenue	234.91
Shahrigian, Rose, 51 Cypress Street	190.97
Shaljian, Annie, 14 Francis Street	277.16
Shamon, Helena M., Boston	255.19
Shanahan, Henry, 65 School Street	3.38
Sharpstein, Joel A., 160 Belmont Street	40.56
Shaw, Bartlett M. Heirs, 27 Oliver Street	319.41
Shaw, Florence McN., 62 Langdon Avenue	187.59
Shaw, James E., et ux, 45 Fitchburg Street	187.20
*Shay, Eleanor H., Hancock, N. H.	234.91
Shea, Casimir et ux, 219 Common Street	89.52
Shea, James P. et ux, 162 Worcester Street	158.86
*Shea, Raymond K. et ux, 154 Robbins Road	90.55
Sheehan, Anna G., 56 Carroll Street	147.03
Sheehan, Bartholomew, 56 Carroll Street	18.59

Sheer, Isaac, 129-A Galen Street 4.06
Sheer, Isaac et ux, 120-A Galen Street 635.44
Sheils, Mary Margaret, 195 Mt. Auburn Street 368.42
Sheldon, Charles L. et ux, 311 School Street 224.77
Shelman, Ruth, 179 Watertown Street 100.00
Sheridan, Theresa A., 5 Theurer Park 310.56
Sheridan, Thomas F., 89 Main Street 59.15
*Sherlock, Edward J., et al, 300 Common Street 140.27
Sherlock, Ruth N., 100 Hillside Road 105.13
*Sherman, Charles F. J. et ux, 24 Purvis Street 102.94
Schick, Mary, 185 Grove Street 253.50
*Shield, Mildred S., 143 Robbins Road 223.08
*Shriver, Arthur Franklin et al, 155 Highland Avenue........ 65.00
Shutt, Mary Ellen, 211 Palfrey Street 158.86
Siegfriedt, Mary A., Allston 213.56
Sigismonte, Nunzio, 71 Winter Street 246.29
Silsbee, Heirs Alice M., 50 Garfield Street 1,858.42
Silvestri, Erminia, 6 Homer Street 211.25
Simcock, Mae, 65 Gilbert Street 148.08
Simone, Salvatore, 123 Galen Street 260.26
Simon, Sophie B., 126 Walnut Street 216.32
Simonds, Lillian L., 93 Palfrey Street 268.71
Simonds, Luther W., 100 Church Street 202.80
*Simone, Heirs, Joseph, 29 Myrtle Street 40.18
Simonetti, Domenic, 47 Prospect Street 58.50
*Simonetti, Domenick et ux, 47 Prospect Street 212.71
Simpson, Bethel W. et ux, 44 Grenville Road 244.35
Simpson, Lorraine C., 165 Standish Road 292.37
Simpson, Mabelle C., 25 Olcott Street 184.60
Siranosian, Setrak, 409 Mt. Auburn Street 62.18
Sjostedt, Oscar M., 136 Highland Avenue 341.38
Skillin, Everett E. et ux, 24 Appleton Street 179.42
*Skinner, Harry, Cambridge 719.94
Skinner, Harry H., Sudbury 270.85
Skinner, Hiram L., 56 Marion Road 239.98
Skinner, Ruth D., 56 Marion Road 347.85
Skuse, George W. et ux, 11 Stearns Road 314.34
Slamin, Mary A., 43 Union Street 518.83
Sliney, Edward et ux, 368 Arlington Street 253.44
Small, Guy V. et ux, 80 Capitol Street 148.72
Smith, Abigail H., 428 Mt. Auburn Street 321.10
Smith, Heirs Annie J., 8 Melville Terrace 179.14
Smith, Carl G., 21 Franklin Street 272.40
Smith, Edna M. B., 10 Mt. Auburn Street 40.56

Smith, Elinor P., 35 Hardy Avenue	167.31
Smith, Hazel D., 20 Wilson Avenue	192.98
Smith, Lottie B., 12 Parker Street	292.37
Smith, Marsden G. et ux, 41 Kondazian Street	232.00
Smith, Martha A. et al, Belmont	545.44
Smith, James S., 74 Capitol Street	158.86
Smith, William C., 85 Spring Street	936.26
Smokler, Sophie, 98 Poplar Street	151.80
Snow, Albert H. et ux, 75 Harnden Avenue	100.00
Snow, Emma C., Chatham	69.29
Snow, Ernest, 312 Charles River Road	85.24
Snow, Mildred E., 90 Harnden Avenue	236.60
Sokolski, Julia E., 31 Adams Street	241.11
*Solan, Mary G., et al, 76 Forest Street	70.98
*Sorenson, Soren, 97 Main Street	10.14
Satera, Salvey, Boston	141.67
Sottile, Nunziata, 44 Dartmouth Street	124.77
*Sousa, Abel, 144 Belmont Street	6.76
*Spalding, Charles W. et ux, 64 Bates Road	260.26
*Sparks, Newman et ux, 6 Stuart Street	165.74
*Spector, Abraham, 148 Belmont Street	6.76
Sperguiro, Vincenzo, et ux, 65 Cottage Street	73.65
*Spinosa, Lena, 20 Merrill Road	312.65
Spiro, Dora, 55 Spring Street	109.85
Splaine, Edward F., 34 Keenan Street	57.45
Stacey, Herbert G. et ux, 11 Dwight Street	123.37
Stagliano, Salvatore F., 11 Norseman Avenue	214.63
Standel, Eva, 65 Morse Street	282.23
Standel, Max, 65 Morse Street	6.76
*Standish, Katherine L., 35 Piermont Street	156.38
Stanley, Bertha M., 71 Whites Avenue	39.92
Stanton, Charles et ux, 16 Charles Street	178.23
Starr, Walter J., Lowell	250.12
Stathaki, Helen P., 58 Boylston Street	102.35
*Stavers, George W., 31 Thayer Road	40.16
Stead, Edna M., 37 Channing Road	196.00
Steele, Ethel M., 808 Belmont Street	229.84
Stefanelli, Antonio, Somerville	13.52
Stepanian, Mugardich, 55-A Dexter Avenue	8.45
Stepanian, Mugerdich et al, 20 Oak Street	267.02
Stepanian, Archaluis et al, 7 Grove Street	165.62
Stephen, Lucy Y., 42 Keenan Street	250.12
Stevens, Edward A., 23 Emerson Road	193.44
Stevens, George W., 354 Arsenal Street	16.90

Stevenson, Harold M. et ux, 124 Lovell Road	337.42
Stewart, Alice H., 105 Langdon Avenue	180.83
*Stewart, Carrie E., 12 Bancroft Street	11.83
Stewart, James A., 164 School Street	263.64
Stewart, Malena E., 165 School Street	1.69
Stewart, Robert C., et ux, 12 Bancroft Street	84.07
Stewart, Sarah C., 54 Olney Street	59.90
*Sticker, Wilhelmina C., 25 Stearns Road	331.24
*Stickney, Lottie C., 32 Spruce Street	50.46
Stiles, Catherine I., 92 California Park	185.54
Stone, Emma G. et al, 128 Barnard Avenue	273.78
*Stone, Gertrude W., 22 Hilltop Road	73.00
Stone, Walter C., 19 Stoneleigh Road	894.01
Stonogo, Peter et ux, 15 Hardy Avenue	234.91
*Strandberg, John Victor et ux, 70 Boylston Street	241.67
Strauss, John M. et ux, 45 Pequosette Street	282.23
Strayhorn, Annie E. et al, 51 Morse Street	147.73
Storm, Signe M., 5 Channing Road	130.00
Strum, Arthur W., 45 Royal Street	177.45
Stryker, John P. et ux, 761 Mt. Auburn Street	108.16
Stuart, Albert T. et al, Trustees, Newton Centre	246.74
*Stuart-Marshall Realty Co., Newton, Mass.	28.73
Stuart, Mary I., 70 Phillips Street	2,972.71
Stuart, T. & Son, Newton	1,690.00
Stucke, C. Fred et ux, 14 Wolcott Road	283.84
Sturnick, Rosalie, 34 Walnut Street	581.98
*Sullivan, Daniel J., 170 Church Street	246.74
Sullivan, Dennis, Cambridge	55.60
*Sullivan, Edward J., 267 Pleasant Street	89.28
Sullivan, Elizabeth R. et al, 71 Bradford Road	286.08
Sullivan, James H., 508 Main Street	479.12
Sullivan, James J. et ux, 194 Orchard Street	228.15
Sullivan, Lillian A., 19 Brimmer Street	47.00
Sullivan, Mabel L., 166 Common Street	292.18
Sullivan, Mary A., Cambridge	28.21
Sullivan, Michael F. et ux, 29 Dartmouth Street	100.00
Sullivan, Minnie J., 102 Fayette Street	181.83
Sullivan, Rose M., 508 Main Street	184.21
Sullivan, Thomas E., Trustee, Cambridge	253.31
Summers, Heirs Fanny, 319 School Street	354.90
Surabian, Kachaddor M., 86 Cypress Street	223.08
Surabian, Sarah, 72 Prentiss Street	152.10
Surabian, Surphouhi, 69 Crawford Street	236.52
Surety Cleansing Shop, Inc., 115-A Galen Street	1.69

Sutherland, Frederick, 8 Bemis Street	202.20
Sutherland, Jessie H., 285 Mt. Auburn Street	365.04
*Sutherland, Mary E., 54 Herson Street	256.88
Swanson, Alma, 361 Orchard Street	87.48
*Swanson, Charles A. et ux, 77 Standish Road	175.47
*Swanson, Lillian, 49 Fairview Avenue	123.43
Sweeney, Francis W., 106 Poplar Street	299.13
*Sweeney, Patrick et ux, 28 Fairfield Street	221.39
Swift, Heirs Marion T., 96 Pleasant Street	324.48
Sylvestre, Frederick N. et ux, Brookline	189.43
*Sylvya, Mary G., 61 Nyack Street	184.82
Taintor, Charlotte Morton, Cambridge	65.18
Takvarian, Zartik, 21 Kimball Road	280.54
Tamburro, John, 24 Wells Avenue	185.98
Tangusso, Laura, 94 Bellevue Road	302.81
Tanoian, Helen, 108 Laurel Street	135.20
Tarbell, Samuel K. et al, 18 Avon Road	151.11
Tardif, J. Paul et al, Belmont	74.58
Tarjian, Cassie J., 143 School Street	236.60
*Tashian, Hovnan, 231 Boylston Street	197.48
Tashjy, Frieda, 35 Coolidge Hill Road	205.30
Taverna, John, 19 Hersom Street	133.51
Taverna, Salvatore et al, 141 Westminster Avenue	108.16
Taylor, Alice F., 146 Spring Street	179.14
Taylor, Bessie I., 89 Harnden Avenue	246.74
*Teletchea, Margaret, 760 Belmont Street	251.81
Tenney, Ellen E., 1 1Cuba Street	91.87
Terhune, William L. et al, Brookline	164.14
Terwilliger, Wynn M., 145 Common Street	261.95
Tessin, Fred G. et ux, 114 Lovell Road	335.49
*Tessmer, Frank R. et ux, 74 Morse Street	179.14
Testa, Pasquale, 2 8New Lexington Street	221.44
Theurer, Mabel M., 12 Theurer Park	199.11
Theodore, Bessie T., Dorchester	236.56
Theurer, Otto A., Contracting Co.	253.50
Theurer, Otto A., Trustee	483.22
Thierry, Adelaide H., Boston	581.36
Thierry, Louis S., Boston	1,859.00
Thoburn, Thomas N. et ux, 35 Copeland Street	7.00
*Thomas, William, 73 Galen Street	270.40
Thomaian, Thomas M., 15 Elton Avenue	167.31
*Thompson, Eldora J., 22 Bartlett Street	109.85
Thompson, Francis E. et ux, 18 Melendy Avenue	252.00
Thomson, Frederick M., 67 Carroll Street	119.55

*Thorsell, Carl G. et ux, 2 Hilltop Road	271.43
Thresher, Grace E., B., Longmeadow	192.66
Thurlow, Mary E., 4 Orchard Street	73.70
Thurston, Cassie, 18 Adams Street	143.72
Thurston, William J. et ux, 31 Lovell Road	279.06
Tiano, Rocco, 50 Pleasant Street	30.42
Tiano, Rocco et al, 50 Pleasant Street	126.75
Tiberio, Joseph et al, 27 Churchill	60.84
Ticobossi, Vincenza et al, 66 Cottage Street	116.20
*Tidewater Oil Co., 619 Mt. Auburn Street	3.38
*Tierney, Martin F., 476 Main Street	182.52
Tione, Rocco, 37 Quirk Street	84.50
Tirabassi, Vincenzo et ux, 19 French Terrace	128.30
Titus, Leroy C., 33 Irving Street	608.40
*Titus, Taknee, 24 Concord Road	251.81
Tobin, James J., 129 Dexter Avenue	91.46
Tobio, Andrew et ux, 4 0Bacon Street	502.36
Tocci, Carmine, 240 Waverley Avenue	59.59
Tocci, Carmine et al, 240 Waverley Avenue	223.20
*Tocci, Edsee, Orchard Street	3.38
Tocci, Lucia, 10 Lowell Avenue	1,205.09
Tocci, Carmine et al, 240 Waverley Avenue	223.20
Tomasian Agavne, 16 Chauncy Street	263.64
*Tomasian, Mugerdick, 219 Dexter Avenue	300.82
*Tomasini, Pierina W., Roxbury	11.83
Tooghmanian, Mary J., 25 Oak Street	179.14
Toomajanian, Harry et al, Medford	490.10
Toomy, Heirs William P., 122 Dexter Avenue	85.34
Toopzian, Paul K., 520 Mt. Auburn Street	84.50
Torosian, Satenig, 24 Porter Street	247.13
Torrens, James B., Boston	256.88
Torres, Marianno DeRego, 32 Whitney Street	174.07
Tortorella, Antonio, 20 Clarendon Street	185.90
Toscano, Nazzareno A. et ux, 3 Langdon Avenue	211.25
*Tovmassian, Mariam, 71 Spruce Street	100.00
Townsend, Herbert M. et ux, 19 Robbins Road	290.19
Tracy, Edith C., 70 Stuart Street	219.70
Tracy, Harry L., 70 Stuart Street	32.11
Tracy, John H., 125 Spring Street	128.44
Tracy, John H. et ux, 16 Broadway	181.12
Tracy, Reuben M., 256 Orchard Street	37.18
Trapelo Road Realty Corp., Belmont	1,614.05
*Travers, John H., 47 Edenfield Avenue	57.50
Treggiari, Giocondo et ux, 186 Walnut Street	86.50

Treglia, Guiseppina, 77 Salisbury Road	196.10
Tremark, Frank, et ux, 33 Bancroft Street	214.22
Treholm, Harriet M., Belmont	43.11
Tricomi, Domenico, 113 Forest Street	167.31
Tripp, Mary E., Boston	6.76
Troiano, Maria, 54 Ralph Street	263.64
*Troiano, Pasquale, 54 Ralph Street	20.28
Troiano, Pasquale et ux, 54 Ralph Street	10.14
*Trow, Paula L., 49 Marion Road	101.20
True, John C. et ux, 37 Partridge Street	88.58
Truesdale, Herbert L., 19 Avon Road	84.77
Tsicoulios, Arthur A. et al, 14 Oak Street	135.20
Tsolas, Rodothea, 27 Berkeley Street	13.46
Tuck,, Harold S. et ux, 27 Richards Road	300.26
Tudino, Antonio, 45 Riverside Street	119.80
Tugman, Heirs Mary T., 131 Summer Street	162.24
Tugman, Heirs Nina C., 131 Summer Street	141.96
Turbini, Samien J., 40 Salisbury Road	291.65
*Tutunjian, Abraham et al, 94 Nichols Avenue	16.90
Tutunjian, Abraham, 94 Nichols Avenue	199.53
Tutunjian, Sarkis, 109 Boylston Street	283.92
Tutunjian, Sarkis et ux, 109 Boylston Street	260.26
Twomey, Daniel D., Trustee, Waltham	332.93
Tydewater Oil Co., 684 Mt. Auburn Street	3.38
Tylor, Nathalea R,, 22 Patten Street	147.03
Tyrrell, Joseph T. et ux, 15 Edgecliff Road	319.41
Tashjy, Frieda, 35 Coolidge Hill Road	21.97
Union Market National Bank	40.27
United-American Soda Fountain Corp., Walnut Street	190.97
*United States Bond & Mortgage Corp.	273.78
Utting, John A. et ux, 39 Marion Road	236.60
Uva, Joseph et ux, 141 Edenfield Avenue	63.31
Union Church of Watertown	15.62
Vachon, R. Alexander, 276 Waverley Avenue	170.69
Vahey, Heirs James H., 14 Palfrey Street	432.64
*Vahey, Mary Etta, 52 Irving Street	90.54
Vahey, Patrick, 13 Ladd Street	150.41
Vail, Norma F., 182 Maplewood Street	290.68
Valacelli, Elpiniki, 24 Merrifield Avenue	158.86
Valchuiso, Attilio et ux, 22 Belmont Street	262.04
Valentine, Zeda I., 16 Orchard Street	908.59
Valentine, Albert et al, 757 Mt. Auburn Street	13.52
Valois, Margaret B. D., 60 Hancock Street	235.15
VanBeslar, Herbert C., 22 Mt. Auburn Street	6.76

VanDyke, Sadie L., Stewartson, N. H.	334.62
Varkas, Alexander D., 144 Pleasant Street	103.09
Varney, Edward A. et ux, Boston	177.63
Varonakis, Anthula C., 17 Berkeley Street	60.84
Vartanian, John, 598 Mt. Auburn Street	43.77
Vartanian, Peter, 233 Boylston Street	273.78
*Vartanian, Peter D. et al, 11 Putnam Street	233.22
Vartanian, Zarouki, 12 Kondazian Street	221.99
Vecchione, Bernice, 219 Watertown Street	192.66
Veronakis, Costas et ux, 31 Berkeley Street	60.84
Vessella, Concetta L., 90 Putnam Street	239.98
Viers, Felice H., 43 Hosmer Street	236.60
Vigna, Fidele et ux, 5 Bromfield Street	279.01
Vincent, Julia Z. et al, 95 Boylston Street	248.43
Vincini, Eugenio, 18 Berkeley Street	187.59
Virgo, Luther H. et ux, 49 Chester Street	189.25
Vitale, Silvio, 25 Merrifield Avenue	180.83
Vivier, Lillian M., 409 Mt. Auburn Street	16.90
Voci, William et ux, 9 Wilson Avenue	255.32
Vogel, Joseph et ux, 174 Worcester Street	100.00
*Vose, LeRoy C .et ux, 104 Standish Road	96.39
Vose & Sons Piano Co., Boston	4,195.29
Vosgerchian, Arsen, 13 Howe Street	246.74
Vahey, Eleanor, 236 No. Beacon Street	157.17
Waite, Wilbert R. et ux, Belmont	255.19
Walker, Margaret, Milton	215.23
Wallace, John E. et ux, 69 Stuart Street	172.38
Wallen, Ebba A., 76 Poplar Street	295.75
Walsh, Albert et ux, 111 Harnden Avenue	234.22
Walsh, John J., 19 No. Beacon Court	72.67
Walsh, John P., 7 California Park	172.38
Waltham Lumber Co., Waltham	66.61
Walton, Parker J., Trustee	92.95
Ward, Benjamin J., 76 Capitol Street	152.10
Ward, George F., 66 Palfrey Street	202.80
*Ward, Grace E., 66 Palfrey Street	126.81
Ward, Ruth E., 120 Bellevue Road	331.25
*Ware, I. Grace, 169 Worcester Street	170.92
Warren, Edmund M. et al, Trustees, Boston	1.69
Waterman, Heirs Maria, 137 Maplewood Street	363.35
*Watertown Amusement Corp., 650 Mt. Auburn Street	101.40
Watertown Apartments, Inc., 29 Hardy Avenue	100.00
Watertown Book Bindery, 81 Spring Street	33.80
Watertown Builders Supply Co., 418 Arsenal Street	2,379.28

Watertown Co-operative Bank, Main Street 897.47
Watertown Electric Co., 29 No. Beacon Street 1,190.55
Watertown Excavating Co., 200 Summer Street 185.90
Watertown 1513 Associates, Inc., 268 Arlington Street 263.64
Watertown K. P. Associates, Inc., 32 Church Street 100.00
Watertown Land Co., 65 Irving Street 1,014.85
Watertown Mfg. Co., Boston 16.90
Watertown Motor Sales Co., Inc., 49 No. Beacon Street...... 16.90
*Watertown Savings Bank, 60 Main Street 34.10
*Watertown Square Theatre, Galen Street 33.80
Watson, Mae F., 12 Longfellow Road 211.78
Watts, Arthur L., 185 Maplewood Street 287.30
Waverley Co-operative Bank, Waverley 6.76
Weatherbee, Dora L., 13 Russell Street 87.88
Webster, Edward C., 124 Marshall Street 182.52
Webster, George H., Belmont 55.77
Wells, Florence O.,34 Maple Street 236.60
Welsh, Charles D., 121 Highland Avenue 170.17
West, Josephine, 23 Chester Street 268.71
Westcott, Ernest W., 655 Mt. Auburn Street 3.38
Wester, John et al, 784 Belmont Street 255.19
Westling, Mary S. et al, 81 Commonwealth Road 277.16
*Westlund, Andrew S., Belmont 313.27
Westlund, Elmer G., 21 Stearns Road 11.83
Westlund, Elmer G. et ux, 21 Stearns Road 346.43
Westlund, Tekla E., Belmont 328.14
West Newton Co-operative Bank, West Newton 106.47
Wetsell, William H., Jr., 51 Harnden Avenue 8.45
Whalen, Patrick E. et ux, 121 Edenfield Avenue 132.35
Whelan, John B., et ux, 173 Worcester Street 170.92
White, Catherine V., 40 Hillside Street 17.12
White, Clara M., 60 Mt. Auburn Street 794.30
White, Edward H., 60 Mt. Auburn Street 92.95
White, George F., Trustee, 31 Quincy Street 158.86
White, James L. et ux, 68 Spruce Street 127.67
White, Lawrence W., 53 Hillside Street 242.58
White, Edward H., 64 Mt. Auburn Street 25.35
White, Patrick, et ux, 16 Stanley Avenue 23.37
White, Peter J., 26 Royal Street 129.07
White, Willard H., 42 Hillside Road 106.99
White, Heirs William L. et ux, 70 Fayette Street 175.76
Whitehead, Karl W. et ux, 79 Bradford Road 216.15
*Whitehead, Mae E., 11 Clyde Road 267.02
Whiting Milk Co., Waltham Street 1,023.30

Whiting, Heirs Moses, 18 Royal Street 241.67
Whitman Savings Bank, Whitman 467.84
*Whitney, Helen R., 29 Hall Avenue 285.61
*Whitney, Heirs Minetta J., 249 Main Street 507.00
Whittemore, Casper M. et ux, 149 Hillside Road 289.33
Whittier, Eva F., 3 Centre Street 100.00
Whittredge, Harry T., 166 Belmont Street 27.04
Wirner, John et ux, 14 Hosmer Street 233.77
Wiggin, Ruth L., 29 Channing Road 288.58
Wiley, Herbert A., 173 Bellevue Road 163.02
Wilkinson, Katherine, 26 Palmer Street 124.49
Wilkinson, Katherine, Trustee 146.74
Willard, George C., Dedham 250.12
*Williams, Heirs Edith J., 180 Boylston Street 256.88
Williams, Florence M., 62 Pearl Street 113.28
*Williams, William A., et ux, 107 Worcester Street 29.95
Wilson, Butler R., Jr., 29 Adams Avenue 30.42
Wilson, Heirs Ida M., 84 Bradford Road 419.32
Wilson, Jennie, 469 Main Street 120.65
Wilson, John I., 50 Harrington Street 143.65
Wilson, Rebecca, 44 Harrington Street 66.46
*Winchendon Savings Bank, Winchendon 462.53
Winchester, Roy. W., Winchester 135.20
Winkler, Philip N. et al, Boston 177.68
Winner, Ellanor M., 26 Russell Avenue 50.00
Winsor Club, Langdon Avenue 273.23
Winsor, Frederick et ux, 29 Partridge Street 89.57
Winsor, Mark J., et ux, 17 Otis Street 166.74
Winter Hill Co-operative Bank, Somerville 199.18
Wohltman, Cora Wells, 317 Common Street 289.91
Wojtulewisz, Julius, et al, 102 Belmont Street 292.37
Wolcott, Paul, Lowell 122.42
*Wood, Alexander et ux, 14 Gilbert Street 127.08
Wood, Alvin D. et ux, 13 Lawrence Street 262.02
Wood, Ernest H. et ux, 10 Avon Road 268.71
Wood, Robert D. et ux, 83 Morse Street 135.20
*Woods, Anna E., 9 Gilbert Street 21.74
Worcester, Josephine C., 34 Irving Street 194.35
Worcester, Ralph, 43 Phillips Street 6.76
Workingmen's Co-operative Bank, Boston 69.29
Wright, Frederick J., Jr., et ux, 22 Middlesex Road 222.22
Wry, H. I., 22 Mt. Auburn Street 8.45
Yanco, Sarah, Newton 260.26
Yantosca, Nellie, 66 Poplar Street 295.15

Yeremian, Garabed K., 97 Lovell Road	204.80
Yerxa, Partlow A., Trustee, 24 Garfield Street	101.33
Yiakoumes, Pandelis et ux, 33 Clarendon Street	160.57
York, Catherine M., 235 Mt. Auburn Street	512.07
Young, Ernest L., 21 Boylston Street	270.56
Young, Madeline B., 175 Church Street	183.92
Young, Ulysses S., 39 Upland Road	1,081.60
Ypsilantis, Nicholas D. et ux, 217 Arlington Street	258.57
Zaccagnini, Pietro, et ux, 91 Fayette Street	145.34
Zaccagnini, Rose, 103 Pleasant Street	290.68
Zacheus, Oscar I. et ux, 85 Robbins Road	238.42
Zakarian, John, 57 Quimby Street	209.84
Zampello, Louis et ux, East Boston	5.07
Zissis, Irene, Somerville	21.97

TAX TITLES

Abbondanzio, Antonio, 28 Quirk Street	256.88
Accetta, Manfredi, East Boston	23.17
Alward, Murray B., Mattapan	25.48
Ananian, Narin, Malden	314.37
Anderson, Maude V., 54 Carroll Street	234.91
Andrews, Frank H., 348 Charles River Road	303.58
Annese, Felice et ux, 66 Sparkill Street	45.63
Arslainian, Samuel, 11 Kondazian Street	223.68
Bacon, Jennie C., 92 Common Street	226.46
Barruzza, Manoel M. et ux, Somerville	265.33
Bartis, Veneita J. et al, 13 Morse Street	256.88
Benfield, Albert J., 33 Franklin Street	196.04
Berry, Casper, Boston	5.07
Berry, Sarah H., 31 Katherine Road	277.16
Berry, Sarah et al, 31 Katherine Road	280.54
Bickford, Sarah E., 71 Walnut Street	241.67
Bittelari, John T., 46 Spring Street	175.76
Bloomer, Mary A., 7 Edenfield Avenue	184.03
Bogosian, Theodore Oscar, 116 Nichols Avenue	282.39
Bond, Charles Wood, 30 Winsor Avenue	234.91
Borden, Lucy B., Allston	168.12
Borges, Joseph, Somerville	3.38
Borges, Mary Leland, 18 Stuart Street	170.69
Botti, Grazia M., 215 Palfrey Street	163.93
Boudreau, Helen L., 27 Maplewood Street	47.32
Boyajian, Bogohos, 69 Laurel Street	218.01
Burbank, Annie E., 44 Katherine Road	196.04
Bruce, Sarah H., 14 Beacon Park	177.45
Burke, Mary Margaret, 120 Westminster Avenue	158.37

Burr, James M., 85 Boylston Street	263.64
Busconi, Mary, 40 Quimby Street	342.23
Butler, Heirs George, 26 Myrtle Street	81.12
Butters, Lucinda, 277 Main Street	172.38
Cacavaro, Mary, 25 Acton Street	162.24
Calf, Jerry, Walpole	35.49
Callinan, Gertrude, 11 Gleason Street	279.90
Camerato, Salvatore et ux, 38 Bradshaw Street	147.03
Cameron, James M. et al, Somerville	33.80
Canady, Oscar M., 18 Channing Road	147.32
*Candido, Joseph, 49 Hovey Street	272.09
*Cappucci, Michele et ux, 23 Bostonia Avenue	155.48
Carbone, Rose, 20 Gertrude Street	260.01
Carboni, Maria, 96 Fayette Street	182.52
Carey, Thomas W., Everett	3.38
Carlstrom, Fannie M., 49 Pequosette Street	250.12
Carr, Catherine A., Hopkinton	6.76
Carrabis, Vincenza, 44 Bacon Street	96.33
Carroll, Pearl A., Trustee, 124 Putnam Street	278.85
Caruso, Concezio et ux, 185 Warren Street	91.26
Caruso, Vincenzo et ux, 27 Myrtle Street	170.69
Caso, Pasqualina, 41 French Street	77.74
Casselman, Louise C., Boston	69.89
Cerrato, Vincenzo et ux, King Street	27.49
Chambers, Margaret M., Andover	322.58
Chooljian, Sarah, 46 Salisbury Road	304.82
Cohen, Samuel J., Newton	104.29
Colby, Maurice D. et ux, 41 Piermont Street	135.65
Connor, Michael V. et ux, 61 Prospect Street	194.35
Corcoran, Frank G., et ux, 123 Arsenal Street	192.66
Costa, Grace F. et al, 14 Bromfield Street	280.70
Cotani, Samuel et ux, 357 Main Street	171.53
Coupal, Frances, 608 Main Street, Wakefield	6.76
Courtney, Heirs Margaret E., 271 Pleasant Street	143.24
Covino, Felice, Milford	209.56
*Crescitelli, Antonio, 90 Edenfield Avenue	148.72
Crosby, Thomas J., et ux, 212 Boylston Street	174.07
Dadaian, Hampar, et ux, 212 Boylston Street	162.24
D'Allanno, Antonio, et ux, 88 Arlington Street	273.78
Dalby, Thomas, Co., 101 Morse Street	964.99
Danikian, John, 26 Porter Street	238.29
D'Antonio, Cesidia, 200 Summer Street	218.01
Davenport, Alfred M., 88 Grove Street	1,096.81
Davenport, Florence M., 88 Grove Street	310.96

Davis, Albert et ux, 29 Lowell Avenue	135.20
*DeFelice, Guiseppe, 45 Melendy Avenue	148.72
Della Rosa, Francesca et ux, 191 Warren Street	16.90
DeNebellis, Guilo et ux, 39 Fairfield Street	119.24
DerBogosian, Maryam K., 21 Melendy Avenue	219.70
DerHovhanesian, Israel, 138 Forest Street	126.75
Derian, Mary, 16 Hazel Street	199.42
Derayian, Arminag, 19 Melendy Avenue	253.50
Devenney, John J. et al, 10 Hillcrest Circle	305.70
DiVecchio, Maria G., 114 Elm Street	202.80
DiVecchio, Mary, 192 Waltham Street	569.70
Dixon, Georgiana A., 24 Quincy Street	260.84
Dolan, Bessie C., 11 Prescott Street	236.60
Donahue, Elizabeth M., 11 Hill Street	94.64
Duffy, Peter D., 15 Prescott Street	141.96
East Cambridge Savings Bank, Cambridge	136.89
Edwards, Margaret, Somerville	182.52
*Egleston, Mary, 29 Winter Street	287.30
Eliot Savings Bank, Roxbury	270.40
Elliot, Elias W., 35 Union Street	287.30
Elliot, Florence E., 35 Union Street	263.64
Esposito, Vincenzo, 18 Chandler Street	179.14
Evans, Frederick E. et ux, 206 Pleasant Street	223.08
Evans, Charles M., 19 Carroll Street	251.81
Farese, Theresa, 264 Warren Street	15.21
Fay, Mary A., 122 No. Beacon Street	158.86
Files, Marion I., 36 Hardy Avenue	167.31
Finance Corp. of New England, Boston	10.14
Flavin, Mary E., 11 Carleton Terrace	269.51
Flecca, Caterina, 231 Arlington Street	211.25
Flitcroft, Albert E., 58 Chapman Street	125.06
Foley, Charles A., Pleasant Street	130.13
Fucci, Pasquale A., 120 Edenfield Avenue	149.29
Galligan, John F. et ux, 5 Clayton Street	245.05
Galvin, Mary A., 110 Brookline Street	136.89
Galvin, Patrick S., 110 Brookline Street	30.42
Geramanes, Costos P., 24 Berkeley Street	6:76
Glanz, Max, 294 Washington St., Boston	476.58
Godwin, Nellie, 17 Chester Street	221.39
Graham, Helen F., 122 Barnard Avenue	298.72
Gray, Robert W., Cambridge	544.98
Gringeri, Salvatore, 24 Holt Street	119.99
*Gullotti, Concetta, 68 Westminster Avenue	119.37
Haddie, James L., 27 Copeland Street	432.76

Haddie, James L. et ux, 27 Copeland Street 15.21
Haddie, Florence.V., 27 Copeland Street 6.76
Hadjinlian, Mary, 92 Nichols Avenue 502.14
Hadley, Mary V., 316 Common Street 278.85
*Haigian, Garabed et ux, 33 Fairfield Street 224.77
Hall, William W., Malden 160.55
Halladjian, Rose, 79 Dexter Avenue 243.36
Hamilton, Charles E. 5.07
Handy, Daisey A., 161 Lexington Street 181.43
Hanson, Elin M., Trustee, 25 Lincoln Street 588.12
Harney, Mary E., 8 Cottage Lane 49.01
Harrington, Ralph E. 28.73
Harrison, Alice, 14 Merrifield Avenue 158.86
Hartung, Paul C., 27 Maplewood Street **958.02**
Hawes, Otis L., 184 Mt. Auburn Street 236.60
Healey, John J., 43 Waltham Street 312.65
Hey, Mary S., Boston 266.14
Hill, Wilfred R. et ux, 11 Quincy Street 58.29
Hodkinson, Elsie M., Worcester 267.02
Hodkinson, George R., Worcester 264.29
Hodson, Ida M., Boston 40.56
Hudson, John R. et ux, 5 Partridge Street 241.94
*Hunsley, Ruth, 135 Templeton Parkway 319.39
Hunt, Mabel M., 281 Arsenal Street 224.77
Iannelli, Nicola, 7 Hearn Street 174.07
Iodice, Clemente, 259 Lexington Street 199.42
Iodice, Domenic, 259 Lexington Street 81.12
Jensen, John K., 572 Main Street 1,653.25
Jacobson, George, 66 Belmont Street 285.61
Johansson, Carl W., Trustee, Boston 535.23
Johnson, Jacob J., 78 Dexter Avenue 348.14
Joseph, Christo, 68 School Street 309.27
Kalfian, Bogos et al, 49 Fairfield Street 233.22
Kane, Elizabeth M., 4 Derby Road 178.85
Kane, Minnie, 161 Mt. Auburn Street 463.06
Kaplan, Bernard et al, Trustee, 545 Mt. Auburn Street........ 244.75
Karalekas, Charles B., 212 Boylston Street 273.78
Kashishian, Almost, 125 Walnut Street 236.49
Kazanjian, Avedis, Cambridge 10.14
Kazanjian, Kenneth K., 135 School Street 229.84
Keaney, William J., et ux, 4 Theurer Park 311.12
Keefe, Mary G., 14 Irving Park 116.61
Keefe, Heirs, Mary V., 14 Irving Park 423.35
Keefe, Michael, Brighton 21.03

Kelley, Anne M., Belmont	209.37
Kelley, Joseph M., 98 Mt. Auburn Street	770.64
Kelley, Margaret A., 549 Main Street	218.51
Killeen, Owen H. et ux, 34 Adams Street	280.41
Kinder, William F., Jr., et ux, 69 Springfield Street	152.10
Konian, Neva, 12 Cypress Street	277.16
Kent, Bert N., 241 Palfrey Street	214.63
Laffey, Annie E., 253 Waverley Avenue	224.77
Laguff, John H. et ux, 45 Hersom Street	170.00
Lally, Raymond et al, 48 Grandview Avenue	5.07
Lally, Joseph M., 48 Grandview Avenue	386.66
Lally, Michael H., 48 Grandview Avenue	5.07
Larkin, M. Isabella, 215 Arsenal Street	256.88
*La Spada, Annie, 70 Westminster Avenue	234.78
LeConti, Charles, 158 Fayette Street	140.27
Leonard, Bryan et ux, 105 Rutland Street	313.09
LePore, Concetta, 26 Keenan Street	250.12
Lindahl, Maude, 20 Prescott Street	118.30
Linehan, Simon J., Brookline	6.76
Lionetti, James et ux, 87 Fitchburg Street	185.02
Loew's, E. M. Theatres Corp., 45 Galen Street	400.00
Lopez, Nancy, Admx., Lowell Avenue	182.52
Lovell, Eva B., 31 Katherine Road	234.91
Lynn Five Cents Savings Bank, Lynn	146.19
MacBeth, George H. et ux, 109 Standish Road	294.16
McDonald, Sarah A., 31 Prescott Street	236.60
MacFarland, Charles J., 618 Belmont Street	311.52
MacGinnis, Allen, 125 Rutland Street	142.72
McMillan, Sterling A., Antigonish, N. S.	12.50
Maggiacomo, Gerardo et ux, 239 Lexington Street	30.42
Magnuson, John, 36 Putnam Street	219.70
Manzelli, Maria, 1016 Belmont Street	459.94
Marderosian, Dick, 140 Nichols Avenue	286.07
Martin, Harriet T., Trustee, 14 Winthrop Street	275.47
Martin, James V., 8 Hazel Street	251.81
Martocchio, Heirs, Pietro, 11 Warren Street	66.85
*Marucci, Pasquale et ux, Newton	3.38
Mason, Vernon et al, Trustees	66.53
Maynard, Henry et al, Waltham	36.39
Mazza, Carmine, 48 Cottage Street	10.14
Mazza, James V. et ux, 66-B Ralph Street	212.94
McCafferty, Heirs, William, 56 Cuba Street	104.78
McCue, Helen C., 293 No. Beacon Street	608.40
McElroy, Laura E., 23 Hunt Street	150.41

McEnaney, Michael, 115 Boylston Street	283.92
McKenna, Charles et ux, 93 California Street	89.57
McMahon, Bridget K., 10 Fifth Avenue	253.50
McMahon, William J. et ux, 24 Springfield Street	188.64
McMurtrie, Lillian, 84 Fitchburg Street	188.40
*Madeiros, Joseph et ux, 200 Sycamore Street	135.16
Menton, Patrick A. et ux, 669 Main Street	210.18
Merullo, Pellegrino et ux, 69 Forest Street	170.69
Miller, Albert E., 136 Orchard Street	260.26
Minty, K. Chesley, et ux, 30 Everett Avenue	224.38
Monaghan, Carroll Y. et ux, 128 Hillside Road	265.33
Moore, Elizabeth G., 61 Marion Road	175.76
Mooers, Heirs, Wilhelmina, 105 Spruce Street	207.87
Mooney, Daniel G. et ux, 124 Nichols Avenue	297.03
Morgan, Mary P., 32 Chandler Street	144.48
Morrone, John et ux, 377 Main Street	528.97
Morse, Arthur L., 24 Chapman Street	273.76
Moscato, Luigi, East Boston	16.90
Muckjian, Herop, 21 Hosmer Street	241.67
Mullen, Joseph P., 181 Walnut Street	145.34
Mullen, Margaret J., 376 Arsenal Street	212.94
Mullins, Hannah L., 117 Lovell Road	312.80
Mulvaney, Ellen, Allston	11.44
Mulvahill, Mary L., 129 Maplewood Street	300.82
Murdock, Charles E., 135 Morse Street	103.09
Murphy, Helen E., 27 Hunt tSreet	148.72
Nahigian, Agnes, 190 Boylston Street	267.02
Nardone, Andrew, 17 Middle Street	18.59
Nelligan, Gertrude H., 69 Hillside Road	282.23
*Neshe, Domenico et ux, 86 Walnut Street	160.55
*Newcomb, William M., 11 Fairview Avenue	264.57
New England Land Co., Boston	3,893.76
Newton Realty Corp., Newton	229.84
Newton Trust Co., Newton	353.21
Noel, Nora K., Roxbury	272.12
Nolen ,Joseph F., et ux, 20 Warwick Road	307.86
O'Brien, Albert A., Newton	15.21
O'Brien, George A., Waverley	15.57
O'Flaherty, Patrick et ux, 354 Arlington Street	50.53
Ohanian, Mary M. et al, 89 Bigelow Avenue	194.35
O'Neil, Abbie C. et ux, 38 Forest Street	98.02
Ormsby. Leslie E. et ux, 78 Fitchburg Street	202.67
O'Shea, Ida McCarthy, 41 Adams Avenue	299.71
O'Sullivan, James H., 154 Belmont Street	246.74

Pappas, Costas, 67 Coolidge Hill Road 294.06
Parr, Thomas, South Boston 6.76
Partridge, William H. 11.83
Pass, Ida, Newtonville 248.43
Patrick, Elstratios, 37 Berkeley Street 60.84
Perkins, Elias A., 73 Fayette Street 30.42
Phelan, Cecelia, 103 Chapman Street 34.90
Phillips, Thomas A., 234 Arlington Street 292.37
Piantedosi, Jennie D. 18.59
Pouliot, Joseph M. et ux, 231 No. Beacon Street 192.00
Putney, Clarence L. et ux, 126 Westminster Avenue........... 165.85
Quaranto, Joseph, et ux, 104 Putnam Street 239.98
Queeney, Catherine T., 21 Gleason Street 218.87
Raimondo, Domenico B., 10 Bostonia Avenue 255.19
*Regan, Miriam C., Cambridge 268.71
Renfrew, Robert A. et al, 26 Hersom Street 125.06
Revere Trust Co., Revere 143.65
Ricci, Angelo 53.82
Ricci, Salvatore, 10 Chadbourne Terrace 185.90
Rich, Everett B., 35 Adams Street 306.13
Ridge, Patrick M. et ux, 191 Boylston Street 265.33
Riggs, Axel J., 50 Bailey Road 750.36
Ringer, Clayton, 54 California Street 99.01
Riordan, Helen M., Quincy Street 11.36
Riverside Trust Co. 722.21
Rizzo, Anna, 114 Forest Street 47.89
Rizzo, Guiseppe, 114 Forest Street 162.65
Rizzutti, Vincenzo et ux, 39 Dartmouth Street 238.29
Rodeo, Homer, Boston 50.70
Rutledge, Harold F. et ux, 70 Chapman Street 135.61
Saboonjian, Anna, 95 Nichols Avenue 109.85
Sallese, Heirs, Guistino, Coolidge Hill Road 79.43
Salvitti, Antonio, 114 Putnam Street 219.70
Santoro, Vincenzo, 83 Fayette Street 344.76
Sarabella, Elisa, 54 Piermont Street 106.47
Sarkisian, Melke M. et al, 90 Cypress Street 151.97
Sattanio, Peter, 14 Everett Avenue 174.82
Savage, Jeremiah J., 142 Palfrey Street 180.83
Schou, David, 16 Lawrence Street 258.27
*Schwabe, H. Marie, 69 Channing Road 308.50
Seaman, Isabel C., East Orange, N. J. 15.21
Semple, Robert et ux, 129 Westminster Avenue 158.37
Sergi, Guiseppe, 19 King Street 13.52
Severino, Bebardino et ux, 110 Edenfield Avenue 252.46

Shahbazian, Nellie E., 1063 Belmont Street	332.93
Sharmat, Lucille B., Boston	215.23
Silvia, Domenico, 75 Pleasant Street	57.46
Smith, George William et ux, 291 Main Street	11.83
Solomon, Lewis et al, Boston	25.48
Soukiasian, Kaloust, 144 Nichols Avenue	286.07
Sparks, Grace A., 31 Fifield Street	260.26
Stephen, Paul, 104 Coolidge Street	380.25
Stone, Edwin L., 100 Russell Avenue	204.49
Stone, Gladys W., Cambridge	314.57
Sullivan, John J. et ux, 96 Boylston Street	262.64
Sweeney, William J. et ux, 25 Russell Avenue	334.62
Sylvester, Julia, 42 Berkeley Street	601.64
Taverna, Pasquale, 141 Westminster Avenue	305.02
Testa, Pasquale, 28 New Lexington Street	82.17
Theurer, Otto A., 171 Watertown Street	920.66
Thierry, Adelaide H., Boston	270.40
Thissen, Hazel Lee, 153 Common Street	248.43
Titus, LeRoy C., et al, 10 Chester Street	309.27
Tobio, Sam et ux, 149 Lexington Street	237.22
Topalian, Victor et ux, 18 Porter Street	239.98
Torri, Cesare, 67 Waltham Street	111.54
Toscano, Guiseppe et ux, 23 Brimmer Street	250.12
Towne, Elizabeth C., 24 Howard Street	270.40
Trapasso, Antonetta	5.07
Trapelo Road Realty Co., Belmont	346.65
Tsloas, James et al, 41 Coolidge Hill Road	277.80
Tuttle, Charles H., Malden	11.44
*Tutunjian, Heirs, Asdoor, 54 Quimby Street	204.11
Usello, Rosa, Trustee, East Boston	278.74
United States Bond & Mortgage Corp., Boston	1,147.65
Vacca, Rose, 28 Bostonia Avenue	238.29
Venetzian, Jasper, 35 Cypress Street	226.46
Vartanian, Kirkor B. et ux, 10 Kondazian Street	220.30
Verducci, Domenico, Brighton	6.76
Vergillo, Carillo, 51 Quirk Street	20.28
Vigna, Fedele et ux, Bromfield Street	54.31
Vincini, Peter, 73 Nichols Avenue	155.48
Vincent, J. Edmund, Cambridge	483.34
Waltham Country Club, Waltham	2,467.40
Warren, Edmund M. et al, Trustees	.85
Watertown Co-operative Bank	111.57
Watertown Savings Bank	73.57
Welsh, Charles D., Highland Avenue	28.22

Welch, John, 27 Quincy Street	158.86
White, Clara M., 60 Mt. Auburn Street	158.86
White, Edward H., 60 Mt. Auburn Street	179.14
Whitney, Emma R., 15 Fifield Street	146.54
Whitney, Lester E., Waverley	3.38
Wilbur, J. W. Company Inc., Boston	101.40
Wilson, Mary B., 118 Marshall Street	196.04
Woodward, Donald E. et ux, 45 Olcott Street	228.75
Wright, Bertha G., 83 Fitchburg Street	201.92
Wright, Edward F., Trustee, 70 Mt. Auburn Street	1,144.47
Wright, Edward F. et al, 70 Mt. Auburn Street	302.51
Wright, Frank E., et ux, 64 Olcott Street	55.37
Young, Hebron E., 65 Hillside Street	34.32
Young, Ulysses S., Trustee	11.83
Youngman, Harry E. et ux, 59 Bradford Road	286.08
Zaccagnini, Pietro, 103 Pleasant Street	218.01
Zakarian, David, 15 Malden Street	109.85
Zakarian, Nevart, 16 Kondazian Street	120.00
Zanco, John, Waltham	79.65
Borges, Joseph, Somerville	5.07
Baboian, Charles, 710 Mt. Auburn Street	218.71
Butterfield, Nettie F., 53 Marion Road	177.74
Caccavaro, Emily, 11 Thurston Road	106.66
Caira, Enrico, et ux, 213 Watertown Street	111.50
Callaway, Annie et al, 152 Hillside Road	127.78
*Camara, Heirs Joseph, 209 Summer Street	117.00
Cambridgeport Savings Bank	239.98
Campagno, Corinne, 25 Hillcrest Circle	116.85
Campbell, Bernice L., 330 School Street	197.44
Capone, Pasquale et al, 26 Waverley Avenue	109.70
Chrakian, Bagdassar et ux, 14 Coolidge Hill Road	181.32
Christianson, Fred J., 11 Wilmot Street	77.40
Christianson, Hilda, 32 Priest Road	100.00
Cianci, Pietro et ux, 22 Elmwood Street	100.00
Ciarlo, Domenico, 61 Lexington Street	23.46
*Cicotelli, Vincenzo, 16 New Lexington Street	89.02
Claflin & Co., 127 Mt. Auburn Street	62.21
*Clay, Walter F., 42 Waltham Street	86.86
Clinton, Edward et ux, 27 Union Street	100.00
Cloonan, Michael, 29 Gilbert Street	138.88
Clougherty, Catherine F., 111 Poplar Street	195.71
*Clouter, William et ux, 230 No. Beacon Street	16.07
Clynes, Martin A. et ux, 8 Green Street	223.08
*Coffey, Julia J., 81 Dexter Avenue	66.37

Cohen, Bessie, 83 Templeton Parkway	244.77
Comella, Josephine et al, 26 Norseman Avenue	48.00
*Comstock, Heirs Albert E., 103 No. Beacon Street	180.65
Condon, Anna B. et al, Newton	30.55
Carr, James F. et ux, 60 Hovey Street	116.67
Caruso, James, 35 Winter Street	96.52
Casavant, Mary A., 232 Watertown Street	73.23
Cossaboom, Annie A., 83 Maplewood Street	93.16
*Cavallaro, Emidio et ux, 15 French Terrace	167.31
*Cavallaro, Rose, 341 Arlington Street	151.72
Cavaretta, Alfonso et ux, 35 Howard Street	212.90
Cendroski, Fawsten, 16 Cottage Street	82.46
Centebar, Charles H., 460 Main Street	550.15
Centolo, John et al, 154 Pleasant Street	216.78
Chapman, Eleanor M., 12 Chauncy Street	162.49
*Cheeseman, Herbert E., 45 Hardy Avenue	177.45
Chevoor, Mary, Boston	72.09
*Chick, Arnold L., 69 Langdon Avenue	68.01
Chilengarian, Arsen, et ux, 23 Porter Street	100.00
*Condon, Elizabeth A., 33 Forest Street	94.64
Conklin, Minnie L., 304 Common Street	128.98
*Connell, Catherine V., 70 Belmont Street	122.09
Connolly, Mary E., Belmont Street	184.21
*Cooke, Mary A., 53 Carver Road	14.06
Corazzinni, Gaetano et ux, 109 Arsenal Street	201.54
*Corazinni, Giovanni et ux, 55 Cypress Street	31.66
*Creamer, Thomas, 113 Winsor Avenue	46.36
*Critchett, Alice M., 158 Spring Street	43.00
Crupi, Domenico et ux, 29 Prentiss Street	152.03
*Cuccinotta, Giovanni, Waverley	120.58
Curtin, Peter, 44 Elliot Street	213.25
D'Amico, Guiseppe, 81 Arlington Street	68.76
D'Amico, Guiseppe, 81 Arlington Street	48.10
*Dana, Bridget, 64 Belmont Street	133.69
Dana, Herman et al, Boston	234.91
*Dangel, Sadie L., 650 Mt. Auburn Street	2,604.36
Danvers Savings Bank	436.84
Davis, Edith M., 9 Gay Road	156.03
Davis, Edna S., 87 Lovell Road	131.39
Dealtry, Eleanor M., 51 Garfield Street	468.13
DeFelice, Edward A., 38 Melendy Avenue	126.24
DeLaney, John C., Jr., 897 Belmont Street	298.38
Della Rosa, Francesca et ux, 191 Warren Street	18.59
DerKazarian, Tourvanda, 31 Elton Avenue	106.78

Desantis, Concetta et al, 13 Howard Street	132.00
DeSimone, James et ux, East Boston	96.47
*DiLucci, Francis D. et ux, 78 Salisbury Road.	104.39
DiMelle, Guiseppe et ux, 40 Waverley Avenue	82.96
*Dixon, Mary M. et al, 21 Templeton Parkway	100.00
DJinivis, Varther, 28 Concord Road	177.55
Donne, Nicola Delle, et ux, 175 Fayette Street	50.12
Duffy, Florence H., 40 Longfellow Road	76.56
Doyle, Isabelle A., 346 Belmont Street	131.31
Duffy, Mary E., 503 Main Street	82.40
Durkin, Edward A. et ux, 10 King Street	196.10
D'Urso, Nicola et ux, 535 Mt. Auburn Street	424.18
Dyer, Jamie et al, 43 Hovey Street	134.28
Eaton, Levi W., 21 Elton Avenue	64.01
Edmunds, Rowena S., 35 Channing Road	195.00
Egan, Alice G., 45 Winsor Avenue	100.00
Egisio, Francseco, 128 Main Street	74.00
Ellis, Mary Helen, 85 Russell Avenue	197.75
Emery, George H. et ux, 41 Wilmot Street	93.50
Emery, Heirs Herorge T., 18 Beechwood Avenue	33.80
Evans, James D. et al, 119 Church Street	150.41
Evans, Kate F., 11 Chester Street	180.52
Everett Brothers Inc., 75 No. Beacon Street	300.00
Fairbanks, Catherine L., 44 Spruce Street	170.05
Falbo, Frank, 15 Berkeley Street	31.81
*Falzarano, Mario, 160 Walnut Street	28.44
Fantasia, Domenick et ux, 6 Hudson Street	72.77
Fantasia, Eugene, 22 Hudson Street	32.49
Faricelli, Donato, et ux, 6 Rifle Court	39.85
Farraher, Margaret, 42 Royal Street	106.47
Farren, Mary A., 5 Bridgham Avenue	51.82
Fay, John J. et ux, 24 Putnam Street	121.94
Fay, Leon F. et ux, 110 Rutland Street	69.11
Fay, Nora E., 13 Copeland Street	211.15
Feeney, Mary A., 26 Elliot Street	267.02
Feinberg, Esther, 78 Rutland Street	144.12
Finlay, Clara, 7 Laurel Street	39.98
Fitchburg Co-operative Bank	59.68
*Fitzgerald, Joseph A., 36 Stuart Street	100.00
Frederick, Fritz W. et ux, 375 School Street	184.61
Freethy, Mildred L., 98 Barnard Avenue	192.72
Frissora, Henry et ux, 86 Waverley Avenue	225.19
Fuller, Carrie M., 7 Chester Street	157.49
*Fuller, Will S., 30 Richards Road	149.39

Fundeklian, Setrak et ux, 18 Lloyd Road	178.80
Furey, Thomas et ux, 121 Arsenal Street	140.00
*Gallagher, Louise E., 42 Irving Street	53.76
Gallen, Mary, 16 Hardy Avenue	76.01
Gallo, Domenico et ux, 210 Palfrey Street	50.27
Garaway, Herbert J. et ux, 3 Morse Street	236.60
Geary, Cecelia G., 17 Bradford Road	297.49
Giacoumakis, Calliope M. et al, 194 Arlington Street	239.98
Giacoumis, Arthur et ux, 30 Adams Avenue	180.00
Gibbons, Edward C., 16 Hall Avenue	145.64
Gilligan, Bartholomew, 291 Arsenal Street	50.56
Giordiano, Pietro, 100 Putnam Street	150.47
Giuliano, Angelina, 143 Fayette Street	47.61
Gjertsen, Ingebret, 33 Chapman Street	79.01
Glancy, Nellie S., Newton	138.73
Goldsberry, John R. et ux, 12 Robbins Road	185.74
Golub, Eva, 82 Beechwood Avenue	190.57
Goodrow, Hattie et al, 83 Spruce Street	182.52
*Grace, Margaret G., 16 Sunnybank Road	254.04
Grade, Oscar W. et ux, 32 Sunnybank Road	253.90
Graham, Inez M., 4 Franklin Street	153.21
*Granville, George A., 65 Carver Road	100.00
Gray, Charles et ux, 358 Arlington Street	109.24
*Gray, James, 60 Fayette Street	60.00
Greene, Catherine et al, 29 Priest Road	25.36
Greene, Joseph M. et ux, 33 Williams Street	83.10
Gregorian Armenian Society of Parma	185.81
Griffin, Sarah C., Waltham	122.82
Guadarette, Michele, 9 Elmwood Avenue	134.44
Gulesian, Abraham, 48 Cypress Street	95.14
*Gulesian, Esther, 203 School Street	255.96
Gustafson, Charles W., 776 Belmont Street	194.29

1933 REAL AND PERSONAL TAXES UNPAID
At Close of Business December 31, 1934

Asterisk (*) paid since close of books or Tax Title

Butler, George F., et ux, Mary F., 45 Main Street	$136.80
Canady, Oscar M., 18 Channing Road	1.71
Chopourian, Harry M., 504 Mt. Auburn Street	11.29
Cohen, Benjamin, 84A Main Street	8.21
Cohen, Dexter S., 4 Mt. Auburn Street	4.28
*Colligan, Mary A., 5 Royal Street	131.67
Crawford, Mattie C., 30 Lincoln Street	224.71

Cucinotta, Giovanni, 66 Beech Street, Belmont	33.12
Cucinotta, John, 66 Beech Street, Belmont	104.49
Dunn, Joseph A., 279 Mt. Auburn Street	91.31
*Files, Walter W., 12 Hardy Avenue	1.71
Haartz Mason Grower Co., Pleasant Street	1,504.80
Healey, John J., Waltham Street	181.26
Hurley, John, 164 Main Street	1.71
Iknaian, Kevork V., 81 Bickford Street, Jamaica Plain	1.28
Jones, David R., Alfred Road	23.94
*Kazanjian, Hagop M., 105 School Street	23.94
Keefe, Joseph, 164 Main Street	3.42
Kelley, Catherine L., 30 Springfield Street	175.49
Landry, Leo P., 42 Bradford Road	20.52
Leacy, Elizabeth, 111 Galen Street	117.55
Leacy, H. Maynard, 55 Galen Street	13.68
*Lovell, Eva B., 31 Katherine Road	3.42
McNamara, Louise A., 5 Lovell Road	350.35
McVey, Thomas, Brighton	42.75
Mooney, Frederic, et ux, 36 Washburn Street	5.12
Natoli, Laurence G., 84 Barnard Avenue	834.48
Natoli, Laurence G., et ux John B., 20 Mt. Auburn Street....	1,535.58
Natoli, John B., et ux, Laurence G.	695.97
O'Brien, Frank, 31 Standish Road	257.47
Richey, William, 25 Queensbury Street, Boston	34.18
Roche, Frank, 124 Galen Street	3.42
Secord, Fred, 65A Dexter Avenue	11.97
Simonds, Luther W., 100 Church Street	208.62
Sokalski, Julia E., 33 Adams Street	5.00
Stacey, Herbert C., et ux, 11 Dwight Street	10.69
Tocci, Lucia, 10 Lowell Avenue	99.84
Torres, Marianno DeRogo, et ux, 32 Whitney Street	39.33
Watertown Grist Mills, Inc., 83 Galen Street	7.70
Watertown Excavating Co., Inc., 200 Summer Street	188.10
*Whiting, Heirs of Moses, 16 Royal Street	20.00
Martocchio, Heirs or Devs of Pietro, 42 Forest Street	17.20

· 1933 POLL TAXES UNPAID
At Close of Business December 31, 1934

Alwis, William, Coolidge Avenue
Amodeo, Anthony, 204 Orchard Street
Busconi, John, 40 Quimby Street
Comfort, Redford, 669 Main Street
Colligan, John J., 5 Royal Street

DeMarino, Michael, 531 Pleasant Street
Glynn, Leo C., 106 Putnam Street
Gretter, W. Plumber, 387 School Street
Grigoreas, Christopher, 31 Kondazian Street
Holland, J. Edward, 16 Stearns Road
Kasabian, Harry, 27 Elton Avenue
Kelley, Daniel, 35 Morse Street
Ladd, Joseph H., 90 Robbins Road
Lavoy, Henry, Jr., 404 Pleasant Street
Lennon, George, 224 Belmont Street
Marchant, Leo, 34 Oakland Street
Marchino, Joseph, 18 Myrtle Street
McDowell, Charles D., 16 St. Marys Street
McGovern, John H., 104 Belmont Street
Moran, Paul C., 56 Gilbert Street
Natsis, Nicolo, 50 Capitol Street
Nichols, Elwood B., 34 Oakley Road
Ounjian, Samuel, 49 Laurel Street
Phinney, Brenton M., 300 Main Street
Photos, Louis, 139 Hillside Road
Proto, Dominic, 50 Riverside Street
Rogers, Chester F., 35 Dexter Avenue
Rooney, Edward D., 110 Riverside Street
Thurber, Donald H., 39 Commonwealth Road
Thurston, John, 18 Adams Street
Tiberio, Carmine, 29 Church Hill Street
Tiberio, Joseph, 27 Church Hill Street
Doyle, John, 344 Belmont Street
Mansell, John J., 1 2Gertrude Street

1933 UNPAID EXCISE TAXES
At Close of Business December 31, 1934

Committed March 15, 1933

English, Dorothy H., 40 Pequosette Street	$3.47
Merry, Charles E., 55 Channing Road	49.85
Moore, Marion E., 16 Dunton Road	3.79
Netos, George, 43 Crawford Street	18.93
Trust, Gasparello, R. E., 143 Fayette Street	10.10
Watertown Excavating Co., Inc., 200 Summer Street	52.38

Committed August 8, 1933

Burke, Thomas F., 78 Chestnut Street	$4.63
Cavicchi, John, 8 Fifth Avenue	.60
Colligan, Charles P., 5 Royal Street	6.81

Ladd, Evelyn M., 90 Robbins Road 8.76
MacBeth, Helen C., 109 Standish Road 21.82

Committed November 27, 1933

Farrar, Catherine, 42 Royal Street $6.70
Gallagher, Thomas H., 126 Worcester Street 2.00
Gamble, Anna L., 141 Edenfield Avenue 2.37
Gately, Mildred E., 36 Bacon Street 2.00
Giaimis, Frances, 141 Galen Street 4.25
Greene, George, 15 Adams Street 2.00
Griffin, Delia E., 8 Fifth Avenue 4.47
Grimm, Charles N., 69 Prentiss Street 2.00
Hogan, Rosemary F., 221 Arsenal Street 1.81
Hurley, John F., 164 Main Street 2.00
Monahan, Helen, 68A Edenfield Avenue 2.00
Murphy, Edmond N., 16 Belknap Terrace.............................. 2.53
Nicastro, Casino D., 428 Mt. Auburn Street 2.21
Oliveto, Frank, Jr., 27 Carroll Street 2.00
Parkinson, Frederick O., 37 Prescott Street 2.00
Piantedosi, Joseph, 183 Fayette Street 4.73
Poillucci, Frank J., 3 Oliver Road 4.21
Riggs, Lewis W., 50 Bailey Road 3.78
Robinson, Herbert E., 25 Palmer Street 2.10
Robinson, R. L. & Co., 12 Church Street 2.00
Sislane, Leo R., 267 Boylston Street 2.00
Volante, William A., 20 Merrifield Avenue 9.67
Watertown Poultry & Cattle Co., 10 Lowell Avenue 4.00

Committed January 17, 1934

Brooks, Robert P., 65 Union Street $2.76
Bunell, Stuart, 40 Marshall Street 2.42
Chapman, William J., 185 School Street 2.00
Coffey, John E., 50 Putnam Street 2.00
Crossman, Chester, 167 Spruce Street 2.00
Dodakin, James, 8 Irma Avenue 4.00
Gallinaro, Cosmo, 37 Boylston Street 2.21
Howland, Allen L., 29 Springfield Street 2.00
Lopez, Agnes C., 484 Main Street 2.47
MacDonald, Richard, 77 Putnam Street 2.00
Moss, Elsie, 12 Bancroft Street 2.00
Piscopo, Cathleen D., 27 Gleason Street 2.00
Ranney, Mabel, 114 Fayette Street 4.47

Riley, William J., 74 Olcott Street 2.00
Robinson, Herbert E., 25 Palmer Street 2.00
Sevigny, Alice G., 149 Spruce Street 2.00
Shulman, Mitchell, 149 Irving Street 2.00
Whalen, Charles J., 30 Morton Street 4.00
Wilson, Charles E., 24 Louise Street 2.00
Zaino, Albert, 51 Crawford Street 2.00

REPORT OF TOWN CLERK'S DEPARTMENT

Watertown, Mass., December 31, 1934.

The report of this department for the year 1934 is herewith submitted.

For report of Town Meetings, which comes under the work of this department, reference is made to that title.

Marriage Records By Months

Months	Number
January	28
February	15
March	12
April	38
May	23
June	61
July	36
August	28
September	54
October	44
November	34
December	28
Total	401

Death Records By Months

Months	Number
January	44
February	36

Months	Number
March	34
April	34
May	28
June	30
July	24
August	28
September	23
October	20
November	31
December	35
Total	367

Birth Records By Months
(Stillbirths Excluded)

Months	Number
January	53
February	30
March	52
April	55
May	43
June	47
July	43
August	40
September	34
October	30
November	27
December	26
Total	480

FEES COLLECTED IN THE OFFICE OF THE TOWN CLERK AND PAID TO THE TOWN TREASURER

503	Fish and Game license fees at 25c each	$125.75
503	Male dog licenses at $2.00 each	1,006.00
61	Female dog licenses at $5.00 each	305.00

178 Spayed female dog licenses at $2.00 each   356.00
Miscellaneous fees, such as marriage permits,
certificates and recordings   1,775.97

                                                 $3,568.72

Fees Collected for Licenses Granted by Selectmen

36 Garages at $1.50 $54.00
83 Victualler's licenses at $1.00   83.00
 9 Pool licenses at $5.00   45.00
 5 Junk licenses at $10.00   50.00
   Liquor license fees   2,397.62
22 Liquor advertisements at $1.25   27.50
 7 Coffee House permits at $5.00   35.00
   Beers and Wines licenses   2,800.76
19 Transfers at 50c each   14.50
17 Auto dealers licenses at $5.00   85.00
64 Renewals at $1.00   64.00
 9 Auctioneer permits at $2.00   18.00
 1 Bus license at $2.00   2.00
 2 Theatre licenses at $1.00   2.00
 1 Employment Agency permit at $2.00   2.00
 5 Taxi permits at $3.00   15.00
 5 Second Hand Dealers' licenses at $1   5.00
   Edison Grants   8.00
   Telephone Grants   2.00
   Boston Elevated Grants   1.00
                                         --------- $5,711.38

Total $9,280.10

I have examined the amount of money received in the office of the Town Clerk for Town Licenses issued by the Selectmen and the receipts of the Town Treasurer for the same; also the money received from dog licenses and receipts from the County Treasurer for same and find them to be correct.

W. W. NORCROSS, Jr.,
Town Auditor.

Fish and Game Licenses Issued in the Office of the Town Clerk

2	Duplicate licenses at $.50	$ 1.00
166	Fishing licenses at $2.00	332.00
228	Hunting licenses at $2.00	456.00
82	Combination licenses at $3.25	266.50
23	Minor Fishing licenses at $1.25	28.75
2	Trapping licenses at $5.25	10.50
2	Minor Trapping licenses at $2.25	4.50
16	Free Sporting licenses	
521		$1,099.25
503	License fees at 25c each	125.75
		$973.50

The sum of $973.50 was sent to the Department of Conservation, Division of Fisheries and Game, 20 Somerset Street, Boston, Mass.

W. W. NORCROSS, Jr.,
Town Auditor.

WM. P. McGUIRE,
Town Clerk.

REPORT OF THE CHIEF OF POLICE

Watertown, Mass., December 31, 1934.

The Honorable Board of Selectmen,

Gentlemen :—

In compliance with the By-Laws of the Town, I have the honor to submit the annual report of the Police Department of the Town of Watertown for the year ending December 31, 1934, together with recommendations for the ensuing year.

Organization of the Department

Chief

JOHN F. MILMORE

Lieutenants

JAMES P. BURKE

JOHN E. McNAMARA   JOSEPH J. REILLY

Sergeants

THOMAS W. DEVANEY   ANDREW J. DONNELLY
JOHN J. IGOE   JAMES M. IGOE

Patrolmen

JOHN F. GLEASON	WILLIAM H. MUNHALL
CHARLES H. GLIDDEN	JOSEPH P. STEAD
ARTHUR F. PERKINS	RUSSELL J. KIMBALL
LAWRENCE C. HANLEY	GEORGE M. CLINTON
STEWART E. SAVAGE	JOHN A. HIGGINS
RICHARD J. OWENS	JOHN J. HANLON
JAMES M. REILLY	JOHN F. McGEEVER
THOMAS J. CULLEN	JAMES P. SHEA
JOSEPH F. LOUGHLIN	EDWARD A. MURRAY
JOSEPH WALSH	EDMUND H. NORTON
PATRICK J. CALLAHAN	WALTER F. FLAHERTY

FRANK L. MANNIX	JAMES J. BURKE
EDWARD J. LISTON	WILLIAM W. CARNES
GEORGE J. FARRELL	CHARLES E. SHEA
EDWARD P. MURPHY	JOHN J. LONG
FRANCIS A. NALLY	JOSEPH C. HARRINGTON
EDWARD J. BOYLE	HAROLD M. PARKER
JOSEPH H. GILFOIL	WILLIAM J. SHEA
HENRY L. WELSH	

Wagonman
FRANCIS A. GARAFALO

Janitor
THOMAS RYDER

Arrests

Total number	1080
Males	1058
Females	22
Native Born	809
Foreign Born	271

Causes of Arrests

Assault with a dangerous weapon	3
Assault with intent to rape	1
Assault and Battery	27
Adultery	2
Abandonment of infant child	2
Accessory before the fact to a felony	3
Accessory after the fact to a felony	1
Breaking and entering and larceny	58
Breaking and entering, attempt	10
Bastardy	6
Burglarious instruments in possession	2
Carnal abuse of female child	4
Conspiracy to rob	3
Conspiracy to break and enter	2
Drunkenness	471

Liquor laws, violating:
Keeping and exposing for sale............................... 1
Illegal sale of liquor 1
Town Ordinances, violating:
Distributing handbills without a permit 1
Not stopping before entering through way 8
Wrong way on one-way street 2
Motor Vehicle Laws, violating:
Allowing improper person to operate 1
Failing to stop on signal of an officer 1
Going away and not making self known after an
    accident 12
Operating without a license 21
Operating under influence of liquor 28
Operating negligently, so that the lives and
    safety of the public might be endangered............ 28
Overspeeding 18
Operating after revocation of license.................... 4
Operating uninsured car 5
Operating unregistered car 4
Operating and not having license in possession.... 3
Operating and not having registration in posses-
    sion 1
Passing red light 5
Passing within eight feet of a street car which
    had stopped for the purpose of allowing pas-
    sengers to board or alight 1
Using an automobile without authority 11
                                                          ——
Total 1080

Valuation of Propery Stolen and Recovered, 1934

Value of property reported stolen $22,231.57
Value of property recovered 16,199.24
Value of property recovered for out-of-town
    Departments 10,805.50

Work of Signal System

Day on duty calls	28,704
Night on duty calls	46,237
Total telephone calls, day and night	9,729
Radio calls	1,836

Miscellaneous

Accidents other than automobile	26
Automobile accidents	409
Autos stolen in Watertown	39
Animals found	2
Animals lost	4
Articles lost	101
Articles found	38
Arc lights reported out	60
Breaking and entering cases	67
Breaking and entering, attempt	11
Bicycles stolen	22
Bicycles recovered	15
Cases investigated	4053
Children found	36
Children reported lost	45
Deaths	16
Defective streets and sidewalks	164
Dogs found	101
Dogs reported lost	218
Dog cases investigated	271
Doors and windows found open and secured	269
Fires discovered by officers	2
Glass broken	69
Houses reported closed	187
Incandescent lights reported out	96()
Larceny Cases	132
Larceny, attempt	3
Murder	0
Manslaughter	4
Officers delivering messages	309

People reported missing 20
Robbery Cases 6
Robbery, attempt 2
Sick and injured assisted 96
Suicides 3
Street obstructions lighted 13

Motor Vehicles

Runs made by ambulance 280
Miles run by ambulance 1,076
Miles run by touring cars 106,121
Miles run by motorcycles 13,995

Changes

Patrolman William J. Shea was appointed to the Department on April 1, 1934.

Patrolman Louis Perkins was pensioned from the Department on October 27, 1934.

Patrolman George M. Clinton was appointed patrolman-mechanic as of September 1, 1934.

Patrolman James M. Reilly was reinstated in the Department by the Civil Service Commission on December 3, 1934.

Wagonman and Janitor Arnold E. Holmes left the service on August 22, 1934.

Thomas Ryder was appointed Wagonman and Janitor on September 17, 1934.

Crime

The number of breaking and entering cases shows a decrease in comparison to last year, which is very gratifying in view of conditions as they are. Much time has been devoted to apprehending those responsible for this type of crime, with an encouraging degree of success.

I am pleased to report that the number of robbery cases for the year is but six, the same as last year. Of this number two have been solved, and at the making of this report have some evidence which may account for two more.

The number of automobiles stolen in Watertown was 39, the same as last year. All of these machines have been recovered and returned to their owners.

It requires constant effort, diligence and patrol to keep major crimes to a low mark.

Liquor Laws

There were two arrests for violation of the liquor laws during the year, as contrasted with 26 last year.

The arrests for drunkenness you will note have increased from 333 in 1933 to 471 in 1934.

This large increase is undoubtedly brought about by the fact, that with the repeal of prohibition, many persons who possibly never tasted the strong beer were unable to guage their capacity, and therefore fell by the wayside. I say this because it is noted by the monthly arrests, that for the first three or four months in the year the arrests for drunkenness were more than doubled what they would be in times of prohibition, and then in the remaining several months the arrests were about the same as they would be in other years.

The licensed places in the Town are under constant surveillance of the Police. In the beginning there was some difficulty in several of these places, probably due to the fact that the proprietors were new to the business. Almost all of these mistakes were corrected, and these places are now being run in as orderly a manner as possible.

Traffic

The ever-increasing traffic requires more and more time on the part of the officers to properly control and conduct it, in order that the streets of Watertown may be safe places in which to travel, and the death and injury to pedestrians may be cut to a minimum.

There has been a decrease in the number of automobile accidents during 1934, the number being 409 as against

442 last year, and 544 in 1932. Many of these accidents this year were minor. There were four persons killed on our highways this year. In all cases the operator of the car responsible was prosecuted for negligent operation and found guilty.

I wish to call attention to the fact that when the new road, under construction on Galen Street, at the intersection of Watertown Street, is completed, it will undoubtedly be the most hazardous place in the Town. I would recommend that the location be studied by traffic engineers with a view to the installation of a set of traffic lights that will properly control the traffic.

Radio

During the year two radio-equipped cruiser cars were added to the Department. These two cars are on constant patrol 24 hours a day. The Buick Sedan attached to the Department was also radio-equipped and is used for patrol duty.

We have an agreement with the City of Newton Police Department whereby they broadcast to our cars. A call received at the Station is immediately relayed to Newton via the teletype, and from there to the cars. In actual timing, from the time a telephone call is received here until it is received by the cars, a period of time of less than one minute has elapsed.

In other words the service received by the citizens is almost instantaneous, and has produced excellent results.

Recommendations

I have, for the past several years, strongly urged that some definite action be taken toward the construction of adequate quarters for this Department. I consider that it is now imperative that action be taken to overcome the handicap under which the Department is working, because of lack of sufficient space.

I would recommend that a new ambulance be purchased

for use in the Department. In a Town of 36,000 people there is not a single ambulance that can be called upon for service, except our combination ambulance and patrol wagon. This is a matter which requires serious consideration, and we have indeed been fortunate up to the present moment that an emergency has not presented itself where the lack of such a vehicle would call for an explanation from those whose duty it is to see that it was installed.

. I recommend the appointment of two patrolmen to the Department, one to fill the existing vacancy in the Department, and one additional man. In order that the routes may be properly patrolled, the services of these men are necessary.

It is recommended that the two Chevrolet cruisers, now in use in the Department, be replaced. These cruisers are on continuous duty 24 hours a day and will not stand up and give efficient service for another year.

Conduct of Officers

The conduct of the officers in the Department has been good. During the year several officers were commended in general orders for meritorious service and were rewarded with extra time off as a result. All men have been called upon to do much extra work which was done willingly.

Conclusions

In conclusion I desire to thank the Justices of the Superior and District Courts, the Clerks of same, the Honorable Board of Selectmen, and all other Town Officers and individuals who have rendered advice and assistance to this Department during the year.

Respectfully submitted,

JOHN F. MILMORE,

Chief of Police.

REPORT OF THE FIRE DEPARTMENT

To the Honorable Board of Selectmen:

Gentlemen:

I herewith submit the following report of the Fire Department for the year ending December 31, 1934.

The membership of the department consists of forty-nine (49) classified as follows: one (1) permanent chief; three (3) permanent captains; four (4) permanent lieutenants; one (1) call captain; one (1) call lieutenant; one (1) mechanician; thirty-eight (38) permanent ladder and hosemen.

Alarms and Losses

The total number of alarms for 1934 was 450, exceeding all previous records by 57. Of these 243 were still alarms and 207 bell alarms. The false alarms exceeded all previous records with a total of 43.

	Values	Losses	Insurance	Insurance Paid
Buildings	$429,350.00	$31,090.48	$400,887.27	$30,365.48
Contents	214,950.00	7,402.70	179,950.00	6,390.70
	$644,300.00	$38,493.18	$580,837.27	$36,756.18

The largest individual loss on buildings was $8,000.00 on an unused and apparently abandoned sand hopper and the largest individual loss on building contents was $1,412.00, the only loss to exceed $800.00 on contents. There were but four fires where the loss exceeded $2,000.00 on the building.

In all, the losses are the lowest since 1925 when the alarms totaled 301. This would indicate that the department has made a reasonably good record during the past year when the great increase of alarms is given consideration, but regardless of this the losses show a reduction.

Some credit should be given fire prevention methods as it is the first full year that a fireman has been detailed to the work of fire prevention and inspection exclusively.

During the year the department suffered the loss by death of three members, who gave untiring of their efforts as faithful servants in their chosen calling. Gilbert Nichols who served with distinction since May 1, 1885 died in the performance of his duty, at a fire on Jan. 3, 1934. Willard E. Streeter, who served from April 1914, died of exertion after returning from an alarm of fire Jan. 1, 1934. Joseph J. Gildea, a veteran of the World War, and a member of the department since April 1924 died after a brief illness April 23, 1934.

Thomas J. Murphy, a member of the department since June 1891, was retired on pension Jan. 1, 1934.

Recommendations

During 1934, from the appropriation of $1,500.00 allowed for the purchase of hose, we were able to purchase 1800 feet of good quality hose. All hose in the department was tested during the year and 2000 feet of hose was found unfit for use, or at least only good for flowing purposes. I recommend an appropriation of $900.00 for the purchase of hose for 1935.

As reported to your Honorable Board in my report of last year our oldest pumping engine of 400 gallon capacity purchased in October 1917 is practically of no value at this time as a pumping unit. The chemical equipment and pumping unit have been of no use to us during the year and cannot be made serviceable only at a great cost which is not advisable due to the age of this engine which is now used only as a hose carrier. I recommend an appropriation of $9,000.00 to replace this engine with one of at least 750 gallon pumping capacity, with booster pump and tank to replace present chemical equipment.

No appropriation has been asked for uniforms for the members of the department since 1931. Many men have been forced to provide their own uniforms, many also at the present time are in need of uniforms and it seems only reasonable that if the men are required to wear a distinctive uniform the town should provide them. The men have been reasonable and have cooperated to the fullest extent in conserving supplies and uniforms and as a reward for their faithfulness I believe the town should provide an appropriation for uniforms for 1935. I recommend an appropriation of $1,200.00, which even though small, will be appreciated where needed.

The supplies, tools and equipment of the department are so depleted that it will be necessary to make many purchases this year that were denied last year because of inadequate appropriation.

The continued use of Fire Station Two by the E. R. A. workers has caused a drain on the appropriation beyond all expectations. Heating, lighting and supplies for the station have almost doubled, with no additional appropriation to take care of it.

With the appropriation granted for toilets and repairs at Fire Headquarters we were able to improve conditions there, but much remains to be done to this old station to make the first floor safe for the heavy apparatus stored there. New floors are needed as well as in the recreation room and I look forward to this work being done as an E. R. A. Project, and so recommend.

I recommend that the New England Insurance Exchange be invited to make a survey of the department as no survey has been made since 1923.

In behalf of the members of the Fire Department I express their appreciation for the very fair consideration given us by the citizens of the Town in the restoration of salaries during the past year, and in return pledge their best efforts in the important work of Fire Prevention and extinguishment.

To the Honorable Board of Selectmen we are very grateful for the full cooperation given and their willingness to do all possible during the past year to make the work of this department a success.

To the members of the department I express my personal thanks for their willingness to cooperate, because with the additional burden of operating the Fire Alarm System many inconveniences were overlooked, devotion to their chosen work was foremost with them at all times.

Respectfully submitted,

JOHN W. O'HEARN,

Chief of Fire Department.

ANNUAL REPORT

OF THE

BOARD OF HEALTH

OF THE

TOWN OF WATERTOWN

FOR THE

YEAR ENDING DECEMBER 31, 1934

THE HAMPSHIRE, PRESS, INC.
Cambridge, Mass.
1935

ORGANIZATION OF THE HEALTH DEPARTMENT
1934

Board of Health

EARL J. WYLIE, M. D., *Chairman*

EUGENE F. GORMAN, M. D., *Secretary*

GUY C. PESCE, M. D.

Agent and Health Officer

FRED W. BODGE

Plumbing Inspector

CHARLES M. HEWITT

Superintendent of Cemeteries

VAN D. HORTON

Inspector of Milk

PERICLES CANZANELLI, M. D.

Clerk

ALICE H. FARNHAM

Board of Health Physician

WALTER N. SECORD, M. D.

Board of Health Nurses

ROSE AJEMIAN, R. N.

AGNES KIRKER, R. N.

HELEN SULLIVAN, R. N.

School Dentists

JAMES E. DONAHUE, D. M. D.

OWEN F. KEEFE, D. M. D.

CHARLES E. KELLEY, D. M. D.

H. VAN BESLAR, D. M. D.

Dental Assistant

IRENE K. DRUMMEY, R. N.

Baby Clinic, Eastern

R. C. LAVRAKAS, M. D.

Western

L. SILVERSTEIN, M. D.

REPORT OF THE BOARD OF HEALTH

To the Citizens of the Town of Watertown:

The Board of Health submits the following report for the year ended December 31, 1934:

The Board organized March 13, 1934 and elected Earl J. Wylie, M. D., Chairman; Eugene F. Gorman, M. D., the new member, Secretary; with Guy C. Pesce, M. D. as the third member.

Walter N. Secord, M. D. was appointed Health Department physician, Pericles Canzanelli, M. D., Inspector of Milk, R. C. Lavrakas, M. D. as physician at the East Well Baby Clinic, and Miss Alice H. Farnham as clerk. All other employees were reappointed.

A much needed receiving tomb and tool house were erected at the Ridgelawn Cemetery. Through the E.R.A. the unfinished roads were resurfaced and are now all in good repair. There has been a great deal of grading done, and with the new wall completed the cemetery takes on a much improved appearance.

The Board wishes to extend its thanks to all departments and department heads and to all others who in any way assisted, for their co-operation in helping this department in carrying out its work.

Respectfully submitted,

EARL J. WYLIE, M. D., *Chairman*
EUGENE F. GORMAN, M. D., *Secretary*
GUY C. PESCE, M. D.

REPORT OF THE HEALTH OFFICER

To the Board of Health, Town of Watertown:

Gentlemen:

I herewith submit the following report of work done by the department during 1934.

The report here presented is necessarily brief, but complete details are on file at the Board of Health office.

Financial Report

Appropriation for 1934:		$33,590.00
General Administration	$8,650.00	
Contagious Diseases	22,000.00	
Dental Clinic	2,500.00	
Well Baby Clinic	440.00	
		$33,590.00
Expenditures:		
General Administration	$8,705.29	
Contagious Diseases	21,713.62	
Dental Clinic	2,489.92	
Well Baby Clinic	428.38	
Gross Expenditures to Town	$33,337.21	
Returned to the Treasurer	252.79	
		$33,590.00
Gross Expenditures per Capita		$ .91
Reimbursements during 1934, Exclusive of Plumbing and Cemetery		$7,511.95
Licenses	$485.50	
Dental Clinic	123.91	
State Subsidy for Tuberculosis	4,348.23	
City Subsidy for Tuberculosis	261.00	
Private for Tuberculosis	39.93	

State Subsidy for Other
Contagious Diseases   144.00
City Subsidy and Private for Other
. Contagious Diseases   1,763.18
County Commissioners for Rabies
Vaccine   346.20

                                        $7,511.95
Net Cost to Town $25,825.26
Net Cost Per Capita $ .71

Summary of Vital Statistics

Population (estimated)   36,500
Births   557
Birth Rate per 1,000 population   15.2

Corrected Death Rate

Note: The corrected death rate is found by eliminating the deaths of all non-residents dying in Watertown and adding the deaths of all residents of Watertown dying elsewhere, as shown by the records of the Town Clerk.

Deaths of residents occurring in Watertown   223
Deaths of residents of Watertown occurring elsewhere   137

Total (Stillbirths not included)   360
Death Rate per 1,000 population   9.8
Tuberculosis Deaths   14
Tuberculosis Deaths per 100,000 population   38.4

Mortuary Report

Age Groups	Male	Female	Total
Under 1 year	12	11	23
From 1 to 2 years	—	1	1
From 2 to 3 years	2	1	3
From 3 to 4 years	—	—	—
From 4 to 5 years	3	—	3
From 5 to 10 years	6	3	9
From 10 to 15 years	2	2	4

From 15 to 20 years	1	1	2
From 20 to 30 years	3	5	8
From 30 to 40 years	11	8	19
From 40 to 50 years	14	10	24
From 50 to 60 years	33	28	61
From 60 to 70 years	34	48	82
From 70 to 80 years	29	53	82
From 80 to 90 years	16	19	35
From 90 to 100 years	1	3	4
	167	193	360

Stillbirths   7

Communicable Diseases

During the early part of the past year measles, whooping cough and chicken pox were very prevalent throughout Town. Aside from these the general health of the Town was on a par with other years.

The following chart shows reportable diseases by months:

	Jan.	Feb.	Mar.	Apr.	May	June	July	Aug.	Sept.	Oct.	Nov.	Dec.	Total
Chicken Pox	32	46	34	15	8	15	5		3	14	37	17	226
Diptheria	1								2		1		4
Dog Bite		3	13	12	14	24	15	10	1	8	9	5	114
German Measles	1	1	1				2						5
Ophthalmia Neonatorum		1											2
Suppurative Conjuctivitis										2			2
Lobar Pneumonia	3	9	11	5	4		1	1		2		1	37
Measles	14	97	302	251	132	8	4	1		1		1	811
Mumps	2	2	4	2	4			2		1	6	8	31
Scarlet Fever	25	23	18	11	16	7	5	2	2	2	8	10	129
Septic Sore Throat	1				1				4				6
T.B. Pulmonary	2	2	6	4	1	1	5	3	4	2	6	4	40
T.B. Hilum		4				1	2		4		1	5	17
T.B. other forms												1	1
*Typhoid Fever						1	2	3		1		1	*8
Whooping Cough	52	33	33	8	7	6	5	2	9	12	21	10	198
Rabid Dog			4	1	1								6

*Five of the cases of Typhoid Fever shown above had their onset elsewhere.

Dog Bites

There were reported 114 persons bitten by dogs. In each case the animal was examined by the Animal Inspector, Dr. H. W. Jakeman and restrained for two weeks.

Rabies

Six cases of rabies among dogs have been reported.

In March a chow dog was captured by the police that was a positive rabid dog, the owner unknown. Due to very good work on the part of a police officer we were able to put in quarantine fifteen dogs that we knew had been exposed to this one dog. Five of these, which had not been inoculated, developed rabies while in quarantine, thereby doing no damage; two were young dogs badly bitten and destroyed; four were given the Pasteur treatment, and the others had been inoculated at our clinic.

Twenty-eight people have been given the anti-rabic treatment in town this past year, due to exposure, for which this department has furnished the vaccine. Due to a new law in effect the first of January, 1935, we will have to furnish vaccine and treatment up to Fifty Dollars for certain dog bites, as recommended by the State Department of Health.

Dog Clinic

In April we held four clinics for the immunization of dogs. It seems a great pity that more people do not take advantage of this clinic, as it is of most importance that all dogs be immunized for the safety of all children, as well as adults. If every dog were immunized, rabbies would be stamped out.

We had 454 dogs at the last clinic, which is about fifty per cent of the number of dogs licensed.

Diphtheria

We have held 48 clinics this past year at which 761 children were immunized, and it is very gratifying that so many parents of children under the age of five years availed themselves of this opportunity.

There were 3218 visits to homes, advising mothers of the importance of immunizing their children either by their family physician or at the clinic.

We had only four cases of diphtheria this year, in unimmunized persons, and no deaths, a decided drop from the past.

Scarlet Fever

There was a slight increase in the number of cases reported over last year. Every case was of a mild nature, only one proving fatal. The result of using scarlet fever serum has proved very successful in every case used, by eliminating secondary cases.

Tuberculosis

The handling of this disease is a very serious and important part of our work. It should be given a great deal more thought by the people of the Town than at present.

We have had this year a decided increase in the number of reported new cases of pulmonary type, which is truly alarming. This increase has been due largely to the fact that more contacts were examined through the newly available facilities placed at our disposal by the Middlesex County Sanatorium, thereby finding a case in the early stages, when a patient has a good chance of recovery.

Our work could be helped substantially if the public bought more tuberculosis seals and donated to our branch of the Middlesex Tuberculosis Association, so that more undernourished and underprivileged children could enjoy the benefits of a summer in camp under supervision. This past summer only fifteen children enjoyed this privilege.

Tuberculosis Summary

Number of cases reported, pulmonary	40
Number of cases reported, hilum (childhood type)	17
Number of cases reported, other forms	1

Number of patients leaving Town	15
Number of patients entering Town	4
Number of patients entering sanatoria	31
Number of patients leaving sanatoria	19
Number of patients who died from tuberculosis	14
Number of cases on visiting list	213
Number of examinations made	262
Number of calls made	897

Patients in Sanatoria

Middlesex County Sanatorium	18
Rutland State Sanatorium	11
North Reading State Sanatorium	5
Lakeville State Sanatorium	1
Mattapan State Sanatorium	2
Tewksbury State Infirmary	1
The Channing Home	1
Plymouth County Hospital	1

Typhoid

We have had eight cases of this disease reported this year, an increase of seven over last year. One instance was of three children returning from a vacation on a farm in Canada, because of illness. The case was found to be typhoid. On tracing this, we were able to locate the carrier in the children's grandmother. Another instance was of two persons in a family from Boston staying temporarily in Watertown, but the onset was elsewhere. This leaves three cases on which we are still working to find the source of infection.

Well Baby Clinic

The Well Baby Clinic is held two afternoons a week, on Tuesdays at the West Junior High School, and on Fridays at the Coolidge School. We have had a total of 1339 babies at these clinics. Advice is given mothers as to feeding and care of babies and their weight is taken and recorded.

School Nursing at St. Patrick's and Sacred Heart Schools

Pre-school work is done during the summer months and 304 visits were made to the two schools during the year. There were 255 home visits to sick pupils.

Dental Clinic

Again we realize the limited amount of work done at this clinic when compared with the amount that should be done, for which there is a crying need. Work during the first four months of the year was done in the first three grades at St. Patrick's School. Two months were given to examination in other schools. In September we started at the James Russell Lowell School and worked for two months, then to the Coolidge School where we are still working.

Results of these clinics are as follows:

Pupils examined	1409
Pupils treated	870
Teeth filled .	1077
Teeth extracted	229
Teeth treated	318
Emergency cases from other schools and classes	104

Instruction in the use of toothbrushes and proper food have been given with distribution of dental literature.

Food Distribution

Sanitary conditions in all stores, bakeries and restaurants are very good. The co-operation of owners in keeping places clean has been very gratifying.

The following inspections have been made:

Restaurants	95
Bakeries	47
Stores	445
Ice cream manufacturing plants	10

Food condemned as unfit for consumption:

5 dozen sun fish

5 dozen frozen mackerel

8 pounds of fowl
30 pounds of beef

General Sanitation

Sanitary conditions have taken very little attention this year. Only a small number of complaints have come in that needed adjusting.

Milk Inspection

The following inspections were made during the year:

Milk samples	149
Cream samples	47
Milk Plants	48

In conclusion, I wish to thank the members of the office and all outside employees in any way connected with the department for their loyal co-operation in furthering the health work now being carried on in Watertown.

Respectfully submitted,

FRED W. BODGE,
Agent.

REPORT OF PLUMBING INSPECTOR

January 15, 1935.

To the Board of Health:

Gentlemen:

I herewith submit my annual report as Plumbing Inspector for the Town of Watertown for the year 1934:

Total amount of fees received for permits	$576.00
Permits issued for plumbing	144
Permits issued for replacements of boilers	35
Total inspections on replacements of boilers	35
Total inspections on all plumbing permits	400
Total sanitary inspections	125

Total inspections and water tests	200
Total final inspections on plumbing and boilers	435
Total permits issued, work not finished	6
Hearings on violations of Plumbing Code	9
Fixtures installed	562

Several changes were adopted and passed by the Board of Health on December 4, 1934, which will appear in the new issue of the plumbing code. Many hours in the office were taken up in consultation and in laying out of plumbing and sanitary installations, also in hearings and adjustments of complaints.

Respectfully submitted,

CHARLES M. HEWITT,
Inspector of Plumbing.

REPORT OF SUPERINTENDENT OF CEMETERIES

To the Board of Health:

Gentlemen:

The report of the Superintendent of Cemeteries for the year ended December 31, 1934, is herewith submitted:

Appropriated for:

Superintendent		$2,000.00
Labor		8,000.00
Contingent		550.00
Total Appropriation		$10,550.00
Expenditures	$10,547.27	
Balance	2.73	
		$10,550.00
Special Appropriation for Tomb and Tool House, Ridgelawn Cemetery		$2,500.00

Expended   2,500.00
_____

Special Appropriation for Lowering Device
and Greens, Ridgelawn Cemetery $250.00
Expended $244.50
Balance   5.50
_____
250.00
_____

Amounts paid to Town Treasurer for sale of lots, graves and general labor from January 1, 1934 to December 31, 1934, $7,084.29.

Number of interments in cemeteries is as follows:

Common Street	17
Ridgelawn	85
Number of removals	4
Number of vaults used	18
Number of foundations placed	37
Number of two-grave lots sold	8
Number of three or more grave lots sold	11
Number of adults' single graves sold	24
Number of children's graves sold	3

I recommend that special amounts be appropriated, as follows:

Eleven Hundred Dollars for fence at Common Street Cemetery, and Three Hundred Dollars for water extension at Rideglawn Cemetery.

Respectfully submitted,

VAN D. HORTON,

Superintendent of Cemeteries.

ANNUAL REPORT OF THE WATER
COMMISSIONERS
December 31, 1934

The fiftieth year of the Water Works of the Town has now closed.

During the year 6881 feet of water mains have been laid, 21 new services have been installed. The active services now total 6142. 1124 meters have been repaired. Twenty-two new hydrants have been added during the year making the total 702 now in use. New mains were laid in Quimby St., Melendy Ave. and Chestnut Park, thereby eliminating bad conditions of dead end pipes. In Laurel St. and Hazel St., the old 2-inch galvanized pipe was removed and replaced by 8-inch cast-iron cement-lined pipe. The extreme cold in the winter 1933-1934 made working conditions unusually hard but our men responded nobly and gave unsparingly of their own time in order to satisfy the demands of the citizens. In addition to our regular work we finished the C. W. A. projects begun in the closing months of 1933 on Coolidge Ave., Dexter Ave. and Arlington Street.

The E. R. A. projects consisted of Dexter Ave., from School to Hazel St., Quimby St., from Cypress to Laurel St., Coolidge Ave., connecting two dead ends, Arlington St., from Elm St. to above Calvin Road, Mt. Auburn St., from Franklin to Parker Street. All piping and materials needed on these projects were laid according to our own methods by regular employees of the department. The Industrial District has been greatly benefitted by these improvements and our pipe system reinforced.

An ever increasing difficulty is the clogging of old services. This means continuous work in order to satisfy our consumers and to give adequate supply to the householders. A large number of old services must be renewed this year.

In order to comply with requirements of the Fire Underwriters as to higher pressure and greater flow of water we propose to install twenty-five new hydrants for 1935. This will decrease the distances between hydrants and afford better protection for homes of our citizens.

The fifty year old 14-inch cement-lined old fashioned main on Pleasant St., from the Waltham line to Green St. and in Green St., to Main Street, now carrying our low pressure service, furnishes a constant threat to our security. The inevitable break in this line would bring calamitous results and would prove a serious handicap in case of a fire. We would recommend an appropriation for a new 12-inch main, 7400 feet, if the Town finances could possibly afford it.

Respectfully submitted,

JOHN P. GALLAGHER, Chairman
ARTHUR C. FAGAN, Secretary
GEORGE J. GAFFNEY

REPORT OF THE WATER DEPARTMENT

The thirty-eighth annual report of the Water Department for the year ending December 31, 1934, is respectfully submitted. The transactions relating to this department are as follows:

Receipts

Appropriation for maintenance	$41,300.00
Appropriation for office	2,125.25
Appropriation for vacations	1,299.00
Appropriation for clerks	2,336.00
Appropriation for superintendent	3,200.00
Appropriation for F. E. R. A.	8,960.00
Appropriation for new 1934 car	625.00

Appropriation for 1934 truck	1,200.00	
	————	$61,045.25

Expenditures

Maintenance account	$41,298.28
Office account	2,122.66
Vacation account	1,299.00
Salary of clerks	2,336.00
Salary of superintendent	3,200.00
New 1934 car	624.00
New 1934 truck	1,200.00
F. E. R. A. account	8,960.00
Balance of maintenance account	1.72
Balance of office account	2.59
Balance of new 1934 car account	1.00

$61,045.25

Report of the Superintendent

To the Board of Water Commissioners:

Gentlemen: In accordance with the usual custom I herewith submit my report for the year ending December 31, 1934.

The extension and renewal of mains for the past year has been as follows:

	Length	Size
Arlington Street	283 feet	6-inch
Arlington Street	54 feet	8-inch
Arlington Street	1408 feet	10-inch
Bigelow Avenue	325 feet	6-inch
Calvin Road	412 feet	6-inch
Chestnut Park	30 feet	6-inch
Coolidge Avenue	456 feet	8-inch
Dexter Avenue	1477 feet	12-inch
Dexter Avenue	16 feet	6-inch
Hazel Street	313 feet	8-inch

Laurel Street	364 feet	6-inch
Melendy Avenue	70 feet	6-inch
Melendy Avenue	182 feet	8-inch
Mt. Auburn Street	196 feet	6-inch
Mt. Auburn Street	23 feet	8-inch
Mt. Auburn Street	43 feet	10-inch
Mt. Auburn Street	717 feet	12-inch
Quimby Street	227 feet	8-inch
Stoneleigh Road	285 feet	6-inch
Total	6,881 feet	

Total number of feet laid, 6,881 feet.

Expenditures

For maintenance of meters	$14,662.03	
For maintenance of mains	12,610.20	
For maintenance of services	7,277.20	
For maintenance of repair shop	755.68	
For maintenance of hydrants	3,645.39	
For maintenance of automobile No. 1	389.70	
For maintenance of automobile No. 2	429.05	
For maintenance of automobile No. 3	353.04	
For maintenance of automobile No. 4	402.37	
For maintenance of automobile No. 5	438.18	
Maintaining air compressor	335.44	
		$41,298.28
For vacations	1,299.00	
Salary of superintendent	3,200.00	
Salary of clerks	2,336.00	
Maintenance of office	2,122.66	
New 1934 car	624.00	
New 1934 truck	1,200.00	
F. E. R. A. account	8,960.00	
		$19,741.66
		$61,039.94

Respectfully submitted,

WALTER E. RUNDLETT,
Superintendent.

Statistics of Consumption of Water

1. Estimated total population to date, 36,500.
2. Estimated population on lines of pipe, 36,500.
3. Estimated population supplied, 36,500.
4. Total consumption for the year, 834,407,000 gallons.
5. Passed through meters, 652,871,000 gallons.
6. Percentage of consumption metered, 78.
7. Consumption for manufacturing purposes, 157,968,-000 gallons.
8. Average daily consumption, 2,286,000 gallons.
9. Gallons per day to each inhabitant, 56.
10. Gallons per day to each consumer, 56.

Statistics to Distribution System
Mains

1. Kind of pipe; cement and cast iron.
2. Sizes, 16-inch to 2-inch.
3. Extended, 1,946 feet during year.
4. Total now in use, 75.58 miles.
5. Number of hydrants added during the year, 22.
6. Number of hydrants now in use, 702.
7. Number of stop gates added during the year, 53.
8. Number of stop gates now in use, 1,711.
9. Range of pressure on mains, 115 lbs. to 30 lbs.

Services

10. Kind of pipe, wrought iron, cement lined, cast iron.
11. Sizes, ¾-inch to 10-inches.
12. Extended, 678 feet.
13. Total now in use, 22,752.7 miles.
14. Number of service taps added during the year, 21.
15. Number now in use, 6,142.
16. Percentage of services metered, 100.

REPORT OF THE HIGHWAY DEPARTMENT

To the Honorable Board of Selectmen:

Gentlemen:

The following report relating to work done and money expended for the year ending December 31, 1934, is respectfully submitted.

Highway Construction

Receipts

Appropriation	$28,672.00
Transferred at Town Meeting	3,000.00
	$25,672.00

Expenditures

Irving Street	$10,432.25
Marshall Street	8,964.52
Morse Street	6,269.29
	$25,666.06
Balance	5.94
	$25,672.00

Highway Maintenance

Receipts

Appropriation	$65,000.00
Transferred at Town Meeting	8,817.40
	$73,817.40

General Maintenance

Expenditures

Building driveway at Town Garage	$88.16

Building Skating Rinks	433.84
Cleaning Catch Basins and Drains	11,795.21
Coolidge Avenue	211.65
Cleaning Gutters	1,929.36
Cutting wood	564.68
Cutting bound stones	123.75
Grading Cook's Pond Playground	71.70
Grading Victory Field	163.50
Garage Keepers	1,600.95
Galen Street Bridge Repairs	104.47
Lanternmen	1,681.41
Mechanics	4,000.17
Painting streets	758.80
Patching streets	5,042.47
Post Santa Deliveries	101.07
Repairing bridges	502.95
Repairing wall in front of Legion Home	49.75
Street Cleaning	7,978.73
Snow	24,224.11
Sanding	1,044.50
Trucking for Welfare Department	171.78
	$62,643.01

Equipment Maintenance

C. W. A. Supplies	$536.75
Equipment supplies and repairs	537.65
Expressing and freight	22.92
Hardware supplies	469.68
Incidentals	9.00
Lighting garage	43.16
Painting equipment	54.60
Painting street and traffic signs	688.74
Roller repairs	414.42
Telephone service	178.82
Traffic Beacon repairs and supplies	256.45
	$3,212.19

Automobile Maintenance

Automobile and truck repairs and supplies '	$7,253.27
Insurance	25.61
Storage of cars and trucks	645.00
Registrations	38.00
	$7,961.88

Summary

General Maintenance	$62,643.01
Equipment Maintenance	3,212.19
Automobile Maintenance	7,961.88
	$73,817.08
Balance	.32
	$73,817.40

Highway Stable

Receipts

Appropriation	$12,000.00
Transferred at Town Meeting	2,000.00
	$14,000.00

Expenditures

Blacksmith and helper	$2,766.36
Cleaning stable	16.33
Grain	1,596.98
Hay and straw	1,300.77
Lighting stable	206.27
Nightmen	2,069.98
Saddler	1,074.75
Saddler and blacksmith supplies	605.91
Stable repairs	98.00
Stablemen	4,206.21
Telephone service	57.76
	$13,999.32

Balance .68

$14,000.00

Highway Stable Special

Receipts

Appropriation $500.00

Expenditures

Hay and Grain $499.68
Balance .32

$500.00

Highway Vacations

Receipts

Appropriation $7,284.00
Transferred at Town Meeting 119.06

$7,164.94

Expenditures

Vacations to Employees $7,164.94

Highway Superintendent

Receipts

Appropriation $3,600.00

Expenditures

Salary of Superintendent of Streets $3,600.00

Highway Clerks

Receipts

Appropriation $2,750.00

Expenditures

Salary of 1st Clerk $1,500.00
Salary of 2nd Clerk 1,250.00

$2,750.00

Highway Office

Receipts

Appropriation	$400.00

Expenditures

Office supplies	$50.18
Printing	214.96
Telephone service	115.54
Advertising bids	6.00
	$386.68
Balance	13.32
	$400.00

Patching C. W. A. Streets

Receipts

Appropriation	$5,000.00

Expenditures

Patching C. W. A. Streets	4,996.16
Balance	3.84
	$5,000.00

Drainage

Receipts

Appropriation	$3,000.00

Expenditures

	Labor	Stock	Total
Bellevue Road	$887.79	$71.10	$958.89
Fayette Street Repairs	956.15		956.15
Drain Repairs	908.06	173.71	1,081.77
	$2,752.00	$244.81	$2,996.81
Balance			3.19
			$3,000.00

Sidewalks

Receipts

Appropriation	$6,000.00

Expenditures

Cinder walks	$114.72
Granolithic walks and repairs	3,590.05
Grading walks	766.54
Grading borders	1,455.88
	$5,927.19
Setting curbing	72.53
	$5,999.72
Balance	.28
	$6,000.00

Sidewalk Special

Receipts

Appropriation	$4,000.00

Expenditures

Granolithic sidewalks	$3,998.09
Balance	1.91
	$4,000.00

Ashes and Papers

Receipts

Appropriation	$25,000.00
Transferred at Town Meeting	1,800.00
	$26,800.00

Expenditures

Ashes and Paper Collection Notices	$189.66
Cleaning Dumps	2,097.15
Collecting	22,098.72

Gasoline and Motor Oils	1,470.62
Storage of trucks	330.00
Supplies	34.60
Truck repairs	579.15
	$26,799.90
Balance	.10
	$26,800.00

Garbage

Receipts

Appropriation	$27,500.00

Expenditures

Collecting	$25,168.57
Gasoline and motor oils	1,652.52
Storage of trucks	330.00
Truck repairs	146.41
Supplies	196.31
	$27,493.81
Balance	6.19
	$27,500.00

Dust Laying

Receipts

Appropriation	$5,000.00

Expenditures

Pay Rolls, dust laying and cleaning streets	$4,522.35
Road Oils	300.69
Sand	168.94
	$4,991.98
Balance	8.02
	$5,000.00

Betterments

Receipts

Appropriation	$4,950.00
Transferred at Town Meeting	635.04
	$4,314.96

Expenditures

Betterment Construction

	Labor	Stock	Total
Hill Street	$2,481.36	$1,006.12	$3,487.48

Betterment Drainage

	Labor	Stock	Total
Hill Street	$718.63	$108.85	$827.48
Betterment Construction			3,487.48
			$4,314.96

Sewer Construction

Receipts

Appropriation	$3,050.00

Expenditures

	Labor	Stock	Total
Bostonia Avenue	$140.61	$38.14	$178.75
Keith Street	85.96	26.16	112.12
Manhole repairs	1,501.81	283.97	1,785.78
Grandview Avenue	900.58	69.00	969.58
	$2,628.96	$417.27	$3,046.23
Balance			3.77
			$3,050.00

Sewer Maintenance

Receipts

Appropriation $15,000.00

Expenditures

	Labor	Stock	Total
Cleaning Galen St. Siphon	$200.14	$30.00	$230.14
House connections	1,929.65	263.56	2,193.21
Stoppages and flushings	7,917.08	381.69	8,298.77
Sewer repairs	4,274.71		4,274.71
	$14,321.58	$675.25	$14,996.83
Balance			3.17
			$15,000.00

Respectfully submitted,

PIERCE P. CONDON,

Superintendent of Streets.

REPORT OF TOWN ENGINEER

To the Honorable Board of Selectmen,

Gentlemen:

I herewith submit the following report of work done by this department for the year ending December 31, 1934.

Assessors' Plans

The Assessors' Plans, in the several departments using same, are being revised and brought up to date as usual. There were one hundred and fifty-nine (159) permits issued for dwellings, mercantile buildings, garages, alterations and removals which are being located on the ground and placed on plans.

Public Works Administration

Under the Public Works Administration Program, the construction of a portion of Mt. Auburn Street and School Street with an asphaltic concrete surface has been completed. Surface water drainage in Elm Street, Bailey Road and Summer Street has also been completed. These projects have kept this department very busy completing plans, and also the layout and inspection of construction.

E. R. A. Program

Under the Emergency Relief Administration Program many plans and estimates of projects were made and lines and grades furnished on the ground. Also under the E. R. A., projects were found for fourteen engineers and architects in this department. This work has been the replacing of worn out plans, survey of street lines, topographical plans of land owned by the Town of Watertown and a large Zoning Map for the Planning Board. This map

548

is about nine feet by four and one half feet showing all lots, each lot having a symbol, which indicates nature of building thereon.

Miscellaneous

Plans and reports have been prepared for accident cases as usual for the Board of Selectmen, Town Counsel and Police Department. We have given street lines and grades to property owners and others as requested. For list of public streets rebuilt, sidewalk construction, curbing laid, sewers and drains built during 1934, please see schedule for same.

Highways

Upon the following-named streets grades have been established, street lines defined, record plans drawn and descriptions written by this department, and they have been made public ways by the Board of Selectmen under the Betterment Act.

Street	From	To	Length Feet	Feet Width	Date
Hill St.	Fayette St.	Palfrey St.	450	20	April 3, 1934

Public Streets That Were Rebuilt During 1934

Street	From	To	Length Feet
Irving St.	Mt. Auburn St.	Charles River Rd.	2200
Marshall St.	Mt. Auburn St.	Oliver St.	2000
Morse St.	Galen St.	Watertown St.	1980
Mt. Auburn St.	Main St.	Walnut St.	2800
School St.	Flint Rd.	Belmont St.	1500

Total 10,480

Total Length of Streets

Public Ways .... 58.63 miles
Private Ways .... 11.82 miles

Total .... 70.45 miles

List of Granolithic Sidewalks Constructed During 1934

Street	No. of Sq. Ft. 4″ Walks	No. of Sq. Ft. 6″ Walks
Avon Road	64	
Bailey Avenue	100	
Beechwood Avenue	96	
Bellevue Road	149	32
Boylston Street East	3060	801
Bradford Road	140	104
Burnham Street	50	
Centre Street	125	
Church Street		50
Common Street	20	
Fairfield Street	2695	943
Frank Street	176	
Franklin Street	50	
Fuller Road	50	
Garfield Street	20	
Katherine Road	75	
Kimball Road	25	
Lovell Road	400	392
Louise Street	43	
Maplewood Street	75	
Middlesex Road	16	
North Beacon Street	59	
Palfrey Street	125	
Porter Street	32	
Rangeley Road	25	50
Robbins Road	50	
Royal Street		108
Salisbury Road	50	
Spring Street	12	
Springfield Street at Fitchburg	886	228
Washburn Street	25	
Total	8693 sq. ft.	2708 sq. ft.

Curbing Laid During 1934

Street	Radius Feet	Straight Feet
Green Street at Green St. Terrace	26	
Hill Street at Fayette Street	70	24
Hill Street at Palfrey Street	74	24
Totals	170	48

Drainage Built During 1934

Street	Length Feet	Size in Inches	No. of M.H.	No. of C.B.
Bailey Road	828	12	4	10
Bates Road	543	12	2	7
Bellevue Road	159	12	1	2
Bridge Street	132	12	1	4
Centre Street	346	12	2	6
Chester Street	515	12	2	4
Cross Street	180	12	1	2
Cushman Street	282	12	1	4
Cypress Street	228	10	1	4
Dartmouth Street	343	12	3	4
Eliot Street	405	12	2	6
Elm Street	1085	12	7	10
Fayette Street	554	12	3	5
Fifth Avenue	304	12	1	2
Fifield Street	346	12	1	6
Hill Street	—	—	—	6
Hillside Road	284	12	2	4
Hudson Street	253	12	1	4
Irving Street	1409	12	8	11
Ladd Street	215	12	2	2
Marshall Street	1657	12	5	14
Morse Street	937	12	4	8
Riverside Street	64	12	—	4
Royal Street	242	12	1	3
Summer Street	1221	12	5	10
Whitney Street	198	12	2	2

Williams Street	234	12	1	4
Totals	12,964		63	148

List of Sewers Laid During 1934

Street	Length Feet	Size in Inches
Bigelow Avenue	153	12
Bostonia Avenue	37	6
Elm Street	320	10
Grandview Avenue	347	6
Keith Street	137	6
Short Street	168	12
Wheeler Court	173	10
Totals	1,335	

Private Sewer Connections During 1934

Number of sewer connections located, 24.

Total length of sewer connections located, 798 feet.

The sewer system of Watertown is now sixty-three and seventeen hundredths (63.17) miles long and has six thousand seventy-four (6,074) sewer connections.

Respectfully submitted,

OTIS D. ALLEN,
Town Engineer.

STREET LIST

TABLE SHOWING LENGTH AND WIDTH OF PUBLIC AND PRIVATE STREETS IN WATERTOWN, MASSACHUSETTS

Name	From	To	Width	Length Private	Length Public	Year Accepted
Acton Street	Howard Street	Rutland Street	40			
Adams Avenue	Mt. Auburn Street	Shattuck Road	50	2,800	900	1895
Adams Street	Mt. Auburn Street	Nichols Avenue	40		505	1927
Allen Road	Belmont Street		62		310	1917
Walsh Road	Galen Street	Private Land	40			
Alfred Road	North Beacon Street	Riverside Street	40	400	385	1930
Alan Road	Main Street	Stearns Road	40		425	1927
Andrew Street	Main Street	Partridge Street	40	200		
Appleton Street	Upland Road	Rangeley Road	40		400	1919
Appleton Terrace	Main Street	Private Land	40		180	1919
Arden Road	Stoneleigh Road	Private Land	40		730	1929
Arlington Street	Belmont Street	Canal Street	40-66		5,090	
Canal Street	Beacon Square	Boston Line	66		900	
Arthur Terrace	Adams Street	Private Land	25	180		
Avenal Terrace	Boyd Street	Private Land	30	30		
Ashland Street	Arlington Street	Private Land	40	190		
Avon Place	Mt. Auburn Street	Private Land	20	150		
Avon Road	Belmont Street	Private Land	40			
Bacon Street	Main Street	Pleasant Street	26-30	900	350	1921
Bailey Road	Belmont Street	Private Land	40			
Abbey Road	Mt. Auburn Street	Bellevue Road	45		345	1931
Bancroft Street	Waverley Avenue	Lexington Street	50	230	1,400	1889-1924
Baptist Walk	Spring Street		40		673	1928
Barnard Avenue	Broadway	Bellevue Road	10	212	215	1875
					1,530	1897-1907

Name	From	To	Wth	Length Private	Length Public	Year Accepted
Bartlett Street	Everett Avenue	Forest Street	40	700		1899
Bates Road	Mt. Auburn Street	Private Land	40		820	1912
Bates Road East	Mt. Auburn Street	Bates Road	40		300	1921
Bay Street	North Beacon Street	Charles River Road	40		270	
Beacon Park	North Beacon Street	North Beacon Street	40	850		
Beechwood Avenue	Charles River Road	Arsenal Street	40-45		1,350	1913-1921 1907-1924
Belknap Terrace	Wn Street	Private Land	20-55	200		
Bellevue Road	Bailey Road	Channing Road	40		2,420	1926-1928 1929
Bellevue Terrace	Bellevue Road	Private Land	20	160		
Belmont Street	Lexington Seet	Wm Line	35-50		2,600	1928
Bemis Steet	Waverley Avenue	Lexington Street	50		938	1922
Berkeley Street	Arlington Street	Private Land	40		398	
Bigelow Avenue	Mt. Aurn Street	Nichols Avenue	65		1,220	1873-1926
Bigelow Terrace	Boyd Street	vMon Line	30	110		
Eith Road	Waut Street	Private Land	40		410	1930
Bostonia Avenue	Mt. Arn Street	B. & M. R. R.	30	530		
Boyd Street	Glen Street	Wm Line	40		1,000	1872
Boylston Street	Mt. Aurn Street	Mt. Arn Street	50		3,500	1900
Bradford Road	Orchard Street	Locke Street	40		1,420	1927
Bradshaw Street	Waverley Avenue	Lexington Street	40	1,060		
Bridge Street	Buick Street	Newton ihe	30-49	270	900	1915
Bridgham Avenue	Burnham Street	Fate Land	30		184	1925
Brigham Stet	Russell vthe	Bailey Road	40		645	1901
Mier Street	Mt. uhn Street	Belmont Street	40		675	1912
Broadway	Russell Avenue	Barnard Avenue	40	265		
Bromfield Street	Nash Street	uBck Street	40	460	690	1930
Brook Street	Bit Street	Metropolitan Park Land	20	360		
Brookline Street	Bel mnt Street	Warren Street	40	1,660		

Street	From	To	Width		Length	Year
Brown Street	Sycamore Street	Waltham Line	40	210		
Buick Street	Evans Street	Edge Street	40	335		
Burnham Street	Chandler Street	Belmont Line	40			
California Park	California Street	Private Land	40-80		400	1925
[?]ia Street	Watertown Street	[?]n [?]e	36-64		270	1930
Calvin Road	Arlington Street	Grove Street	40	640	1,575	1720
Capitol Street	Glen Street	Union Street	40	430	1,055	1897
Carey Ave	Chapman Street	King Street	40			
Carlton Terrace	Carroll Street	Town [?]nd	40		200	1930
a[?]ll Street	Orchard Street	Belmont Street	40		1,425	1874
Carver Road	Belmont Street	Clyde Road	40-46		850	1918
Carver Road East	Carver Road	Maplewood Street	40		670	1918
Centre Street	[?]t. Street	Franklin Street	40		515	1874
Chadbourne Terrace	Elm Street	Pate Land	30	145		
Chandler Street	Sycamore Street	Belmont Line	40		545	1925
Channing Road	Orchard Street	George Street	40		1,480	1929
Chapman Street	Main Street	Madison Avenue	40		600	1923-1929
Charles Street	Olney Street	Gilbert Street	40	810		
[?]es River Road	Watertown Square	North Beacon St.	50	700	5,000	1905
Chauncey Street	Mt. [?]rn Street	Boylston Street	40		730	1886
[?]ler Street	Mt. Auburn Street	[?]rn Street	24-30	235	660	1862
Chestnut Street	Main Street	Cuba Street	40	210	800	
[?]nut Park	Dexter Avenue	Quimby Street	40			
[?]th Street	Main Street	Orchard Street	40			
[?]th Hill Street	Main Street	Roman [?]c	40		2,920	1851-1891 1906
Church Lane	Pleasant Street	Roman Catholic	22	155		
Church Place	Church Street	Private [?]d	12-19	200		
Clarendon Street	Arlington Street	Glen Road	20	320	375	1930
Clayton Street	Lloyd Road	Irma Ave	41		165	1914
Clyde Road	Carver Road East	Commonwealth Road	40		430	1918
Coker Street	Sycamore Street	Waltham Line	40	75		

Name	From	To	Width	Length Private	Length Public	Year Accepted
Columbia Street	Russell Avenue	Common Street	40-50		860	1896
Common Sreet	Mt. ...in Street	Belmont Street	40-50		4,250	1917
...th Road	Belmont Street	Maplewood Street	40		1,070	
...t Road	Pleasant Street	Private Land	40-60	320		
Concord Road	Boylston Street	...rop Street	50		640	1920
Coolidge ...ve	...al Street	Cambridge Line	40		2,900	1854-1874
Coolidge Hill Road	...ton St...t	Grove St...t	40-50	850	850	1890
...ld Street	...in Street	Warren St...t	40	780	830	1927
Cottage Lane	Cottage Street	Molloy Street	30	195		
Cottage Street	Mt. Auburn Street	Roman Catholic Cemetery	30		980	1923
Cozy Street	Summer Street	Faye t... Street	40			
...ford Street	Arlington Street	Kondazian Street	40	280	985	1921-1931
Cross Street	Pleasant St...t	Winter Street	24-38		600	1794-1854
Cuba Street	...in Street	Myrtle Street	40		775	1830-1856
Cushman Street	Fayette Street	Oak Place	40	330		
...ss St...t	Mt. St...t	Quimby Street	40		2,000	1897-1921
Dana Terrace	Summer Street	Private ...d	20	200		
Dartmouth Street	Dexter ...ue	Boylston Street	40		740	1916-1920
Derby Road	Watertown St...t	Jackson Road	40		275	1929
Dexter Avenue	Mt. Auburn Street	School Street	40-50		2,800	1897
Dewey Street	...in St...t	Prentis Street	40		490	1930
Downey Street	Waverley Avenue	Westminster ...ue	40	550		
Duff Street	Belmont Street	...te a...d	40	1,020		
...n Road	Carroll Street	Private Land	40	190		
Dwight Street	Sycamore Street	Waltham Line	40	205		
Edenfield Avenue	Main Street	Orchard Street	40-50	1,237	2,058	1926-1927-1931
Edgecliffe Road	Maplewood Street	Hillside Road	40		1,275	1927-1928-1930

Street	From	To	Width		Length	Accepted
Edith Avenue	Beechwood Avenue	Pequossette Street	40	200	850	1897
Eliot Street	Galen Street	Union Street	40		1,500	1868
Elm Street	Arsenal Street	Arlington Street	50		440	1930
Elmwood Avenue	Bancroft Street	Warren Street	40		990	1873
Elton Avenue	Mt. Auburn Street	Nichols Avenue	40		1,040	1932
Emerson Road	Main Street	Highland Avenue	40		250	1931
Essex Street	Main Street	Nash Street	40		1,780	1930
Evans Street	Elm Street	Waltham Street	40		600	1925
Everett Avenue	Palfrey Street	Palfrey Street	40	700		
Fairfield Street	Dexter Avenue	Boylston Street	40		700	1913-1920
Fairview Avenue	Bradford Road	Wilson Avenue	40		1,035	1928-1929
Falmouth Road	Wm Street	Private Rd	40	440		
Farnsworth Street	Galen Street	Middle Street	21		130	1922
Fayette Street	Spring Street	Waverley Avenue	40		2,875	1836-1856-1901
Fifield Street	Irving Street	Perkins Street	40		500	1894
Fifth Avenue	Watertown Street	... Street	45-60		500	
	Waverley Avenue	Lawrence Street	23		1,243	1928
Flint Road	Patten Street	Private Land	40	200	407	1926
Florence Terrace	School Street	Private abd	30	170		
Forest Street	Spring Street	Springfield Street	40	450	1,560	1886-1887
Francis Street	Main Street	Belmont Street	40		530	1912
Frank Street	Mt. Auburn Street	Louise Street	40		530	1913
Franklin Street	Beechwood Avenue	Mt Street	40		1,385	1873
French Street	Mt. Auburn Street	Homer Street	32		600	1922
French Terrace	Main Street	B. & M. R. R.	40		368	1932
Fuller Road	Orchard Street	George Street	40		775	1929
Galen Street	Main Street	Newton Line	70		2,480	1850
Garfield Street	Mt. Auburn Street	Bellevue Road	40		1,605	1882
Garnet Street	Irving Street	Parker Street	40		425	1870-1874
Gay Road	Sunnybank Road	Flint Road	40		136	1926

Name	From	To	Width	Length Private	Length Public	Year Accepted
George Street	Orchard Street	Channing Road	40		925	1930
Gertrude Street	Kney Avenue	Westminster Ave	40		440	1930
Gilbert Street	Main Street	Grandview Avenue	40		885	1923
Gilkey Court	Patten Street	Private Land	12-22	220		
Gill Road	Sycamore Street	Waltham Line	40	265		
Glen Street	Main Street	Highland Avenue	40	200		
Glen Road	Coolidge Avenue	Clarendon Street	40	355	555	1931
Kie Street	Kney Avenue	Elmwood Avenue	40	850		
Grandview Avenue	Copeland Street	Bitt Street	40	250		
Grant Avenue	Duff Street	Waltham Line	40	910		
Glen Street	Min Street	Bitt Street	40	1,330		
Green Street Terrace	Green Street	Private Road	15-40		1,050	1854
Nelle Road	Common Street	Marcia Road	40	167		
Guild Street	Edenfield Avenue	Lexington Street	40		840	1929
Grove Street	Agton Street	Coolidge Ave	30-52	200	3,120	1850
Hall Avenue	Belmont Street	Fairview Ave	40		875	1915-1928
Hamilton Street	Warren Street	Grandview Ave	40	520		
Hancock Street	Winthrop Street	Chauncey Street	50		256	1928
Hardy Avenue	Belmont Street	Fairview Ave	40		715	1920-1929
Harnden Ave	Lexington Street	Private Land	40		1,880	1874
Harrington Street	Belmont Street	Perry Street	40		410	1905
Hawthorne Street	Hall Street	Private Land	40	795		
Hazel Street	Kirby Street	Boylston Street	20		1,000	1897-1928
Hearn Street	Cottage Street	Peite Land	40	300		
Hersom Street	Main Street	Highland Avenue	20		820	1923
Highland Ave	Lexington Street	Min Ave	40	1,755	1,500	1929
Hill Street	Fayette Street	Palfrey Street	40		455	1934
Hillcrest Circle	Hillside Road	Private Land	40-80		450	1930

Street	From	To	Width	Length	Accepted
Hillside Street	Belmont Street	Private Land	40	1,000	1930
Hillside Road	Mt. Auburn Street	Belmont Street	40	2,150	1906-1919-1920
Hop Road	Whitney Street	Hovey Street	40	765	1980
Holt Street	Harrington Street	Belmont Line	40	1,270	
Homer Street	Mle Street	Fish Street	40	280	1919
Hosmer Street	Boylston Street	Putnam Street	40	630	1874
Hovey Street	Orchard Street	Belmont Street	49.5	1,320	1818
Howard Street	Main Street	Pleasant Street	40	90	1919
Howe Street	Putnam Street	Hazel Street	40	260	
Hudson Street	...an Street	Whites Ave	40	480	
Hunt Street	Galen Street	Maple Street	40	430	1912
Irma Avenue	Mt. Auburn Street	Maplewood Street	40	730	1914-1921
Irving Street	Mt. Auburn Street	Charles River Road	40	2,200	1856-1908
Jackson Road	Morse Street	Newton Line	40	520	
James Street	Holt Street	Perry Street	40	360	
Jefferson Avenue	Brookline Street	Waltham Line	40	440	
Jewett Street	Boyd Street	Morse Street	40	275	
Katherine Road	...in Street	...th Street	40	950	1906
Keenan Street	Mt. Auburn Street	Belmont Street	40	820	1912
Keith Street	Prentiss Street	...n Street	20-30	490	
Kimball Road	Mt. Auburn Street	...l Street	40	590	1925
King Street	...on Ave	...w Ave	40	615	
Knowles Road	Belmont Street	Belmont Line	40	1,300	1928
Kondazian Street	Coolidge Hill Road	Grove Street	40	800	1931
Ladd Place	Ladd Street	Private Land	20-40	205	
Ladd Street	North Beacon Street	Riverside Street	40	525	1910
Langdon Avenue	Mt. Auburn Street	Belmont Street	40	2,100	1901-1917
Laurel Street	School Street	Melendy Avenue	40	1,480	1897
Laurel Street	Knowles Road	Belmont Line	40	234	1928

Name	From	To	Width	Length Private	Length Public	Year Accepted
Lawrence Street	Orchard Set	Worcester Street	40		437	1928
Lexington Stree t	Aton Street	Belmont Stree t	40-50		4,150	1930
Lincoln Street	Mt. Auburn Street	Spruce Set	40		1,085	1887-1922
Linden Way	Summer Street	Private Land	20	100		
Linden Street	Waverley Avenue	Wn Property	50	160		
Lloyd Road	Mt. Auburn Street	Clayton Street	40		445	1914
Eke Street	Common Set	Poplar Street	40		807	1927-1928
Longfellow R ad	Main Street	Waltham Line	40		900	1932
L omes Avenue	Downey Street	Orchard Set	40	1,030		
Louise Street	North Beacon Street	al Street	40		420	1913
Dill Road	Orchard Street	Belmont Street	40		2,500	1926-1927-1928
Dll Avenue	Orchard Street	George Str et	40		1,710	1874-1929
Lyons Court	Watertown Set	Private Land	20	350		
Lyons Stree t	ge Set	Private nd	20	300		
Mn Ave	Ele Street	King Street	40	580		
Min Street	n Square	Wm Line	6600		7,460	
Malden Street	Forest Street	tt Avenue	40	380		
Me Street Set	G Set	Newton Line	46-50		700	1813-1854
Marcia Rd	Arlington Set	Private Land	40		2,670	1917-1920
Marlboro Terrace	Bellevue Road	Grenville Road	40		504	1928
Marion Rd	pd Street	Private Rd	40	245		
Marion Rd	Spring Street	Orchard Set	40		2,050	1891
Ml Street	Mt. urn Street	Oer Street	40		2,000	1874
Mn Rd	Channing Road	Fuller Rd	40		200	1929
Mly Avenue	Mt. an Street	Laurel Set	40		1,500	1897-1898
Me Terrace	Morse Street	Private nl	12	95		
s w	Min Street	Private nd	30		175	1917
Merrifield Avenue	Arlington Set	Bigelow Avenue	40	460		

Street	From	To	Width		Length	Date
Merrill Road	Bel mt Street	Ike Street	40		784	1928
Middle Street	Main Street	Myrtle Steet	21		418	1922
Middlesex Road	Common Street	i on Steet	40		450	1929
Mnd Road	Falmouth Road	Private Land	40	180		
Mloy Steet	Hearn Street	Private Land	12-25	300		
Me Steet	Galen Street	Watertown Street	40		1,980	1875
oMon Street	Main Street	Acton Street	40		565	1931
Mt. Aurn Stret	Glen Steet	Cambridge Line	80		10,380	
Munroe Avenue	Elm Street	Private Land	40	143		
Myrtle Steet	Main Steet	Elnt Street	40		1,010	1852
Nash Street	Evans Street	Essex Street	40		340	1931
Nichols Ame	Arlington Street	Boylston Street	40		2,071	1881-1912-1928
Norseman Avenue	Mt. Auburn Steet	Private Land	40-50	300		
North Beacon Street	North Beacon Street	Boston Line	72		6,500	1868
North Beacon uft		Fate id	30	285		
North Irving Park	Irving Street	Royal Street	40		285	1891
North Park Street	Morse Steet	Boyd Steet	30		270	1888
Nyack Street	Belmont Street	Private id	40	990		
Oak Place	Private Land	Private Land	30	215		
Oak Street	Ly Avenue	Laurel Street	40		410	1897
Rand Street	Main Street	Private Land	40		515	1930
Oaley Road	Mt. Steet	Stoneleigh Road	40	365	460	1927
Oltt Street	Main Steet	Highland ahe	40		890	1922
Oler Street	Church Street	Marshall Street	40		830	1891
Oliver Road	Adams Street	Dexter Avenue	20	300		
Olney Street	Din Steet	Highland Avenue	40			
Orchard Street	Barnard Avenue	Lexington Street	35-40		800	1910-1923
Ola Aaue	Elm Street	Private Land	25		4,820	
Otis Street	Washburn Street	Mt. Auburn Street	40	175	555	1856
Palfrey Street	Mt. Auburn Street	Waverley Avenue	40		3,605	1851-1924-1931

Name	From	To	Width	Length Private	Length Public	Year
Palmer Street	9th Beacon Street	afies River Road	40		475	1927
Parker Steet	Mt. Aern Str e t	Private Land	40		855	1873-1897
Partridge Street	Main Street	Private Land	40	1,100		
Patten Street	Mt. Auburn Street	Arsenal Street	25-33		610	1838
Paul Street	9th Beacon Street	Charles River Road	40		675	1913
Pearl Street	Siner Street	Oner Street	40		1,030	1903
Pequosette Street	9th Beacon Street	Charles River Road	40		860	1913
Perry Street	Sycamore Street	Russell Street	40	565		
Phillips Steet	Mt. barn Steet	B. & M. R. R.	40		800	1913
Piermont Str et	Belmont Street	Tappan Avenue	40		860	1929
Pleasant Steet	Galen Steet	Waltham Line	40-50		8,510	B71
Prentiss Street	Mt. Uan Street	Belmont Street	40		1,025	1889
Pond Street	Watertown Street	Watertown Street	40	475		
Poplar Steet	Bent Steet	Loke Street	40		790	1926
Porter Street	Boylston Street	School Street	40		610	1920
Prescott Street	Main Str et	Giles Street	40		670	1921
Priest Road	Riverside Street	ifles River Road	40		501	1928
Priscilla Gile	Arlington Street	Arlington Street	40	785		
Prospect Street	Belmont Stree t	Private And	40		980	1931
Purvis Steet	Main Steet	Giles Street	40		565	1919
Pram Street	Hazel Steet	Boylston Street	40		1,710	1920-1921
Quimby Street	Cypress Street	Nichols Avenue	40		1,080	1897-1930
Quincy Street	Fitchburg Street	Palfrey Street	40	760		
Quirk Street	Waverley Avenue	Private Land	40	680		

Street	From	To	Width		Length	Year
Ralph Street	Belmont Street	Private Land	40	1,000	500	1927
Rangeley Road	Hillside Road	Irma ...ue	40		450	1927
Richards Road	Mt. Auburn Street	Stoneleigh Road	25	160	2,000	1886-1890
Rifle Court	Sawin Stre ct	Private Ind	40		1,915	1922-1924
Riverside Street	Beacon Square	Perkins Institute	40			
Rhins Road	Columbia Street	Private Ind	40			
Rosedale Road	Min Street	Waltham Street	40	1,300	665	1891
Royal Street	Mth Beacon Street	Riverside Street	40		2,070	1882-1884-1907
Russell Avenue	Mt. Auburn Street	Bellevue Road	50			
Russell Street	Holt Street	Perry Street	40			
Rutland Street	Main Str ct	Waltham Street	40	290	1,710	1931
St. Mary Street	Mt. ...n Street	Belmont Street	40		385	1912
Salisbury Road	Belmont Street	Maplewood Street	40		660	1929
Sawin Street	Cottage Street	Spring Court	30	265	5,200	1889
Sch col Street	Mth Beacon Street	Belmont Street	50-60			
Sexton Street	Cottage Str ct	Private Land	20	250	770	1895-1928
Shattuck Road	School Street	...th Road	50-100		270	1922
Sheldon Road	Belmont Street	Private Land	40		115	1926
Sh et Street	Bigelow Avenue	Elton Avenue	60		230	1891
Sidney Street	Marshall Street	Wn Property	40	90	285	1891
South Irving Park	Irving Street	Royal Street	40		275	1888
South Park Street	Morse Street	Boyd Street	30			
Sparkill Street	Belmont Street	Madison ...ue	40	1,080		
Spring Court	Sawin Street	...te Land	25	230		
Spring Street	Main Street	Common Street	40		2,150	1812
Springfield Street	Orchard Street	...cy Court	40	650	460	1928
Spruce Street	Mt. ...n Street	School Street	40		2,460	1905-1915-1921
Standish Road	Orchard Street	Belmont Street	40		2,380	1928
Stanley Avenue	Waltham Street	B. & M. R. R.	40	1,250		
Stearns Road	Mt. Auburn Street	Stoneleigh Road	40		550	1927
Stoneleigh Circle	Bailey Road	Stoneleigh Road	40		620	1905-1928
Stoneleigh Road	Bailey Road	Shattuck Road	40		1,588	1905-1927-1931

Name	From	To	Width	Length Private	Length Public	Year Accepted
Stuart Street	Main Street	Highland Avenue	40		883	1813-1856-1877
Summer Street	Mt. Auburn Street	Waverley Avenue	40-50		3,000	1920
Summit Road	Maplewood Street	Rangeley Road	40		260	1926
Sunnybank Road	School Street	Private Land	40		424	1921
Sunset Road	Common Street	Avon Road	40		325	
Swetts Court	Waltham Street	Private Land	50-60	180		1896
Sycamore Street	Belmont Street	Belmont Line	50		1,524	
Tappan Avenue	Nyack Street	Sparkill Street	40	430		1850
Taylor Street	Mt. Auburn Street	Arsenal Street	35-40		225	1920
Templeton Parkway	Mt. Auburn Street	Belmont Street	40-75		1,785	1924-1925-1928
Thaxter Street	Main Street	Town Land	40	200		
Thayer Road	Brown Street	Town Line	40	50	335	1929
Theurer Park	Watertown Street	Jackson Road	40		445	1928
Thurston Road	Riverside Street	Charles River Road	40			
Union Street	Galen Street	Morse Street	40		1,350	19 50
Upland Road	Mt. Auburn Street	Hillside Road	40		670	1910
W alltt Road	Fuller Road	Elg Road	40		430	1930
Walnut Street	Mt. barn Street	School Street	40		2,570	1875
W allm Street	Ent Street	Wm. Line	20-40		3,575	1928-1930
W an Street	Waverley Avenue	Waltham Line	27-50		3,950	20-1929
Warwick Road	Belmont Street	Fairview valle	40		560	1886-1897
Washburn Street	Franklin Street	Parker Street	40		635	1851-1873
Water Street	Galen Street	alen Street	19-3 0		1,515	1874
Watertown Street	Galen Street	Newton Line	60		2,870	1899-1907
Waverley vaue	Main St.	Belmont Street	40-50	880		
Webster Street	Warren Street	Waltham Ine	40		3,900	

Street	From	To	Width			Year
Wells vde	Arlington Street	Bigelow Avenue	40		460	1932
Westland Road	Belmont Street	Edgecliffe Road	40		400	1921
Westminster Avenue	Main St	Orchard Street	40-50	1,440	1,700	1928-1930
...er Ane	Riverside Street	Private Ard	30	440		
Wheeler Court	Elm Street	Pate Land	40	200		
Whitcomb Street	Knowles Road	Belmont Line	40			
Whites vue	Main Street	Palfrey St	20-40	470	86	1928
Whitman Road	Tain St	Wm Line	40	300	900	1886
Wiley Street	Orchard Street	Belmont Street	40		685	1874
Williams Street	Aden St	Newton Line	30		500	
Mot Street	Main Street	Highland Avenue	40		839	1919
Wilson Avenue	Belmont Street	Channing Road	40		850	1925-1929
Winsor Avenue	Mt. Arn St	Belmont Street	50		2,090	1901-1917
Winer Street	Fifth St	Fayette Street	26-30	800	250	1850
Winthrop Street	Mt. Vlan St	Boylston Street	50		730	1905
...gh Road	Belmont Street	Edgecliffe Road	40		541	1924
Winer Lane	Myrtle Street	French Street	20	270		
Worcester Street	Waverley Avenue	Wn Land	40		1305	1929
Yukon Avenue	Elm Street	Private Land	40	153		

TOTAL AREA OF WATERTOWN, 2,664.58 or 4.163 square miles
TOTAL LENGTH OF STREETS: PRIVATE WAYS 11.82
PUBLIC WAYS 58.63

TOTAL 70.45

TREASURER'S REPORT

For Year Ending December 31, 1934

Borrowed in 1934
Anticipation of Revenue

Jan.	16.	Bank of the Manhattan Co.		
		of New York @ 4½		$100,000
		The National Shawmut Bank @ 4½		100,000
		Union Market National Bank @ 4½		100,000
Mar.	19.	Union Market National Bank @ 3		65,000
		The National Shawmut Bank @ 3		70,000
		Bank of the Manhattan Co. of		
		N. Y. @ 3		65,000
May	18,	Whiting Knowles & Weeks	.75	200,000
June	14.	Faxon, Gade Company	.89	200,000
Aug.	8.	Union Market National Bank	1.	25,000
		The National Shawmut Bank	1.	20,000
		Bank of the Manhattan Company	1.	20,000
Sept.	13.	Faxon, Gade Company	.93	100,000
Dec.	18.	Whiting, Knowles, Weeks	.69	200,000

$1,265,000

Bonds 1934

Nov.	1.	Estabrook Company @ 100.57-2¼	
		Sidewalks	$11,000
		Street	28,000
		Drainage	16,000
Dec.	1.	Tyler, Buttrick, Company @ 100.43-2½	
		School Addition	115,000
		Library Addition	29,000

$199,000

Bonds Paid 1934

Jan. 1.		Sewers	$2,000	
		Drains	5,000	
				$7,000
Feb.	1,	Administration Building	11,000	11,000
Mar.	1.	School (Outside)	30,000	
		School	1,000	
				31,000
Apr.	1.	Schools	35,000	
		Hosmer School (Outside)	5,000	
		Drains—Sewers	6,000	
		Playgrounds (Outside)	1,000	
		Streets	14,000	
				61,000
May	1.	Water (Outside)	1,000	
		Refunding	2,000	
		Schools	31,000	
		East End School (Outside)	2,000	
		Streets	17,000	
				53,000
June	1.	Athletic Field	1,000	1,000
July	1.	Water (Outside)	5,000	
		West Watertown School (Outside)	12,000	
		Schools	3,000	
		Land	2,000	
		Sewers	2,000	
		Street	7,000	
		Fire Alarm Signal	8,000	
				39,000
Oct.	1.	Sewers—Drains	1,000	
		Water (Outside)	1,000	
				2,000
Nov.	1.	No. Beacon St. Bridge (Outside)	3,000	
		Drains and Sewers	2,000	
				5,000

Dec.	1.	Sewer	6,000	6,000
				$216,000

Notes Paid 1934

Apr.	16.	Anticipation of Revenue	$100,000
May	15.	Anticipation of Revenue	100,000
May	31.	Anticipation of Revenue	300,000
Aug.	20.	Anticipation of Revenue	250,000
Nov.	9.	Anticipation of Revenue	300,000
Nov.	21.	Anticipation of Revenue	200,000
Dec.	28.	Anticipation of Revenue	200,000
Dec.	17.	Anticipation of Revenue	65,000
			$1,515,000

Bonds Due 1935

Jan.	1.	Sewers	$2,000	
		Drainage	4,000	
				$6,000
Feb.	1.	Administration Building	11,000	11,000
Mar.	1.	School (Outside)	30,000	
		School	1,000	
				31,000
Apr.	1.	Hosmer School (Outside)	5,000	
		Playground (Outside)	1,000	
		Drains—Sewers	6,000	
		Street	14,000	
		Schools	35,000	
				61,000
May	1.	Refunding	2,000	
		School E. End (Outside)	2,000	
		Schools	31,000	
		Street	10,000	
		Water (Outside)	1,000	
				46,000
June	1.	Athletic Field	1,000	1,000

July	1.	School W. Watertown		
		(Outside)	12,000	
		Schools	3,000	
		Land	2,000	
		Sewers—Drains	2,000	
		Fire Alarm Signal	. 8,000	
				27,000
Nov.	1.	No. Beacon St. Bridge		
		(Outside)	3,000	
		Drainage (PWA)	2,000	
		Drains, Sewers	2,000	
		Sidewalks (PWA)	3,000	
		Street (PWA)	6,000	
				16,000
Dec.	1.	Sewers	6,000	
		School Addition (PWA)	12,000	
		Library Addition (PWA)	3,000	
				21,000
				$220,000

Notes Due 1935

Mar.	28.	Anticipation of Revenue	$200,000
May	18.	Anticipation of Revenue	100,000
Sept.	11.	Anticipation of Revenue	100,000
Oct.	11.	Anticipation of Revenue	100,000
			$500,000

The indebtedness of the Town and on what account it was incurred is as follows:

Fire Alarm System	$24,000
New Administration Building	172,000
Water Loans	9,000
Refunding Loan	4,000
Sewer and Drains	119,000
North Beacon Street Bridge	15,000
Athletic Field	6,000

Street Loans	100,000
School Loans	976,000
Land	11,000
Playground	6,000
Sidewalk	11,000
Library Addition	29,000
	$1,482,000

Statement required by Chapter VI, Town By-Laws, Article 4.

State of debt and total cash Expenditures of the Town for thirty years:

Year	Total Expenditures	Town Debt
1905	$601,365.35	$788,800
1906	569,814.38	766,000
1907	789,735.64	792,800
1908	671,282.59	757,025
1909	702,274.31	724,725
1910	676,377.48	790,225
1911	811,158.18	761,625
1912	800,488.71	766,225
1913	795,500.10	802,225
1914	884,248.80	767,525
1915	978,082.53	775,725
1916	1,010,473.76	807,925
1917	1,165,912.95	809,500
1918	1,116,816.30	767,500
1919	1,525,651.33	1,003,000
1920	1,788,282.40	1,087,000
1921	2,083,986.77	1,319,000
1922	2,037,672.76	1,238,500
1923	2,144,143.57	1,183,500
1924	2,571,082.55	1,679,000
1925	3,015,407.96	1,914,000
1926	3,010,470.05	2,079,500
1927	3,384,965.67	2,023,000
1928	3,378,589.10	2,172,000

1929	4,011,343.85	2,171,500
1930	3,903,795.26	1,982,000
1931	4,282,947.52	1,947,000
1932	4,923,029.72	1,742,000
1933	4,171,875.82	1,499,000
1934	3,908,434.08	1,482,000

Financial Statement

Total Debt, December 31, 1934		$1,482,000
Outside		
Water	9,000	
East End School, Chap. 272, Acts 1915	20,000	
Hosmer School, Chap. 299, Acts 1917	25,000	
No. Beacon St. Bridge, Chap. 780A-1914	15,000	
Senior High School, Chap. 372-A-1923	300,000	
Playground	6,000	
W. Watertown School, Chap. 27A-1921	84,000	
Sidewalk (P.W.A.)	11,000	
Street (P.W.A.)	28,000	
Drainage (P.W.A.)	16,000	
School Add (P.W.A.)	115,000	
Library Add (P.W.A.)	29,000	
	$640,000	$640,000
		$842,000
Valuations 1932	$57,923,155	
Valuations 1933	55,447,850	
Valuations 1934	55,079,515	
	$168,450,520	168,450,520
Abatements 1932	2,044,976	
Abatements 1933	826,893	
Abatements 1934	479,744	

	————	3,351,613
	3)	165,098,907
		55,032,969
	3%	1,650,989
		842,000

Borrowing capacity for January 1, 1935 $808,989

The indebtedness of the Town matures as follows:

1935	$220,000
1936	211,000
1937	193,000
1938	168,000
1939	140,000
1940	122,000
1941	101,000
1942	79,000
1943	79,000
1944	75,000
1945	18,000
1946	14,000
1947	13,000
1948	13,000
1949	13,000
1950	12,000
1951	11,000
	———— $1,482,000

The following is a list of all moneys and securities which have been placed in my charge by virtue of any gift, devise, bequest or deposit:

The Martha Sanger bequest in the shape of a fund deposited in the Watertown Savings Bank.

Balance on hand December 31, 1933	$686.36
Interest for year 1934	24.23
Balance December 31, 1934	$710.59

The Templeton Fund, $2,500 which is represented by two $1,000 four per cent first mortgage gold bonds of the New York, New Haven and Hartford Railroad, Harlem River and Port Chester Division, and an account in the Watertown Savings Bank for $500. The interest on same $97.64 paid to the Associated Charities for distributing at Christmas time as per order of the Board of Selectmen.

The several sums of money turned over to me on account of perpetual care of lots in the cemeteries have been deposited in the Watertown Savings Bank and now amount including interest to:

Balance, December 31, 1933	$45,753.13
Interest for the year 1934	1,623.42
	$47,376.55
Interest withdrawn on account of cemetery department 1933	1,581.66
	$45,794.89

Names and amounts collected since last report:

John Johnson	$15.00
T. Gallagher (Askanaz)	15.00
Mrs. George Owens	37.50
George H. Gregg & Sons (Cross)	15.00
Mabel Powers	37.50
W. G. Rockwell (Secord)	37.50
Alice Capers	15.00
A. Kambagian	15.00
Ed. Doherty	15.00
W. G. Rockwell (Fielding)	15.00
George H. Gregg & Sons (Kimball)	37.50
Violet D. Young	50.00
J. Johnson (Barsom)	75.00
J. Johnson (Boghosian)	150.00
Laura Crocker	30.00
Charles B. Watson (Barkman)	37.50

Lavinia Middleton	126.50
Wm. Hughes	15.00
Z. Dagavarian	10.00
K. Pesherian	50.00
Magdalena Hughes	15.00
C. H. Oxner	7.50
David Ross	75.00
K. Vagaretian	15.00
Harry Calvert	15.00
J. W. Duvall	37.50
J. J. Johnson (Arisian)	7.50
J. J. Johnson (Misserian)	15.00
H. F. Cate (Sutherland)	50.00
E. H. Johnson	112.50
E. H. Johnson	15.00
Norman Sevigney	15.00
Henry Doherty (Hyland)	15.00
Jean Sutherland	75.00
W. G. Rockwell (Cepurneek)	7.50
H. Derkazarian (Perelzian)	50.00
W. G. Rockwell (LeShana)	62.50
John Johnson (Boghigian)	15.00
Estate Irene Lathrop	80.00
Wentworth Sosn (Chase)	37.50
J. J. Johnson (Badlian)	15.00
Tenni-Sements (Magerian)	30.00
Short, Williams (Mayer)	37.50

Total December 31, 1934 $47,398.89

I have also in my charge the following property of **the** public Library, which are not direct gifts or bequest **to** the Town:

Bonds from the Pratt bequest, amounting to $5,000.

Bonds for $2,000, invested from accumulated interest received from above funds. Interest due semi-annually and paid to Mr. Otis L. Hawes, who represents the committee in charge of the fund.

The Benjamin Hosmer Pierce Fund, represented by a deposit in the Watertown Savings Bank, amounting to, including interest $1,307.28.

The Barry fund, deposited in above savings bank, amounting to $1009.77.

Mary D. Emerson Mead Fund, account Watertown Public Library deposited in Union Market National Bank, savings department, amounting to, including interest $3116.36.

No sums can be drawn from the above accounts except upon written order of a majority of the Trustees of the Public Library.

Receipts and Expenditures

Balance, December 31, 1934	$130,337.66	
1934 Receipts	4,051,037.78	
		$4,181,375.44
1934 Paid Treasury Warrants		3,908,434.08
Balance December 31, 1934		$272,941.36

W. W. NORCROSS, Jr.,

Approved   Auditor

LIST OF TOWN NOTES, TIME OF MATURING

Date	Amount	Rate	Annual Interest	Interest Due	Maturity	Borrowed on account of
May 1, 1906	2,000	4	80.00	May and Nov.	May 1, 1935	Refunding Debt
1, 1906	2,000	4	80.0	"	1, 1936	"
1, 1915	2,000	4	80.0	"	1, 1935	East End School
April 1, 1916	1,000	4	40.0	Oct. and April	April 1, 1935	Surface Drainage
1, 1916	1,000	4	40.00	"	1, 1936	"
1, 1916	1,000	4	40.00	"	1, 1937	"
1, 1916	1,000	4	40.0	"	1, 1938	"
1, 1916	1,000	4	40.0	"	1, 1939	"
1, 1916	1,000	4	40.0	"	1, 1940	"
1, 1916	1,000	4	40.0	"	1, 1941	"
1, 1916	1,000	4	40.00	"	1, 1942	"
1, 1916	1,000	4	40.0	"	1, 1943	"
1, 1916	1,000	4	40.00	"	1, 1944	"
1, 1916	1,000	4	40.0	"	1, 1945	"
1, 1916	1,000	4	40.00	"	1, 1946	"
May 1, 1917	1,000	4½	45.0	"	May 1, 1935	High School Land
1, 1917	1,000	4½	45.0	"	1, 1936	"
1, 1917	1,000	4½	90.00	"	1, 1937	"
April 1, 1919	5,000	5	250.0	April and Oct.	April 1, 1935	Hosmer School
1, 1919	5,000	5	250.0	"	1, 1936	"
1, 1919	5,000	5	250.0	"	1, 1937	"
1, 1919	5,000	5	250.00	"	1, 1938	"
1, 1919	5,000	5	250.00	"	1, 1939	"
April 1, 1919	1,000	5	50.00	April and Oct.	April 1, 1935	Spring Street Drain

Issue Date	Amount	Rate	Interest	Payable	Due Date	Purpose
1, 1919	1,000	5	50.00	"	1, 1936	"
1, 1919	1,000	5	50.00	"	1, 1937	"
1, 1919	1,000	5	50.00	"	1, 1938	"
1, 1919	1,000	5	50.00	"	1, 1939	"
1, 1919	1,000	5	50.00	"	1, 1940	"
1, 1919	1,000	5	50.00	"	1, 1941	"
1, 1919	1,000	5	50.00	"	1, 1942	"
1, 1919	1,000	5	50.00	"	1, 1943	"
1, 1919	1,000	5	50.00	"	1, 1944	"
1, 1919	1,000	5	50.00	"	1, 1945	"
1, 1919	1,000	5	50.00	"	1, 1946	"
1, 1919	1,000	5	50.00	"	1, 1947	"
1, 1919	1,000	5	50.00	"	1, 1948	"
1, 1919	1,000	5	50.00	"	1, 1949	North Beacon Street Bridge
Nov. 1, 1919	3,000	4½	135.00	May and Nov.	April 1, 1935	"
1, 1919	3,000	4½	135.00	"	1, 1936	"
1, 1919	3,000	4½	135.00	"	1, 1937	"
1, 1919	3,000	4½	135.00	"	1, 1938	"
1, 1919	3,000	4½	135.00	"	1, 1939	"
April 1, 1920	1,000	5	50.00	April and Oct.	April 1, 1935	Drain and Sewer
1, 1920	1,000	5	50.00	"	1, 1936	"
1, 1920	1,000	5	50.00	"	1, 1937	"
1, 1920	1,000	5	50.0	"	1, 1938	"
1, 1920	1,000	5	50.0	"	1, 1939	"
1, 1920	1,000	5	50.0	"	1, 1940	"
1, 1920	1,000	5	50.0	"	1, 1941	"
1, 1920	1,000	5	50.0	"	1, 1942	"
1, 1920	1,000	5	50.0	"	1, 1943	"
1, 1920	1,000	5	50.	"	1, 1944	"
1, 1920	1,000	5	50. 0	"	1, 1945	"
1, 1920	1,000	5	50. 0	"	1, 1946	"
1, 1920	1,000	5	50. 0	"	1, 1947	"
1, 1920	1,000	5	50. 0	"	1, 1948	"

LIST OF TOWN NOTES, TIME OF MATURING—*Continued*

Date	Amount	Rate	Interest Annual	Interest Due	Maturity	Borrowed on account of
April 1, 1920	1,000	5	50.00	April 1, 1936	April 1, 1949	Drain and Sewer
1, 1920	1,000	5	50.00	"	1, 1950	"
June 1, 1920	1,000	5½	55.00	June and Dec.	June 1, 1935	Athletic Field
1, 1920	1,000	5½	55.00	"	1936	"
1, 1920	1,000	5½	55. 0	"	1, 1937	"
1, 1920	1,000	5½	55. 0	"	1, 1938	"
1, 1920	1,000	5½	55.00	"	1, 1939	"
1, 1920	1,000	5½	55.00	"	1, 1940	"
April 1, 1921	1,000	5	50.00	April and Oct.	April 1, 1935	Drainage
1, 1921	1,000	5	50.00	"	1, 1936	"
1, 1921	1,000	5	50.00	"	1, 1937	"
1, 1921	1,000	5	50.00	"	1, 1938	"
1, 1921	1,000	5	50.00	"	1, 1939	"
1, 1921	1,000	5	50.00	"	1, 1940	"
1, 1921	1,000	5	50.00	"	1, 1941	"
1, 1921	1,000	5	50.00	"	1, 1942	"
1, 1921	1,000	5	50.00	"	1, 1943	"
1, 1921	1,000	5	50.00	"	1, 1944	"
1, 1921	1,000	5	50.00	"	1, 1945	"
1, 1921	1,000	5	50.00	"	1, 1946	"
1, 1921	1,000	5	50.00	"	1, 1947	"
1, 1921	1,000	5	50.00	"	1, 1948	"
1, 1921	1,000	5	50.00	"	1, 1949	"
1, 1921	1,000	5	50.00	"	1, 1950	"
1, 1921	1,000	5	50.00	"	1, 1951	"

July 1, 1921	12,000	5¼	630.00	Jan. and July	July 1, 1935	West Watertown School
1, 1921	12,000	5¼	630.00	"	1, 1936	"
1, 1921	12,000	5¼	630.00	"	1, 1937	"
1, 1921	12,000	5¼	630.00	"	1, 1938	"
1, 1921	12,000	5¼	630.00	"	1, 1939	"
1, 1921	12,000	5¼	630.00	"	1, 1940	"
1, 1921	12,000	5¼	630.00	"	1, 1941	"
July 1, 1923	1,000	4¼	42.50	Jan. and July	July 1, 1935	School Plans
1, 1923	1,000	4¼	42.50	"	1, 1936	"
1, 1923	1,000	4¼	42.50	"	1, 1937	"
1, 1923	1,000	4¼	42.50	"	1, 1938	"
July 1, 1923	2,000	4¼	85.00	Jan. and July	July 1, 1935	School Lands
1, 1923	2,000	4¼	85.00	"	1, 1936	"
1, 1923	2,000	4¼	85.00	"	1, 1937	"
1, 1923	2,000	4¼	85.00	"	1, 1938	"
1, 1923	1,000	4¼	42.50	"	1, 1939	"
1, 1923	1,000	4¼	42.50	"	1, 1940	"
1, 1923	1,000	4¼	42.50	"	1, 1941	"
1, 1923	1,000	4¼	42.50	"	1, 1942	"
1, 1923	1,000	4¼	42.50	"	1, 1943	"
1, 1923	2,000	4¼	85.00	"	1, 1935	Barnard Block
1, 1923	2,000	4¼	85.0	"	1, 1936	"
1, 1923	1,000	4¼	42.50	"	1, 1937	"
1, 1923	1,000	4¼	42.50	"	1, 1938	"
1, 1923	1,000	4¼	42.50	"	1, 1939	"
1, 1923	1,000	4¼	42.50	"	1, 1940	"
1, 1923	1,000	4¼	42.50	"	1, 1941	"
1, 1923	1,000	4¼	42.50	"	1, 1942	"
1, 1923	1,000	4¼	42.50	"	1, 1943	"
Mar. 1, 1924	1,000	4	40.0	Mar. and Sept.	Mar. 1, 1935	Senior High School
1, 1924	1,000	4	40.00	"	1, 1936	"
1, 1924	1,000	4	40.00	"	1, 1937	"
1, 1924	1,000	4	40.0	"	1, 1938	"

LIST OF TOWN NOTES, TIME OF MATURING—Continued

Date	Amount	Rate	Annual Interest	Interest Due	Maturity	Borrowed on account of
Mar. 1, 1924	1,000	4	40.00	Mar. and Sept.	Mar. 1, 1939	Senior High School
1, 1924	1,000	4	40.00	"	1, 1940	"
1, 1924	1,000	4	40.00	"	1, 1941	"
1, 1924	1,000	4¼	42.50	"	1, 1942	"
1, 1924	1,000	4¼	42.50	"	1, 1943	"
1, 1924	1,000	4¼	42.50	"	1, 1944	"
1, 1924	30,000	4	1,200.00	"	1, 1935	"
1, 1924	30,000	4	1,200.00	"	1, 1936	"
1, 1924	30,000	4	1,200.00	"	1, 1937	"
1, 1924	30,000	4	1,200.00	"	1, 1938	"
1, 1924	30,000	4	1,200.00	"	1, 1939	"
1, 1924	30,000	4	1,200.00	"	1, 1940	"
1, 1924	30,000	4	1,200.00	"	1, 1941	"
1, 1924	30,000	4	400. 0	"	1, 1942	"
1, 1924	30,000	4¼	1,275.00	"	1, 1943	"
1, 1924	30,000	4¼	1,275.00	"	1, 1944	"
April 1, 1925	1,000	4	40.00	April and Oct.	April 1, 1935	Playgrounds
1, 1925	1,000	4	40. 0	"	1, 1936	"
1, 1925	1,000	4	40. 0	"	1, 1937	"
1, 1925	1,000	4	40.00	"	1, 1938	"
1, 1925	1,000	4	40.00	"	1, 1939	"
1, 1925	1,000	4	40. 0	"	1, 1940	"
April 1, 1925	6,000	4	240. 0	"	April 1, 1935	High School Equipment
1, 1925	6,000	4	240. 0	"	1, 1936	"
1, 1925	6,000	4	240.00	"	1, 1937	"
1, 1925	6,000	4	240.00	"	1, 1938	"

Date of Issue		Amount	Rate	Interest	Interest Payable	Maturity		Purpose
	1, 1925	6,000	4	240.00	"		1, 1939	"
	1, 1925	6,000	4	240.00	"		1, 1940	Coolidge School
	1, 1925	11,000	4	440.00	"		1, 1935	"
	1, 1925	11,000	4	440.00	"		1, 1936	"
	1, 1925	11,000	4	440.00	"		1, 1937	"
	1, 1925	11,000	4	440.00	"		1, 1938	"
	1, 1925	11,000	4	440.00	"		1, 1939	"
	1, 1925	11,000	4	440.00	"		1, 1940	"
July	1, 1925	2,000	4	80.00	Jan. and July	July	1, 1935	Sewers
April	1, 1926	10,000	4	400.00	Oct. and April	April	1, 1935	North End School
	1, 1926	10,000	4	400.00	"		1, 1936	"
	1, 1926	10,000	4	400.00	"		1, 1937	"
	1, 1926	10,000	4	400.00	"		1, 1938	"
	1, 1926	10,000	4	400.00	"		1, 1939	"
	1, 1926	10,000	4	400.00	"		1, 1940	"
	1, 1926	10,000	4	400.00	"		1, 1941	"
	1, 1926	7,000	4	280.00	"		1, 1935	Streets
	1, 1926	7,000	4	280.00	"		1, 1935	"
	1, 1926	3,000	4	120.00	"		1, 1936	Pavements
April	1, 1926	3,000	4	120.00	April and Oct.		1, 1936	"
	1, 1927	8,000	4	320.00	"		1, 1935	West Junior High School Ext.
	1, 1927	8,000	4	320.00	"		1, 1936	"
	1, 1927	8,000	4	320.00	"		1, 1937	"
	1, 1927	2,000	4	80.00	"		1, 1935	Sewers and Drains
	1, 1927	2,000	4	80.00	"		1, 1936	"
	1, 1927	2,000	4	80.00	"		1, 1937	"
	1, 1927	4,000	4	160.00	"		1, 1935	Streets
	1, 1927	4,000	4	160.00	"		1, 1936	"
	1, 1927	4,000	4	160.00	"		1, 1937	"
May	1, 1928	11,000	3¾	412.50	May and Nov.	May	1, 1935	Hosmer School
	1, 1928	11,000	3¾	412.50	"		1, 1936	"
	1, 1928	11,000	3¾	412.50	"		1, 1937	"
	1, 1928	11,000	3¾	412.50	"		1, 1938	"

LIST OF TOWN NOTES, TIME OF MATURING—Continued

Date	Amount	Rate	Annual Interest	Interest Due	Mat'ity	Borrowed on account of
May 1, 1928	10,000	3¾	375.0	May and Nov.	May 1, 1935	Arsenal Street
1, 1928	10,000	3¾	375.0	"	1, 1936	"
1, 1928	10,000	3¾	375.0	"	1, 1937	"
1, 1928	10,000	3¾	375.0	"	1, 1938	"
May 1, 1928	1,000	3¾	37.50	May and Nov.	May 1, 1935	Water Mains
1, 1928	1,000	3¾	37.50	"	1, 1936	"
1, 1928	1,000	3¾	37.50	"	1, 1937	"
1, 1928	1,000	3¾	37.50	"	1, 1938	"
1, 1928	1,000	3¾	37.50	"	1, 1939	"
1, 1928	1,000	3¾	37.50	"	1, 1940	"
1, 1928	1,000	3¾	37.50	"	1, 1941	"
1, 1928	1,000	3¾	37.50	"	1, 1942	"
1, 1928	1,000	3¾	37.50	"	1, 1943	"
Dec. 1, 1928	6,000	4	240.0	Dec. and June	Dec. 1, 1935	Sewer
1, 1928	6,000	4	240.0	"	1, 1936	"
1, 1928	6,000	4	240.0	"	1, 1937	"
1, 1928	5,000	4	200.00	"	1, 1938	"
May 1, 1929	14,000	4¼	595.0	"	May 1, 1935	West End School
1, 1929	14,000	4¼	595.0	"	1, 1936	"
1, 1929	14,000	4¼	595.0	"	1, 1937	"
1, 1929	14,000	4¼	595.0	"	1, 1938	"
1, 1929	14,000	4¼	595.0	"	1, 1939	"
1, 1929	12,000	4¼	510.0	"	1, 1940	"
1, 1929	12,000	4¼	510.0	"	1, 1941	"
1, 1929	12,000	4¼	510.0	"	1, 1942	"

Date	Amount	Rate	Interest	Interest Payable	Date Due	Purpose
1, 1929 Jan.	12,000	4¼	510.00	" "	1, 1948	" "
1, 1929	12,000	4¼	51.0	" "	1, 1944	" "
1, 1930	2,000	4½	9.0	Jan. and July	1, 1935 Jan.	Sewer
1, 1930	5,000	4	200.00	"	1, 1935	Lowell School
1, 1930	5,000	4	200.00	"	1, 1936	"
1, 1930	5,000	4	200.0	"	1, 1937	"
1², 1930 Jan.	5,000	4	200.00	"	1, 1938	"
1, 1930	5,000	4	200.0	"	1, 1939 Jan.	"
1, 1930	5,000	4	200.0	"	1, 1940	"
1, 1930	4,000	4	100.0	"	1, 1941	"
1, 1930	4,000	4	160.00	"	1, 1942	"
1, 1930	4,000	4	1f0.00	"	1, 1943	"
1, 1930	4,000	4	160.0	"	1, 1944	"
1, 1930	4,000	4	f0.0	"	1, 1945	"
1, 1930 Jan.	2,000	4	80.00	Jan.—July	1, 1935 Jan.	Drainage
1, 1931	5,000	4	200.00	"	1, 1935	"
1, 1931 Feb.	4,000	4	16.00	Feb. and Aug.	1, 1935 Feb.	New Administration Building
1, 1931	11,000	4	440.00	"	1, 1936	"
1, 1931	10,000	4	400.00	"	1, 1937	"
1, 1931	10,000	4	400.00	"	1, 1938	"
1, 1931	10,000	4	400.00	"	1, 1939	"
1, 1931	10,000	4	400.00	"	1, 1940	"
1, 1931	10,000	4	400.00	"	1, 1941	"
1, 1931	10,000	4	400.00	"	1, 1942	"
1, 1931	10,000	4	400.00	"	1, 1943	"
1, 1931	10,000	4	400.00	"	1², 1944	"
1, 1931	10,000	4	400.00	"	1, 1945	"
1, 1931	10,000	4	400.00	"	1, 1946	"
1, 1931	10,000	4	400.00	"	1, 1947	"
1, 1931	10,000	4	400.00	"	1, 1948	"
1, 1931	10,000	4	400.00	"	1, 1949	"
1, 1931	10,000	4	400.00	"	1², 1950	"

LIST OF TOWN NOTES, TIME OF MATURING—Continued

Date	Amount	Rate	Annual Interest	Interest Due	Maturity	Borrowed on account of
Feb. 1, 1931	10,000	4	400.00	Feb. and Aug.	Feb. 1, 1951	New Administration Building
July 1, 1932	8,000	4¾	380.00	Jan. and July	July 1, 1935	Fire Alarm System
1, 1932	8,000	4¾	380.00	"	1, 1936	"
1, 1932	8,000	4¾	380.00	"	1, 1937	"
Nov. 1, 1934	3,000	2¼	67.50	May and Nov.	Nov. 1, 1935	Sidewalk (P.W.A.)
1, 1934	2,000	2¼	45.00	"	1, 1936	"
1, 1934	2,000	2¼	45.00	"	1, 1937	"
1, 1934	2,000	2¼	45.00	"	1, 1938	"
1, 1934	2,000	2¼	45.00	"	1, 1939	"
Nov. 1, 1934	6,000	2¼	134.00	May and Nov.	Nov. 1, 1935	Street (P.W.A.)
1, 1934	6,000	2¼	134.00	"	1, 1936	"
1, 1934	6,000	2¼	134.00	"	1, 1937	"
1, 1934	5,000	2¼	112.50	"	1, 1938	"
1, 1934	5,000	2¼	112.50	"	1, 1939	"
Nov. 1, 1934	2,000	2¼	45.00	May and Nov.	Nov. 1, 1935	Drainage (P.W.A.)
1, 1934	2,000	2¼	45.00	"	1, 1936	"
1, 1934	2,000	2¼	45.00	"	1, 1937	"
1, 1934	2,000	2¼	45.00	"	1, 1938	"
1, 1934	2,000	2¼	45.00	"	1, 1939	"
1, 1934	2,000	2¼	45.00	"	1, 1940	"
1, 1934	1,000	2¼	22.50	"	1, 1941	"
1, 1934	1,000	2¼	22.50	"	1, 1942	"
1, 1934	1,000	2¼	22.50	"	1, 1943	"
1, 1934	1,000	2¼	22.50	"	1, 1944	"
Dec. 1, 1934	12,000	2½	300.00	June and Dec.	Dec. 1, 1935	School Addition (P.W.A.)

Date	Amount	Rate	Value	Payable	Due	Purpose
1, 1934	12,000	2½	300.0	June and Dec.	1, 1936	Library Addition (P.W.A.)
1, 1934	12,000	2½	300.0	" "	1, 1937	"
1, 1934	12,000	2½	300.0	" "	1, 1938	"
1, 1934	12,000	2½	300.0	" "	1, 1939	"
1, 1934	11,000	2½	275.0	" "	1, 1940	"
1, 1934	11,000	2½	275.0	" "	1, 1941	"
1, 1934	11,000	2½	275.0	" "	1, 1942	"
1, 1934	11,000	2½	275.0	" "	1, 1943	"
1, 1934	3,000	2½	75.00	June and Dec.	1, 1944	"
1, 1934	3,000	2½	75.0	Dec.	1, 1935	"
1, 1934	3,000	2½	75.0	"	1, 1936	"
1, 1934	3,000	2½	75.0	"	1, 1937	"
1, 1934	3,000	2½	75.0	"	1, 1938	"
1, 1934	3,000	2½	75.0	"	1, 1939	"
1, 1934	3,000	2½	75.0	"	1, 1940	"
1, 1934	3,000	2½	75.0	"	1, 1941	"
1, 1934	3,000	2½	75.0	"	1, 1942	"
1, 1934	3,000	2½	75.0	"	1, 1943	"
1, 1934	2,000	2½	50.0	"	1, 1944	"

1,482,000

LIST OF TOWN NOTES, TIME OF MATURING—Continued

Date	Amount	Rate	Annual Interest	Interest Due	Maturity	Borrowed on account of
	200,000				Mar. 28, 1935	Anticipation of Revenue
	100,000				May 18, 1935	"
	100,000				Sept. 11, 1935	"
	100,000				Oct. 11, 1935	"

Watertown, December 31, 1934

HARRY W. BRIGHAM, *Treasurer.*

Insurance

	Amount	Due
City of New York	$36,000	Sept. 1, 1936
Imperial	33,000	Sept. 1, 1936
Home	29,000	Sept. 1, 1936
Home	20,000	Sept. 1, 1936
Caledonian	25,000	Sept. 1, 1936
Liverpool London Globe	25,000	Sept. 1, 1936
Travelers	33,000	Sept. 1, 1936
Home	42,000	Sept. 1, 1936
Mercantile	20,000	Sept. 1, 1936
Boston	33,000	Sept. 1, 1936
Aetna	33,000	Sept. 1, 1936
National Fire	33,000	Sept. 1, 1936
Massachusetts	12,000	Sept. 1, 1936
Boston	30,000	Sept. 1, 1936
Liberty	22,000	Sept. 1, 1936
Continental	15,000	Sept. 1, 1936
Firemens	20,000	Sept. 1, 1936
North America	53,000	Sept. 1, 1936
Pennsylvania	25,000	Sept. 1, 1936
Springfield	53,000	Sept. 1, 1936
National Fire	25,000	Sept. 1, 1935
Aetna	25,000	Sept. 1, 1935
N. Y. Underwriters	38,500	Sept. 1, 1935
Penn	26,500	Sept. 1, 1935
Queen	20,000	Sept. 1, 1935
Reliance	20,000	Sept. 1, 1935
Connecticut	42,000	Sept. 1, 1935
Liverpool-London Globe	26,000	Sept. 1, 1935
Hartford	45,000	Sept. 1, 1935
Norwich Union	19,000	Sept. 1, 1935
North River	36,000	Sept. 1, 1935
Firemen's	35,000	Sept. 1, 1935
Anglo-American	70,000	Sept. 1, 1935
Norwich Union	80,000	Sept. 1, 1935
National Fire	30,540	Sept. 1, 1935

	Amount	Due
Atlas	15,000	Sept. 1, 1935
Aetna Auto Ins., Hartford	25,000	Sept. 1, 1935
Mass. Fire-Marine	36,000	Sept. 1, 1935
Liverpool, London	25,000	Sept. 1, 1937
London-Lancashire	7,790	Sept. 1, 1937
Continental	35,000	Sept. 1, 1937
Travelers	15,000	Sept. 1, 1937
Home	10,000	Sept. 1, 1937
Home Fire-Marine	27,000	Sept. 1, 1937
Benjamin Franklin	36,000	Sept. 1, 1937
Superior	21,000	Sept. 1, 1937
Mercantile	127,800	Sept. 1, 1937
Penn	26,000	Sept. 1, 1937
Queen	46,000	Sept. 1, 1937
Home	38,000	Sept. 1, 1937
Penn	13,000	Sept. 1, 1937
St. Paul	135,000	Sept. 1, 1937
Springfield Ins. Co.	485,870	Sept. 1, 1939
	$2,265,000	
Boiler Mutual	10,000	Feb. 1, 1935
Employer's Liability	10,000	Jan. 8, 1937
	$20,000	

HARRY W. BRIGHAM,

Treasurer.

APPRAISERS' VALUATION

Highway Department

Building	$9,520.00	
Contents	11,226.00	
Oil Shed	921.00	
Contents	1,150.00	
Toolhouse and Shed	4,429.00	
Contents	7,474.00	
Smith Shop	1,440.00	
Contents	1,387.00	
Dwelling House	7,006.00	
Garbage Transfer Station	2,085.00	
Four acres of land, including dump	8,000.00	
Gravel Pit	8,200.00	
		$62,838.00
Sewer system	$525,000.00	
Drainage system	400,000.00	
		$925,000.00

Moth Department

Automobile	$100.00	
Tools	200.00	
		$300.00

Infirmary and Equipment

Almshouse Building	$34,229.00	
Contents	2,505.50	
5 Acres of Land	10,000.00	
		$46,734.50

Administration Building

Building	$243,899.00	
Contents	51,712.20	
		$295,611.20

Old Town Hall, Annex and Land

11,595 square feet of land	$34,785.00	
Town Hall and Annex	67,582.00	
Contents	2,073.00	
		$104,440.00

Poles and Wires Department

Automobiles and Equipment	$2,000.00	
		$2,000.00

Park Department

Athletic Field	$50,000.00	
Whitney Hill Park, 6 acres	10,000.00	
Saltonstall Park, 5 acres	57,250.00	
Howe Park, 1½ acres	2,000.00	
Cooks Pond, 4½ acres	10,000.00	
Playground equipment, tools, etc.	900.00	
House	200.00	
Equipment	400.00	
Miscellaneous land, deltas, etc.	3,000.00	
Marion Rd. and Orchard St., 6 acres	20,000.00	
West End Playgrounrd	20,000.00	
Land in Delta	62,600.00	
		$236,350.00

Water Department

Dwelling house and barn	$10,753.00	
Contents	12,964.25	
803,378 square feet of land	40,000.00	
10,000 square feet of land	1,500.00	
Water mains	650,000.00	
		$715,217.25

Public Library

50,240 square feet of land	$25,120.00	
Building	78,076.00	
Contents, books, furniture, fittings, etc.	71,563.40	

12,230 square feet of land, East End 3,100.00
East End Public Library   23,581.00
Contents   18,425.35
15,648 square feet of land   3,000.00
North End Library   9,237.00
Contents   8,622.40
                              ——————— $240,725.15

Health Department

Automobiles (2) $600.00
                                  ——————— $600.00

East Junior High School

Land, 142,900 square feet $40,000.00
Buildings   281,834.00
Contents   39,688.13
                               ——————— $361,522.13

High School Land and Building

Land $34,000.00
Building   408,940.00
Contents   103,539.90
                               ——————— $546,479.90

Phillips School

57,010 square feet of land $11,400.00
Building   34,340.00
Contents   7,304.10
                                ——————— $53,044.10

Spring (West) School Land

17,599 square feet of land $8,000.00
                                 ——————— $8,000.00

Bemis School Land

48,120 square feet of land $4,800.00
                                 ——————— $4,800.00

Grant School

Building	$30,209.00	
Contents	4,816.00	
		$35,025.00

Marshall Spring School

Land	$10,000.00	
Building	92,925.00	
Contents	8,910.63	
		$111,835.63

James Russell Lowell School

Building	$167,557.00	
Contents	18,583.43	
4½ acres of land	15,000.00	
		$201,140.43

Francis School

55,208 square feet of land	$11,400.00	
Building	87,327.00	
Contents	8,072.04	
		$106,799.04

Hosmer School

80,530 square feet of land	$16,000.00	
Building and addition	192,340.00	
Contents	27,822.31	
		$236,162.31

Coolidge School, Arlington Street

Land	$24,000.00	
Building	189,969.00	
Contents	21,632.51	
		$235,601.51

Browne School, Main Street

Land	$17,225.00	
Building	150,318.00	
Contents	17,895.75	
		$185,438.75

Old Parker School Land

38,496 square feet of land	$19,000.00	
		$19,000.00

West Junior High School

Land	$10,000.00	
Building	208,277.00	
Contents	36,628.54	
		$254,905.54

New Parker School

126,453 square feet of land	$13,000.00	
Building	88,027.00	
Contents	9,958.72	
		$110,985.72

Central Fire Station and Police Station

13,000 square feet of land	$26,000.00	
Building	50,719.00	
Contents, including apparatus	50,187.90	
		$126,906.90

East End Fire Station

Land	$5,000.00	
Building	32,616.00	
Contents	19,078.85	
		$56,694.85

Veterans' Memorial

Building	$16,744.00	
Contents	1,342.70	
		$18,086.70

Total	$5,302,244.61

MAURICE H. O'CONNELL,
JAMES H. SHERIDAN,
EDWARD D. HOLLAND,
Selectmen.

For year ending December 31, 1934.

REPORT OF PARK COMMISSIONERS

To the Citizens of Watertown:

The Board of Park Commissioners herewith submits its annual report for the year 1934.

Considerable work has been accomplished this past year toward improving present playground and recreational areas as well as the construction of five new tennis courts on the land adjoining Victory Field. These new courts will be ready for use in the early summer.

The area adjacent to the cinder track and old tennis courts has been resurfaced and graded and will be used as a playground this year. These new additions to our popular recreation center were sorely needed and will go a great way toward relieving the already greatly overburdened tennis courts and ball field.

The work on Saltonstall Park is nearing completion and will improve considerably the appearance of the grounds around the new Administration building.

Cement borders were built around each of the three sections which form the Watertown Square Delta. This work was made possible by the bequest to this Department of the late Mrs. Hiram McGlauflin.

Handicapped by ruthless slashes in its budget, brought about undoubtedly by that form of public hysteria which apparently has "Economy at any price" as its sole motive, this department has, nevertheless, kept its parks, deltas and playgrounds in such condition that they have reflected credit upon the town. Much work remains to be done however, in order that our children may have adequate room where they may play in safety.

The cost of maintaining this department has never added but a few cents per thousand to the tax rate, yet that few cents represents many times itself in actual value to the younger generation whose future is the welfare of every community, and of the nation as a whole. Tax dollars should be saved by other means than the handicapping of the boys and girls who constitute the future hope of all of us.

WINTHROP G. ROCKWELL, *Chairman*
GEORGE B. WELLMAN, *Secretary*
ARTHUR L. MORSE,

Park Commissioners.

CONTENTS

Lightning Source UK Ltd.
Milton Keynes UK
UKHW020217260219
337978UK00012B/1127/P